HARDPRESS.NET
HOME OF HARD-TO-FIND BOOKS

The Westminster Review
by Unknown

Address:
HardPress
8345 NW 66TH ST #2561
MIAMI FL 33166-2626
USA
Email: info@hardpress.net

THE

WESTMINSTER

REVIEW.

JANUARY AND APRIL,
1864.

"Truth can never be confirm'd enough,
Though doubts did ever sleep."
SHAKESPEARE.
Wahrheitsliebe zeigt sich darin, daß man überall das Gute zu finden und zu schätzen weiß.
GÖTHE.

NEW SERIES.
VOL. XXV. 81

LONDON:
TRÜBNER & CO., 60, PATERNOSTER-ROW.
MDCCCLXIV.

CONTENTS.

THE

WESTMINSTER

AND

FOREIGN QUARTERLY

REVIEW.

JANUARY 1, 1864.

ART. I.—THE LIFE AND WRITINGS OF ROGER BACON.

1. *Fratris Rogeri Bacon, Ordinis Minorum, Opus Majus, à Samuele Jebb. Londini editum.* 1733.
2. *Fratris Rogeri Bacon: Opus Tertium, Opus Minus, Compendium Philosophiæ.* Edited by J. S. BREWER. London, 1859.
3. *Roger Bacon: sa Vie, ses Ouvrages, ses Doctrines.* Par ÉMILE CHARLES. Paris, 1861.

ROGER BACON is one of the few really great men who have been equally neglected by their contemporaries and by posterity. All who have looked into his writings, Leland and Selden no less than Humboldt and Victor Cousin, point to him as the most original thinker of the middle ages. His anticipations of the course of scientific discovery, yield only in importance to the justness of his conceptions of the method and purposes of science itself. First among the schoolmen, he pointed out the evils of that blind subservience to authority which is the cardinal defect of scholasticism. First in an age almost wholly devoted to metaphysical speculation and logical dispute, he realized the value of the study of nature, and insisted on the importance of experiment as an aid to it. The language in which this great reform is advocated, is in the highest degree striking and original. There are passages which recall, if they did not suggest, some of the most brilliant aphorisms in the "Novum Organum" of his illustrious namesake. These facts sufficiently mark the interval which separated Bacon from the current thought of the thirteenth century; and therefore we cannot be surprised that in his lifetime he should have shared the ordinary fate of those who presume to differ from the world around them. What is remarkable is, that of all the mediæval doctors, the one who approaches most nearly to the spirit of modern science should have obtained the smallest share of postumous renown.

The bibliographical history of his 'works shows clearly how little attention they have received. Bacon is known to have been a most active writer. Yet, with the exception of six minor treatises printed between the years 1541 and 1614,* his writings remained buried in manuscript until 1733. For four centuries and a-half these manuscripts, the sole evidences of the most advanced thought of the middle ages, were at the mercy of such accidents as those which destroyed Sir Robert Cotton's library in 1731, or Lord Mansfield's library in 1780. It appears indeed that in the time of Selden, some "juditious friends" of Langbain's "were very much taken with sundry passages in fryar Bacon's 'Epistle to Clement and suitors for a Publication.'" They certainly did not obtain their suit, for it was only in the middle of the eighteenth century, that Dr. Jebb published the text of the "Opus Majus," the very Epistle to Clement with which Langbain's judicious friends were so much taken. This edition, chiefly founded on a manuscript known as the "Codex Dubliniensis," presents but an imperfectly collated text. It includes nearly one hundred pages of a treatise "De Multiplicatione Specierum," which undoubtedly forms part of the "Opus Tertium;" and it omits the important chapters on Ethics which are found in the MSS. of the Bodleian, and of the library of Trinity College, Cambridge, as well as in the "Codex Dubliniensis" itself. Notwithstanding these defects and some lesser inaccuracies, it is a most valuable and scholar-like work; the earliest as well as the most important edition which has yet issued from the British press.

It is strange that the curiosity of scholars was not roused to know more of Bacon's works, and that the "Opus Minus" at

---

* These treatises are the following:
1. "Speculum Alchimiæ." 1541.
2. "De Mirabili Potestate Artis et Naturæ." Parisiis, 1542.
3. "Libellus Rogerii Baconis, Angli Doctissimi Mathematici et Medici, de Retardandis Senectutis accidentibus, et de Senibus conservandis." Oxoniæ, 1590.
4. "Sanioris Medicinæ Magistri D. Rogerii Baconis Angli, de Arte Chymiæ scripta." 1603.
5. "Rogeri Baconis Angli viri Eminentissimi Perspectiva." Francofurti, 1614.
6. "Specula Mathematica." Francofurti, 1614.

least, the contents of which are described by Dr. Jebb in his preface (not very accurately, by the way), should never have been printed. Yet nearly a hundred years passed before the subject was again brought prominently forward. At last, in the year 1847, M. Victor Cousin, who was engaged on his "Fragments of the Philosophy of the Middle Ages," discovered in the library at Douai an inedited manuscript of Bacon's. Becoming interested in it, he applied himself to the task of mastering its contents, when he found that it contained, under a false title, the important treatise known as the "Opus Tertium." He communicated this discovery to the learned world in the *Journal des Savans* for March 1848, addressing at the same time an eloquent appeal to the Universities of Oxford and Cambridge for a continuation of the work commenced by Dr. Jebb. We regret to say that this appeal was made in vain. Cambridge may plead that she was not immediately interested in the matter; but Oxford was, and is without excuse. Roger Bacon is one of the most illustrious of her sons. In the Bodleian, in the Ashmolean, and in two at least of her college libraries, invaluable materials for a complete edition are to be found. The task is one for which many Oxford scholars are eminently fitted, and which seems naturally to devolve upon a wealthy and learned corporation. To borrow Bacon's own language, "impossibile est quod aliquis de his qui modo vivunt solus hoc peragat nisi expensas habeat pro sua voluntate." Unfortunately, Oxford men at the present day seem more interested in convicting one another of heresy than in making common cause for the advancement of learning and the honour of their University.

The bread which M. Cousin cast upon the waters in 1848 has returned after many days, in the shape of a monograph on Bacon by M. Émile Charles; and an edition of the "Opus Minus," "Opus Tertium," and "Compendium Philosophiæ," by Mr. Brewer. The latter volume, published some three years back, forms one of the valuable series of mediæval chronicles and memorials, now in course of publication by the authority of the Treasury, under the direction of the Master of the Rolls. So far as we are able to judge, the editor has done the work put into his hands with judgment and care. To say this is to say all that can be said. The preparation of a text by the collation of MSS. is a task which requires knowledge and critical feeling; but these qualities do not appear on the surface, and only those who go over the same ground can fairly judge of them. Mr. Brewer will gain no popular applause by what he has done, but he will be remembered by whoever understands the difficulty of his task, and will look into the manner of its execution.

M. Charles' work is more recent, more elaborate, and is immediately due to the appeal made by M. Victor Cousin.   It is the fruit of six years' unremitting labour in a field which few would have had the courage to enter.   The object which its author proposed to himself was no less than to exhibit in a connected form the life, works, and doctrines of Roger Bacon.   Inasmuch as with the exception of the six treatises mentioned above, the "Opus Majus" was the only work of Bacon's already printed when M. Charles commenced his labours, it was, in the first place, necessary for him to undertake a critical examination of the MSS. then in existence.   This cardinal task has been most conscientiously performed.   The MSS. of the British Museum, of the Bodleian, of the Sloane collection, of the Ashmolean, of the Imperial Library, of the Mazarine Library, as well as those of Amiens and Douai, more especially indicated by M. Cousin, have all been examined.*   The result is a book full of information, well arranged, agreeably written, and in every way most creditable to the ability and zeal of the Professor of Logic in the Lycæum of Bordeaux.   One thing, however, perplexes us.   We do not understand how so diligent an author, writing in 1861, could be ignorant of Mr. Brewer's work, published in 1859. Certain it is that M. Charles nowhere alludes to it, and occasionally places himself on false ground from his want of acquaintance with the labours of his predecessor.

   Such is a brief history of what has hitherto been done to make Bacon known to the world.   It is clear that much remains to do. In the first place a uniform and perfect edition of his works is called for.   Dr. Jebb's book is scarce and expensive; its Venetian reprint,† and the various editions of the "De Mirabili Potestate," and the "De Retardandis Senectutis Accidentibus," scarcely less so, while several of the MSS. have not been printed at all.   It may be admitted, that to prepare such an edition would be a most difficult and laborious task, but it is not creditable to English letters that it should not be undertaken.   Bacon's great contemporaries, Albert of Cologne and Thomas Aquinas, have long since been canonized by the printing-press; it is full time that justice should be done to one who was as much their equal in mere learning, as their superior in originality and speculative insight.

   The oblivion which has fallen on Bacon as a writer rests also on his history as a man.   Neither the time of his birth nor of his death is certainly known.   A few salient facts——his meeting

---

   * M. Charles does not seem to have seen the Cambridge manuscripts. There are several well worth looking into, especially those in the library of Magdalen College, and some fragments included in the Gale MSS. in the library of Trinity College.
          † Venetiis, 1750. Apud Franciscum Pitteri.

with Henry III. at Oxford, his correspondence with Clement, his enforced retreat at Paris, his long imprisonment—have been transmitted to us by contemporary authorities; but the main story of his life has to be constructed from conjecture, and from the random allusions to be found in his own works. If the results so arrived at are not, historically speaking, very important, they are at least interesting, from the light they throw on the manners and opinions and literary life of the thirteenth century. For this reason we shall attempt to exhibit them in a connected form.

Roger Bacon was born near Ilchester, in the county of Somerset. There is traditional authority for placing his birth in the year 1214: it is at least certain that he must have been born in the early part of the thirteenth century. We have little information respecting his family beyond the assurances of old writers that it was of some consideration. Ross, in a passage quoted by Mr. Brewer, describes Bacon as "de generosa prosapia incolarum comitatus Dorsettiæ;" Wood says he came of a "good" family; M. Charles, on what authority we know not, makes them wealthy and noble. His immediate relations seem to have taken the side of Henry III. in the long contests between the king and his nobles, and they were either wealthy enough, or powerful enough, to have incurred the displeasure of the de Montfort party, and to have been exiled in consequence of their partisanship. It has been supposed that Robert Bacon, the friar mentioned by Wendover as having spoken his mind so boldly to Henry with regard to the Bishop of Winchester, on the occasion of the king's visit to Oxford, was a brother of the philosopher. A shade of probability has been thrown on this supposition by an allusion in the "Opus Tertium," to "my brother the scholar." But Robert Bacon died, an old man, in 1248. He can scarcely, then, have been less than seventy years of age, which, if Roger Bacon was born in 1214, would make thirty-six years' difference between them—a greater disparity than is usually found between two brothers.

A younger son and a student, the Church was the only career open to Bacon. At the age at which most boys now go to a public school, he was sent to Oxford. That university was, in the thirteenth century, in the height of its fame; its reputation was European. In spite of the disadvantages of its position on the confines of the intellectual world, it was the successful rival of Prague and Bologna, and only inferior in general estimation to Paris. Thirty thousand students, we are told, were assembled within its walls.* Italy, France, Germany, Scotland, and Wales

---

* These numbers are given by Matthew Paris. Of course they are not to be relied on.

found representatives in the active throng which was collected on
the banks of the Isis, and which daily crowded into the Franciscan
lecture-room at St. Ebbe's.   It requires a little imagination for
those whose recollection of Oxford teaching resolves itself into
a picture of some dozen undergraduates languidly translating the
" Ethics " to a gentlemanly man in an arm-chair, to realize the
life and vigour of the mediæval prelections.   The schools were
public class-rooms in which all members of the University without
distinction were taught.   They were presided over by the regent-
masters in the several faculties.   The privilege of teaching was,
however, confined to those who had given evidence of their fitness
for it ; and as such teachers were authorized to take a fee from
each pupil, it became, in the hands of an able and popular lecturer,
a valuable one.   No restriction of any kind seems to have been
imposed on entering the University, nor was freedom of choice
between various masters in the same faculty interfered with.

In this state of things, with an intense interest in speculative
discussion, and with a common language — Latin — for the
exchange of ideas, with the fact that distinction in law and
philosophy opened out the readiest path to the honours of the
Church, and therefore of the State, it is not surprising that the
number of students in a given university should be in proportion
to the fame of its public teachers.   In order, therefore, to account
for the popularity of Oxford in the thirteenth century, we have
only to look at the names of those who taught in her schools
during that period.   Duns Scotus, and Occham, are even now
remembered as among the greatest of the schoolmen ; the former,
while regent of philosophy at Oxford, is said to have been lis-
tened to by 30,000 students.*   But there were many others as
highly thought of in their day, and whose reputation was equally
sure to attract ; such were Alexander of Hales, Thomas Wallis,
Richard of Cornwall, Peocham, Baconthorpe, Burley, Middleton,
Bungay, Bradwardin, Adam de Marisco, and Grostête—names
unfamiliar in modern ears, but associated with the profoundest
learning of those times.   So great was the fame of some of these
doctors, that they were called from England to deliver lectures
on the Continent.   Three at least of the most celebrated teachers
at Paris, Alexander of Hales, Thomas Wallis, and Richard of
Cornwall, had been students of the English University.   We
learn from Eccleston, that shortly after the introduction of the
Franciscans into England in 1224, the general master of the
order sent to Oxford for two brothers to read at Lyons; and there
is evidence to prove that the practice was not uncommon.   But,
from a higher point of view, Oxford's title to the reputation she

---

* Brucker, Hist. Crit. iii. 826, quoted by Hauréau ; De la Philosophie
Scholastique, ii. 308.

enjoyed will be found to rest neither on the number of her scholars, nor on the celebrity of her professors. Like many kindred establishments on the Continent at the present day, it was the rallying-point of the popular party in politics, and the centre of the liberal party in opinion. Grostête, its chancellor, was the intimate friend of Simon de Montfort. From his letters, as well as from the contemporary correspondence of Adam de Marisco, it clearly appears that a strong anti-monarchical feeling prevailed among the students. Most of those who, during this century, protested against the authority of Aristotle, and the still more intolerable authority of his commentators, were Oxford men. The most celebrated of these, beyond doubt, were to be found in the ranks of the Minors, and, if we may believe Bacon, the learning of the Minors culminated in two brothers of the order—Robert Grostête and Adam de Marisco. Both these men were original thinkers, and both were innovators on the studies which then prevailed. While Paris was ringing with disputes on the interpretation of the Third Book of the *De Anima*, they were devoting themselves to mathematical and physical science. It was due to them that lectures on Optics were delivered at Oxford, at a time when that subject was read nowhere else. Although it would be incorrect to represent them as entirely opposed to Logic and Metaphysics, or inclined to shelve these studies for the sake of Physics, yet it is certain that they read differently from their contemporaries—more independently, and more at first hand; while at the same time they found a place for branches of knowledge then of no account, but destined in the future to modify the whole scope both of learning and teaching.

An anecdote related by Bacon of Adam de Marisco, may serve, in the absence of more definite information, to illustrate what we suppose to have been the attitude of these teachers towards the prevailing studies. There was a very celebrated controversy as to whether the active intellect was part of the human soul or not. The question arose out of the Aristotelian distinction between the active and the potential intellect; and if the existence of the soul itself had depended on its solution, it could not have been more keenly debated. This point was submitted to the judgment of Adam de Marisco, then a leading teacher at Oxford. His answer was conveyed in the following lucid sentence, which we leave in its native simplicity—*Intellectus agens est corvus Eliæ.* "He was unwilling," adds Bacon, with perfect gravity, " to explain himself because the question was put to tempt him, and not for the sake of knowledge." It certainly looks as if he did not care to explain himself, from want of interest in the discussion itself.

Robert Grostête occupies so large a place in the history of

Bacon's life and writings, that he requires more than a passing notice. He was, as has been said, Chancellor of the University. On the establishment of the Franciscans in England, in 1224, he was appointed their first rector at Oxford. He became Bishop of Lincoln in 1235, in which office he continued until his death, in 1253. He is now chiefly remembered for his zeal as a Church reformer, and for the boldness with which he resisted Innocent IV., when commanded to induct the Pope's nephew into a canonry at Lincoln. The letter containing his refusal has been printed, and fully deserves the celebrity it has obtained. Apostolic mandates, Grostête observes, cannot be opposed to the doctrine of the Apostles. But the command of the Pope is not only not consonant to apostolic sanctity, but most dissonant and discordant therewith. For since the sin of Lucifer, there has been no sin more odious, detestable, and abominable than the destruction of souls by robbing them of those spiritual aids by which they were intended to be saved ; and therefore, since the commands of his Holiness evidently tend to that great sin, with the utmost obedience, and in the most filial manner, he must utterly refuse to obey them :—"*filianter et obedienter non obedio contradico et rebello.*" He managed the affairs of his diocese in the same uncompromising spirit. "He was," says Matthew Paris, "a manifest confronter of the pope and the king, the blamer of prelates, the corrector of monks, the director of priests, the instructor of clerks, the support of scholars, the preacher of the people, the persecutor of the incontinents, the zealous student of all scripture, the hammer and despiser of the Romans."

Everything that we know of his life points to him as a man, bold, energetic, and not to be moved either by fear or favour. In addition to these qualities, which constitute the active side of his character, he was one of the most voluminous writers and deeply read scholars of the age. "*Solus unus scivit scientias ut Lincolnensis Episcopus,*" says Roger Bacon. His known works comprise physical treatises, such as the "De Iride" and "De Cometis ;" books on Agriculture ; French poems and commentaries on Aristotle. But although distinguished for his knowledge of mental and natural philosophy, he is more particularly known for his linguistic attainments. It is impossible to conceive anything lower than the general state of scholarship in that day. Bacon declares that there were not four men of his time who knew anything of Greek. Neither Albertus Magnus nor Thomas Aquinas knew a word of that language. Hugutio and Papias, the chief grammatical authorities, make mistakes which we are almost afraid to print. For instance, they derived *parasceve* from *paro* and *cœna*, "*Et dicunt quod dicitur preparatio cœnæ.*"*

---

* Bacon, "Compendium Studii," c. vii.

Brito, another grammarian, who takes upon himself to criticise some of their performances, is not much better when it comes to his turn. Brito, says Bacon,* *"Asserit quod Deus etymologizatur quasi dans æternam vitam suis."* This is a fair average sample of Brito's powers as an etymologist.

Into this mass of ignorance Grostête boldly plunged. He translated Suidas' Lexicon ; he sent to the East for the Greek texts, and had them transcribed under his own eye ; he invited Greek teachers from Italy, and by precept and example enforced the study of the Greek philosophers in their own language.

Under these two men, Grostête and Marisco, Bacon read when at Oxford. This is an inference merely, but it is an inference justified by strong probability. We may believe that a youth of Bacon's promise would seek and be sought by the most eminent teachers of his day. We know who these men were. They were Robert Bacon, Richard Fitzacre, Adam de Marisco, and Robert Grostête. The two former are never once mentioned by Bacon, the two latter are quoted with enthusiastic admiration in almost every page.

" It is not clear," says one of the biographers, in which doubt he is followed by M. Charles, " whether Bacon was of Merton College or Brazenose Hall." We think it abundantly clear that he was at neither the one or the other, for the reason that neither was founded till long after he went to Oxford. It was not at that time necessary for the members of the University to become members of a college. The innovation by which a great public body has been transformed into an aggregation of private establishments had not then taken place. The colleges which, from time to time, were opened by the liberality of founders, for the benefit of a particular class or locality, long retained the special character imposed upon them ; their object was not to teach, but to lodge, feed, and clothe their members. The University, on the other hand, was a public institution, and its function was not eleemosynary but educational. Membership of a college was what the logicians would have called a separable accident of an Oxford man. With it, he no doubt enjoyed some peculiar and personal privileges ; but without it he was equally a member of the University, and a sharer in all the advantages which the state of membership conferred.

After a residence of some five or eight years at Oxford, Bacon went forward to Paris. An education in the thirteenth century was hardly considered complete without a course of study at one of the Foreign Universities. Salerno was still the chief school of medicine as Bologna was of law ; but in the theological and moral sciences Paris was supreme, and no ambitious Churchman

---

* "Compendium Studii," c. vii.

could afford to dispense with a course of study in the Rue Fouarre. The editors of the "History of French Literature" have taken advantage of this circumstance to place the name of Bacon on the roll of their own worthies.   Against this assumption we must beg leave to protest.   French literature, in a national sense, had no existence till the fourteenth century; but even if this were not so, France has no title under which she can claim Bacon as one of her sons.   He was by birth, by education, by temperament, essentially English.   The character of his mind and of his philosophy was formed not in Paris but at Oxford.   It was from Grostête that he learned to study Greek, Arabic, and Hebrew, and to apply himself to the investigation of natural phenomena. It was under the influence of the somewhat lawless and republican spirit which pervaded Oxford that he learned to distrust authority, and the accident of his family having made sacrifices for the royal cause, probably contributed to that profound dislike of popular opinion which his writings disclose.   Although he cannot have been more than twenty-one when he left England, he carried with him the germs of all his after-beliefs, together with some moral and intellectual peculiarities, which the conditions of his previous education were especially calculated to engender.

It seems pretty well established that Bacon made two visits to Paris.   The length of the first is uncertain; but it was not less than three or four years, and very likely was much more.   Perhaps bearing in mind that eight years' residence was usual as a qualification for the Doctorate, and that Bacon took the degree of Doctor at Paris, we shall not be wrong in presuming that he spent as much as eight years in France on the occasion of his first residence in the University.   Never were the schools in that distinguished seat of learning more flourishing than when the young Oxford student visited them for the first time.   His countryman, Alexander of Hales, "the irrefragable doctor," still occupied the chair of Theology; the Bishop of Paris, William of Auvergne, was combating with all the ardour of a Crusader the Pantheism of Averroes, and maintaining against the authority of Aristotle the spiritual nature of the soul.   The keen interest which these subjects excited had lately been heightened by the labours and genius of Albert of Cologne, who, together with his illustrious pupil, Thomas Aquinas, visited Paris shortly afterwards.   The translation of the Arabian texts, and notably of the Commentaries of Averroes, executed some fifteen years before by Michael Scot at Toledo, had given a new impulse to philosophical discussion; and, in Bacon's own phrase, "had magnified the philosophy of Aristotle among the Latins."   That philosophy, checked by the Council of Paris in 1209, and formally proscribed by Robert de Courçon's statutes in 1215, had just been re-established in the schools after a sharp struggle.   All those vast and indeterminate problems which metaphysics and psychology open out were eagerly discussed, and the zeal of the new orders who, partly from conviction and partly from rivalry, interpreted in a different sense the thought of Aristotle, gave additional quickness to the life which had been breathed into the body of scholasticism. In short, several causes aided in making Paris the centre of a vigorous intellectual movement; and therefore within its walls were assembled not only several of the most prominent teachers of the day, but a crowd of scholars from every nation in Europe, eager for knowledge, but loving nothing so much as excitement and dispute.

Bacon seems to have regarded these signs of awakening life with anything but hope. Indeed he was almost equally dissatisfied with the men, with the studies, and with the methods which he found in vogue. He attached himself to none of the celebrated teachers who swayed the schools of Paris. Their ways were not his ways, nor their thoughts his thoughts. He looked to the future for a possible realization of his dream of a perfect science : they held that philosophy had run its course, and that it would change only to go back. He believed that intellectual advance had no deadlier enemies than authority and custom, and that an instauration of the sciences on the double basis of philology and physics was the only remedy for the evils of the times. This was his creed—the idea which had taken possession of him —an idea to which he passionately clung through years of persecution and neglect, and which forms the substance of his earliest as of his latest teaching. The practice of the Paris schools when Bacon joined the University was one continued contradiction of this philosophy: authority reigned supreme, language was universally neglected, and the study of nature was unknown. This must have been discouraging to the pupil of Grostête, fresh from the physical studies of Oxford, and anxious to bring them into prominence elsewhere : and perhaps his own teaching was not received in such a manner as to conciliate a temper somewhat haughty and impatient; at any rate, the terms in which he describes the state of learning in Paris in the "Opus Majus" imply something of irritation as well as of disappointment. "There was," he says, " a great appearance of wisdom, much studious energy, a host of doctors and students, but nowhere have I met so much ignorance. Neither teachers nor learners seem to care about knowledge, if only they can get the reputation of it with the ignorant." Everything seemed over-ridden by custom and authority ; he could not find four scholars who knew anything of Greek. Wretched Latin translations furnished the text from which Aristotle was read. So bad were these, that Bacon declares that if he had the power he would cause all the books of Aristotle to be burned, as it was, in his opinion, a pure waste of time to study them. Nor does he confine himself to terms of merely general reprobation. He boldly attacks the most esteemed authorities of the day in language not to be mistaken. Among these no one held a higher rank than Alexander of Hales, the irrefragable doctor. At the request of Innocent IV. this venerable man had composed a "Summa," or compendium of theology, which was submitted to the judgment of seventy divines, and, having been approved by them, was recommended to masters in theology as a canonical treatise. As to Alexander himself, Bacon classes him with Albert of Cologne, as one of those through whose influence the whole course of study was vitiated. Of his "Summa" he says, that "it is so full of mistakes and philosophical twaddle, that no one thought it worth while to copy it."* This irreverent criticism of the greatest Franciscan authority is followed by an estimate of Albert the Great, not more flattering to the vanity of the Dominicans.

"A hard-working man," observes Bacon, with calm superiority; "but he has never been thoroughly grounded; and therefore is necessarily ignorant of the common sciences. His works are full of mistakes and emptiness. True, this is more his misfortune than his fault; nor should his ignorance be imputed to him as a crime, since there are many men of ability and skill who are very ignorant, and yet useful in their generation."

This is Albert, who was looked up to by the whole Dominican order as an almost supernatural authority: "*cui adhæret sicut angelo totus ordo;*" and Bacon can find nothing better to say of him than that he is a useful, plodding man, and that his ignorance ought not to be considered a crime! St. Thomas was not as yet in the zenith of his fame, so Bacon does not waste many words on him: he merely alludes to him in passing, as "a well-known man, and a blunderer,"† and says that he became a teacher of philosophy without ever having learned it. These details indicate the light estimation in which Bacon held even the most revered names, and while they prove how little he was indebted to Parisian teaching, they go far to explain, if not to justify, the treatment which he afterwards received from his superiors. We may be sure that if he used the language we have just quoted, in his old age, in a philosophical treatise addressed to the head of the Church, his discourse with his companions in his youthful days at Paris could not have been very guarded; and when every allowance is made for the freedom of expression usual in a mediæval university, we can scarcely wonder that the

---

* "Ejus autem Summa plures habet falsitates et vanitates philosophiæ, cujus signum est, quod nullus facit eam de itero scribi."
† "Vir erroneus et famosus."

trenchant criticism of the young Oxford student should have raised up against him many powerful enemies.

The necessity of obtaining some sort of protection against the odium so incurred, was, in all probability, one motive which prompted him, about this time, to take a step which he ever afterwards regretted. At a date not exactly known, but in all probability during his first visit to Paris, Bacon entered the Order of St. Francis. It is certainly, at first sight, rather difficult to understand why a man of his character and temperament should have voluntarily subjected himself to the restraints which the rule of the Order imposed, and of which he afterwards complained so bitterly to the Pope. M. Charles observes that " there were only three powers able to aid Bacon—the King, the Pope, a religious corporation such as the Mendicant Orders, or an educational one such as the University." What specific aid Bacon sought for, or was likely to obtain by becoming a Franciscan, M. Charles does not say, nor can we imagine. The friar Minor was bound to absolute poverty. He was forbidden to possess books or instruments, or to use ink or parchment. That these restrictions were sometimes enforced, we know on the best possible authority. Years afterwards, when Clement IV. wrote to Bacon, requesting an account of his discoveries, the latter excused his delay by reminding the Pope of his poverty and of his want of books. " I have, as you know, no money, nor can I have any, and consequently I am unable to borrow, as I can find no security." And again :—" I have not been commanded by my superiors to write ; nay, I am strictly enjoined to the contrary, under a penalty of losing the book, and being made to fast on bread and water many days." These regulations must have been perfectly well known to Bacon before he assumed the frock of St. Francis, but they are not conditions under which a philosopher, as such, would be anxious to work. Why, then, we may ask, should Bacon have voluntarily adopted a course of life from which he could gain so little, and by which he would lose so much ? Why, of the two Mendicant Orders, did he associate himself with that one which laid the least store by those intellectual gifts which are his own best title to fame ? Bacon's character was decidedly rugged, self-asserting, and intolerant. He had nothing of that gentle mysticism which endeared St. Francis to his Order and to the world. It is not easy to fancy him in an access of religious exaltation. It is still less easy to suppose that his natural impulse would lead him to seek a field of labour among the uneducated poor—that rabble for whom he is ever expressing such unmeasured contempt. If virtually compelled, as M. Charles supposes, to enter the ranks of the Mendicants, why should he not have become a Dominican, the more cultivated and least rigorous of the two, rather than a Franciscan? It is not easy to give a satisfactory answer to these questions; but we incline to think that what Bacon required, was not so much aid in his studies as protection for his opinions. His uncompromising denunciation of received authorities and accepted systems, cannot have failed to render him unpopular and suspected. The new Orders stood high in the papal favour, and once enlisted in their ranks, he might count on being able to say and do many things which would expose him to danger as a simple clerk. Assuming this to be so, there is comparatively little difficulty in accounting for the choice he actually made. Notwithstanding its asceticism and apparent devotion to the Roman See, the Franciscan school stands prominent in the history of the thirteenth century as the head-quarters of the Rationalistic and Liberal party. That this should be so is not what we should expect, but of the fact there is no doubt; and as it is important in its bearings on the philosophical history of the time, it may be well to attempt to explain it.

The intercourse with the East, which sprang from the Crusades, and was afterwards fostered by the commercial activity of Venice, led to results little within the view of those zealous Churchmen who had preached to Christians the duty of securing the Holy Sepulchre. A dangerous disease and a still more dangerous heresy—leprosy and Manicheism—were the immediate fruit of the relations which had then for some time been established between the Eastern and Western empires. The bad food, bad clothing, damp and unwholesome houses, in which the town population of the thirteenth century lived, aggravated the leprosy, until, if we may judge from the precautions taken against it, it rose to the dignity of a national scourge. The infected person lost his civil rights, and all ecclesiastical privileges; he was at once cast off by society, and excommunicated by the Church. The physician held out to him no hope of being cured, and the priest no hope of being saved. What wonder that, out of sheer desperation, he should contract habits which ended in his being little less unwholesome in mind than he was in body. The treatment of these miserables presented a difficulty which no statesman of that day was able to grapple with. Not less critical for those whom it concerned was the question of heresy. The condition of the Church in Languedoc was full of anxiety for whoever was interested in the welfare of the Papacy. That province constituted one of the most civilized and wealthy portions of Europe. But its people had imbibed strange doctrines. They held the eternal antagonism between mind and matter—they spoke blasphemously of God and Christ—they despised outward ceremonials, priests, and temples. It was not that these opinions were held by a few isolated sectaries: it was that a sectarian Church was formed within the bosom of the Catholic Church.

The honour of having devised a remedy against these two pressing dangers belongs to St. Francis and St. Dominic. The Church certainly owes a debt of gratitude to the religious orders. In the time of Gregory VII., when men could no longer tolerate the overbearing sacerdotalism of the priesthood, it was saved by the monks. But the feminine virtue of these recluses was of little avail when Christendom was swarming with infidel preachers, and when cities were being ravaged by a frightful disease. In this emergency rose St. Francis and St. Dominic, with new weapons, forged for a new warfare. Each may be said to have chosen a separate field of mission. St. Dominic addressed himself, in the main, to the spiritual difficulty—to the question of heresy. He perceived that the state of religious opinion in Languedoc was produced, in great measure, by the fact that an educated laity was brought face to face with an uneducated and careless priesthood. He accordingly created a class of men versed in science, especially trained to preach, and imbued with a large measure of his own fervid spirit. To the eloquence of the Albigenses and Waldenses, the Dominican opposed an eloquence to which his learning and poverty lent an additional charm. He did not believe that anything would come of the foolishness of preaching. He aspired to an intellectual supremacy, to be exercised in the education and conversion of mankind. The plan was only moderately successful as regards the heretics of Languedoc ; but one result of it was that, in a few years, the preachers filled the chief places in the great Universities of Europe—in Bologna, in Cologne, in Paris, in Oxford. Before long they counted in their ranks the greatest of the schoolmen—Albert of Cologne and Thomas Aquinas.

St. Francis, on the contrary, set out with a belief in the uselessness of all learning in matters spiritual. He read in their most literal sense those passages of Scripture which draw the line between human means and divine ends. He would preach that gospel which was foolishness to the Greeks ; he would subdue the world by the works of the Spirit. To this theory he joined, however, an aim as practical and benevolent as that of Howard. He was willing to do anything, or to endure anything, for the sake of the flock of Christ ; but there was one work to which he felt himself especially called—that of ministering to the distresses of the unhappy class for whose wants no one else would care. To attend the leper-hospitals was his own work, and the duty especially enjoined on all his brethren. The discipline was a necessary preliminary to admittance into the Order. The motive with which it was framed was, no doubt, a mixed one—partly humane, partly penitential, but its effect was to familiarize the Franciscans with the treatment of disease, to encourage physical studies as a means of alleviating the sufferings to which they were compelled to minister, and to create, in the midst of the metaphysicans and canonists, a school of pure experimentalists, whose labours were a necessary preliminary to the scientific revival of the sixteenth century. This was one great result—a result undoubtedly not contemplated by the founder of the Order—of the injunction laid upon every Franciscan to devote himself to those who were under the ban and scourge of leprosy ; and it affords a striking example of the necessary antagonism between the scientific and theological spirit. Here was a religious corporation, established for purposes purely spiritual, but whose members in the course of carrying out those purposes, were compelled to observe facts, to devise remedies, to adopt methods which were not the methods of the schools, and to breathe an atmosphere infected, indeed, with physical disease, but intellectually purer than that of the University, because more free from the taint of authority. The traditions of the Church, and the assertions of Aristotle, were alike useless in the sphere in which the Franciscan habitually worked ; he could not cure a man of leprosy by quoting the " Organon," or referring him to the Latin fathers. He therefore came to see that, side by side with these authorities, which even the most hardy thinkers of that age were not prepared altogether to reject, there was a wisdom, as Bacon himself says, " exterius expectata,"—without, if not above, and won by observation and experiment.

The foundations of independent inquiry being thus laid on physical studies, it accords with all we know of the history of the human mind, that it should seek to extend its newborn freedom. Now, to the English Franciscans of the thirteenth century, two fields lay open into which they were not slow to carry the standard of revolt. Innocent III. and his successor, Gregory IX., adopted a tolerably uniform line of conduct towards England. They treated its people as vassals of the Apostolic See, its clergy as the *locum tenentes* of the Italian priesthood, and the country itself as a tributary province, belonging as of right to the Roman Church. "Surely," writes Gregory to the Archbishop of Canterbury, "the English people cannot complain if foreigners living among them should attain to wealth and place, since God is no respecter of persons." What was complained of was not so much that alien residents should be promoted, as that strangers should spend in luxury at Rome the emoluments of offices whose duties they neither pretended nor were able to fulfil. The insolent denunciation of the Great Charter by Innocent, and the demand of Honorius that two prebends in every cathedral and conventual church should be assigned in perpetuity to Rome, may be taken as examples, and not the worst examples, of a policy which caused such universal indignation, that Matthew Paris began to fear "ne immineret generalis discessio"—in plain English, lest the nation should anticipate by three centuries the date of its separation from the Papal See.

The men who most vigorously protested against this policy were found almost exclusively in the ranks of the Minors. Nor was this all. Speaking generally, the Franciscans exhibited a far greater independence in dealing with philosophical and religious problems, than the Dominicans. The Minorites were, in the Church, the stronghold of Averroism—that is to say, of that party which maintained the theory of Aristotle, pure and simple, against those who sought to reconcile the forms of the peripatetic doctrine with the spirit of Christian theology. The position of the Franciscans among the religious parties of the thirteenth century, is analogous to that of those who, in our own day, accept the conclusions of natural science without reference to the question how far those conclusions are logically reconcilable with their other opinions. What geology and history are now, that was Aristotle then. It would have been as shocking to Albertus or to Aquinas to have been compelled to admit a radical discrepancy between the third book of the *De Anima*, or the eleventh book of the " Metaphysics," and the " Epistles of St. Paul," as to an English bishop to be obliged to reject the Mosaic cosmogony or the account of the Noachian deluge. Now Averroes, who may be considered as the representative of the Arabian teaching, brought into strong relief the differences which the orthodox party were anxious to conceal. Take, for example, the theory of individuation—the explanation of the process of thought in a given person. The Aristotelian doctrine amounts to this:—Just as to all existence the concurrence of two elements—matter and form—is necessary ; so we find that the fact of knowledge implies two principles—an active principle, which gives *form* to our thought ; and a passive one, which affords the *material* of it. And while the passive material element differs in different individuals and is transitory, the active formal element is eternal, and constitutes an universal intelligence, a central mind, by participation in which we have our rational being. It is obvious that this theory, implicitly at least, denies the immortality of the soul ; for that alone which does not die is, according to it, the universal intelligence ; and it is equally obvious that it tends to lower the power of the human will, since it considers man as a mere element in the cosmical order. It was in this light that the Arabian commentators interpreted the doctrine of Aristotle—it was against this interpretation that St. Thomas employed all the resources of his somewhat heavy dialectics. It is clear, however, from the manner in which the angelic doctor conducts his attack, that his real adversaries are not so much the Arabians, or the

Greeks, as a school of contemporary philosophers, who disguised a more than suspected orthodoxy under the names of Averroes and Aristotle.

Who were these men ? It is not difficult to guess. Those who theorize on the constitution of the universe and of the human mind invariably give prominence to one of two kinds of explanation; resting either on the doctrine of law, of necessity, of the relative nature of the intelligence, or on the doctrine of a personal God with determinate attributes, and of an absolute self-existent soul. Knowing the philosophical rivalry which existed on these questions between the friars Preachers and Minors, and knowing how strongly the Dominican doctrine, as set forth by Aquinas, inclined to absolutism, we should have little difficulty in determining *à priori* the general tendency of the Franciscan teaching. But we are not left entirely to an inference of this kind. Bacon tells us that he had twice heard William of Auvergne maintain, at Paris, the doctrine of the active intellect; and not only does he give-in his own formal adherence to the theory, but his works abound with references to Avicenna and Averroes, and with general commendations of the teaching of the Arabian school. It must be remembered what this implies. Although the name of Averroes was not, as yet, the symbol of incredulity which it became in the fourteenth century, it was still associated with an essentially anti-Christian belief. If the Mussulman doctor was not credited with the authorship of that imaginary book, the "Three Impostors," at any rate he was denounced as the chief of the Materialists. To profess the Averroistic doctrine was then as great an offence against strict Catholic orthodoxy, as it is now to accept M. Rénan's views of the life and character of Jesus Christ. Yet neither William of Auvergne nor Bacon hesitated to give to that doctrine a general support, and in particular to endorse an opinion which St. Thomas wondered that any one calling himself a Christian could hold.

For these reasons, we are not without warrant in saying that in the thirteenth century the Franciscans were the representatives of the freest speculation, and the most liberal politics that were to be found within the Church; and therefore, notwithstanding the wide differences which separated Bacon from the boldest of his order, there are sufficient reasons why so uncompromising a thinker, if compelled to make his election, should have chosen the Franciscan in preference to the Dominican body. His subsequent history proves that he little foresaw the consequences of the step.

After having spent some seven or eight years at Paris, where, as we have seen, he became a friar and took his doctor's degree, Bacon returned to his old home at Oxford. Wood tells us that

his University readily confirmed the distinctions bestowed upon him in France. This is very likely; but we have no means of knowing whether it was so or not. To say the truth, our knowledge of this part of Bacon's history consists of a series of guesses, bounded by two tolerably well-ascertained facts. We know that he left Paris for England in 1250, or shortly after; we know that he must have returned again to France about 1257, as he says, writing in 1267, that he had been ten years in exile. But of what took place in this interval of seven years, which he spent in Oxford, we know nothing certainly. We may conjecture that during the first three or four years he was free to indulge in his favourite pursuits; that he accordingly employed himself in physical research and experiment—that he became acquainted with Thomas Bungey, whose name is so closely associated with his own in legend, and that together with Bungey he matured the views afterwards set forth in the "Opus Majus," some twelve years later. It is, moreover, probable that his devotion to sciences which were little understood, gave an opportunity to those who suspected his orthodoxy, and disliked his liberalism, of preferring against him the charge, so dangerous in those days, of magic; that during the lifetime of his friend Grostête, whose influence at Oxford was deservedly great, no immediate measures were taken against him; but that on the death of Grostête in 1253, and the election of St. Bonaventura to the generalship of the Franciscans, two years later, his superiors placed him under restraint, and that the remaining years which he spent at Oxford before his next visit to Paris (1255-7) were passed in confinement more or less strict, from which he was not completely freed till 1267.

Had Bacon been imbued with the true feeling of Monasticism, he would have taken this punishment very contentedly: he might have spent the fourteen years during which he was forbidden to write, in illuminating a missal: he might have expiated, by fasts and vigils, the fault of differing from the church on the theory of the active intellect. By a sufficiently severe self-discipline, he might even have brought himself to accept the claims of authority as a ground of scientific belief: as it was, his enforced silence only soured his temper, and exaggerated his confidence in his own opinions. He believed that he held the key to a storehouse of invaluable truth : he was burning with impatience to open these treasures to the world. The sentence which condemned him to inaction was particularly galling to a man of his disposition and acquirements, and the language in which he refers to it in his letter to Clement shows how heavily it weighed upon him. But, though we may pity Bacon, we must be just to his superiors. Now it does not appear that they did more than enforce as against him the rules to which he had deliberately subjected himself, and to which every Franciscan stood pledged. Their views were narrower than his, but then his were greatly in advance of the age. No one can fairly be blamed for not seeing farther than his contemporaries, or for not acting as the majority of enlightened men about him would have acted. Bacon preached a philosophy of which not half-a-dozen men in Europe saw the value, and of which the majority of really good men feared the results. He was accordingly punished (by no undue straining of the law), and only suffered as everyone suffers whose misfortune it is to be unable to agree with his neighbours on important and difficult subjects. M. Charles seems to lose sight of this, when he denounces the treatment of Bacon as iniquitous, and blames St. Bonaventura for having sanctioned it. The General of the Franciscans acted according to his lights. He was, constitutionally and by education, very little fitted to sympathize with Bacon's habit of thought. We have no reason to impugn his motives; all that we can say against him is, that he was intellectually inferior to the man he had to rule, and that he had not learned the lesson of tolerance, which Cardinals and Bishops in our own day have equally failed to understand.

In 1257, Bacon was compelled to return to Paris. This was, perhaps, not the least part of his punishment. We know that he had little in common with the spirit which prevailed there. At Oxford, on the contrary, something of the influence of its late Chancellor had entered into the teaching of the University; and, intellectual sympathy apart, Bacon must have felt freer and more at home in England than in France.

He had been in Paris about eight years when an event occurred which seemed to open out to him a brighter prospect. This was the elevation of Guy de Foulques to the Papal chair. The new pope, who assumed the title of Clement IV., was already acquainted with Bacon. While Bishop of Sabina, the philosopher's name had been favourably mentioned to him by one Raymond of Laon, and the curiosity of the Cardinal Bishop seems to have been roused by the account given him of Bacon's investigations and discoveries. He even went so far as to request Bacon to send him some of his writings for perusal. This took place between 1260 and 1264. We may gather that Bacon was not permitted to reply to this communication—at all events, before he replied to it, the Bishop of Sabina became Pope. On this, Bacon despatched a messenger named Bonecor, to explain the reason of his delay, and to inform Clement that his position as a Franciscan had made it impossible for him to comply with the request which had been previously preferred by his Holiness, without an express dispensation to that effect. This dispensation Clement sent in the second year of his pontificate, by Raymond of Laon, commanding Bacon, on his apostolical authority, notwithstanding any rule of his order or prohibition of his superiors, to transmit to him, secretly and without delay, the work which had been the subject of their correspondence.*

Bacon was beyond measure delighted at this request. He saw in it the realization of his most earnest wishes. The philosophy of which he was the apostle particularly demanded the encouragement of the great; wealthy patronage — intelligent support—these were the aids without which his reform could not possibly be carried out. Not to mention ordinary expenses, there were instruments to be made, observations to be recorded, a staff of trained assistants to be created. He had himself spent two thousand French pounds already, and the most valuable results were still behind. It was idle to expect the general public to take any interest in the matter; but could he fairly enlist the Pope in his cause, he might count not only on material assistance, but on the more valuable aid which would be given by the sympathy of the acknowledged head of European opinion.

Full of these hopes, he at once set to work on the "Opus Majus." Clement's letter is dated in the July of the second year of his pontificate, that is in 1266. The "Opus Majus" was written, finished, and despatched in the course of 1267. We learn from the "Opus Tertium," that no part of it had been composed before the receipt of Clement's letter.

"When I was in another state of life," says Bacon, "I had written nothing on philosophy, and since I became a friar I have not been required to do so by my superiors. The contrary, indeed, has been expressly enjoined, on pain of forfeiting the book, and many days' fasting on bread and water, if I should communicate to others anything written within the cloister walls.† And certainly had I been able to

---

* The following is the text of Clement's letter, printed by Mr. Brewer from Martene. Dr. Jebb, in his Preface, substitutes "esse" for "occasione" at the end, and this at all events makes sense.

"Dilecto filio, Fratri Rogerio dicto Bacon, ordinis Fratrum Minorum.

"Tuæ devotionis litteras gratanter recepimus: sed et verba notavimus diligenter quæ ad explanationem earum dilectus filius G. dictus Bonecor, Miles, vivâ voce nobis proposuit tam fideliter quam prudenter.

"Sane ut melius nobis liqueat quid intendas, volumus et tibi per apostolica scripta præcipiendo mandamus, quatenus non obstante præcepto Prælati cujuscunque contrario vel tui ordinis constitutione, quacunque, opus illud, quod te dilecto filio Raymundo de Landuno communicare rogavimus in minori officio constituti scriptum de bona littera nobis mittere quam citius poteris non omittas; et per tuas nobis declares litteras quæ tibi videntur adhibenda remedia circa illa quæ nuper occasione tanti discriminis intimasti. Et hoc quanto secretius poteris facias indilate.

"Dabam Viterbii, x. Cal. Julii, anno ii."

† "Si aliquod scriptum factum apud nos aliis communicetur." Mr. Brewer translates these words:—"If any work written by me or belonging to my

have communicated freely what I wrote, I should have composed much for my brother the scholar, and other dear friends of mine. But since I had no hope of making anything known, I neglected to write. Hence, when I represented myself to your Holiness as being ready, be assured I referred to works to be written, not to works already written. Therefore, Raymond of Laon, your clerk, was altogether mistaken in the mention he made of me."

Having sent the "Opus Majus" by a messenger to the Pope, Bacon began to consider the risk which his treatise ran of being lost by the way, and the probability that his correspondent might be too much engrossed to read so lengthy a letter. He also recollected some statements inadvertently made, and some explanations which he thought might be useful. Accordingly in the same year (1267), he proceeded to compose an introductory treatise — the "Opus Minus;" and not content with this, he added a third work, usually known as the "Opus Tertium," in which there were further additions and explanations. These three works, the matter of which would occupy at least one thousand pages of this review, were composed, fair-copied, and sent to Rome within eighteen months of the first commencement of the undertaking.

This must be regarded as a remarkable literary feat. The "Opus Majus" is not only highly original in its general conception and plan, it is an encyclopædia of mediæval science, full of curious research and ingenious experiment. Its style is more lively and sustained than that of any contemporary author. It is enriched with quotations from Cicero, Pliny, Seneca, and the Latin poets—now and then a phrase of Livy, or a line of Juvenal, is incorporated into the text. In point of literary merit, we cannot pay it a higher compliment than in saying that it invites criticism. As for the "Compendia" and "Summulæ," of the Dominican doctors, one would as soon think of criticizing them as of objecting to the style of "Euclid's Elements."

---

house should be communicated to strangers." He adds the following note : "By the classical words *apud nos* Bacon does not mean that the prohibition was exclusively directed against himself, but that it was a rule of his order that no friar should be permitted the use of writing materials or enjoy the liberty of publishing, without leave first had from his superiors." We are unable to agree either with Mr. Brewer's rendering or his explanation. *Scribere apud aliquem* is very good Latin for " to write at a man's house ;" *scriptum factum apud nos* is, " a work composed in our house :" that is, in the Franciscan convent in Paris, and certainly not "a work written *by me or belonging to my house.*" Bacon was not an elegant Latin writer, but he knew better than to say *apud nos*, either for " by me" or for " belonging to my house." Why Mr. Brewer should go out of his way to impute to him this double barbarism, we cannot tell, especially as his words give a much better meaning when interpreted in their usual sense.

This work is divided into seven parts.* It opens with an introduction, which describes in detail the causes which delay the progress of true knowledge. These are four in number:— (1.) The influence of authority. (2.) The force of custom. (3.) The ignorance of the vulgar. (4.) The pride of false and seeming knowledge. The three first Bacon considers together, and in the first place; the fourth is important and deadly enough to require separate treatment.†

The second part consists of an Essay, addressed to the proof of the proposition, that all wisdom is implicitly contained in the Holy Scriptures, but that it can only be evolved therefrom by the aid of the Canon Law and philosophy. In the discussion of this subject Aristotle is made to play a very important part. Indeed, Bacon does not hesitate to affirm that, in common with Pythagoras, Socrates, and Plato, he was a specially inspired authority. The Dominican doctrine of the active intellect, the same, it will be remembered, which Aquinas opposed to the theory of Averroes, is vigorously criticized, and shown to be inconsistent with the idea of all human wisdom existing as a direct revelation from God. Having pointed out, in this manner, the source of knowledge, and the instruments by which alone it can be obtained, and so harmonized, after a fashion, the rival claims of philosophy and faith, Bacon next turns to grammar and language, studies necessary to the understanding of the sacred and philosophical writings. His remarks on this subject are especially interesting. He first observes that languages are connected with one another, and that it is necessary to know several before we can fully understand any. He justifies the study of philology by the joint authority of the Latin poets and the saints, especially St. Jerome, whose enthusiasm was so great that he filed his teeth, in order that he might give the proper breathing to certain Oriental words.‡

Next follows a plea for a critical revision of the text of the Bible. The Paris Vulgate is declared to be so hopelessly corrupt, especially in its figures, that no educated man can conscientiously read it or preach from it. But this is not the worst. Bacon complains that the clergy, both regular and secular, have taken upon themselves to make corrections at their pleasure. With so much effect have they exercised their powers of emendation, that they have succeeded in outdoing the blunders of the Paris copy itself. " Clamo ad Deum et ad vos," he says, " de ista corruptione

---

* The 7th part, " On Moral Philosophy," is not printed in Jebb's edition, but it certainly forms part of the " Opus Majus."

† " Separavi hanc ab illis propter malitiam principalem. Hæc enim est singularis fera quæ depascit et destruit omnem rationem."—Op. Maj. c. 9.

‡ " Dentes suos aptari fecit ut anhelantia verba formaret."

litteræ.". In the thirteenth century this appeal for a critical revision is not a little noticeable, and it marks a turn of mind quite peculiar to Bacon, and which was no doubt owing to his habits of accurate scientific research.

A long treatise on grammar may seem somewhat out of place in a strictly scientific treatise ; but it should be remembered that it was not merely as models of literary style that Bacon wished the ancient masters of philosophy and eloquence to be studied. He considered that their writings contained many facts highly necessary for the observer and experimentalist. Notwithstanding his antipathy to authority, he does not hesitate to accept facts on the authority of authors of established reputation.* The effects of this inconsistency will hereafter appear.

The fourth part of the " Opus Majus" is devoted to mathematics. Considerable acuteness is shown in describing the relation of this study to the other natural sciences. Bacon explicitly declares, not only that a familiarity with mathematics is necessary for the purposes of experiment, but that it is necessary as a *preliminary* for such purposes—that other branches of knowledge are grounded in numbers, and that an acquaintance with numbers must precede their rational study. These canons are applied at great length to celestial and terrestrial physics, and also, it must be confessed, to some physiological and metaphysical questions, with which mathematics have very little to do.

Bacon tells us in the " Opus Minus," that the fifth part of his greater work—the " Treatise on Perspective"—was, in his opinion, one of the most valuable portions of the whole.† In this judgment we are not easily induced to agree. The " De Perspectiva" is very long, and somewhat encumbered with scholastic distinctions and divisions. It describes, in the first place, the instruments of sight, *i.e.*, those parts of the brain which are concerned in vision ; the optic nerve and the anatomy of the eye ; the nature of the medium through which light is transmitted, and some of the qualities of visible objects are next considered ; then we have an analysis of what are called modes of vision—in fact, a description of the different lines which rays take in passing through media of varying density. The arrangement is not unscientific ; several facts are recorded which prove accurate and original observation, but there is also a great deal of error which the slightest observation would have corrected. Bacon trusted rather too much to his " solid and true authorities."

In the sixth and last division of the " Opus Majus" Bacon enlarges on the dignity and importance of experimental science,

---

* " Sed quamvis auctoritas sit unum de istis (sc. impedimentis sapientiæ) nulla ratione loquor de solida et vera auctoritate."—Op. Maj. c. 1.

† " Æstimo multum de prima parte et totum quod est in quinta parte." Op. Min. p. 316. (Edit. Brew.)

"the mistress and ruler of all."[*] He accurately distinguishes observation from experiment, and points out the greater certainty of the conclusions arrived at by that means than by a merely ratiocinative process. The latter, he pithily remarks, terminates the discussion, the former settles the fact. Instances are given of the errors which have arisen from the unfortunate habit of trusting to report rather than to experience : for example, there is the common belief that adamant can only be split by goat's blood, that hot water freezes sooner than cold, and many others. Nothing can be more admirable than the first twelve chapters of this Essay ; but presently Bacon betakes himself to his " solid authorities," to Pliny, to Solinus, to Avicenna, to Basilius, Ambrosius, and the poets. Then we get the story of a man who lived several centuries by smearing himself with some ointment which he found in a jar, and who carried about with him a letter from the Pope to certify the truth of his statement ; and the story of the kingfishers, who are able to quell the winter storms till such time as they have laid their eggs and their young are fledged. Bacon hopefully conjectures that these facts will be of great service in converting infidels who deny the truths of faith because they are not able to understand them.

It will be seen from this rapid sketch, that the " Opus Majus" is written on a plan conspicuously different from that of the commentaries and compendia most in vogue, and that it differs from them not more in the form in which it is cast than in the object kept in view. It must, nevertheless, be confessed that its value lies rather in the spirit in which it is written than in the facts it records, or in any merit which it may have as a scientific whole. The state of knowledge in Bacon's time was not such as to enable even the most far-seeing man to carry out the object proposed—that of methodizing and relating the various branches of human learning. So far as the " Opus Majus" aims at classifying the sciences, proceeding, as it did, on a misapprehension inevitable at the time, it produced and could produce no useful effect ; but before any true philosophy could expand itself there was a false philosophy to be cleared away. "There are three very bad arguments which are perpetually in use : this has been shown to be so ; this is customary ; this is universal—therefore we must hold to it."[†] This was the real incubus which weighed down the finest and most subtle intellects of the middle ages, and it is Bacon's especial merit to have laid his hand on the root of

---

[*] Nam hæc se habet ad alias, sicut navigatoria ad carpentariam, et sicut ars militaris ad fabrilem, hæc enim præcipit ut fiant instrumenta mirabilia et factis utitur, et etiam cogitat omnia secreta propter utilitates reipublicæ et personarum, *et imperat aliis scientiis, sicut ancillis suis.*"—Opus Majus, ad fin.

[†] "Semper utimur tribus pessimis argumentis : scilicet, hoc exemplificatum est ; hoc consuetum est ; hoc vulgatum est—ergo tenendum."—Opus Majus, c. i.

the evil, and to have been constant in his efforts to eradicate it. Though containing many striking passages and many remarkable anticipations, it is, we think, as a propaideutic work that the "Opus Majus" best justifies its name.

It is not known what Clement thought of the triple reply which his letter called forth. No allusion to the subject is to be found either in his own lengthy correspondence, or in Bacon's works. It would seem, however, that the Pope sufficiently appreciated Bacon's labours to procure for him a remission of his sentence of exile, and of the strict surveillance to which he was subjected, and that the philosopher was permitted to return to his own country and university. Internal evidence suggests that the latter part at least of the "Opus Tertium" was written at Oxford. And Bacon distinctly says, in that work, that the restrictions which had formerly interfered with his writing had been removed, "whereby," he adds, "I have been able to add certain necessary matters which I could not put down before."

The whole of this transaction is highly creditable to Clement. Not many men of his time placed in his position would have cared to demand of a simple friar his plan of reform ; fewer still would have rewarded a work conceived in the spirit of the "Opus Majus" with a token of approbation even so slight as the remission of an ecclesiastical sentence. While therefore we may regret, with Mr. Brewer, that Clement did no more, we ought, in reason, to be grateful to him for having done so much.

In 1268, shortly after Bacon had returned to Oxford, Clement died. The accession of Gregory X. after an interval of three years of intrigue and confusion, destroyed any chance of protection or countenance from the head of Christendom for the new philosophy. Nor was the state of things at home or abroad calculated to inspire hope of the co-operation of men in place and power, in a scheme of intellectual reform. The long contest between Henry III. and the popular party had lately turned in favour of the king by the death of de Montfort at Evesham three years before. But the dispossessed nobles were maintaining a guerilla warfare throughout the length of the country : at Chesterfield, at Kenilworth, in the Isle of Ely, at London, the king's troops were held in check. When at last, through the energy and good fortune of Prince Edward, the leaders of the insurrection had been finally driven from these strongholds, it was just a question whether the objects for which they had so long contended had not been surrendered also. In the midst of this confusion Prince Edward sets out on the Crusade, and while he is abroad, no one knowing whether he was alive or dead, the king dies.

It was at this critical time—in 1272—that Bacon wrote his fourth work—the "Compendium Studii Philosophiæ." The confusion and misery around are accurately reflected from its pages. The treatise is designed to show the necessity of wisdom—the means by which it may be acquired, and the impediments to its acquisition. It is the last head, however, which chiefly occupies the author. The following passages seem to point directly to the state of England during the concluding years of Henry's reign :—

"The princes, barons, and soldiers mutually oppress and spoil one another, and ruin those who are below them by wars and exactions without end. . . . . No one cares what is done or how, whether justly or unjustly, if only he can work his will; they are slaves withal to luxury and the pleasures of the palate, and to other deadly sins. The people thoroughly incensed by its rulers hates them, and therefore keeps no faith with them if it can be avoided. As to traders and artificers, there is no question of them, for in everything they say and do, boundless fraud, cheating, and lying prevails."

The same desponding tone is preserved throughout. The four great impediments on which he enlarges in the "Opus Majus"—authority, custom, popular opinion, and the pride of knowledge—are referred to, but the corruption of the times is made the first and principal count of the indictment. The picture he draws is sufficiently gloomy :—

"Let us diligently consider," he says, "every state of society, and we shall find infinite corruption everywhere, which first of all shows in the head. The Court of Rome is torn in pieces by deceit and fraud; justice is no more; all peace is broken in upon; the scandals which arise are infinite. As a consequence, morals are perverted, and pride reigns supreme; avarice is rampant, envy eats into the heart of individual men, while all are ruled by the pleasures of the palate, and luxury depraves the whole of that Court. Nor is this enough. A Vicar of God is denied us through the negligence of his church, and the world is left without a ruler, as has lately been the case for several years, owing to the envy and desire of honour which rule the Court of Rome."

On the state of the clergy he is equally explicit— ·

"Let us consider the religious bodies; I exclude no order. Let us see how far each one has fallen from his proper state, and how the new orders have already lapsed terribly from their former dignity. The whole body of clergy gives itself up to pride, luxury, and avarice. Wherever the clerks are collected in any number, as at Paris and Oxford, they scandalize the whole lay body by their brawls and disturbances and other vices."

These extracts show the profound impression which the state of Europe and England produced upon Bacon's mind. They also indicate pretty clearly the deadening influence of cloister-life even upon a thinker as original as he. Nowhere does he betray the slightest thought or care for the great political revolution which was being enacted before his eyes. It is solely in its reference to the welfare of his philosophy that he deplores the anarchy which he describes. The wars of Henry and de Montfort are an " impediment to knowledge." The crusade in which Louis of France and Prince Edward were engaged, is an ineffectual means of advancing the works of wisdom. Bacon does not so severely confine himself to the subject in hand as to prevent his remarking on some of the other bearings of these events, if it had occurred to him to do so. It is evident that he had no thought for them. He considered reform in speculation to be the determinant of all practical improvements. " If men are corrupt in their studies, they will be corrupt in their lives." " Such as a man shows himself in the study of wisdom, so he must always be in life." Hence, his one, sole, all-including object was the proper direction of studies ; speculative reform being the necessary preliminary of practical improvement.

The gloomy anticipations with which the "Compendium Studii" was written were shortly afterwards realized with respect to himself. In 1274, two years after the appearance of that work, Jerome of Ascoli succeeded to the generalship of the Franciscans, on the death of St. Bonaventura. The leaders of the Church party felt strongly that repressive measures should be taken to check the growing spirit of liberty. They could not see why men should want to know anything which Aquinas did not know, or why they should not accept, as their fathers had done, the "Book of Sentences" as a rule and code of faith. Accordingly, in 1277, the Bishop of Paris, one Stephen Tempier, convened a synod, at which more than two hundred philosophical propositions were formally condemned. In the succeeding year, the Dominican Chapter held at Milan decreed severe punishments to those brothers who presumed to differ from the doctrine of St. Thomas. The Franciscan General was determined not to be outdone by his Dominican rivals in vigour of action. He assembled his own order at Paris in the same year as that in which the Synod of Milan was held ; and brought Bacon before them, charged with entertaining new and dangerous views—" propter quasdam novitates suspectas." Neither his age, nor his learning, nor his undoubted fidelity to the Papal See, protected him—his doctrine was formally condemned, and he himself thrown into prison.

In prison he remained for fourteen years, to the great comfort of the religious world. At last, in 1292, he was released by the authority of a Chapter General of his order held at Paris, under the presidency of the humane Ganfredi. He was in his seventy-eighth year. One would think he had had enough of writing. However, with an energy and determination which nothing could subdue, he immediately made use of his freedom to compose a fifth and last work—the " Compendium Studii Theologiæ." This treatise adds little that is new either to Bacon's doctrine or his method : it is a commentary on the old text—a dying lament on the causes of human ignorance, the neglect of useful knowledge, and the unreasoning obedience to authority.

After this we know nothing authentic of Bacon. The time, place, and manner of his death are nowhere mentioned. Tradition only relates that he died at Oxford, and that he was buried within the walls of the Franciscan cloister at St. Ebbes.

It is unfortunate that Bacon's printed works afford such slender materials for a judgment on his personal character. A man so original in speculation must have had many curious points of contrast with ordinary Englishmen, in his habits and in his every-day mode of regarding various current events. But we are not able to fill-in those little touches which complete the character of the man. It is solely as a thinker that he exhibits himself to us. No writer with whom we are acquainted is so carefully reticent as regards his actions and feelings in all things which lie outside his philosophy. When he warms into gratitude, it is to Clement, for having deigned to notice his scientific labours ; when he breaks out, as is too frequently the case, into a torrent of bitter invective, it is against ignorant grammarians, like Hugutio, Brito, and Papias, or against the leaders of the two new orders, or against the administrative abuses which rob the Church of its head and Science of its legitimate support. We have already remarked how curiously inobservant he seems to have been of political and social changes. To merely human interests—those which concern the sentient and suffering man—he was, to all appearance, more indifferent still ; at least, we cannot recal a single passage which reveals a fellow feeling with the hopes and fears, the joys and griefs, which make up so large a part of actual existence. It is not because of their irrelevancy to the object of his writings that such subjects are avoided. The truth of the matter is this : Bacon cared very little about the human race as such, or about anything which did not directly bear upon his philosophical system. His whole nature was absorbed in speculation. He himself made considerable sacrifices to science, and he was prepared to sacrifice in its cause the interests of any other person or class whatever. The poor and ignorant—those for whom his vows as a Franciscan especially bound him to care—were precisely those with whom, as a thinker, he was least concerned. When it became a question between St. Francis on one side and Aristotle or Averroes on the other, Bacon had not much doubt which side to take.

A man of this temper may command our respect, but must fail to draw us to him by any closer feeling. To say the truth, the impression left by a perusal of Bacon's writings is not favourable to him as a man. He is somewhat arrogant ; he is intensely self-confident ; he is apt to assume motives ; he is frequently hasty in his judgments and unnecessarily severe in his criticisms. Above all, he is infected with a bitter class spirit. His contempt and aversion for those who are not members of his own intellectual aristocracy are boundless : in his eyes, the people which knoweth not the law is cursed indeed.

But whatever may be thought of Bacon in a moral point of view, there can be no doubt of his intellectual power. In what proportion truth and error are mingled in his doctrine is another matter. The consideration of this question demands a more detailed examination of his philosophical writings than our present limits allow. We shall hereafter return to the subject, and attempt to trace the outlines of Bacon's system in connexion with the physical philosophy of the thirteenth century.

Art. II.—The Tunnel under Mont Cénis.

1. *Senato del Regno. Rapport du Bureau Central, composé de Messieurs les Senateurs de Brignole-Sala, Plana, Mosca, De la Marmora, et Jacquemoud, sur le Projet de Loi pour la percée du Mont Cénis, et l'Approbation du nouveau Cahier de Charges de la Compagnie Victor Emmanuel.* Turin : 1859.

2. *Discorso del Ministro dei Lavori Pubblici, Conte Menabrea, pronunziato alla Camera dei Deputati nella tornata del 4 Marzo, 1863, sul Traforo del Montcenisio.* Torino : 1863.

3. *Traforo delle Alpi tra Bardonnèche e Modane : Relazione della Direzione Tecnica alla Direzione Generale delle Strade Ferrate dello Stato.* Torino : 1863.

FANCIFUL speculators have often amused themselves with the question, What would remain of London were it abandoned for two or three thousand years, like the cities of Assyria? Lord Macaulay figured to himself a New Zealander musing over a vast heap of bricks at some period in the far future, but perhaps by the time A.D. 4000 or 5000 had arrived, even bricks might have disappeared, and nothing be left but a gigantic mound of dust, which the one near Euston-square, lately sold for a vast sum, may represent to our fancy, in spite of its diminutive scale. This image is certainly not calculated to give us a grand idea of the nineteenth century, especially if we compare it with the splendid ruins which still attest the power of Nineveh and Rome. But a little reflection may perhaps help us to salve over the wound to our vanity. The remains of bygone days are the memorials of individuals ; the palaces of old recall the name of some dead tyrant, and even the most useful works of antiquity—the Roman aqueducts—were but the presents of emperors to their subjects ; whereas now the object for which we labour has been displaced, and the advantage of millions, instead of the gratification of units, is the aim we strive after. If our cities are no longer adorned with buildings of a material and massiveness calculated to resist the assault of ages, it is not that our engineers are incapable of producing works worthy to excite the admiration of posterity. We no longer, indeed, build pyramids to shroud the bones of some dead Rameses, or erect a cathedral like that of Glasgow to the memory of an obscure St. Mungo ; but in this very island we have spanned arms of the sea with railway bridges under which the largest line-of-battle ship can pass, all sails set ; our nearest neighbours are toiling, despite a short-sighted and ungenerous opposition, to open a canal between the Mediterranean and Red Sea, while another scion of the Latin race is working equally hard to pierce the natural barrier of the Alps, and put their railway system in direct communication with that of the rest of Europe. To the present generation the Menai tubular bridge is a nine days' wonder ; the Suez canal has been discussed until the subject has been worn threadbare, and must now be left to the practical test of success ; but the third great engineering work of the day is almost unknown in England, at least in its details, and we therefore propose to devote some pages to an account of this marvellous tunnel—marvellous, not so much from its great length, though that will be between seven and eight miles (12,220 mètres), as from the scientific interest attached to the employment of natural forces not hitherto utilized.

At the late meeting of the British Association at Newcastle, Sir William Armstrong startled, and probably alarmed, many of his hearers by imparting his opinion that the seams of coal in these islands would be exhausted in little more than two centuries. Posterity will have to judge of the accuracy of this calculation. It may perhaps be found that as coal becomes dearer by the working out of the upper veins, it will be profitable to sink the shafts down to the lower ones, now left untouched because the market price is not such as to cover the expense to be incurred, and a supply be thus obtained for a considerably longer period. Be this as it may, however, there can be no doubt that we are now expending coal at a rate far more rapid than that at which it was formed by the decay of primeval vegetation ; and it would therefore be a discovery of no small benefit to our race were it possible to find some power capable of setting all our manufacturing machinery in action, other than steam, to generate which in sufficient quantities so vast an amount of coal is daily consumed ; and the advantage would be all the greater if the new force we desiderate could be one sure not to be exhausted so long as the physical conditions of our globe remain unchanged, or indeed fit for the habitation of such creatures as ourselves. The only two forces of which this can be predicated with any safety are *air* and *water*, and the use that may be made of them is the great lesson to be learnt from a consideration of the tunnel under Mont Cénis.

Scarcely had the importance about to be assumed by the railway system of Europe been acknowledged, than a tunnel under the Alps became the dream of engineers, especially those of Italy. It is indeed evident, that even supposing the Peninsula suddenly endowed with a railway net as complete as that which intersects the manufacturing districts of the West Riding or Lancashire, Italy must be cut off from the great flow of transit and traffic so long as no direct communication exists between her railway system and that of other nations. The difficulty of creating one was, however, enormous, and the Alps presented an obstacle as difficult to turn as to overcome. Apart from all engineering impediments, the Corniche line implied so great a circuit, that the railroad journey from Paris to the Valley of the Po by this route would have cost more in time and money than the twelve or fourteen hours' passage over Mont Cénis in a carriage ; and the same might be said of the circuit round the upper end of the Adriatic, without adding that the problem would not have been in any degree solved even thus, before the construction of the remarkable ascending lines over the Bocchetta Pass and the Simmering. Nor when these were made, did the question seem nearer to a real solution. The Alps were too high to be crossed by this system, even had the snow which covers them for half the year not opposed an invincible obstacle, and the same double objection presented itself to the construction of a tunnel on any method hitherto employed, for shafts could not be thought of, and yet no tunnel of even a quarter the length had hitherto been considered possible without them. Nevertheless, as a tunnel seemed the only resource, engineers continued to devise schemes for piercing it, more or less impracticable, very much like those we periodically hear of for bridging over or boring under the Channel.

To add to the difficulty, it so happened that Mont Cénis, the shortest and most frequented of the Alpine passes, the one by which it was soonest possible to reach the plain and the railway system on either side, and which the genius of Napoleon had marked out as the true line of communication between France and

Italy, was in the hands of a third-rate State, counting scarcely five millions of inhabitants. Fortunately, however, though the kingdom was small, its destinies were directed by the greatest statesman of our day—one whose eagle glance took in far more than the interests of the moment, and who, foreseeing the time when Piedmont would be Italy, was steadily bent on preparing her to play the part of a great Power. As it happened, also, the Minister was not only a skilful politician, but he had received an admirable scientific education, and when three engineers, whose names deserve to be chronicled for all ages, MM. Grandis, Grattoni, and Sommeiller, supported by the authority of M. Ranco, whose views gained weight from the distinguished part he had taken in the construction of the Genoa and Turin Railway, presented their invention to him, Count de Cavour did not turn away with disdain, because no tunnel had ever before been pierced by machines impelled by compressed air * produced by the action of water, but rather saw in the novelty of the idea a ground for hoping that difficulties insuperable by any means usually practised would thus be overcome. To the above-mentioned four engineers, in the first instance, and secondly, but no less perhaps, to Count de Cavour and his two illustrious friends and colleagues M. Paleocapa and General de Menabrea, who concurred and sympathized in his opinion of the feasibility of the scheme, will the world owe lasting gratitude for breaking down the barrier of the Alps, and still more for introducing a new motive power into mechanics.

The whole scheme was so new, that the first thing to be done was to test the models of the proposed machines. A Commission of five persons was therefore appointed by the Piedmontese Government to try a series of experiments, to prove the possibility of compressing air by water-power, and then conveying it to a distant spot there to put a perforating machine in motion, and also to determine whether so long a tunnel without shafts could be ventilated.

The report of this Commission was so favourable as fully to answer to the farsighted anticipations of the Minister. Much doubtless remained to be done, for the machines tested were mere models, requiring to be greatly modified and increased in size before they could be used on a large scale; still the principle was so well established, and the whole scheme appeared so far superior to any other that either had been, or was likely to be presented, that the commissioners did not hesitate to recommend its immediate adoption. At the same time a favourable conjuncture presented

---

* An Englishman, Mr. Bartlett, had previously adopted a perforating machine for boring holes for mines, eight or ten times quicker than by hand; but this machine was impelled by steam, a method evidently inapplicable, from the want of air in a tunnel of great depth and without shafts.

itself by the absorption of the companies running the lines between Susa and the Ticino into the Victor-Emmanuel Railway, and when the Bill for this fusion was brought in, the Government added clauses authorizing the construction of the tunnel by the State, and the necessary expenses, to which the Company agreed to contribute a sum of 20,000,000 francs (800,000*l.*) besides premiums on the shares, and so great was the faith inspired by Counts de Cavour and Menabrea, that the Piedmontese Chamber of Deputies actually passed this audacious law by a large majority.

The practical difficulties of the enterprise now began. But it was much that the project should have been approved, and the confidence of the Government and the Parliament would have been a spur to the energy of the engineers had not the grandeur and glory of the undertaking itself been sufficient to excite their utmost zeal. No sooner had the Bill passed into law than the works were begun, in the autumn of 1857. The trigonometrical survey necessary to obtain an accurate tracing of the axis of the future tunnel was in itself no slight task, if we consider that its extreme points could not be made visible from one another without placing them at a distance which would have rendered any accurate observation impossible, and also that all the operations had to be carried on at heights varying from 3000 to 10,000 feet above the level of the sea, and amidst the constant atmospherical changes characteristic of such elevated regions. The first difficulty was overcome by establishing an observatory on the very summit of Grand-Vallon, the highest peak in that part of the Alps, and two extreme points of the axis in the same vertical plane with it and one another, having been determined by turning the theodolite 180° it was comparatively easy to fix the intermediate signal points on each side one by one, always keeping the extreme point in view, and then lowering the instrument perpendicularly until a site for an observatory had been found in each of the two opposite valleys of Rochemolles and Fourneaux, exactly on a level with and opposite to the respective entrances to the tunnel, so that the signals received from the outside could be repeated underground, and the works kept on the correct line necessary to ensure the junction of the two halves under the very centre of the mountain. To increase the difficulties to be contended with, it was found that the valley of Rochemolles was more than 700 feet higher than that of Fourneaux, on which account it was determined to give a slope of 22 in 1000 to half the tunnel.

Nor were the obstacles presented by the ground confined to the trigonometrical survey. Every single article required for the works, or for the persons engaged in them, from the chief engineers to the lowest labourers, had to be conveyed from the plains below. Fourneaux, indeed, though itself a wretched hamlet, was not very distant from Modane, a considerable village situate on the main road into France; but Bardonnèche, the opposite end, is not only distant from Susa, the nearest railway terminus, but nearly 2500 feet above it. Yet it was requisite here to assemble vast bands of workmen, with their foremen and directors; to provide dwellings and daily food for so vast an increase of population in a place the resources of which barely sufficed for the wants of its own inhabitants; to construct canals, huge reservoirs, workshops and engine-houses; and finally to set up an immense system of machinery with which no one could boast himself practically acquainted, and every portion of which had to be separately brought from Seraing in Belgium, where it was originally constructed.

All this required time; and that not a moment might be unnecessarily wasted, it was resolved to begin boring the tunnel at both ends by the ordinary methods. The progress made might not be great; still, every yard gained was always something, and it was the only resource until the machines were constructed and fairly set in motion. So the works began in 1857 itself, and were continued at Bardonnèche (at Fourneaux even longer) until January, 1861, for owing to various reasons, chief among which may be mentioned the war of 1859, which stopped all the transports for nearly a year, it was not till then that the mechanical perforation could be inaugurated. Nor will this lapse of time seem excessive if we reflect how much had to be done before attaining this first result. Not only had the machinery to be designed and constructed, with the improvements suggested by the experiments made by the Commission, to arrive from Belgium, and be put together in the engine-house, but two large reservoirs, one twenty-six, the other fifty mètres above it, had to be prepared, and a supply of water sufficient to keep the former constantly full brought through a canal from a torrent more than a mile distant, and all these works in solid masonry had to be roofed in, to preserve the water from the influence of the frost. And when all this was done, the machinery had to be tried repeatedly and for a considerable time before it could be employed with safety to the mechanics entrusted with it, or with advantage to the works in the tunnel itself.

After repeated trials, the machinery was at length brought into working order, the pipes for conveying water and compressed air from the machine-house where it is produced, to the further end of the tunnel where the works were proceeding, were laid down in a trench which, in the finished section, is built in to serve as a main drain, as well as a third pipe for gas, which is fabricated in a gasometer just outside the entrance, and the additional light of which is found greatly to facilitate the manœuvres of the workmen, while, not being affected by the explosions, &c., constantly going on, the whole apparatus gives less trouble than a single lamp. At last, the perforating machines were pushed in on a framework along rails prepared for the purpose, and since that time they have continued to be employed. At first there were many interruptions, owing to various causes, and especially the awkwardness of the workmen in dealing with machinery of which they had not the slightest experience, and many days were of course lost; still the Report before us testifies to the general satisfaction of the engineers, and also to the fact that every succeeding month of increased practice sees the work proceed with greater facility and regularity.

Nothing can be more curious than the account M. Sommeiller gives of the manner in which the works proceed. The section of the tunnel which the machines are employed to excavate is about eleven feet wide and eight high; a double rail runs along the centre, upon which a framework upon wheels is rolled forward, carrying the ten perforators, of which nine are usually kept at work at once, close up to the face of the rock. Once there, the distributing pipes for air and water which are fixed on the frame are put in connexion with the main tubes, carried along under the floor of the tunnel from the machine-house outside by means of flexible pipes, and each perforator is then supplied with air and water by turning the cocks belonging to it in the distributing pipes. Pressed forward by the compressed air, the augers then strike the rock, which they pierce very much as a gimlet bores a plank, only that by a special contrivance they recede after each blow, that a jet of water may be impelled into the hole being bored, in order to clear it of dust, and to keep the auger itself cool. This retrograde motion is produced in a manner very similar to that in which the same movement is given to the piston of a steam-engine. In the perforating machine the auger is fixed to the end of a piston moving backwards and forwards in a cylinder. Compressed air enters this cylinder at both ends; but as it is contrived that the front surface of the piston (the one towards the rock) upon which it presses should have only half the size of the other end, it follows that at an equal pressure of six atmospheres, the pressure received from behind is twice as potent as that in the contrary direction, and the auger strikes the rock, although less violently than if there were no compressed air in front of the piston to resist its forward motion. As soon as the blow has been given, however, this relative proportion of the strength of pressure is reversed. The valve by which the compressed air enters the portion of the cylinder behind the piston closes; and another, communicating with the outer atmosphere, opens. This escape being afforded, the forward pressure is immediately reduced to the strength of one atmosphere, which is of course overcome, and the piston recedes, while the compressed air which has just escaped resumes its primitive volume, and thus fulfils its second purpose, by driving out the mephitic air, which naturally collects in so small a space with no draught through it, and supplies the workmen with fresh air to breathe. The augers of the perforating machines continue their work until eighty holes have been bored, each from twenty-seven to thirty-two inches in depth, an operation often accomplished within six hours, though, in the beginning especially, it took a good deal more—ten, or occasionally even fourteen hours. The connexion with the main pipes is then cut off, and the whole framework, with all its apparatus, is rolled away by the workmen to a distance of a hundred and fifty to two hundred yards, behind great gates made of thick planks and beams, called "safety doors." A fresh gang of workmen, the miners, then appear on the scene, whose duty it is to load the mines thus prepared, and then to fire them. No sooner have the mines been exploded, those in the centre, where they are closer together, first, then the ones on the circumference, than a burst of compressed air is admitted into the farthest end of the tunnel, to clear it from smoke and the gases produced by the explosion, and a third set of workmen arrive, with a number of little trucks running upon side rails laid for this special service, in which they cart away the fragments of rock brought down by the explosion. In this way about a yard of progress is generally attained.

At first this operation could only be attempted once in the twenty-four hours, owing to the inexperience of the workmen, of whom only a small number could be taught to use the machines at once; but gradually it was found possible to organize a second gang, and after that, whenever a series of manœuvres such as those above described was effected within twelve hours, it was immediately repeated; and as improvements are gradually introduced into the machinery, and the workmen acquire greater facility in employing it, M. Sommeiller and his colleagues express their hope that it will be possible for them either to make three breaches in the rock every twenty-four hours, or else to attain a more rapid rate of progress by boring deeper holes each time, if two attacks only be found more advantageous.

After the small section of the tunnel has been excavated by the perforating machines, it is enlarged by the ordinary method—a work which it is always the endeavour of the directing engineers to keep at a certain proportionate distance from the front of attack; while the masons who build in the part of the tunnel already enlarged to its full size, follow close upon the workmen who have been digging it out with their picks, for it is of course desirable to leave as little as possible to be done towards completing the tunnel after the mountain shall once have been pierced.

But we need not dwell on this part of our subject, which offers no peculiarity worthy of remark : we will rather say something of the special machinery employed, and particularly of the two systems at work for obtaining the necessary supply of compressed air.*   The Report of M. Sommeiller is accompanied by a series of drawings, with detailed descriptions, without which it would be of course impossible for any one to master all the intricacies of these machines; but we may perhaps be able to give our readers some notion of the system employed.   The first idea was that of what is called a column compressor. It had been calculated that a tension of six atmospheres was required for the compressed air to be employed in the tunnel, and to produce this, a fall of twenty-six mètres (eighty-five feet four inches) was found necessary to give a sufficient impetus to the descending rush of the volume of water which was to compress a certain amount of common atmospheric air to this extent.   This fact once having been theoretically ascertained by calculation, the means of reducing it to practice were simple enough.   At Bardonnèche there was no difficulty in procuring any quantity of water with which to fill a reservoir eighty-five feet above the machine-house, and this reservoir serves to feed ten compressing columns in the shape of syphons, each of which communicates with a chamber filled with atmospheric air, of such a height and size that the impetus of the water when turned on is just sufficient to carry it to the top.   This is effected by opening a valve in the column, through which the water in the upper part (previously, as it were, suspended) rushes, pushing before it the water at rest below the valve in the lower part of the syphon formed by the column.   Rapidly rising above its original level at the bottom of the chamber, the invading water thus compresses the air therein contained, until it has attained a tension of six atmospheres, at which point it has acquired strength sufficient to raise a valve at the top of the chamber, and thus escape into a recipient specially prepared for it.   Every particle of compressed air is driven out by the pursuit of the water, which continues to rise until it touches the top of the chamber, when, at the very moment, the valve in the column is shut, so as to cut

---

* In 1862 the production of the ten compressors at Bardonnèche was no less than 1,404,000 cubic mètres of compressed air, and it is found that a still greater quantity will be required as the works advance farther from the outer air.

off the downward rush; another valve* situated in the lower part of the column is then simultaneously opened, to allow the water in the compressing chamber to run off until it has sunk to its normal level in the syphon, after which fresh atmospheric air is admitted into the vacuum above it, through a series of suspended valves at the side of the chamber, which are shut by the water as it rises, and open again by their own weight as it recedes, and the operation is thus indefinitely repeated, at the rate of three pulsations per minute. At Bardonnèche there are ten compressors constantly at work, every one of which can be stopped for repairs without interfering with the rest, and each impels the air it has compressed into its own recipient. The ten recipients of compressed air, however, communicate together, and a very simple and beautiful contrivance has been resorted to in order to keep the tension in them invariable, independently of the production going on in the compressors, and of the quantity drawn off for use through the pipe carried into the tunnel. To effect this, a vast reservoir of water was constructed, 50 mètres (163 feet 5 inches) above the recipients, connected with them by a long pipe. The static weight of the water thus superimposed on the compressed air being exactly sufficient to maintain it at a tension of six atmospheres, when the supply of air is low, the water enters the recipients, when on the contrary it is superabundant, the water is forced back up the pipe into the reservoir.

When this system was first proposed there were innumerable objections urged against it in the scientific world. It was declared impossible to construct recipients strong enough to hold a supply of compressed air, which was thought capable of bursting the vessel in which it was enclosed, and perhaps even of oozing out through the pores of the cast-iron plates of which it was made. The practicability of conveying compressed air to any distance through pipes, without a loss of tension rendering it utterly useless, was even more strongly and generally insisted on. Fortunately, the experience acquired at Bardonnèche affords a full refutation of these unfavourable predictions; for we learn that not only is there no escape of air from any part of the machinery or pipes, sufficient to stir the flame of a taper, but experiment shows, that the loss of tension liable to be incurred in the transport of compressed air would not equal one-tenth of an atmosphere in any distance less than 25,000 mètres, or nearly four times that which it can be required to traverse for the works under Mont Cénis! Another fear also expressed by the opponents of

---

* The alternate play of these two valves—one of which is always open and the other shut—is regulated by a contrivance called an aërometer, also set in motion by compressed air.

the tunnel was, that from want of shafts the workmen employed must necessarily be suffocated; it is, however, found, that though the temperature is somewhat higher, it is as easy to breathe at the further end of the tunnel as on the hillside itself, since a quantity of compressed air is daily impelled into the small section seventeen times greater than its cubic capacity, and this rush of compressed air not only renews the atmosphere, but also tends to moderate the heat generated by the presence of a large number of workmen in a small space, in which a number of gas-lights are perpetually burning; for it has been demonstrated by experience, that when air is compressed it loses a portion of its natural caloric, whence it follows, that when it resumes its primitive volume on being allowed to escape, it is ready to absorb an amount of heat equal to that which it had previously emitted. From what we have already said, our readers will readily perceive that there need be no fear of the workmen being suffocated; nevertheless, the directing engineers proposed at least to double the supply of compressed air before the end of 1863.

At the northern entrance, the system employed for compressing air is different, and of greater general interest, since it is more readily applicable than that of the column-compressor, which requires a quantity of water and a fall by no means attainable everywhere, as was soon found to be the case at Fourneaux, where one torrent at a sufficient height above the engine-house had not the necessary supply of water, and another, which was abundant, had but an insignificant fall. To combat this difficulty, the first device was to raise water to the requisite height by means of hydraulic wheels, when a new invention, the pump-compressor, afforded a real solution of the problem, so satisfactory, that it will supply three times the amount of compressed air, while the machinery costs one-third less than the column-compressor. In this machine the compression is effected by a piston, which an hydraulic wheel causes to move backwards and forwards in a chamber communicating with two vertical columns, supplied with water in such a way and such a quantity, that when one is full the other must be empty, and this occurs alternately as the piston moves. Each time a vacuum is left in the one, it is filled with air from the outer atmosphere, which the water on its return compresses until it acquires sufficient tension to raise a valve and escape into a recipient, just as in the column-compressor. In this machine, however, the air is driven into the vacuum by water flowing from an outer basin. This water serves a double purpose; when the column is full of air, it accumulates over the valve by which the latter has entered, and the superimposed weight prevents any leakage through this valve when the air begins to be compressed by the return of the piston ; when, on the other hand, the column is empty, the water flows in, entering with the air, and makes up for the loss of the water in the column caused by evaporation.   Any extra amount which may thus enter escapes with the compressed air into the recipients, at the bottom of which it accumulates until it is enough in quantity to raise a concentric float, under which it makes its way out, and which then closes again over the orifice. It is calculated that each pump-compressor is able to supply the works with thirty litres (nearly seven gallons) of compressed air per second, and when six of them shall be at work, according to the declared intention of the engineers, it is evident there will be no difficulty in obtaining a quantity of compressed air amply sufficient for the perforating machines, for renewing the atmosphere in the tunnel, and for speedily clearing it of smoke after the explosion of the mines.

At Fourneaux, two other contrivances of considerable interest are in use.   We have already said that the valley of Rochemolles is at a level considerably higher than that of the Arc ; so much so, that the tunnel, which at the south entrance is at the bottom of the one valley, issues out at the north end at a height of 186 mètres (347 feet 10 inches) above the opposite one, in spite of the slope given to half of it.   To obviate the inconvenience of having to drag everything required for the works in the tunnel up so considerable a perpendicular height, the engineers bethought themselves of constructing an automatic plane between the platform at the mouth of the tunnel and the valley below, sufficiently wide for a double line of rails to be laid on it.   At the top stands a large drum with a cable, each end of which is attached to a truck, one of which is at the top while the other is at the bottom. When the latter has been loaded, the former is filled with water, and descends by its own weight, dragging up the other as it moves ; a contrivance by which a weight of 1500 kilogrammes (not far from a ton) can be raised in a few minutes, and the water being emptied out of the truck which reaches the bottom, it is ready to convey another load to the top in its turn.

The second contrivance, peculiar to Fourneaux, concerns the ventilation. When the tunnel shall be completed, in order to allow the railway lines from each side to run into it, it will be necessary to make it take a curve up the valleys on each side, and a branch from the main tunnel is already being excavated for this purpose at Bardonnèche, in addition to the straight one, which will be kept open, as it facilitates the work and the admission of air. In spite of the straight line observed at Fourneaux, the slope inwards of 22 per 1000 is found to be a great obstacle to the entrance of a current of fresh air, in spite of the difference of temperature which had been counted on to promote it.   A special contrivance has therefore been devised for sucking out the bad air which accumulates in the tunnel, through a large wooden conduit hanging from the roof. The torrent of Charmaix has been made to supply a small quantity of water with a fall of 70 mètres (in round numbers 230 feet) which, by means of a wheel, sets two enormous pistons in motion. These alternately raise and let fall a mass of water enclosed in two chambers, communicating with the conduit from the tunnel ; as the water sinks in each alternately the vacuum thus produced is filled by the bad air, which is immediately afterwards expelled into the outer atmosphere by the return of the piston; and it is calculated that in this way all the mephitic air likely to be generated will be drawn off without difficulty, even when the works shall be under the centre of the mountain.

We have now sketched the peculiar machinery employed for tunnelling Mont Cénis. The perforators we will not attempt to describe minutely, partly because the extreme complication of parts necessary to fit them for their various functions is such as to render them unintelligible without the assistance of drawings on a large scale, and also because the great singularity in them that we wish to impress on our readers is quite independent of their arrangements and form—viz., that of their being kept in motion by compressed air, conveyed from a distance which even now exceeds a mile, and will be considerably more before the works are terminated. For the first time since the application of steam to machinery, a great engineering work is being carried on without its assistance ; and the accounts given of the success attained in the employment of compressed air, as well as the small cost, calculated per dynamic horse power, ought to commend this great enterprise to general attention. Air is a commodity to be obtained everywhere, water is neither scarce nor dear, especially if we remember that it is by no means necessary to produce compressed air at or even near the spot where it is to be employed, for even supposing it has to be conveyed to a distance such as to occasion a considerable loss of tension, (and experience, confirming the tables of the Commission, shows that this would not occur at any moderate one), it would suffice slightly to raise the degree of the original compression, a result which it is found can be attained by the same water power, provided the quantity of air to be operated upon be reduced in proportion to the additional tension it is desired to give it. The column-compressor, indeed, was not generally applicable, owing to the great fall required to make the water used for compression descend with sufficient impetus, but this difficulty is removed by the invention of the pump-compressor, for which but a very small quantity of water, and no fall, is required, and in which, if necessary, another motive power, such as the wind, we conceive, or steam, might be substituted for the hydraulic wheels used to move the compressing pistons at Fourneaux. A review intended for general perusal is not the place in which to discuss the applications which may be made of the working power contained in compressed air, nor to enter on the abstract scientific advantages it presents; nevertheless we cannot refrain from expressing our hope that engineers will take advantage of the works now going on at Mont Cénis to make themselves practically acquainted with this new motive force, and to study the use that may be made of it elsewhere.

The scientific interest in the tunnelling of the Alps, excited by the employment of compressed air, though in our eyes the chief, is by no means the only one connected with this great enterprise, the importance of which, owing to the political events of the last seven years, has enormously increased since the project was first presented to Count de Cavour. When the bill authorizing the tunnel passed, both slopes of the Alps belonged to the same State, the two parts of which it was to connect, while it put the Mediterranean port of Genoa in communication with France, Switzerland, and Germany; but, owing to the restrictive commercial policy of the governments that then ruled all the rest of Italy, its influence did not seem likely to extend further south. Three years, however, sufficed to bring great changes. The southern half of the Italian peninsula had fused itself with the northern, and the frontier of France was on the crest of the Alps. Savoy having thus passed into the power of another State, a special convention was concluded on the 7th of May, 1862, to regulate the interests concerning the tunnel. The Italian Government insisted on retaining the exclusive command and direction of the works, which it had begun at its own risk and cost; but it was agreed that when they were terminated, France should pay for half the length at the rate of three thousand francs per mètre; and, moreover, that for every year less than twenty-five—the extreme limit of time fixed by the convention—she should pay an additional sum of 500,000 francs, a premium to be raised to 600,000 per annum if the works be terminated within fifteen years.

Our readers thus see how great an interest the Italian Government has even financially in the speedy termination of the tunnel; an argument made use of by General de Menabrea, in his interesting speech of the 4th of March last, to induce the Parliament to grant additional sums for the works, showing that to spend now is true economy, since every year gained will increase the proportion of the general expense to be borne by France. According to the calculations of the Minister, twelve and a half years may be looked to with confidence as the ultimate term of the undertaking; in January last, the works were already 1274 mètres, or rather more than a tenth of the whole distance, from the entrance on the side of Bardonnèche, and of this, 550 mètres (170 in 1861, 380 in 1862) were, owing to the mechanical system, which, there is every reason to hope, will every year afford increasingly satisfactory results, not less at any rate than a yearly progress of 400 mètres. At Fourneaux, where it was only inaugurated in January, 1863, at a distance of 925 mètres from the entrance, the progress made in the first two months was such as to afford ground for the confident expectation that the works on that side will soon be in as forward a state as those at Bardonnèche; and if these calculations be not falsified by encountering some fresh obstacle in the centre of the mountain, and the expected total advance of 800 mètres (400 at each end) be attained each year, it will follow that France will be liable by the treaty for a sum which will go far to acquit the obligations of the Italian Government with respect to the tunnel; since, including the interest on the sum spent on the French half, it will exceed 31,700,000 francs (1,268,000*l.*). Besides this an additional sum of 13,000,000 francs (520,000*l.*) will have to be reimbursed by the Victor Emmanuel Railway Company, leaving little more than 20,000,000 francs out of the 65,000,000 francs the tunnel is computed to cost, to be finally paid by the Italian Government, in which sum is included the cost of the railway between Bardonnèche and Susa.

As long as the opening of the tunnel could be deemed problematical, it would have been idle to speculate on the advantages to be derived from its existence—advantages incalculably multiplied by the fusion of the greater part of Italy into a single state, blessed, moreover, with freedom of commerce. Less than twenty-five miles (forty kilomètres) of railway will suffice to connect the southern entrance of the tunnel with the iron net which covers the valley of the Po, and though the whole descent is little less than 2500 feet, the engineers promise that in no part of this line will the slopes exceed 27 per 1000, nor will the curves have a radius of less than 500 mètres; and as only a sixth of this line will be underground, computing the whole of the eighteen tunnels of different lengths through which it will have to pass, we need not fear but what it will be completed in time to give its full value to the tunnel as soon as it shall be opened. On the northern side there are but a few miles of railway wanting to connect St. Michel, where it at present stops, with Modane, the works for which are already progressing, and we cannot doubt that the French authorities, who co-operate so heartily with the Italian engineers, that, as it is pleasant to hear from the Report of the latter, not a single dispute has arisen in the course of three years, nor a day been lost to the works by the transfer of the province, will make it a point of honour to terminate them before the tunnel can be completed.

We are, therefore, safe in considering that as soon as the Mont Cénis tunnel is open, a train will be able to run direct from Chambéry to Turin. Let us now see what advantages this will imply : Chambéry, as most of our readers are doubtless aware, is in direct railway communication with Paris and Switzerland, and scarcely thirty hours distant from London, and when once the barrier of the Alps shall be broken down, the enterprising statesmen of Italy hope to see their country once more the high road between Europe and Asia. For this purpose they are busily engaged in the construction of railways, and the repair and enlargement of long-neglected harbours. Already a line of steamers is running between Ancona and Alexandria, the starting place of which it is proposed to transfer to Brindisi (the Roman Brundusium), and perhaps in time to Taranto, when the railway which now stops at Foggia shall be successively open to these ports, an event which may reasonably be expected to occur within a very few years, certainly before the completion of the tunnel. If we look to the consequence of this we shall find that when Brindisi is in direct communication with Boulogne, the journey from London to Egypt, and therefore to India, by this route, will be shorter by at least three days and nights than it ever can be through Marseilles, and that the sea passage will be reduced to less than half what it is at present. This fact only requires to be stated to give an idea of the great advantage this road will possess for the Indian mails, for passengers, and all the lighter and more valuable species of merchandize, in regard to which greater rapidity of transmission will more than compensate for any additional expense incurred by the substitution of railway for sea carriage, while as for travellers, we conceive there would be few unwilling to abbreviate a journey oftener undertaken from necessity than pleasure, and to substitute a railway route down the Adriatic coast for the constant tossing of the now inevitable Gulf of Lyons.

To our merchants, too, the opening of the Mont Cénis tunnel, and the railway system of which it may be regarded as the crown and keystone, should be a matter of no small interest, especially now that the commercial treaty just signed will entail a great reduction of the tariff. The southern provinces of Italy afford a field for commercial enterprise hitherto neglected, and necessarily so, from the utter want of means of communication between it and the rest of Europe ; and yet, while Manchester mills stand idle for want of cotton, there is perhaps no soil more capable of producing it than the plains of Taranto and the southern shores of Sicily,* while it would be tedious to attempt even the most

* We believe that in the course of the winter it is intended to open an exhibition at Turin of this cotton cultivated in different parts of Italy.

cursory enumeration of the many objects of use or luxury that might be obtained from these rich but long-abandoned lands. The portals leading to them have now been closed by a barrier which seemed insuperable to human skill, and every day which brought places connected by the iron bond of the age more closely together, appeared proportionately to isolate and doom to atrophy all such as had no part in the great community of interests.

All honour then is due to those who have rescued a country so fertile and so progressive as Italy from the moral and commercial suffocation to which she seemed condemned, by the Alpine girdle which cut her off from the rest of Europe, both to the engineers who devised, and the statesman who encouraged, the enterprise. In whatever light we look at the tunnel, it cannot fail to do the highest credit to Italian genius and Italian perseverance. Count de Cavour never lived to see the works which owed so much to his fostering care, for on the very 6th of June, 1861, which had long been fixed for him to visit Bardonnèche, and inspect the new machines in motion, the great Minister expired; but while the department of public works is in the able hands of General de Menabrea, we may be very sure that nothing will be omitted to favour an undertaking of which he may justly be held one of the principal authors, owing to the share he took in the labours of the original Government Commission, and the zeal with which he has always upheld it, against every objection, both in the Parliament of his own country, and in the scientific assemblies of other nations.

For the directors of the works, and the engineers carrying them out under their orders, no praise can be deemed extravagant. The glory of utilizing a force hitherto without employment, and of contriving means for executing a work which seemed to defy the utmost resources of art, belongs entirely to the former; but the great merit of the latter cannot fail to be appreciated, if we consider the extraordinary difficulties with which they have had to contend. At no time, and in no circumstances, would the task of inaugurating an entirely new system of machinery, constructed on purely theoretical principles, the action of which was totally unknown, and whose every defect had to be discovered, and a remedy devised by the light of the experience practically acquired day by day, without any data, either in books or in engineering traditions, which could be of the slightest use as a guide, while a whole series of complicated manœuvres had to be taught to a large band of workmen all at once, have been an easy one; but in the case before us the inherent difficulties were incalculably increased by adventitious ones. They would have been great enough in the centre of an industrial district, with workshops and tool manufactories close at hand, with a choice of intelligent mechanics, trained to turn their attention to different kinds of work—what must they have been in an Alpine region, buried in snow for nearly half the year, far away from even a village offering the smallest resource, with only such workshops on the spot as could execute small repairs or slight modifications in the machinery, while every alteration of real importance had to be made in Belgium by the original constructors? If we consider, moreover, that all the requirements, and the very daily subsistence of great numbers of workmen* collected together from distant places had to be provided for—that bridges had to be built, and roads constructed, before even a cart could arrive at the scene of the works, besides the reservoirs and canals we have already mentioned, and that all this was accomplished in a country and by a nation among which all industrial enterprise had been unknown, and political and commercial liberty had only just sprung into life, we think it must be conceded that no panegyric can exceed the deserts of such men as M. Borelli, local director at Bardonnèche, and MM. Mella and Copello, who have successively occupied the same post at Fourneaux. It is indeed their highest praise to say that they have overcome difficulties like those we have briefly hinted at above, leaving it to such of our readers as are practically acquainted with engineering enterprises to appreciate their magnitude, and brought the works and the machinery to a state of such forwardness and perfection, as to make it possible approximatively to calculate the time and cost still requisite to assure the completion of this extraordinary work.

All the persons concerned in it have given such proof of their capacity and energy, that it would be unjust to doubt that they will continue to the end equal to themselves, and we therefore look with confidence to their final success at the period they have assigned for the conclusion of their labours. The annual Report the chief directors are bound to present to the Italian Parliament, and of which the one now before us is the first (since none could be made until the mechanical perforation had been sufficiently tried to attest its powers), must be looked for each spring with increasing interest, and engineers will be glad to learn, that the present volume holds out a promise of a technical work already in course of compilation, giving a detailed description of the different machines, and an account of their action, both in a theoretical and practical point of view, as well as accurate data, illustrating the phenomena connected with the compression of air, besides various studies on the use that may be made of it as an industrial force, which it is hoped may be given to the public in the course of the next two years.

---

* On the 1st January, 1863, 900 workmen were employed at Bardonnèche, and 720 at Modane, a number intended to be increased during the past year.

To this future work, and in the meanwhile to the Appendix of the present Report, with its excellent illustrations, we must refer whosoever wishes to acquire an exact knowledge of the state of the works under Mont Cénis, and especially of the means employed for boring the tunnel. If we have succeeded in giving our readers any clear general notion of this great undertaking, and of the vast commercial interests involved in its success, we have done all that lies within the province of a reviewer, and can but rejoice in having had the opportunity of paying our tribute of admiration to the men who are at once doing so much for the honour of the Italian name and the advantage and prosperity of the world at large.

Art. III.—Astrology and Magic.

La Magie et l'Astrologie dans l'Antiquité et au Moyen Age ; ou Etude sur les Superstitions Païennes qui se sont perpetuées jusqu'à nos Jours. Par L. F. Alfred Maury. London: Williams and Norgate. 1860.

TILL the sixteenth century, says Liebig, the earth was regarded as the centre of the universe, and the life and fortunes of men were believed to stand in the closest relation to the motions of the celestial spheres. Roger Bacon held the opinion that, from all the ends of heaven the creative forces radiated towards the earth, and determined earthly destinies. Paracelsus taught, that when a man ate a bit of bread he therein consumed heaven and earth and all the heavenly bodies, "inasmuch as heaven by its fertilizing rain, the earth by its soil, and the sun by its luminous and heat-giving rays, have all contributed to its production, and are all present in the one substance." In short, the dominant idea was, that "all that happened on earth stood written in starry characters."* This belief in the influence exerted on our tiny world by every member of the stellar system was annihilated by the introduction of the Copernican theory of astronomy, which, in depriving the planet Tellus of her importance as the centre round which the universe revolved, created a suspicion, soon to ripen into a conviction, that our modest little globe could hardly be of such paramount consequence as to enjoy the peculiar care

---

* Liebig's "Letters on Chemistry," p. 28.

of the entire Cosmos. Before this period the history of astronomy had been pretty nearly, though not exclusively, identical with that of judicial astrology, the stars being consulted principally for the sake of their supposed power of prognostication, by all except the old Greek observers of the heavens. Of this subordination of the real to the fictitious, we have a noteworthy instance in an age so recent as that of Sir Isaac Newton, for the first lunar tables constructed on the Newtonian theory were designed, it is said, to facilitate the calculation of nativities.

In an earlier time the planetary positions attracted attention chiefly as they affected the destinies of the human race. The twelve divisions into which the astrological heaven was distributed were called Houses. There was the House of Life, the House of Riches, the House of Parents. Health, Death, Religion, Friendship, Enmity, had also their separate establishments. Of each of these Houses one of the heavenly bodies was lord. Besides his original inheritance above the clouds, his lordship had manorial rights in certain countries, animals, plants, and minerals below.

The signs in the sun, moon, and stars were of the utmost importance to mankind. Mercury being in an *airy* sign, foretold the suspension in the air of a distinguished gentleman, who, born June 24, 1758, at eight minutes past eight, A.M., and in process of time coming to years of discretion, had the misfortune to commit a murder. After casting and rectifying his nativity, the Zadkiel of that day brought up the direction of death with great nicety and precaution, " and found that his illustrious client would be plunged into eternity when the sun came to the anaretical point of the mid-heaven and met the noxious beams of the moon and Mars in opposition ;" a concurrence which, it appears, is ever productive of a violent death. We presume the starry prediction in this case was fulfilled. But the planets sometimes prophesied quite wide of the mark. In the fifteenth century Stöffler foretold a universal deluge. This second edition of the great aqueous catastrophe was to come off in 1524, at the instance of three rascally planets then in conjunction in a watery sign. " All Europe," says our informant, " was in consternation, and those who could find the means built themselves boats in readiness." Foremost among these boat-builders was a doctor of Toulouse, who actually made an ark for himself and his friends.* Morin, the last of the astrologers and the opponent of Gassendi, had no reason to bless his stars when he consulted them, for he was always predicting Gassendi's death, and was always wrong. When he announced that of Louis XIII., he was equally unsuccessful. This preposterous faith, however, died hard. Kings and other eminent

---

* See " Penny Cyclopædia," article, " Astrology."

persons resorted to astrology down to a very late period. In the fifteenth century, Pope Calixtus IIL anathematized an heretical comet that had in some way aided and abetted the infidel Turk. In the sixteenth, Catherine de Medicis presented Henry IV. to the famous Nostradamus. In the seventeenth, Charles I. took counsel of Lily, the Sidrophel of Butler. Dryden not only cast the nativities of his sons, but singularly enough lived, or ought to have lived, to see one of them positively verified. At the present day there are few, perhaps, among the educated classes who would profess a belief in judicial astrology, but we have still a Zadkiel, whose almanack is popular, whose exhibitions are attended by the "great and good," and whose character for disinterested credulity can secure the protection of the law. Wise in our generation as we unquestionably are, we are, nevertheless, not universally entitled to borrow the Homeric vaunt, that we are better than our forefathers. If our mediæval ancestors were weak enough to discuss the age and dress of the celestial hierarch who brought the message to the Blessed Virgin, or to inquire how many angels could stand without crowding on the point of a needle, are there not potent, grave, and reverend signiors in our own day who believe that men float in the air without sensible agency, who fancy that they are the favoured recipients of good news from the land of souls, and for whom millions of spiritual beings walk the earth—disembodied blockheads who speak bad grammar and write infamous poetry—unmannerly goblins that almost make us wicked enough to hope that the future state— which is the only state they ought ever to be in—is as baseless a figment as their own nonsensical existence?

But we will not be too hard on these last infirmities of the human mind, remembering that the brave have their fears and the wise their follies. If men are not always sane, there is at least a method in their madness. The recurrence of the same aberrations, the perpetual rencontre of old friends with new faces, indicates the operation of some cause, implying not indeed a chronic or incurable lunacy on the part of mankind, but a continued liability to disease, for which, however, we may one day effectually prescribe. For the mischief originates mainly in that ignorance which our great national poet calls the curse of God, while the remedy will be found in the knowledge which he glorifies as the wing wherewith we fly to heaven.

To the earliest ancestors of the human race the world must have been an almost wholly unintelligible riddle. In "the dark abyss of time" man began, unaided and undisciplined, to make those guesses at truth, which he has continued to make ever since. The first explanation of nature was inevitably incorrect and fictitious. Systematic observation requires time; to institute comparison or experiment argues a degree of mental enlargement which did not exist in the infancy of the race, and without observation, experiment, and comparison, no true science can possibly be constructed. In the absence of real knowledge a sham knowledge sprang up. Mankind, like children, began life with fairy tales. Misunderstanding natural phenomena, man founded his explanation of the universe on a fiction. He assumed that the operations of nature were the actions of beings resembling himself. Motion suggested life, and to his distempered fancy thunder, lightning, storm, and hail were occurrences dependent on the arbitrary will of conscious agents, capable of being influenced by motives similar to those which influenced himself. His religion thus became the counterpart of his philosophy. To command nature by obeying her laws is the practical issue of modern science; to coerce the supernatural powers, spirits, gods, or genii whom an imaginative faith had created, was the illusive aim of primitive speculation. Hence prayer, entreaty, adulation, to persuade the more compliant divinities. Hence offerings, spells, charms, in a word, *magic*, to extort what the god seemed reluctant to give. The enchanter, says M. Maury, held the world in his hand. He could, at his pleasure, reverse the order of the universe, for he could compel the beings on whose volition all the processes of nature depended to surrender their own and to execute his will.

As the same principle of interpretation was universally applicable, every province of nature and every corresponding branch of knowledge were necessarily subjected to the same treatment. Thus the study of the stars was conceived as a study of human-like passions and impulses, and as their empire became subjectively predominant, all territorial objects and events were modified by their malign or beneficent influence. And not only was the fictitious science of astrology the offspring of early cogitation, but in virtue of a general interdependence, or more frequently, perhaps, of the same common characteristic, primitive physiology was a fictitious science. So was the earlier chemistry: so was the elementary psychology. But as the simple phenomena of nature came to be better understood, this fictitious philosophy found its area restricted. Banished from the earth, it took refuge in the skies—driven from the material world, it retreated to the spiritual. Its empire is proportioned to our ignorance of law. It rules in the unexplored territories of nature. Its residuary domain is an ever-decreasing *terra incognita*. Animal magnetism and modern spiritualism are the impotent representatives of this philosophy of fiction. Miracle is everywhere receding, both in time and place. It is content to limit itself to the Apostolic age or to the Holy Land—it resides in the region of the anomalous or the yet unexplained. It preserves its existence by the sophistry "which confounds empirical laws with the absolute and ultimate law of universal order."* Modern miracle-workers and miracle-defenders are the real though unacknowledged successors of the astrologer, the alchymist, the soothsayer, and their vindicators. The episcopal rain-and-fine-weather-maker in England differs little from his humble competitor in equatorial Africa. Henry IV. was justified in directing the clergy to search for the philosopher's stone; "for since they could change bread and wine into the body and blood of Christ, they might also," argued the royal logician, "by the help of God, succeed in transmuting the baser metals into gold."

This filiation has perhaps been often sketched with a more or less steady pencil, but we doubt if anywhere it has been more satisfactorily traced than in the two little volumes by M. Alfred Maury, one on Magic and Astrology, the other on Sleep and Dreaming. In these interesting expositions the author shows, convincingly as we think, the close interconnexion of all the several ramifications of superstition. In describing the rise and progress of this fanciful philosophy, he has delineated the family likeness as it re-appears in astrology, in medicine, and in physiology; he has explained various psychological phenomena that arise out of mental disturbance; he has illustrated the subject of hallucination, ecstasy, presentiment, and dreaming; he has facilitated the comprehension of so-called cases of miraculous cure; he has connected Catholic miracle with Pagan prodigy; he has called in Iamblichus to illustrate Chardel, and Paracelsus to interpret Mesmer; he has shown how the same delusions repeat themselves in Greece, in Judæa, in England, in the centuries before and the centuries after Christ; he has pointed out the links in the great electric chain of fact, emotion, and fancy which darkly binds the different human families in one common unity of superstitious practice and belief. This multifarious task M. Maury has discharged with considerable ability, and with a philosophic impartiality which is alike remote from the extremes of scepticism and from those of credulity. The research and erudition displayed in the prosecution of his enterprise are highly creditable, and if a reader in pursuit of special knowledge on certain points has to complain of omission or to resent a diffuseness that excludes what he would regard as more valuable matter, he should remember that these little volumes do not profess to exhaust the subject, and that in such a maze of speculation the due proportion of space to which each topic is entitled is not very easy to deter-

---

* See Mackay's "Tübingen School," p. 386; also the section on "Absolute Miracle," p. 32.

mine. Perhaps he might like to hear more of Cardan and Agrippa, or perhaps he would willingly dispense with some of the pages on the Catholic stigmatics. M. Maury, however, is not writing a biography of magicians, but a history of magic, and the question of stigmatization has some aspects so peculiar that we readily pardon the author for multiplying facts and accumulating evidence.

Taking this accomplished writer for a pioneer, we will now try to penetrate some little way into the wild labyrinth of primitive, though still surviving or yet unexhausted superstition, tracing with him some of its most striking manifestations in the Old and New World, amongst Chaldæans, Persians, and Egyptians, amongst the worshippers of fetishes and adorers of the dead; wandering in the land alike of the black and the white, and glancing into the twilight realms of dream, possession, nervous malady, mysticism, anæsthesia, and somnambulism.

Passing from that rude form of nature-worship which recognises all objects as gifted with a mysterious life or power to a more refined and discriminating religion, we detect in Assyria, one of the centres of ancient civilization, the dawning sense of cosmological speculation and the growth of a truly theological conception. In Asia, the serenity of the sky and the splendour of the constellations early favoured observation and stimulated fancy and emotion. The order, the universality, the inaccessibility and fascinating beauty of the heavenly bodies, made them the pre-eminent objects of human adoration. If in our own age a poet can sing of their wild spiritual brightness, if he can ask—

> " Whoever gazed upon them shining,
> And turned to earth without repining,
> Nor wished for wings to flee away,
> And mix with their eternal ray ?"*

we can have no difficulty in conceiving that the grown children of the dark fore-time could kiss their hand in the rapture of devotion to the moon that walketh in brightness, or in comprehending that even the wise Aristotle and the large-hearted Origen believed that the stars were living beings—angels, spirits, gods.

Star-worship then, it is inferred, early became the religion of the pastoral tribes who, descending from the mountains of Kurdistan into the plains of Babylon, were ultimately represented by those CHASDIM or CHALDÆANS, who seem to have constituted a sacerdotal caste. Of this caste the appropriate function was to study the heavens, in order to obtain a deeper insight into the nature of the gods. The temples which they erected thus became

---

* Byron, "Siege of Corinth."

the first observatories, and the legendary Tower of Babel, in the
Book of Genesis, is probably but the mythical equivalent of a
real edifice consecrated to the pious contemplation of the seven
planets, or perhaps, as the *Bab* (court or palace) of Bel, to the
brilliant star of good fortune alone. By a long succession of
observations, the Chaldæans became possessed of a theological
astronomy. The pretenders to this chimerical knowledge, called
by the Greeks astrology, or the apotelesmatic science, which
means the science of the starry influences, undertook to show
what effects the celestial luminaries exert on human destiny,
either individual or collective.

In the Assyrian Pantheon the sun and moon had the precedence. Their daily positions were referred to the constellations
in the zodiac—a mental construction which we, perhaps, owe to
the Chaldæans. The zodiac, in fact, with its twelve signs, represented the *aggregate residency* of the sun, throughout the
year. Each of these twelve signs was ruled by a god, whose
office could have been no sinecure, since he had to look after the
corresponding month, as well as to keep his own house in order.
Each of these months was subdivided into three parts, so that
there were three dozen in all. Each of these subdivisions was
superintended by a deity. Thirty-six in number, these sublime
overseers formed a sort of deliberative assembly, under the title
of *Counsellors.* Half of them attended to business above the
earth, while the other half kept an eye on the state of affairs
below. The sun, the moon, and the five planets, occupied the
most elevated rank in the celestial hierarchy, and as their daily
march was supposed to indicate the course of the world and the
succession of events, they bore the proud title of *Interpreters.*
Saturn or *old* Bel, regarded as the highest, because it is the most
distant of the planets, was the object of peculiar veneration, being
the revealer or interpreter in chief. *Young* Bel, or Jupiter, Mero-
dach, or Mars, Nebo or Mercury, were considered to be of the
worthier gender, while Sin or the Moon, and Mylitta, Baalthis
or Venus, were reputed to be of the more beautiful sex. These
starry ladies and gentlemen presided (so fancy taught), over the
destinies of mortals. The astronomical state of the sky at the
moment of birth determined the fate of every individual. Nor
was man alone subordinated to the planetary powers. Fortuitous
or frequent coincidences led the observer to conclude that there
was an intimate connexion between each of the planets and the
phenomena of meteorology. There is even some reason to suppose that among the priests of Babylon mysterious relations
were assumed to exist between planets and metals, in virtue of a
certain resemblance between the lustre of the former and the
colour of the latter. At any rate, the Sabæans, who inherited the

Babylonian traditions, maintained the correspondence of gold with the sun, silver with the moon, lead with Saturn, iron with Mars, tin with Jupiter: and in this doctrine originated an alchemy analogous to that taught and practised in Egypt.

The nature-worship of PERSIA was still more refined and spiritual than that of Assyria. Intelligent and invisible beings there replaced the material gods of primitive idolatry, the sun, the stars, the earth, the water, and the plants being adored only as manifestations of unseen powers. Ahoura-Mazda or Ormuzd, the maker and master of the world, was in the belief of the Persian, the wise and good being whose beneficent action was perseveringly counteracted by his natural enemy Angra-manyou, or Ahriman, the ill-intentioned. Associated with Ormuzd were the Amschaspands, or immortal saints, the idealized personifications of the solar forms; the Izeds who presided over the phenomena of nature, and the Ferouers, genii who represent the living forces, or as Maury still more precisely defines them, hypostases of life and intelligence, yet having their ideal origin in the imaginary existence of the souls of the departed. The attendants of Ahriman were the Dews, perhaps the conquered and degraded gods of the Aryans (Daeva). In the struggle thus organized between good and evil, conservation and destruction, light and darkness, the worshippers of Ormuzd were vitally interested. To secure the protection of the Amschaspands, or spirits of light, and to avert the malignant influence of the Dews, or the spirits of Darkness, was the end and aim of their religious observances. To the more scientific Greek, the Persian *cultus* seemed a tissue of enchantments and evocations, and after the Macedonian conquest, the priests of that ancient creed began gradually to assume a new character, till in the Western world the magi were transformed into magicians, and their holy service was secularized into magic.

The EGYPTIANS dispute with the Chaldæans the honour of the discovery of astrology. Noting the influence of the atmospheric changes on the physical constitution of man, they attributed to the different stars a special action on the several parts of the human body. Their funeral rituals are quoted in illustration of this practice. From their testimony it appears that the divinities shared among them the entire body of the dead. To Ra or the Sun was assigned the head, to Anubis the nose and the lips, to Hathor the eyes, to Selk the teeth, and so on. To ascertain a nativity, the astrologer had only to combine the theory of the influences thus exerted by these star-related gods with the appearance of the heavens at the moment of birth. It was an element of the Egyptian as well as of the Persian astrological doctrine that a particular star was interested in the natal hour of

every human being, and the prevalence of this belief, even in the
Christian community, is shown by the legend of the Magi, who
had seen the birth-star of Jesus in the East, and had followed its
guidance till they arrived at his home in Bethlehem.   In Egypt
as in Assyria the chemical properties of bodies were referred to
divine or sidereal influences.   The shores of the Nile were the
classical country of chemistry, or rather of alchemy, and the false
and the true science equally derive their name from *Chemi*, the
Black Land.   Thus in Egypt, as in Persia and in Chaldæa,
natural philosophy, resumes M. Maury, was a sacred doctrine, of
which magic and astrology were branches, and which represented
the phenomena of the universe as directly dependent on the genii
and divinities with which it was supposed to be peopled.

If at a late period Greek culture was adverse to astrological
pretension, ANCIENT GREECE was by no means exempted from
the influence of the common superstition.   To charm serpents, to
lay the winds, to change men into animals, to prepare poisons and
love-philtres, were old and recognised practices in Hellas.   At
Cleonæ, a sacerdotal order called *Chalazophulakoi* was employed
to watch the clouds and give notice of the coming hailstorm, that
those " great goddesses to lazy folks," as Aristophanes terms them,
might be propitiated by the sacrifice of a lamb or chicken.*   And
though the state religion in general discountenanced sorcery, the
extraneous *cults* of Thrace, of Phrygia, of Egypt, found their way
into Greece, and there assumed a sort of magical character.   The
foreign divinities, as dæmons, genii of a secondary order, though not
legally established in the country, yet enjoyed a private and secret
recognition.   One decidedly magical cultus appears to have had
considerable popularity in Greece—that of Hecate.   This goddess,
who personifies the moon projecting her mysterious rays into the
darkness of the night, was the patron deity of sorcerers.   As one of
the Powers of the under world, she was regarded as a spectral being
who sent from the realms below the phantoms that taught witchcraft, that dwell on tombs and near cross-roads and places
drenched with the blood of murdered persons.   The Mormo, the
Cercops, the Empusa, were among the goblin-crew that did her
bidding.   Accompanied by the souls of the dead, the terrible
goddess, with her ever-changing form, wandered over the earth,
while the howling and whining of dogs announced her approach.
She presided over the rites of purification and expiation ; reptiles
and loathly animals and all repulsive mixtures were associated
with her service.   The vervain and the root of the rue were hers,
myrrh and storax flavoured the lizard-mash set in her honour
under the crescent moon, when, constrained by some barbarous spell

---

* Seneca, " Natur. Quæst.," lib. iv. cap. 6.

or archaic word of power, she revealed herself in dream to her expectant adorers. The hell-broth of Macbeth's witches was thus anticipated by a classical brew of a somewhat similar description. Indeed, Hecate appears as the witch-queen in modern no less than in ancient times. Our own poets, Middleton and Shakespeare, equally with Virgil and Horace,* acknowledge her sinister sovereignty ; and while Hippolytus in the third century, preserving an old heathen incantation, shows how her pagan votaries did homage to the infernal, heavenly, and terrestrial Bombo, Shelley, in the nineteenth, translating Goethe's *Walpurgisnacht,* re-echoes the name in apostrophizing the modern Hecate, unless we err in presuming identity of appellation from similarity of form and circumstance :—

> " Honour to her to whom honour is due,
> Old mother Baubo honour to you,
> An able sow with old Baubo upon her,
> Is worthy of glory and worthy of honour."

But Greek sorcery is exemplified not only in the uninviting *cuisine* of Hecate, but in the mysterious cave of Trophonius, in the necyomanteia, or evocation of the dead, described in the *Odyssey* and in the ceremonies of the Orpheotelestæ. In fact, the acute and sagacious Greek did not escape the universal epidemic, though he had the disease in a mild and favourable form. Indeed, when the seat of government in Assyria was transferred from Babylon to Seleucia, and the free institutions of Greece proving prejudicial to Asiatic theocracy, the Chaldæan magi lost their credit, the science of the starry influences was eagerly welcomed by the versatile Hellenes. Nor was the Egyptian astrologer in less repute with them than his Assyrian rival. The former was honoured as the Mathematicus, or Learned Man *par excellence.* The latter, as the Chaldæan or Constructor of Horoscopes, still recalled by his name the historical importance which had once attached to him as the priest of an ancient religion.

Following in the wake of Greek and oriental speculation, magic properly so called penetrated into ROME about two centuries before the Christian era. Previous to that time it was represented by Tuscan divination, the worship of the dead, the evocation of the lemures or phantoms sent by them, and the celebration of the mysteries of Mana-Genita, a divinity who bore some resemblance to the terrific goddess that made night hideous in Greece. With the progress of philosophical scepticism the augural art fell into

---

* Virgil, Eclogue viii., " deducere Lunam." Horace, Epode v., " Nox et Diana."

disesteem, but as the native superstition declined, the Eternal
City began to look for the unveiling of the future to the illusory
promise of the Chaldæan charlatan. *Chaldæis sed major est
fiducia,* is the bitter exclamation of the indignant satirist.* These
new prophets unfortunately soon became fashionable. Patrician
families retained them in their service. If a son was born or a
daughter married, the mathematician was summoned to draw their
horoscope. On the birth of Octavius, the learned Pythagorean
Nigidius Figulus, predicted the splendid destiny of the future
master of the world. Tiberius, his imperial successor, took
lessons in astrology from the renowned Thrasyllus, and thus,
himself an expert in the art of the Chaldæans, foretold the brief
tenure of power enjoyed by the consul Servius Galba. Of this able
master and his dexterous pupil a curious anecdote is found in
Tacitus. The slave who conducted him into the presence of the
future lord of the world over steep and scarcely accessible rocks,
was instructed, if Tiberius entertained any suspicion of his
having trifled with or deceived him, to fling him into the sea that
rolled below his rock-built residence. During the visit in which
he announced to Tiberius his coming greatness, he was asked, in
return, if he was acquainted with his own horoscope. The
Sidrophel of Rhodes, after observing the position of the stars, and
simulating surprise and terror, declared that some mysterious and
almost fatal misfortune menaced himself. His adroitness saved
him. Tiberius embraced him, regarded him as an oracle, and
numbered him among his most intimate friends.†

Tiberius was far from being the last of the emperors who read
his destiny in the stars. The son of Thrasyllus predicted Nero's
elevation to the throne of the Cæsars, Ptolemy that of Otho ; the
astrologers whom Vitellius ordered to leave Italy by a certain
day, retaliated by ordering their persecutor to leave the earth
first. Before the year was over, Vitellius was dead.

Though the emperors practised astrology privately, magic,
generally speaking, was officially discountenanced at Rome.
Augustus, Tiberius, Nero and Vespasian, as well as Vitellius,
prohibited the residence of magicians in Italy. Pituanius, less
fortunate than his contemporary Thrasyllus, was precipitated
from the Capitol, and Martius, a brother offender, was executed,
to the sound of the trumpet, in accordance with ancient prescription, beyond the Esquiline gate.

The progress of philosophical speculation tending to unity of
conception, while under the influence of Rome the world was
tending to political and social unity, ended in a complete transformation of classical polytheism. In the interest of the monotheistic

---

* Juvenal, Satyr. vi. 553.　　　　　　　† Taciti Annalium, vi. 21.

idea, the Neo-Platonists subordinated to the Supreme God a whole hierarchy of supernatural powers, whose genesis is traceable to the original fetishistic notion of the posthumous existence of the dead. According to Hesiod, thirty thousand guardian dæmons, souls of departed heroes, continually wandered over the earth, clothed in darkness, noting the actions of men and dispensing weal and woe to mortals. This doctrine of the existence of spirits, of intermediate beings between God and man, as Plato described the dæmons, played an important part in the speculative reform of the Neo-Platonic school. By its aid the monotheistic idea enjoyed a theoretic supremacy, and a dæmonological polytheism was invented, which maintained a certain respect for traditional and established sanctities. In this metamorphosis of the old creed, the dæmons reappeared as the principles that animate various agents and phenomena of nature. Man was thus brought into close relation with the Good Genii. Through music, through dialectics, through love and prayer, the Neo-Platonist attained to a state of ecstasy or intuition, and through ecstasy or intuition to the comprehension of the deity. At a later period, acts of homage to the Good Spirits were followed by the exorcism of the Bad Spirits, or by protective ceremonies of purification. Gradually old magical practices, collected from various parts of the Roman Empire, were revived and readjusted to the exigencies of the new dæmonology, till, in the last representatives of the new school, Religion degenerated into theurgy, or divine magic. It is only just to add that this magic was not wholly irrational, inasmuch as it was founded on what were assumed to be laws of nature. Fictitious entities, however, supplanting mechanical and physiological forces, the natural philosophy of the Neo-Platonists terminated in a narrow superstition. By enchantment it was held men might obtain power over the dæmons and souls of the dead, though to constrain the bad spirits to aid the applicant in any criminal object was severely reprobated.

Dæmonology in one shape or other had now become universal. The Jews and Christians supported and extended it. Among the Jews magic had always existed. In an obscure antiquity they had their pythonesses or Oboth : they pretended to raise the dead, they interpreted dreams, they believed that the divine will was made known in vision. Rhabdomancy, or divination by wands, was a Jewish practice that an ancient prophet had reproved.[*] Under the influence of the Persian religion, a Jewish angelogy early developed itself. Satan assumed the proportions of Ahriman, and the celestial hierarchy, headed by Michael, was but a reflex of the Amschaspands, the Izeds, and Ferouers. Like

---

* Hosea, iv. 12.

the Persians, the Jews now peopled the universe with malignant or beneficent spirits. Illustrious historical personages acquired an adventitious importance from the attributes with which they were invested. Solomon figured as a distinguished exorciser. Noah, Ham, Abraham, and Joseph were the reputed authors of the books of magic which inundated the East. Even the mythical world was put under contribution. Beelzebub, Ashtaroth, Belial, and Lucifer, foreign and degraded deities, were promoted to a bad eminence as the principal potentates of the infernal realms.

The Christians, notwithstanding the superior purity of their creed, accepted and propagated similar dæmonological ideas. The miracles which the pagans attributed to their gods, they referred to evil dæmons. With the Neo-Platonists and the Jews they maintained the intervention of supernatural powers. Pestilence, tempest, and hailstorm were regarded as the operations of malignant spirits, whose pernicious efforts required to be counteracted by the agency of good angels. While they rejected the employment of magical expedients, they yet continued to believe in their reality and effectiveness. Pagan magic, indeed, was not tolerated either by the secular power or by the Church. Though Constantine had permitted, Constantius absolutely proscribed the art of divination. Towards the close of the fourth century, Theodosius prohibited the Pagan ceremonial altogether. Henceforth no fire was to be lighted in honour of the Lar, no wine to be poured to the genius, no incense to be offered to the Penates. The sacrifice of a victim was to be considered as high treason, and the decoration of a tree or an altar was punished with confiscation. The persecuted polytheists retired from the city to the village, from the open country to the desert and the valley. The worship of the divinities of Greece and Rome ceased to be that of the great and noble, and acquired the expressive designation of *religio paganorum.**

Primitive Christianity, however, was only unfavourable to *Pagan* magic. Repudiating polytheistic theurgy, it practised a theurgy of its own. At an early period of its history a mysterious virtue was supposed to reside in the name of its founder, and the shadow of a favoured apostle, or the handkerchief of a successful rival, was invested by popular superstition with preternatural properties. To cast out devils, and heal the sick by imposition of hands, to take up serpents and drink deadly beverages with impunity, were the fancied privileges of the convert in the days

---

* "Qui ex locorum agrestium compitis et pagis pagani vocantur."—Quoted by M. Maury from "Orosius," lib. i. p. 2.

when the closing sentences of St. Mark's gospel were written. At the commencement of the Christian era exorcism was an established practice with the Jews. Jesus himself appears in the Synoptics as exercising the power of casting out devils. His countrymen undoubtedly shared the prevalent belief of orientals that madness, nervous derangement, and other diseases, were the immediate effects of supernatural agency. In the book of Job, Satan is allowed to affect the patient sufferer with the frightful malady of elephantiasis (?), and in one instance at least, his intervention is directly recognised by the great Nazarene prophet himself (Luke xiii. 11—16).

It is believed that Jesus, no less than his disciples, conceived epilepsy, hypochondria, and other forms of madness, to be occasioned by corporeal dæmoniacal possession. It is probable that the Gergesenes of St. Matthew's narrative were violent madmen. The youth of St. Mark's compilation was afflicted with epilepsy. The attack, it is said, usually commences with a loud cry; the muscles of the face contract: the patient falls suddenly to the ground: he grinds his teeth: he foams at the mouth: the tongue moves convulsively: the body is bathed with perspiration: and finally, insensibility supervenes. In addition to the coexistence of most of these symptoms, the Jewish youth is said to have had a dumb spirit, just as among the Persians blindness and privation of hearing are ascribed to the malevolence of the *dews.*

With such precedents as these, we cannot wonder that possession and exorcism were accepted facts in the early church. Theophilus, a bishop of Antioch in the second century, identifies these indwelling devils with the spirits who inspired the poets and prophets of the heathen world, and affirms that when they were exorcised in the name of the true God they confessed as much themselves. Origen declares that lost senses were restored and madness cured by the invocation of the same holy name, or by the recital, in the presence of the possessed, of some passage in the life of Jesus; while Tertullian describes how the devils which had insinuated themselves into the bodies of men, lashed, burned, and tortured by the Christian exorcists, with human words but divine power, howled, groaned, entreated, and ultimately retired. The efficacy of exorcism was formally recognised by the church itself in A.D. 367; when, by a decree of the Council of Laodicea, it was ruled that none should practise it but those who were appointed by the bishop. Nor let modern Christians, in their intellectual self-sufficiency, condemn this antique superstition as an exploded folly which characterized only the uninstructed childhood of Christianity. The reformed Church of

England had once,* has it not still, an official faith in the reality of exorcism? nor have the people of this country long abandoned their belief in the miraculous power of that royal touch in the case of scrofula. As late as the reign of Queen Anne, a *Form of Touching for the Evil* was actually printed in the service-books of the period; and so eminent a divine as Bishop Bull vindicated the reality of this royal magic.

The exorcism of devils was far from being the only theurgical practice of the earlier Christians. The faithful enjoyed, as they maintained, a general therapeutic qualification, and even boasted the possession of a power by which they could raise the dead. St. Augustine, the bishop of Hippo, whose testimony is surely as authoritative as that of most Christian apologists, asserts that the relics of St. Stephen not only cured the gout and restored sight to the blind, but renewed life in no fewer than five (dead) persons. (*De Civitate Dei*, xxii. 8.)

Another variety of what we may regard as early Christian magic, was the recourse had to vision and ecstasy. Justin Martyr, referring probably to some one of the many forms of seizure with which modern science is acquainted, compares the inspired recipient of divine knowledge to an instrument struck by the plectrum; and Tertullian assures us that he who is the subject of celestial communication must necessarily be deprived of his natural senses. To the ecstatic maid whom this ardent writer celebrates, it was revealed in trance that the *soul was tangible, tender, lucid, and of an airy colour.* To another sweet enthusiast an angel disclosed the exact dimensions of the veil that it became a Christian woman to wear. The great Cyprian himself believed in divine intimation, and ruled the church in conformity with suggestions made in vision. Thus, in obedience to a heavenly admonition, he ordered water to be mixed with wine in the Eucharist; and, authorized by what he termed the *divine suffrage*, he conferred ordination " without the previous consent of his clergy and people."†

---

* "Constitutions and Canons Ecclesiastical," 72: "Neither shall any minister not licensed as is aforesaid, presume to appoint or hold any meeting for Sermons, commonly termed by some Prophecies or Exercises. in market-towns or other places, under the said pains: nor, *without such licence*, to attempt, upon any pretence whatsoever, either of possession or obsession, by fasting and prayer to cast out any devil or devils, under pain of the imputation of imposture or cozenage, and deposition from the ministry." N.B.—This Canon is headed: *Ministers not to appoint public or private Fasts or Prophecies, or to exorcise, but by authority.* The Canons of 1603 do not in general bind the laity of these realms; but, according to Lord Hardwicke, the clergy are bound by all the Canons which are confirmed by the King. How far does this decision apply to the present time?

† Middleton's "Inquiry"

Under the influence of the Palestinian Reform, the gods of Greece and Rome were degraded to devils—their temples were destroyed and their worship proscribed. But the old instinct still survived ; the old rites, under some thin disguise of orthodox belief, still lingered in Greece, in Asia Minor, and in Italy. The Christian procession replaced the Pagan theoria : the sacred lamp burnt before the image of the Virgin instead of that of the Lares. In Sicily the Virgin appropriated the sanctuaries of Ceres and Venus ; at Naples the popular worship of the Madonna emanated from that of Vesta and Demeter ; while the rural festivals of Bacchus and his divine consort are still recalled by the dancing pilgrims of the South, who, with ivy wreaths, garlanded thyrses, and leaf-covered chariots, celebrate the fête of the Madonna del Arco.

In modern Greece the Virgin, supplanting the star of Aphrodité, opens the gates of the morning ; the forty saints bring back the nightingale and the returning spring ; the shepherds commit the care of their flocks to Demetrius instead of Pan ; St. George watches over the harvest-field ; St. Nicholas calms the tempest ; St. Elias has succeeded to the adoration of Helios, or the Sun. In the East, a horrible tragedy at Pergamos proved that, seven hundred years after the birth of Jesus, the art of the Aruspex was not wholly discredited. In the sixth century, the Delta of the Nile was still believed to be haunted by the colossal river-god. Menas, the governor, is said to have beheld this awful presence, and Isidorus of Gaza, if we may take his own word for it, was likewise favoured with a personal interview. If the gods were no longer directly worshipped, their names were at least honoured in the rites of evocation. Their fountains, their fields, their groves, were still held sacred. The thunders of the Church rolled in vain ; in vain was the strong arm of the secular power uplifted. The people could not be persuaded to abandon the old magical practices altogether. Curiosity, revenge, avarice, supplied motives too strong for piety to resist or power to subdue. Rejected by the Church, magic, astrology, and witchcraft were secretly favoured and supported by popular prepossessions. Dæmons were invoked to reveal the secrets of the future. The devil was supposed to take the form of a black dog, a pig, a wolf, a bull, a rat ; and unclean animals were excommunicated as agents of the Prince of Darkness. Hecate was still the protecting deity of sorcerers ; the cross-road, the rendezvous of ghost and evil spirit. The witches' SABBATH itself, with its licentious ceremonies, was a relic of the old festival of Bacchus Sabbazius, and as a goat was consecrated to the heathen god, " the cloven-foot" of modern mythology very properly appeared in the form of that animal. The sorcerer still summoned the storm or called down the rain. Jupiter, Belus, or Janus, had not " all died" when Gregory III. prohibited the *paganam consuetudinem.* The poetical and pictorial representations of the Greek Tartarus or the Egyptian Amenti supplied materials for the popular or artistic delineation of the Christian hell ; and the craters of volcanoes were perseveringly regarded as the entrances to the infernal regions. The consecration of the Yule-log carries us back to the days of heathen ceremonial, and the bale-fires of St. John's Eve refer us for their origin to the ancient feast of the summer solstice, to the rites of Baal or the mysteries of Adonis. In the *Indiculus Superstitionum et Paganiarum,* a work of the eighth century, and in a similar catalogue drawn up four hundred years later, we have evidence of the ethnic origin of the magic of the time. The more recent of these two productions, in effect, specifies the existence of astrology, sorcery, oracular practices, offerings to the Parcæ, and *carmina diabolica,* or, in other words, the old hymns addressed to the gods. A certain white magic was even sanctioned by the Church, or resorted to by her children, though not of course under that name. The storm was laid by the use of holy water, or by the revolution of the Cross, whose mystic virtue was celebrated by early patristic writers. The *agnus Dei* protected from lightning, fire, flood, and sin. The random consultation of the sacred volume foretold the coming event; the recital of the Lord's prayer was prescribed for the cure of wounds; the relics of a female saint were dipped in the river to procure rain ; while the skin of some wild beast over the Christian door, recalled the *rostrum lupi* which the pagan householder nailed up as a defence against witches. Some of these practices, however, were forbidden by the Church, though, *out of church,* they were not unfrequently prosecuted.

But above all, the celestial sphere continued to publish its predictions to the Christian as to the Pagan world. To Tertullian the stars with " fiery tresses" announced pestilence, war, and revolution. Mediæval Christianity shared the sentiment of Tertullian. An eclipse threatened our devout forefathers with some dreadful disaster. To their excited vision an electric storm was a heavenly army ; a meteor, a sign of divine displeasure; and a hurricane the manifestation of an evil spirit's anger. If the soldiers of Germanicus clashed the ringing brass and blew the echoing trumpet during a sudden eclipse of the moon, rejoicing or lamenting as *the goddess* darkened or brightened, the servants of Him whose kingdom is not of this world resorted to similar artifices to prevent the magicians from *hurting the* obscured luminary whose helplessness they sought to protect.

That the belief in ghosts survived the fall of Paganism, and was even encouraged by Christianity, is no more than we should have expected. The death of Jesus was accompanied by numerous instances of spectral visitation. Evodius, the correspondent of Augustine, testifies that the dead had been seen to come and go in private houses, and to assemble for devotional purposes in churches. Other forms of old superstition also flourished in the Middle Ages. The grotesque fancy of classical lycanthropy was transmitted in the fables of the were-wolf of Germany and the loup-garou of France. In the Morea, the peasants even now believe in the Naïad and Nereïd of the old Greek waters. In Crete the fisherman sees the local divinity standing on the bank. The Morai still live in Hellas, and attend at the birth of an infant, or the union of bride and bridegroom. In Wallachia, Diana is honoured as a goddess. The fays of France (if they are not yet all vanished) represent the Fata of Latium; and though the *Dusius,* or night genius of the ancient Celt, no longer haunts our English island, " the Deuce is in it" to this very day; and the devil, good-humouredly assuming the name of Old Nick, still reminds us of the extinct Water Nix from whom he borrowed it.

Thus, the astrology and magic of the Christian world were derived from primitive philosophy and pagan superstition. The pretensions of the sorcerer were recognised in the Middle Ages; his power over the dæmons was never called in question; his imagined leagues with the spirits of darkness exposed him to the most terrible imputations and the most tremendous penalties. Unfortunately, all intellectual independence and mental superiority were subject to similar suspicions, and included under the fatal category of sorcery. The meetings of the Valdenses, the Cathari, and the Templars were ominously compared with the witches' sabbaths. Even science and art were accused of magic. Virgil was transformed into an enchanter: the favourite black dog of Cornelius Agrippa was regarded as a familiar dæmon; and the people fled before the approach of the heretical magician, who knew perfectly eight languages, and denied that St. Anne had three husbands. Pope Gerbert himself did not escape the imputation. Against Albertus Magnus, Roger Bacon, Arnauld de Villeneuve, and Raymond Lully, the like charge was preferred. The revival of learning was far from being unfavourable to the traditionary faith in the might of stars and of angels, of spirits and gods. In Greece, Michael Psellas published his version of the Neo-Platonic dæmonology. Paracelsus and Agrippa employed the names of pagan deities in their mystical nomenclature. The alchemists assimilated the forces which, as they supposed, governed nature, to the dæmons of the ancient philosophers, and, like their prototypes, endeavoured to acquire a mastery over them. The astrologers, asserting the interdependence of all phenomena, pretended to read the fate of men and empires in the bright *leaves* of the stars, and to explain by their help the nature of the human constitution and character. Cardan acknowledged the reality of the stellar influences. Pica de Mirandola and Gerson argued against them. Kings and Queens shared the common frenzy. Rodolph II. was surrounded with astrologers, magicians, and sorcerers. Even Tycho Brahe and Kepler did not wholly escape the contagion. The early natural philosophers indeed, were, equally with the vulgar, the dupes of their own ignorance, sanguine hope, and excited imagination. Paracelsus has left us a receipt for making a fairy ; and Baptista Porta does not deny the possibility of manufacturing creatures which, at their full growth, should not exceed the size of a mouse, though he disparagingly adds, they would be nothing more than pretty little dogs to play with. Porta believed himself to be a prognosticator, but warned by the Pope, that "magical sciences were great hindrances to the study of the Bible," he took the hint, it would seem, and henceforth appears to have limited his genius to a sort of natural thaumaturgy. "On entering his cabinet, some phantom of an attendant was sure to be hovering in the air, moving as he who entered moved : or he observed in some mirror that his face was twisted on the wrong side of his shoulders, and did not quite think that all was right when he clapped his hand on it ; or passing through a darkened apartment, a magical landscape burst on him, with human beings in motion ; the boughs of trees bending, and the very clouds passing over the sun : or sometimes banquets, battles, and hunting parties were seen in the same apartment."

A great English poet had heard of these, or similar ocular illusions, and in his "Franklin's Tale" immortalized the impressions which the natural magic of the *Juggler* or *Tregetour* had produced on his mind.

> "For I am siker that there be sciences
> By which men maken divers apparénces,
> Such as these subtle tregetourès play.
> For oft at feastes have I well heard say
> That tregetours, within a hallè large
> Have made come in a water and a barge,
> And in the hallè rowen up and down.
> Sometime hath seemèd come a grim lioún,
> And sometime flourès spring as in a mead,
> Sometime a vine and grapes white and red ;
> Sometime a castle all of lime and stone,
> And when them liketh, voideth it anon :
> Thus seemeth it to every mannès sight."

This was a very innocent magic. After our poet had long ceased to sing, a black art, to which the patriotic Maid of Orleans and Eleanor, the wife of good Duke Humphrey, were believed to be addicted, called down the censure of the Church. In the native country of the virgin-martyr of Arc, an ordinance was issued against charmers, diviners, invocators of evil spirits, and necromancers, A.D. 1493; and in England an Act of Henry VIII. pronounces magic and sorcery to be felony; while under James I. death was the adjudged penalty of the same imaginary crime.

During four centuries, says Carrière, European jurisprudence sacrificed thousands of human victims to the belief in the existence of compacts between men and the evil one. Dr. Sprenger, in his admirable Life of Mohammed, computes the entire number of persons who have been burned as witches during the Christian epoch, at nine millions, an estimate which he regards as not exaggerated. When treatises on procedure for sorcery were written by men learned in the law, and reason itself was cowed by a theological, legal, and social reign of terror, it was useless to defend, as Gabriel Naudé defended, the illustrious men whose superior knowledge was regarded but as a sign of their intercourse with supernatural agents. The unhappy victims of this horrible infatuation came themselves to believe in their own wonder-working powers. Dæmonology, once an attenuated form of expiring Polytheism, ended in becoming a psychological epidemic that absorbed all phases of mental alienation; so that in spite of the thunders of the Church and the baring of the red right-hand of secular power, in spite of reason, and in spite of rhyme, magicians continued to practise and dupes to be practised upon.

But here, breaking off from our historical survey of idolatrous magic and astrology, we proceed, with M. Maury's continued assistance, to give some account of the proximate causes of the superstitious beliefs of the Pagan and Christian past.

The parent source of these delusions, as we have already seen, lay in the instinctive predisposition of the unlessoned mind to ascribe mental activity or supernatural virtue to external objects; to infer volition where it sees motion; to make gods of beasts or stars, and talismans of trees and stones. A powerful auxiliary of this primitive naturalism was supplied by a conviction of the posthumous existence of deceased friends or illustrious chiefs, grounded on their return in dream or their appearance to the mind's eye, in moments of intense excitement, and issuing in a formal adoration of dead ancestors. To evoke the spirits of the departed was the special function of the early priest or sorcerer. To procure vivid *narcotic* dreams, in which the sleeper might fortify his belief of the continued existence of his friends by retracing the old familiar features, was a principal part of his sacerdotal office. In the religion of barbarous tribes dreams

F 2

assumed a paramount importance. With the Red Indians, in particular, they were the great mainstay in the belief of magic. Even with more civilized communities dreams have been held in high esteem as expedients for determining the secrets of the future. In Egypt, in Assyria, in Judæa, the dream was the favourite instrument of divination. Egypt was preserved from a famine by a dream. The Book of Daniel asserts that coming events were clearly disclosed to the King of Babylon by a dream; and the conveyance of the promised land, with a recital of its ultimate boundaries, was made in a dream to the great Hebrew expectant in Genesis (xv. 12). Even at the dawn of a more spiritual dispensation the miraculous conception of Jesus was announced in a dream to Joseph; and Peter's warrant for the admission of the Gentile converts into the Christian Church was " of such stuff as dreams are made of." The dream of Agamemnon and the vision of Achilles will recur to the mind of every reader of Homer.

Certain remarkable phenomena in dreaming sufficiently account for the sacred or prophetic character with which it was invested. Its fantastic representations are often the reflex of internal sensations actually experienced. Dreams indicate the natural qualities or disposition of the sleeper—they furnish data for the diagnosis of the physician. In dreams latent ideas are developed, and mental operations, including literary composition and even scientific discovery, performed. Dreaming intensifies the memory: forgotten facts return in sleep with an emphasis and a reality that seem well-nigh miraculous. It is a peculiarity of dreaming that we attribute to others the acts which really emanate from ourselves. We translate our thoughts into words, and receive them back as extraneous utterances from the airy interlocutors whom we encounter in our dreams. Thus invalids having sometimes a dim presentiment of the means to be adopted for their restoration to health, have, in their dreams, affiliated their own medical prescriptions on the appropriate deities—in Pagan times, on Apollo, Jasonius, or Cyzicenus, a therapeutic god; and after his temple on the shores of the Bosphorus had been re-dedicated to St. Michael, to that archangelic physician of the Christian world. The subsequent employment of the means prescribed, and the actual restoration of the patient, supplied a triumphant argument to justify the faith of the devout few in the divine efficacy of dream-revelations; while in all ages that fruitful source of fallacy, fortuitous coincidence, which records fulfilment and overlooks failure, must have powerfully sustained, as it primarily founded, the belief of the credulous masses in the prognosticatory significance of dreams.

This natural tendency of mankind was of course inflamed and

augmented by the artificial devices of the professed interpreters of dreams. To render these sacred apparitions more startlingly real, the *oneirocritist* had recourse to inhalations of carbonic acid, to sulphurous vapours, to narcotic beverages, and the like, selecting appropriate localities as the scene of the vision, gloomy caverns from whose mysterious depth the thermal fountain rose, and whose dismal aspect had procured them the ominous names of the Gates of Hell, the Charonium, the Plutonium. The gaseous exhalations of these grim regions superinduced delirium ; and the illusions which presented themselves to the patient's mental sense, were mistaken for divine communications.

A singular variety of dreams, illustrated at some length by M. Maury, under the title of hypnogogical or sleep-inducing hallucinations, satisfactorily accounts for the belief in the apparitions of devils, angels, and spirits, recorded in old lives of saints and books of magic. In these dreams, fugitive, grotesque, and frightful shapes appear before the closed or half-closed eyes, as the precursors of approaching sleep. "They come," says our author, " unbidden, and sometimes remain several seconds. Like the dreams to which they furnish materials, they are evoked by the images which have impressed themselves on the organ of vision during our waking hours, by the fanciful thoughts that have traversed, and the reflections that have preoccupied our minds." These illusions, very common in the case of persons of morbid sensibility, proceed from a plethora of the little vessels of the brain and over-excitement of the nervous system. Standing in close relation to certain forms of disease, and particularly that in which the senses are affected, some of them enter into the category of hallucinations properly so called—the second of the four great divisions of M. Maury's PATHOLOGICAL MAGIC ; those that precede, or, as is sometimes the case, survive sleep, being the first.

The ignorance of the ancients as to the true character and real origin of disease appropriately corresponded with their ignorance of the constancy of the phenonema of the external world. The same impulse which led them to substitute personal beings for regulating forces, made them attribute malady and death to the supernatural action of gods and genii. To the primitive man death, particularly sudden death, appeared the immediate act of some invisible power, and his first impression must have been very similar to that which Byron supposes Cain to have had when he makes him speculate on the nature of " this Almighty Death."

> " I thought it was a *being :* who could do
> Such evil things to beings, *save a being ?*"

Next to the fatal and mysterious death-stroke the epidemic, or
the nervous malady no doubt presented to the untutored mind
evident signs of supernatural derivation. The unexpected appearance, the contagious character, and deadly effects of the former,
and the obscure origin of the latter, the excessive mental agitation
which it produces, the muscular movements and the heightened
sensibility which accompany it, are so many presumable indications of divine intervention.   Madness, epilepsy, catalepsy,
hysteria, and the cognate varieties of disease, long excited the
wonder and superstitious terror of mankind.   The hallucinations
to which the patient is liable, the cries and the strange words
which he utters, the sinister and terrific aspect which his features
assume, his loss of reason and self-control, and the voluntary
ascription of his own words and actions to invisible persons who
beset or pursue him, seem all so many proofs of a literal seizure
and possession by an evil spirit.   In *hysteria* the sensation of a
ball rising in the throat suggests the notion of the positive intrusion into the human frame of some personal agent.   In *canine
madness* the periodical return of the crisis of the disorder, the
frantic ebullitions of the epileptic or the maniac, the sensations
of pricking, tingling, and of a weight under the skin, so common
in hypochondria and mental alienation, the muscular contractions
and convulsive movements, and the irresistible impulsion of ideas,
which are symptomatic of certain maladies, were in old times conclusive arguments for the reality of dæmoniacal possession.   Accordingly, in Rome the hallucinations of madmen were attributed
to the goddess Mania, the mother of the Lares, and the Manes or
souls of dead men, and the sufferer was called larvatus, *haunted*,
or Cerritus, from the goddess Ceres, who guarded in the bosom of
the earth the shades of the departed.   In the classical lands of
Greece and Rome, epilepsy, under the name of *lues deifica*, was
respected as a sacred disease.   Plato himself tells us that no ma
in possession of his senses ever obtained the gift of true divination : it was the privilege of the sleeper, whose understanding
was shackled, or of the sick, or of the subject of some divine
rapture.   Porphyry attributes the inarticulate sounds, the sobs,
the sense of oppression, the difficulty of breathing, characteristic of
mental disease, to dæmons dispersed in the air; though Hippocrates,
long before his time, had protested against the folly of making a
dæmon responsible for the phenomena of the *Morbus sacer*,
wrongly so called.   Corybantism, a kind of mental epidemic, is
recognised by Aretæus as a malady of the imagination curable by
music.   In Egypt, Circassia, India, China, Oceania, among the
tribes of North America, in Ethiopia, in the Soudan, and among
the Caffres and Hottentots, the absurd superstition which refers
disease to dæmoniacal possession and endeavours to remove it

by exorcism or enchantment, prevailed in the past, or exists in the present time. Pagan and Christian equally recognised the supernatural origin of different forms of nervous derangement, and alike resorted to similar expedients for their cure. Human reason, however, was not without its champions. In antiquity Hippocrates and Aretæus, probably Cælius Aurelianus, the Neo-Platonist school in spite of its dæmonology, and Plutarch in spite of his vindication of the prophetic power of madness, referred all such morbid affections to natural causes. In modern times Montaigne and Cyrano de Bergerac expressed their doubts of the reality of possession, while in 1684 Bonet showed that the explanation of this mystery, as of magic in general, was to be sought in the pathological state of the subject. The special dissertation of J. S. Semler (1770-1779) was written expressly to show that the Biblical dæmoniacs were merely sufferers from nervous disease. In the preceding century Lightfoot had started the same theory in England, and Teller and Farmer, about the same time as Semler, vindicated the heterodox teaching of common sense. M. Maury, after stating that the hypothesis received its *coup de grâce* from Lædinger's Treatise *De Veterum Hebræorum, Arte Medica,* &c., adds that the demonstration offered was so conclusive, that even theologians could not refuse to accept it. Thus the Abbé Bergier acknowledges that the evil spirit of the Bible is the conventional designation of unknown and incurable disease; and Debreyne, a Trappist physician, while inconsistently excepting the New Testament cases of possession, admits that all other instances imply either disease or imposture.

The third determining element in M. Maury's pathological theory is the influence of imagination. The imagination, he says, is affected by the senses, and, in turn, reacts upon them. His doctrine, if we rightly apprehend it, is identical with that of Mr. Alexander Bain, with us a *clarum et venerabile nomen.*[*] "In the recovery of objects as ideas when they are no longer present as realities, the same nervous circles and the same organs of sense and movement are occupied as in the original perception during the actual presence" (p. 560). "We see that when the revival is energetic, it goes the length of exciting even the surface of sense itself by a sort of back movement. We might think of a blow in the hand until the skin was actually irritated and inflamed. The attention very much directed to any part of the body, as the great toe, is apt to produce a distinct feeling in the part, which we account for only by supposing a revived nerve-current to flow there, making a sort of false sensation—an influence from within mimicking the influences from without" (p. 336).

---

[*] "The Senses and the Intellect."

In hypochondria, and in cases of excessive sensibility, very singular phenomena occur.

"I have seen," says Hufeland, "not only people who, with features perfectly regular, supposed that their noses stood awry; and who, though slender, and sound in every respect, could not get rid of the idea that they were in the last stage of the dropsy; but I have seen a lady who, if asked whether she had not this or the other local disorder, felt in a moment every symptom of it. Having asked her if she had the headache, she was instantly seized with it; and on asking in like manner respecting the cramp in the arm, and the hiccup, both these affections immediately took place. . . . . Nay, we have had the instance of a person who imagined himself to be actually dead, and who therefore would have been starved had not a friend, who pretended to be dead also, persuaded him that it was customary in the other world to eat a sufficient quantity daily."—(p. 164).

A curious instance of spectral illusion, which Mr. Lewes explains as the effect of suggestion acting on an over-excited brain, is supplied by Professor Stevelly, who, being in weak health, had gone out to his brother-in-law's seat in the country for a few weeks, and who, while there, had become greatly interested in the habits and economy of the bees.

"One morning, soon after breakfast, the servant came in to say that one of the hives was just beginning to swarm. The morning was a beautiful, clear, sunny one, and I stood gazing at the insects as they appeared projected against the bright sky, rapidly and uneasily coursing hither and thither in most curious and yet regular confusion, the drones making a humming noise much louder and sharper than the workers, from whom also they were easily distinguished by their size, but all appearing much larger in their rapid flight than their true size. In the evening, as it grew dark, I again went out to see the beehive, into which the swarm had been collected, removed to its stand. Soon after, I was much surprised to see, as I thought, multitudes of large flies coursing about in the air. I mentioned it to my sister, who said I must be mistaken, as she had never seen an evening in which so few flies were abroad. Soon after, when I retired to my chamber and knelt to my prayers before going to rest, I was surprised to see, coursing back and forward between me and the wall, what I now recognised as the swarm of bees, the drones quite easily distinguishable from the workers, and all in rapid whirling motion as in the morning. This scene continued to be present to me as long as I remained awake, and occasionally I awoke in the night, nor had it entirely faded away by the next night, although much less vivid."

The spectral illusion now described, Mr. Lewes considers to be somewhat similar to that of mania or of dreaming; and he seeks to explain the latter phenomenon by analogies drawn from our waking experience, combined with a correct interpretation of nervous action in general.* In this explanation he appears to have been in part anticipated by St. Basil, who, however deficient in physiological knowledge, proposed, somewhat hazardously we should have thought, a similar method of interpreting what we will take the liberty to call the Prophetic Hallucination. The vision in which God communicates his thought to men, when awake, must, he suggests, bear some analogy to that which visits them in sleep ; and just as in dreams we believe that we hear sounds, though none are produced by the action of the vibratory medium on the auditory nerve, so, or nearly so, do the prophets hear, in their waking hours, that mystical utterance which is called the voice of God. In this suggestion, which the originator of course applied no further than was consistent with the orthodox faith, lies a virtual explanation of the mystery. The scene which the mind appears to contemplate as an independent spectator, is in reality its own fantastic creation. Miracles and enchantments (imposture are apart) are the works not of angels or devils, but of the deluded senses and the excited imagination. Seething brains and shaping fancies body forth the forms of things known and unknown, the cerebral reflexes being uncontrolled by the reflexes from sense, during the temporary abdication of " cool reason."

Positive evidence of this despotic power of the imagination is adducible. To say nothing of this second sight of Swedenborg, Goethe, Tasso, or Shelley, the realizing fantasy of William Blake strikingly attests it. This glorious visionary persuaded himself into a belief in an ante-natal existence. He formed friendships with Homer and Moses, with Pindar and Virgil, with Milton, who recited to him an unpublished poem, with Dante and others, describing them as majestic shadows, grey but luminous, and superior to the common height of men. Sometimes he beheld less imperial shapes. Nothing can be more graceful than his account of a fairy funeral which he witnessed.

" I was walking alone in my garden ; there was great stillness among the branches and flowers, and more than common sweetness in the air. I heard a low and pleasant sound, and I knew not whence it came. At last I saw the broad leaf of a flower move, and underneath I saw a procession of creatures of the size and colour of green and grey grasshoppers, bearing a body laid out on a rose-leaf, which they buried with songs, and then disappeared."

As a morbid state of the nervous system acts upon the mind, so the mind reacts upon the physical constitution. A strong conviction that certain maladies will break out—nay, the very

---

* " Physiology of Common Life." By G. H. Lewes.

fear of being attacked by some of them—has been known to bring about the very evil apprehended. The origination of unusual muscular movements can be effected at will by a process similar to that which, in some exceptional cases, controls the circulation of the blood and even arrests the action of the heart.

Again, as there are certain reflex movements which are produced unconsciously, though in conformity to some natural requirement, so are there reflex acts automatically determined, independently of the will and without the knowledge of the person experiencing them. This is precisely what happens in dreams. The dreamer expressing his thoughts with a sort of mental speech, or, it may be, in articulated words, fancies that he is conversing with other persons, while he is really talking only with himself. The same peculiarity occurs in hallucination, only on a grander scale. Desire, fear, enthusiasm, provoke an unconscious action in the organism which we "by an inevitable tendency of our nature to convert every sensation into an external cause," refer to a foreign agent; and as the responses of the imagination harmonize with our wishes, or correspond to our wants or our fears, we become all the more completely the dupes of this involuntary imposture. Every one of the senses, moreover, being accessible to the effects of this pathological sorcery, the illusion acquires a strange consistency and perfection from the simultaneous enchantment of two or more of them. For "the ghost" may be present not only to the eye but to the ear, to the smell, to the taste, to the touch. Under the influence of some cerebral agitation, some tyrannizing emotion, spectral objects have been seen with all the vividness of actual vision. It was thus Maupertuis was seen, after his death, by the German *savan* Gleditsch as distinctly as if he had been really there. It was, perhaps, with like distinctness that Catherine of Genoa, revisiting the glimpses of the moon, was seen by the sisters of her convent; or that the celebrated visionary Jane Leade was beheld by her co-religionists some time after she had ceased to live. But, in general, these hallucinations have not the clearness or force of the real images: they are the reflection not the reality, the shadow, not the figure, of the persons long loved, tenderly regretted, and unconsciously evoked by the invisible wand of the magician,—Imaginative thought. One of the most extraordinary forms of mental malady acting on the physical constitution is that which has the somewhat vague title of stigmatization. It is probable that Protestant incredulity would explain this mystical disorder and its singular phenomena, by referring them exclusively to the operation of imposture. But after making certain deductions on the score of deception and self-delusion, and admitting the complementary action of the imagination, which under the influence of emotion can make " a bear out of a bush," and translate a fancied resemblance into an actual and designed likeness, M. Maury still claims a large amount of good faith for the stigmatic invalids, and of reality for the theory of corporeal impressions implied in this concession. Nor does he stand alone here. This peculiar form of religious disease is not the exclusive possession of the Catholic. As if to divest it of its value as a celestial credential, the marks of the Lord Jesus in the body of Christian men have, according to Dr. Sprenger, a parallel in the reproduction of the battle-wounds of Mohammed in the body of the faithful sons of Islam. Stigmatization, then, may be regarded as the result of a real *Morbus sacer.* The consequence of a mental disturbance attributable to an excess of religious meditation, to the abuse of asceticism, and prolonged abstinence, in constitutions predisposed to nervous disease, it shows itself in the reaction of the ideas on particular organs, and in the downright creation of the disorder for which they have, so to speak, a natural affinity. The persons who, as they fancy, have received wounds in their sleep, have, on waking, or some days after, under the influence of this conviction, exhibited traces of inflammation or ulceration on the parts of the body which they suppose to have been injured. The hermits of the *Thebaïd* and certain other visionaries, have shown on their skin the red marks left by the airy whip of the dæmon or angel who seemed to administer the flagellation. Of all these holy stigmatics the most celebrated was doubtless the famous St. Francis of Assisi, whose case, as related at length by M. Maury, may be briefly reported here. The proud pre-eminence of being regarded as a second Jesus Christ was accorded to this pillar of the Catholic Church, in virtue of his exact imitation of the career of his great Exemplar. The events of his own life were often in strict correspondence with those in the life of his Divine Master. Like him, he was announced by prophets; like him, he had twelve apostles, one of whom, to make the coincidence more striking, fulfilled the part of the traitor Judas ; like him, he was tempted by the devil, and, like him, he vanquished his subtle enemy. The miracles attributed to this *new* king of the Jews—for so was the Saint of Assisi considered—were the counterparts of those of Jesus, and the transfiguration of the Son of Mary was repeated in the case of his favoured representative. The semi-deification of which St. Francis thus became the subject is not, however, to be attributed to deliberate imitation only. It was due still more to a remarkable circumstance which occurred towards the decline of life, and which seemed to mark him as with the seal of a divine election. Buried in his mountain retreat near Camaldoli and Vallombrosa, St. Francis dedicated himself to ascetic practices, religious meditation, and pious ecstasy. In the year 1224, during the forty days which separate the feast of the Assumption from that of St. Michael, attenuated by fast and rapt in the ardours of devotion, the saint imagined that he heard the voice of God bidding him open the gospel and read therein the divine will. Three several times the volume was opened; and three several times the passage at which it opened, was that which contained the narrative of the last sufferings of Christ. Hence, St. Francis inferred that his imitation of Jesus must be carried further than it had yet been. Prolonged fasting, increased absorption, extreme asceticism, brought him still nearer to the ideal perfection to which he aspired. On the day of the elevation of the cross, this ' second son of God,' surrendering himself with unusual ardour to ecstatic contemplation beheld, or fancied that he beheld, a seraph descending from heaven and approaching him. Between his luminous wings the angelic visitant bore a human figure, attached by the hands and feet to a cross. After a while the vision passed away, but the pious anchorite was sensible of a strange shock and of a profound disturbance of his entire system. In particular, he experienced painful sensations, soon succeeded by ulcerations or quasi-wounds. These wounds were regarded by St. Francis as the *stigmata* or marks of the passion of Christ. Nor was St. Francis the only one who so regarded them. The fame of the miracle rang through the world. The sanctity which environed the saint augmented. The father of the faithful in Christendom—the type or organ of infallibility—pronounced this natural operation to be the miraculous effect of divine grace; and the spiritual children of the unerring pontiff, observing that the impression of the stigmata had occurred on the very day of the elevation of the cross, easily convinced themselves that the welcome prodigy was a peremptory demonstration of the mystery of the sacred redemption.

The preference thus accorded to the *Seraphic Doctor* excited the jealousy of his Dominican rivals. Opposing miracle to miracle, they set up a female stigmatic, and the divinely-inspired Catherine, who taught that the mother of our Lord was conceived in sin, was selected to confute the divinely-inspired Bridget, who maintained the immaculate conception of the Virgin-parent. In both cases the result was the same. The votaries of either order (and nearly all the stigmatics of the seventeenth and eighteenth centuries are found in one or other of these two orders) made it the end and aim of their religious career to renew in their own persons this grotesque expression of celestial favour. With the images of St. Francis or St. Catherine ever before their eyes, the candidates for this divine privilege succeeded, by the force of mystical reverie, in effecting the same or a very similar prodigy. The slight variation observable in the form of the imprints is not uninstructively traceable to the diversity of the circumstances in which the subject was placed; the stigmatic emblazonment being modified in conformity with the representation in the portraits. Thus Madeleine de Pazzi, Hieronyma Caruaglio, Anne Catherine Emmerich, Columba Rocasani, Mary of Lisbon, Stephana Quinzani, and others, received on their bodies marks resembling rays of blood mingled with fire. The explanation is easy. They were all Dominicans, and they reproduced the stigmatization of this Dominican model, St. Catherine, on whom Jesus himself stamped the impression of his divine wounds by means of the blood-coloured rays which emanated from them. We may add, that to outdo the opposition saint, Francis of Assisi, who was only marked on the feet, the neck, and side, the pious maiden had the traces of the crown of thorns distinctly visible on her brow; a distinction which did not fail to attract the attention of Ursule Aguir, who wore, as she affirmed, an *invisible* diadem to match it. In a somewhat similar way Walter of Strasbourg, meditating on the sorrows experienced by the Holy Virgin at the foot of the cross, felt his side pierced by a sword; that is, as M. Maury explains it, his imagination availed itself of the image adopted by Catholic iconography, in its representation of the Mater Dolorosa.

To such an excess did these religious histrionics proceed, that all the phases of the passion were represented on the person of one or other of the performers. In their ambition to bear, literally, the cross of Christ, one, as Veronica Giuliani, drank the cup of bitterness presented by the angel to the Saviour on Gethsemane, while another, as Catherine Ricci, preserved on her tender person the marks of the scourge which had flogged alike her and her Lord. These illustrations of pathological magic, it is noticeable, were nearly always women. For one man who received the divine favours, there were at least ten of the more impressionable sex.

Between this morbid affection and the mysticism which in some measure suspends both mental and corporeal action, there is a close connexion. In its extreme or ecstatic form, mysticism endeavours to effect an entire self-conquest, to annihilate nature, to rise beyond this visible diurnal sphere, and to realize an absolute devotion to God. In India this mystical self-immolation has matured into a positive religion. In Catholic countries this spiritual *felo de se*, except in individual cases, has never been systematically practised. Among those honoured with the stigmata, however, some ecstatics have been found, as Marie de Mœrll, whose limbs have stiffened and whose muscles have lost their flexibility and even the power of motion. The hallucinations peculiarly characterizing the Christian mystics are the persuasion that they are suspended in the air, like Thomas de

Villanova and St. Theresa, and the fancy that they visit distant lands, while really at perfect rest, as St. Lidwine, renowned for his visionary travels to the Holy Land, and Marie d'Agreda, who took an imaginary journey to Mexico. The additional power which the memory of the ecstatic mystics acquires, and which enables the devotee to recall long passages from sermons and discourses; the tact with which they form a style in keeping with their prophetic pretensions, their ardent imagination and their lavish use of metaphor as an instrument for revealing the secrets of the future, necessarily seem to themselves and their uninstructed adherents so many proofs or presumptions of the reality of their claims. The misfortune was that in all this divine rapture there lay extreme peril. The love of God is not easily separable from the love of man; and the sensuous passion of "the Song of Songs," a favourite poem with the brides of Christ, tended to reproduce itself in these elect souls. For them, so at least says M. Maury, Jesus was a beautiful youth whose personal charms encouraged rather amorous affection than moral improvement. Margaret Alacoque, founder of the order of the "Sacré Cœur de Jesus et Marie," may be cited as an exemplary instance of mystical attachment. This object of the particular attentions of Jesus Christ, is said to have written with her blood the synallagmatic contract dictated by her distinguished lover, when he pronounced her the heir of his heart and all its treasures for time and eternity. St. Theresa, who, as we have seen, was not far from illusion herself, but whose fine intellect constitutes her "the metaphysician of feminine mysticism and ecstatic illumination," saw the dark side of all this romance of the soul, confessing that the love of God had its allurements of pride and vanity, and that in this subjective phantasmagoria there were elements that were not divine.

The summary with which M. Maury concludes this part of his subject affords a still less favourable view of this rapturous piety. Ecstatic mysticism, he says, is a long chain of moral and physical hallucinations, which in the case of the more delicate and excitable organisms end in stigmatization, and eventually in death. It is the most startling proof of the influence of thought and imagination on the human system. Actions, words, written compositions, everything in short, reflects the physical derangement which accompanies it, which sustains it, and by which it is in turn sustained.

This ecstatic mysticism, continues our author, has its natural application in magic. What the visionaries believed they saw and felt, and what they really did see and feel, as the consequence of their persevering meditation, the sorcerers felt and believed under other forms. Instead of the marks of God, they bore on their desecrated bodies the stigmata of the devil; the pictures which were disclosed to their eyes were not pictures of paradise and its joys, but horrible or burlesque scenes of hell, of the witches' sabbath, of disgusting or flagitious ceremonies— the tracings of their dissolute imagination. The psychical phe- nomenon in both cases was identical; the light which the study of mysticism throws on beatific vision falls with equal effect on the hideous and terrifying images of magical evocation.*

The pathological phenomena above described were known from a very early period to the professors of magic. It was quite natural that they should turn this knowledge to account, and seek to produce by artificial processes those abnormal con- ditions which originate, as it were spontaneously, in undue emotional excitement or a perversion of mental activity. Accordingly, to determine hallucination, ecstasy, and the reac- tion of the imagination on the organs, they constructed a species of rudimentary physics or magical chemistry, without, however, possessing any appreciation of its true character, their object being to establish a communication between the human inhabi- tants of the visible, and the divine or infernal powers of the invisible world. To this magical chemistry M. Maury refers us for an explanation of a large residuary class of pathological prodigies.

We have already indicated the interdependence supposed to exist between the starry powers, the different provinces of nature, and the various parts of the human body. It is easy to see, then, that in an astrolatrous age and country, curative operations would be directly referred to the gods. In such a case, there might even be an astrological *materia medica.* In Persia, where the high rank accorded to the planetary bodies attests an Assyrian lineage, we find the sacred plant *Hom* or *Soma* regarded as the source of life, health, and beauty, the averter of death, the talisman that defends men against evil spirits, and the passport to the celestial regions. But art-magic does not grow primarily out of star-worship, though it grows with it, and is encouraged by it; nay, what may be considered as its most practical or representative form, the old sacerdotal *medicine* rose *remotely* from the instinctive conviction of the residence of mysterious powers in the various objects with which we are surrounded, and *directly* in the ascertainment of the qualities possessed by cer- tain plants, gaseous exhalations, and perhaps minerals. Thus, the sorcerers among the North American Indians administer medicaments to produce factitious delirium, and to heal wounds and diseases, attributing the cure to the Manitous, or spirits. In Africa, the rain-doctor still boasts that he has the knowledge of

* " La Magie et l'Astrologie," p. 413.

certain medicines by which he can charm the clouds and avert
the consequences of drought.   The negroes have their fetish
water ; the Egyptians their singing potions, their talking,
dancing, and dreaming potions.   In the East, the magician
invariably has recourse to the burning of narcotic substances.
The fakeers, dervishes, kalenders, and bonzes superinduce ecstasy,
nervous crisis, sacred delirium, and fantastic vision with the pills
of Esrar, the opiate of Persia, and similar preparations.   In
ancient Greece, the worshippers of Hecate employed various narcotics to generate that state of hallucination in which the fearful
goddess of the night revealed herself to the half-dreaming adept.

Thus, in its directly practical form, magic, as Pliny remarks,
had its point of departure in popular medicine.

The same factitious philosophy prevailed in the mediæval and
post-mediæval period.

· " The pharmacopœia of those times," says the elder Disraeli, " combined more of morals with medicine than our own.   They discovered
that the agate rendered men eloquent and even witty ; a laurel-leaf
placed in the centre of the skull fortified the memory ; the brain of
fowls and birds of swift wing wonderfully helped the imagination. . . .
Lentils and rape-seed were a certain cure for the small-pox, and very
obviously—their grains resembling the spots of this disease.   They
discovered that those who lived on ' fair' plants became fair, those on
fruitful ones were never barren—on the principle that Hercules
acquired his mighty strength by feeding on the marrow of lions."

The principle which the accomplished author of the " Curio-
sities of Literature" thus illustrates, resolves itself into the
logical fallacy which assumed that " the conditions of the phenomenon must resemble the phenomenon itself."   Thus, if a
charm was required to prolong life, all animals of real or fancied
longevity contributed to the magician's mystical broth—as, in
that of Ovid's Medea, the tortoise, the stag, and the crow, all
presumed to be long-living animals—formed the appropriate
ingredients.   This notion became ultimately embodied in the so-
called doctrine of Signatures, according to which the yellow
turmeric was a cure for the jaundice ; the euphrasia or eye-
bright, for eye complaints, because it exhibits a black spot on its
corolla resembling the pupil : the bloodstone for a bleeding in
the nose, and nettle-tea for urticaria or nettle-rash ; just as " the
influences of the planets were supposed to be analogous to their
visible peculiarities, " as Mars, being of a red colour, portended
fire and slaughter, and the like."*

In the thirteenth, fourteenth, and fifteenth centuries, says
Liebig, all knowledge of nature and her powers was concentrated

---

* See Mill's " System of Logic," vol. ii. pp. 224—227.

in alchemy, magic, and astrology. In the first of these three centuries arose the idea that the philosopher's stone, originally the imagined instrument of the transmutation of metals, " possessed the power of healing disease and restoring youth. This idea was developed from the opinion that the vital process was nothing else than a chemical process. With the philosopher's stone it was possible to heal metals of their maladies, to render them healthy, to convert them into gold ; and the idea that it must have a like effect on the human body naturally suggested itself." Accordingly Hollandus recommends the universal panacea by the assurance that the patient shall think he is no longer a man but a spirit: he shall feel as if he were nine days in Paradise, and living on its fruits. Another of these alchemical doctors, " Solomon Trismosin, maintains . that, when an old man, he renewed his youth by means of a grain of the philosopher's stone. His yellow, wrinkled skin became smooth and white ; his cheeks rosy, his grey hair black ; his back, bowed with age, became erect." Nor was this all. He restored, as he asserts, perfect youthfulness to ladies ninety years of age. Even his great namesake had no such enchantments as this !

With the progress of chemistry, which has banished for ever the belief in the philosopher's stone, we have lost our faith also in the spells of the enchanters, who pretended to evoke the spirits of darkness, to disclose future events, and to reveal the hiding-place of priceless treasure. As early as the sixteenth century enlightened men saw that the illusions of magic had their source in the employment of fumigations, unguents, and narcotics. Cyrano de Bergerac, Malebranche, and Gassendi (who actually swallowed a sorcerer's pill, and had the nightmare afterwards), all came to this opinion. In a later day, Sir Humphry Davy, while inhaling protoxide of azote, fell into a kind of ecstasy or delirium. Still more recently the discovery of the properties of ether, chloroform, and amylene, conclusively establishes the possibility of artificially inducing the state of hallucination. We may conclude with tolerable certainty, then, that while under the influence of a stupefactive or anæsthetic, the sorcerer or the person subjected to his artifices, beheld spirits or dæmons, the insensibility of his body naturally suggested the idea of a *bond fide* death, and induced the belief that his soul had really been withdrawn from its tenement of clay, to become a temporary denizen of the invisible world. The magical operation itself, independently of the tortures inflicted on the victim by his exasperated persecutors, during this state of suspended animation, thus came to be regarded as the effect of diabolical agency. Instances of this suspension occur in old chronicles. In a similar way, too, we may explain the resuscitation of Jeremiah

Wilkinson, a religious sectary, in whose case cataleptic lethargy was mistaken for death, but who, luckily for him, awoke just in time to prevent his being buried alive ; and the partial recovery of a young man of Hinwyl, whose comatose state was accompanied with visions.

A still more conclusive illustration of the perfectly natural character of these *magical* processes and conditions, is supplied by the scientific establishment of the long-observed phenomenon of Hypnotism. A person of feeble constitution and nervous temperament, who fixes his eyes on a brilliant object, as a plate of polished metal, placed directly opposite and at a short distance from him, falls into a cataleptic state analogous to that produced by the inhalation of anæsthetics. His limbs assume a rigid or lax appearance ; the sensibility is weakened or altogether suspended, while the special senses, as the sense of hearing or of touch, acquire an extraordinary vivacity. The slightest sounds are then perceived, and dreams and hallucinations, such as those which occur in some cataleptic attacks, present themselves to the consciousness of the person thus affected. This was a secret not unknown to the ancient professors of the magic art. Divination by mirrors, or catoptromanteia, divination by water, or hydromanteia, in which the bright surface of a liquid replaced that of metals or glass, were methods of revealing the unknown resorted to in classical antiquity. The imagination, duped by a dream or hypnotic hallucination, evoked some shape or figure ; and as in the spontaneous dream, latent suspicions, fears, and hopes are rendered palpable by an ill-defined half-conscious feeling, so in the artificially-produced dream, a similar sentiment intrudes itself with a similar result—the supposed transformation of the figure into a real person or object. To foresee the event of an impending battle with Severus for the empire of the world, Didius Julianus consulted one of these magic mirrors, employing a child on whom he had previously operated according to the prescriptions of the magic art. A child, too, was the chosen agent of Mithridates in a similar transaction. Children, in fact, were preferred as interpreters in such cases then ; and the now known fact that women and children are the best, because the most excitable subjects, for hypnotic experiment, explains the reason of the preference. The prophetess of antiquity was an hysterical female.

The somnolent state into which the hypnotic subject is thrown resembles that of magnetic somnambulism : the body and mind become strangely susceptible to external influence. In some, though only exceptional cases, the person hypnotized obeys the orders given him, and experiences genuine sensations corresponding to the attitudes which he is made to assume, in the same way that the somnambulist does. This effect is produced, as Mr. Braid has shown, by a kind of suggestion, which converts into seemingly spontaneous experiences impressions that are really communicated from without. The so-called *media* of the present age of credulity are included by M. Maury in the same category; and though he is far from assuming that we have attained a sufficient knowledge of all the related phenomena, he is certainly disposed to regard the excited imagination as *the* agent in their production. In particular, he protests against the hypothesis which identifies the nervous force with electricity, regarding it as a force distinct and unique, but at the same time allowing that, as nervous maladies, paralysis, and blindness, have been cured in a moment in thunderstorms, similar effects may be determined by a violent and sudden *reflux* of the nervous force in some part of the system. The miracles of animal magnetism he resolves into legendary exaggerations which cluster round some simple physiological fact. The somnambulist, he says, does not see with the epigastrium or nape of the neck; but, possessing an owl-like faculty of vision, in a partial obscurity perceives the light through the closed eyelids, and probably refers the sensation to this or that particular part, because the excess of sensibility which accompanies hysteria or hypochondria, gives that part unusual prominence in the consciousness of the patient. The intuitive knowledge and prescient power ascribed to the somnambulist are really attributable to the greatly enhanced force of the memory and a singular power of concentration—of attending only to the thought that has a special interest for him. The case of the young Englishman recorded by Desessarts, who was deprived of his senses by an attack of fever, and who, during his ecstatic crisis, employed himself in solving mathematical problems with which he had never previously occupied himself, admits of an explanation in accordance with these data.

Following Berard, M. Maury supposes ecstasy itself to consist in the vivid excitement of ideas, which so absorb the attention that the external sensations are suspended, the voluntary movements arrested, and the vital action retarded. According to M. Havrot, ecstasy has three different states: the mystic, the cataleptic, and the prophetic. The mind of the ecstatic does not reflect, it simply contemplates; and the more it contemplates the more absorbed it becomes. His own conceptions appear to him as a picture which he views as an indifferent spectator. His reminiscences and his ideas assume the semblance of external realities. More closely considered, ecstasy, there seems some reason to think, is to the brain what catalepsy is to the nervous and muscular system. A *form* of catalepsy, it differs from what is properly understood by that name; for whereas catalepsy

G 2

consists in *muscular* rigidity, such that the patient has no power over his limbs, ecstasy implies a *mental* tension and arrest—the encephalic fibres continuing to be affected by the movement which the idea that has produced the ecstatic state has impressed on it. Ecstasy is, in fact, a waking dream, which generally, though not always, arises under the influence of emotion of a mystical or religious character. Thus a young female ecstatic of Niederbronn, in the rapturous excitement of devotional exercises, drawn irresistibly towards the ideal divinity to which she aspired, gradually lost all consciousness of the surrounding world, and saw and heard only the objects of the visionary sphere into which she had projected herself. Though the patient was decidedly hysterical, the determination of this state was accompanied by no observable nervous symptoms or spasmodic movements. She used to announce, two hours previously to their occurrence, the period at which these transports would take place. A similar announcement was made by the young visionary of Vonay. Her expression, that *she was going away*, was her vernacular equivalent for the Greek-derived word ecstasy.

With the different states of body and mind now described, the artificial somnambulism, or animal magnetism, of our own day has obvious affinities. This scientific heresy, though it has for an alternative designation a name derived from that of Mesmer, is traceable to Paracelsus, a really remarkable man, of whom Liebig says that " he had the instinct but not the full consciousness of the right path." Though wise enough to proclaim to the world that " the true use of chemistry was not to make gold, but to prepare medicines," Paracelsus was the first to broach the modern magnetic doctrine. He taught that man attracted the stars and was nourished by them ; that he attracted the grosser elements and was renovated by them. To the former he referred the senses and the intellect ; to the latter the flesh and the blood. He taught further that the magnetic force differed according to the sex. The mutual attraction of beauty in lovers is a phenomenon still witnessed ; but we can hardly allow that it establishes the existence of the Paracelsian duality of magnetism.

This double attraction, entitled by its advocates magnetic sympathy, constituted the distinguishing peculiarity of the doctrine of the Rosy Cross, which numbered among its adherents Tentzelius, Rumilius, Pharamond, Kenelm Digby, Oswald Croll, Bartholin, and others. The new theosophy was successfully propagated. It took root in Germany, where a system of magnetic medicine was inaugurated. In England, Robert Fludd, the author of " The Philosophy of Moses," espoused the cause of the Rosicrucians. According to this conciliator of the claims of the Bible with the pretensions of the new science, every terrestrial body had its attendant planet : that of the magnet being the polar star. The " magnetic afflatus " was caught by the " long-stoled " Mesmer, the " antique Egyptian Hierophant" of our latter days, as Carlyle, with strict philosophical propriety, designates him. Mesmer, like his greater predecessor, re-asserted the influence of the heavenly bodies on the bodies of men, thus indicating the astrological character of his physiological speculations. " For so, under the strangest new vesture, the old great" *falsehood* " begins again to be revealed." Old friends with new faces return. The magic and astrology of to-day are at bottom the magic and astrology of how-long vanished yesterdays! Egypt and Chaldæa still legislate for the world of the credulous. " O women, O men, great is your infidel faith !" But we hasten to a conclusion.

M. Maury, while fully allowing that there is much in this natural magic of muscular and nervous disease that science is still inadequate to interpret, has, in his interesting exposition, brought together a number of facts, more or less authenticated by science, which, in our judgment, furnish materials for the formation of a complete theory of that pathological magic which is the principal subject of his investigations.

As there is a strong presumption against the reality of ancient magic, arising from the circumstance that it had its origin and development in the dark ages of primitive ignorance ; so is there a strong presumption against the reality of modern magic, of a precisely similar character. The delusions of our own time have the same point of departure. Both equally assume fictitious virtues, whether those virtues be attributed to invisible agents or metaphysical entities. All the old religions, and all their lineal or collateral descendants, carry the prestige of suspicion about them. They all indicate the same foregone conclusion, for they all rest on a basis of feeling or fancy. All miracle is a species of magic, whether the cause of the miracle be a star or star-god, a hero, or a personal antecedent " out of nature and beyond reason."* To assume miraculous intervention before we have exhausted natural explanation is an unnecessary and illicit process. The anomalous facts are continually being included in the category of orderly existences ; and it is far more easy to believe that in the ignorant " background of time," dæmoniacal possession, the cure of disease, prophetical vision, and the like, were pathological phenomena, hypothetically attributed to divine or diabolical agency, than to accept a theory which does not harmonize with physical or sensible truth, which disparages science or systematized experience in favour of the " second-hand assurance" of indi-

---

* Baden Powell, " Essays and Reviews."

vidual testimony, which substitutes confusion for order, dethrones reason and calls into question the principle on which rest the entire education and discipline of the human race—the constancy of Nature's operations.

That this explanation of irregular physiological phenomena is that which alone will ultimately satisfy all enlightened men may be fairly presumed from an important concession made by one of the authors of a book intended to supply " Aids to Faith," but which seems rather to furnish " Aids to Unbelief." In a striking passage in this adroit and sophistical volume, William Fitzgerald, Bishop of Cork, thus writes :—

" It is quite true, and should always be distinctly allowed, that nervous excitement, the strong tonic of a powerful faith and a lively imagination, perhaps also some subtle influence, such as animal magnetism, are capable of producing wonderful cures of some disorders ; and that if some of the narratives of miraculous cures in the Gospels and the Acts were all the miraculous narratives relating to the first planting of Christianity that we had, it might be reasonable to suppose the cures effected by some such agencies as these."*

It is true that in this statement animal magnetism, no less than Christian thaumaturgy, may be understood to have episcopal sanction ; but the concession which it embodies, notwithstanding the accompanying qualification, is really a virtual deathblow to the doctrine of supernaturalism ; and if the advocate of Palestinian miracle thus glides into the suggestion of surrender, what chance have the astrologer, the spiritualist, and the other miserable masqueraders of effete superstition, of maintaining *their* authority in the reign of Chaos and Old Night ?

The sole remedy for the fatuous misbeliefs which are the intellectual scandal of the age will be found in the philosophical cultivation of science, in the general diffusion of the knowledge of its methods and principles, and in the corrective influence of a sound public opinion. The process, if slow, is a sure one. In proportion to the advance of truth will be the retirement of error ; for it is just where science has not yet succeeded in effecting an entrance that faith insinuates herself, and imagination displays her dazzling spells. Interpreting morally the pregnant description of Tacitus, we may apply what he says of the Roman populace, wandering in unreasoning exultation through the dark streets of the mighty city, to the bewildered multitude that in our own day stand hoping, fearing, fancying, in the benighted regions of unexplained fact and "disorderly mystery"—*juvit credulitatem nox et promptior inter tenebras affirmatio.* Undue bias to believe, and precipitate forwardness to assert, characterize that intellectual night which

---

* " Evidences and Aids to Faith," p. 75.

at once conceals and distorts reality, which predisposes us to see ghosts, and aids and abets the emotion that creates them.

Our starting-point in the great mental evolution was ignorance, or rather, perhaps, an instinctive guessing at truth. Our progress has been through fiction, and even by fiction, to knowledge. It would be unjust to overlook the merits of this tentative but inevitable process—a process which not only served to stimulate, refine, and discipline the intellect, but which has been, at the same time, a positively fruit-bearing process : for alchemy and astrology were the direct precursors of chemistry and astronomy, and under their presidency observations were made and facts established which constituted valuable material for the growth and development of a sound natural science. In the first stirrings of the ardent speculation of the world's grey forefathers we see the necessary troubling of the waters of the mind. The storm of thought, which of old agitated the great sea of life, threw up on the shore what prove to be shells of truth, now that the winds have died away, and we can examine them in quiet and leisurely security.

Man, moreover, is not all intellect. Often what is not scientifically true has in it a truth of feeling. The past is dead ; but without much exaggeration we may say, that " nothing of it that doth fade " is incapable of conversion into " something rich and strange," under the transforming power of the sovereign magician-art. In the exquisite fairy tale of Goethe, the shining jewels into which the body of the snake* breaks up, make the piers of the royal bridge which spans the river of Time, and the giant Superstition is petrified into a strong colossal statue of reddish glittering stone, while his shadow serves as an index to point out the hours—to indicate, shall we say, " the long results of time." The old witch is happily extinct, but she has a beautiful and innocent successor in the Lady Geraldine of Coleridge's musical lay, whose shrunken serpent eyes, represent, without harming us, " the fascinating tendencies of fear." Passion is still a potent enchanter, and

> " Fable is Love's world, his home, his birthplace :
> Delightedly dwells he 'mong fays and talismans,
> And spirits ; and delightedly believes
> Divinities, being himself divine."

Hecate and all the rest of the faded hierarchy of the old religion live no longer in the faith of reason, but the goddess of the night, with her Stygian retinue, may still sweep by in the poet's world, where witches, with royal prerogative, " can do no

---

* Mechanical science ; (?) or, let us say here, fictitious philosophy.

harm." The cublike Caliban and the dainty Ariel still do their ministry in the charmed verse of a divine *Tempest*, though you would explore in vain the once-haunted shores of the still-vexed Bermoöthes for a trace of the " delicate spirit " or the " ridiculous monster." Prospero has buried his staff and drowned his book ; but MAN, the great enchanter, still practises the white magic of science, which conquers nature by the subtle spells of genius, and of art, which, charming and transfiguring life, carries us into the presence of the primæval powers that, in the silent realms of Fancy, still retain an immortal privilege :—

> " *For* to *her* starry world they now are gone,
> Spirits or gods that used to share this earth
> With man as with their friend ; and to the lover
> Yonder they move : from *yon invisible* sky
> Shook influence down, and even at this day
> 'Tis Jupiter who brings whate'er is great,
> And Venus who brings everything that's fair."

ART. IV.—THE DEPRECIATION OF GOLD.

1. *Cours d'Economie politique—De la Monnaie.* Par M. CHEVALIER. Paris: Chapelle, 1850.
2. *On the probable Fall in the Value of Gold.* By M. CHEVALIER, translated from the French, with a Preface, by RICHARD COBDEN. London : Smith and Son, 1859.
3. *Manual of Political Economy.* By H. FAWCETT, M.A. London : Macmillan, 1863.
4. *A serious Fall in the Value of Gold ascertained, and its Social Effects set forth.* By W. S. JEVONS, M.A. London : E. Stanford, 1863.
5. *The Drain of Silver to the East, and the Currency of India.* By W. NASSAU LEES, LL.D. London : W. H. Allen and Co., 1864.

THE attempt to estimate the effect of the unprecedented increase in the supply of gold, which has followed on the discovery of new sources of its production in California and Australia, has resulted in a variety of opinion that is one of the most remarkable and, at first sight, most unaccountable phenomena of modern times. The interest which all economists feel in its solution is accurately balanced by the profound dis-

I

regard with which it is met by almost all those who are engaged in the active prosecution of the details of commerce ; nor is this to be wondered at, for the question is more scientific than practical. The consequences which flow from any increased supply of the precious metals require a lengthened period for their full manifestation, and but slightly affect the daily transactions of trade. A capital that is usually renewed within six months is but little, if at all, affected by any alteration which can possibly occur within so short an interval in the standard by which it is estimated. The disregard of all such questions by those who are engaged in productive industry is supported by an absolute want of relation to their personal interests. The effects of an increased supply of the precious metals act upon them merely as a stimulus to further exertions, and it is long before those exertions lose their reward. It is quite otherwise with those whose inquiries lead them to investigate ultimate and remote effects, and whose investigations are not limited to the ascertainment of a chance of immediate profit. Among those authors who have addressed themselves to the theoretical solution of the question, the names of M. Chevalier, Mr. Jevons, and Mr. Fawcett have, either from their reputation or powers, attracted most public attention. The first of these authors well deserves his great and European reputation, but we imagine that the true grounds of it are not very accurately appreciated. In his work on Money he has brought together, with admirable discrimination, all the extant information on this much vexed topic. Though substantially a compilation, its merits are so great, and are so much enhanced by his personal investigations in Mexico, that it is, without a rival, the best manual on the subject. Original views will be looked for in vain in this volume, but sound and comprehensive information will always reward those who refer to its pages. In 1857 he treated, in the *Revue des Deux Mondes*, the question with which we are concerned ; but, too much excited by the novelty of the facts he had to criticise, and carried away by that tendency to push a theory to its ultimate results—a national bias to which he has always betrayed a great personal leaning—he was led to anticipate an effect which he exaggerated both in magnitude and proximity. Though full of valuable statistical matter on the topics connected with its subject, and in spite of its accurate representation of the predominant impressions of 1857, it has been refuted by the progress of events. The six years which have passed since the first promulgation of his views have advanced on the path he indicated at a pace so different from that which he anticipated that many have disputed the existence of any movement whatever. This is to fall into the opposite extreme. It is impossible that the annual production of gold can have risen from 6 millions sterling, at which amount it was estimated in 1848, to 35 millions in 1850, at which rate it has, with but little variation, continued up to the present time, without in some degree affecting its value. This consideration has pressed so strongly upon all who have endeavoured to investigate the question, that the recent attempt at its solution by Mr. Jevons has met with a popularity and general acceptance which is but a just tribute to the great labour involved in the method he has pursued, and to the unquestionable insight which he displays into every collateral branch of his subject. Indeed, it appears at first sight somewhat difficult to question the adequacy of the test by which he has endeavoured to determine the extent of the fall in the value of gold, while in everything else connected with the matter in hand he shows so great a mastery of every detail.

The process by which he assumes that he has demonstrated a most serious fall in the value of gold consists in comparing the average price of a great variety of articles before and after the gold discoveries, which commenced in 1848. It is, however, abundantly evident that the articles in his list are exposed to causes of fluctuation in price from so many and such different sources, that a comparison of plus and minus cannot give a pure resultant that may be attributed to the increased supplies of the metal in which those prices are quoted. Before any such operation upon the prices of various commodities can be effected with any chance of a true result, a full insight into the conditions of production of each is requisite, and the necessary allowance for such changes must be made. Such an insight is manifestly unattainable, and even if it were, another equally perplexing inquiry into the circumstances which have, in the given interval, effected their consumption must likewise be gone into, and a corresponding allowance be made on this side also. We have no doubt that, if two periods anterior to 1848 were compared in this manner, a similar resultant might be brought out, which, however, could not then be attributed to any change in the value of the precious metals. The progress of population, and the increase of national wealth, are, and must alway sbe, attended by a rise of price in all commodities which are consumed as food or which form the raw material of manufactures. Constant improvements in machinery and the constructive arts may, and constantly do, bring about a fall in the price of a variety of manufactured goods, in spite of an increased demand ; but the resources of agriculture will bear no comparison with such causes of increased cheapness as these. A great part of those articles which show an advance in Mr. Jevons' tables can be either shown to belong to this category, or have been notoriously affected by peculiarities which have influenced their supply. The assumption that the favourable and unfavourable circumstances which have affected the production of thirty-nine selected commodities would so balance one another that any general rise displayed by their averages can only be accounted for by some influence on the conditions of the production of that commodity on which their prices are quoted, is too hazardous, and its precariousness vitiates, in our opinion, the very basis of Mr. Jevons' calculations. The influence of speculation and credit on prices, in periods of active trade, tends also to exaggerate a result arrived at by these means. Price, too, though it has a constant tendency to identify itself with value, never exactly does so ; and in its constant oscillations on either side of the cost of production, which constitutes value, maintains, on the whole, an average rather above than below the natural price. It cannot be too often repeated that value is dependent upon the conditions of production, and price upon the proportion between the amount of money and the mass of commodities which are exchanged by its intermediation. Considered by itself, gold has no *price* ; were there no other metal used as money, it would absolutely have none, but only a local and a natural value, which in every country that admits of trade with foreign nations could not long remain very different the one from the other. This is very clearly shown by the case of Japan, which having so long withdrawn itself from the influence of European commerce, had no other standard by which to determine the value of gold than the relative difficulty of its production in that country when compared with silver. Its cost of production in those islands caused it to circulate there at less than half the value it maintained in Europe. Some of our first difficulties with the Japanese Government arose from the eagerness of the first traders to take advantage of this relative depreciation of gold, which was a consequence of their policy of isolation, and could of course be no longer maintained as soon as that policy was relinquished.

In spite of the enormous increase in its production during the last twelve years, it may be maintained that the cost of gold is as great as ever ; that the average gains of all those who are engaged in gold-mining rather fall short of than exceed the remuneration of more regular trades. An ounce of gold now probably costs as much as ever it did. Any disturbance in its value must be traced rather to its indestructible character as a commodity, so that the yearly additions to the existing mass tend to disturb the old relations between the mass of commodities to be exchanged and gold as the instrument of those exchanges. This tendency is so manifest that the counteracting agencies of extended trade are very apt to be under-rated. If the imports and exports of all countries in 1848 could be compared with their amount in 1862, it would be found that the disproportion between the wealth of the whole world and the commodity by which it is measured is not nearly so large as at first sight the great increase in the production of gold would lead any one to suppose. The increased trade of late years not only calls for more gold, but has in a great measure been called forth by the increased supplies of the metal itself. The extent of trade between any two countries depends upon the strength of their desire for each other's commodities, and trade with the East has been hitherto limited by the small market they have afforded for European productions. The poverty and apathy of the Indian population, and the settled habits of the Chinese, have made it extremely difficult to extend our commerce with them. How great has been the difficulty is well shown by the history of the opium trade with the latter, and by all the lamentable consequences which have indirectly flowed from it. But no sooner are we enabled to go to them with money in our hands than the most enormous expansion takes place: we are no longer at our wits' end to discover what we can offer in exchange for such of their productions as we require ; we can offer them an universal equivalent, and in the shape they most appreciate. The silver, which formerly maintained itself current in Europe at a certain relative proportion with gold, can do so no longer, and this silver is precisely what all Eastern nations most desire. There is no longer any need to discover the means of acting upon their dormant needs, or of inoculating them with new tastes which will induce in them an increased energy in the production of articles of European consumption : we can offer them the means of satisfying their existing desires, known and unknown, and may safely rely upon their speedy growth and on the beneficial effects which must follow on their exertions to gratify them.

In spite of our troubles in India, and a state of chronic warfare in China, the increase of our trade with the East during the last ten years has been enormous. This, too, may be looked upon as only the beginning of a commerce that must grow to proportions which cannot be estimated. The most important feature, too, of Eastern trade, is the manner in which it absorbs the precious metals. This is a peculiarity so intimately bound up with the social condition of the East that it is likely to last as long as their ignorance and mutual mistrust. Until a system of credit can grow up among them like that which in Europe dispenses with the use of gold and silver for almost all things but retail transactions and the payment of labour, the East must ever remain a perfect sink for the precious metals. What amount of money would be sufficient to saturate the hoarding propensities of these hundreds of millions of men, who believe in nothing but the little store they know of under some hearthstone or other favourite hiding-place ? There is no practical limit to the demand of the East for the precious metals, except the industry that they can develope in its acquisition, and that industry is susceptible of indefinite development.* Nor are the countries of the East the only ones whose industrial development stands in need of the spur which is supplied by the increased abundance of the precious metals. Indeed, it may be said that only those whose civilization has enabled them

---

* This view is supported by the following extract from a work just published by Dr. Nassau Lees, on the Drain of Silver to the East:—" Will," he says, "the drain of silver to the East continue? After what has been stated above, it is hardly necessary to state that a demand for an increased supply of the precious metals *will* continue; and not only continue for a very long time, but, judging from that future progress of the country which present events foreshadow, the demand will yet be enormous. The experience of America gives us some data on which to found an estimate of what the demands of an intelligent and enterprising people, rapidly forming themselves into a great nation, on the precious metals of the world *may* be; and though it cannot be asserted that the circumstances and prospects of India are precisely similar, they are nevertheless such as fully to warrant the above conclusion. Indeed, since 1857, it may be said that India has entered on a career of progress the limits to which no living man can define. Regarding the amount of gold and silver afloat as currency in the various countries of the civilized world there are very conflicting opinions; but estimating the amount of gold and silver circulating as coin in Great Britain—the country in which, perhaps, the greatest economy of the precious metals consistent with the maintenance of proper safeguards is observed—at 80,000,000*l*.,† and the population at 30,000,000, and estimating the currency of India in 1857 at an equal amount‡—an estimate I venture to think high—and the population at 180,000,000, it requires but very little calculation to show that India is capable of yet absorbing silver to the amount of Rs. 4,000,000,000, or 400,000,000*l*. in addition to this amount, for the purposes of currency alone. Nor must it be forgotten that India is able to support a population many millions more numerous than she at present possesses; nor, on the other hand, that England has many means of economizing the use of coin which, in consequence of her immense extent of area, will be denied to India, if not for ever, for many years to come. If, then, it be admitted that there is even a shadow of truth in these estimates, it may not be unreasonable to conclude that there is a possibility—distant it may be, yet still a possibility—of the requirements of India for currency purposes approaching the enormous sum of 500,000,000*l*. in silver coin."

---

† It has been estimated by various authorities at seventy, seventy-five, and even ninety millions, and that of France at one hundred and forty millions sterling.

‡ Mr. Wilson estimated the quantity of coin in circulation in India, in 1860, at 100,000,000*l*.; and though this estimate was based upon very uncertain data—viz., the aggregate of the amounts coined in the preceding twenty-five years—it may not be far wrong.

to supply the place of gold by different systems of credit, have been enabled to develope their resources to anything approaching the extent which their other circumstances admitted.

Let it not be thought that in these remarks we are confusing money with capital ; far otherwise ; but money is the first form in which capital displays itself, as is abundantly evident from the history of Europe. The commercial education of the world will call for much greater masses of the precious metals than have been supplied by the late unprecedented productions of California and Australia.

These considerations are sufficient to display the universality and strength of the demand for the precious metals, and this strength and universality tend constantly to maintain their purchasing power unimpaired. It is true that time is required to produce these effects, and the question still recurs whether at any particular moment the production of gold outstrips the powers of production in other things which would maintain the old ratio at which they exchanged for one another. It seems to us that there is but one way of answering this question, and that so simple a one that we can only suppose it to have been considered insufficient from its very obviousness. We have said before that gold considered in itself has no price, and the same may be said of silver, were there no gold in which its price could be quoted.

As both metals are equally used as standards of value, they each afford a means of quoting the price of the other. The only *price* of gold is the number of ounces of silver which are given in exchange for one of gold, and, conversely, the *price* of silver is determined by the quantity of gold which is obtainable for a given amount.

Up to 1848 the annual production of gold barely compensated for the annual waste incurred by that metal in the various uses to which it was put. This is manifest by the constant premium it maintained, which was the measure of its increased value since the period when the relative rate (15½ to 1) at which it should circulate in common with silver was established. The first effect of the new gold discoveries was the disappearance of this premium and the establishment of a greater relative value in silver. In 1848 the price of an ounce of silver, calculated in gold, was 59½, and in 1862 it had risen to 62½, or about 3 per cent., and this rise in relative value was sufficient to withdraw from France, which had almost exclusively employed a silver currency, an amount of that metal which has been estimated at sixty millions sterling,—every ounce of which, together with the greater part of the silver from the producing countries of America, has gone to the East. Is it not also evident that so long as any silver remains in Europe, while there is so great a demand for it elsewhere, that this, its present price in relation to gold, furnishes an accurate instance of the existing depreciation of the latter metal, unless some altered circumstances can be shown in the production of silver, which would of themselves have a tendency to lower its cost of production also? The change of the circulating medium in France from silver to gold has been called by M. Chevalier (in a phrase that has acquired much currency) a parachute, from the action which he contends that it has had upon the fall in the value of gold. Had he called it a barometer, we think it would have been a better simile. The rise in the price of silver forms the only safe point of departure in an attempt to estimate the depreciation of gold; if there were no changes in the conditions of its production it would form an absolutely accurate measure of that depreciation. It remains, then, to inquire whether there are any new circumstances connected with the production of silver which are calculated to affect its value. The following table gives the annual imports from the silver-producing countries into England, which is very nearly synonymous in this case with Europe, from 1848 to 1862 inclusive, with the average of the yearly prices which silver commanded in the London market. It will be observed that the annual export from Mexico and South America has only during the last year regained the proportions of that of 1859. The disturbed state of society in Mexico is accurately displayed by the decreased exports of the intervening years :—

		oz.		s.	
1848	.	17,337,226	at	$59\frac{1}{2}$	per oz.
1849	.	20,486,600	,,	$59\frac{7}{8}$	,,
1850	.	14,715,247	,,	60	,,
1851	.	16,304,403	,,	61	,,
1852	.	18,848,521	,,	$60\frac{5}{8}$	,,
1853	.	17,421,714	,,	$61\frac{1}{4}$	,,
1854	.	16,797,442	,,	$61\frac{1}{4}$	,,
1855	.	14,868,935	,,	$61\frac{1}{4}$	,,
1856	.	17,041,761	,,	$61\frac{3}{4}$	,,
1857	.	16,798,163	,,	$61\frac{3}{4}$	,,
1858	.	9,017,458	,,	$61\frac{5}{8}$	,,
1859	.	11,909,246	,,	$62\frac{1}{16}$	,,
1860	.	16,624,696	,,	$61\frac{11}{16}$	,,
1861	.	19,954,001	,,	$60\frac{13}{16}$	,,
1862	.	20,828,538	,,	$61\frac{1}{16}$	,,
1863	.			$61\frac{1}{2}$	,,

It is to be observed that these quantities include both bar silver and dollars, in the proportion of about one-third of the former to two-thirds of the latter. This arises from the duty on silver being levied at the Mint in Mexico, so that all exports of the metal from that country are necessarily in coin.

The prices given are those of bar silver. Of late the demand for dollars in China has caused them to command a price above their intrinsic worth; but as this is only a consequence of Chinese barbarism, it cannot be taken as entering into the price of silver, any more than the still more excessive premium they were content to pay for Spanish pillar dollars, which amounted to nearly 20 per cent. on their value. Indeed, it is only the absolute exhaustion of that once almost universal currency that induced the Chinese authorities in 1855 to publish a tariff at which the Mexican dollars should circulate in China. No stronger proof can be required of the absorbing power of the East than the fact that the Chinese demand has absolutely swallowed up the most extensively known silver coin that ever existed in the world. This celebrated piece-of-eight, from its consisting of eight reals, which we all know, from "Robinson Crusoe" and the tales of the buccaneers of the Spanish main, has now almost entirely disappeared from commerce, and will soon become a numismatic curiosity. But to return to the table. It is manifest that silver has not undergone any depreciation from an increased supply. The present exports scarcely exceed those of 1849, while there has been a rise of 3 per cent. in their value. It remains to be ascertained whether the reduced exports of the intervening years have been procurable by the Mexicans and Peruvians at a lessened expense, in spite of the disturbed state of the country, which must have exercised so hostile an influence on every branch of productive industry. M. Chevalier, in the work on Money of which we have spoken, gives the following results of some calculations made by M. Dupont on the distribution of the expenses of silver-mining:—

	Per Cent.
Salt and magistral	6·1
Mercury	11·2
Trituration	17·1
Subsequent labour	7·2
Wages and superintendence	3·8
Taxes and Mintage	14·5
Melting, carriage, and freight	3·5
Leaving, for mining and profit	36·6
	100·0

For the proper understanding of this calculation it is necessary to enter into some details of the processes which are employed for the extraction of silver from its ores. These charges are all incurred after the ore is drawn from the mines, the average expense of which it is very difficult to determine, owing to the great variety of situations in which the mines are worked. They are usually situated in very mountainous districts, at considerable distances from the spots to which the ore has to be carried that it may be subjected to the necessary manipulations. The conveyance of the means of life and of the necessary implements from these spots to the scene of the miners' labours must be very costly, as it has to be performed by men, the expense of maintaining mules and horses being too great. Of course, the preparatory expenses vary very greatly; but this estimate shows us the limits beyond which the working of any mine could not be profitably carried on. When the ore is brought down to the locality where it has to be treated, it is first reduced to a fine powder in a stamping mill, which, where water-power is not to be had, is worked by mules and horses. As soon as this is accomplished, the triturating process is completed. The ore is then spread over a paved court called a patio, about a foot deep. Salt and magistral, or roasted copper, are then added, to assist the chemical action of the mercury, which is at the same time mixed with the ore. The whole mass is then stirred about either by hand-labour or by driving mules over it. The mass is then left to allow the process of amalgamation to take place, being turned over again at intervals, the number and frequency of which are determined by the state of the weather—heat being favourable to the chemical actions by which the metal is separated from the ore. This stage of the proceedings may vary from six weeks to three months. When, from tests afforded by a sample taken from the mass, it is ascertained that the process is completed, the whole is washed over. The light and earthy parts of the ore are thus separated from the heavier amalgam, which is collected and subjected to mechanical pressure for the purpose of recovering a part of the quicksilver. The silver then presents a spongy appearance, in which state it is called pina, from the resemblance of the moulds, in which it is often pressed, to a pine-apple. A considerable part of the quicksilver will not yield to the pressure thus employed, but is recovered by roasting the pina in properly constructed ovens. The vapour which it then gives off is condensed in the chimney through which it is made to pass, and a further portion of the quicksilver recovered. In this condition the silver sometimes, but not usually, appears in the London market. The almost universal practice, however, is to melt the pina into solid bars, which are then ready for home use or foreign exportation.

It is evident from the enumeration of expenses given above, that many of them are susceptible of great reduction. The high price of almost all the materials used cannot maintain itself in the face of improved means of communication; when something better than mule tracks, or absolutely no tracks at all, has lessened the present enormous charges incurred for carriage, both salt and fuel will not enter, for the large comparative proportion that they do at present, into the cost of production. It is true that by the time the country has acquired such material improvements as these, we may expect the wages of labour to rise in a proportion that will fully meet any economy that may result from them. There is, however, one item of these charges which has undergone a complete revolution. Before 1850, the production of quicksilver was almost confined to the mines of Almaden in Spain and those of Idria. After the revolt of the Spanish Colonies the Government of the mother-country, which had been accustomed to furnish the Mexican miners with this indispensable requisite at a fixed and moderate charge, granted a lease of these quicksilver mines to a European firm, which, being thus in possession of a powerful monopoly, drove the price of quicksilver to such a height that many of the poorer mines in Mexico could no longer be profitably worked. Shortly after the discovery of gold in California, however, most extensive mines of cinnabar (the ore of quicksilver) were discovered in the same country. These mines have proved so productive, that the price has fallen from 5s. per lb., at which it stood in 1850, to 2s. per lb. in 1862. This is an effectual saving of more than 6 per cent. in the cost of the production of silver, which cannot fail not only to encourage the existing enterprises, but greatly to extend the field of silver mining, by enabling the poorer ones to be profitably worked. A more settled state of society in Mexico and South America will, in all probability, be followed by a great increase in the production of silver, which is found universally in the chain of the Andes, from Mexico to the borders of Patagonia, and probably still further south. The enormous geographical extent of this argentiferous chain opens an almost inexhaustible field for the production of silver. Indeed it may be said that it is only limited by the incidental expenses. On this ground many have argued that silver supplies a more equable standard of value than gold, and there is much to be said in support of their opinion. Gold, however, so far surpasses it in the prime excellence of a medium of exchange—viz., that of possessing great value in small bulk—that it will always be able to maintain itself in spite of the sudden inequalities in the rate of its production which are occasioned by every fresh discovery of auriferous regions.

It must not be forgotten, in the surprise attendant upon the enormous gold production of late years, that every site is soon exhausted, that the profitable localities are those in which nature has for centuries been quietly performing the miner's work. By frost and chemical disintegration of the quartz rock, the gold it contained has been set free to be washed by every rain to the foot of the mountains which are its native source. As soon as these alluvial deposits are exhausted, gold-mining is subjected to all the chances which attach themselves to mining in general, and is by no means exempt from the highly speculative character which is proverbially attached to all such enterprises.

It would thus appear that the only change in the circumstances affecting the production of silver has a direct tendency to lower its value; but the decreased production of late years, by greatly diminishing the amount of the annual supply from Mexico and South America, has, no doubt, to a large extent counterbalanced this tendency. The fact that silver has not risen more than 3 per cent. since the discoveries in California and Australia could not, of course, escape the attention of so well-informed a person as Mr. Jevons; but he avoids the necessary inference by assuming, that as he has conclusively, as he fancies, established a general rise of prices of 9 per cent., that silver must have fallen 6 per cent., and reconciles himself to the assumption by the supposed decreased value of silver. incident on the large supplies of it which have been drawn from France during the substitution of gold for it in the circulation of that country. Gold, however, is the standard of price in all the laborious calculations of which he has given us the result. They are founded on the quotations of the English market, and are expressed in sterling. To establish a special fall in silver, not shown in the tables, a fresh series should be constructed, on the basis of a silver standard, from the returns of such countries as use that metal alone. But even then, though we have no doubt hat the desired result would not be attained, the calculation would be vitiated by the same misconception which renders Mr. Jevons' tables so inconclusive, that he hesitates himself between 9 and 15 per cent. as the true measure of the fall in the value of gold. It is not any fall in the value of silver which has brought about the drain of this metal to the East, but simply the nature of the Indian and Chinese demand for our manufactures, which is very small compared with ours for their productions, but which is immense for silver, which represents to them everything desirable in their conceptions of luxury, comfort, and security. All the efforts which have been made to estimate the fall of value in gold by calculating the effect of the annual additions to the existing stock of the metal err by ignoring the immense effect of the additions themselves upon the productive industry of the world, and by overlooking the direct tendency of such a stimulus to re-establish the old ratio between the circulating medium and commodities, upon which ratio prices ultimately depend.

But it would be well if this were the only deficiency in these calculations. The most enormous differences exist in the estimate both of the stock to be affected, and in the allowance that must be made for the increased consumption and wear and tear of the metal itself, before the true annual addition can be determined. Is it not enough that in the first case the amount of gold existing in the world in 1848 has been variously estimated at from 350 to 560 millions sterling; and that the annual consumption has been calculated by M. Chevalier at 17,856,000*l.*, while Mr. McCulloch maintains that it ought to be considered to amount to at least 29,500,000*l.*? While so much is uncertain about the two factors of any such calculation, it is as well to wait for further and more definite knowledge before they are made the basis of any calculations at all. One thing, however, is certain—that should the unappropriated surplus of the annual production of gold long continue as large as that of the last ten years, and nothing is less probable than that it should do so, its effect on price must be less with each year, as an equal yearly addition represents with each succeeding year a lessened per-centage upon the mass indicated by previous accumulations of a like kind. This is excellently shown by Mr. Jevons in a *pro formâ* table, on an assumed stock of five hundred and sixty millions in 1848, increased by annual additions of twenty millions, in which he conclusively refutes the notion entertained by Mr. Cobden, and expressed in the introduction to his translation of M. Chevalier's pamphlet, that the change in the value of gold would be effected by leaps and after struggles which would tend to derange and convulse the relations of capital and labour. But whether the fall in the value of gold be a passing phenomenon or one that may be expected to continue for many years, whether its rate per annum be great or small, it cannot but be welcome to every one who fully understands its consequences. To all the vital part of the population of the world—to every member of the productive classes—it is an unmixed good; it is a harvest of increased ease that they are the first to reap; and not only they, for even the unproductive classes, who live upon fixed incomes and salaries, or who draw their means of life from fees and settled payments, experience some relief in the diminished weight of taxation in a country where nearly one-half of the national revenue is collected for the purpose of paying the interest on a debt the capital of which would be so greatly reduced in value. Every capital that is invested in a non-productive manner would be lessened in its power of commanding the means and enjoyments of life; a fresh and lively spur would be applied to every form of active exertion, and if the fall should progress at anything like the rate anticipated by so many who have prophesied on the subject, it cannot fail to have the greatest influence on the moral sentiments with which commerce is regarded, and to hasten the inevitable day when feelings drawn from a departing form of society will give place to others founded on the interests of a far greater number, and consequently more really moral and honourable to mankind at large.

ART. V.—GILCHRIST'S LIFE OF WILLIAM BLAKE.

Life of William Blake, " Pictor Ignotus," with Selections from his Poems and other Writings. By the late ALEXANDER GILCHRIST, Author of the " Life of William Etty." Illustrated from Blake's own Works, in fac-simile, by W. J. LINTON, and in Photolithography, with a few of Blake's original Plates. In 2 vols. London : Macmillan and Co. 1863.

THERE is no name connected with English art, which, in the scope and interest of the questions connected with it, is any way comparable with that of William Blake. Not only does his whole life constantly thrust upon its readers a consideration of the true relations between an artist and the public ; but his practice and methods can only be judged in relation to the fundamental conceptions of Art itself. It is to be regretted that the otherwise valuable biography of this great and original painter, by the late Mr. Gilchrist, should be conceived in a spirit of hero-worship which incapacitates the writer for a dispassionate statement of the few events which marked Blake's life, or for anything but an indiscriminate and vague laudation that partakes much more of rhetorical advocacy than critical judgment. This amounts to a complete reversal of the method to be desired in treating such a life. This kind of advocacy was not needed ; for it can neither add to the estimation of those who appreciate the painter, nor awake a fresh capacity in those who are blind to his beauties or revolted by his extravagance. It is a very one-sided method of treating Blake's reputation which consists in declaiming against the ignorance and want of sympathy of that generation in which the English school rose to its greatest height, and which included Reynolds, Gainsborough, Flaxman, and Fuseli. It cannot be contended that Art was neglected. The prevailing theories of that time may be criticised, and grounds shown by which their shortcomings can be estimated ; but blindness to the beauties and want of sympathy with the productions of Art cannot fairly be brought forward as characteristics of the period during which Blake lived.

The true sources of the comparative neglect of this painter are to be sought for in the peculiarities of his personal character, and

in the nature of the works he produced.   A right insight into the
causes of this neglect would in no way detract from the reputation
Blake deservedly enjoys, either as a man or as an artist : as soon
as the man is understood, his works are explained, and their
greatness stands forth in the light of a clear comprehension of
the states of mind they represent.   However lofty and noble,
however sweet and pure, they are even more interesting as
psychological studies than as independent works.   It cannot be
denied that they are among the most markedly individual and
peculiar productions that the world has ever seen ; and it may
fairly may be contended that few, if any, of his cotemporaries
could have found the true point of view from which they ought to
be judged.   How few are there, even at the present day, who look
upon painting as anything more than an ornamental art, a kind
of superior upholstery—the chief value of which is found in its
capacity to gratify a desire of display.   That painting has anything to say that could not be otherwise said, that it is the only
language for certain delicate thoughts and feelings, would even
now be treated as a paradox.   How, then, can Blake's cotemporaries be inconsiderately blamed, when they failed to read his
language on subjects that were so remote from their every-day
thoughts and habits !   Blake's art springs from his conception of
the universe, and is rendered obscure not merely by the nature of
the conception itself, but by the necessary incoherence and arbi-
trariness which are involved in it.   This conception is no new
thing : it is found in the literature of all mystical religions.   It is
impossible that any one with the slightest acquaintance with the
works of Behmen, or William Law, can fail to be struck with the
exact parallel between their treatment of morals and religion, and
Blake's conceptions of art.   The manner in which these writers
set aside every form of historical religion, and elevate themselves
above all established doctrines of morality ; the prominence, and
almost exclusive validity which they gave to the influence of the
Third Person of the Holy Trinity ; the methods of life they advocated, their scorn of learning, the wrathful fires in which they
burn up all things which do not come before them with the seal
of immediate personal inspiration ; their quietism and Antinomian
freedom, are the exact counterpart of Blake's exaltation of the
imagination above all other gifts which adorn his art.   If any one
would take up one of Law's books, " The Spirit of Love," for instance, or a volume of his Letters, and then a folio of Blake's
wildest prints, he will find himself reading the same language and
surrounded by the same atmosphere of thought, if that can be called
thought which is but passive contemplation of an accustomed
strain of imagery and feeling.   When once the theory is accepted,
that this is a deformed world, that it is but a blasted image of the

fair conception of the Creator, that it is an obstacle to the attainment of truth, rather than the only means by which it can be arrived at, there exists no longer any standard by which the opinions of mankind at large can be tried, or to which the productions of Art can be referred.   A reliance upon the guiding spirit which is supposed to manifest itself exclusively in the secret depths of conscience, speedily results in a kind of self-worship, of a quiet and unobtrusive character so long as it meets with no resistance from without, but venting itself in terms of the most lofty contempt so soon as it is called upon for a reason for the faith that is in it.   These men have the evidence in themselves, and feel the impossibility of making it intelligible to others.   They content themselves with the assertion that their doctrines are spiritually discerned and transcend the bounds of human reason.   However lofty and pure their conceptions of duty, they have no foundations on which any ethical system can be constructed.   The world starts afresh with every individual. The race of men, as such, has no future and no continuous progress.   In their view, God's providence and love are confined to those who have received insight into the nothingness of this life— a gift incommunicable from man to man, and entirely personal to its possessor.   This spiritual life bears no relation to morality, and often expresses itself in Antinomian vagaries, which, were it not for the religious tone of thought that is almost always found in its professors, would, and sometimes does, lead to the strangest incoherences of doctrine and conduct.   With these religionists, more than any others, is it true that *wie ein jeder ist so ist sein Gott.* It is clear, from almost every line that Blake wrote after he had come to manhood, that he had adopted these views of God and Nature ; and the singularity, in his case, is the thoroughness with which he carried his principles into practice in the region of his art.   The pre-eminence given by his conceptions of religion to the workings of the spirit, he gave in his art to the promptings of his imagination.   The effects of this conviction are strange enough in morals where they often go no further than the mind that entertains it ; but in art could they not but engender monsters. Art is the interpreter of Nature, and not a new language of the imagination.   The images which presented themselves to Blake's imagination were accepted by him as direct inspirations, from that source to which alone he looked for guidance in conduct as well as art.   Nothing but a feeling of religion prevents him asserting that imagination is creative rather than inventive ; and, indeed, by the intermediation of a direct inspiration, with which he believed himself endowed, he constantly assures the world that he brings it news from spheres beyond its ken.

Is it, then, surprising that his communications met with but little sympathy? They were conveyed in a language of their own, and necessarily understood, even by those who had a feeling for its music, in a sense quite different to that intended by the prophet.

It may be questioned whether any of his oracular utterances were ever understood by any human soul in the sense they conveyed to himself. On a ground of taste, or as suggestive of something different to each reader or beholder, they have been admired and wondered at by all who have any feeling for Art or Literature. But his vagueness is so great, that as many different judgments may be given, as there are judges to give them. This is what made him, what Fuseli called, " so d—d good to steal from." Each man gives a personal interpretation to his lovely clouds; with one it is a weasel, with another a camel, and with a third, very like a whale. In short, Blake was a quietist or mystic, who, having accepted the vague promptings of his mind as immediate inspirations given to direct his conduct, received the images of his imagination as emanations from the same source—as little regarding the world and the ways of men in the one case as in the other : this is the secret of his life and works. The beauty of both consists in the fulness of his faith, and in the noble sacrifices he made to it. These sacrifices, however, were rendered comparatively easy to him by many peculiarities of his mind and circumstances. In the first, he had imbibed from education no notion of Science that could trouble convictions grounded on his feelings ; and, in the second, his happy marriage and its childlessness enabled him to dispense with that portion of the world's goods which he must have striven for had he had a less loving partner, or a family to bring up.

This is very clearly brought out by Mr. Gilchrist, from whom we shall collect the chief features of his life. He was born on the 28th November, 1757, the second child in a family of four. His father was a hosier in Broad-street, Golden-square ; at that time a much more fashionable quarter of the town than it is at present. He can scarcely be said to have had any education in the usual sense of the word. At ten years of age he was sent to Mr. Par's Drawing-school, in the Strand, to qualify him for entrance into the Academy of Painting and Sculpture in St. Martin's-lane, which Hogarth had helped to found. In this the boy's own tastes and feelings were consulted by his parents in a way that speaks highly for their kindness of heart and good practical judgment.

The father bought casts for him to copy, and young Blake, before he was thirteen years old, was a frequenter of Art auctions, at which he would buy, when his means sufficed, prints from the old masters—displaying precocious good taste in their selection.

At this period of his life, too, he began to write verses : one very remarkable poem Mr. Gilchrist is able to determine as written before he was fourteen.   In 1771, he was apprenticed to James Basire, engraver to the *Archæologia*, and *Vetusta Monumenta*, of the Society of Antiquarians. While in his studio he became more or less acquainted with Strange, Woollett, Vivares, and Bartolozzi, and was much employed by his master in making studies from the monuments in Westminster Abbey.   A great deal of artistic and literary gossip connected with these years is got together by Mr. Gilchrist, and many gratuitous suppositions indulged in as to how many of the events narrated could, or might, have had an influence on the young apprentice.

It was during these years that those remarkable poems were written which, by the help of friends, were published in 1783. When the artificial style of the prevailing taste is called to mind, the originality and simple beauty of such a song as the following, shows at once how strong and individual a character was required for its production.

The taste displayed in it is manifestly the result of a style of reading and study to which he would have found but little external encouragement.

> " My silks and fine array,
>   My smiles and languished air,
> By love are driven away,
>   And mournful, lean Despair
> Brings me yew to deck my grave—
> Such end true lovers have.

> " His face is fair as heaven
>   When springing buds unfold ;
> Oh why to him was't given,
>   Whose heart is wintry cold ?
> His breast is Love's all-worshipped tomb,
> Where all Love's pilgrims come.

> " Bring me an axe and spade,
>   Bring me a winding-sheet ;
> When I my grave have made,
>   Let winds and tempests beat :
> Then down I'll lie, as cold as clay,
> True love doth pass away."

This is a sufficiently remarkable production, and but little influenced by any contemporary models ; whether the reader recognise or not what Mr. Gilchrist calls its " shy evanescent tints and aroma, as of pressed rose leaves." In spite of its sweetness and harmony, it is, in our opinion, rather the contemplation of a passion than the expression of any personal experience of it.

On the expiration of his apprenticeship in 1778, Blake returned to his father's house.　He pursued his studies in the "Antique School" of the Academy, neglecting the living model; "mere natural objects," as he said late in life, "always did, and do, weaken and deaden imagination in me."　At this period began his connexion with the booksellers, as an engraver, sometimes of his own designs, but much more frequently of those of other painters. This through all his life was his only connexion with the bustle of external affairs—a feeble, and then a most unremunerative one. Mr. Gilchrist traces his productions with enormous industry through all the fugitive and forgotten literature of the day, and supplements the utter absence of directly biographical matter by sketches of the neighbourhood in which he lived, and by notices of cotemporary events.　These collateral studies greatly increase the interest of the biography, and give it a life and movement that could not be extracted from the uneventful tenor of the artist's days.

One of the most pleasing of these sketches is that of the circle which used periodically to assemble at the house of "the celebrated Mrs. Mathew," a distinguished bluestocking of the day, who had always a ready welcome for promising genius of every kind.　Smith, the biographer of Nollekens, has preserved a picture of the artist at one of these reunions, singing his verses to melodies of his own composition.　The connexion, however, did not last very long : he appears to have been lionized until it was found that he was by no means inclined to "roar like any sucking dove;" his natural note of self-assertion was soon found incompatible with the conventional proprieties as conceived by the *habitués* of 27, Rathbone-place.　This was in the nature of things. Blake was in earnest, and such circles seek only amusement ; but after all, it was amusement of an intellectual character, and Mrs. Mathew seems to have displayed an amount of amiability and good feeling in her relations with the poet and painter that should have saved her from Mr. Gilchrist's scornful simile : he likens Blake among the bluestockings to Phœnix amid an admiring circle of cocks and hens.　At this time he made the acquaintance of Stothard, and, through him, of Flaxman, both for many years attached friends.　The balance of obligations, which should never be held by friends, is somewhat unfairly weighted by his biographer in Blake's favour.　Of the ultimate breach with Stothard we shall have to speak presently.　These, too, were the days of courtship and marriage.　There is some account of a previous flirtation, which we will give in Mr. Gilchrist's own words :—

"A lively little girl, in his own, or perhaps a humbler station, the object of his first sighs, readily allowed him, as girls in a humble class will, meaning neither marriage nor harm, to 'keep company' with her; to pay his court, take mutual walks, and be as love-sick as he chose;

but nowise encouraged the idea of a wedding. In addition to the pangs of fruitless love, attacks of jealousy had stoically to be borne. When he complained that the favour of her company in a stroll had been extended to another admirer, 'Are you a fool?' was the brusque reply, with a scornful glance. 'That cured me of jealousy,' Blake used naively to relate. One evening, at a friend's house, he was bemoaning his love crosses. His listener, a dark-eyed, generous-hearted girl, frankly declared she pitied him from her heart. '*Do* you pity me?' 'Yes, I do most sincerely.' 'Then I love you for that,' he replied, with enthusiasm :—such soothing pity is irresistible, and a second more prosperous courtship began. At this, or perhaps a later meeting, followed the confession, I dare say in lower tones, '*Well, and I love you,*' always, doubtless, a pretty one to hear."

Thus commenced a connexion which closed forty-five years later by Blake's words to her on his death-bed—"Stay, you have ever been an angel to me,"—and this, indeed, she had been; for, as during all those years they seldom had the means to keep a servant, she not only performed all the household work, but became his helpmate in the fullest sense, aiding him in the mechanical parts of his art, and above all accepting with the greatest cheerfulness a poverty that many would have made a source of misery to their husbands; seconding his high ideas of scrupulous probity by every effort of domestic economy. Yet when they were married in 1782, he being then in his twenty-fifth and she in her twenty-first year, the bride could neither read nor write, and had to sign the parish register with her mark. This was, perhaps, the cause of his father's displeasure at the match. The young people established themselves at 23, Green-street, Leicesterfields. Two years later his father died, an honest shopkeeper of the old school—a Dissenter, we suppose a Wesleyan, among whom the kind of religious literature to which we have alluded was always very popular. His elder brother continued to live with his mother, and succeeded to the business in Broad-street. It is said of him that he used to talk *Swedenborg*, which we take to be a sort of popular cant phrase of the time for any expressions of mystical religion.

At this time Blake removed to the house next door to his brother, in Broad-street (No. 27), at which, in conjunction with an engraver named Parker, he opened a shop as printseller, not without kindly pecuniary assistance from friendly Mrs. Mathew. His younger brother, Robert, for whom he had the most ardent affection, came to live with them as his apprentice. The only noteworthy incident of his life here is thus told by Mr. Gilchrist with an aridity that is somewhat surprising :—

"One day a dispute arose between Robert and Mrs. Blake; she, in the heat of discussion used words to him, his brother (though a husband too) thought unwarrantable. A silent witness thus far, he could now bear it no longer, but with characteristic impetuosity when stirred—rose and said to her, 'Kneel down, and beg Robert's pardon directly, or you never see my face again.' A heavy threat uttered in tones which, from Blake, unmistakeably showed that it was *meant.* The poor thing ' thought it very hard,' as she would afterwards tell, to beg her brother-in-law's pardon when she was not in fault. But being a duteous, devoted wife, though by nature nowise tame or dull of spirit, she *did* kneel down and meekly murmured, '*Robert, I beg your pardon—I am in the wrong.'* 'Young woman, you lie!' abruptly retorted he, '*I* am in the wrong.'' "

Surely it demands a large amount of hero-worship to tell a tale like this without one word of indignant protest. In 1787, this brother died, tenderly nursed by Blake, and we doubt not by his wife ; in the same year disagreements with his partner put an end to what Mr. Gilchrist calls the curious sight of William Blake behind a counter. The poet throws off the yoke and resolves to satisfy himself with that inheritance in the heavens which Jove's bounty to other men had left as his sole resource. He removed to Poland-street in the immediate neighbourhood ; and from this time, with the exception of his three years' sojourn at Felpham, the history of his life is one with that of his works. He was now thirty-one years old ; and in the utter absence of any extant correspondence, from which some picture of his mental life could be drawn, Mr. Gilchrist has very happily availed himself of memoranda made in a volume of Lavater's Aphorisms. Blake had accepted the somewhat pedantic advice that Lavater gives to his readers, to select such of his aphorisms as attracted or repelled them at the first reading, and afterwards to reflect on the collection, promising them increased self-knowledge from the contemplation. Many of Blake's remarks are, as might be expected, very characteristic. This book seems to have incited him to the composition of his own " Proverbs of Hell," and " The Marriage of Heaven and Hell." From this last we extract the following most significant of Antinomies, as Blake conceived them.

The Voice of the Devil.

"All Bibles or sacred codes have been the source of the following errors :—

"1. That man has two real existing principles, viz., a body and soul.

"2. That energy, called evil, is alone from the body, and that heaven, called good, is alone from the soul.

"3. That God will torment man in eternity for following his energies.

"But the following contraries to these are true :—

"1. Man has no body distinct from his soul ; for that called body is a portion of the soul discerned by the five senses, the chief inlets of the soul in this age.

"2. Energy is the only life, and is from the body, and reason is the bound or outward circumference of energy.

"3. Energy is eternal delight."

We must make room for two of his proverbs:—

"The fox provides for himself, but God provides for the lion.

"The tigers of wrath are wiser than the horses of instruction."

These extracts are alone sufficient to support that view of the origin of Blake's hallucinations to which we have referred them above, and a multitude of equally strong passages might be collected which lead to the same conclusion.

With the year 1788, we enter on the strange series of Blake's original productions as an artist. The first of these, the "Songs of Innocence," is in many respects the most charming and delightful of his works: their meaning is more accessible, and the illustrations with which he accompanied them are most original in conception and beautiful in execution. The collection of poems printed in 1783 had met with so little success, that there was but small chance of his finding a publisher for this new venture. He determined, in this as in all other things, to be self-sufficing, and invented a method of execution by which he could be his own printer and publisher. With some modifications this became the form in which all his subsequent works were produced. It consisted in a reversal of the usual process of engraving. Those parts of the plate which are usually bitten in with acid were protected by the design itself, executed in a kind of stopping-out varnish. The parts untouched were then eaten away with aquafortis, so that ultimately the impression was taken by surface printing, in the same manner as from a woodcut. This necessarily implied some delicacy of manipulation in taking off impressions, but in this process Mr. Blake soon became an adept. From these plates was printed off the prevailing ground tone, the letterpress being usually red; the print was then coloured by hand, in imitation of the original drawing. This method admitted of any degree of elaboration in single copies. In the second volume of the present life will be found seven of the twenty-seven which the volume contained, being all of which the copper plates are known to exist; of course, they are uncoloured, and give no notion of the strange beauty of the finished works. There is a fine copy in the print-room of the British Museum, which is accessible to every one, and many others scattered about in the collections of intelligent connoisseurs. Indeed, those of his friends who, at any time, wished to assist Blake, found an order for this charming book the most easy way of doing so, without wounding the susceptibilities of the

artist.   At this point it will be perhaps most appropriate to say
something on Blake as a colourist.   He was, in a certain sense,
unquestionably one of the greatest that ever lived.   The harmo-
nious effect of his best works cannot be surpassed;   but in
colour as well as in design, he cared so little for the external
world, that he thought nothing of the most glaring departures
from local truth.   It is impossible to give any idea of these works
by language, without the use of vague similes, which, after all,
leave no determinate impression on the mind.   Mr. Gilchrist
has made the effort, in our opinion, necessarily unsuccessful.
The following poem we extract for its beautifully graduated cry
of distress, and for the obviousness of its symbolism.   In
dramatic power it is equal to Goethe's "Erl König."   The picture
in which it is set represents a child decoyed by an *ignis fatuus.*

THE LITTLE BOY LOST.

"Father, father, where are you going? '
   Oh, do not walk so fast;
Speak, father, speak to your little boy,
   Or else I shall be lost."

The night was dark, no father was there,
   The child was wet with dew;
The mire was deep, and the child did weep.
   And away the vapour flew.

Some few years later a second series, called the " Songs of
Experience," was added to this volume.   They are now usually
found together.   Six plates of this series have been discovered
by Mr. Gilchrist, and are given in his second volume. The poetical
tone is more bitter, and the harmony between the pictures and
poetry not so great.   About this time he designed and engraved
the plates to Mary Wollstonecraft's "Tales for Children," published
by Johnson of St. Paul's Churchyard.   Some interesting particulars of the circle which used to meet at this excellent man's
house are well brought together by Mr. Gilchrist.   In 1793
Blake removed from Poland-street to Hercules-buildings, Lam-
beth; and the next seven years of his life are marked by the production of those strange works to which he owes the imputation
of madness often brought against him.   These are—" The Gates
of Paradise," "Visions of the Daughters of Albion," " Europe,"
"Urizen," "The Song of Los," and "Ahania."   They are certainly
more incoherent than the " Prophecies" and " The Marriage of
Heaven and Hell," which had preceded them; but they by no
means imply madness : they are the legitimate results of his
notions on inspiration, which precluded his affecting to criticise
any vivid images that offered themselves to his imagination.   The
belief in an immediate personal influence of the Spirit of God on

the mind of man was accepted by him with a child's simplicity, and these books are the direct result of such a belief in an entirely uncritical mind. ✓ The notion of morals as a science manifestly never occurred to Blake, or would have been rejected by him, had it done so, as an instigation of Satan. He walked alone with his God, and trusted to that guidance which he believed would be granted him. In this he presented no isolated phenomenon. There are many who still adopt this course, but it is one that only such entire faith as Blake's can render harmless ; the nobleness of his spirit and the honesty of his heart alone preserved him from the terrible pitfalls with which this conception of life abounds. These works of Blake's are, we suppose, never read, except as studies of his state of mind. The designs which accompany their text are the wildest and most incomprehensible of his productions —only to be accounted for by that theory of his, that the suggestions of the imagination are truer than the facts of external nature. The legends of saints and anchorites abound in similar phenomena, except that they are seldom inspired by a spirit of beauty. It was while living at Hercules-buildings that he and his wife were one day discovered in a state of nature in their back garden, reading Milton. Eccentricity and contempt of the world's usages could surely go no further than this !

To endeavour, as Mr. Gilchrist does, to rationalize this caprice by a gradually diminishing series of similar practices, so that he at last brings it into the same category as taking a cold bath every morning, is merely to betray the conflict in his own mind between outraged propriety and unqualified admiration. The story is too valuable as a striking symptom of the divorce from all external things in which he chose to live during this period of his life. It is not more violent than his departure from all recognised models in his literary efforts of the same period ; and both do but show the natural effect of isolation from the common current of human thought. This story rests on the report of Mr. Butts, his most constant patron and friend. In the second volume of his life a few of Blake's letters to this gentleman are printed : it is much to be regretted that the answers to them are not extant, as they would throw great light upon the grounds of so constant an admiration. We cannot help surmising that it was not all founded upon a love of art, but that a secret sympathy with Blake's religious views entered greatly into its fervour. Mr. Butts' constant readiness to purchase his drawings, and the sale, as may be imagined, a very small one, of the works of these years, did not relieve him from the necessity of working for the booksellers. In 1797 appeared his illustrations to Young's " Night Thoughts," of which we shall speak in connexion with those to Blair's " Grave." Three years later he was introduced by Flaxman to the poet

Hayley, who was then engaged on his Life of Cowper and the Memoirs of his son.   At Hayley's invitation he left London for the first time in his life, to reside near his new patron at Felpham, near Bognor, in Sussex.

He was to engrave the illustrations to Hayley's projected works. At first sight it would appear that two more uncongenial names could not possibly be connected ; but the poet's gentlemanly consideration for the painter's eccentricities, and the goodwill displayed by his constant efforts to serve him, kept Blake at the seaside for three years, in spite of every discrepancy between the men.   On the whole, they were happy years for Blake, and fortunate ones for those who would understand his life.   Here only was it necessary for him to write to his friends ; the great majority of his letters which are preserved are dated from Felpham.

The chapters in which Mr. Gilchrist describes the sojourn in the country are among the most pleasant in his book.   He does full justice to Hayley ; and has drawn a charming portrait of the fussy and vain, but substantially amiable man, whose efforts to push his friend's fortunes among his aristocratic acquaintance were ultimately frustrated by Blake's utter antipathy to those walks of art by which alone he could have seconded them.   Art and liberty were too ardently worshipped by the painter for him to sacrifice an iota of his conceptions of either for riches and reputation.   After a sojourn of nearly four years at the seaside, Blake returned to London and settled in South Molton-street. The first works he published were the "Jerusalem" and "Milton," a continuation of that train of thought—if thought it may be called—which inspired him at Hercules-buildings.   To criticise these works is impossible ; that which is thoroughly purposeless cannot be criticised.   This would be manifest, if not true of itself, from the fruitless attempts which Mr. Gilchrist makes at extracting any meaning from their pages.   Their leaves are turned over like those of an artist's sketch-book, for the beautiful forms which are found in them : the attempt is futile to connect them with the text or to attach any definite meaning to them in themselves. They are "songs without words," depending for their effect as much upon what is brought to their study as upon anything they themselves furnish to the student.

Their vague grandeur appeals exclusively to the imagination, and can only be appreciated by a feeling in harmony with the source from which they sprung.   In 1804-5 began his connexion with Cromek, who had given up his profession as engraver for the business of printseller and publisher.   He was a very energetic and pushing man.   His first venture was the publication of Blake's illustrations to Blair's "Grave."   It appears that when he bought the designs by which Blake is most known, he promised the artist that he should engrave them for the forthcoming edition of the "Grave." That *he* should have made any such promise surprises us; and we would willingly see some more complete evidence of his having done so. Blake's engravings of his own designs to Young's "Night Thoughts" had already been published, and the publication had not gone farther than the first part. Even Mr. Gilchrist is compelled to admit of this performance, that it is far from attractive, that both in treatment and handling it is monotonous; that it has but little individuality; that the artist expresses his meaning by typical forms and faces and abstract impersonations; that "everything—figures, landscape, costume, accessory—is reduced to its elemental shape, its simplest guise—bare earth, bare sky, and ocean bare."

Cromek must have been acquainted with this work, and could not have wished his venture to share its fate. It is by no means clearly made out that he "*jockeyed*" Blake out of his copyright, putting aside all question of whether a copyright in design existed at the time. Blake does not appear to have quarrelled with him until long after his designs were in Schiavonetti's hands. That Cromek displayed a good judgment in confiding their execution to that accomplished engraver, cannot be denied, nor can it be asserted that in his hands Blake's designs lost any of their characteristic beauty. The result is certainly somewhat different to what we might have expected had Blake been commissioned to engrave the plates, but nothing is lost save certain peculiarities of execution that can hardly be called excellences. Blake's powerful imagination was satisfied by the merest suggestion; the indication which was sufficient for himself he at once assumed to be all that could be required by the public. Cromek knew better, and determined that Blake should for once be presented to the public in an intelligible dress. The result did credit to his judgment. The illustrations to Blair's "Grave" are, and always have been, the most popular of Blake's works, the only one, in fact, which is not really scarce. The work was well advertised and brought before the public by every publishing device. The Queen allowed it to be dedicated to herself, and a host of literary and artistic testimonials were printed in the prospectus. Apropos of the dedication to the Queen, Blake had composed a vignette which should enclose it: he sent it to Cromek, demanding four guineas for the design—he had received only twenty for the twelve compositions in Schiavonetti's hands. The fact of his sending it to Cromek.at all seems to us to imply that up to that period, 1807, there was no breach between them, in spite of the employment of another engraver. In the letter that accompanied this vignette (which may be seen at the British Museum, and is one of Blake's most finished drawings), he accuses Cromek with having imposed upon him, as may be gathered from the reply printed by Mr. Gilchrist. This reply, manifestly written in a moment of exasperation, is on the surface intended to wound the feelings of his correspondent, and was the more calculated to do so from a certain amount of truth in the most offensive of its paragraphs. The vignette was curtly refused. What Mr. Gilchrist calls the low affronts of Cromek's letter, cannot be properly judged in the absence of the letter which provoked them. Cromek undoubtedly did Blake a service, and he calls upon him to acknowledge it—an attitude which is never graceful, nor likely to be at all more becoming when assumed in the height of passion. Another cause of grief is alluded to, viz. the "Canterbury Pilgrimage," by Stothard. Cromek had been the means of estranging these two old friends. He had admired a drawing of Blake's on this subject, and wished to possess it, but Blake refused to sell unless he were allowed to engrave the plate for which Cromek wanted the design. Failing in this negotiation, he suggested the subject to Stothard, and again made a successful speculation. He may have also suggested to the painter some of the ideas which he had derived from Blake's drawing. But it appears that Stothard was innocent of all direct plagiarism in the matter: this was the opinion of Flaxman, a friend of both artists. The exhibition, however, of Stothard's picture led to a breach between the two artists which was never closed. Many years later, Blake made repeated offers of reconciliation: once he called when his old friend was ill, and was refused admittance to him. In this, his amiable character shows to great advantage. Irascible but forgiving, he had to suffer from the effects of his own sharp arrows of wrath, and to experience how much more easy it is to wound with angry words than to efface the remembrance of them.

The whole history of Blake's business relations with Cromek is told by Mr. Gilchrist in a spirit of such uncompromising partisanship, that it requires to be read with the greatest caution, and the more so as he does not scruple to support his views by an endeavour to fix the stigma of positive theft on Cromek's memory. If the case between him and Blake had been otherwise sufficiently clear, there would have been no occasion to look out for collateral support for the view he takes of it. Justice can be done to Blake without the sacrifice of another's reputation. This connexion, however, led Blake to undertake the task of bringing his own works before the public in an exhibition he opened in a room in Broad-street, over his brother's shop. He had no doubt reflected on the attention that had been drawn to his designs for the "Grave" by Cromek's advertising arts, and had perhaps admitted to himself that the explanatory and laudatory testimonials which accompanied the prospectus to that work were in some sort needed. He consequently published a catalogue of his works exhibited in Broad-street, concluding with characteristic simplicity, that no one was so capable of pointing out their meaning and beauty as he was himself—that all the public wanted was to be shown the truth ; and who, he thought, was so capable of pointing it out in this matter as himself ?

The force of a testimonial lay, with him, in the justice of the remarks contained in it, and not in the position or reputation of the person giving it : no greater mistake could have been made. One hardly knows whether to laugh or weep at such single-mindedness. What man, though he speak with the tongue of angels, can expect to be heard in his own praise ? The commendation of a fool is a better passport to public appreciation than the most well-grounded self-justification. This interesting document will be found in the second volume of his life. The account of his picture of the " Canterbury Pilgrims" is one of the most masterly criticisms on the Prologue to the Tales that has ever been written. The picture itself, though much more full of character than that of his rival, is, to judge from the engraving which he published a year later, wanting in that general gracefulness which has long rendered Stothard's amongst the most popular of English prints. The exhibition added but little to his reputation. It was visited by the curious, and by his friends, but the general public seemed hardly aware of its existence. As Mr. Gilchrist candidly admits—" The public competition with Stothard placed him in a false position, and, in most people's eyes, in a wrong one. It left him more tetchy than ever, more disposed to wilful exaggeration of individualities [we suppose peculiarities is what is meant] already too prominent, and more prone to unmeasured violence of expression."

The next seven years of his life, from 1810-17, were passed in an increasing isolation and neglect. It is said that he never left his house for two whole years except to fetch his beer for dinner. He continued writing in the old style, but without hope of finding a publisher for his reveries, and would console himself with the reflection—" Well, they are published in heaven." In those days his chief associates were Varley, Richter, and Holmes, the water-colour painters. The first of these had been introduced to him by John Linnell (a name which in those years had not reaped its rich harvest of reputation). Varley was himself almost as eccentric as his new friend, a professional astrologer, as well as a clever but somewhat mannered painter : he was a sincere believer in the science he professed. Several stories are told of lucky hits among his numerous predictions. At Varley's house were drawn those visionary heads of which most have heard who have heard anything of Blake. Some of them are engraved in Mr. Gilchrist's volumes. It is only necessary to say of them that they all look so like natural children of the artist that it is surprising even Varley could have believed they had any other suggestion than his own request, or any other origin than the well-known generic conceptions of Blake's mind.

After seventeen years' residence in South Molton-street, Blake removed to 3, Fountain-court, Strand. This was the last of his changes of residence. He was now sixty-four years of age, and was chiefly visited by a circle of young and enthusiastic admirers. His old patron, Mr. Butts, after the purchases of so many years, had his house full of Blake's designs, and Blake would have found difficulty in supplying even his moderate wants, had it not been for the friendship of Mr. Linnell, who, himself at that period by no means wealthy, gave him commissions, which, with such employment as he still got from the publishers, enabled him to live.

Among the young men who at this time surrounded him was that Thomas Griffiths Wainwright whose story has been told by Talfourd in his "Final Memorials of Charles Lamb," and who supplied the material for the well-known character in Bulwer's "Lucretia." Some additional particulars are gathered together by Mr. Gilchrist of the career of this man whose name has so ominous a reputation.

One of the last works bought by Mr. Butts of Blake was the original series of twenty-one "Inventions" from the Book of Job. These Mr. Linnell gave the artist a commission to engrave. These plates were the consolation of his age. They are undoubtedly what Mr. Gilchrist calls them, "the most remarkable series of etchings, in a scriptural theme, which has appeared since the days of Albert Durer and Rembrandt." They are all reproduced in Mr. Gilchrist's second volume. It is to be regretted that the means employed does but imperfect justice to the originals. The photolithographic process gives them a rather indistinct appearance, which conveys no notion of the beauty and clearness of the originals ; so great, indeed, is the drawback, that the expression is often ludicrously marred by it. The First Person of the Trinity has certainly never been so majestically conceived as in these pictures. The variety and originality of the compositions is miraculous. The sublime spirit of the Book of Job is reflected as in a mirror, while the delicate beauty of the execution is beyond praise.

Mr. Gilchrist's handsome volumes, which are filled with woodcuts from the best examples of Blake's powers as a draughtsman, contain nothing so valuable as these inadequate repetitions of his "Inventions" from the Book of Job. If the biography were not so good as it is, from the care with which every available resource has been exhausted which would throw light upon the painter's life, the fine collection which it contains of examples of his art would always make it a most desirable possession.   In a chapter which he entitles " Personal Details," Mr. Gilchrist collects the testimonies of those who knew the artist in his last days.   These are most interesting, and show how the character of the man made sunshine for his friends in that shady place, an alley in the Strand ; how completely the poverty and poor accommodation—he had but two rooms to live in—was outshone by the simplicity and nobleness of their inhabitant.

The last designs he executed were illustrations to Dante, also a commission from Mr. Linnell.   One of these, the " Circle of Traitors," when compared with Gustave Dóré's treatment of the same subject, shines with all the lustre of a poetical conception, seen beside a merely realistic treatment however clever.   At this period he used sometimes to dine at the house of Mr. Aders, a German merchant : here he came in contact with Mr. Crabb Robinson, who has preserved memoranda of his conversation. These are chiefly remarkable for the strong light they throw upon Blake's practice of at once outraging what he supposed to be the feelings of his interlocutor, as soon as he fancied that he was being " drawn out."   This is a common resource with any one who suspects that the inner sanctuary of his favourite thoughts is about to be profaned by an unsympathetic intruder.   Many of his wildest sayings may be thus accounted for ; when sure of sympathy, nothing could be milder or more quiet than Blake's manner of expressing his opinions.   That these opinions were often strange, and even inconsistent, is the natural result of the mode in which he formed them.   Anything that pleased his feelings or imagination was true to him, as accordant with the only standard to which he ever referred as a proof of genuineness. In 1826, his health began to fail ; he became subject to constant attacks of cold and dysentery.   The walks he had so much enjoyed to the friendly house and circle which was always open to him at Hampstead, had to be given up.   Some of his letters to Mr. Linnell have been preserved.   In August, 1827, he took to his bed, attended solely by that faithful wife who had, as he then said, always been an angel to him.

"On the day of his death, 12th August, 1827," writes Smith, who had his account from the widow, " he composed and uttered songs to his Maker, so sweetly to the ear of his Catherine, that when she stood to hear him, he, looking upon her most affectionately, said—' My beloved, they are *not mine—no ;* they are *not* mine.'   He told her they would not be parted ; he should always be about her to take care of her."

And, in a certain sense, he was so ; he died owing no man anything, and the copious artistic inheritance he left her, supported her in comfort for the four years she survived him. He was buried in Bunhill-fields Cemetery, whither his father and mother had gone before him. There was no monument put up to his memory, and the exact spot can now no longer be certainly identified.

The sad suddenness of Mr. Gilchrist's death in the prime of life, left this biography in some degree incomplete; but his friend, Mr. Dante G. Rossetti, has done it the service that Goethe long desired to do to Schiller, by completing the "False Demetrius."

The supplementary chapter by this accomplished artist is a masterpiece of critical appreciation : himself the most poetical and ideal of modern painters, he, while describing the technical methods pursued by Blake, discusses the question of his general conception of the sphere of art. Sympathizing to the full with Blake's doctrine of the supremacy of the imagination, he yet, in passages of the greatest insight, disputes its omnipotence.

The passages in which he maintains the absolute necessity for the constant presence of Nature as the only means by which variety and fulness can be given to any work of art, are as important in doctrine as they are persuasive in expression.

He also traces the signs of Blake's influence on art through the works of many neglected or half-forgotten artists with a completeness which is in itself a valuable contribution to the history of modern painting. Nor are his good offices confined to this valuable chapter. The whole of the second volume, which contains a selection from Blake's poems, the most important of his prose writings on art, and a *catalogue raisonné* of all Blake's known works, by Mr. William M. Rossetti, has been arranged and brought together by his care. No one who is acquainted with the rare union of masculine good sense and delicate appreciation of beauty displayed in Mr. Rossetti's translations from the early Italian poets, can doubt that in the selection from Blake's poems we have all that is truly excellent in them. In his introduction Mr. Rossetti follows their influence on modern poetry as he had done that of Blake's designs on modern art, and with the same fulness of knowledge and delicacy of taste.

Nothing more graceful and appropriate than this, his offering, has perhaps ever been laid on the tomb of a departed friend.

ART. VI.—PARTIES AND PROSPECTS IN PARLIAMENT.

DURING the last session or two the position of parties in the House of Commons has been thoroughly exceptional. The almost total disappearance of great questions of domestic interest has partly caused and partly been caused by the sudden and singular subsidence of the old divisions which kept asunder party and party. Abandoning their proverbially insular peculiarities, the people of England have begun of late to be almost exclusively occupied in the consideration of foreign politics. Of course, the absence of any exciting topic of domestic concern greatly favoured this change of feeling. But there have been many seasons during which all the same excitement that might have attended the discussion of some great domestic question was evinced in relation to a topic of utterly insignificant character. In the absence of a Reform Bill, or a Church and State question, parties in the House and out of it have often fought quite as fiercely about some petty interest of a purely parochial or a strictly administrative nature. Not so for the last two or three sessions. There has been something like a tacit understanding that all domestic affairs were either to be settled quietly or put aside altogether. It would seem as if the leaders had resolved that there should be no battle, because no leader was quite certain on which side, if it came to a struggle, his usual followers might be found. Some sham battles were fought, and many displays of rhetorical fireworks were exhibited, just to show the public that something was going on; but it was understood all the time by those concerned in the manœuvres that the season was quite unsuited for any serious struggle. Parties are just now in a curious transitional state. The old divisions have disappeared, and the new camps have not yet been formed. One is inclined to compare the present state of the House of Commons to that of the armies of the German Confederation during some of the diplomatic interludes which interrupted the Holstein struggle of 1848. The Federal troops had been doing duty for the insurrection and against the King of Denmark. But if the diplomatic *pourparlers* should come to anything, it was almost certain that the same forces would have to operate for the King and against the insurrection. During the pause, therefore, the Federal captains must have felt somewhat puzzled, and must have been rather anxious that they should not be compelled to act before it became quite clear whom they were to act for. Thus a steady-going old Tory of the average dulness must of late have felt considerably perplexed with regard to his future course. Here is the Opposition, and yonder are the Ministry. There, then, one would have thought, are the natural antagonists clearly defined as ever. But whenever the Ministers are opposed with anything like earnestness, or even criticised with anything like severity, the opponents and the critics address the House from the Ministerial side. The leader of the Cabinet is seldom so loudly applauded as from the benches of the Opposition. The leader of the great Conservative party is sometimes assailed by one of the Ministry ; and the attack provokes cheers and chuckling laughter from the lower benches of Opposition. No wonder one of the older Tories is a good deal bewildered by this condition of things, and would gladly see a return to the good old intelligible state of affairs, when the opposite rows of benches were hostile camps, about whose occupants there could be no more mistake than there is about the principles and the purposes of the followers of General Meade and the followers of General Lee.

"There are no more Pyrenees," exclaimed Louis the Great. There are no longer Whigs and Tories, many a man in our day is perhaps tempted to exclaim. But the Pyrenees became natural and political barriers again, despite of the Great Monarch, and Ministry and Opposition will be enemies once more, when the present transitional state has passed away. At the present moment there is nothing necessarily demanding a party struggle; and there is no leader sufficiently ardent and fresh to provoke a battle for mere enterprise, or even mere conquest. Lord Palmerston evidently desires no longer anything more than that the machine should outlast his time. His parliamentary position is one of serene comfort. He is in the peculiar position of having hardly any enemies, except a very few whom their political principles nevertheless compel for the most part to fight on his side. His personal popularity is immense. He enjoys the almost unqualified support of the Conservative party. He has the devoted adhesion of five-sixths of the Liberals. His position furnishes the most amusing contrast to that of Mr. Disraeli, who is only supported with downright cordiality by a few on his own side, and is regarded merely as an intellectual gladiator by nearly all who sit on the opposite benches. Therefore it may be said that the Ministerial leader gives too much satisfaction, and the Conservative leader gives too little, to allow any chance of a real contest for power. The Tories are not willing to unseat Lord Palmerston. Even if they were so, they would not be particularly anxious to instal Mr. Disraeli. As regards the latter, the Conservative party seem to think there is no living with him or without him. If, then, Lord Palmerston could only live, and if

Providence did not bestow on Toryism—a very unlikely contingency—a leader as able as but more congenial than Mr. Disraeli, there seems no reason why this condition of things should not outlast our generation. But as even Lord Palmerston cannot last for ever, as somebody else must take the place of Prime Minister, and as, moreover, any such change will in all probability sound the close of the present truce, and call all the sleepy belligerents to their arms and their camps again, it may be interesting to consider, now on the eve of a new session, what capacity of fresh combinations the House presents, and what men are likely to lead the divisions of the next great parliamentary campaign.

Certainly we cannot expect to find in our day one other man capable of assuming and retaining the position of ascendancy over the House of Commons which Lord Palmerston has for many years enjoyed. If he has not ruled that House as absolutely as Count Cavour, towards the close of his splendid career, ruled the parliament of Turin, it is only because the English Commons could not, in our day, be induced to bear an absolute dictatorship. But the personal influence of Lord Palmerston has been long supreme. Anything which he cannot do in England, nobody can do. Not alone is he a perfect master of the arts by which the House of Commons can be led and governed, but he is an equally perfect master of the very different arts by which the people at large can be led and governed. It is doubtful whether the most popular democrat living could be more popular among the very classes to whom he chooses to appeal than is Lord Palmerston. This vast influence, this almost unbounded popularity, must be considered a marvellous moral phenomenon in any case. But it will seem marvellous almost beyond understanding to any one who fairly criticises the conditions under which and despite of which it has been obtained. For the Prime Minister who is now, and has been for years, far more influential in England than ever Bolingbroke was ; wielding a political power as great as any ever owned by Chatham or Pitt ; as supreme in his own country as Cavour was in Sardinia ; holding a position such as no French statesman has held for generations in France, has scarcely any pretension whatever to be considered an orator, and has not, during the whole of his long career, affixed his name to any grand act of successful statesmanship.

A declaration of this kind may seem to many a startling heresy—a paradox—a piece of self-contradiction. It is none the less a simple fact. In no sense in which the word is used among educated men can Lord Palmerston be pronounced an orator. He seems rather to make the very best of his debating powers by carefully avoiding all pretension to oratory. Neither in language

nor in thought does the character of his public speaking ever rise
for a moment beyond the level of commonplace. His manner is
singularly ungraceful, his utterance often hesitating, his action
quite ungainly. He takes no view of any public question
but that which is the most obvious. He does not penetrate, or
care to penetrate, beyond the external of anything. None of his
speeches would ever be read except for the present or the historical
interest of the subject. No separate passages of them dwell in
the memory to inspire orators and to animate the national heart.
No lofty thoughts shine out through the sentences. No great
political doctrine is expounded in them. No splendid phraseology,
no brilliant rhetoric delights one class of mind ; no masterly,
comprehensive, irresistible power of reasoning charms another.
No special morsels are quoted and passed from mouth to mouth.
No writer fortifies himself with any authoritative maxim gathered
from the speeches of Lord Palmerston. It may be doubted
whether (apart from the jocular and humorous hits) the most constant observer of the Prime Minister's career remembers anything more of his eloquence than the general fact that on such a
night he defended this measure, and on such another occasion he
denounced that. Having heard or read the greater number of
Lord Palmerston's speeches during recent years, we can recall but
one single sentence which seems to us to have risen above the
level of the merest commonplace. We cannot understand how
anybody who believes that Fox and Pitt and Burke, Canning
and Peel and O'Connell, Gladstone, Ellenborough, and Bright,
were or are orators, can apply the title of orator likewise to Lord
Palmerston.

Having said all this, does it seem a paradox to say immediately
after that the Prime Minister is the most effective speaker now in
the House of Commons ? Paradox or not, it is the actual truth.
The average of Lord Palmerston's speeches are more successful
than those of any other man in the House. He never delivers a
speech which can be termed a failure. A remark which we heard
made in reference to the late Lord Lyndhurst applies with equal
force, different as the two men are, to Lord Palmerston. The
claims of Lord Lyndhurst to be considered an orator, in the
higher sense, were being discussed. It was observed that one of
the best and most discriminating of the biographical notices which
appeared after his death described Lord Lyndhurst as the most
equal of speakers, as one in fact who never made a failure.
"Then," was the shrewd comment, "I am satisfied that he was
not a great orator. Great orators are especially unequal." And
great orators are not always very successful as practical debaters.
It seems doubtful whether a mere partisan, caring only for a

division, would not often have preferred that Edmund Burke should be against and not for him. In our own day it may have happened that a division would show better for the Liberal side had John Bright not spoken, or spoken against the Ministry. We have heard orations from Mr. Gladstone which undoubtedly injured rather than served the cause which the orator had at heart. A great rhetorician has almost always something of the nature of the white elephant in him. Not so Lord Palmerston. Like Homer's or Pope's Nestor, he says no more than just the thing he ought. He always selects, and as if by a sort of instinct, not the arguments which are most logically cogent, but those which are most likely to suit the character and the temper of his audience. He speaks always for his hearers, and never for himself; always to affect those he addresses, never for the sake of arguing out any convictions present and passionate in his own mind. He earns the positive affection of the House of Commons by never becoming a lecturer or a bore. He never stands alone, or nearly alone, on any question. No sudden impulse, no irresistible conviction, ever drives him to take up any position which might bring him into antagonism with the average mind of the country. He never talks over the heads of his audiences; he never compels them to strain their intellects in order to keep pace with him; he never fails to harmonize with the general intelligence of the English people. Even those who are forced into a political antagonism with him on special topics, are likewise compelled to acknowledge that they are pleased with his way of viewing the subject. He employs always just the kind of reasoning which addresses itself to the moderate party on either side. Having a thorough knowledge of the varying tempers of the House, he never thinks of addressing Philip excited as he would reason with Philip in his calmer moments. Very seldom does Lord Palmerston say a really witty thing. Few of his satirical touches are likely to be remembered; scarcely any of his sarcastic hits will be quoted hereafter, as so many of Disraeli's now are; but his jests are invariably much better adapted to time and place and temper than the repartees of any other debater in the House. His shots hit, as Burke said of Charles Townshend's wit, just between wind and water. No man can interpose so skilfully as he can, just before the division, to break and dissipate the effect of a telling speech against him, and to induce the House into a frame of mind for regarding all that has been done by the Opposition as a mere harmless conventionality gone through in deference to the formal necessities of party, on which it would be a waste of power to bestow a serious thought, and a waste of time to hunt up a reluctant vote. The secret of his success lies in his consummate cleverness; his thorough knowledge of English temper; his absence of any of the aspirations or the caprices of genius. He has the happy art of seeming to lead where in reality he takes good care only to follow. The Doctor in one of Dickens's novels obtains the repute of supreme skill because he prescribes just the remedies which he knows the lady of the house has been already preparing. Thus with Lord Palmerston. He knows exactly what the general voice of the country will demand under given conditions; he shapes his course accordingly, and thus he secures all the honour while avoiding all the responsibility of leadership. Lord Palmerston represents, under all circumstances, the feelings, the judgments, the inclinations, the prejudices, and the passions of the average British character. He represents the average head and heart of an age singularly devoid of high aspirations or constant earnest purpose; an age peculiarly intolerant of eccentricity, especially if it be that of genius; an age averse to having its feelings long strained in any one direction, delighting only in easy and ephemeral pleasures, interests, and excitements, practical in so far as to be reluctant to risk or sacrifice much means to be practical, and hostile to anything which draws heavily on the intellect, whether in art, in literature, or in statesmanship. That is the England which Lord Palmerston admirably represents. Future generations can best understand what sort of people were the Englishmen of our day by studying the life and character of our most successful statesman. To serve the purpose of the hour is Lord Palmerston's policy; to succeed in serving it is his triumph, to have succeeded in serving it will be his fame. In the strictest sense may his political reputation be called a national possession, for it is the reputation of his country during his period of success.

When Lord Palmerston passes away, he will leave no man behind him capable of attempting to take his peculiar place. Chatham, Fox, Burke, were far greater men than our present Prime Minister; yet we should sooner expect to see another Chatham, or Fox, or Burke, than another Palmerston. Not having settled any great domestic question—not even having brought, or tried to bring, any such question into a fair way towards settlement, Lord Palmerston has done nothing whatever to render the task of his successors less difficult than his own; while he cannot possibly bequeath to any successor the peculiar qualities which made difficulties so light to him. Even in foreign politics, his own special and favourite sphere, he has done nothing towards reducing into shape and natural coherence the confused heaps of ill-assorted combinations which are threatening every day to fall asunder. " Where I did begin," says Cassius, about to die, " there now I end." So with Lord Palmerston. Nor does he seem to have cared about bequeathing his policy and his character to any successor. No Canning, no Gladstone, continues his work and mirrors his reputation. We look around, and discern no rising statesman who seems to have moulded himself upon the model of Lord Palmerston. One member of the Government alone is supposed to cultivate what he conceives to be an imitation of Lord Palmerston's style and bearing. Even that imitation is not successful, for the supposed imitator is Sir Robert Peel.

The removal of Lord Palmerston will unquestionably bring to a close the present lethargic and purposeless truce. But who, after Lord Palmerston, will lead the House of Commons? Two or three years ago every one would have pointed to the late Sidney Herbert. No man could be more admirably fitted for the task. Possessed of a ready easy eloquence; of large acquaintance with the world of politics and the world of society; having the most genial, graceful, and conciliatory manner; certain to make friends wherever friends could possibly be made, and unlikely to make enemies of any whose friendship was honourable or worth having—Sidney Herbert seemed designed by fortune and by nature to be the English Prime Minister of an untroubled era. What he or anybody else might have proved if fate had designed that England should pass through any stormy and trying period, no one can pretend even to conjecture. Any such speculation would be as futile as to attempt to conjecture what some one of our friends, who has never quitted his own quiet ingle nook for a week, might do if he were placed in the position of Pizarro, or Clive, or Robinson Crusoe. Our long era of peace at home, and only rare and moderate trial abroad, has rendered us unaccustomed even to contemplate a serious emergency arising to test the resources of an English statesman A Premier has his troubles and trials ; but they are only like the troubles and trials which are always attendant upon the administration of a vast and splendid property. They involve no years of terrible anxiety, no exhausting struggle, no crisis of vital danger. The task which devolves upon an English Prime Minister of our generation is no more like that which fell to the lot of Pitt, or Cavour, or Louis Napoleon than the duties of a county surveyor are to those of an African explorer. Even the statesmen of Russia and Austria have of late had functions of infinitely greater anxiety and peril devolving upon them than fortune has assigned to our Aberdeens and Derbys and Russells and Palmerstons. That English statesmen would rise up equal to any task imposed by necessity, no one can doubt for a moment ; but the necessity has certainly not been sent in our day, and does not seem likely soon to present itself. Therefore, when we speculate upon the character of Eng-

land's future Premier, we demand nothing more than a man fairly
equal to the conduct of the country's ordinary business, and
capable of leading the House of Commons. This latter part, which
may seem the less important, is really the one essential which
at present must be asked of any one who would fill the post of
British Prime Minister. Sidney Herbert was qualified beyond
any statesman of his party now living to perform this service.

Sidney Herbert dead, people thought of Lord Canning. The
English public found out, when it was just too late, that in the
great Indian viceroy England had a statesman of the highest class :
a man capable of acting and succeeding in the most sudden, unexpected, and terrible emergencies ; a man to whom the aspect
of the danger always suggested the means of averting it. But
Canning only came home to die. Then the attention and the
expectations of politicians fixed themselves upon Sir George C.
Lewis. There was a man who, although not possessed of that
great personal influence and weight which are desirable qualities
in an English Prime Minister, was well able to command
the respect of all parties in the House by the noble impartiality
of his character—by his thorough disinterestedness—his reliability
—his great, although not brilliant, talents—his vast, although
not showy, acquirements. He, too, passed away prematurely,
regretted sincerely by all parties. Had he lived we should
probably witness the unusual spectacle of an English Parliament and public accepting, without hesitation, without objection, and without a sneer, the leadership of a man who did
not personally belong to any of the great hereditary ruling
families, and who had not even large resources of wealth to
recommend him. Apart from the merits of the man himself,
this would have been a sight worth seeing, and a worthy precedent
for a new generation to follow. Because it is an indisputable
fact that, with all our political equality, there is no country in
Europe which guards with a more superstitious jealousy its highest
political places against the incursions of the men of mere talents
and personal character. But Sir George Lewis, too, is dead, and
England is again on the look-out for a successor to her premier post.

Have we forgotten that the present Cabinet possesses a man
of far greater political abilities than Sidney Herbert or Sir George
Lewis ? In the present Ministry there is at least one man of
genius. Mr. Gladstone is incomparably the greatest parliamentary orator of the day. Lord Derby's faculty of debate is
narrow compared to the range of the Chancellor of the Exchequer ; Mr. Bright shows most effectively on the platform ;
we have never been able to believe that even partisanship can
seriously compare Mr. Disraeli with Mr. Gladstone as a speaker ;
and there is nobody else whom any one would think of comparing

with him at all. If Mr. Gladstone be the most brilliant orator,
he is, beyond all doubt, the most brilliant financier of the House
of Commons. Brilliant may seem an odd epithet to bestow upon
a financier, and yet we can think of none other which so peculiarly characterizes Mr. Gladstone's financial career. In finance
alone he is always bold and enterprising—never hesitating and
cautious. When his schemes are successful, they are always brilliant; and when they fail they are brilliant likewise. But it does
not seem as if any party were looking with great satisfaction to
the prospect of having Mr. Gladstone for Prime Minister. In
the ordinary course of things, and supposing that there does not
spring up some new man of extraordinary political aptitude and
personal influence within the next few years, Mr. Gladstone must
inevitably lead the country before very long. Yet nobody seems
anxious to anticipate the moment. Perhaps Mr. Gladstone is
not exactly what people are fond of calling a thoroughly English
character. It is not, perhaps, a mark of great national enlighten-
ment to desire that our leaders in politics should be all of the
same general pattern; but there is undoubtedly such a tendency
in the British mind, as Burke knew yesterday, and Mr. Disraeli
knows only too well to-day. Mr. Gladstone is too hesitating,
perhaps too sensitively conscientious, studies too carefully all
the sides of every question, and discovers too many sides in it,
to be just the mould of man whom the English public loves,
and trusts, and applauds. Much of his character bears a close
resemblance to that of Halifax, at least to that of Halifax as
Macaulay has pictured it. The amount of enterprise with
which Providence has endowed him seems wholly to expend itself
in schemes of finance. In ordinary politics he appears never
quite to make up his mind; and he has a tendency—generous in
the man but inconvenient for the leader—always to find out that
there is much to be said for the weaker cause just when everybody else is giving it up as lost. The popular cry which would
suggest to Lord Palmerston a happy opportunity for shouting
with the strongest would probably remind Mr. Gladstone of a
duty incumbent upon him to uplift his voice on behalf of the
silenced faction. What does Mr. Hawthorne, in his late work, say
about Englishmen and their practical success? "The secret,"
declares this shrewd and not very genial critic, "of English practical success lies in their characteristic faculty of shutting one
eye, whereby they get so distinct and decided a view of what immediately concerns them that they go stumbling towards it over a
hundred insurmountable obstacles, and achieve a magnificent
triumph without ever being aware of half its difficulties." In this
attribute, at least, Mr. Gladstone is thoroughly un-English—save
in his finance alone. "When a man," remarks Hawthorne,

" opens both his eyes, he generally sees about as many reasons for acting in one way as in any other, and quite as many for acting in neither." Mr. Gladstone generally opens both his eyes in this way to look at every subject, and generally opens them widest at the very moment of critical importance when it is essentially necessary to take one view or the other, and act accordingly. Decidedly there are national emergencies when the very worst thing a man can do is to consider too long before doing anything.

Moreover, Mr. Gladstone is deficient in many of the qualities which make a man successful as a leader of the House of Commons. One of the sources of Lord Palmerston's popularity is his unfailing good temper and courtesy towards opponents. Nothing ever puts Lord Palmerston out. Of late years he has even abandoned the half-insolent *insouciance* with which at one time it was his habit to answer arguments and dispose of opponents. All that the Premier of to-day retains from the pert Palmerstonian banter of earlier years is a joyous *bonhommie* kind of satirical humour which never offends those upon whom it plays. Mr. Gladstone, although not naturally given to the satirical, is terribly apt to offend his opponents in debate. He is too earnest, too sensitive, too impressionable—too hot tempered, his severer critics say—to display much parliamentary tact when he has to defend any cause which lies at his heart. Moreover, he is, to some extent, the slave of his splendid eloquence. Once he mounts his hobby, he is apt to let the steed run away with him. His rhetoric sometimes overwhelms himself and his opponents alike. It is impossible to observe the rush of that torrent of eloquence without feeling occasionally convinced that the orator is being carried away by the flood. One result of this is, that while the speaker bears all opposition resistless before him, he makes permanent antagonists of many of those whose ephemeral arguments he sweeps away. Dull men especially do not like being literally drenched in overpowering rhetoric. Honest Conservative gentlemen do not by any means enjoy being singled out as the mark for such an onslaught as the Chancellor of the Exchequer loves to make. To refute arguments is by no means the great end which a debater, and more especially a leader, in the House of Commons must keep in view. Even as a mere debater, Mr. Gladstone's impetuosity often leads him wildly astray. He is apt to meet the objection of the moment by some argument which covers indeed the point assailed, but, at the same time, includes a vast deal which the orator would never have thought of defending. Few men are more often charged with inconsistency, although none can be less open to the charge of deliberately trifling with any question, great or little. Mr. Gladstone is looked upon by solid people as not quite reliable, as wanting ballast, as an unsteady man. It is not unfair to say that there is no character which secures so much general confidence in England as that of steady, solid mediocrity. Nothing better proves the consummate cleverness of Lord Palmerston than the success with which he humoured his countrymen out of this weakness as regarded his own political character. The highest attributes, no less than the most obvious deficiencies of Mr. Gladstone's character, alike forbid his ever achieving a similar triumph. Every one in the House of Commons admires Mr. Gladstone's genius. Every one acknowledges his entire disinterestedness, conscientiousness, and sincerity. Yet it would be scarcely possible for a statesman of his renown and his character to have a smaller personal following in the House of Commons. Where is the party —where is even the knot of persons—whom any one could confidently point out as the pupils and the adherents of the brilliant and high-minded Chancellor of the Exchequer? In this respect he is even less fortunate than the rival who sits just opposite to him. Mr. Disraeli is not regarded with implicit confidence by the country. His own party is not absolutely devoted to his guidance. There are plenty of grumblers in his own ranks who think he has been captain quite long enough. But there is always in the House a certain group of persons—young men, generally—who look up to Mr. Disraeli with a positive enthusiasm—a personal devotion. In and out of the House Mr. Disraeli's political character, with all its outward coldness and cynicism, seems to have a peculiar charm for the young and the ardent. Were he to suffer any political humiliation whatever, he would always have his faithful body-guard ready to close around him like the staunch youths who gathered round Pitt when troubled and pained by the Dundas impeachment, to protect him from the taunts of his enemies. Mr. Gladstone, whose superb and impassioned style might naturally be supposed the very gift to awaken personal enthusiasm, seems to have individually no distinguishable following in the House of Commons.

Mr. Gladstone, therefore, does not seem to us, or, we suppose, to anybody, the *beau idéal* of a future Premier. Even with a Prime Minister in the Lords, and the Chancellor of the Exchequer leader of the House of Commons, we cannot help thinking that talents far less splendid than those of Mr. Gladstone might serve the purpose better. But, after him, what remains? An infinite deal of nothing on the Liberal side—at least, among those who alone are ticketed for office. There are plenty of respectable men of decent abilities—men who, whether thrown by fortune into a parish vestry or an Imperial Parliament, would alike approve themselves respectable; but there is nothing available of a higher stamp. The Granvilles, Argyles, Cardwells, Greys, and all the rest, are, in their several places, highly commendable. Their abilities are considerable—their intentions unexceptionable—their services, on the whole, useful. The high special talents of men like the present Lord Chancellor or Sir Roundell Palmer are, of course, only available in their own sphere; and no other sphere seems at present to promise much of brightness. On the Liberal side we see very few rising young men of promise, even if in England rising young men unpossessed of distinguished rank were likely ever to fill the highest political place. Indeed the Whig side of the House shows at present a singular dearth of rising talent. Where are the young men who are to succeed when the reign of their sires has concluded? Even among the ranks of the Radicals there seems the same deficiency. That generation, too, appears to have exhausted itself, and left nothing behind. Where are the followers who are to succeed Bright and Cobden? How comes it that these eminent men seem to have no pupils capable of hereafter taking their places? The Radical party is still considerable and thoroughly respectable. But after Bright and Cobden who are its orators? Mr. Stansfeld is absorbed into administrative detail; and even he did not give much promise of the readiness and spontaneity so essential to parliamentary success. Mr. Forster is a man of ability, and a fair debater. There is, so far as we are aware, nobody else to be mentioned. From Mr. Bright to the very ablest of his parliamentary followers there is all the distance between genius and promising mediocrity. Not the least conspicuous among the many singular parliamentary phenomena of our day is the manner in which the extreme Liberals of the House of Commons have allowed their influence to glide from their hands. Partly, no doubt, this was owing to the peculiar reaction which took place in the public mind, and to the distracting effect of great wars and momentous crises abroad; but it is likewise due in a great degree to the singular want of fresh talent in the ranks of the party itself. To reorganize the Liberal party would require, in the first instance, a constant and vigilant devotion on the part of the leaders to all the labour and drudgery of leadership in the House of Commons. This kind of attention neither Mr. Cobden nor Mr. Bright is, we should think, qualified by physical condition any longer to give; but were the leaders endowed with superhuman resources of *physique*, they could not do much with the Liberal party in its present condition. Respectable mediocrity has done it to death.

How stands the position of the Conservative party? It has fallen into a state more peculiar still than that of the Ministerial body, or of that which once used to be styled the great Liberal party. It is distrustful, divided, uncertain, disaffected; unable to look steadily forward, not much encouraged, perhaps, when it glances casually back. It has a leader whom it scarcely trusts, and yet whom it cannot replace. So far as the Conservatives proper are concerned, they may be described as utterly devoid of Parliamentary talent. The respectable country gentlemen who form the most influential portion of the party are not indeed, in any sensible degree, like to the English country gentlemen of the days of Fielding, or even of the days of Pitt. They are men of high character, moderate views, and for the most part excellent college education. They have very little of the coarse spirit of faction in them, and they have learned to admire intellect and respect noble character even though the force of intellect and character be put forth against them ; but they do not furnish at the present moment to the Opposition in the House of Commons one single individual who could be called a statesman—one solitary being whom even the partiality of his friends could describe as a brilliant debater. Even the hero-worship which elevated into a great leader a man so moderate in abilities as the late Lord George Bentinck, could do nothing to exalt into states-manship any one of the country gentlemen who follow, more or less reluctantly, the guidance of Mr. Disraeli. Not that ability is wanting on the Conservative side of the House. Nothing could be more unjust than to suppose that Mr. Disraeli is the only great debater on that side. But the ability is all, or nearly all, exotic and imported. Mr. Seymour Fitzgerald is a very promising politician ; a man thoroughly acquainted with foreign politics, where the Conservatives are generally weakest, and gifted with admirable skill in debate. Sir Hugh Cairns is one of the ablest speakers in the House, and, unlike almost all other lawyers, is able to address himself to general subjects with the temper of a politician. Mr. Whiteside, despite all the old-fashioned college debating-society floridness and rotundity of his rhetoric, is a powerful influence in debate. But these men, we need hardly say, belong to the English Conservative party only as the O'Donnells and MacMahons and O'Sullivans and O'Reillys belong to the various European courts and armies to which genius and fortune attach them. Yet these are in debate the sole sustaining power on which Mr. Disraeli can rely. The two or three tolerable speakers who appear in other parts of the Conservative benches are just as likely to be against him as for him. So little of native ability is there about the Tory party, that there is even a sort of inclination to look up with admiration and hope to the small cynical cavilling, the incurably narrow mind of Lord Robert Cecil. Of course we purposely omit, in considering the general power of Toryism, all reference to Lord Stanley. In Lord Stanley would be combined at once the ability, the influence, and the character to make a leader. But we should be grieved to think that there was the slightest chance

K 2

of Lord Stanley's ever becoming a leader of such a party as that
represented by the Conservatism of our day. Somebody well
remarked, not long since, that the Conservatives have one and only
one objection to the leadership of Lord Stanley, but that one
objection is insurmountable—if he led at all, he would lead the
wrong way.

In truth, the Tory party are perplexed at present. They seem
to have nothing to fight for. They hardly know from day to day
on which side to fight. The politics of the age have outgrown
them. Their education is for the most part purely a college
course. Their travel is little better than a feeble imitation conducted on the traditions of the grand tour which formed so indispensable a part of the education of an earlier generation. The
country gentleman of that day, when he had completed his college
course, set off upon his travels, furnished with letters of introduction to the British Ministers at half the courts of Europe. He
went there to educate himself, and he was shown all that it was
thought might help to educate him. He obtained some slight
knowledge of political science, in the miserably narrow limits to
which it was then restricted. It was then the acquirement of the
wealthy and illustrious ; and the country gentleman strove at
least to understand its elements. He conversed with Ministers
and diplomatists at Versailles and the Hague and Vienna, and he
acquired at least some of the jargon of *la haute politique.* This
quite sufficed him for his future career in the House of Commons.
This, and the knowledge that, being a Tory, he was bound to oppose
the Whigs, carried him smoothly along, and enabled him always
to understand what was going forward, to see his way and to
keep his place. But about the time of the younger Pitt all this
began to change. The political basis began to widen immensely,
and bewildering complications commenced to exhibit themselves and to distress the ingenuous, easy, downright mind of
Toryism. Not merely did all the old sacraments of England's
policy begin to be questioned, but political creeds grew up which
were as difficult to understand as they were dangerous to acknowledge. Legitimacy, the balance of power, the doctrine of England's
hereditary antagonism to France—all these and various other
political superstitions faded away. Then came political economy
and free trade, and the terrible entanglement of politics with tariffs,
and prices, and Customs' duties, and productions, and corn, and
sugar, and tallow, and various other bewildering and vulgar
objects and considerations. With all this, too, came the inevitable melting away of the political monopoly so long in Tory
hands. The manufacturer, and the shopkeeper, indifferent to the
balance of power, and perhaps not knowing the name of any one
of our foreign ambassadors, were perfectly at home when tariffs

and Customs' duties came to be discussed. Conservatism roused itself up for one desperate and final battle with the encroaching novelties. The struggle against free trade was the last gigantic effort of the Tory mind. Fearful and wonderful will that effort seem to an amazed posterity. Conservatism resolved to enter the arena with its new enemy, and do battle with that enemy's own weapons. It bent its utmost energies to the mastery of the horrid subjects. It racked its brain to comprehend all about demand and supply, prohibitive duty and restrictive duty, tariffs and customs, corn, sugar, and navigation. Not unworthy of a certain sort of pitying admiration is this last effort of the Conservative genius to grapple with its relentless enemy. It propounded the most astounding theories; it backed them up with the most appalling facts. One grand principle it kept firm hold of, and for the support of that it devoted itself to the most exhausting labours and sacrifices. It was plain as day to the Tory mind that to allow a foreigner to come into our own ports and undersell our own growers must be to undermine our own interests. This seemed so self-evident a fact that only maniacs or revolutionists could dispute it. Yet, seeing that it was disputed, the Tories devoted themselves to die in its defence. Ludicrous, fantastic, preposterous, yet not without a certain pathos and pitiable dignity, were the efforts to repel free trade by economic arguments. To read the debates of that day is the oddest of studies. From Lord Derby and his famous Tamboff argument down to the drollest theories of the dullest country squire; from Lord George Bentinck on the sugar duties to Mr. Ferrand on the manufacturing question, the whole is pervaded and assimilated by one unvarying stream of nonsense. No man could read these debates now without frequent laughter. When all proved a failure, when the last lingering adherent acknowledged at least a present defeat, the foundations of Toryism seemed to be utterly shaken. No faith in anything seemed any longer secure. We are far indeed from saying that the doctrine of Protection has been wholly banished even yet from the Tory mind. Only too often does some argument turn up in debate which shows that the dear old delusion is cherished still, and that Toryism still involuntarily strives to build its houses upon the beloved sandbank which it once thought a rock. But the political doctrine is no more a recognised power. Free trade must be professed now even by the slowest of Tories; even by those who would still fain believe that it is only a fallacy; even by those who have never been able really to bring themselves to understand what it means at all. We have a secret conviction that this is not confined even to the slowest of Tories. We much doubt whether the fulness of Sir John Pakington's faith is given to the new theory.

" Lost in the depths of heresy on the gold question," Mr. Glad-stone last session pronounced the right honourable baronet. We doubt whether the heresy is limited to the gold question. But free trade has to be acknowledged as a principle even by those who only acknowledge it as Mrs. Pendennis professed to admire Shakspeare. The acknowledgment has left the Tory party proper without a political creed, without even a political *mot d'ordre*. Most of them have passed the time for constructing a new political faith, and drilling themselves and their pupils into it. In the exhaustion and perplexity of the condition which followed the free-trade struggle they even allowed the old time-honoured standard of legitimacy to be taken down and furled and flung in the dust. Greater political stupor there surely could hardly have been than that in which the Tory party allowed this sacrilege to be perpetrated, quietly, unresistingly, without even an intelligible or coherent protest. Nay, so utter has been the confusion of ideas that the Opposition now talk as frequently and as glibly as the Whigs about the right of people to choose their own rulers. This is indeed Toryism's pet argument in favour of the Southern Confederacy, taking precedence even of that other cherished argument about the right of a people to rebel against a protective tariff. The British Protectionists now profess to hold their own economical principles so accursed that even rebellion against them is honourable and just. The British Legitimists rally almost to a man in favour of the sacred and inalienable right of a people to assert that choice of ruler which Edmund Burke wrote his Essay on the French Revolution to stigmatize as the frenzied dream of maniacs or the guilty ambition of anarchists. Surely the Tory mind must be sadly perplexed, or have undergone some complete revolution, when it can exhibit itself in such fantastic attitudes. Obviously, either Toryism must come to an end altogether, or it must in some manner reconstruct itself in better accord with the relation between the old principles and the new practices. This reconstruction is clearly not to be the work of the elders who were once the leaders. We must look to the younger race of Conservatives for any stout and genuine battle against their opponents ; we must wait until the hereditary struggle can be taken up by those who are able to choose their ground with a perfect recognition of established realities. In plain words, the Opposition must remain as at present, weak, staggering, and uncertain, until it can clearly make up its mind as to what object it now considers worth fighting for, and what leader it can have to conduct the struggle.

But are the Whigs, the old Whigs, any better than their opponents ? Have they much to boast of as regards leaders or principles ? Truly, we think not. Forlorn, indeed, is now the aspect of that great party once led by him—

> " On whose burning tongue
> Truth, peace, and freedom hung."

The Capua of office has ruined our Whig party; it is worse off than after many defeats ; the poor remnant and wreck of its once noble host is the victim not of overthrow, but of success. Not an earnest, not even an eloquent man left. The few political debaters of intellect and power who attach themselves to its banner are drawn from the ranks of those who were once its enemies. The Whigs, too, want a new creed and a new man. They have worn to death the old principles of peace, retrench-ment, and reform. Indeed, they have brought these principles into sad contempt. They have effected no peace which was not inglorious and debasing, like the abject submission with which England the other day was made to grovel in the dust before the cold and cutting insolence of Prince Gortchakoff. They have done so much for retrenchment that the military and naval ex-penses of England are greater during the period of that singular condition which we have fallen into the habit of calling peace, than in the ordinary times of heavy war. If expense is to be a consideration, and the economy of an administration its highest praise, then we cannot help remembering that some of England's grandest military triumphs were won with less of military and naval expenditure than it now costs us to sit at home and eat our meals in quiet. This is, indeed, peace at any price ; certainly, at the highest price in figures which the commodity ever before cost any nation on the earth. Reform, the last of the principles which were once watchwords, the Whigs have at length reduced to that condition that it requires high moral courage for any man to profess himself a Reformer. Even Mr. Bright seems to allude with something of hesitation to the unpleasant subject. For, after the memorable session of 1860, it has become positively ludicrous to suggest the idea of a political reform. Here, too, we have the peculiar Whig notion of peace emphatically realized. A Reform Bill was once a lightning conductor : now it is only a laughing-stock. Once men fought for or against it : now they chuckle compla-cently over it. The noble art of letting things alone is the highest effort of our home policy. To realize the splendid condition when Ministers will actually be allowed to do nothing, appears to be the present Whig ambition. The whole creed of Whiggery in our day was admirably summed up in the concluding phrase of Earl Russell's closing speech at Blairgowrie—the memorable "Rest and be thankful" motto. Earl Russell at present is likely to make

one believe that England has grown very, very old.   If we were
to measure the change in the sentiments of the nation by the
change in the political tendencies of this leading statesman, we
might really begin to think there was some sense in the polite
and flattering suggestion of the Rev. H. W. Beecher, at Exeter
Hall, that England, having fallen into a quiet decrepitude and
decay, had better seek a retreat, quite out of the way of disturbance and harm, in some far-off Western region.   Earl Russell
certainly is not very old, as statesmen are measured in our days.
He is nearly ten years younger than Lord Palmerston.   He is
more than ten years younger than Radetzky was when the latter
set about the series of campaigns which crushed Italian revolution.   He does not appear to have suffered the slightest decay in
mental faculties ; he gives no other indication of failing physical
power than just so much as is absolutely inseparable from advancing years. Yet he seems to have made up his mind that he must
not be harassed any more by severe political duty. Nay, he seems
to think that because he is tired of real work, all the nation ought
to be tired as well·   One of the reasons he gave for declining to
espouse more warmly the cause of Poland was, that at his time of
life he could not undertake the responsibility of conducting so
critical a policy.

The younger political observers of our day must be rather
puzzled to comprehend Earl Russell, and to reconcile him with
the traditional Lord John.   They must wonder what on earth
Sydney Smith could have meant by his famous illustration of
the headlong temerity and self-confidence of the Whig leader
who then bore the name of Russell.   Did not Thomas Moore
once liken Lord John to the eagle soaring at the sun ?   Did not
the poet write of the " strife," and the " mighty arena," where

> " All that is grand,
> 'Tis for high-thoughted spirits like thine to command ?"

The present generation must be a good deal puzzled about the
application of lines like these.   Perhaps some youthful political
students take refuge in the conviction that as there were an elder
and a younger Pitt, an elder and a younger Canning, so likewise
there must have been an elder and a younger John Russell.   It
may be that the present sensation of languor and disinclination
to active work which Earl Russell so frankly acknowledges is not
a peculiarity, but a sort of epidemic spreading itself over many
of our politicians.   Certainly, when we find men so energetic as
Mr. Bright talking in the desponding strain which that gentleman
lately adopted at Rochdale—talking as if the wine of political life
were drunk and nothing but the lees were left—as if farther
effort were hopeless and only calm surrender remained — we

feel less inclined to blame Earl Russell and more disposed to doubt whether, after all, the quietness of unreasonable content is not better than the quietness of unreasonable despair. Happily for England she cannot adopt, even if she would, the new political philosophy of the Whigs. She cannot long rest, merely thankful for what has been done. Mr. Froude, in his " Life of Elizabeth," speaks well when he says that there are in the English nature two great antagonistic tendencies, " visible in our laws, our institutions, our religion, and in the thoughts and actions of our greatest men :" the one a disposition to live by rule and precedent, to distrust novelties, to hold the experience of the past as the surest guide ; the other " a restless, impetuous energy, inventing, expanding, pressing forward into the future, regarding what has been already achieved only as a step or landing-place leading upwards and onwards to higher conquests ; a mode of thought which in the half-educated takes the form of a rash disdain of earlier ages, which in the best and wisest creates a sense that we shall be unworthy of our ancestors if we do not eclipse them in all that they touched." Mr. Froude is still right when he affirms that in healthy ages the two tendencies co-exist, and, co-existing, " produce that even progress, that strong vitality, at once so vigorous and so composed, which is legible everywhere in the pages of English history." This is especially true in politics. The season we have just passed through has not been healthy, for it wholly lacked the operation of one of the two tendencies. It has not been healthy, even though it may have been inevitable and necessary. The languor which follows fever, the exhaustion which succeeds over-exertion, may be unavoidable, and may be necessary conditions ; but they are not in themselves healthful stages of existence. So with our recent season of political quietude. After over-excitement and long and heavy struggles, it was an inevitable reaction. But it was not in itself a satisfactory or desirable condition. Only that fate summoned up some great and noble interests abroad, the British political mind of this generation would have been stunted and stupified by it. As it is, the great House of Commons has degenerated under its influence to the capacity of a parish vestry. All manner of mediocrities have been brought up to the front along with the small questions which suited them. A placid, sleek, stultifying kind of self-content began to steal over the nation. We were arriving fast at that most imperfect and dangerous of all conditions, when men begin to consider themselves quite perfect and safe. Even our foreign policy became tainted by it. Always when Great Britain is inclined to degenerate, she seeks, as if instinctively, the companionship of Austria. We have had this ominous indication of our condi-

tion forced somewhat unpleasantly upon our notice once or twice
of late. Our social condition has certainly not been improving.
We have had more of that kind of poverty which is a national
disgrace (unlike the Lancashire poverty) exhibited throughout
England of late, than for a whole previous generation. We have
been careless and unconcerned everywhere ; looking with cynical
eye upon the decay of great principles which once made our creed
and our battle-cry ; seeking only easy excitement, and shunning
deep political thought. We have been resting, if not thankful.
All this will soon end. There are plenty of grievances in English politics, English social life, English laws, which demand
redress. The time will never come when an earnest, conscientious, faithful Englishman can feel himself at liberty to rest in
the belief that there is no more reforming work to be done. When
the English public feels this kind of sensation stealing on, it
should be strongly shaken off as delusive and dangerous. It is
to healthy political and social vitality what the tendency to sleep
is to the traveller who has lost his way in some snowy Alpine or
Pyreneean pass, a tendency which, if not resisted, stupifies the
victim wholly, and leaves him to perish.

Therefore, when we look forward to great political struggles
once again, we look to them, not with dread, but with hope. An
early uprousing of the nation's political activity we do not indeed expect ; even if immediate questions of great interest were
not wanting, there is no probability of any stirring scenes being
enacted under our present leaders. The rest-and-be-thankful
policy having stupified some, they sit contentedly, like grey old
pensioners in Chelsea, looking meditatively back on the events
of early struggles, and quite content if an audience can be got
now and then to listen to the often told story of their Torres
Vedras and their Waterloo. They have, moreover, acquired all
the honours and all the pensions they can possibly have. Earl Russell has gone as high in the peerage as he can expect to go ; Lord
Palmerston could not possibly be more popular than he is ; the Earl
of Derby is, on the whole, rather a greater man out of office than
in. There are, indeed, among the men now resting, some who do not
yet seem doomed by fate and years to a contented self-compla-
cent rest. Mr. Disraeli, for instance, is surely not thankful for a
quietude which resembles the ease of Lethe's wharf. But the
great mistake of Mr. Disraeli's political career is one which he
will now scarcely find time to retrieve. That grand and capital
mistake was, the subjection of his peculiar genius and temperament to the doctrines of Conservatism. A genius like his—so
bold, so self-reliant, so little inclined to have its course held in
by the ancient ruts and grooves, so rarely under the influence
of the feelings which invest the past with a superstitious

reverence, so apt for criticism, so specially fitted to do the destructive work which must, after all, ever be the pioneer of progress in an old system like ours ;—such a genius as this finds an uncongenial place among minds whose only clear political principle is the faith which opposes a dull *vis inertiæ* to all intrusive novelty.   Unhappily, Mr. Disraeli has of late years only rendered his recovery from the cardinal error of his life more difficult than before.   For with an eccentricity for which even his political career furnished no precedent, which even his caprices of political whim would not have led us to expect, he has identified himself with the present condition of the Church of England.   He has marked himself out as the very foremost of those who obstinately and vehemently resist all and any reform in the political relations of that Church to State and people.   This is to be regretted for many reasons.   For Mr. Disraeli's own sake, one must regret that so keen and brilliant an intellect should have given itself up to the uncompromising support of so great an anomaly.   The reactionary course to which the Conservative leader has pledged himself does not seem to secure for him the unstinted confidence even of those dogged anti-reformers who oppose a leaden immobility and dead weight to all intellectual and political movement. It is particularly unfortunate too, as any prospect which we can now see of an earnest and inspiriting political struggle lies in the direction of the Church questions.   The Church rate dispute has still to be fought out to some end.   There is, moreover, just arising on the horizon the prospect of a struggle about the Irish Establishment.   It will be a hard fate for Mr. Disraeli if he has to fight a second great losing battle in the course of his career, to become absolutely identified with another grand political *fiasco*.   He has saved himself with regard to questions of Reform. He can always plead that he did his best for that question ; that he shaped out a reform scheme of some kind, and that he did more to carry it through than those who claimed the parentage and monopoly of all Reform movements did to redeem their life-long pledges to the country.   But on Church questions Mr. Disraeli has pledged himself to the stolid *non possumus*.   No one who has watched the growth of public feeling in these countries can entertain any serious doubt of the fate which threatens the Irish Church Establishment.   Whenever a really great effort is made to procure its fall, it falls.   A cordial and complete understanding remains to be formed between two parties in the House of Commons, whom, oddly enough, it has of late been very hard to bring together—the English Radical Dissenters and the Irish Roman Catholics.   This understanding does not seem near at hand just now, but it must be ultimately the result of natural affinities.   Once that co-operation were attained, the Irish Church

Establishment would really begin to be in some danger, and of course the Conservative spirit would wake up for its defence. We have often wondered at the absence of all inclination for co-operating action, which seems now to keep asunder the English Radicals and the Irish Roman Catholics. This disposition is only the growth of recent years. There are surely points of affinity sufficient to hold these two parties together. The English Radicals are always ready to listen to the demands and the grievances of Ireland. Some of them are quite inclined to favour even any substantial Irish appeal for a separate national representation. They are nearly all ready to insist upon the fullest religious equality for Catholics. They have scarcely any ill-feeling towards the Pope; nay, it is a remarkable, but an indisputable fact, that the principal leaders of the English Radical party are not particularly enthusiastic about the independence of Italy—the great stumbling-block over which English and Irish fall into collision. Except Mr. Stansfeld, and one or two others, the English Radicals and Dissenters in Parliament (we speak now of those under the leadership of Mr. Cobden and Mr. Bright) have never manifested any particular interest in the Italian movement for national independence. The only connecting link which at present holds together the English Conservatives and the Irish Catholics, is the mutual sympathy with the cause of legitimacy in Italy. Every month weakens this frail link. Italian unity being settled, the futile, ignoble cabal in England must quickly dissolve. The Irish Catholics will see that they have been befooled, and will have to seek new alliances. Should they form any kind of expressed or tacit understanding with English Radicalism once again, it is almost certain that a vigorous attack will be made upon the stronghold of the Irish Church. Mr. Disraeli leading the forlorn defence of such a struggle as this will be a sorry sight; but a sight which, if political conditions do not take some sudden and remarkable change very soon, we shall probably be fated to look upon. No political spectacle could well be more unpleasing to an admirer of Mr. Disraeli's genius than that presented by the statesman himself, when on the Wednesdays of recent sessions he used to labour with an eloquence strained and thin and hollow, with an emphasis of gesture apparently destined to cover like a powerful accompaniment the false notes of the argument, in defence of what certain fanatics from rural districts believe to be the interests of the Church against the ultimately resistless tendency which would bring her within the influence of reform, and harmonize her with the altering conditions of English society.

But, for the present, political movements are clearly at a deadlock. We expect nothing from the next Session; nothing, that is to say, which in parliamentary history deserves to be called an event. The leaders of the Tory party (Mr. Disraeli, and one or two younger men, like Sir Stafford Northcote, excepted) are not anxious to come into office, because they would hardly know what to do if they got there. They are not anxious to go to the country, having a painful memory of the astonishing and overwhelming victory which Lord Palmerston achieved when he appealed to the constituencies on the memorable Chinese question. The present Parliament, it must be remembered, is a Derby Parliament; and the Opposition do not, therefore, expect much good to arise from a course which would appeal to the country for a new House elected under Palmerstonian auspices. No doubt there could be no difficulty in forming a combination which would unseat the present Cabinet, or necessitate the appeal to the country. We do not know whether anybody except Mr. Buxton and a certain portion of the more high-minded and consistent Radicals, is really in earnest about the Japanese operations. If the country, in its present condition of reaction and languor, could be stirred up to genuine interest in any question affecting the honour and character of our own nation, here, surely, is a subject upon which Englishmen might be roused to earnestness and even to passion. If the Opposition could make up its mind and see its way, here is a path into power and credit at once. But the Opposition will probably not make up its mind, and, more probably still, will not see its way. The wrong done in Japan will perhaps be explained away, or disavowed, or condoned for, or allowed to escape unexpiated, because nobody knows well what might be the result if any serious expiation were enforced. The portentous warning phrase of the Duke of Wellington about the necessity, above all things, of carrying on the Queen's Government, will operate potently, although dimly, on many minds. Somebody must carry on the Queen's Government. No one seems inclined or able to take the responsibility of the task but Lord Palmerston. It is all very well to condemn this or that detail of policy—this or that unwarranted massacre. The people in Japan may have been hardly used; but then, even supposing they did not deserve all they got, being barbarians and such like—what is to be done if nobody is ready to govern but Lord Palmerston? It is easy to complain of his Government, but who is to replace it? Outvote him, and he goes to the country. The country, partly influenced by the conviction that Lord Palmerston's officials have done nothing which Lord Derby's would not do under similar circumstances, and partly carried away by the admiration for an old favourite and a determination to rally round him in all difficulties, returns Lord Palmerston at the head of an overwhelming majority. This sort of performance results in nothing. Mr. Buxton's enterprise will,

we fully believe, lead to no serious results whatever. The difficulty at the present moment is not to find any one who can
govern better than Lord Palmerston. That might be, under
certain circumstances, a very healthy condition. The difficulty
is to find any one who can govern but Lord Palmerston. That
could not be a healthy condition under any conceivable combination of circumstances. There is not a country in Europe so
peculiarly situated as England is in this respect. She is tied to
the administration of Lord Palmerston by a bond far stronger
than the mere fetter of Royal will which binds the government of
Prussia to the ankle of Von Bismarck.

Whatever becomes of the present Parliament—whether it is cut
off by a sudden dissolution or drags out to its last legal gasp—its
memory will be equally inglorious. So barren and wearying a Parliament has not been seen for generations. The best that could
be said of it is that it did no great harm. Even that negative
commendation must be qualified when we remember Sir Minto
Farquhar and the Game Laws. Happily for the country it did
not put its hand to many tasks, for it seemed to have the faculty
of touching nothing without marring it. Many complications it
found waiting to be solved, and it only twisted them into more
perplexing convolutions. When it found a Sisyphus toiling
with his burthen heavily up the hill, it approached to help, and
immediately sent the load rolling down faster than before. It
removed no difficulty whatever out of the way of its successors,
but it added some fresh perplexities, to render the work of the
future harder. When this Parliament began, there was good
hope that it might at least settle two of the standing vexations
of parliamentary existence, the Church-rate question and the
Reform Bill. It had not gone far, when it reduced both questions to a condition far·more distressing and dangerous than
either had suffered from during the whole generation. It talked
a great deal, but the talk was not even good of its kind. The
orators who had a reputation when the Parliament opened added
nothing to their renown, and the successive Sessions gave no new
reputation to the country. Looking back over the four or five
Sessions, and the long, drear, dead level of debates upon French,
and Italian, and American, and German, and Danish, and
Turkish, and Polish questions, which stretched on from first to
last, can any one point out, among the legions of mediocrities
who pushed themselves forward, one solitary first-class reputation
won by any man who had not earned it long before? It was for
the most part a mirthful Parliament—mirthful although by no
means witty, laughing much over the smallest of jokes, and
finding food for merriment in subjects which rational men do not
commonly regard as jocular. The House laughed inextinguish-

able laughter over the Reform Bill, chuckled at the Ballot, tittered at the Church-rate question, screamed with mirth over the American War, and exploded with drollery at the hint of Irish grievances. There seemed to be a tacit understanding to treat all home questions as bores which must be laughed down, and to regard the two or three great foreign questions which presented themselves as heaven-sent themes for the explosion of a little empty and superfluous rhetoric. In its highest hours the House seldom rose, during the present Parliament, above the level of a debating society, discussing for sheer discussion's sake : in its most practical moments it conducted no business of a character superior to that which usually occupies the attention of a local town council. Perhaps the most earnest moments it ever knew were called into existence by the great national question concerning the disposal of a huge brick shed at South Kensington. It treated great questions as if they were small, and had not the gift to make small questions show as if they were great. It did nothing at home, and when its attention wandered abroad, it was only as a gadding woman goes out to tattle about everything and settle nothing. It kept up a condition which had not the economy of peace, or what the French Emperor termed the "happy chances" of war. At enormous cost it maintained a kind of truce which may end at any moment, and which leaves England scarcely a friend in the world whose friendship is worth having. Surveying the career of the present Parliament, only one satisfactory reflection arises to the mind ; and that is, the consoling recollection that, however it is fated to terminate, that career cannot possibly be protracted much longer.

Art. VII.—The Inspired Writings of Hinduism.

1. *Rig-Veda-Sanhitâ : the Sacred Hymns of the Brahmans,
   together with the Commentary of Sâyanâcharya.* Edited
   by Max Müller, M.A.   Volume IV.   London : 1862.
2. *The Taittiriya Brâhmana of the Black Yajur Veda, with
   the Commentary of Sâyanâcharya.* Edited by Rajendra-
   lala Mitra, with the Assistance of several learned Panditas.
   Vol. II.   (In the "Bibliotheca Indica," published under the
   Superintendence of the Asiatic Society of Bengal.)   Calcutta : 1862.
3. *Original Sanskrit Texts on the Origin and History of the
   People of India, their Religion and Institutions.* Collected,
   translated into English, and illustrated by Remarks, by
   J. Muir, D.C.L., LL.D.   Part IV.   London : 1863.
4. *A Contribution towards an Index to the Bibliography of the
   Indian Philosophical Systems.* By Fitzedward Hall, M.A.
   Calcutta : 1859.
5. *Report of the Mâhâraj Libel-Case.* Bombay : 1862.
6. *The Mâhârajas.* By Karsandass Mooljee. Bombay: 1861.

THE beginning of the year 1862 was marked by an occurrence
of great importance in the social and religious history of
India.   Little notice was taken of it by the European press, and,
to superficial observation, it has floated away on the current of
contemporary events.   We will briefly recall it to the memory of
our readers.   In a native newspaper, *The Satya Prakâsa,*
that is, "the Light of Truth," published at Bombay, there
appeared, on the 21st October, 1860, an editorial article headed
"The Primitive Religion of the Hindus, and the present
heterodox opinions."   It began with stating that the Purânas and
other sacred works of the Hindus predict the rise of false religions
and heresies in the Kaliyuga, or the present mundane age, which
according to Hindu theory dates from 3101 B.C. ; it then went on
to relate that the religion of the Vallabhâchâryas is one of these
heresies, and wound up by emphatically calling on the Mahârâjas
or high priests of that sect to desist from the propagation of
their faith until they had renounced the gross immoralities countenanced or directly inculcated by it.
   The sect in question, we may remark, was founded by a
Brahmin, Vishnu-Swâmin, but derives its name from its principal
teacher and saint, Vallabhâchârya (or the spiritual teacher

Vallabha), who was supposed to be an incarnation of the god Vishnu, and lived towards the end of the 15th and the beginning of the 16th century of our era. Its doctrinal tenets are a fantastical mixture of pantheism and mysticism, and its worship is that of Krishna, one of the incarnations of the god Vishnu, particularly in his juvenile forms, and commemorating his amorous sports with the cowherdesses amongst whom he passed the earlier stage of his earthly career. There is this remarkable feature, however, about this sect, as compared with other Hindu sects based on Brahminical tradition—that its teachers, rejecting abstemiousness as not conducive to sanctity, enjoin the worship of the Deity, not by means of mortification, or an austere ritual, but by indulging in the pleasures of society and the enjoyment of the world.

The members of this sect are very numerous and opulent, the merchants and bankers, especially those from Gujarat and Malva, belonging to it. Their temples and establishments are scattered all over India, and their spiritual chiefs are the supposed descendants of Vallabha, veneration being paid to them, not on account of their learning or piety, but for their family connexion with that arch-saint of the sect.*

One of their actual chiefs—now styled Mahârâjas—the Mahârâja Jadunathjee Brizrattanjee of Bombay, felt highly incensed at the article we have alluded to. The respectable journal in which it was contained had imparted to it more than the ordinary weight of a controversial production of the native press, and the name and position of its author, Karsandàss Mooljee, renowned amongst his countrymen for his undaunted zeal in the cause of their social and religious reform, had impressed on it the stamp of purity of motive and a strong presumption of trustworthiness. Had the Mahârâja vented his indignation by assembling the members of the caste to which the writer of the article belonged, and had he made them excommunicate the obnoxious reformer—as with his social and spiritual influence he could doubtless have done—it is more than probable that the world at large would have heard nothing of the actual state of this Vallabhâcharya creed, and that native apathy—in this case, as in others—would have little heeded the appeal made to their better selves. But the Mahârâja acted otherwise, and India, we hope, will have to thank him for the course he took. He sued the writer of the article in the Supreme Court of Bombay for having "caused to be printed and published a false, scandalous, malicious, infamous, and defamatory libel" on the religion of his sect in general, and on the conduct and character of the Mahârâjas in particular.

---

* See H. H. Wilson's Works, vol. i. p. 119. ff.

Hence ensued a spectacle which is unique in the history of India.   An English tribunal had to decide whether the charges made by the editor of the *Satya Prakása* were founded in fact and justifiable on public grounds.   It was nominally a question whether Mr. Karsandáss Mooljee was a libeller and should be mulcted in the amount of 5000*l.*, the damages laid, but in reality, whether the actual religion of the Vallabháchárya sect ordained those immoral practices which the defendant had imputed to it, and whether it was, or was not, in keeping with the spirit of the ancient Hindu faith, " one of the different ways," as was alleged in favour of it, " into which the courses of the Vedas and Puránas have diverged, just as some one goes from the gates of the fort to proceed to Walkeshwar and some one to Byculla."

The Spirit of History seems to have had one of his turbulent fits of impatience and weariness.   He must have grown tired at the slow pace of reforming benevolence and antiquarian research ; for, as we see, he suddenly called upon Justice to engrave with her sword on the skull of a religious community that which Science with her pen had not yet been able to write into its intelligence.

The task of Justice was, we must acknowledge, well performed by her substantially acquitting the defendant in the suit : her verdict is recorded in the elaborate and lucid judgment of Sir Matthew Sausse and Sir Joseph Arnould, and it henceforward belongs to the annals of the judicial history of India.   But though twenty-four days of a rigidly scrutinizing trial is no mean amount of time to be allotted to the settlement of a legal point, though the light thrown by it on the social and moral condition of a large and interesting portion of the Hindu community will advance our knowledge of modern India, we cannot share in the sanguine hope of those who entertain the belief that this trial has materially advanced the solution of the problem of the religious future of India.   That the facts disclosed by it may become a stimulus to rouse the activity of the indolent, and to impress every thinking Hindu with a sense of his personal duty towards his nation at large, we are willing to admit ; but we do not believe that it will bring us nearer the desired end, unless the real question at issue in the trial and its true importance be fully understood by the followers of the Sástras.

That importance does not lie in the startling disclosures which the world has received concerning the doctrinal immoralities of the present Vallabháchárya sect and its leading priests.   Disclosures like these need as little surprise us as attract our attention on behalf of their novelty.   Every one, however slightly acquainted with the history of religions in general, knows that there is no religious stem without its parasitical priesthood sucking its sap, if allowed to cling to its bark. Who will denounce Christianity because Mormonism has sprung from its soil? or who will question the morality of its tenets, because, so recently as twenty-seven years ago there existed, at Königsberg, in Prussia, the sect of the *Muckers*, which held its conventicles for the procreation of a new Messiah, and, though yielding nothing in mysticism and lewdness to the sect of the Vallabhâchâryas, was so highly respectable as to count amongst its members some of the first families of the land?

To lay stress on aberrations of this kind would be unjust as well as unwise. But the very comparisons we have alleged involve the point on which we *must* lay stress. Mormonism must hide its profligacy in the deserts of America, and a few Prussian police-constables proved strong enough, with the applause of the good people of Königsberg, to check the new Messiah in his career of incarnations.

The Vallabhâchârya creed, however, continues to flourish all over India, and to feed, we believe, its fourscore of saints; no professor of it is looked upon by a Hindu as a heretic, with whom it is not permissible to associate; no Brahmin ceases to be one, though he eat the dust of the feet of the Mahârâja. Do, then, the Hindus really believe that this creed is a true Hindu creed? Or—since there is no necessity for singling out this special sect from among numerous others, the practices of which would startle us as much as those of the followers of Vallabha—do the Hindus really assume that all these sects are healthy branches of their original religious stock? and, as to all appearance, their reply is in the affirmative,—on what grounds does the assumption rest?

Some answers to those questions have been given by "The Mahârâja Libel Case;" and because this case, if stripped of its specialties and personalities, is in reality no other than the case of Hinduism itself as it now stands, we will once more cast our eyes on it.

The defendant in that trial had charged the sect of the Mahârâjas and their chiefs—to use his own words—with "perpetrating such shamelessness, subtilty, immodesty, rascality, and deceit," as have never been perpetrated by other sectaries; and, convinced that the committal of such acts could not be countenanced by the true Hindu faith, he accordingly stigmatized the persuasion of the Vallabhâchâryas as a "sham, a delusion, and a heresy." The plaintiff, on the other hand, stoutly denied ever having been "guilty of heterodox opinions in matters connected with his religion, or of the offences or improper conduct imputed to him."

The denial, we may see at once, does not meet the charge.

For, supposing the life of the Mahâraja had been as spotless as one could desire, it does not follow from his words that he had abstained from licentious acts, *because* his religion declared them to be sinful ; nor, *if* his religion enjoined or encouraged such acts, does it necessarily follow that it must be a heterodox faith; since, for aught we know, it might derive its tenets from the old and authoritative Brahmanic source. It is true that by his evidence the defendant fully proved that acts of the grossest immorality were not only committed by the Mahârâjas, but committed by them with the full knowledge and connivance of their followers ; it is likewise true that he proved that " the Mahârâjas are considered by their followers as incarnations of the god Krishna," that " their managers give the sectaries water to drink in which the Mahârâja had bathed ;" and that " drinking the nectar of the feet, swinging, rubbing, and bathing the body with oils, or eating the dust on which they have walked, are not practised towards the Gurus of other sects." But evidence like this obviously does no more than establish the fact, that such customs are the actual practices of a particular sect and of certain individuals professing to be their high priests and chiefs. It will induce no one to charge the faith of these people with inculcating these practices, or to say whether they are or are not in harmony with the ancient religion of the Hindus, the supposed foundation of all present creeds, unless further evidence be produced to that effect from the sacred works of both.

What means, then, did the defendant and the plaintiff possess, the one to denounce the heresy of the Mahârâja sect, the other to vindicate its orthodoxy ?

The text-books of the sect are the works of its principal teacher, Vallabha; they are all written in Sanskrit; and a leading commentary on one of these works, by Gokulnâth, a grandson of Vallabha, is likewise written in Sanskrit. Some of these works are translated in the Brij-Bhâshâ language ; but, as the Mahârâja very properly observed, these versions have authority so far only as they exactly render the original ; and, for himself, he seemed to scorn the idea of reading his sacred books in such versions at all. That the groundworks of the ancient Hindu faith are likewise written in the sacred language of India, and some in that archaic form of Sanskrit, which differs in many respects from the Sanskrit of the classical literature, it is almost needless to say; but it may perhaps not be superfluous to add that several of those works—the Vedas, for instance—and the principal Purânas, are not accessible to a Hindu except in that language, since no translation of them exists in any of the vernacular tongues.

Now, as to Mr. Kursandâss, the spirited editor of the Bombay journal, who in this noteworthy case courageously staked his property, and probably his personal liberty, who had to brave not only the obloquy of his countrymen, but an organized conspiracy —what does he say as to his trustiest weapon, this Sanskrit tongue, when he enters the arena to struggle for the restoration of the pure ancient religion of India? He frankly and honestly confesses that he has no knowledge whatever of it. He does his best to supply that defect by resorting to a young native who seems to have a smattering of it, and provides him with the translation of a passage of the commentary of Gokulnâth; but beyond the result of this trifling assistance, given only for the purposes of his defence, his ascertaining the authoritative sense of a Sanskrit work does not go. He had taken up the cause of religious reform, because he had heard, and felt convinced, that the ancient Hindu creed must be pure, and different, therefore, from the unclean shape in which it is paraded before his eyes; but it had never occurred to him, when appealing to the Vedas, that the Vedas could not talk to him unless he mastered the language in which they were composed.

And the Mahârâja? When we quote the words of one of the judges, who said—"That the plaintiff has allowed his personal interests to overcome his respect for truth while on his oath in the court," and those of the other judge, who declared "the oath of the plaintiff as utterly valueless," and "the whole framework of his evidence as conceived in a spirit of hypocrisy and falsehood," —we may be spared the necessity of scrutinizing the knowledge of which he makes profession in regard to the original works of his own and the ancient Hindu faith. Yet some of his own statements are, nevertheless, too curious not to deserve a passing notice. Sanskrit, he says, on one occasion, he knows "for the most part;" and on another, he owns that he "knows more of Sanskrit now than he did before the libel." In his plea he classes the "sacred books of the Hindus" as, first the Purânas, then the Vedas and Shastras; but, when cross-examined, he can neither give the names of the four Vedas, nor had he any idea whatever as to the number of that part of them called the Brâhmanas. He has heard the name of the Brahma-vaivarta-Purâna, but he has not read it. His opinion was that if the Shastras allowed it, remarriages of widows might take place, but not otherwise. He had seen no authority in the Shastras for remarriages, but personally he had no objection thereto; in his sect, indeed, remarriages took place, and he did not prohibit them. He likewise informed the Court of a fact which as yet rests on no other authority than his own— viz., that the name of the god Krishna occurs in a portion of the Vedas. Of the other Mahârâjas he cannot say whether a few only can read Sanskrit; but the witness most friendly to him did not hesitate to say that " the plaintiff was an exception amongst them, the rest being ignorant persons."

We have shown enough, we think, of the scholarship of these high priests and preceptors of the Vallabhâchârya sect. Yet, though the specimen of saints introduced to us by this trial is perhaps merely an illustration of the adage that there is but one step from the sublime to the ridiculous, we cannot conceal from ourselves the reality that that step may be an extremely unpleasant one.

In the worst days of Roman Catholicism, when the multitude professing that religion was steeped in ignorance and its worship was no better than idolatry, there was still a considerable portion of its priesthood fully acquainted with the text-book of Christianity. It was, no doubt, with its priests a question of policy whether their flock should be admitted to the knowledge which they possessed, and restored to a purer faith ; but that they had the power to work that change is borne out by the history of Protestantism. Yet, without fear of contradiction, we may assert that the vast majority of all Hindu priests are as ignorant of the ancient faith of their nation as the Mahârûja of Bombay ; nay, this Mahârâja himself is not merely a fair average specimen of a Hindu priest, but his knowledge, however miserable, exceeds that of most priests of other Hindu sects. Amongst the hundred million and more who profess Brahmanism, there are perhaps a few thousands who may be able to read an easy Sanskrit book ; but those who can master a philosophical or grammatical work are scarcely to be found except at the high seats of learning, such as Benares, Calcutta, and Poona, while as to those who can understand a Vedic text, like the venerable author of the great Cyclopædia, Râjâ Râdhakânt Deb, or the learned editor of one of the Vedas, Babu Rajendralâla Mitra, or like the accomplished Dr. Bhau Dajee, a gentleman whom Sir Joseph Arnould describes as " one who in learning, freedom from prejudice, and general superiority of mind, is among the foremost, if not *the* foremost of the native citizens of Bombay,"—their number is indeed so infinitely small that it disappears in the mass of their co-religionists.

And yet every Hindu, high or low, is eager to persuade himself, that his actual worship is founded on inspired texts : for he knows that it would be worthless unless it could trace its tenets to the " inspired" words of the Vedic hymns ; he clings to it because he is penetrated with an instinctive feeling, that if he abandoned a religion based on the Vedas, he would abandon that which is dearest to a man, his nationality. It is this instinctive feeling alone that arms him against any attempt at conversion ; for, even though the intelligent native may recognise the superiority of

Christianity as taught by the New Testament over the sectarian worship practised by himself, yet, rather than profess a religion foreign to his instincts, habits, and nationality, he will console himself with the hope that he may one day possess in his old faith, when restored, one as good and as pure as any other faith.

Whether that hope be justifiable or not is a question that admits of different answers, according to the mental and social condition of the inquirer. But Hindu and European must alike agree that a nation which cannot examine and understand the foundation of its own existence is on the high road to the loss of that existence altogether. And because we are well aware that the intelligent portion of the present generation of India has raised its political aspirations, and has the proud ambition of conquering for its country the same position which is occupied by the other parts of the British Empire, we must remind them that the first and most efficacious means for attaining that end is boldly to attack the deplorable religious condition of their countrymen, and that this is to be done only by imparting to them a knowledge of their own literature, and more especially of those sacred works which mark the brightest epoch of their national life. There are some amongst them, we know, who consider the religious question as insignificant compared to the great political questions of the day, and who judge of the different forms of their present worship by the standard which a celebrated historian applied to the various forms of Paganism in ancient Rome : that they are all alike sublime to the vulgar, all alike useful to the politician, and all alike ridiculous to the philosopher. But these modern Hindu statesmen seem to forget the downfall of ancient Rome, and that masses sunk in religious degradation can never become the political equals of those to whom their sublime is the ridiculous. Nor must they imagine that their favourite appeal to the argument of Sankaráchárya can avail in these days. When that great reformer and philosopher—probably about a thousand years ago—made his crusade against the heresies then rampant all over India, he is said to have himself established several sects, and to have sanctioned the worship of any acknowledged deity, " for the sake of those whose limited understandings rendered them incapable of comprehending and adoring the invisible Supreme Being." Hence they conclude, that if so stanch a defender of " a sole Cause and Supreme Ruler of the universe" considered the worship of Vishnu and Siva in its various forms compatible with the monotheistic doctrine he was preaching to his countrymen, no objection need be taken to the present creed as answering the same ends.

An appeal to authorities, instead of an argument, is in itself a confession of defeat ; but those who are in the habit of using this appeal as their argument do not seem to apprehend that it could be turned against them as one of the strongest condemnations of the practices which they palliate.   Sankara, one of the most renowned and influential scholars of mediæval India, was himself one of the most zealous denouncers of all worships if repugnant to the Vedas.   His aim was the propagation of a belief in one immaterial Cause.   In his chief work, the Commentary on the text-book of the Vedânta philosophy, he endeavours to prove that the celestial beings named in the Vedic writings are but allegorical personifications of that Supreme Being, and in his Commentary on the Upanishads he compares such gods even to demons, or foes of the human race.   If tradition therefore be correct, that he tolerated the modern worship of the sectarian gods,—for, let it be remembered, that it is only a vague tradition which ascribes that toleration to him—it is obvious that this admission on his part, was, if not an act of weakness and inconsistency, at the best, an educational experiment, supposed by him to lead to the end which engrossed his mind.   A thousand years, one would think, are a sufficient space of time to prove the error of Sankarâchârya.   The experiment has had its test, and it has lamentably failed.   Another thousand years of a similar experiment, and we feel convinced that no Brahmanical Hindu will then be found to whom it could be denounced as fallacious and mischievous.

But let us ask what those writings are which the orthodox Hindu is called upon by his creed to consider as inspired, and what are those other works which in the course of time his priests have foisted as such on his credulity?

The oldest tradition is very precise in the answer it gives to the first of these questions.   So far from leaving it to the option of a believer to declare at will any book inspired, and so far from recognising any gifted individual who might at some future period pretend to receive inspirations from divine apparitions or intuitions, it has carefully defined the personages who alone had been favoured by the Deity, and the revelations they had obtained. The former, it says, are the old Vedic Rishis or saints; and the latter are the hymns of the Rigveda, which, dating from eternity, were " *seen* " by them, and the number of which is one thousand and twenty-eight.   Passing, then, over the doubts as to the genuine antiquity of some of these hymns—and we could show that even the most orthodox authorities of India looked upon some as spurious —it is certain that the inspired writings of the Hindus do not exceed the limits of those one thousand and twenty-eight hymns.

The Hindu priesthood, however, has managed to demonstrate that one thousand and twenty-eight hymns mean in reality a very ponderous mass of divinely revealed works. "These hymns," it says to the people, "you must be aware, speak of ritual acts which are unintelligible to you, and they make allusion also to events, human and divine, which are shrouded in obscurity; hence you must admit that those works called *Brâhmanas*, which explain the origin and the proper performance of rites—which give illustrations of those events and legendary narratives, and which contain philosophical speculations to boot—are a necessary complement of the inspired Rigveda hymns. And," say the priests, "there are three other Vedas besides the Rigveda, viz., the Yajur-, Sâma-, and Atharva-Veda; but, as the contents of these Vedas," they continue, "are bodily taken from the Rigveda, their inspiration can as little be gainsayed as that of these hymns themselves;" and as the Brâhmana portion of these Vedas stands in the same relation to *their* hymnic part as the corresponding portion of the Rigveda stands to the hymns of the latter, the Brahmins conclude that the inspired works of the Hindu religion are the hymns of the four Vedas and the Brâhmana works attached to each of them. The theologian, moreover, adds:—And because in the hymns, as well as in the Brâhmanas, there are many hints of extreme mysteriousness—allusions to the production of the world, to the qualities of a supreme God, and to the nature of the human soul—those works which contain the authoritative explanation of these mysteries, the *Upanishads*, cannot be disconnected from the inspiration of the hymns and Brâhmanas.

Those who have followed the course of the religious development of mankind in general will not feel surprised at this luxuriance of inspired texts: the instincts and the history of a priesthood are alike everywhere. One thousand and twenty-eight hymns, of a few verses each, are but a poor livelihood for a fast-increasing number of holy and idle men: but expand these hymns into a host of works which even the most diligent student could not master in less than several years; apply to their teaching the rule that the pupil must never study them from a manuscript, but receive them orally from his spiritual guide; make them the basis of a complicated ritual, which no one is allowed to perform without a host of priests, and handsome presents to each of them —and what a bright perspective opens itself to a member of the Brahminical caste, and to those who follow in his track!

That the Brâhmana portion of the Vedas which is entirely ritual and legendary, has no claim whatever to be considered by an orthodox Hindu as dating from eternity, like the hymns of the Rigveda, and as supernaturally composed, results from the tradition to which we have referred; for, though the doctrine of their divine origin has been current in India for more than two thousand years, no Rishi has ever been mentioned into whom they were divinely inspired, except, perhaps, in the case of one, the Satapatha-Brâhmana. But the sanctity of this very Brâhmana was so little acknowledged by common consent when it was composed, that it marks, on the contrary, a great schism in the ancient religion of India ; in fact, when compared with the hymns of the Rigveda, it is so late that there is strong reason to surmise that it did not exist in Pânini's time. This grammarian himself, when teaching the names of some Brâhmanas, gives us rules for distinguishing between ancient and modern Brâhmanas ; and even if, contrary to the evidence supplied by him, a single one of those ancient Brâhmanas had come down to us, his rules would bear testimony to the fact that in his time the authors of those works were not yet looked upon as inspired. A very learned writer on Sanskrit literature, indeed, has asserted, on the authority of those rules, that the affix *in* which terminates the name of such ancient Brâhmanas as the Sailâlin, Karmandin, &c., is " a mark that the name to which it is added is that of an author considered as a Rishi, or inspired writer." But such is not the case ; for, Pânini, who distinguishes between works that were " seen " or are inspired, between works that were " made" or composed, and works that were " promulgated" or taught, states in the clearest possible manner that those " ancient" Brâhmanas were not " seen," but only " promulgated" by the personages after whom they are named.

Of the inspired character of the Upanishads still less need be said. It is, in India itself, upheld only either by those theologians who—like their commentator, the celebrated Sankarâchârya, or the translator of some of these theosophical works, the late Ram Mohun Roy—endeavoured to give a stamp of sacredness to the Vedânta philosophy founded on them, or by those adherents of other philosophical schools, which appeal for the truth of their axioms to passages from these works. At the time when the priests had succeeded in laying down the law that instruction in sacred works could be imparted only by them, and was to be " heard," or orally received by the pupil from the teacher, they gave currency to a term, " *Sruti*"—" hearing"—implying by it that the texts which the pupil heard from their mouth were inspired works ; but in the early literature even this term comprises merely hymns and Brâhmanas. It is only at a late period of Hinduism that we meet with " Sruti" as applied also to the Upanishad literature.

The inspired network of the hymnic portion of the three Vedas, called the Yajur-, Sâma-, and Atharva-Veda, is apparently closer drawn than that of the other writings just named : but now that it is laid open before the investigating mind of modern Europe and India ; now that the spell is broken which made the study of the Veda consist of intonating its verses to the melody of the Guru, and mechanically committing them to memory; now that native and European industry has given us in print not merely the obscure words of the hymns, but also the commentaries which lead us into their inner meaning, no Hindu can shrink from the duty of examining the grounds on which the inspiration of these three Vedas rests.

He will probably not offer much resistance when he is asked to reject that of the Atharvaveda. He possesses abundant evidence that no Atharvaveda was known at an early period of Hindu life. The old and orthodox authorities of India speak of three Vedas only—the Rig-, Yajur-, and Sâma-Veda; even late commentators, though the Atharvaveda existed at their time, pay little attention to it; it is ignored by the ritual-philosophers, the Mîmânsists, whose influence is felt wherever a sacrificial fire receives pious offerings. *Trayi vidyâ*, "the *threefold*," not the fourfold, "wisdom" is in the mouth of every learned Hindu. Will he then contend for the inspired origin and the eternal existence of those incantations and charms which aim at "the attainment of wealth, the destruction of evil influences, the downfall of enemies, success in love or play, the removal of petty pests, recovery from sickness, and even the growth of hair on a bald pate"? Yet, though the character of the hymns of this Veda differs from that of the Yajuz- and Sâma-Veda, the causes whence all these three Vedas arose, are similar; and the test by which a Hindu may judge of the claims to inspiration of one of them, is the test which he may apply to the claims of the remaining two.

The hymns of the Rigveda are essentially poetical: they make frequent allusion, it is true, to pious and sacrificial acts; but so far only as the latter are the concomitants of the pious and poetical feelings of the poet, or as they are connected with events in his personal life. We meet, therefore, with many hymns which have nothing to do with religious performances: thus, some describe the grandeur of natural phenomena; here a gambler "laments over the passion that beguiles him into sin," and there a Rishi even ridicules the worship performed by the priests. In short, these hymns, if taken as a whole, are the genuine product of the poets' minds: they reflect the gradual growth of a nation's life; they were not composed for any ritual purposes. On the other hand, there is nothing genuine in the Yajur- and Sâma-Vedas. These Vedas are arranged and written merely to serve as prayer-books at various sacrificial acts. The collection of the Rigveda hymns, as one may *a priori* conclude from their very character, did not admit of any arrangement answering systematically the order of an elaborate ceremonial; the arrangement of the two other Vedas, on the contrary, is entirely adapted to it, and therefore throughout artificial. Thus, the verses of the Sâmaveda were intoned at the sacrifices performed with the juice of the Soma plant, and the order in which these verses occur is that of the sacrificial acts of which the Soma sacrifices consist. Again, those of the Yajurveda are arranged according to the rites of a great variety of sacrifices, at which the officiating priests had to mutter them inaudibly.

Now, so firmly rooted is the belief in the divine origin of these Vedas, that it seems almost to have overshadowed the belief in the sanctity of the Rigveda itself; not indeed in spite of their unpoetical character, but on account of it. For, judging from the opinions met with in the most orthodox writers, the Brahmins seem to have concluded that the Rigveda, however beautiful from an æsthetical point of view, was, after all, more an ornamental than a useful book; that its real destiny is fulfilled in those two other Vedas, taken from it, which a contingent of sixteen officiating priests, supported by butchers, ladle-holders, and choristers, could turn to practical account at ceremonies regulated in their minutest detail, and some of them lasting as many as a hundred days. And, as the sacrifices requiring the muttering of the Yajurveda were even more imposing and more elaborate than those which fall within the range of the Sâmaveda rites, we find that the sanctity of the Yajurveda ultimately outstripped that of the rival Veda too. "The Yajurveda," says Sâyana, the great commentator on the Vedas, "is like a wall, the two other Vedas like paintings [on it]." Yet, as we before observed, the inspired character of these later Vedas rests on the assumption that their verses are borrowed from the Rigveda; that they are, in fact, portions of it. So far as the Sâmaveda is concerned, this assumption is justified; for, though in the present edition of this Veda there are some verses which do not occur in the present text of the Rigveda, we must remember that this text is but one of the recensions of the principal Veda, and that the missing verses may have existed, and probably did exist, in some other recension of it. But a comparison of the Yajurveda with the Rigveda does not allow us to stretch probabilities to this extent. There are portions of the Yajurveda which can at no time have belonged to any recension of the Rich,—we mean those passages in prose, called Yajus, whence the Yajurveda derives its name; for, there is no hymn in the Rigveda that is not composed in verse. Here then this question obtrudes itself—Who are the Rishis who "saw" these passages in prose? Tradition, so far as we know it, is just as silent respecting them as it is respecting the authors of the Brâhmanas. But as little as these latter works can become inspired because they are tacked to the hymnic collection which was "seen" by the Rishis of old, so little can inspiration pass like the electric fluid from the Rigveda verses, found in the Yajus, to those passages in prose which, from ritual reasons, had been joined to them. Yet, setting aside these pseudo-revealed passages, and those verses of the Yajurveda, too, which do not occur in the actual recension of the Rigveda, we shall be at once enabled to judge, by even a superficial glance at how the inspired poetry of the Rigveda found its way into the Sáma- and Yajurveda, on what grounds the Brahmins invite the nation to recognise the last two Vedas as inspired texts.

We open at random two hymns which form part of the first book of the Sámaveda and three chapters of one recension of the Yajurveda. The first hymn of the Sámaveda which meets our eyes consists of eleven verses (370—380) ; and with the exception of its third verse (372), every one occurs amongst the verses of the Rigveda ; but what is the mutual relation of the verses in both Vedas ?

				Book.	Hymn.	Verse.
Sámav., verse	370 is Rigveda	...	8	...	86	...	10
,,	,,	371	,,	10	...	147	...	1
,,	,,	373	,,	1	...	57	...	4
,,	,,	374	,,	3	...	51	...	1
,,	,,	375	,,	10	...	43	...	1
,,	,,	376	,,	1	...	51	...	1
,,	,,	377	,,	1	...	52	...	1
,,	,,	378	,,	6	...	70	...	1
,,	,,	379	,,	10	...	134	..	1
,,	,,	380	,,	1	...	101	...	1

The second hymn we happen to choose is the opening one of the Sámaveda. It consists of ten verses, nine of which are likewise contained in the present recension of the Rigveda, but those nine verses correspond respectively with the following Rigveda verses :—

				Book.	Hymn.	Verse.
Sámav., verse	1 with Rigveda	...	6	...	16	...	10
,,	,,	2	,,	6	...	16	...	11
,,	,,	3	,,	1	...	12	...	1
,,	,,	4	,,	6	...	16	...	34
,,	,,	5	,,	8	...	73	...	1
,,	,,	6	,,	8	...	60	...	1
,,	,,	7	,,	6	..	16	...	16
,,	,,	8	,,	8	...	11	...	7
,,	,,	9	,,	6	...	16	...	13

We turn to any chapters of the Yajurveda, say the 22nd to the 25th. They contain verses and passages in prose, which were muttered at the horse sacrifice. Of chapter 22, which has 34 divisions, only four verses occur in the Rigveda, viz. :—

			Book.	Hymn.	Verse.
Yajurveda, verse 10 in Rigveda ...	1 ...	22 ...	5
,,	,,	15	,,	5 ...	14 ...	1
,,	,,	16	,,	3 ...	11 ...	2
,,	,,	18	,,	9 ...	110 ...	8

Of chapter 23, which consists of 65 divisions, there correspond :—

			Book.	Hymn.	Verse.
Yajurveda, verse 8 with Rigveda ...	10 ...	121 ...	2
,,	,,	5	,,	1 ...	6 ...	1
,,	,,	6	,,	1 ...	6 ...	2
,,	,,	16	,,	1 ...	162 ...	21
,,	,,	32	,,	4 ...	39 ...	6

Chapter 24, being entirely in prose, is foreign to the Rigveda; and of chapter 25, with 47 divisions—

		Book.	Hymn.	Verse.
Yajurveda, verse 12 is Rigveda ...	10 ...	121 ...	4
,,	,,	13	,,	10 ...	121 ...	2
,,	verses 14—23 are	1 ...	89 ...	1—10
,,	,,	24—45 ,,	1 ...	162 ...	1—22

and   ,,   verse 46 is the first-half of the Rigveda verse 10, 157, 1, the first half of 10, 157, 2, and the latter half of 10, 157, 1.

There is unhappily nothing so irreverent as statistical prose. A Brahmin will tell his nation that the verses of the Sâma- and Yajurveda are the same as those of the Rigveda, and, if need be, he may perhaps show that a good number of them do really occur in the original Veda. We, however, are impertinent enough to test that sameness by book, chapter, and verse; we marshal side by side the figures which mark the position of these verses in their respective Vedas—and what do these figures reveal? A Rigveda piecemeal : verses of the same hymn transposed, verses of different hymns shuffled about, and even verses of different authors strung together, as if they had proceeded from the same mind. We expected to find, in the later Vedas, the feelings and thoughts of the ancient poets, but we hear only the sounds of their words ; we were promised possession, in these Vedas, of a living portion of the Rigveda, but we discover there only its scattered remains. In short, the Brahmin juggles before our eyes what he calls an identity of these Vedas with the Rigveda, yet what we really obtain is but a miserable counterfeit of it.

Well may the disciples of Loyola feel humiliated when they look at the consummate skill with which this Brahminical legerdemain was performed, long before their master had taught them how to govern the world by obfuscating its intellect ; for there is no priesthood in the universe which, by a stratagem like that we have described, can boast of so splendid a success in metamorphosing its most sacred book into a dull attendant on artificial rites, and in diverting the stream of the national life from its original course.

While acknowledging, however, the intellectual capacity of those Brahmins who fashioned the hymns of the Rigveda into a series of "inspired" texts, we ought not to forget that they were powerfully assisted in their task by an invention which, though some may imagine to be of recent date, those Hindu priests are fully entitled to claim as theirs,—we mean the invention of writings without a writer—anonymousness. Pride in his personality is the natural feeling of a man whose work proceeds from the promptings of his own genius and will; and nations likewise have the instinctive feeling that they uphold their own individuality by guarding from oblivion the memory of their deserving men. Unless, therefore, this innate feeling be intentionally subdued, it is merely an accident—political or literary—when works that merit to be remembered go down to posterity without the names of their authors, since so many names of authors survive without their works. We do not know, it is true, the authors of the Nibelungen and of the Kutrun ; we can speak only of the compiler of the Edda ; but it is exceptions like these that prove the rule ; for even a name like Homer—probably devoid of a personal reality—shows that the nation which put it forward was eager to possess an individuality in the poet of the Iliad and Odyssey.

But, when man is not the agent of his own acts, or if, for good or evil purposes, he wishes or is forced to personate more than his own self, he sinks his individuality into a brotherhood : he becomes anonymous. To assume it to be a pure accident that the authors of the Yajus and of the Bráhmanas have remained unknown, would be assuming that all those artificial and elaborate works were of unintentional origin, and that the Hindu mind is an exception to the general law. But that the proud feeling of individuality was as strong in India as it is everywhere else, and at all times too, is evidenced by the long list of proper names which represent the authors of her greatest poetical, philosophical, grammatical and other works ; and it is borne out by the fact that the Hindus remember the names of their oldest Rishis, the "inspired seers" of the Rigveda hymns : for, whether these personages existed or not, whether they *were* the authors of the works or hymns ascribed to them, matters not. To the Hindu mind they are realities : and since, on the other hand, Hindu tradition supplies us with a full account of the names of those who "collected" or arranged the Vedas, and who "promulgated" or taught the Bráhmanas and Upanishads, the very jealousy it betrays in perpetuating the memory of merits inferior certainly to those of authorship, proves that the names of their "inspired" authors cannot have remained unknown through chance or carelessness.

The anonymousness of these Vedic writings is, however, up to this day the staple argument in proof of their sanctity. In a spirited drama, written probably six hundred years ago, a Jaina mendicant apostrophizes a follower of Buddha who intends to persuade him of the superiority of his creed over that of the Jaina sect, in the following terms :—" But who has laid down these laws ?" " The omniscient, sacred Buddha," is the reply. " And whence know ye that Buddha is all-wise ?" " Why," says the Buddhist, " because it is written so in his sacred books." The Brahminical author of this satire is obviously alive to the more solid basis on which the sanctity of his own revelations rest. The belief in *their* genuineness does not depend on the testimony of those by whom they were composed. Public opinion has never heard of any author of them; hence they must be of superhuman workmanship.

In surveying the origin of the three later Vedas and that of their liturgic and theosophical appendages, we stand, as it were, on the heights of Hinduism; but the descent from them to the region of its actual condition is easy, and scarcely requires a guide. For, once acquainted with the spirit that engendered these Vedas and Bráhmanas, with its method of fabricating inspired texts, and the conclusion wrought by its powerful engine, anonymousness, we may feel curiosity as to the turnings and byways of the road; but the journey itself is monotonous. There is one reflection, however, which may arrest our steps.

It must seem a matter of course that so fertile a soil as the sacrificial Vedas, and the ritual, legendary, and mystical Bráhmanas could not remain without an abundant crop of works ;— human works, to be sure, with their authors' name duly recorded and recognised, but works as indispensable to a proper use of those " inspired" texts, as they were indispensable to turn the ornamental Rigveda into a book of practical utility. They are the Kalpa works. But even these writings could not do justice to the store of services that might be rendered by a Brahmin to his countrymen. The Kalpa works merely treat of those great and public ceremonies which, for a time, may handsomely stock the budget of the officiating priests, but which are too sporadic and too select to be a permanent and solid livelihood. A number of daily and household ceremonies was evidently needed to bring the whole life of a believer under the control and into the grasp of his spiritual master, the priest. These ceremonies, then, were regulated by the Grihya books; but as the life of even the most pious society cannot be entirely filled up with rites that take place at conception and birth, tonsure and investiture, marriage and the like, it was prudent to impart a religious stamp also to habits and customs—in one word, to the whole organism of society. A special class of works—the Sâmayâchârika rules—was therefore devoted to the ordinary practices of life; and from these resulted ultimately the so-called legal works, amongst which Manu's law-book is known as the most prominent. Everything was now as complete as it could be. Social and religious duties are henceforward synonymous; *dharma* is the word which designates both. All the institutions of society have now become of Vedic origin; for the laws of Manu and others are founded on the habits and customs laid down in the works complementary to the Grihya works; these complete the Kalpa works; and without the Kalpa works the practical Vedas would be unpractical. The chain which links religion and politics together is, on several occasions, brought home to the Hindu mind by a reasoning like this:—Society cannot perform the duties prescribed in these sacred books unless it possesses a king, who watches over the safety of the people; but a king cannot exist without the produce of the land; land, however, yields no produce without rain; rain is sent down by the favour of the gods; such favour is obtained by means of sacrificial acts; but where there is no Brahmin there is no sacrificial act: king and Brahmin thus close the circle within which the people has to obey the behests of both.

There is, then, that difference between the Vedic works and those which are the present foundation of the Brahmanic belief—that the former were inspired for the exclusive interests of the priests, whereas the latter were inspired for the combined benefit of priests and kings. But the latter, the *Purânas*, have this in common with the three "practical" Vedas and the Brâhmanas—that they are likewise "inspired," because they are anonymous; for, tradition, which knows all about Vyâsa, their wonderful compiler, has concealed the names of the holy personages who received them direct from the Deity. If comparison wants to go beyond this, it must hold the Vedic texts before a mirror which reflects a caricature. There is no trace of Vedic poetry or of Vedic thought in all those Purâna works composed in glorification of the epical Pantheon of India, and more especially in that of the Hindu triad—Brahmâ, Vishnu, and Siva. There is scarcely a legend or myth narrated by them which can claim the remotest connexion with a Vedic myth. There is no ceremony they teach which, put even against the ceremonial of the Brâhmana and Kalpa works, does not appear devoid of all that may please the imagination or elevate the mind; and with the exception of a few of them, their style even is tedious, slovenly, and to some extent ungrammatical. Considered as a whole, these Purânas contain cosmogonies, which are a superstructure of epical and modern legends on the creative theories propounded in some of the systems of philosophy ; theogonies, which expand the myths of the great epos, the Mahàbhàrata, in favour of the particular god whom it was the intention of the writer to place at the top of the Pantheon ; they profess to know the genealogies of patriarchs and the chief dynasties of kings ; they are bits of law-books in imitation of Manu and Yâjnavalkya ; they pretend to explain ancient ceremonies, and abound in the description of rites which vie with one another in the absurdest detail ; they prophesy. And as it is plain, from this summary of their contents, that they aimed at being the books that teach everything, and with the weight of religious authority, we cannot feel surprised that some of them considered it necessary also to expatiate on sacred geography or the description of places where there is a special chance of attaining to eternal bliss, on medicine and astronomy, on archery, rhetoric, prosody, and grammar. But the low position which these works occupy in the household of Sanskrit literature, is nowhere more manifest than when they attempt to meddle with those scientific branches of human knowledge, where every student can test the kind of omniscience by which they were inspired.

The modern date of the existing Purânas has long ceased to be matter of doubt to any one who reads them without prejudice ; but even an orthodox Hindu must shut his eyes to all evidence, literary, historical, and grammatical, if he attempt to assert their antiquity. From the abundance of disproof which is open to him, we need, for curiosity's sake, only point to one. That works called Purânas—*i.e.,* " old,"—may have existed at ancient times, and that they may have combined some portion of the matter embodied in the actual works bearing this name, is not improbable ; for, the word itself, as designating a class of writings, occurs as early as in the law-book of Manu, though this book itself, as we have seen, may be called recent when compared with the Vedic texts. A definition, however, of what such Purânas are, does not occur before the beginning of the Christian era, when the lexicographer Amarasinha says, that a Purâna is a work which has " five characteristic marks." This definition is again explained by the commentators on the glossary of Amarasinha ; and the oldest of them did not live earlier than about four hundred years ago. He says that these five characteristic portions of a Purâna are—primary creation ; secondary creation, or the destruction and renovation of the world ; genealogy—viz., of gods and patriarchs ; reigns of the Manus ; and history—viz., of the princes supposed to derive their pedigree from the sun or moon. Now, in applying this definition to the actual Purânas, Professor Wilson, the distinguished Sanskrit scholar, who translated the whole Vishnu Purâna, and was thoroughly conversant with these works, observes, "that not in any one instance do they exactly conform to it: that to some of them it is wholly inapplicable; whereas to others it only partially applies."* Whatever, therefore, may have been the nature of the original Purânas, and whatever scope one may give to the assumption that the actual Purânas have borrowed part of their contents from some older works of the same name, it is obvious that, in their present shape, they cannot reckon their age by many centuries.

When, by priestcraft and ignorance, a nation has lost itself so far as to look upon writings like these as divinely inspired, there is but one conclusion to be drawn : it has arrived at the turning-point of its destinies. Hinduism stands at this point, and we anxiously pause to see which way it will direct its steps. For several centuries, it is true, its position has seemed stationary ; but the power of present circumstances, social and political, is such · that it can no longer continue so. All barriers to religious imposition having broken down since the modern Purânas were received by the masses as the source of their faith, sects have sprung up which not merely endanger religion, but society itself ; tenets have been propounded, which are an insult to the human mind ; practices have been introduced, which must fill every true Hindu with confusion and shame. There is no necessity for examining them in detail, by unveiling, for instance, the secrets of the Tantra literature ; nor need we be at the pains of convincing the intelligent portion of the Hindu community ; for, the excellent works which it sends forth from Calcutta, Benares, and Bombay, and the enlightened views which it propagates through its periodical press, fully prove that, equal in mental accomplishments to the advanced European mind, it requires no evidence of the gulf which separates the present state of the nation from its remote past.

But what we do hold is, that all the activity of that learned portion will not avert the danger which threatens the future destiny of Hinduism, unless it boldly grapples with the very root of the disease. The causes of the gradual degeneracy of Hinduism are, indeed, not different from those to which other religions are subject, when allowed to grow in the dark. In Europe, religious depravity received its check when the art of

---

* A translation into English of the most interesting portion of these works was made in India many years ago, under the personal direction of this celebrated and learned scholar. With the consent of his widow, and by the liberality of Government, this important MS. collection—the only one which enables the English student, not conversant with Sanskrit, to examine the principal contents of the Purânas—forms now part of the library of the India Office.

printing allowed the light of publicity to enter into the book whence her nations derive their faith; and no other means will check it in India than the admission of the masses to that original book which is always on their lips, but which now is the monopoly of that infinitesimal fraction of the Brahminical caste able to understand its sense; and admission, also, to that other and important literature which has at all periods of Hinduism striven to prove to the people that their real faith is neither founded on the Brâhmaṇa portion of the Vedas, nor on the Purânas, but on the Rigveda hymns.

If those intelligent Hindus of whom we are speaking have the will and the energy to throw open that book and the literature connected with it, to the people at large, without caring for the trammels imposed on caste by the politicians of late ages, we have no misgivings as to the new vitality which they will impart to its decaying life. The result is foreshadowed, indeed, by what their forefathers attempted to do, but did not succeed in accomplishing, because they had not the courage to break through the artificial bonds which had already in their day enslaved Hindu society. We will briefly advert therefore to their views and to the light in which they must have read their most ancient text.

The hymns of the Rigveda, as we observed before, are of an entirely poetical stamp. "They almost invariably combine," as Professor Wilson writes, "the attributes of prayer and praise. The power, the vastness, the generosity, the goodness, and even the personal beauty of the deity addressed, are described in highly laudatory strains; and his past bounties or exploits rehearsed or glorified; in requital of which commendations, and of the libations or oblations which he is solicited to accept, and in approval of the rite in his honour, at which his presence is invoked, he is implored to bestow blessings on the person who has instituted the ceremony, and sometimes, but not so commonly, also on the author or writer of the prayer. The blessings prayed for are, for the most part, of a temporal and personal description,—wealth, food, life, posterity, cattle, cows, and horses. . . . There are a few indications of a hope of immortality and of future happiness, but they are neither frequent nor, in general, distinctly announced, although the immortality of the gods is recognised." The following verses taken from the second Octade of the Rigveda—in the literal translation of it by Professor Wilson—may afford an idea of the general tenor of these hymns. They are addressed, the first four to Púshan, the nourishing Sun; the five latter to Heaven and Earth:—

"1. The greatness of the strength of the many-worshipped Púshan is universally lauded; no one detracts (from his praise); his praise displeases no one. Desirous of happiness I adore him, whose protection is ever nigh; who is the source of felicity; who, when devoutly worshipped, blends with the thought of all (his worshippers) ; who, though a Deity, is united with the sacrifice.

" 2. I exalt thee, Pùshan, with praises, that thou mayest hasten (to the sacrifice), like a rapid (courser) to the battle ; that thou mayest bear us across the combat, like a camel ; therefore do I, a mortal, invoke thee, the divine bestower of happiness, for thy friendship ; and do thou render our invocations productive (of benefit) ; render them productive (of success) in battles.

" 3. Through thy friendship, Pùshan, they who are diligent in thy praise and assiduous in thy worship, enjoy (abundance), through thy protection ; by (assiduous) worship they enjoy (abundance) ; as consequent upon thy recent favour, we solicit infinite riches ; free from anger, and entitled to ample praise, be ever accessible to us ; be our leader in every encounter.

" 4. Free from anger, and liberal of gifts, be nigh to us, for the acceptance of this our (offering) ; be nigh to those who solicit food : we have recourse to thee, destroyer of enemies, with pious hymns. I never cease, Pùshan, acceptor of offerings, to think of thee ; I never disregard thy friendship."

" 1. Those two, the divine Heaven and Earth, are the diffusers of happiness on all, encouragers of truth, able to sustain the water (of the rains), auspicious of birth, and energetic (in action) ; in the interval between whom proceeds the pure and divine Sun for (the discharge of his) duties.

" 2. Wide-spreading, vast, unconnected, the father and mother (of all beings), they two preserve the worlds. Resolute, as if (for good) of embodied (beings), are Heaven and Earth, and the father has invested everything with (visible) forms.

" 3. The pure and the resolute son of (these) parents, the bearer (of rewards) [the sun], sanctifies the world by his intelligence ; as well as the milch cow (the earth), and the vigorous bull (the heaven), and daily milks the pellucid milk (of the sky).

" 4. He it is, amongst gods (the most divine), amongst (pious) works the most pious, who gave birth to the all-delighting heaven and earth : who measured them both, and, for the sake of holy rites, propped them up with undecaying pillars.

" 5. Glorified by us, grant to us, Heaven and Earth, abundant food and great strength, whereby we may daily multiply mankind ; bestow upon us commendable vigour."

As with the exception of a few hymns which have no reference to the praise or worship of the elementary gods, the scope and tenor of all the lays of the Rigveda are similar to those we have quoted, the first question suggested by them is whether they contain any laws or injunctions concerning sacrificial rites. The answer is in the negative. They allude to such rites, some with less, and others with more detail ; but these allu-

sions are no more than a record or a narrative of the practices of
the poets of the hymns. We are told, it is true, that the practices
of those holy men are tantamount to a law ordaining them;
but it is clear that such an inference is purely arbitrary. That it
was strenuously opposed, moreover, by the highest authorities of
ancient and mediæval India is borne out by the works and efforts
of that influential school which professes the Vedânta tenets, and
which counts Sankarâchârya amongst its teachers and divines.
No Hindu doubts of the thorough orthodoxy of that school, and
yet all its writings reject "work," that is, the observance of the
sacrificial rites, as a means conducive to eternal bliss. It rejects,
therefore, implicitly, the sanctity or authority of those "sacrificial"
Vedas, the only object of which is the institution of such rites;
and with them, as a matter of consequence, the binding power of
the Brâhmanas and the worship founded on them.

The next important question relates to the doctrine professed by
those poets who are supposed to have received the Rigveda hymns
from a deity. The answer to it is complicated from a European,
but simple from a Hindu, point of view. To the European inquirer
the hymns of the Rigveda represent the product of various epochs
of Hindu antiquity : in some he will recognise a simple, in others
a complex, ritual; some will reflect to his mind a pastoral
and, as it were, primitive life, others a' people skilled in several
arts and engaged in mercantile and maritime pursuits. And, in
investigating the religious views expressed by these hymns, he
will find accordingly, in some, the worship of the physical powers,
whereas he will discover in others the idea of a Supreme Creator
of the universe. He will perceive in them, in short, a progressive
religious thought, beginning, as everywhere religion began, with
the adoration of the elements, proceeding to an attempt at understanding their origin, and ending with the idea, more or less
clear, of one creative cause. The last stage of this development
is indicated, for instance, by a hymn which has already acquired
some celebrity, as attention was drawn to it by so early a
Sanskritist as the illustrious Colebrooke, and as it has found its
way into several European works. It runs as follows :—

" Then was there no entity nor nonentity ; no world, nor sky,
nor aught above it ; nothing anywhere in the happiness of any
one, involving or involved ; nor water, deep or dangerous. Death
was not ; nor then was immortality ; nor distinction of day or
night. But THAT breathed without afflation, single with (Swadhâ)
her who is sustained within him. Other than him, nothing existed
(which) since (has been). Darkness there was ; (for) this universe
was enveloped with darkness, and was undistinguishable (like fluids
mixed in) waters ; but that mass, which was covered by the husk,
was (at length) produced by the power of contemplation. First,

desire was formed in his mind, and that became the original productive seed; which the wise, recognising it by the intellect in
their hearts, distinguish, in nonentity, as the bond of entity. Did
the luminous ray of these (creative acts) expand in the middle?
or above? or below? That productive seed at once became
providence (or sentient souls) and matter (or the elements):
she, who is sustained within himself, was inferior; and he, who
heeds, was superior. Who knows exactly, and who shall in this
world declare, whence and why this creation took place? The
gods are subsequent to the production of this world; then who
can know whence it proceeded? or whence this varied world
arose? or whether it upheld itself or not? He who in the
highest heaven is the Ruler of this universe does indeed know;
but not another can possess that knowledge."

The orthodox Hindu mind does not admit in these hymns of a
successive development, like that which we must assert. It considers, as mentioned before, all the hymns of the Rigveda as being
of the same age; as dating from eternity. The Upanishads, and
still more explicitly the Vedânta writers, cannot therefore allow
any real discord to exist between the adoration of the phenomena of nature and the belief in one Supreme God. They solve
the difficulty by concluding that the elementary gods are but
allegorical personifications of the great soul, the primitive cause
of the universe. And even Upanishads and Vedântists were
already preceded in this view by Yâska, the oldest exegete of
the Vedic hymns, who, on one occasion, says:—"There are three
deities (Devatâs): Agni (Fire), who resides on earth; Vâyu (Wind),
or Indra (Firmament) who resides in the intermediate region (between heaven and earth); and Sûrya (Sun), who resides in heaven.
. . . . Of the Devatâ there is but one soul; but the Devatâ having
a variety of attributes, it is praised in many ways: other gods are
merely portions of *the one Soul.*"

Upanishads, therefore, and Vedânta, the type of Hindu orthodoxy, will by no means allow that Hinduism, represented
by the Rigveda, was at any period idolatry; they maintain that
all the Rishis intended to inculcate the standard tenet of Monotheism. Whether they are justified in this theory does not affect
the practical conclusion at which we aim. For, this much is certain, that they interpret the Vedic hymns so as to derive from
them the belief in one God, and that they quote numerous passages
by which they intend to invalidate all doubts to the contrary.

But, what is remarkable, too: during the long period of Hindu
theology which is comprised by the Upanishad and Vedânta literature, there is no attempt on its part at expanding this tenet of
Monotheism into any doctrinal mysticism. They abound in the
most pious phraseology: they show that the Vedic text inculcates

the idea of the immateriality, the infiniteness, and the eternity of the Supreme Spirit ; they expatiate on its qualities of goodness, thought, and beatitude ; but they are entirely free from any tendency to justify the notion of a mystical incarnation of that Spirit such as is taught, for instance, by the votaries of Brahmâ, Vishnu, and Siva. From the words of the Veda, it must be granted, they endeavour to prove that the human soul having been created by that One Spirit, it is bound to maintain its original purity, and if it lose it by its acts in the] world, it must renew its earthly existence until it is capable of commingling with the divine source whence it sprang. But beyond this doctrine of transmigration—which is incidental to all the Monotheistic religions of mankind—it does not even try to found any religious dogma on the Rigveda hymns. In one word, the pre-eminently orthodox schools demonstrate that *the* Veda imposes no observance of a superstitious ritual ; that it enjoins no law regulating for all eternity social or political life, no dogma except the belief in One God, no duty except that of living in conformity with the nature of that God from whom the human soul has emanated.

The bane of the social edifice within which these schools had to live and to teach *Vedánta,* that is, the " purport *(anta)* of the Veda," thwarted their full success, which would have stopped the degeneracy of Hinduism they foresaw ; but, however powerful, it could never entirely crush their existence, or completely stifle the influence which they exercised on the nation. The adherents of these schools always fostered a spirit of investigation, and, by it, threw doubts, at least, into the mind of the masses as to the authority of those law-books which profess to regulate society for all eternity. To their influence, in our days, we must ascribe the quiet disappearance of the practice of Sati after they were shown that the injunction of burning the surviving widow on the funeral pile of her deceased husband had arisen from a misreading of a Rigveda verse. Their learning is active in convincing the masses that the remarriage of widows is not prohibited by the Vedic text; and to them are due the progressive changes which mark, for instance, the laws of inheritance, propounded by the existing legal authorities, as compared with those presented by Manu.

We may, therefore, still entertain the hope that the regeneration of Hinduism will proceed from these schools, provided that they possess the energy to refuse any compromise with the sectarian worship, which has brought Hinduism into contempt and ridicule. The means which they possess for combating that enemy is as simple as it is irresistible ; a proper instruction of the growing generation in its ancient literature ; an instruction, however wholly different from that now constituting the education of

a Hindu youth ; to whom reading the Veda is jabbering thought-
lessly the words of the verse, or intoning it to the melody of a
teacher as ignorant as himself of its sense ; who, by studying
grammar, understands cramming his memory with some grammatical forms, without any notion as to the linguistic laws that regulate them ; who believes that he can master philosophy or science
by sticking to the textbook of one school and disregarding its
connexion with all the rest of the literature. That such a
method and such a division of labour do not benefit the mind is
amply evidenced by the crippled results they have brought to
light. The instruction which India requires, though adapted to
her peculiar wants—religious, scientific, and political—must be
based on the system which has invigorated the European mind ;
which, free from the restrictions of rank or caste, tends to impart
to it independence of thought and solidity of character.

ART. VIII.—RUSSIA.

1. *Organisation Sociale de la Russie.* Par un Diplomate. Paris :
   1863.
2. *La Vérité sur la Russie.* Par le Prince PIERRE DOLGOROU-
   KOW. Paris : 1860.
3. *Essai sur la Situation Russe.* Par N. OGAREFF. Londres :
   1862.
4. *La Russie sous l'Empereur Alexandre II.* Par M. CHARLES
   DE MAZADE. Paris : 1862.
5. *Essai sur l'Histoire de la Civilisation en Russie.* Par NICOLAS
   DE GEREBTZOFF. Paris : 1858.
6. *Russische Fragmente.* Von F. BODENSTED. Leipzig : 1862.

"A LONG slavery," says M. Herzen, "is not an accident; it
naturally corresponds to some element of the national
character." We would carry this idea still further, and say that
national institutions and manifestations of extraordinary national
effort are always strongly tinged with both mental and moral
national characteristics. If we look at the present state of
Russia, we shall find a striking confirmation of the truth of this.
The curious institutions, if they may be so called, that have been
laid bare by the fever of reform which seized the Russians just
before the outbreak of the Polish insurrection, show unmistake-
able marks of a character exclusively national; and the same may

be said of the insurrection itself, which has so abruptly put to flight the amiable dreams of a theoretic and unsubstantial Liberalism. The frightful passions and degrading propensities which the Russians have displayed in this deadly struggle are eminently characteristic, and are even in a certain measure indicative of the better side of the national character. The acts committed under their influence are, beyond question, atrocious and revolting in the last degree ; but at the same time they often imply the existence of those good qualities which, in every nation as in every individual, supplement, and to a certain extent explain, the bad ones. The ingenious idea which M. Eugène Sue has made the foundation of one of his novels, that vices are only exaggerated virtues, is not without truth, and has found practical application in many of the incidents of this most terrible of wars.

Those who know Russia will freely admit, for instance, that the heartless subserviency which, in Poland, makes men the unscrupulous instruments of a bloodthirsty satrap in the commission of crimes at which Europe shudders with horror, may become in Russia, under other circumstances, subordination and respect for authority ; that the ardent patriot in Russia, may be, in Poland, the bitter persecutor of the race which strives to deprive his country of some of her richest possessions ; and that even such repulsive tools of power as the Mouravieffs and the Bergs, with their warped ideas of the rights and duties of rulers, show a disregard of public opinion which in another position might make them capable of the most heroic sacrifices. Respect for authority, a strong feeling of patriotism, and dogged perseverance in a given course of action, are well known and strongly-marked elements of the Russian character. The bad qualities of the nation are, however, by no means only to be found in that portion of it which hangs, transports, and insults in every possible way the unfortunate population of Poland. The Russian, by the nature of the country he inhabits as well as by his social and political characteristics, is an Asiatic, and he has the bad qualities of Asiatics, though in many respects he is far their superior. The violent efforts made by Peter the Great and his successors to transform him into a European, have produced many unfortunate results, but have certainly not been successful in attaining their object. To all intents and purposes the average Russian of the present day has as little of the European about him as had the boyars who felt themselves lowered to the very extreme of degradation when, in obedience to Peter's orders, they were forced to shave off their beards. Even European manners and the European dress have penetrated but little below the higher strata of society, and European ideas have as yet not been assimilated at all by the Russian mind. The language of European Liberalism is indeed freely used ; but the ideas it conveys are, as a rule, utterly incomprehensible to the majority even of well-educated Russians. The present state of Russia is the best proof of this. Is it possible to believe of a people in any perceptible degree penetrated with the great principles of European civilization, that it can allow itself to be deluded into regarding the horrors now committed in Poland as not only necessary, but admirable, and that a notion so monstrous should be actually developed and enlarged upon *ad nauseam* by its greatest politicians and its most distinguished writers ?— that the few of its enlightened patriots who, "on another shore," venture to raise their voices in the cause of right and of humanity, are at home bespattered with the foulest calumnies, and stigmatized as traitors to their country ?—and finally, that it submits almost without a murmur to the tyrannous rule of a degraded bureaucracy, which exists only by a system of bribery unprecedented in any nation, and is practically placed above every law and every right, both of person and of property ? If the attempts of the Czars since Peter to make Russia a European power have been the origin of much of her greatness, they have also caused her much misery. We shall not stop here to speculate on the probable position which Russia would now have occupied in the world if this unfortunate policy had not been adopted and systematically carried out by her Czars ; but it seems to us clear that nothing but advantage could have resulted both to Russia and to humanity if, instead of being forced into an unnatural connexion with races and ideas with which she had nothing in common, she had been left free to develope those germs of national institutions which are deeply rooted in her organization, and which alone are congenial to her national character. If not by race, at least by national characteristics and by geographical position, Russia belongs to Asia.

The Asiatic tendencies of Russia,* which lie at the root of all her most important social institutions, are best understood by a reference to their origin. Without touching on the debated ques-

---

* That the characteristics and tendencies of the Russians are Asiatic is acknowledged by all who have given any attention to the subject. "Un Diplomate," who writes with a great partiality for Russia, says — "Le Russe est Asiatique par tempérament, Européen par accident." Haxthausen, another philo-Russian, speaks of the "Oriental civilization" of the towns of Russia Proper, such as Moscow, Jaroslaf, Wladimir, and Nizni Novgorod. A review of St. Petersburg, published under the title of *Wremia* (The Time), which was conducted by some of the most distinguished writers and politicians of Russia, and has since been suppressed, in its April number characterises the struggles of the Poles with the Russians as "struggles of the European spirit with Asiatic barbarism." "The Russians, though they speak French quite well, are more or less Tartars at bottom," says M. Ivan Golovin. This reminds one of the well-known saying of Napoleon :—" Grattez le Russe, et vous trouverez le Tartare." See also Custine *passim*, for illustrations of this idea.

tion of the non-Sclavonian origin of the Russians, which we may safely leave in the hands of such distinguished ethnologists and historians as Duchinski, Viquesnel, and Henri Martin, it will be sufficient here to extract a few facts of the internal history of Russia from the writings of men notorious for their strong bias on the side of Czarism. According to the official historians, the history of Russia begins with the inroad of the Norman Rurik and his followers into the territory of the Sclavonian Republic of Nowgorod, in the year 862. What was then, according to these writers, the Russian people, was a race widely differing, both in character and disposition, from that which now forms the dominant nationality of the Russian Empire (the Great Russians or Muscovites). It was a warlike, agricultural, and liberty-loving race, with a republican government and free institutions, presenting a striking contrast to the servile, unprincipled nation of traders and officials, with no attachment to the soil or conception of political freedom, which constitutes the Great Russia of the present day.* Nor did the State formed by Rurik occupy any portion of the territory of what is now called Great Russia. It extended southward from the Baltic, and its eastern frontier was the Dnieper, while Great Russia was then a vast plain far to the east of that river, overgrown with primitive forests, and inhabited by savage tribes of the Finnish and Ouralian races.† This wilderness was not penetrated by the Russians until 1155, when George Dolgorouki, a descendant of Rurik, crossed the Dnieper with his followers, established a town at Wladimir, on the Klasma, and subdued one by one all the tribes around him. That in this process the Norman George and his followers eventually became Finnized, as the Normans who conquered England became Anglicized, is of course denied by the Russians, in opposition to M. Duchinski and his friends; the Russian view being that the Sclavonian element became the dominant one, in consequence of the establishment of colonies of Sclavonians in the land which had been conquered by the invaders of their own country.‡ Be this as it may, it is certain that

---

* Lest we should be thought too hard on the Muscovites, we will here quote the words of Gerebtzoff, whose blind partiality to his country and its government is remarkable, even among the most extravagant effusions of the venal writers of the official press:—" Les défauts principaux du peuple Russe (Moscovite) sont la ruse, le manque de persevérance, l'indolence, et la convoitise du bien d'autrui." The best of the good qualities he has to set against this somewhat startling selection of defects are " la piété, la résignation, et l'amour du prochain." The view of the Russian character taken by Haxthausen and other admirers of the Russian people is even more unfavourable than the above.

† Karamsyn, Nestor.

‡ For an exposition of M. Duchinski's theory, see M. Régnault's "La Question Européenne improprement appelée Polonaise." Paris: Dentu. 1863.

George was very much more successful in establishing a dynasty in his new possessions than his ancestors had been on the other side of the Dnieper. It is well known that the State founded by Rurik fell to pieces not quite three hundred years after the first Norman invasion, chiefly in consequence of frequent insurrections of the Sclavonian inhabitants against their Norman rulers.

Nowgorod and Pskow became two great Sclavonian republics, and being Hanse Towns, were connected with the European commercial system ; and the remainder of the country was ruled by princes of the Rurik dynasty, who had become almost completely Sclavonianized, and had very limited powers over their peaceful, but high-spirited and independent subjects. George, on the other hand, exercised absolute authority in the State he had founded, and the most bitter antagonism soon sprang up between him and the Free States of the West. In 1155 he captured Kiew, one of the earliest of the conquests of his ancestors, and after his death his son Andrew carried his aggressions into Nowgorod. These and subsequent wars with the peoples west of the Dnieper were marked by cruelties on the part of George and his followers which excited universal horror even in that barbarous age. The infant state of Wladimir was already an autocracy, displaying many of the characteristics of its maturity when, as the Russian Empire, it became the terror and aversion of its western neighbours.[*] Then came the Mongol invasion, which involved the whole of the Russian States in one common ruin. But the Khan found a very different reception in Wladimir to that which was given him in the territories on the other side of the Dnieper. The dukes of Wladimir, true to the Asiatic tendencies which were already developing themselves in their rising State, not only submitted to the Mongol yoke, but even ministered to the cruelties of their new master. "They took," says Karamsyn, "the humble title of servants of the Khan, and by so doing became powerful monarchs." The States west of the Dnieper, on the other hand, presented a sturdy resistance to their invaders. Though their united armies were defeated at the river Kalka, in 1224, the victory cost the Mongols so dear that they were obliged to retire, and did not again make their appearance in the country for several years, when they were repulsed by the Poles at the battle of Lignitza, in 1241. This victory, and the necessity for a strong barrier against the torrent of Mongol invasion, led to an alliance between Poland and the other States west of the Dnieper, which lasted for two centuries, and eventually resulted in a voluntary union of those States with Poland. Meanwhile the dukes of Wladimir assisted the Mongol

* Karamsyn.

forces in their constant attacks on the West, asked in marriage the daughters of the Mongol chiefs, and punished those who were visited with the displeasure of the Khan. The inhabitants of Nowgorod having refused to pay tribute to the Mongols, the Duke of Wladimir entered the city, seized upon the principal citizens, and cut off their noses and ears. The elevation or deposition, and even the life, of a duke of Wladimir, depended upon the good pleasure of the Chief, or Czar,* of the Golden Horde, who also became the arbiter in the family quarrels of the Wladimirians, and encouraged informers by offering them the property of those whom they denounced as ill-disposed to his rule. But the cup of the infamy of this servile State was not yet full. Having conquered the whole of the territory between the Oural and the Dnieper, the Khan assembled all the princes whom he had subjected to his rule, and after forcing them to swear allegiance to him, commanded them to prostrate themselves before the Tartar idol. Most of the Christian princes hesitated. One of them, the Duke of Tchernigoff, refused, and was killed on the spot ; but George, the Duke of Wladimir, hastened to obey the order of the Khan, and received as the price of his venal subserviency, the title of Grand-duke, and priority of rank over the other princes. It was this base act that laid the foundation of the future greatness of Russia. Shortly after, in 1328, the Grand-duke of Wladimir seized Moscow, made it his capital, and assumed the title of Grand-duke of Muscovy. The Muscovites, however, remained subject to the Mongols until 1492.

Thus, during a period of nearly three centuries, did the inhabitants of the State now known as Russia purchase a precarious security for their lives and properties against the depredations of their Mongol masters by submitting themselves to a slavery such as we see only among savages. So lengthened an exposure to the most corrupting influences cannot but have produced some impression on the character of the Russian people ; and that such has been the case is admitted by many Russian writers. " Cunning," says an author† whose *naïves* admissions of the inward rottenness of his idol we gladly quote—" cunning, which is generally a trait of the Russian character, is the fruit of the times of the Mongol dominion, during which every one *was obliged to deceive habitually for his own preservation.* . . . Indolence arose from the same reason. When one is not sure of the morrow, why sacrifice one's repose to the acquisition of a property one may never enjoy ? The coveting another's property proceeds from the difficulty which

---

* The word czar, or tzar, is of Tartar origin, and signifies "lord of the steppes."

† Gerebtzoff, vol. ii. p. 574.

existed in securing one's own from the exactions of the oppressor. *When my right of property is not sacred in another's eyes, I can see no difference between* meum *and* tuum." Our readers will wonder at these transparent sophisms; but we can assure them that such argument is by no means rare in the literature of a country whose most striking characteristics have always been plausibility and deceit. The same writer treats of another defect of the Russian character, traceable to the time of the Mongol invasion, with so outrageous a contempt of our Western notions of decency and common sense, that we cannot resist quoting the passage :*—

"There is another marked trait of the manners of the Russian people which is energetically condemned by strangers : it is that of not considering corporal punishment as more degrading than any other. It is a fact, that in the eyes of the Russian people, corporal punishment is even less sensibly felt than a verbal insult; a penal detention is regarded as much more degrading than corporal punishment; especially when the latter is inflicted in secret. *This idea has a religious foundation : a good Christian cannot admit that the punishment of fustigation, which has been inflicted on the Saviour of humanity, can be, for a man, a stain of infamy ;* he believes that a verbal insult affects the immortal part of man, whereas a blow only produces suffering in the least noble part of his being."

It is easy to understand how a nation with such debasing faults of character should have become the submissive tool of an unprincipled and cruel military autocracy. The many excellent qualities of the private character of the Russians, their kind-heartedness, their charity, their hospitality—virtues which are admirable in individuals, but which have little influence on the character of nations—did nothing to counterbalance these grave defects. Without honour, without honesty, without individual initiative, or a consciousness of individual dignity—cunning, idle, and servile— what could Russia become but a huge material machine, with no internal forces capable of stirring it to social action, and no power of movement but what is given it by the lawless hand of an autocrat? Her deliverance from the Mongols only left her in the power of another master, who borrowed from them his title and the boundless authority attached to it. Nor were the men charged with the guidance of this powerful, but inert instrument of despotism unequal to the task. Bloodthirsty, cruel, and unprincipled as were the earlier Czars, they had the virtues which sustain absolutism, as well as the vices which are its consequences; and by their frequent conquests, which flattered the national vanity and increased the national wealth, they firmly established their

---

* Gerebtzoff, vol. ii. p. 575.

power, and laid the foundations for that idolatry of Czardom which is deeply implanted in the breast of every true Russian. In the eyes of this unfortunate people, nurtured amid oppression and crime, the rapid growth of material prosperity and power was cheaply purchased by the deprivation of a liberty they had never known, and that blind obedience to a tyrant's rule which had become habitual to them. Thus, both in its form and in its tendencies, Russia remained an Asiatic State—not, however, stagnant and enervated, like the effete Empires of modern Asia, but powerful, aggressive, and faithless, like the Persia of Xerxes or the Tartary of Genghis Khan.

The official revolution introduced by Peter the Great only served to confirm this Asiatic character in the nation. The poorer classes, in whom all the higher feelings of humanity had long perished under the deadening influence of Czarism, went with touching simplicity to a certain death at the bidding of their stern master. Tens of thousands perished in the marshes of Ladoga, to satisfy what most Russian historians now regard as an imperial caprice; yet not a voice of complaint was raised against the barbarity, and the bereaved families wept in silence. A new city rose in ghastly splendour over the dead bodies; the ancient capital, the awe and veneration of all good Russians, was neglected, and the seat of government transferred to a new acquisition of Russia; the national feeling was outraged in every way; the national manners and dress were proscribed, and European customs made compulsory; the national religion was placed under the direct control of the sovereign; the nobility were degraded, and the peasantry turned into slaves; yet all, nobles and peasants, priests and patriots, obediently accepted the decrees of their Czar, and did their best to adapt themselves to their new position, as if it had been forced upon them by a fate which it would be useless to resist and criminal to accuse. What was this but the result of the Mongol invasion over again? Not having the spirit to rise against the tyranny that oppressed it, the nation fell back into a state of greater debasement than ever. Nor was there anything European about Peter, except the institutions and the customs of which he attempted to introduce an apish imitation into his own country. This very imitation had something barbarous about it, strongly resembling in its grotesqueness and want of adaptation the attempts at European costume of the savages of the South Sea Islands. As hypocrisy is the homage which vice pays to virtue, so is unmeaning imitation that which barbarism pays to civilization. It is true that this imitation was forced by Peter on the Russians with a set purpose. But this very purpose was that of an Asiatic despot. It was not, as

M. Herzen and his followers seem to think,* the development of the moral and material prosperity of the country by the introduction of European institutions; it was the re-organization of the people so as to make them more effective tools of the Czar. Peter saw with admiration the power which a well-organized bureaucracy and a regular military administration gave to European States, and by substituting these institutions for the cumbrous machinery which had clogged the action of his predecessors, he only swept away the obstacles which had made their despotism less directly felt. Where are we to look for a single act of Peter's that was calculated to promote the moral or material happiness of his people? In his murder of his own son? In the hecatombs of poor workmen that were sacrificed to his caprices? In the enslavement of the peasantry? Or in the stifling and corrupt net of officialism he has spread over the whole country? His whole reign is a series of pitiless cruelties at home and of brilliant conquests abroad, all having but one object—the systematic compression of the nation to an inert mass moving at his will, and the firm establishment of his empire in a position whence at any moment it might spring upon Europe.

The system introduced by Peter has now been on its trial about a hundred and fifty years. During that period the material progress of the Russian Empire has been beyond question very great. But with this progress the system of Peter had little to do. The boundless resources of the country, and the versatile and roving disposition of the people, naturally increased the national wealth to an enormous degree. Virgin territories of fabulous extent and fertility have been put under cultivation, and their produce disposed of to the best advantage by Russian merchants, whose commercial acuteness is proverbial; manufactures of all kinds have sprung up, and although generally inferior to those of Western Europe, they suffice to provide for the ordinary wants of the country. All this is traceable to natural causes, independent of any Government action, which, indeed, usually hinders more than it developes the material prosperity of a nation. But if we look at the moral and political progress of Russia during the above period, it is impossible to admit that it has in any degree kept pace with the spread of civilization in the other countries of Europe. The subject is an interesting one, and deserves a much more extended investigation than we can give it here. A general review, however, of the present state of thought and feeling in

* See his " Idées Révolutionnaires," and an admirable article, entitled "The Princess Catherine Romanovna Dashkova," in the last number of the *Kolokol.*

Russia, and of the social condition of the various classes of the nation, will enable our readers to judge for themselves.

It is well known that the Russian official world is divided into fourteen classes, or *tchins.* Every noble is liable to be called upon to serve the State ; and his rank in the civil or military service, when he is employed, depends on his *tchin.* Thus a nobleman belonging to the twelfth *tchin* may become a lieutenant in the army, a midshipman, a secretary to a governor, or a deacon, if he can obtain any of these appointments ; but his *tchin* will not allow him to be a lieutenant-colonel, a captain of a ship, or a court councillor, because those ranks are reserved only for noblemen of the seventh *tchin.* *Tchinovniks* below the ninth *tchin* are not nobles ; and hereditary nobility is only the right of those in the first five *tchins.* This cumbrous organization, which strikingly resembles the official system of the Chinese, derives its origin, like everything else that is bad and corrupt in Russia, from the times of the Mongol invasion. When the first Russian Czar assumed the reins of power over a people stupified and degraded by three centuries of slavery and hypocrisy, he found it impossible to work the machine of Government, and to keep up an army large enough for the preservation of his dominions from attack, without a large staff of officials. Accordingly, two classes of public func-tionaries were established : the first, usually selected from the military chiefs, were rewarded for their services with grants of land, and formed the nobility ; the second, recruited from the body of the people, lived by pillage on the inhabitants of the district to which they were posted, and eventually, by flattering the Czar, obtained grants of land, and thus also became nobles. The chivalrous element which, in the feudal nobility of Western Europe or the democratic aristocracy of Poland (as it is happily called by Lelewel), restrained the power of the sovereign and paved the way for the liberties of the people, was in Russia entirely absent. The Russian noble had no claim on his country for services rendered either by himself or his family, nor could he arrogate to himself any moral superiority on the ground of his own deeds or those of his ancestors. His title was usually the reward of sycophancy and intrigue—his reputation that of an un-scrupulous agent of oppression—his wealth the fruit of bribery or pillage. His class was called in Russian *dvorianstvo,* that of the courtiers ; he had no rights or privileges except that of treating the slaves (or, in the official phrase, souls) in his possession like cattle ; he was liable to corporal punishment like every other Russian ; and when in the Czar's presence, he was obliged to prostrate himself before him and kiss his hand, as in former times the Russian princes knelt to do homage to the Great Khan. As in other countries the nobility transferred from father to son their titles and estates, so in Russia the *dvorianins* left to their descendants the offices they had filled in the State and the lands attached to them. It is obvious that a class like this could never have any *esprit de corps*, any sense of individual dignity, or any aspirations after public liberty, and it naturally had not the smallest influence with the mass of the people, by whom it was hated and despised.

The transformation of this class of hereditary officials into a hierarchy of *tchinovniks* was the greatest and most radical change introduced into the social organization of Russia by Peter the Great. We have already observed that the real character of this measure was not that of a great national reform, but simply of an improvement in the machine of autocracy. The old hereditary system, besides making the nobles to a certain degree independent of the Czar, led to endless law-suits and quarrels, which greatly impeded the working of the service ; and by making offices only tenable during pleasure, Peter not only bound the already corrupt nobles to him body and soul, but put a stop to all further differences arising from disputed hereditary rights. The numerous foreigners with whom he loved to surround himself were also, by this summary measure, provided with posts under the State to which, under the old system, their rank and nationality would have been an insuperable bar. It was, in fact, sweeping off the last of the scanty rights, absurd and corrupt as they were, which the nation still enjoyed, and subjecting every Russian to the control of an arbitrary and irresponsible power. The system established by Peter practically exists to this day, and has produced the most lamentable effects on the character of the nation, on which it has acted like one of those cosmetics which, while giving a superficial outward polish, develop to a frightful extent the seeds of internal corruption. The modifications introduced by Catherine, who, acting on the *divide et impera* principle, tried to play off the territorial nobility against those who still remained officials by granting to the former certain political rights, produced little or no effect in remedying the evil. The system of *tchins* is nothing less than the perpetuation of the enslavement of the people by the total corruption and abasement of their moral nature. The first thing that every *tchinovnik* learns, on entering the service of the State, is how to deceive his superiors and rob those who are under him. His salary is ludicrously insufficient for his wants; the printed regulations issued by the Government for his guidance he soon finds it impossible to carry out ; he breathes an atmosphere of venality and hypocrisy ; and even the people who are to be his victims contribute to his corruption by offering him bribes. In other countries the official fears to do wrong ; in Russia he fears to do what will not tally with the caprice or pleasure of his superiors. The Russian official is not the servant of the State, but the slave of the Czar. All notion of duty to his country is, of course, entirely extinct in his breast; he holds office at the good pleasure of the Czar, or his own immediate superior who represents him, and so long as he can contrive to keep his situation by making himself agreeable to his chief, he considers he has a perfect right to enrich himself at the expense of the people. It is an old remark that to a foreigner one of the most striking characteristics of the Russian people is their love of show. This characteristic, harmless and very pardonable in itself, appears in the *tchinovnik* in its most hideous and repulsive form. The unhappy official, whose place—nay, whose very life—depends on the caprice of the Czar, naturally strives to exalt in the eyes of his master the value of his services, and thereby to come in for a share of the harvest of rewards which falls from the Imperial hand. Hence the superficial and deceptive nature of most of the work of Russian officialism; details and forms are carefully looked to, as they come under the immediate eye of the Czar, while things which are really important are either neglected or hurried over. The painted canvas erections made to resemble villages which were posted at some miles' distance on either side of the high road while Catherine was travelling through her dominions, are but a single example of multitudes of deceptions equally silly and outrageous. When the sovereign has to trust to a written report, the dissimulation is still more unblushing—statements are sent in from various officials, almost every one of which is a series of untruths. Well may Prince Dolgoroukow say that "Russia is the country of official and organized falsehood." Nor is the Czar the only object of terror. Every petty official who has others employed under him is a little Czar, as capricious and almost as redoubtable as the great one. We have already alluded to the code of rules by which every official is supposed to be bound. It is quite impossible to observe these rules, most of which relate to mere formalities, on all occasions; and accordingly the functionary is obliged to be constantly on the watch lest he should be suddenly caught by his superior in a contravention of the regulations. He must, therefore, be always ready with his masquerading dress, and have acquired sufficient proficiency in the arts of Tartuffe to put it on so as to give it all the air of reality. But, with all his caution, there are still numberless points of form which no one ever thinks of observing, besides real crimes which every one commits, that place him completely in the power of his superior, who consents to look them over for a certain fixed bribe, regulated according to his position. The *ispravniks* (district chiefs of police) pay in bribes of this kind from 1000 to 1500 roubles (160*l.* to 240*l.*), the chiefs of towns 500 to 3000 roubles (80*l.* to 480*l.*), and the *gorodnitchyi* (commissioners of police) a sum varying according to the importance of the towns in which they are stationed. We need hardly add that these large sums are not paid by the officials out of the scanty salaries allowed them by the Government.

Another evil, more directly traceable to the influence of Czarism, is the sickening servility of manner and language with which every official that cares to keep his place must approach the Czar or his representative. Thus, on certain occasions, such as the Czar's birthday, not only the officials, but also the chief inhabitants, everywhere pay an official visit to the chief local functionary to express their sentiments of loyalty to the Czar. At these visits the Czar only is the subject of conversation ; stereotyped forms of language are used, from which the visitors depart at their peril, to express the most fulsome adulation of his moral, mental, and even personal qualities ; and the mention of ideas and sentiments that have been reproved by the Government invariably rouses a loyal indignation, couched in terms prescribed for the occasion.

Toadyism and hypocrisy are, however, the least important of the vices of the Russian official. What makes him a real curse to the country, and a nucleus of gradually extending corruption, is his venality and rapacity. The stories illustrative of this canker of Russian society which may be seen in most books on Russia, disclose a state of public morality that is perfectly astounding. It is a mistake to suppose, as is done by some writers, that the Czars know nothing of this ; the evil is too great and universal even to escape their ears. Peter the Great used to say that only those Russians who have hair growing on the palms of their hands did not steal ; and the well-known saying of Nicholas, that there was but one man in his dominions who did not steal, and that was himself, will still be fresh in the memory of many of our readers. These sayings, paradoxical as they appear, are almost literally true. Every one steals in Russia, from the highest to the lowest, from the high official who stole three millions of roubles in the reign of Nicholas, to the petty *tchinovnik* who grows rich on the peasants of his commune. Perhaps the most gigantic specimen of official fraud on record is that which was perpetrated by an entire public department in 1844. At the general survey of the Empire under Catherine II., the country was divided into districts (datcha), whose limits were accurately marked out and registered in a public office belonging to the Department of Justice. As several of these districts contained the estates of more than one proprietor, it was determined, in 1835, to register the limits of these estates also. According to the then existing law, the limits of estates of this kind were settled on the basis of actual possession combined with the usual decennial term of prescription.

This, however, did not suit the views of the Ministry of Justice, who wanted to make money by the transaction—a very general feeling of the judicial authorities in Russia. Accordingly, a law was passed, with the concurrence of the Emperor Nicholas, abolishing the decennial prescription, and putting back the prescription for the estates in question eighty years, *i.e.*, to 1765, the date of the first survey. The unfortunate proprietors were now obliged to hunt up the title-deeds of their estates previous to 1765, but the officials politely saved them the trouble. By one of those miracles known only to the Russian bureaucracy, the missing title-deeds, which were supposed to have been lost or destroyed long ago, suddenly made their appearance just at the right moment in the Moscow archives. Of course, it would have been contrary to all the principles of official tradition to be allowed to inspect these valuable documents without payment of a consideration; but this condition was cheerfully complied with by the proprietors, who were only too glad to close with the officials at their own price, and even, by the judicious administration of sundry gratuities, obtained large additions to their estates, which the accommodating *tchinovniks* surreptitiously introduced into the alleged title-deeds. This last manœuvre, however, somewhat complicated matters, and five years ago there was a curious trial, in which three gentlemen presented title-deeds delivered to them by the Archive-office at Moscow, each of which clearly established the right of its owner to the same piece of land!

The evils of the *tchin* system do not, however, stop here. Everything in Russia being under Government control, the corrupting influence of the *tchinovnik* penetrates into the smallest and most obscure branches of the social organization. The oppression exercised by the country officials, from the highest to the lowest, on the population of the towns and villages, for instance, is almost inconceivable. Some idea of the extent of the arbitrary power they wield may be conceived from the fact, that so recently as 1859 a Governor-general of a province obtained authority to punish serfs for disobedience to their masters according to his own pleasure, without any regard to the limits fixed by the law. There is practically no appeal to these arbitrary acts. Once at a municipal council, one of those bodiless forms of European organization with which Russia abounds, a merchant ventured to express an opinion which was opposed to that of the governor. He was immediately summoned to the presence of the irritated representative of the Czar, roundly abused, and put under arrest. With a spirit which is but too rare in Russia, the merchant complained to the Senate, which respectfully asked the governor for an explanation. This proceeding on the part of a body which is, next to the Czar, the principal estate of the realm, was surely of a very mild character; but it was sufficient to alarm the official dignity, wounded in the person of a *tchinovnik.* The champion of the bureaucracy on this occasion was the Minister of Justice, who severely reproved the Senate in a despatch, and at the same time informed the merchant, through the Director of Police, that if he did not let the matter drop he would at once be sent into exile without trial. The tradesmen in towns are even more at the mercy of the officials than the wealthier part of the population. The forms which the law requires them to go through are so numerous and minute, that they have no alternative but to purchase exemption from them by bribing the *gorodnitchy,* or commissary of the town police. This functionary is empowered suddenly to close the shop of any tradesman who does not comply with these forms, so that the trading class must do its best to secure the good graces of the *gorodnitchy* at the penalty of absolute ruin. But beyond all comparison the class which most feels the oppression of the *tchinovnik,* is that of the peasants of the Crown, or, as they were called before the emancipation, free peasants. The grievances of these unfortunate people are so great that most writers on Russia regard them as considerably worse off than were the serfs, who, though they had no civic rights, were at least subject to the caprice of but one master, while the Crown peasants are oppressed by hundreds who have no interest in their prosperity.

The approaching reduction of the serfs by the project of emancipation to a position similar to that of the Crown peasants gives a peculiar interest to this large section of the Russian people, and we shall endeavour, in a subsequent portion of this article, to make our readers clearly acquainted with their social condition. We wish here only to show by a few facts the nature of their relations with the Government officials. These officials are elected by the peasants themselves; but once elected, their electors have no power over them, and they become servants of the Government, which alone can dismiss them. The result is, of course, to all intents and purposes the same as if the Government had the appointment in its own hands. The peasant functionary is exposed to the same temptations as any other, and dismissal and punishment equally hang over his head if he does not rob his inferiors and deceive his superiors in the same manner as his fellows. He is under the control of a secretary, nominated by the Government, who usually takes a truly official pleasure in setting the law at defiance. Thus nothing is more common than for an official of this kind to order a peasant a greater number of lashes than is allowed by law, and then to forge a report in which it is stated that the peasant was tried by a regular court of justice, and sentenced to receive the regulated number of lashes. The peasant has no redress, for he can only complain against one official to another ; and all the officials play into one another's hands. As to the pretexts for extorting money from the peasants, they are innumerable, and often very ingenious. In a certain field belonging to Crown peasants there was a large piece of stone, weighing several hundreds of tons. One day the resident official assembled the peasants, and informed them that he had received orders from the Czar to direct them to take the stone to St. Petersburg. The peasants remonstrated, and begged the official to intercede for them with the Czar, adding the usual golden inducements. The intercession was of course successful, and the lucky official made a little fortune by his ingenuity. Another expedient, which is very frequently resorted to, is the following :—At the most busy time of the agricultural season, two or three officials arrive at a village on pretence of a political investigation, send for the wealthiest of the peasants, and keep them for days under examination. The peasants, to whom a day's delay at that season is worth a large sum, give the officials a handsome present, and the investigation is of course closed immediately.

It must not be supposed that in all these cases the peasant is the dupe. The Russian peasant is remarkably sharp and intelligent, and is particularly clever at detecting a fraud ; but there is a sort of fatalism and want of initiative in his nature which prompts him to accept his sad lot as irremediable, and even to contribute to the maintenance of a state of things which he feels himself powerless to oppose. We cannot give a better illustration of the characteristics of both peasant and official than by relating an incident which occurred some years ago in a Russian commune. This commune had just built some very expensive edifices in a certain spot, when a functionary arrived with directions to pull them down and have them re-erected elsewhere, as their present situation was wanted for a new high road. The peasants resisted, and even threatened to appeal to the Czar. The scandal was tremendous, and the functionary determined to crush out the opposition without delay. Accordingly, he assembled the chief men of the place, and called upon them to proceed with the demolition at once. They pleaded inability : he gave them each several hundred blows with a stick. The argument was irresistible ; the buildings not only vanished like magic, but were soon built again in another place, and the peasants actually expressed their gratitude to the official for the embellishments executed by his orders. The stick, however, did not quite complete its cure. A short time after, the same functionary wanted to elect a friend of his to a vacant communal appointment. He accordingly proceeded to the spot where the election was to take place, and loudly sang the praises of his friend. The peasants bowed repeatedly, and answered that what he said was for the best ; notwithstanding which, when the official candidate's name was put up, the balloting-urn was found to contain nothing but black balls—he had been unanimously rejected. This decision, according to the law, was final; but in Russia the public functionary is above the law. The patron of the defeated candidate became angry and abusive, declared the first voting null, and ordered the electors to vote again. They bowed and obeyed : but when the urn came to be examined, the black balls were again found to be in a majority, although a few of the more timid had put in some white ones. But this, far from disconcerting the *employé*, only increased his rage. He declared that the electors, by refusing to elect his candidate, had been guilty of disobedience to the Czar's representative, and that therefore he would teach them obedience—by electing him himself. This decision was received with marks of the greatest satisfaction by the peasants, who hailed their new official with immense applause, and were evidently highly delighted at their escape from an awkward dilemma.

There is much that is instructive as well as curious in this little scene of Russian peasant life. The truculent, unprincipled official, with his flagrant nepotism and reckless disregard of the law, and the sulky and discontented but obsequious peasant, are characters that may be met with in every Russian village. It is seldom, however, that the opposition to the oppression of the *tchinovnik* presents itself in such a determined form. The strongest sentiment that is felt by the Russian peasant with regard to all officials is generally a vague, unreasoning terror. This is of course chiefly due to the unlimited authority with which every *tchinovnik* is armed ; but much of it is also attributable to that constitutional inertia and passive endurance of wrong which a long course of uninterrupted slavery has strongly engrafted on the character of the Russian people. The Russian peasant, moreover, though hating the *tchinovnik* because he beats, robs, and abuses him, does not feel for him that contempt with which thieves and parasites are regarded in the other countries of Europe. Dishonesty, though punishable by the law, is so common in Russia that the moral sense of the people has become corrupted, and the Russian, like the Spartan of old, generally thinks himself perfectly justified in stealing, so long as he does it cleverly enough not to be found out. The fact that the law forbids it, does not in the slightest degree appeal to his sense of duty, for he knows perfectly well that there are numberless vices which the Russian law not only sanctions but encourages. The result is that people are more frequently condemned for theft in Russia than for any other crime. A curious instance of the manner in which the peasantry connive at the peculation of the officials is related by a *tchinovnik*, who was once sent for the first time to a country district. The law requires that all peasant officials shall receive their pay from the superintendent appointed over them by the Government ; but this pay is never issued, and the peasants give a receipt for it to the superintendent, which is forwarded by him to head-quarters —the money of course going into his own pocket. The *tchinovnik* above alluded to, who was new to his business, on receiving the money for the pay of the peasant officials, summoned them to his office, and tendered the amount due to each. The peasants looked at each other in astonishment, and no doubt supposing that their new superior was possessed with an extraordinary desire to save appearances, bowed humbly like slaves before a master who likes to have his joke. When, at length, he succeeded in making them understand that the money was really for them, their surprise was changed into terror. They accepted their pay, but could not be made to believe that this simple act of common honesty did not conceal some diabolical contrivance for imposing upon them a new and more onerous contribution.

The whole of the judicial administration in Russia being under the direct influence of *tchinovniks*, it will be easily understood that this rapacious and dishonest class exercise to the utmost the powers which are thus placed in their hands. We have already alluded to the merely formal character of the Russian laws. They are contained in fifteen volumes with several appendices, but the first of them, which places the Czar above the law, nullifies all the rest, for the officials are, *de facto* if not *de jure*, as much above the law as their master. The laws themselves, as might be expected of a code drawn up by a series of cruel, fanciful, or imbecile despots, are a strange farrago of heterogeneous fragments of legislation, some purely Utopian, some ridiculously minute, some base and inhuman to the last degree. The penal code published in 1845 is an example of the latter class. By it any one convicted of having knocked down a bust of the Czar is to receive the punishment of high treason ; every faithful subject is recommended to perform the office of a common informer, and those who fail in this duty are declared also guilty of high treason. The administration of justice has, however, been somewhat reformed in the present reign. The frightful venality which, until last year, placed the Russian courts of justice on a par with those of Turkey, has now, to a certain degree, ceased under the influence of the ukase of the 14th October, 1862, although it still runs riot in the inferior country tribunals. By this ukase, judges were to be in future appointed for life ; trials were to be public, and conducted orally ; the accused were allowed the privilege of counsel ; no case was to be tried more than twice ; the Chamber of Requests was abolished, and the right of pardon was reserved for the Emperor alone. All the subjects of the Empire were to be tried by the same tribunals, which are divided into two classes—the superior tribunals, whose judges are appointed for life by the Government, and the inferior, whose judges are elected by the district inhabitants from a list of candidates who are Government nominees. Appeals against the decisions of these Courts lie with the general body of the judges of corresponding rank. Even juries were to be introduced in criminal trials. Political trials, however, are still to be conducted in secret, although the accused is allowed the privilege of having the marshals of the nobility of his province among his judges—a privilege that is almost worthless, if we consider the arbitrary manner in which these trials are always conducted. These reforms, however, excellent as they undoubtedly are, have as yet extended but little beyond the written law, and it is known how wide an interval usually separates a good law from its execution in Russia. As yet we can only regard them as representing the theory of the future ; let us now cast a glance at the practice of the present. We recollect reading in a number of the Russian paper, *The Northern Bee*, published not three months ago, an extract from an article communicated to the local newspaper of the Government of Kherson by a Russian pope named Tchemenn, describing a strange scene in which he was one of the principal actors, and which throws a mournful light on the present mode of administering justice in Russia. M. Tchemenn had been summoned by the police to perform the last rites of religion on the body of a dead man in the dead-house of the town. He found the corpse stretched out on a deal table, a small tallow candle casting a dismal light in the wretched room. The only person in the house besides himself and his assistant was an old woman whose duty it was to dress the dead in their funeral garments. The body was that of a well-built man, wasted by disease, and with an indescribable aspect of suffering on his face. The expression was mild and touching ; he had evidently been an honest workman, whose death had been caused not by crime, but by severe illness brought on by mental suffering and over-work. And yet he was alone in the dead-house, without a friend to mourn by his body, like a criminal and an outcast. The burial-service commenced ; a few pale and frightened faces of women peered in through the window, and then flitted past like shadows. One of these faces was paler and more haggard than the rest, and a stifled sob was heard as it disappeared, after casting an eager glance into the room. A few days after, a poor woman, whom M. Tchemenn recognised as the one who had thus given audible vent to her grief, came to him to relieve her conscience of a great burthen. She was the widow of the dead man, she said : they were poor, hard-working people, and the deceased had killed himself in his efforts to support a large family. His axe had fallen from his hands while he was at work, and he had sunk dead on the sod. Her first impulse on hearing the dreadful news had been to fly to the spot ; but the other inhabitants of the village had dissuaded her. They had told her that the corpse of her husband had been laid in a retired spot near the road ; that the police would find it and bury it in due course ; that if she were found by the body she and all the inhabitants of her village would be ruined by a lengthy cross-examination, from which they could only escape by paying large bribes, and that even then many of them would probably be thrown in prison on suspicion of having murdered her husband. The poor woman had allowed herself to be convinced by these arguments ; but she could not resist going to the dead-house to take a last look at the remains of him who had died for her and her children's sake. Even then her tears had betrayed her ; she had been pursued by the police ; and she had fled without even knowing where her husband had been buried. M. Tchemenn adds that cases of this kind frequently come under his notice ; and that on one occasion, as he was reading the burial-service over a dead man whose name was unknown, a peasant stepped forward, whispered the name in his ear, and then disappeared. This fear of being implicated in a criminal trial is universal all over Russia, and often produces the most lamentable results. It is notorious that a man who has been attacked by robbers and left wounded on the highway has no chance whatever of obtaining assistance, except from the police, the passers-by always giving him a wide berth for fear of being implicated in the affair. Haxthausen tells a story of a Votiak peasant who conceived such a violent hatred towards an inhabitant of his village, that he surreptitiously entered his house and hanged himself, knowing that the mere fact of a dead man having been found on his premises would bring down on his enemy's head the severest punishment his vengeance could desire. In another part of the country a *tchinovnik*, who was in want of money, proceeded to some rich villages with which he was in no official connexion whatever, and summoned them to pay him a certain sum. The peasants having refused, the *tchinovnik* looked about for means to compel them to grant his demand. Having heard that a Government horse had died in an adjoining wood six months before, he opened an inquiry into the matter. The facts of the case were clear enough ; the horse had run away, and afterwards died in the wood of starvation. But the *tchinovnik* wanted money, and his inventive faculties raised up so many difficulties, that the peasants, whom he had called as witnesses, were glad to escape further detention by paying the sum originally asked. Fraudulent judicial investigations of this kind are indeed so common and lucrative, that the officials have coined a word (*vziontka*, a catch) which they generally use to express their good fortune in being engaged in a criminal inquiry. Where such abuses as these exist, it must be evident that nothing but. a radical change in the whole official organization can remove them. We confess we have no faith in the efficacy of the judicial reforms already alluded to, even if they are honestly and fully carried out. What guarantee is there that the judges, even though they are appointed for life, will not be open to bribes in a country where bribery and extortion have become recognised institutions? The juries, too, will probably be not incorruptible; and even supposing that both judge and jury fulfil their duty in the spirit of a Solomon, the Czar, or rather his Minister of Justice, is still empowered to modify or aggravate the sentence. The evil lies deeper than the number and constitution of the Courts or the permanency of the judges; and while giving all due credit to the good intentions of the present Emperor, we fear that his judicial reforms will do little to ameliorate those evils of the criminal procedure which most urgently call for a remedy.*

Perhaps the most fatal manifestation of that curse of slavery which has for so many centuries undermined the moral instincts of the Russian people, is to be found in the condition of the clergy of Russia. History abounds with instances where a nation sunk in ignorance and oppression has yet had the seeds of true morality kept alive among its people by the example of the pure-minded ministers of even a bigoted and superstitious religion. But this faint ray of light, where all else is darkness, has long been extinguished in Russia by the universal repression which is the characteristic of Czarism. The Russian clergy, never very independent in a country where everything was always subject to the unlimited power of the sovereign, lost their only safeguard against the direct control of the Czar in religious matters by the abolition of the patriarchate under Peter I. The synod which was then established for the direction of church affairs soon degenerated into a ministry for carrying out the orders of the sovereign, and Nicholas gave it one of his generals for a president. The effect of this policy has of course been to convert the Russian clergy into a body of spiritual *tchinovniks*, who, like their civil brethren, flatter and cringe before their immediate superiors, make every duty of morality and religion subservient to a blind obedience to the wishes of the Czar, and eke out their scanty salaries by fleecing those who are

---

* We may add, as a significant commentary on the above remarks, that the Emperor has recently decreed, on the recommendation of the Minister of Justice, that newspapers, when exposing the abuses of the judicial administration, are not to publish the names of the culprits.

placed under their charge. This extraordinary body of clerical officials constitutes a sort of caste, all the sons of popes (priests) being compelled by law to adopt their fathers' profession; and although, by money and interest, people frequently obtain exemption from this law, it very rarely happens that a layman voluntarily becomes a clergyman, the profession of the church being regarded with very general discredit in Russia. Like the civil officials, every ecclesiastic holds his appointment only during pleasure, and the hardship of his position is still further aggravated by the circumstance that he may at any time be dismissed on the mere order of the civil authorities, and even be sent to serve in the army as a common soldier. This somewhat abrupt transition from the ecclesiastical to the military state is so much a matter of course, that the pupils of the ecclesiastical seminaries have often been actually drafted off into the army for no other reason than that there were no vacancies for them in the church. As if to complete the degradation of the Russian ecclesiastic, the education in the seminaries is of the rudest description, and the mere elements of knowledge are taught in books which are written by paid scribes of the Government, and which are full of falsehoods and sophisms, all directed to prove the truth of the official religion, and the infallibility of the Czar. The distinction between the black clergy, or the monks, who are not permitted to marry, and the white clergy, who are forced to marry, is another great evil, which reacts in the most pernicious manner on the lower classes of the Empire. The bishops are exclusively selected from the black clergy; and the married popes, who can only fill the inferior offices of the church, are accordingly looked down upon and oppressed by the bishops, who have unlimited power over them, and use it to its fullest extent, the two classes of forced bachelors and forced Benedicts being naturally antipathetic. The result of all this may be easily imagined. The pope is not only the slave of the Czar, but of his bishop, who naturally hates him, and whose good-will he can only obtain by the basest servility and obsequiousness; his personal dignity is thus lost, his character becomes corrupted, and he loses all independence of thought and feeling. His nature, rendered plastic by the crushing weight of an irresistible oppression, feels no repugnance to deeds most unworthy of a minister of religion. He becomes an agent of the temporal power, and considers it his duty to divulge political secrets communicated to him under the seal of confession. Being forced to embrace the clerical state, and initiated from his earliest youth in the fraudulent arts of his brother ecclesiastics, he regards his sacred profession only as a means of making a fortune by robbery and extortion. Knowing the violent means employed by the Government in its so-called conversions to the orthodox faith, he uses his interest or his powers of flattery to obtain a parish where the inhabitants belong to a recently-converted sect, and reaps a rich harvest of bribes in return for his non-interference in the secret rites of their old and still practised faith. He requires payment for everything : for baptism, for marriages, and for confessions ; and in the latter he regulates, according to the number of roubles he receives, the amount of penance he chooses to impose. During the celebration of Divine service, the prayers which occupy most time and are most carefully read are those for the Czar and his family. These prayers are repeated several times during the service, and on each occasion they are accompanied by a complete enumeration of all the members of the Imperial family, with all their christian names, titles, and dignities. When the priest blesses the bread, he divides it into seven portions, the first of which is in honour of the Czar, and the rest of Christ, the Virgin, and the Saints. Can it be wondered at that, with such teachers, the religion of the Russian peasant should have been reduced to a series of empty forms, and one dominant idea—the Czar ? As for the principles of religion and general morality, they are entirely absent. A Russian peasant will discuss with great ingenuity, and a certain force of argument of the scholastic kind, the question whether the sign of the Cross should be made with two fingers or with three ; but ask him whether it is a greater crime to drink milk on Fridays, or to steal, and he will laugh in your face, with an expression of wonder that a common offence against man can for a moment be compared with the gravest of offences against God, the non-observance of a fast-day. When he speaks of his saints, he is silent as to their virtues, and only enumerates the number of days they passed without food and their numerous acts of self-mortification. A case is recorded of a peasant who, finding that a traveller to whom he had given hospitality had eaten forbidden food on a fast-day, cut off his head with a hatchet while he was asleep, and next morning boasted of the deed as an act of justice. There is, in truth, no such thing as religion in Russia, so far as those professing the orthodox faith are concerned. The educated classes, seeing the corruption and ignorance of the clergy, and the senseless and unmeaning materialism of the religious rite, scoff at the former and completely neglect the latter ; while the mass of the people, taught to regard forms and ceremonies as articles of faith, and with the example of the most frightful venality in those whom they look up to as the ministers of the Divinity daily before their eyes, are attacked by their Church in the very foundations of morality, and find corruption and servility where they have a right to look for virtue and salvation.

As in most young countries, the middle class of Russia is as ye: very imperfectly organized. It comprises, according to the Russian law, all persons not belonging to the class of nobles, clergy, or country people, and is divided into the members of guilds and "notable citizens;" the townsmen; the artisans, or members of trade companies; and the labourers. The guilds and trade companies were established by Catherine II., who also gave municipal bodies to the towns, consisting of all the inhabitants that were merchants, traders, or householders. These bodies elect a mayor and other municipal officers, but, like all other corporate bodies in Russia, are entirely at the mercy of the Government and the officials. The town corporations are responsible for the payment of the taxes due by their members, and for furnishing the regulated number of recruits. Any person wishing to be inscribed on the list of a corporation must produce a certificate from the one to which he formerly belonged, showing that it has consented to his departure, after which the corporation decides whether it will receive him or not. Certain classes of persons, however, who could not have belonged to a corporation before, have the right to be inscribed on the list of any corporation they please. Townsmen may acquire land or house property in their town provided its value does not exceed 7000 roubles (1120*l*.). Corporations may expel such of their members as have been tried for an offence entailing the loss of civil rights, even if they have been acquitted, and the law entertains only a suspicion of their guilt. The corporations of Moscow and St. Petersburg have also the right to order any townsman convicted of bad conduct, or improper delay in the payment of his debts, to be imprisoned in the House of Correction for a term not exceeding two years. These corporations have within the past year obtained a very complicated municipal organization, the details of which we will not inflict on our readers, merely stating that it is based on the principle of a general municipal council for the town, and special sections for the various classes of townsmen, consisting of hereditary nobles; life-nobles, "notable citizens," and strangers; merchants; townsmen inscribed in trade companies; and townsmen not so inscribed. The merchants and traders are divided into three guilds, admission to which is procured by the proved possession of a certain amount of capital. Thus, a capital of 15,000 roubles is required for admission to the first guild, of 6000 for the second, and of 2400 for the third. The members of the first guild have the privilege of trading wholesale in home and foreign goods in all parts of the empire, of founding banking-houses, exchange-offices, and insurance companies, of acting as shippers, and at the same time of retail-trading in the town or district in which they reside. The same privileges, except that of founding banking-houses or exchange-offices, and of importing goods to the value of more than 90,000 roubles, are granted to the merchants of the second guild. The third guild only allows of retail-trading for home or foreign goods, the latter being bought from the merchants of the higher guilds. The members of these guilds are exempt from military service and from corporal punishment, and the sons of merchants of the first guild are admitted to the service of the State on the same footing as nobles. Foreigners are now permitted to enter all the guilds on the same conditions as Russian subjects, and are admitted to the full enjoyment of all the commercial rights conferred on their members. The class of "notable citizens" was founded by the Emperor Nicholas. It comprises the children of life-nobles, and persons of all classes and professions who have acquired a certain standing, and the privileges it confers may be made either hereditary or only tenable during life. These privileges are, exemption from military service, capitation-money, and corporal punishment, and the right of election, on the same footing as the merchants of the first and second guilds, to municipal assemblies. There is, in fact, but little distinction between the "notable citizens" and the nobility, except that the latter have some special privileges in the civil service, which is the career marked out for them by the law. This career, however, still continues to present such advantages to the merchant and citizen class, and the entrance to it is so easy, that it might be almost said the institutions we have above described exist only in name. Their essentially German character, moreover, makes them very ill-adapted to the. Russian, who, as is well remarked by a recent writer,[*] " has remained morally a nomad and an Asiatic, notwithstanding a physical rubbing of Europeanism." The cumbrous guilds and trade-corporations established by the homely Germans only repelled the restless and versatile Russian, who, finding that commerce offered nothing but obstacles to his love of constant motion and change, naturally sought the higher privileges and surer gains of the nobility. Here, again, we find the natural development of the country stopped by the plague of officialism. So long as the system of *tchins* continues, it is hopeless to look for a middle class in Russia.

The abolition of serfage is undoubtedly the glory of the present reign. But nothing short of the exercise of the greatest energy and tact on the part of Alexander II. and his advisers can prevent this glory from being converted into disgrace. Discontents which it was thought necessary to crush by armed force were the ill-omened harbingers of the dawn of liberty in Russia; and although the peasants are now quiet, it is the quiet of sullen dissatisfaction rather than that of contentedness. The causes of this disposition

---

[*] "Organisation Sociale de la Russie." Par un Diplomate.

on the part of the peasants have hardly been justly appreciated in
Europe. It has become the fashion to wonder at the evident
reluctance of the Russian serf to be made a freeman, and much
blame has been very unjustly laid to his charge in consequence.
His saying, that he belongs to his master, but the land belongs to
him, has been quoted over and over again as proving his little
regard for the highest privilege which is possessed by man; and
he has been charged with cupidity and narrow-mindedness in
refusing to accept what is in itself a gain, except with the addition
of material advantages. We shall find much, however, to justify
the Russian peasant in his opposition, if we consider that what is
called freedom in Russia we should call in England only another
kind of slavery. It must be, indeed, obvious, that in a country
where all are the slaves of the Czar and his Government, it matters
very little to a man, so far as his liberty is concerned, whether he
is under the direct control of a noble or a *tchinovnik.* The moral
effect is the same; a freeman must cringe to his superior, place a
guard on his tongue, and often perform the most servile offices,
much in the same manner as the serf. On the other hand, the
serf is often much better off, materially, than the free peasant. We
have already pointed out the greater advantages of his being under
a master who has a personal interest in his prosperity, than under
a *tchinovnik* who cares only to enrich himself at his expense. But,
we shall be told, the free peasants have rights and privileges
accorded them by the law. It may be well here to point out what
these rights and privileges are, both in theory and in practice,
there being usually a wide divergence between the two in Russia.
It is a curiously significant fact, that the promulgation of the law
giving the Crown peasants the rights of freemen was accompanied
by disturbances similar to those which broke out at the first
announcement of the project of emancipation. The reason of these
disturbances was the same in both cases. The Crown peasants
did not object to be made free; but they objected to be granted
rights, which they knew well are in Russia but another name for
endless and vexatious forms, without the slightest value except to
afford a pretext for that sort of persecution which the Russian most
dreads—the oppression of the *tchinovnik.* Their opposition to
being invested with "rights" only too soon showed itself well
grounded. By the law of 1838 the peasants of the Crown domains
acquired similar privileges to those which are to be given to
the emancipated serfs. Their communes acquired a species of
self-government, were to elect their own functionaries, to be responsible for the payment of the taxes to the Government, and to
have absolute control over the distribution of the lands in
their occupation. Nothing could be more liberal or theoretically
just. Everything was provided for; even buildings were erected

for the deliberations of the communal deputies, and fitted up with all the requirements of a free deliberative assembly, including the balloting-urns. But unfortunately the paternal Government of the Czar, fearing, no doubt, that these tremendous preparations would turn the heads of the poor peasants, sent them a functionary or two to keep them in order, and prevent them from taking too large a dose of liberty all at once. This was what the peasants had feared ; and, with their usual suspicion of the official element, they declined to use their privileges on such terms. But it was too late. The Government had given them liberties which were now theirs by law ; and the officials, who were there to execute the law, insisted on making them use their liberties in spite of themselves. We have already shown the working of these liberties in practice. The communal functionaries have become the humble servants of the *tchinovnik*, who oppresses and plunders the commune at his pleasure. The chief of the commune, though elected by the peasants, has no real authority, for the latter only select those in whom they have little or no confidence for an office which is virtually under the orders of the *tchinovnik*. So much is this the case, that the functionary does not treat with the elected chief (*golowa*) in matters of importance to the commune, but with the member of their body in whom they have the most confidence, and who is entrusted by general consent with the care of their interests. Even the elections, though nominally free, are really under the control of the *tchinovnik*, who soon contrives to have both the person and property of every peasant of the commune in his power, by the infractions of the innumerable and vexatious regulations which are constantly occurring, and the real crimes and acts of dishonesty to which the peasants are often driven by his own example or at his own instigation.* Such have been the results of the grant of so-called rights to the Crown peasants ; and a glance at the main features of the emancipation scheme will show that it contains no provision whatever against the occurrence of a similar state of things in the free communes now to be established.

The serfs were divided into two classes, those attached to the soil (*krepostnye*), and the household serfs, or slaves (*dvorovye*). The former cultivated a certain portion of land for their own support, and owed to their masters either a certain number of days' labour in the week, or a money payment in lieu (*obrok*) ; the latter were either employed in the household of their masters, or worked elsewhere on their own account, paying to their masters

---

* The system of recruiting also places immense power in the hands of the country officials. It is conducted nominally by lot, but really by selection, the official giving the good numbers to his friends and the rich peasants, who pay him liberally for exemption from a service which is justly dreaded in Russia.

an *obrok* regulated according to the profits of their labour. The emancipation of the household serfs was of course an easy matter, it being only a question of the amount of compensation to be awarded to the master for the loss of his serf's *obrok*, or personal service. This compensation has been fixed at the very low sum of sixty roubles (9*l*.), payable in two years, after which period the household serf becomes a freeman, with exemption from service in the army and from the payment of taxes for two years, which period is increased to four years if he becomes inscribed on the list of a city commune, or six if on that of a country commune. These privileges are given to check the spread of proletarianism, of which there is some danger when so large a body of men are thrown on their own resources. The measure is a liberal one if we look upon it as an emancipation of the serf from the personal control of his master, although it presses very hard upon those nobles whose serfs, as not unfrequently happened, made large incomes by trade. But it would be very incorrect to speak of it as a transition from slavery to freedom. Having a constitutional dislike to agriculture, and there being nothing to bind him to the soil, the emancipated *dvorovy* will probably become a small trader in a town, and there find that his boasted freedom is nothing but a change of masters, the *gorodnitchy* being as cruel, as rapacious, and as oppressive as his late lord had been. Nor is this all ; as a townsman and a freeman, he is obliged to exercise his right of election to the posts of mayor or assessor at the provincial tribunals. Appointments to these offices are universally avoided, as it is known that the holders of them are treated with the grossest indignity by the Government officials. The municipal assessors are expected to receive the orders of these officials with blind obedience, and it is by no means rare to see an assessor pulling off a *tchinovnik's* boots or lighting the fire in the hall where he is supposed to take part in the deliberations. Let us now turn to the serfs attached to the soil. It is known that their case presented great difficulties, in consequence of the land on which they work being claimed both by themselves and their masters. We shall not enter into the question which of these claims was just ; but it seems to us that the Government having once laid down the principle that a portion of the land, though belonging to the master, should be appropriated to the support of the serf, would have settled the question equitably and to the satisfaction of both parties by giving the serf a certain allotment of land unconditionally, and compensating the master by grants from the State Treasury. As it is, the transitory period fixed by the law of the 19th February (3rd March), 1861, extends to nine years, and even then the *krepostny* does not necessarily become emancipated. During the whole of this time he continues to owe service, or its equivalent, to his master, and he is said to be "under a temporary obligation." The first two years were given to enable the peasants to come to a voluntary agreement with their masters, without the intervention of the Government, with regard to the amount of rent they were to pay in lieu of giving service or paying *obrok;* in the next four years the Government was to step in, for the purpose of enforcing such contracts as had been made, and of fixing the amount of rent in the cases where such amount was not agreed upon; and the last three years were to be dedicated to arranging the purchase of the soil by the peasants, and thus finally converting them into free proprietors. This complicated arrangement has naturally given great dissatisfaction both to the peasants and the proprietors, the former being only offered the prospect of a doubtful liberty after a long series of years, and the latter finding their property depreciated by the unsettled condition of their serfs. The peasants, who have extracted out of the voluminous regulations for their emancipation but one impression—that they are promised their freedom—refuse to accept anything in the shape of a compromise, and work as little as they can, under the persuasion that complete emancipation must come sooner or later. The result has been the appointment of a multitude of officials to compel the peasant to become a sort of tenant farmer, paying a fixed rent in money or work for his house and garden and his piece of arable land, instead of giving a variable amount of work or paying *obrok* to his master. This task will be a difficult one; but the next step, the transformation of the farmer into a peasant proprietor, is so totally opposed to the character and disposition of the Russian people, that it is a marvel the Government should ever have contemplated it. There is no institution so popular in Russia, or whose principle is so firmly adhered to among the lower classes, as that of the commune. This principle may be briefly stated as the equal division of the property of an organized corporation among its members. Thus in a Russian village, constituting a commune in itself, the land is equally divided among the *tiaglos* (a married man and his wife and children under age) every year. This primitive institution, faulty and bad in principle as it undoubtedly is, exists in every Russian village and in many of the artisan companies or *artells* for which the Russians are so famous. The Government, however, not only destroys the communal system at one blow by making the peasants purchase their allotments separately, but makes this purchase so onerous that it is obliged to aid them by a loan, which they will have to repay by yearly instalments, and further forbids them to alienate any portion of their property until the loan is paid. As if to create the greatest possible dissatisfaction both among nobles and peasants on the eve of the final emancipation, the Government has also decided, in the very numerous cases where the nobles are debtors to the State, to deduct the purchase-money of their peasants from the amount of their debt. The absurdity of this arrangement is so evident, that several modifications of it have been under consideration, but as yet we believe without any result.

While the serfs are thus being forced into liberty, "rights" have been given them, similar to those of the Crown peasants. The communes are to have their self-elected chiefs, and a certain number of them is to form a district (*volost*), which is also to have its self-elected president, and a judicial tribunal elected among its members. The formation of these *volosts*, however, depends on the decision of a committee composed of nobles and functionaries; and as the proper union of certain communes in *volosts* is of high importance to the peasant, he becomes at once exposed to a certain degree of official influence. Moreover, as in the Crown communes, the communal officials are really at the mercy of the *tchinovnik*. A justice of the peace, appointed from among the nobles by the Governor of the province, exercises judicial and administrative functions in the commune, deciding differences between landlord and peasant, dismissing at his pleasure the chief of the commune, and acting under the orders of the higher functionaries of the district.

We are now in a position to form an exact estimate of the benefits which have so far accrued to the serf from the system of emancipation. Those household serfs who have paid the fixed amount of compensation to their masters are, in the Russian sense, free; that is to say, they are no longer the property of a noble, are enabled to work on their own account, and have exchanged private for political oppression. The position of the agricultural serfs is not quite so clear. They are still bound to work for their masters, and are subject to his rule, but under Government superintendence. They are offered their freedom (still in the Russian sense), but at the cost of sacrifices they are unwilling to make; and they have been given rights and institutions which are neutralized by official interference. Their position does not appear an enviable one; but it is right to quote here the words of the Imperial manifesto, describing the state of things for which it has been substituted:—"The faculty of acquiring personal rights over the peasants and of giving up those rights to other persons; of moving peasants from one estate to another; of engaging peasants, by order of their actual proprietor, in the service of strangers; of putting out minors as apprentices, or in educational establishments; and, of shutting up the peasants in houses of correction, or placing them at the disposal of the Government;" *i.e.* sending them to Siberia at the absolute pleasure of the master.

Compared with this, the present position of the serf is at least tolerable, immeasurably removed as it is from that of a freeman. The truth is, that more credit is due to the present Emperor for the idea of emancipation (although he was by no means the first, either on the throne or among the people of Russia, to conceive it), and for the determination with which he acted on it, than for the manner of its execution. The development of that idea has at length aroused the Russian people from their long slumber, and has stirred thoughts and feelings in them such as they had never before known.

What will be the result of this awakening of the Russian nation ?—is a question which has been often put during the agitation of the last four years, and which none who were acquainted with Russia could answer to their satisfaction. Those who saw, in the discontented speeches of the nobles and the indefinite utterances of the press, the expression of the determination of a whole people to free themselves from the bond of a secular slavery, mistook the weak and trembling accents of the infant for the decided language of the full-grown man. The history of the Russian people had never before offered an instance of a national movement which could in any sense be called liberal ; and ideas of liberty do not spring like full-grown Minervas from the brain of those who have lived among slaves, and been themselves slaves, ever since they have constituted a nation, even after a course of liberal literature and a six months' tour in the free countries of Europe. The greatest despotism on the Continent is, compared with that of Russia, a democracy, and yet even on the Continent we find liberal ideas still in a very crude and undeveloped state. Unlike the other nations of Europe, Russia never had an aristocracy to curb the power of the Sovereign, or a middle class to fight the battle of public right and of civic liberty. Born in the midst of carnage and rapine, she passed the stormy days of her lawless youth in incessant wars with neighbouring nations, and while the vassal of the Great Khan, was little better than a Tartar horde under a despotic chief. This state of things continued after the Mongol yoke was shaken off ; the States-General, being composed of the official nobility, were entirely at the command of the Czar, except during the six years which followed the national rising against the Poles in 1612 ; and there were not at that time even the elements of a middle class. Since 1618 the only shadow of a popular institution that ever existed in Russia, the States-General, has been assembled but once, in 1767, by the Empress Catherine, for the alleged purpose of reforming the laws and the institutions of the country. A conversation which took place on that memorable occasion was characteristic and significant :—" When we have prepared the code of laws and it is in full

execution," inquired a deputy, "will there still be ukases?"—
"Certainly," was the reply.—"In that case," said the deputy, "it
is perfectly useless for us to lose our time in making laws." This
is, after all, the rock on which every reform in Russia must eventually break. However excellent and liberal the law may be, an
ukase can always reverse or nullify it. This state of things, which
would be unendurable to any one living under our Western civilization, has only been exceptionally objected to by the Russians.
"The Russian," says M. Ivan Golovin, "is a despotic animal."
Every village and every family has a self-imposed Czar, who rules
despotically over his submissive subjects. The eminently Russian
principle of the commune, by equalizing the property and the rank
of all, and thus preventing a gradation of authority, forces the
many to be subject to the individual. The Russian peasant hates
the official, but he reveres the Czar as a sacred being placed above
the petty passions of this world—as a beneficent divinity, watching over his prosperity, and protecting him against his enemies.
He will murder without scruple an oppressive proprietor or official; but he would as soon think of rebelling against God as
against the Czar. Call upon him to fight for his freedom, and he
will not understand you; but tell him you will avenge his wrongs
upon the nobles and the officials, and he will follow you to the
end of the world. All the popular revolts have had this object;
and the most important of them all, that of Pugaczew, in the
reign of the Empress Catherine, owed its extraordinary success to
the further circumstance that Pugaczew gave himself out to be the
Czar Peter III. The present discontent among the lower classes
of Russia has arisen solely from the fear that their material prosperity will be injured by the emancipation. Even the Association
which the more extreme of the malcontents have formed, proclaims
its object by its title: "*Zemlia i Volia*"—our own land and our own
will. By their own will they say that they mean their will to have
daily bread assured to them. There is here, no doubt, the germ
of an idea of liberty; but it is only a very small germ after all. If
we look higher, we shall find finer phrases, but, stripped of their
rhetorical ornaments, they will be seen to convey much the same
sentiments and ideas. There is, it is true, a sort of jargon of
liberalism which every Russian gentleman thinks it his duty to
use on certain occasions. It enables him to display his civilization to Europeans, and to amuse himself by playing at sedition
with his intimate friends in the seclusion of his study. It is
even thought quite proper and gentlemanlike to have belonged
to a real conspiracy in one's youth, and people boast of their
achievements in this way as they boast of their duels, amours, and
other youthful follies. Mouravieff himself was a conspirator when
he was a young man. But all this masquerading leads to nothing.

As the Russians grow old, they cast off the liberalism of their youth as they do their horses and their mistresses, and enter upon the seriousness of life with a boundless veneration for the Czar, and an eager desire for a good *tchin.* We are told by a profound and witty writer on Russia, that the Polish exiles have frequently met with Russians in Siberia who, while expressing the profoundest sympathy for their sufferings, said to them with touching simplicity: "You have suffered much, your hair begins to grow grey ; it is time you gave up your exalted ideas." At the same time it cannot be said that there are no real liberals in Russia. There are some such, noble and generous men penetrated with a deep sorrow for the state of their country ; but they are lost in the crowd. The first appearance of these men in Russia dates from the return of Alexander I. from his European campaigns. Many of the more intelligent of the officers who had accompanied him had been struck with boundless surprise and admiration at a freedom of which they had until then had no idea. These men brought the language and ideas of liberalism into Russia, where they soon became popular, and were even encouraged by the Czar. No practical consequences, however, ensued ; much was said, but nothing was done. At length the death of Alexander, by raising a question of disputed succession, seemed to favour the projects of the liberals, who fondly imagined that the whole country only awaited their signal to rise in insurrection. They were miserably deceived ; even their own troops refused to aid them until they were told they were to fight for Constantine and the Constitution, the latter being Constantine's wife ; and the insurrection of 1826 was crushed in a few hours after a military riot, the great body of the people not knowing to this day when it occurred, what were its objects, or who were its leaders. The next public appearance of liberalism in Russia was in 1859, when the nobles of the principal provinces of the Empire petitioned for a reform of abuses, and even hinted at a Constitution. The causes of this phenomenon—the disasters of the Crimean war, the accession of a liberal Emperor, who inaugurated his reign by an amnesty and a relaxation of the passport and censorship systems, and finally, the disorganization of society caused by the abolition of serfage, are well known. The agitation of the whole country was tremendous ; the cumbrous machine of Government seemed to be yielding to the irresistible force of a determined national will ; and blinded by the rapidity with which events succeeded each other, deafened by the noise, even the experienced and the thoughtful believed for a moment that the regeneration of Russia was at hand. But the blow soon came that was to test the solidity of the liberal professions of the Russians. The Polish insurrection broke out, and dashed all the glittering but unsubstantial liberalism of the Russian nobles and the Russian press to fragments. The Goddess of Liberty was replaced in the worship of liberal Russia by Mouravieff; the circulation in Russia of the *Kolokol*, which before the insurrection was counted by thousands, has dwindled down to eight hundred, simply because it has remained true to its principles; and the enslavement of a neighbouring country is openly advocated by the very men who, two years ago, were the most clamorous in vindicating the freedom of their own. The sad truth has been forced upon the world, that Russia's liberalism is not seriously meant, and that she is therefore as yet powerless to disentangle herself from the corrupt mass of officialism which sucks the life-blood from her body. The prospect is not cheering; for the longer the country is denied the blessings of liberty, the more deeply must the corruption of officialism eat into the national character, and the less fitted will the nation be to achieve its freedom. Whether Russia will pass through her present state of transition without a revolution, must depend on circumstances which it is at present impossible to foresee. One thing, however, is clear—that a revolution, if it really and seriously breaks out, can only degenerate into a jacquerie; for there are no popular grievances in Russia but such as are founded on purely material wants. The dissatisfaction of the higher classes of society, purged of those speculative elements which are merely the product of the example and the teachings of a civilization they are yet unable to understand, reduces itself to an unwillingness to be deprived of a portion of their property in order to compensate the peasants for the losses they would suffer by the scheme of emancipation; while the peasants openly proclaim that nothing will satisfy them but the unconditional grant of the land which they and their ancestors have always occupied. On the other hand, there is the constitutional indolence and want of initiative of the Russian character, combined with the unqualified adoration of the Czar, which has always hitherto prevented popular insurrections from becoming general. Much will depend on the course that will be adopted by the Government. It has been well remarked that, to save Russia, it is necessary to begin by amending the character of her people. Obviously the first step in this direction must be, to cut away the root of the evil, by completely abolishing the system of *tchins,* and calling to the councils of the sovereign men who have shown themselves true liberals, with a sincere desire for reform. Popular institutions might then be introduced, without any fear of their being nullified by the reactionary spirit of the officials. It is true that, for a long time, the people will not be fit to exercise their new liberties; but there is no such improver of the morals of a nation as freedom. When Naples was annexed to Piedmont, the corruption of the Neapolitans was found to be so great, that it was proposed to give them a separate Government with more limited liberties than those of the Piedmontese. The proposal was summarily rejected by Cavour, who said that it were better to give the Neapolitans complete liberty even at the cost of some inconvenience, than to deprive them of what is every man's hereditary birthright. We recommend these noble words of the great Italian Minister to the statesmen of Russia. It is certain that the gradual extinction, by a corrupt and debasing political system, of all sense of individual freedom and moral principle in a powerful nation of seventy millions of kind-hearted and intelligent people, must expose to the gravest dangers, not only its own moral and material interests, but also the liberties and the civilization of the other nations of Europe. But if, as we hope and believe, it is not yet too late to raise the Russian people from their moral degradation—if honesty and the sense of personal dignity are the sure accompaniments of true liberty—if free institutions always bring moral happiness in the train of material wealth, Russia, under a firm but discerning ruler, may yet be saved the disgrace of becoming either the soulless tool of an autocrat, or the home of socialism in its worst and most repulsive form.

ART. IX.—THE PHYSIOLOGY OF SLEEP.

1. *Le Sommeil et les Rêves. Etudes Psychologiques sur ces Phénomènes et les divers Etats qui s'y rattachent.* Par M. L. F. ALFRED MAURY. Paris: 1862.
2. *On Sleep.* By Sir H. HOLLAND. In "Chapters on Mental Physiology." 2nd edit. London: 1858.
3. *The Physiology of Sleep.* By ARTHUR E. DURHAM. In "Guy's Hospital Reports." London: 1860.

THERE is much about sleep that is familiar to all: there is much that is at present known to none: there is much also that to many seems mysterious, which nevertheless, when rightly considered, is clear and comprehensible. We propose in the following pages to discuss especially certain of the phenomena of sleep, which have been the subjects of recent scientific investigation, and to refer to the more familiar phenomena only as they are associated with processes of internal change hitherto little thought of or altogether unrecognised. With respect to the many deeply interesting points upon which we have neither information to give, nor explanation to suggest, we would only say, that these, like all other phenomena and laws of nature as yet beyond our ken, although unexplained hitherto, must not be regarded as therefore inexplicable for ever; nor because uninvestigated and unknown at present, as therefore mysterious and beyond our future powers of research. It seems to have been —nay still to be—very generally supposed alike by physiologists and metaphysicians, that the nature of sleep is peculiarly inexplicable, and veiled in impenetrable mystery. Such a supposition is erroneous and mischievous. Erroneous—inasmuch as it attributes to assumed obscurity of the subject difficulties which arise from our own ignorance and inaptitude: mischievous —inasmuch as it necessarily tends to chill the spirit of inquiry, and to stay at their very commencement researches fraught with scientific interest and practical importance.

Now, in order to arrive at a full conception of the nature of sleep, and to learn from its phenomena all we may of the secrets of our being, we must study thoroughly both its anatomy and physiology, so to speak; and not confine our attention to its psychology alone, as most philosophical writers have hitherto been content to do.

Every one has some general idea, founded on personal experience, of what is meant by sleep. And yet, strange as it may seem, it is by no means easy to give a satisfactory description, much less an accurate definition, of this familiar but truly wonderful state. It is even difficult, as Sir H. Holland observes, "to distinguish that which is its most perfect condition—the condition furthest removed from the waking state." Some maintain that we are conscious, others that we are unconscious, during sleep. Some assert that we always dream when asleep, others that dreams occur only between sleeping and waking, or during imperfect sleep. Indeed, on these and many other points connected with our subject, the greatest possible diversity of opinion prevails among different writers. Such diversity of opinion may be to a certain extent explained by the following considerations. First—the sleeping experiences of differently constituted individuals differ in the same way, though by no means in the same degree, as their waking experience; and hence different observers, judging each from his own experience, may have arrived at somewhat different conclusions. Secondly —"Sleep is not a *unity of state*, but a series of fluctuating conditions;" and thus it may have happened that some have regarded one *phase*, and some another phase, as the most perfect. Thirdly—Many theories of sleep have evidently been adopted because of their conformity with favourite metaphysical creeds, rather than because of their accordance with the simple teachings of experience and observation.

Sir H. Holland and Mr. Durham, regarding the subject from perfectly distinct points of view, express their opinions as to the nature of sleep in very different terms. The former considers sleep in its most general, the latter in its most special, acceptation. Sir Henry Holland writes as follows:—

" Sleep, in the most general and correct sense of the term, must be regarded not as one single state, but a succession of states in constant variation—this variation consisting, not only in the different degrees in which the same sense or faculty is submitted to it; but also in the different proportions in which these several powers are under its influence at the same time. We thus associate together under a common principle all the phenomena, however remote and anomalous they may seem;—from the bodily acts of the somnambulist; the vivid, but inconsequent trains of thought excited by external impressions; the occasional acute exercise of the intellect; and the energy of emotion—to that profound sleep in which no impressions are received by the senses;—no volition is exercised; and no consciousness or memory is left, on waking, of the thoughts or feelings which have existed in the mind. Instead of regarding many of these facts as exceptions and anomalies, it is sounder in reason to adopt such definitions of sleep as may practically include them all."—p. 15.

Mr. Durham, on the other hand, says:—

" Considered *psychologically* I think sleep may be best defined to be a state in which volition, sensation, and consciousness are suspended, but can be readily restored upon the application of some stimulus. 'That sleep alone is healthy,' says Dr. Wilson Philip, ' from which we can be easily aroused. If our fatigue has been such as to render it more profound, it partakes of the nature of disease.'

" Considered *physiologically*, sleep may be most correctly regarded as that particular state of cerebral inactivity which is essentially associated with the nutrition and repair of the brain substance."

These descriptions—we can hardly call them definitions—of sleep are by no means opposed to one another, as they may at first sight appear. Both, we think, may be accepted as true, though neither conveys the whole truth. Their apparent difference manifestly arises from the fact that Sir H. Holland speaks of *actual*, Mr. Durham of *typical* sleep. The one, therefore, describes sleep as it ordinarily occurs; the other, the most perfect sleep that can be conceived. The observations and experiments which Mr. Durham adduces, and the line of argument he pursues in his interesting paper, not only fully support his own hypothesis, but tend also to show, *a priori*, why sleep must necessarily be, as Sir H. Holland rightly maintains, " a succession of ever-varying states."

Every part of the body the office of which is vital, not simply mechanical, passes through alternate periods of rest and action. " The heart pauses after each pulsation, and every breath we draw is followed by a period during which the nerves and muscles of respiration repose before they are again aroused to action." Every one knows that it is impossible to maintain very long any particular position by unaided muscular exertion. After a certain period of action the muscles require a proportionate period of rest. So also with the organs of sense—the brain and every other vital part. These alternating periods of rest and action vary in duration in different parts. Thus the heart acts and rests seventy or eighty times, and often more, in a minute. The voluntary muscles can be made to maintain their active condition for several minutes ; and the organs of sense and brain for longer periods. But in all cases the due proportion of rest to action must be accorded, or the health of the part inevitably deteriorates. Every-day experience teaches us that this is true : physiology shows us why it must be so.

During each period of action the tissue of the part (that is to say, the material substance of which it is made up) is consumed and wastes ;—during rest the tissue is nourished, and the waste repaired. Temporary inaction appears to be essential to perfect repair. Different parts of the same organ, as for instance different parts of a muscle or of the brain, may no doubt be in different conditions at the same time. One part may be in action and undergoing waste, while another part is at rest and undergoing repair ; but there is reason to believe, as we shall by and by be able to show, that in the same part the two conditions of action and waste, on the one hand, and of rest and repair on the other, cannot co-exist ; or at any rate, if they do, only for a time, inasmuch as, sooner or later, the waste outruns the repair. We do not know—we cannot even guess—the precise nature of this intimate connexion between waste of tissue, and development of function (or action) of a part ; but that such a connexion exists we have ample evidence.

We sometimes hear the expression, " the lamp of life." The simile is by no means a bad one. When a lamp is duly prepared and lighted, chemical action is started. This action goes on for a time ; the oil is consumed ; heat is developed, and light is manifest. By and by fresh oil must be added and the lamp trimmed. While it is burning, the products of its combustion— the new substances formed by the chemical action going on— must be got rid of, or they would speedily extinguish the flame. Just so is it with the tissues of our body. Let the proper stimulus be supplied to any living, healthy part—say brain, or say muscle —and it becomes as it were lighted up. In this as in the former case, chemical action is started, chemical change goes on, the material is consumed, and the products of its destruction must be conveyed away. But in this instance instead of heat and *light,* we have developed heat and the *manifestation of the life*—or, in a word, the function—of the part. Whether the chemical changes which take place in the flame of the lamp are the cause of the heat and light, or whether the heat and light are the cause of the chemical changes, we cannot tell. Neither can we tell whether the chemical changes which go on in certain organs of our body are the cause or the consequence of their functional activity. This much is certain in both cases—the particular chemical changes are inseparably associated with the more visible phenomena ; and when the material is exhausted, or from any other cause the normal processes of chemical action are interfered with or stopped, the other phenomena are modified or altogether cease.

Consciousness, Sensation, Volition, Emotion, and Intelligence, are all manifestations of the brain's functional activity. Concomitantly with the manifestation of these—the highest attributes of our being, and to a proportionate extent, chemical changes take place in the brain which necessarily involve the destruction of certain portions of its substance. In order that the waste may be repaired, temporary cessation from action is, as we have seen, requisite. Functional activity of the brain, then, as manifested by sense and intellect, emotion and will, together with destruction of brain-substance, may be regarded as the essential psychological and physiological conditions of perfect wakefulness ; and rest of the brain (suspension to a greater or less extent of those faculties which are the manifestations of its activity), together with repair and nutrition of brain-substance, may be regarded as the corresponding conditions of perfect sleep.

Now, if what has already been advanced be true, it is evident that great and palpable differences must exist between the state of the brain during sleep and that which is associated with the performance of its marvellous functions during waking life. " It is plain," says Sir Benjamin Brodie,* "that in some respects the condition of the nervous system must be different during sleep from what it is when we are awake ; but it seems impossible that we should know in what that difference consists, when we consider that neither our unassisted vision, nor the microscope, nor chemical analysis, nor any analogy, nor any other means at our disposal, enables us to form any kind of notion as to the actual changes in the brain or spinal cord on which any other nervous phenomena depend." From the opinion thus expressed, Mr. Durham does not hesitate to dissent ; and he appears, as far as we are able to judge from

---

* " Psychological Inquiries," part i. p. 134.

his paper, fully to justify the belief he expresses :—" that the
examination of the living brain [exposed as he describes, especially when the eye is aided by the microscope], together with the
careful consideration of certain obvious analogies, may do much
towards enabling us to penetrate the mystery of the subject, and
to advance some steps in the right understanding of the true
nature of sleep, and of some other conditions of the nervous
system."—p. 2.

Considered *anatomically*, so to speak, sleep may be described,
in accordance with the views of Mr. Durham, as a state in which
the bloodvessels of the brain are occupied by a comparatively
small quantity of blood moving at a comparatively slow rate.

"During sleep the brain is in a comparatively bloodless condition;
and the blood in the encephalic vessels is not only diminished in quantity, but moves with diminished rapidity."—p. 24.

That such a state of the circulation in the brain is actually
present during sleep has been proved by observation and experiment.   A case is recorded by Caldwell,[*] and quoted by Durham,
of a woman at Montpellier, who " had lost part of her skull (from
disease), the brain and part of its membranes lying bare.   When
she was in a deep or sound sleep, the brain lay in the skull almost
motionless ;   when she was dreaming, it became elevated ;   and
when her dreams (which she related on waking) were vivid or interesting, the brain was protruded through the cranial aperture."

Blumenbach also describes cases in which, portions of the skull
having been lost, " he witnessed a sinking of the brain during
sleep, and a swelling with blood when the patient awoke."

Similar cases have been, and are to be, met with from time
to time—indeed, there is one such under the writer's observation
at the present time ;   but the evidence afforded by them is
necessarily more or less incomplete and unsatisfactory.   The
brain and its membranes, when exposed in the human subject, by
accident or disease, have always more or less lost their normal
appearance before accurate comparative observations can be made
with safety to the patient.

Now it occurred to Mr. Durham, " that the artificial exposure
of the brains of living animals might afford opportunity for more
definite observation" than could be made in such cases as those
alluded to.   Accordingly he performed numerous experiments
upon different animals.   " The results obtained were uniform
when the necessary and accidental difficulties of the case were
successfully overcome."

Mr. Durham describes his method of proceeding, and what he
witnessed, as follows :—

---

* " Psychological Journal," vol. v. p. 74.

"A dog having been thoroughly chloroformed, a portion of bone about as large as a shilling was removed from the parietal region of the skull by means of the trephine, and the subjacent dura mater partially cut away. The portion of brain thus exposed, seemed inclined to rise into the opening through the bone. The large vessels over the surface were somewhat distended, and no manifest difference in colour between the arteries and veins could be distinguished. As the effects of the chloroform passed off, the animal sank into a comparatively natural and healthy sleep. Corresponding changes took place in the appearance of the brain; its surface became pale, and sank down rather below the level of the bone; the veins were no longer distended. Small vessels containing blood of arterial hue, could be distinctly seen, and many which had before appeared congested and full of dark blood, could scarcely be distinguished. After a time the animal was roused; a blush seemed to start over the surface of the brain, which again rose into the opening through the bone. As the animal was more and more excited, the pia mater became more and more excited, and the brain-substance more and more tinged with blood; the surface was of a bright red colour; innumerable vessels, unseen while sleep continued, were now everywhere visible, and the blood seemed to be coursing through them very rapidly; the veins, like the arteries and capillaries, were full and distended, but their difference of colour as well as their size rendered them clearly distinguishable. After a short period the animal was fed, and again allowed to sink into repose; the bloodvessels gradually resumed their former dimensions and appearance, and the surface of the brain became pale as before. The animal slept in a perfectly natural manner. The contrast between the appearance of the brain during its period of functional activity and during its state of repose or sleep was most remarkable."

In order to obviate certain objections, actual or possible, Mr. Durham, in some of his experiments, "replaced the portions of bone removed by accurately fitting watch-glasses, and rendered the junction of their edges with the bone air-tight by means of inspissated Canada balsam." The different appearances of the brains of animals thus treated could be satisfactorily observed through the windows in their skulls, and "were found to correspond as nearly as possible with the above description."

Whatever may be the opinion of Anti-vivisectionists as to the justifiability of Mr. Durham's operations, there can be no doubt that the results he obtained are most interesting and valuable. They place beyond question what might possibly have been *a priori* supposed, but certainly could never have been so satisfactorily proved in any other manner.

Now the skull cannot alter in capacity from time to time so as to adapt itself to the ever-varying state of its contents; neither can the brain itself (as far as its proper substance is concerned) be supposed to undergo any notable changes in bulk in the course of a few minutes or seconds; and yet the cavity of the skull must always be completely filled. How, then, it may be asked, can there possibly be more blood in the vessels of the brain at one time than another? The consideration of the difficulty thus indicated has led many physiologists into the error of supposing that the total quantity of blood in the encephalic vessels must always be the same, but is differently distributed between the arteries, capillaries, and veins during different states of the brain. But the fact is, the brain and its membranes, their bloodvessels and contents, *never* entirely fill the interior of the skull. There is, in addition, a fluid, called the cerebro-spinal fluid, which occupies to a greater or less extent certain cavities in the brain (the ventricles), and also the space between two of the membranes of the brain— viz., the visceral layer of the arachnoid and the pia mater. This fluid appears, as far as we at present know, to be subservient to mechanical purposes only. It has been proved by experiment to be very variable in quantity. It can very readily be taken up into the bloodvessels or driven out of the skull into the spinal canal, on the one hand, or, on the other, under changed conditions, equally readily secreted, or rather simply exuded from the bloodvessels, or forced up from the spinal canal into the skull, by atmospheric pressure acting through the soft parts of the body. Magendie, Hilton, Ecker, and other physiologists, have demonstrated experimentally the great rapidity with which this fluid can be absorbed and produced according to circumstances; and, as Mr. Durham observes, " it is evident, from the anatomy of the parts, that as the encephalic bloodvessels become distended, the fluid can easily pass from the ventricles to the base of the brain, and from the sub-arachnoid spaces within the cranium into that of the spinal canal. When, on the other hand, the amount of blood in the vessels undergoes diminution, the pressure of the atmosphere on the surface of the body (transmitted by the soft tissues) causes the reascent of an equivalent amount of cerebrospinal fluid." It may further be added, that for purely physical reasons—in other words, in accordance with the recognised laws of endosmosis and exosmosis of fluids—the distended state of the vessels and the rapid movement of the blood through them, which we have seen to be associated with functional activity of the brain, favour absorption, whereas the opposite conditions of the vessels and their contents associated with repose favour secretion, of the cerebro-spinal fluid. Thus the constant repletion of the cranial cavity is maintained, and at the same time the necessary variation in the quantity of blood circulating through the vessels of the brain is permitted.

The correctness of the conclusion at which we have now arrived as to the comparative state of the cerebral circulation during sleeping and waking, although most clearly established by methods which few have opportunity or inclination to pursue, is nevertheless confirmed by every-day facts patent to the observation of all.

It is further supported by the experience of the physician in the treatment of patients whose chief complaint is their "want of sleep."

First, there is a beautiful experiment, ready prepared by nature, of which almost every one may make use. The bones of the skull of a newly-born infant are, as is well known, so far separated that variations in the state of the cerebral circulation and the comparative quantity of blood within the cranium may be to a certain extent appreciated by the touch, for the superficial structures are thin and yielding. If these openings in the skull (or fontanelles) are carefully examined, it will be found that, corresponding to them, there are slight depressions of the surface when the infant is asleep, slight elevations when the infant is awake, and proportionately greater elevations during periods of unusual excitement. Again, every one knows that a hot head with "flushed cheeks and throbbing temples, but cold clammy hands and feet, and a general pallor and sense of chilliness over the surface of the body," are conditions very unfavourable to sleep. In such a case the vessels of the brain are manifestly full and the cerebral circulation active. On the other hand, it is equally well known that coolness of the head with warmth of the extremities are invariably associated with easy sleep ; and such conditions imply a comparatively large supply of blood to the general surface rather than to the brain. In many cases of sleeplessness from over-excitement of the brain, Mr. Durham tells us—and general experience will bear out his statement—that "a warm bath, or even immersion of the feet and legs in hot water, acts like a charm." He adds, "The explanation is obvious. An increased quantity of blood is drawn to the surface of the body, even to the extremities, and proportionate relief is given to the long-distended vessels of the brain." The atmospheric boot of Junot, and the centrifugal bed of the elder Darwin, two instruments designed to induce sleep (by processes apparently very uncomfortable, to say the least), owed their efficacy to the fact that they drew or diverted the blood from the head towards the extremities, and thus tended to diminish the activity of the cerebral circulation. But perhaps some of the most striking practical illustrations of the correctness of Mr. Durham's views regarding the nature of sleep are afforded by certain results obtained by Dr. John Chapman, to which we would for a moment allude.

In the *Medical Times and Gazette* of 18th July, 1863, Dr.

Chapman published a paper, since reprinted,* on " A New Meth
of treating Disease by controlling the Circulation of the Blo
in different parts of the Body." In this paper he says :——

"I have discovered that a controlling power over the circulation
the blood in the brain, in the spinal cord, in the ganglia of the nervo
system, and, through the agency of these nervous centres, also
every other organ of the body, can be exercised by means of cold a
heat applied to different parts of the back. . . . If it be desirable
increase the circulation in any given part of the body, this I ha
found myself able to effect by exerting a soothing, sedative, depressir
or paralysing influence (according to the amount of power require
over those ganglia of the sympathetic which send vaso-motor nerves
the part intended to be acted on. This influence may be exerted
applying ice to the central part of the back, over a width of from fo
to four inches and a-half, and extending longitudinally over the par
cular segments of the sympathetic and of the spinal cord on which
is desired to act. For example, intending to direct a fuller and me
equable flow of blood to the brain, I apply ice to the back of the ne
and between the scapulæ. . . . The thoracic and abdominal visce
can be influenced in like manner ; while the legs and feet can have th
circulation so increased that they become thoroughly warm by
applied to the lower part of the back."

On the other hand, the application of heat to the same pa
(by means of hot-water bags) produces opposite effects, lessenii
the circulation in the parts under the control of those portions
the nervous centres along the back over which it is applied.

Now the bearing of Dr. Chapman's discovery upon the subje
we are discussing is at once obvious. He has already publish
evidence† that cold applied to the back of the neck increases t
cerebral circulation, and with it the functional activity of t
brain. He has, moreover, most kindly furnished us privately wi
the details of numerous cases under his observation but not
published, which show, in the most striking manner, that he
applied to the back of the neck palpably diminishes the circu
tion in the head, and at the same time favours, or rather, actual
induces, sleep. We cannot forbear adding that we consider E
Chapman's observations deserving of the most attentive consider
tion, both of the scientific physiologist and the practical ph
sician.

We may next proceed to inquire, why comparative fulness
the bloodvessels of the brain and rapidity of the circulation a

---

* See Appendix to "Functional Diseases of Women : a New Method
treating them through the Agency of the Nervous System by means of C
and Heat." By John Chapman, M.D. London: Trübner and Co.—So
account of this pamphlet is given in our review of the Contemporary Lite
ture of Science (Section 3).

† Op. cit.

thus associated with waking activity, and why the opposite conditions are associated with sleep.

We have already alluded to the fact that peculiar chemical changes go on in the brain concomitantly with, and in a measure proportionate to, its functional activity. These chemical changes appear from recent investigations to consist principally in the oxidation of certain portions of the brain-substance. If this be true, it is plain that a rapid and large supply of arterial or highly oxygenized blood must be to the brain what a large and free current of air is to a lamp or furnace. It affords a due supply of the element essential to the particular chemical changes which have to take place. And further, much in the same way as a good blast not only supplies oxygen abundantly, but also serves to carry off from the furnace or lamp the products of combustion, so the rapidity with which the blood courses through the vessels during functional activity not only supplies oxygen to the tissue, but favours absorption into the vessels of the products of disintegration, and materially contributes to their speedy removal from parts where their presence would be injurious.

On the other hand, absence of distension of the vessels, and comparative slowness of the current, are conditions which do not supply sufficient oxygen for functional activity, but which, according to simple physical laws, favour that exosmosis of nutrient material into the tissue which is necessary for repair.

Whatever may be the nature of the vital processes by which nutrition (or the incorporation of fresh material with living tissue) is effected, there can be no doubt that nutrient materials pass from the capillary vessels into the tissue, and the products of the disintegration of the tissue from the tissue into the vessels by the recognised physical process called osmosis.

The causes to which are immediately due the changes in the character of the cerebral circulation we have been discussing, are by no means easy to discover. We know that the arteries are kept *en rapport* with the particular state of the organ to which they are distributed, through the medium of the sympathetic nervous system, and that through the same medium their calibre is regulated in accordance with the changing requirements of the part they supply. We know also that " the interchange of relations" between the blood in the vessels and the tissue outside, has much to do with the development of the peculiar forces of the circulation which act in the capillary portions of the vascular system. It may, therefore, be that Mr. Durham is not far from correct in suggesting that—

" When the brain is stimulated (by whatever means) to action, its affinity for oxygen is increased, or at any rate is especially permitted to come into play. The *vis a fronte* thus developed causes the oxygenized blood to be drawn very rapidly onwards. The increased afflux of blood produced necessarily distends the capillaries by mechanical action. Many vessels which, during the unstimulated state of the organ, admitted only the liquor sanguinis, now permit the passage of oxygen-bearing corpuscles, while those through which corpuscles previously passed now admit them in vastly increased numbers. The quantity of blood and its velocity are both increased. The 'circulation of function' becomes established, and the most favourable conditions for the mutual reaction of oxygen and tissue are supplied. Again, when the stimulus to action ceases to operate, or when from any other cause the tendency to oxidation of tissue is diminished, the *vis a fronte* undergoes a corresponding diminution, and the blood that flows onward is lessened both in quantity and velocity. As a necessary consequence, the capillaries (no longer subject to a powerful distending force) reassume, in virtue of their elasticity, their original dimensions. The 'circulation of nutrition' supervenes, and the conditions most favourable to repair of the tissue are supplied.''

Mr. Durham adds a suggestion which from its practical bearing appears especially worthy of note. He says :—

" If, from continued functional excitement of the organ, the distension of the capillaries has been unduly protracted, their walls—like all other elastic bodies kept long on the stretch—are slow to recover themselves. Under such circumstances, the circulation of nutrition is not readily established. *Some explanation is thus afforded of the difficulty we experience in obtaining sleep after excessive mental activity.*''

There would appear to be a strong *a priori* probability that the brain-substance itself varies in susceptibility, and that its readiness to undergo the normal chemical changes of functional activity bears a certain relation to the degree of nutrition attained, and to other possible influences, at the existence of which we can only guess, and of the nature of which we are absolutely ignorant. And thus it may be that a high degree of susceptibility and great proneness to chemical change on the part of the brain-substance are essential conditions of wakefulness, while the reverse are essential conditions of sleep. But we have not yet advanced beyond the *a priori* probability that such differences may exist at different periods in the healthy brain-substance. We have no idea in what they can consist, nor how they can be brought about. We are acquainted, however, with one fact, a consideration of which may help us to explain why functional activity of the brain is normally succeeded by quiescence, wakefulness by sleep, altogether independently of any supposed alteration from time to time in the susceptibility of the brain or in the chemical stability of the brain-substance.

It is well known that, as a general rule, the products of any chemical action interfere by their presence with the continuance of the process to which they owe their origin, long before the necessary materials are exhausted. For example, butyric and lactic acids, unless neutralized, or otherwise got rid of, almost as rapidly as they are formed, check, or even completely stop, the processes of fermentation by which they are severally produced. Again, the sulphate of zinc, as it accumulates in the cells of a galvanic battery, diminishes the chemical action by which correlatively electricity is developed, long before the acid is exhausted. And so in numberless other instances. Now, bearing all this in mind, and at the same time recognising the indubitable fact that the same laws of chemical action prevail in the living body as out of it, we cannot resist the conclusion that the products of oxidation of the brain-substance, or of other chemical changes in the brain, when they have accumulated to a certain extent in the tissue or the blood, must, by their presence, tend to diminish the chemical action by which they have been produced. We have, it is true, no direct evidence that the products of brain-disintegration are ever formed in a state of health faster than they can be got rid of; but we have such evidence in the analogous case of muscle. Immediately after prolonged or violent muscular exertion, the products of oxidation of the tissue (Kreatin, Kreatinin, &c.,) can readily be found in the part experimented upon in much larger proportion than after a period of rest. It is interesting to consider that thus, by the very functional activity of the brain, there are generated compounds which, after a certain period, interfere with the mutual reaction of oxygen and tissue, and by so doing, tend *directly* to prevent over-exhaustion or too great consumption of material ; and further, tend *indirectly*, to induce at the right moment that state of repose which is essential to repair. "This view," it may be remarked, "is supported by the fact that retention in the body of the products of its waste is almost invariably associated with peculiar lassitude and drowsiness."

If what we have advanced be admitted, it becomes manifest *why* sleep, as we actually experience it, *must be* "a succession of ever-varying states."

In the first place, certain periods of time are obviously requisite for those changes to take place in the character of the circulation which we have seen to be the necessary accompaniments of changes in the physiological condition of the brain. Such periods may be longer or shorter, according to circumstances. They correspond to the intervals between sleeping and waking, and are associated with intermediate conditions of the circulation such as were distinctly observed in Mr. Durham's experiments.—"When we are soundly asleep, we do not instantaneously awake to full possession of our faculties ; still less do we pass at once from perfect wakefulness into a state of healthy sleep." During such intermediate periods occur those dreams (of all dreams the most common) which we experience between sleeping and waking.

In the second place, the progress from the state in which material is, to a certain extent, expended, and products of disintegration are, by their presence, diminishing the activity of vital affinities, to the state in which expended material is replaced, and waste products are got rid of, must necessarily be *gradual.* The condition of the brain itself also, and its consequent susceptibility to influences (external and internal) must pass, during such progress, through a series of variations.

In the third place, it is easy to understand, in accordance with the views expressed, that different portions of the brain may be in very different conditions at the same time. For example, some portions may pass either more slowly or less perfectly; others more rapidly or more completely from the active and wasting, to the quiescent and repairing condition. There is every reason to believe that different parts of the brain perform different functions, or, in other words, are subservient to the development of different faculties. If, then, some parts can continue in action while others are at rest, we may advance a step in our explanation of the continuous dreaming which is familiar to some during habitually recurring hours of imperfect sleep, when the will is in abeyance and the consciousness awake—not to material objects acting through the senses—but to mysterious processes of internal change; when faded pictures, photographed, as it were, in the memory are restored, and, it may be, displaced and distorted by the imagination. Such continuous dreaming may almost be regarded as imperfect waking rather than as imperfect sleep. It is, at any rate, a condition of constant change.

Very much might be added in support of what we have stated as to the physiological nature of sleep and the anatomical conditions associated with it. It would, however, be impossible to exhaust the subject; and we think we have said enough to commend the views we have expressed to the consideration of our readers. We cannot but give our general assent to the opinions both of Sir H. Holland and Mr. Durham upon the several questions we have been discussing. Sir H. Holland's admirable essay cannot fail to be read, even more extensively than it has yet been with pleasure and advantage; and Mr. Durham's observations and suggestions merit the attention both of the psychologist and practical physician as well as of the student of physiology.

M. Maury puts forward, on certain points, very different opinions to those we have been maintaining. He believes, for example, that during sleep the brain is in a state of " passive congestion." His opinion, however, is based on theoretical grounds rather than on correct observations carefully interpreted, and is manifestly opposed to well-known facts. Congestion of the brain, passive as well as active, is common enough as a morbid condition, and it not unfrequently proceeds so far as to produce a greater or less degree of insensibility and unconsciousness. In such a case, if the patient recovers, instead of waking up refreshed and invigorated as he would from sleep, he is depressed and exhausted.

M. Maury, however, is a psychologist rather than a physiologist, and appears to have directed his attention to phenomena of the mind rather than to conditions of the brain. His book is very interesting, and contains matter of considerable value. Perhaps the most important facts are those which relate to a very extensive series of experiments and observations made upon himself, by the aid of a friend, with the view of learning something of the nature of sleep, and especially of the mental phenomena associated with it. His method consisted in causing himself to be suddenly roused up, under different circumstances and in different ways, at various stages in the transition from waking to sleeping. His own experiences, and the observations of his assistant, were immediately noted down. The general results at which M. Maury arrived have, as he states them, apparently much more to do with the psychological than with the physiological aspect of sleep. We reserve them, therefore, for discussion in a future article on the "Physiology of Dreaming."

CONTEMPORARY LITERATURE.

THEOLOGY AND PHILOSOPHY.

THE Biblical studies of M. Nicolas have now brought him to inquire into the origin and primitive condition of Christianity.[1] The principal questions to which the present volume is intended to supply the answers are three—The first concerns the four Gospels, their mutual relations, distinctive characters, and the mode of their composition. The second turns upon the form which the preaching of the Gospel took relatively to the personal views of the Apostles themselves; and the third is engaged with the formation of the Canon of the New Testament. These questions are indeed intimately connected, for critical investigation into the primitive Christian writings implies critical inquiry into the primitive Christian history, and *vice versâ*. But it is very important to observe that even the narrative portions of the New Testament do not stand in the same relation to the Gospel history that the books of Herodotus, much less of Thucydides or of Clarendon, stand to the events described in them. In the first place, they are not writings contemporary with the supposed events; and secondly, they are not primarily and directly records of the events, but records or justifications of opinion. They were not to the primitive Christians sources of belief in facts, or sources of Christian conceptions and sentiments, but products. Nor in the first ages had they that authority as writings which afterwards came to be ascribed to them. Tradition was preferred to them. Thus Papias says, that "if he met anywhere any one who had been a follower of the elders, he made it a point to inquire what were the declarations of the elders—for he did not think that he derived so much benefit from books as from the living voice of those who were still surviving."— *Eus. E. H.*, iii. 39. And this he said at a time when all the books of the New Testament must be supposed to have been already written. And thus, observes M. Nicolas, with his characteristic impartiality, the absence of citation in the Apostolical Fathers from any book of the New Testament would not prove that such writing was non-existent, or its authority disallowed; but, on the other hand, citation did not imply such an authority in the New Testament writings as came afterwards to be ascribed to them. Nor do the New Testament writers themselves, whether of the Gospels or Epistles, make any pretension to supplying an inspired Scripture—containing all Christian truth, and nothing but essential Christian truth, as a possession for all time. For their writings were only occasional, suggested for local and temporary purposes; the authors expected a speedy consummation of the

---

[1] "Etudes Critiques sur la Bible : Nouveau Testament." Par Michel Nicolas. London: D. Nutt. 1864.

earthly scene—at least a speedy return in person of the Son of Man; and it was only after the event had proved these expectations to be fallacious that the Church began to set the writings of the New Testament on the same footing with those of the Old. M. Nicolas brings out very clearly the different manner in which the earlier Fathers cite the Old Testament and New Testament writings (pp. 298, 299); that is to say, they refer to 'words of the Lord' or to 'words of the Apostles,' but use the term 'Scripture' only of the Old Testament. But an oral communication of the words and deeds of Jesus could not long retain its superiority over written records. Those who had access to an Apostolic oral tradition at second or third hand, might be justified in setting it for themselves on at least an equal footing with written histories, of which many were notoriously spurious and untrustworthy. But, as time went on, the relative value of the orally transmitted and written evidence would rapidly change. It is important to notice that this change would only be one of relative value. For the lapse of time in each generation would weaken the trustworthiness of tradition; while it would neither add to nor diminish the credibility of that which was already fixed in writing. Hence the suddenness with which, after the middle of the second century, the Christian Church engaged itself in settling the Canon of the New Testament writings, and hence the suddenness with which they rose to an authority which they had not possessed before; for they seemed to have acquired an absolute superiority over tradition, though it was only a relative one. But in truth, if time was necessarily enfeebling the authority of tradition, it would add nothing to the weight of the written Scripture: no supplemental information could be given, nor could the uncertainties which hung about the origin and composition of the different books now be dispelled. Henceforward the books must be received with all their historical accidents: and although the several classes of 'acknowledged' and 'doubted' books came to be included in one Canon, that canonical acceptation would confer no additional character upon them. So that whenever criticism came to re-open the questions concerning the authorship and credibility of the New Testament writings, it would find the material presented to it just in the same condition that it was left at the beginning or middle of the second century. Now this written material cannot be rightly treated in bulk or in its crude state; nor can its real value to us be ascertained unless we can ascertain to some considerable extent the manner of its deposition, the state of mind and religious sentiment of those to whom it was addressed, and, by implication, the mental and religious condition of those from whom it issued. It is only thus we can arrive at the facts which were behind the writing—behind the beliefs and opinions by which the writing was suggested. It may be said now, as it used to be, that the authority and value of the New Testament depends upon 'external' and 'internal' evidence—but by 'external' evidence used to be meant that there was actual proof of the four Gospels having been written by the persons whose names they bear; and the question as to the literal credibility of the narratives which they contain was supposed to be reducible to this: Are we, or not, to receive the testimony of eye-witnesses—of contemporary writers, who could not be deceived as to the facts which they had witnessed, and who sealed their testimony with their blood? It is now becoming generally known that our present Gospels are not cited by the names they bear before the middle of the second century ; and the bringing external evidence to bear upon the story which they contain is a much more delicate and difficult proceeding than such persons as Porteus and Paley imagined. Again, as to internal evidence, it is not now sufficient to appeal to a supposed ' analogy of faith,' or to assume a *necessity* for a preternatural revelation, or to argue that the facts and doctrines of the New Testament *must* be true, because if they were true they would satisfy some real or supposed wants of human nature. It is now requisite for the critic to investigate in detail the literary structure of the writings, and to analyse the modes of thought which they indicate. If these are found to correspond with what our external evidences or investigation of the external circumstances of such writers would lead us to expect, we may be confident we are on the right track, and may hope to solve the problem of the origin of the New Testament writings without having recourse to a miraculous intervention. It is, therefore, necessary to distinguish carefully between the composition or authorship of the several books of the New Testament, and the formation of them into the Canon. M. Nicolas distributes his subject accordingly. He first treats of the Synoptics, which he places in the following order— Mark, Matthew, Luke. Or rather, he supposes that, with respect to its narrative portions, the Gospel according to Matthew shows signs of additions or interpolations in a composition originally like that of Mark, or, as it is called by M. Réville, the "proto-Marc." As for instance the miracle of Peter walking upon the water, Matt. xiv. 28—31, is evidently an insertion between two verses which correspond precisely with Mark vi. 50, 51 : so, again, the passage containing the miracle of the didrachma, Matt. xvii. 24—27, cuts in two the verse Mark ix. 33. But then, again, in Mark as we now have it, are added traits and developments which are not met with in the first Gospel. Moreover, the discourses of the first Gospel, especially the Sermon on the Mount, are evidently from another and independent source ; there can be little doubt that they represent the λόγια spoken of by Papias, written, it is said, originally by Matthew in Aramaic. But if this evidence of Papias be sufficient to connect Matthew with the discourses of Christ, there is no evidence to connect him with the authorship of the rest of the Gospel; and we come to these two principal general conclusions—1. That no one simple theory, as of oral or written origin, is adequate to account for the phenomena presented by the Synoptic Gospels. 2. That they contain no personal voucher of an eye-witness to the truth of the history related in them; they contain only secondary, hearsay evidence and *on dits*—the ἐγένετο δὲ of their relations is only equivalent to ἐλέγετο δὲ. Further, with respect to our present second Gospel, it is said, indeed, by Papias, that Mark, having become a follower of Peter, used to note down what he said of the miracles of Christ, but *without order ;* so that the Mark's Gospel we now have, which is written *in order*, cannot represent these original notes, and if any of them are comprised in it, we have no means of identifying the apostolic matter. Hence also, as Bishop Colenso observes with respect to the insertions and additions made to the original Elohistic matter of the Pentateuch, those who made the additions and modified in various ways the original material which had come down to them, could not have considered that original material as preternaturally sacred, infallible, or suggested by an immediate Divine inspiration. Nor do the Gospels any of them make any such claim for themselves, or for any portions in them. It is clear that the compiler of the third, speaking in the first person, makes no assumption of that kind; and as the composer of the first Gospel interpolated in the proto-Mark, as well as the composer of the existing Mark made additions to the narratives as they appear in our Matthew, so Luke, professing to follow a *plan*, dislocates the material already existing in Matthew; as may be seen especially on comparing the Sermon on the Plain (Luke) with the Sermon on the Mount (Matthew.) He cannot have held the two previously-written Gospels to have been infallibly inspired, otherwise he would not have deviated from them. As he classed himself with the "many" who had taken in hand the same history, he must have classed Matthew and Mark with them likewise, and felt himself at liberty to vary from or supersede them, according to his own particular design. But the great question of all respecting the Gospels concerns the differences between the fourth and the three others. M. Nicolas is inclined to give the preference to the fourth, and treats that portion of the subject with his accustomed clearness and moderation. On the capital point of difference that the Synoptists place the Crucifixion after the celebration of the Paschal Supper, and the fourth Gospel before it, M. Nicolas observes not only that the statements are irreconcilable, but that of the two the latter must be accepted, because no such transaction as the execution of malefactors could take place at that sacred season (comp. Acts xii. 3, 4). It is to be remarked, also, that we have no description of the Last Supper in the fourth Gospel, nor of the institution of the sacrament of the Supper, and may reasonably think that the accounts in the other Gospels have been shaped in order to give a historical form to the doctrine of the sacrifice of Christ himself as mystically the true Paschal offering: and as the third Gospel gives the institution of the Eucharist almost in the words of St. Paul to the Corinthians, that the tradition of other particulars of the Passion became modified according to the speculative views of primitive Christian preachers. The fourth Gospel repeats things less striking than this which had been already related in the Synoptics; and it is inconceivable that the "beloved disciple" should have omitted all allusion to the origin of so touching and significant a ceremonial, if it really took place as recorded elsewhere. But to what extent can John himself be supposed to be the author of the Gospel which goes by his name? M. Nicolas does not consider that it claims more than to rest at second hand upon his authority. The first Epistle of John, he argues, and the Gospel, appear to be by the same hand; nor, he thinks, is there any sufficient reason to sever the second and third Epistles from the first. The two smaller Epistles are written by some one calling himself an "elder" ($\pi\rho\epsilon\sigma\beta\acute{v}\tau\epsilon\rho\rho\varsigma$), and to this same elder —probably the successor of John in the superintendency of the Church at Ephesus—M. Nicolas consequently attributes both the first Epistle and the Gospel. The Apostle himself might or might not be cognisant of the work of his disciple : whether he were or not, the Gospel might fairly be considered as representing his theological and metaphysical views concerning the person of Jesus Christ ; and whether he were or not, he would not be responsible for the literal truth of all facts related. But then it will follow that we have not the voucher of an eye-witness for all facts recorded, some of which may be due to distortion or misunderstanding of what the Apostle said, others to inventions on the part of the actual writer for the purpose of representing tangibly and historically the conceptions of his master concerning the nature and work of his Lord. As to the capital point, however, of the irreconcileable discrepancy between the Synoptics and the fourth Gospel concerning the day of the month on which Jesus suffered, even such a thorough vindicator of the truth of the Gospel history as Ebrard candidly acknowledged it in his second edition. A translation of Ebrard's work has just been published by Messrs. Clark of Edinburgh. where his fair review of this question may be seen at pp. 395–405.[*] We cannot follow our author any further in a work which is highly to be recommended both for its spirit and execution. We will make room only for one observation from the Chapter on the ' Christianity of the Apostles.' M. Nicolas is speaking of the conciliatory tendency manifested in the Acts of the Apostles, the Epistle to the Hebrews, and the first of Peter—a tendency which, looked at from the point of view of pure Pauline Universalism, was reactionary, and he very strikingly says :—

"Il n'y a rien là que de conforme aux analogies de l'histoire. Dans toutes les batailles, dans quelque sphère de l'activité intellectuelle qu'elles se livrent, c'est toujours le parti des idées les plus avancées et les plus vraies qui s'incline devant celui qui représente les erreurs du passé. Il faut des siècles pour reconquérir ensuite laborieusement le terrain dont un homme de génie avait pris possession, et que la faiblesse ou l'incapacité de ses disciples avait abandonné. Du reste, saint Paul n'eut aucun successeur digne de lui. (p. 265.)

Dr. Hanna, in his "Forty Days after our Lord's Resurrection," endeavours to give some substance to that extremely shadowy period.[2] He does not seriously undertake to fill it up with a consecutive narrative, nor to reconcile the apparent contradictions which the Gospels and Acts present respecting it. As to the accounts, for instance, of

---

* "The Gospel History : a Compendium of Critical Investigations in support of the Historical Character of the Four Gospels." By Dr. J. H. A. Ebrard, Prof. of Theology in the University of Erlangen. Translated by James Martin, B.A., Nottingham. Revised and edited by Alexander B. Bruce, Cardross. Edinburgh : T. and T. Clark. 1863.

2 "The Forty Days after Our Lord's Resurrection." By the Rev. William Hanna, LL.D., author of the "Last Days of Our Lord's Passion." Edinburgh : Edmonston and Douglas. 1863.

the appearances after the Resurrection, he acknowledges that, if it cannot be said that the attempts at reconciling them "have all absolutely failed, it must be said that not one of them is entirely satisfactory." He thinks that if missing links were supplied we should be able to harmonize what now seems conflicting. He does not appear to us to see clearly the difference between the "discrepant" and the "fragmentary." The fragmentary can in idea be restored into a whole, but not the discrepant: a few *frusta* of a single cone will enable us to reconstruct it, but portions of dissimilar solids can never be combined. Such discrepancies as that pointed out in the previous notice between the Synoptists and the fourth Gospel as to the day of the Crucifixion, or that between the first and third Gospels as to the place of Ascension, which the former places at a mountain (undefined) in Galilee, and the latter at Bethany nigh to Jerusalem, are not to be hypothetically explained away on the ground of the "fragmentary" nature of the accounts. They cannot both be true, and therefore may possibly both be incorrect. Dr. Hanna's work does not indeed aim directly at reconciling these fragmentary or conflicting narratives. But his object is to throw such questions into the background by means of surmises which seem to us gratuitous, but which may suffice to feed the imagination and sentiment. It is, in fact, an employment of the rhetorical fallacy of δείνωσις; in forensics, enlist the sympathies of the jury against the crime or for the sufferer, they will allow you to infer the fact: here the appeal is to another department of the feelings—this portraiture of the Saviour is touching—there is a deep significance in that miracle—therefore they are thoroughly historical. Dr. Hanna does all this in a masterly way, and with the air of being deceived by his own artifice, or by his own devotional feeling. He is, however, at other times evidently perfectly aware that the evidence for the truth of the Gospel history properly so-called must be dealt with according to a stricter method. In his Preface to the present volume he makes some observations as to the effect on the mind of the critical inquirer of a visit to the localities in which the events described in the Gospel histories are said to have occurred. He thinks that in the case of a person like M. Renan, already a doubter, such a visit may be of the greatest use in giving freshness and vividness to one's conceptions of the incidents narrated by the Evangelists; but he goes on to say of himself:—

"I had the strongest possible desire to plant my foot upon some portion of the soil of Palestine on which I could be sure that Jesus had once stood. I searched diligently for such a place, but it was not to be found. Walking to and fro between Jerusalem and Bethany, you have the feeling—one that no other walks in the world can raise—that He often traversed one or other of the roads leading out to the village. But when you ask where, along any one of them, is a spot of which you can be certain that Jesus once stood there, you cannot find it." (p. x.)

"Jacob's Well," he says, "is sure," though it evidently occasioned him great disappointment; he had to scramble over old buildings, stones, and rubbish, and through two or three small apertures, to "look down into the undiscoverable well." But then

"It is impossible to determine the site of that house in Nazareth under whose roof for thirty years Jesus lived. Of Capernaum, the city in which most of his wonderful works were wrought, scarcely a vestige remains. Travellers and scholars are disputing which is Capernaum among various obscure heaps of ruins on the north-western shore of the Sea of Galilee. No one, I believe, can tell the exact place where any one of our Lord's miracles was wrought, or any one of his parables was spoken. The topographical obscurity that hangs about the history of Jesus reaches its climax at Jerusalem. Bethany is here, *but the house of Lazarus is a fable.*" (p. xiii.)

Perhaps so, in another sense from that which Dr. Hanna intends. So again you " cannot err as to the ridge on which the Temple stood;" but what of " the new sepulchre in which they laid his body?" No doubt further research will determine, as Dr. Hanna foresees, what is doubtful and what is sure. Dr. Stanley, indeed, fondly imagines that topographical research in the Holy Land will enable the winning back to faith much of the Gospel history which a remorseless criticism seems at present to have carried away; but Dr. Hanna perhaps rather anticipates that " it shall appear that the most wonderful of all earthly lives has left the fewest visible marks of itself in recognisable localities;" and this may be intended to make " manifest that the ties of Jesus of Nazareth were not with places but with persons." Now let us remember, also, that modern research has verified the accuracy of the Homeric descriptions of the plain under the roots of Ida, watered by the Simoeis and Skamander; and yet such topographical identification is no evidence of the truth of the tale of the fall of Troy, of the wrath of Achilles and its episodes, of the intervention of the gods in the heroic combats, or of the colloquy of Hector and Andromache. Doubtless, the Homeric poet, whatever the source of his drama, had seen the sites on which he set his actors. On the other hand, there is a remarkable absence in the Gospels of those characteristic features which an eye-witness of events, or a frequenter of well-known scenes supplies unconsciously—no expressive epithets dropped as if unawares, no well-remembered traits, as if the narrator had the locality before his mind's eye. In the older annals of the Jews we have some details of the background of historic events identified, occasionally supplied, as the " conduit of the upper pool," " by the way of the garden-house;" we meet with nothing of the kind on occasion of any of the visits of Jesus to Jerusalem. Compare the particular description (Jerem. xxxv.) of the introduction of the sons of the Rechabites by the Prophet into one of the chambers of the Temple with the vagueness of the description of " an upper room" (Luke xxi. 8—13). This sort of background would have been distinct if the histories had been composed by eye-witnesses. The pictures which are preserved to us are copies, not originals; the distances and shadows are blurred, but not filled in. Now, in the few lines in which Dr. Hanna refers to the recent work of M. Renan, he evidently treats the Gospels as if they were the depositions of witnesses—as if the sole question were as to the trustworthiness of certain known persons concerning things of which they must have been capable of judging. When he has gone further into the matter, he will perceive that the question is far more complicated, and that there is no inconsistency in admitting an *historical element* in the Gospels, and yet in withholding assent from particular parts of the history, where the narratives are either inconsistent with each other or with the likelihood of things.

The Commentary on the Old Testament by Keil and Delitzsch includes in its present volume, which is by Dr. Keil, the Books of Joshua, Judges, and Ruth.[3] In this Commentary the literal history is maintained as far as is possible, but in a manner from which defenders of the faith in our own country might well take example. As to matters of speculation and hypothesis, Dr. Keil considers himself free to maintain the credibility in themselves of the miraculous narratives in the Books of Joshua and Judges. But he does not maintain the contemporaneity of the books with the events of which they contain the history. He thinks that the Book of Joshua may have been written twenty or thirty years after the death of that leader, although the actual limits of time he finds in it only require the supposition that it was written before the time of David; thus the Jebusites were dwelling in Jerusalem "unto this day" (Josh. xv. 63), which would not have been true after David had taken Zion (2 Sam. v. 6—9); the Gibeonites were hewers of wood and drawers of water "unto this day" (Josh. ix. 27), which could hardly have been said after Saul had sought to exterminate them (2 Sam. xxi. 1). It appears, however, that the phrase "unto this day" implies a much greater lapse of time than Dr. Keil supposes, nor do we think he has attached sufficient weight to the reference in Josh. x. to the "Book of Jasher" as a pre-existing authority; and the compilation of the Book of Joshua, whatever earlier materials it may contain, can with greater reason be brought down to about the age of Samuel. With respect to the Book of Judges, Dr. Keil again finds that it was compiled, or at least a portion of it, subsequently to the establishment of the kingdom, as is evident by the references " in those days there was no king in Israel, every man did that which was right in his own eyes" (xvii. 6, xviii. 1, xix. 1, xxi. 25); so that it must have been as to those parts written after the election of Saul. But then the Jebusites are dwelling in Jerusalem "unto this day" (i. 21), so that the limits of composition appear to lie between the first year of Saul and the reduction of Zion by David (2 Sam. v. 6). Hence, says Dr. Keil, the intimation of the Talmud (*Bava Bathra*, f. 14b 16a), that Samuel composed the Book, may be founded in fact, or at least it may have been written, if not by himself in his advanced age, by some younger prophet of his school at his suggestion (p. 185). The Book of Ruth was evidently written subsequently to the establishment of the kingdom (i. 1, iv. 22), and forms a kind of appendix to the Book of Judges. Dr. Keil having vindicated the comparatively early authorship of these Books against those who would bring them down to the period of the exile, is, nevertheless, far from vindicating the authenticity of all their contents. There may be a general truth in

---

[3] " Biblischer Commentar über das Alte Testament." Herausgegeben von Carl Friedr. Keil und Franz Delitzsch. Zweiter: Die Prophetischen Geschichtsbücher. Erster Band. Josua, Richter, und Ruth. London: D. Nutt. 1863.

the history of the conquest of Canaan by the Israelites, and yet 1
truth in the story of the walls of Jericho falling down at the sound
the trumpets, or of the sun and moon standing still at the battle
Beth-horon. The Book of Judges may give a generally fair descriptic
of the constant struggles of the Israelites with the neighbourir
people, and of their own internal disorders previous to the erection
the monarchy, and yet there may be not a whit of truth in the mag
of Samson's locks. The truth of the ordinary history would not carr
with it the truth of the extraordinary or miraculous events; nor do
the falsehood or inconceivableness of the preternatural stories dra
down that part of the narrative which otherwise fits into the world
history. Whatever part the Hebrews had to play in history, ar
especially in the religious history of the world, though it might 1
necessary for them to win the battle of Beth-horon, or some batt
which that tale represents, it could not be necessary that it shoul
be won for them by supernatural means. The maintaining th
description of the hailstones showered down from heaven, and th
arrest of the earth's motion, raises a prejudice against the peopl
themselves, against the religion they professed, and, if we may so sa
against the very Being who is represented as so unworthily an
unfairly intervening. Schoolboys always feel themselves on the sid
of Hector and the Trojans; because it strikes them as unfair tha
Achilles should be invulnerable and invulnerably armed, and becaus
the strongest gods fought on the side of the Greek heroes in thei
battles. It was natural that the Greeks should pride themselves o
traditions which gave expression in that way to their self-esteem; i
was natural the Hebrew people should do the like. But we are no
bound to believe the traditions as relating authentic facts in the one cas
more than the other. Dr. Keil does admit the possibility indeed of th
miracle in Joshua x. having been only subjective—that is, that Joshu
and the people said to themselves, "Would God this day might last lon
enough for us to extirpate our enemies;" and it did last long enough
though how long in duration of actual time they knew not. Dr. Kei
however, prefers to accept the supernatural narrative, and endeavours t
answer objections to it by alleging the sufficient store of " powe
which there is in the Almighty to accomplish that or any such phen
menon. " Nor," he says, "is it an insurmountable objection that a sudd
arrest of the earth's rotatory motion would cause it to fly into fr
ments, for the Power which arrested it could prevent that consequence
It might be said, perhaps, that if it were so prevented, it would ca
the conflagration of the globe, to which probably Dr. Keil would rep
as before. Now, without denying at all this store of " power," it is
least evident, from these and similar considerations, to what extent t
miracle ramifies, and how inconceivable it is that a story should
true which requires us to believe such recourse to be had to th
central " power," for the purpose of destroying a few hundreds
human lives, supposing it fit they should be destroyed, and when th
might have been destroyed by the descent of a few more of those gr
hailstones, which, as it was, are said to have killed more than t
children of Israel slew with the sword. Dr. Keil's book, however,

as we have said, far superior both in learning and temper to our English productions on the Conservative side in such inquiries.

The eloquent addresses pronounced by M. de Montalembert at the Roman Catholic Congress at Malines last summer, were at the time hastily supposed by some to indicate that Catholicism was about to enter on a new phase, or, at least, that a party was forming itself within its bosom on principles of civil and religious liberty.[4] They contain, in fact, the exposition and eloquent recommendation of a policy somewhat new, and a policy of which all the co-religionists of the distinguished and accomplished author may not perceive the wisdom. In our own country, when, after the passing of the Reform Bill, a certain number of the more obtuse Tories were dreaming of winning back again what they had lost, Sir Robert Peel, in his famous " Register— Register—Register," suggested the only available policy to the Conservatives—namely, to fight their battle with the weapons which altered circumstances enabled them to seize. M. de Montalembert recommends a similar course in the interests of the Romish Church itself. Formerly, political despotism was the natural and most effectual ally of Catholicism—its own days are now numbered ; and it is becoming obvious to the shrewder observers in the Roman Church that they may lose more than they can gain by perpetuating an offensive and defensive alliance with it. It is not, says M. de Montalembert, that there is nothing to admire in the old *régime*, but since it is passing away, there is nothing which the good Catholic need regret ; nor, he says, is there nothing to contend against in the new order of things, which he calls the Democracy, but there is nothing in it to fear. The object to be aimed at, therefore, is to gain possession of the new political system, and of the new social order, and to mould them and work them so as to promote the advancement of the designs of the Church. Hence the existing political despotism in France is peculiarly obnoxious to M. de Montalembert, for he sees that if his Church were to lean upon that despotism, and to make common cause with it, at no distant day it might, so far as France is concerned, be involved in its downfall. Moreover, although the present head of the French nation is, for reasons of his own, maintaining the Pope in possession of his temporal power, he will not allow any transgression on the part of the French prelates of the limits which separate the spiritual and political domains. A despotic government is not so easy to deal with as a constitutional one. In Catholic France the Romish priesthood cannot take so many liberties as in heretical England. The law, which is sufficiently stringent in a Protestant and constitutionally-governed country for the guidance of a people who give it strength by their own willing submission, is a feeble barrier against spiritual encroachments, which invade at once the senate, the jury-box, and the family hearth ; and the result of the spread of modern democracy or constitutionalism, not obscurely

[4]" L'Eglise Libre dans l'Etat Libre." Discours prononcés au Congrès Catholique de Malines. Par le Comte de Montalembert, l'un des Quarante de l'Académie Française. London: D. Nutt. 1863.

indicated by M. de Montalembert, if watched with due wisdom by those who wield the great Catholic organization, will be this—that there will remain one true monarchy in the West, namely, that of the Vicar of Jesus Christ. And it is shown at length how liberty of instruction, liberty of association, liberty of the press, and, above all, liberty of religious profession, are the very levers with which Catholicism will henceforth work to its great end ; for with liberty of instruction it will instruct in that which is the *sole truth ;* with liberty of association it will organize its religious orders, bound together by vows, circulating like armed bands among an unarmed population ; with the liberty of the press—it will be free to argue and to denounce, free from all civil restraints which should impede the Roman propaganda among Protestants, but subject to that spiritual restraint which forbids the reading by Catholics of Protestant arguments, or even of English Bibles ; finally, with liberty of religious profession, propagation, and development—the Romish priest will ultimately be the judge of what belongs to religion, and what belongs to moral and political duty.

A portion of the results of the Biblical studies of one Herr Wirmer, apparently of Bremen, entitled " Adam and his Race,"[5] is not worthy of any particular remark, except to notice the author's theory, that the early chapters of the Bible were *written* by the Patriarchs before and after the Flood, beginning with Adam himself. The author is strongly convinced that "if the narratives of the ten first chapters of the Bible do not relate historical facts there is an end of Law and Gospel, and of Jesus and all Religion too." He seems to feel strongly two things— that the " evangelical" conception of Sin and Redemption would lose a great support if the historical truth of the " Fall" were to be given up ; and that traditions, and even Mosaic authorship, are insufficient guarantees for the truth of the narratives—and so far he is surely right. Whose testimony but that of Adam himself could be sufficient to induce a belief in the story of the speaking Serpent ?

The " Lectures" of the late Dr. Scheckenburger,[6] of Berne, on the doctrines of the smaller Protestant sects, supply, to a certain extent, a want often sensibly felt in the perusal of the larger works on the history and development of doctrines. For in these smaller sects we observe both historically and logically the points of divergence and transition, where Christian conviction or sentiment has left an old path and started off in a new direction. The minor dogmatisms here passed in review are, Arminianism, Socinianism, Quakerism, Methodism, Moravianism, Swedenborgianism.

In order to complete Dressel's edition of the " Apostolical Fathers," published in 1857, a complete collation of the Epistle of Barnabas,

---

[5] " Adam und sein Geschlecht." Versuch einer Geschichte der Menschheit aus ihrer ältesten Urkunde. Resultate fünfzigjähriger Bibelforschung. Von G. A. Wirmer, Evangel. Prediger. London : Williams and Norgate. 1863.
[6] " Vorlesungen über die Lehrbegriffe der Kleineren Protestantischen Kirchenparteien." Von Dr. Matthias Scheckenburger, weil. Ordentl. Prof. der Theol. in Bern. Aus dessen handschriftlichem Nachlass herausgegeben von Dr. Karl Bernhard Hundeshagen Geh. Kirchenrath u. Prof. d. Theol. in Heidelberg. London : D. Nutt. 1863.

and of a portion of Hermas, is now supplied from Tischendorf's edition of the Sinaitic Codex. These papers can be bound up with Dressel's original work.[7]

A new edition of "The Friend" is reduced conveniently to two volumes.[8] With the exception of a re-numbering of the essays, there is no alteration from former editions. The papers still read freshly, and long will, although the philosophical portions are no longer deemed so profound as they once were, and the political opinions are too much coloured with the prejudices of the author's own day.

A work of some interest for those who concern themselves in liturgical and ritualistic questions is that of Dr. Denziger, of Würtzburg.[9] It is intended to exhibit, in Latin versions, the order of administration of the Sacraments in the Eastern Churches, properly so called—that is, as distinguished from the Greek. These churches are—1. The Alexandrian, comprising the Coptic and the Ethiopian, or Abyssinian ; 2. The Syrian Church, including the Jacobites and the Maronites ; 3. The Eastern Syrians, or Nestorians. The purpose of this work is, by diffusing information as to the points of resemblance between the rituals of those Churches and that of the Church of Rome in the sacramental ordinances, to assist the project which the Court of Rome has so much at heart, of absorbing them in the Papal unity—a project vigorously pursued of late years, by the usual methods.

Those who wish for an exposition of the essential parts of the doctrine of Swedenborg, without plunging into writings which, unaccompanied with a key, contain so much that is repulsive or unintelligible, will do well to read Mr. Henry James's "Substance and Shadow."[10] It is characterized, no doubt, by a truly American thoroughness ; but when the author's definitions are once mastered, will be found to contain a coherent exposition of a system of the universe.

The work of M. Emil Schlagintweit has for its object to describe the present condition of Buddhism in Tibet, where it has existed for more than twelve centuries.[11] The materials have been collected

[7] "Patrum Apostolicorum Opera," &c. &c. Instruxit Albertus Rud. Max. Dressel. Editio altera aucta Supplementis ad Barnabæ Epistolam et Hermæ Pastorem ex Tischendorfiana Codicis Sinaitici editione haustis. London: D. Nutt. 1863.

[8] "The Friend: a Series of Essays to aid in the Formation of Fixed Principles in Politics, Morals, and Religion, with Literary Amusements interspersed." By Samuel Taylor Coleridge. With the Author's last corrections and an Appendix, and with a synoptical Table of the Contents of the Work. By Henry Nelson Coleridge, M.A. In two volumes. A new edition, revised. London: Ed. Moxon. 1863.

[9] "Ritus Orientalium, Coptorum, Syrorum et Armenorum, in administrandis Sacramentis." Ex Assemanis, Renaudotio, Trombellio aliisque fontibus authenticis collectos. Edidit Henricus Denziger, Ph. et S. Th. Doc. et in Univ. Wirceburgensi Theol. Dogmat. Prof. Tom. I. London: D. Nutt. 1863.

[10] "Substance and Shadow; or, Morality and Religion in their Relation to Life." An Essay upon the Physics of Creation. By Henry James. London: Trübner and Co. 1863.

[11] "Buddhism in Tibet." Illustrated by Literary Documents and Objects of Religious Worship. With an Account of the Buddhist Systems preceding it in India. By Emil Schlagintweit, LL.D. With a folio Atlas of twenty Plates and twenty Tables of native print in the text. London: Trübner and Co. 1863.

principally by the author's three brothers, Hermann, Adolphe, and Robert, in the course of a scientific mission during the years 1854—1858. Buddhism has undergone great modifications, as other religions have, in the course of centuries, and particularly so in its transfer from its original seat to the inhospitable regions of Tibet. There it seems to have settled into a dead and harmless superstition. It has none of the characters of a Reform, which belonged to its first rise, for it is now, on the contrary, an established religion ; nor does it encourage any speculative mental activity—it has degenerated into a mere formalism. Its more philosophical aspects have been covered over by a belief in magical contests between Buddhas and evil spirits. In China proper, Buddhism is said to have been preached as early as 217 B.C., and to have been generally received there in the year 65 A.D. Into Ladak it was introduced within about the like period. In the Eastern Himalaya the conversion of the inhabitants to Buddhism did not take place till our sixteenth century. According to the historians of Tibet, the propagation of Buddhism in that country ranges from the seventh to the tenth century of the Christian era ; and in the fourteenth century we come to the name of Tsonkhapa, an extraordinary reformer, whose design was to re-unite the various schools into which Tibetan Buddhism was divided in his day, and to eradicate the abuses introduced by the charlatanism of the priests. Tsonkhapa is reported to have had some intercourse with a stranger from the West, who was remarkable for a long nose ; and chiefly from the peculiarity of this feature, Huc argues that he must have been a Roman Catholic, and that hence may be accounted for the resemblances between the Romish and Buddhist rituals. "But," says M. Schlagintweit, "the rites of the Buddhists enumerated by the French missionary can, for the most part, either be traced back to institutions peculiar to Buddhism, or they have sprung up in periods posterior to Tsonkhapa" (p. 70). Since the time, however, of the Reformer, the rigour of his ordinances against the priests has been greatly relaxed, and they derive a considerable part of their revenues from the performance of ceremonies for the purpose of driving off the evil spirits.

As in the original Indian Buddhism, blessedness consists in deliverance from existence, which is illusion, and from the necessity of metempsychosis, or re-birth. The Tibetans make two grades of this emancipation ; the one, Nirvána, or absolute deliverance, which is not easily distinguishable from a cessation of consciousness ; the other is the entering into Sukhavati, obtained by those who have accumulated much merit by their virtues, but are not perfect Buddhas, although delivered from metempsychosis. This distinction, however, between Nirvána and Sukhavati is not much dwelt upon by the Tibetan teachers, with whom the essence of blessedness is simply comprised in the exemption from metempsychosis. Thus, a Lama of Bhutan had been at Lhassa during the residence there of the Jesuits Huc and Gobet, and had seen some coloured prints of Jesus Christ, and scenes in the Bible history :

"The Lama alleged against the creed of these missionaries, that it does not afford final emancipation. According to the principles of their religion, he said, the pious are rewarded with a re-birth among the servants of the supreme God, where they are obliged to pass an eternity in reciting hymns, psalms, and prayers to his glory and honour. Such beings, he argued, are consequently not yet freed from metempsychosis : for who can assert, that in the event of their relaxing in the duty assigned them, they shall not be expelled from the world where God resides, and in punishment be re-born in the habitation of the wretched ? Buddhist doctrines, the Lama concluded, are certainly preferable to this theory : they do not allow a man to be deprived of the fruits of the good works performed during life ; and if once arrived at final perfection, he is never again, under any circumstances, subjected to metempsychosis, although, at the same time, if desiring to benefit animated beings, he is at liberty to re-assume the human form, whenever it pleases him, without being obliged to retain it or to suffer from any of its disadvantages."—p. 100.

The chief object of adoration on the part of the Tibetans is Padmapani, and the chief observance of their worship consists in the repetition of the prayer, "Om mani padme hum." Padmapani is the representative to mankind of the last Buddha Sakyamouni, and will continue so to be, being incarnate in successive Dalai Lamas until the advent of the next Buddha Maitreya. Of Padmapani is given the following legend :

"Once upon a time Amitabha (seated enthroned in the wonderful region Sukhavati), after giving himself up to earnest meditation, caused a red ray of light to issue from his right eye, which brought Padmapani Bodhisattva into existence ; whilst from his left eye burst forth a blue ray of light, which, becoming incarnate in the virgins Dolma, had power to enlighten the minds of living beings. Amitabha then blessed Padmapani Bodhisattva by laying his hands upon him, when by virtue of this benediction he brought forth the prayer, 'Om mani padme hum' (O the bright jewel of the Lotus !). Padmapani, moreover, made a vow to rescue all living beings from existence, and to deliver all the wretched souls in hell from their pains ; and in token of his sincerity, he added the wish, that his head should split into a thousand pieces did he not succeed. To fulfil his vow he gave himself up to earnest meditation ; and after remaining absorbed in contemplation for some time, he proceeded, full of wisdom, to look into the various divisions of hell, expecting that its former inhabitants had ascended, by virtue of his meditations, to the higher classes of beings, which indeed had taken place. But who can describe his amazement on seeing the compartments of hell again as full as ever, the places of the outgoing tenants being supplied by an equal number of newcomers ? His head instantly split into a thousand pieces ; he fainted, and fell heavily to the ground. Amitabha, deeply moved by the pains of his unfortunate son, hastened to his assistance. He formed the thousand pieces into ten heads, and assured him, for his consolation, as soon as he had recovered his senses, that the time had not yet arrived to deliver all beings, but that his wish should yet be accomplished."—pp. 84, 85.

Whatever monstrosities may characterize the Tibetan theology, it is at all events free from the representation of the Supreme Being willing to keep alive the rational creatures who have offended him in an everlasting hell ; its religious ideas are not founded upon the notion of sanguinary Atonements, nor its worship framed upon the supposition of the good God being pleased with the bloodshedding of man or beast. The morals of Buddhists appear to be amiable, with a tendency to asceticism ; and if it is somewhat discouraging to find a religion whose followers amount to 340 millions (Christians of all denominations make a sum of 335 millions) so little enlightened on some points which appear to ourselves self-evident, on some others they may have the advantage of us, and we may be thankful, at all events, that it is no worse.

M. Littré observes, with entire justice, that it is impossible rightly to judge the Philosophy of Comte in its several phases without an acquaintance with his personal history. His present critique, accordingly, combines a history of the man with a history of his opinions.[12] In executing his task we do not doubt that it must have occasioned much pain to M. Littré, both to unveil the infirmities and maladies of his friend, and to point out the incoherence of his later opinions with his original doctrine. The work is divided into three parts. In the first, a certain affiliation is traced between M. Comte's Positivism and some opinions of Turgot, Kant, and Condorcet. An account is given of his early connexion and subsequent rupture with Saint Simon ; and his personal history is traced from his marriage to the period of his insanity, attempted suicide, and recovery. These painful circumstances of his life are necessary to be known in order to vindicate the devoted conduct of Mdme. Comte, and to account for the subsequent eccentricities of various kinds which he exhibited. The second part comprises an account of the publication of the " Philosophie Positive," of his struggles to maintain himself in his public appointments, and of the difficulties of his private circumstances ; it terminates with his separation from Mdme. Comte, which appears to have been due to his own morbid egotism. The third part commences with his passion for Mdme. de Vaux, and closes with his death from cancer of the stomach. As to the development of his opinions, this part is occupied with his abandonment, as M. Littré conceives it, of the positive method, and his return to a theoretical and subjective one, and even to a caricature of the old theological hypotheses. It is difficult here to say whether the original positivism did logically exclude, or only keep in abeyance, a theistic hypothesis ; and whether it must not all along have tacitly presupposed an observer according to whose laws of thought the whole universe of existence must be observed; moreover, whether the positivist hierarchy of the sciences is not itself constituted according to a subjective order. Other questions remain to be discussed, as to the influence of Comte's own subjectivity, his own personal estimation of himself, the colouring of his intellect from his own passions, and the warping of it into the forms derived from Roman Catholic belief. The appreciation, in fine, of the Comtean Positivism itself—how far original, not only to Comte himself but in the history of thought—would far surpass our present limits, and we hope the whole subject will be discussed on a future occasion in another part of this Review by a person especially qualified for that undertaking. It should be noticed that the volume of M. Littré derives great part of its interest from the original correspondence which it contains between M. Gustave d'Eichthal, Mr. J. S. Mill, and Miss Martineau and M. Comte.

[12] "Auguste Comte, et la Philosophie Positive." Par E. Littré. London : Williams and Norgate. 1863.

Dr. Buchanan's work on "Analogy" forms a ponderous volume of more than 600 pages.[13]   Dr. Chalmers on that argument was an illustrated and diffuse Butler; Dr. Buchanan is a feeble and diluted Chalmers.   The ground of his speculations appears to lie in a theory of universal correspondences :—

"It thus appears that a real ground exists in Nature for analogical illustration, as well as for analogical reasoning, and that it mainly consists in the marvellous correspondence which has been established between material and mental, sensible and spiritual, earthly and heavenly things—a correspondence which extends to every department of thought, and enables us to find in one of them fit signs or symbols of things belonging to another." (p. 89).

Thus a preordained harmony lies at the root both of the imagery of the poet and the analogical reasoning of the philosopher or theologian. The application, however, of all this apparatus to the real object of his book is extremely inconclusive.   Take, for instance, the chapter, *Analogy between the Volumes of Nature and Revelation.*   After some triviality suggested by the words "volume" and "interpreting," we are to start with the assumption that "it is not unreasonable to suppose that on a comparison between the Works and the Word of God we may discover such a resemblance as may materially contribute to confirm our belief in the scheme of Revealed Religion" (p. 285).   The assumption is thus made that there is such a thing as a "Word of God."   We then are told that, on a general survey of their contents, the two volumes correspond in "the amazing variety and fulness of each;" yet, with all this, "a simplicity of plan."   A third point of analogy is, that their contents, though not presented in a systematic form, "yet admit of being reduced to system."   Then there is a similar mixture in both of "light and shade, of clearness and obscurity."   Further, "each reveals a scheme or system regulated by laws," and "carried on by a long series of means."   It amounts to about this—As the organism of a man is to the functions and end of man, so is the organism of a hippogriff to the functions and end of a hippogriff; as the legs and arms, head and body of a man, show a wonderful adaptation to the life of a man, so do the beak, claws, and wings of a hippogriff to the life of a hippogriff; and therefore we may fairly conclude that a hippogriff exists—at least, we should receive it by faith founded on analogy, if we cannot prove it by reason from observation.   Dr. Buchanan is utterly unaware, as far as we can see, that to the validity of any inference from Analogy, three terms must be given to find a fourth.   Elsewhere he puts it in this way : "Scripture is to Theology what Nature is to Science; and as Science recognises the authority of Nature as supreme and final, Theology must equally recognise the infallible authority of the Word of God" (p. 580).   No ;— not until the immediate Divine authorship of the Bible has been shown to be as certain as the immediate Divine authorship of Nature; nor

---

[13] "Analogy, considered as a Guide to Truth, and applied as an Aid to Faith.' By James Buchanan, D.D., LL.D., Professor of Systematic Theology, New College, Edinburgh; Author of "Faith in God and Modern Atheism compared," &c. &c.   Edinburgh : Johnstone, Hunter, and Co.   1864.

until the Divine Voice in the one speaks to us as directly as the Divine Voice in the other.

Mr. Neale's work on " The Analogy of Thought and Nature"[14] is of much less bulk than the preceding, and of less literary finish, but of a far higher order of merit. It is an attempt to show " a unity between the power manifested in the phenomena of sense and the power exercised in the operation of thought." The method is to analyse the process of thought in our own minds, and to compare it with the observable results of an unknown power in natural phenomena. These are the two members of the comparison; but there is interposed between the parts of the book in which they are treated a second part, tracing the history of the chief metaphysical systems of ancient and modern Europe. We think this portion, though well executed in itself, might have been omitted with advantage to the author's design. His object is to show, or render highly probable, that thought and force, or power, are identical—that they are identical in us, and identical in the universe. All thought in ourselves is found to be either constructive or destructive—either an operation of composition or resolution; in other words, an act of power. For that the materials of thought are presented to us through sensation does not constitute thought passive, it is the activity which gives form to that material. " Our conceptions of the objects of sense appear at first to be fetters on our will, imposing upon us a necessity of conforming our thoughts to them; but this is not the case. We sit constantly in judgment on the instinctive assertions of our consciousness, affirming or rejecting them" (p. 85). Our perceptions, indeed, act upon our will, are not produced by it; they present a something which can only become *known* by the action of a power capable of constructing, of resolving it—of timing it, locating it, quantifying and qualifying it; and this power is the Will. For the Will is to be distinguished into the *practical* and *theoretical* Will. " The Will originates knowledge as the condition of exercising itself; and it carries into its practical dealing with the world of sense the principles through which it produces the world of theory" (p. 86). And hence Mr. Neale derives the *Law of Thought*, which he expresses : " The action of thought consists in producing a unity of subject and object through a perpetual process, wherein the subject continually distinguishes itself from itself, to form its own object, setting itself over against itself as the other of itself, in order to use this other as the means of its own realization" (p. 87). This sounds, it must be confessed, something like a man standing on his own shoulders. It is elsewhere expressed : " We have seen that it is the essential character of thought to set itself over against itself, as the ' other' of itself, which yet is itself. All our *thoughts* have this character. They are a something set over against our *thinking being* by its own actions—different from itself and yet one with itself" (p. 205). That is, apparently, our particular thoughts are products of Thought as a power or phase of Will. And

---

[14] " The Analogy of Thought and Nature Investigated." By Edward Vansittart Neale, M.A. London: Williams and Norgate. 1863.

in these, its products, Thought becomes conscious of itself. Recollecting now that Schopenhauer has employed the term Will to designate the sustaining Force of the Universe, and bearing in mind that Mr. Neale includes in his conception of Will (both the theoretical and practical) the conception of consciousness, we perceive that he has prepared the way for inferring that as our Thought, conscious of its own operation, produces our own particular thoughts, which are its creations, so the Divine Thought or Will produces, by a like conscious energy, all natural existences; and the practical and theoretical Will, which in us divide from a common root, are in the Divine Will entirely one. There are many subdivisions of this book which are extremely suggestive; but, speaking without any anti-dogmatical design, we think Mr. Neale has not rendered any service to a theistic argument of considerable force by undertaking to show that his speculations are reconcilable with a doctrine of the Trinity.

Dr. Geddes's "Phædo" is remarkable as being apparently the first edition of a Platonic dialogue proceeding from Scotland.[15] We wish Dr. Geddes all success in his endeavours to enlist the interest of his pupils in this masterpiece of Greek philosophy. The notes and illustrations with which it is accompanied seem well adapted for that purpose. Some of the translations appear to us to be deficient in *stringency*.

As we are going to press we receive the fourth part of Bishop Colenso on the Pentateuch.[16] It is likely that the appearance of this work in successive parts makes the Bishop's adversaries rather angry. They would have preferred to have seen his whole case at once, that they might then pick holes in it at their leisure. As he has wisely preferred to deal his blows *seriatim*, the defenders of Evangelical orthodoxy resemble the barbarian in Demosthenes—they follow each stroke as it is delivered, incapable of guarding themselves against that which is to succeed. We think those critics must now be heartily ashamed of themselves who represented the whole issue raised by Bishop Colenso to be solvable on the supposition of the corruption of a few numbers in an ancient document; although contradictions in numbers alone would be fatal to the inspiration theory of the "every jot and tittle" men. But although the point of attack has been varied in each successive "Part," the same simple issues, most pregnant as they are in their consequences, have always been kept clearly before the mind of the reader—whether Moses could really be considered the author of the books which are popularly ascribed to him, and whether the whole history of the Pentateuch is to be considered as matter-of-fact truth. In Part III. it was shown to be in the highest degree probable that the entire Book of Deuteronomy is of a much later age than the supposed time of Moses; consequently, we have not Moses' voucher

---

[15] "Platonis Phædo. The Phædo of Plato." Edited, with Introduction and Notes, by W. D. Geddes, M.A., Professor of Greek in the University of Aberdeen. London: Williams and Norgate. 1863.

[16] "The Pentateuch and Book of Joshua critically examined." By the Right Rev. John William Colenso, D.D., Bishop of Natal. Part IV. London: Longmans. 1863.

for any of the narratives peculiar to it. In the present volume the proof of the Elohistic and Jehovistic constituents in the Book of Genesis is drawn out in a manner which will be most striking and thoroughly convincing to every unprejudiced English reader. The first eleven chapters are gone through in the most thorough and detailed manner: the one set of passages, the Elohistic, are shown, when taken by themselves, to form a complete and consecutive narrative; the Jehovistic passages, when set by themselves, do not present completeness and continuity to the same extent, but are evidently incorporated with the other from some independent source. It is shown, also, that these sets of passages not only differ in literary characteristics, but vary in their points of view, as in the two accounts of the Creation; and are discrepant in the narration of particular facts, as in the accounts of the pairs of animals said to have been taken into the ark. Now, if the Bibliolaters will absolutely still maintain that the Pentateuch was wholly written by Moses, they must adopt some such hypothesis as this—that he was inspired to write it in such a way as to make it look as if he had not written it: very much as if one should maintain that the earth as we now know of it was created in one moment or in one week, but made to look as if its geological phenomena had been produced in millions of ages. Absurdity to this extent will be met with here and there. But there are signs that the views of Biblical inspiration built by the dominant Evangelical party upon the phrase "Word of God" will shortly be abandoned by the general common sense of England. One of these indications is pointed out by the Bishop in his Preface. In a recently published article in Smith's "Dictionary of the Bible," the Rev. J. J. S. Perowne both adopts the supposition of a *partial* deluge, and acknowledges the distinction between the Elohistic and Jehovistic sources in the Book of Genesis. Now, we are not disposed to triumph over this circumstance, nor, we are sure, is Bishop Colenso, as if some mighty conversion or new conviction had been operated in Mr. Perowne's mind, for we have no means of knowing how long he has been of the same opinion on those particular points. But there is this curiosity, that when the late Dr. Donaldson published his "Jashar," Mr. Perowne came forth as a champion of orthodoxy. We did not ourselves defend the eccentricities of "Jashar," and expressed the opinion at the time that it was a book which would rather tend to retard than advance the progress of free theological inquiry. In the controversy which ensued between Dr. Donaldson and Mr. Perowne, neither combatant did himself any credit by the manner in which he carried it on. Shortly afterwards, Mr. Perowne became Examining Chaplain to the Bishop of Norwich; and it is thus very curious that a person who with these antecedents might have been expected to be perfectly free from "Neology," and a perfectly "safe" successor to Dr. Rowland Williams as Vice-Principal and Hebrew Professor at Lampeter, should be one of the first to admit openly, speaking as a scholar, that the unity of authorship of the Pentateuch is not tenable, nor the literal accuracy of all its narratives. The concession of the principle is all which is necessary for the free inquirer. Whether the diversity of authorship in the Pentateuch is to be limited to its earlier portions, or whether a whole Book like Deuteronomy is to be severed from the rest, is a question of detail to be determined by the evidence. But in either case it follows that the mere circumstance of a statement occurring in the Pentateuch, is not of itself a sufficient authority for its being received as a fact. And it seems now about to be decided, after solemn argument, that in the great Church of England there is laid down no doctrine of inspiration obliging its members or ministers to receive as *de fide* every narrative in the Bible as literally and historically true merely because it *is* in the Bible; and this liberty has, in fact, existed all along, for the Ecclesiastical Court and the Privy Council do not make the law, they only declare it. " O fortunati nimium sua si bona nôrint *Anglicolæ!*" In his present " Part," Bishop Colenso has exercised this liberty in respect of the narrative of the Deluge, of the Confusion of Tongues, of the story of Eden, and various portions of the patriarchal history. These and other incredible Biblical traditions must be deposed from the rank of genuine history, which they have too long usurped, because their right to that rank is unsupported by sufficient evidence. Neither Moses nor any one else says anywhere that he was inspired by the Almighty to describe the garden of Eden, the creation of the man and woman, their temptation and expulsion, nor whence he derived the account, nor what he takes it to be worth : it is not even such a case as that of Herodotus giving a voucher for his own care in preserving from extinction the traditions of the ancients, while yet not vouching for their truth. For there is not only no one that we know of personally inspired to write the Pentateuch, but no one that we know of personally responsible for it as a literary production. The caution with which Bishop Colenso has hitherto proceeded in his great undertaking is in nothing more admirable than in the manner wherein he has dealt with such of the prodigies of Genesis as have hitherto come in his way. He has shown that there is reason for rejecting them because the accounts given of them are self-contradictory, and because they rest on anonymous, that is, on no substantial authority. It will be seen, we think, in the end, what a large amount of Biblical miraculous narrative may be tacitly removed in this way, without entering upon abstruse metaphysical discussions as to the nature and possibility of miracle in the abstract. In fact, now that the anonymous and multifarious authorship of the Pentateuch has been demonstrated, the onus of *primâ facie* proof is effectually shifted on to the shoulders of those who would maintain the actual occurrence of any particular miraculous event described in those books. We do not in this volume meet with any questions directly touching on the New Testament; it is, however, obvious that the Pauline doctrine of the corruption of human nature, and his antithesis between the first and second Adam, are greatly affected by the ascertained unhistorical character of Gen. ii. iii., and the Evangelical doctrines, more Pauline than Paul himself, which likewise rest on those chapters, must come to the ground. Even Paul cannot sustain that which is groundless in itself; nor does he ever claim for himself that his own expositions of doctrine are infallibly true, or his own appreciation of Old Testament narratives infallibly correct. If subsequent Christian Confessions have done so, they will have in course of time to be repealed. There is one other matter indirectly touching the New Testament upon which a single word may be said. A large number of readers will learn for the first time of the existence of an Apocryphal Book of Enoch, which may probably be the same as that from which a quotation is made in the Epistle of Jude. Bishop Colenso refers to it in connexion with the traditions of the Jews respecting the Patriarch Enoch. The Book exists in an Ethiopic version, from which a translation was made by Dr. Laurence, afterwards Archbishop of Cashel, when he was Regius Professor of Hebrew at Oxford. He supposed it, as other scholars do, to be of about the second century before Christ. Now, the remarkable thing is the extent to which the phraseology of the Book is found to be reproduced in the New Testament; the eschatology of the writings—the scenic judgment, the Heaven and Hell, are painted in precisely the same colours. The Bishop touches on this subject incidentally, as we have said, but we are mistaken if this portion of the present volume does not awaken the liveliest attention. For there is thus manifested unmistakably the circle of religious thought out of which the primitive Gospel itself grew, and the inference will be unavoidable that Christianity arose in the world without any break in the continuity of the world's history.

POLITICS, SOCIOLOGY, VOYAGES AND TRAVELS.

ENGLISH society, as it appears to other than Englishmen, has perhaps never been so well described as in the two volumes just published by Mr. Hawthorne,[1] and, in spite of some strong expression of national feeling on his part, never with greater intelligence and sympathy. The title itself is a kind of compliment, and indicates how unwillingly any educated American would cut himself away from the only ancestors he can claim.

It is curious what a strong hold Americans lay upon everything English that dates earlier than the middle of the sixteenth century. We remember taking an excursion with a celebrated American poet, who seized upon anything that could be supposed cotemporary with the Pilgrim Fathers, and with an exclusive partiality exclaimed, "Ah! this is ours; you have never done such things since we left you." However true this might be, the remark might have been answered, "But what have you to show of a like kind since you left us?" This kind of controversy, however, is of little worth; the Americans have had other work to do, and no one can say that they have not laid valiant hands on the immediate task before them. Indeed, the most interesting side of Mr. Hawthorne's book is the clear insight it gives into what America has made of Englishmen. In describing us, he throws the clearest light upon the moral sentiments of an educated democrat, and

---

[1] "Our Old Home." By Nathaniel Hawthorne, Author of "The Scarlet Letter," &c. 2 vols. London: Smith, Elder, and Co. 1863.

shows us what we must, in many respects, prepare for, if we are not to stop in that social progress which has been the chief significance of the century. In many quarters Mr. Hawthorne's criticisms on English women have exposed him to unfair, if not malicious, retorts. A moment's reflection would have made it evident that he could hold no other opinions. Somewhat a Puritan, and a great deal a patriot, he could not but display a national taste on that point where all pretend to be judges. What the American women are, the Americans have made them, and of course the effects of a different social organization, which show themselves with more force in women than in anything else whatever, could not but clash with the republican ideal. Mr. Hawthorne does not flatter his fellow-countrywomen, as has been insinuated; but simply expresses an opinion which is the rational result of all his former life. His lively onslaught on the bulky proportions of a middle-aged English-woman has been quoted in every notice of his book, and we think it but proper that he should have the benefit of his after-thoughts. In his humorous account of our civic banquets, which is as kindly as it is humorous, he says :—

"I saw much reason for modifying certain heterodox opinions which I had imbibed in my transatlantic newness and rawness as regarded the delicate cha- racter and frequent occurrence of English beauty. To state the entire truth (being at this period some years older in English life), my taste, I fear, had long since begun to be deteriorated by acquaintance with other models of feminine love- liness than it was my happiness to know in America. I often found, or seemed to find, if I may dare to confess it in the presence of such of my countrywomen as I now occasionally meet, a certain meagreness (Heaven forbid that I should call it screwishness!), or deficiency of physical development, a scantiness—so to speak—as the pattern of their material make, a paleness of complexion, a thinness of voice—all of which characteristics, nevertheless, only made me resolve to uphold these fair creatures as angels, because I was sometimes driven to a half acknowledgment that English ladies, looked at from a lower point of view, were perhaps a little finer animals than they."

After this, the English ladies may be satisfied, for this homage is cer- tainly drawn from the most unwilling lips. But, after all, American man- ners and American climate are producing a new race, with great and noble qualities of their own, and he would be but a poor American that did not fully appreciate them. What is really beautiful and becoming in an American woman would not be so in an English one; and one of the strongest proofs of the genuineness of American civilization is the effect it has had upon the women of the country. A new type of female excellence is no small thing to boast of, and though not wholly an American production (for, morally and intellectually, English Quakeresses are very close cousins of theirs), it would be far better to attempt to understand the social forces which have made them what they are, than to indulge in the expression of an ignorant dislike which cannot give a rational account of itself. The physical peculiarities of American women are simply the effect of the dry climate and the unwholesome cuisine which all Americans affect. That these pecu- liarities should be pleasing on their native ground is not surprising. In South Africa quite other graces are not without a charm in the eyes of those who have been from their infancy accustomed to them.

But all this is very trifling, and Mr. Hawthorne himself says, with the greatest truth, that—

" The only value of such criticisms lies in their exemplifying the proneness of a traveller to measure one people by the distinctive character of another— as English writers invariably measure us, and take upon themselves to be disgusted accordingly, instead of trying to find out some principle of beauty with which we may be in conformity."

The American ladies may fairly crown their knight, and every impartial judge must allow that his retort on English criticism is not discourteous. After all, it is a little laughable that this single point in Mr. Hawthorne's book should have such prominence given to it. The substance of Mr. Hawthorne's complaints of the English character resolves itself into this—that an Englishman is provokingly difficult to get at and has a very rough rind : in no case does a closer intimacy fail to produce a kindlier appreciation, and when he turns from its inhabitants to the country itself, nothing can exceed the happy appreciativeness of the author's pictures of English landscape. An English village, with its church, probably dating from the thirteenth century, stirs up the feelings of an American in a way that is, to us who are so familiar with such objects, far from common. To those who have the good sense to welcome rather than tolerate the expression of a national feeling that is not their own, these volumes will be the source of the greatest pleasure. The world has long since made up its mind on the remarkable abilities of the author, and his account of the Old Home of the Americans displays, in some place or other, all his well-known merits, together with this new one—that they make us better acquainted with Mr. Hawthorne himself, an advantage that few will fail to avail themselves of, and fewer still will be the competent judges to whom better acquaintance will not also bring a better liking.

La Sorcière⁹ is certainly the least able of those rhapsodical books to which M. Michelet has lately devoted himself. The vein of poetry which unquestionably traversed " L'Amour " here gives place to a rhetoric which is so extravagant that it seems to distrust itself. However ingenious his genesis of the mediæval witch may be, it rests upon a fundamental moral misconception. When he treats her as a natural product of ecclesiastical obscurantism and feudal oppression, as the despairing refuge of a nature morally and physically outraged, he assumes in the minds of the women of the Middle Ages a susceptibility and delicacy of self-respect that can only be born of a set of external circumstances which he fully shows were impossible in the age in which they lived. The barbarism and brutality at which his own feelings revolt when he comes across their evidence in his historical studies must, he assumes, have produced analogous effects on those who were exposed to them. But this is a radically false conclusion. The feelings of every generation are moulded by its circumstances, and there can be no doubt that some Michelet of a future age will write, if not too well instructed to do so, a similar harrowing picture of the miseries of our

---

⁹ "La Sorcière, the Witch of the Middle Ages." From the French of J. Michelet, by L. J. Trotter. London : Simpkin and Marshall. 1863.

own. The Gold-coast African does not look upon himself as outraged when he is maimed and disfigured by the caprice of his savage chief, but rather accepts it as a natural misfortune. That which can be expected, however horrible in its own character, never produces half the effect of a far smaller injury which violates some acknowledged right. The poetry of the peasant's home exists much more for the poet than the peasant. The reflective self-consciousness which alone would produce the results to which M. Michelet attributes the origin of witchcraft was in direct opposition to the spirit of the ages which witnessed its birth and growth. In the attempt to rationalize the growth of ignorance and superstition, he does more violence to his evidence than the most mystical interpreter ever did to the letter of Scripture. In effect this book is but a party pamphlet in a new guise. The author attacks in it his enemies of to-day, and has been well understood. Nothing but this purpose could have induced him to introduce the stories of Gauffridi, Grandier, Madeline Baset, and La Cadiere, which fill out half this volume, after its professed object had been completed, and which have but the slightest possible connexion with witchcraft, however close a one with priestly dissoluteness and ecclesiastical tyranny. Though we do not think this volume deserved the pains which have been devoted to it, by Mr. Trotter, we should do wrong if we did not acknowledge the success with which he has reproduced the striking peculiarities of his author's style, and overcome difficulties at first sight most formidable.

From table-rapping to mediums, from mediums to Mesmerism, from clairvoyants to Revenants, from ghosts to their means of communication with mankind, and from that means an explanation of inspiration, the Word of God and the New Jerusalem—this is the excursion to which its readers are invited by a book called " From Matter to Spirit."[3] Any one who was some years since, during the temporary rage on the subject of Mesmerism, induced to look into Jung Stilling's Pneumatology, or Kerner's Seherinn von Prevorst, may spare himself the trouble of opening this book. He will find nothing fresh in it, but directions for the new method of knocking at the door of the spirit world. These directions are sufficiently significant: we will extract a few :—

" It is certain that great activity in the brains of those concerned interferes with the experiment.—It is *well*, on first trying the experiment, to have one person in the party who is accustomed to all the various phases of the phenomenon.—When parties form circles without the presence of a practised medium, great wonders must not be expected at once."

It would be thought that simplicity could no further go ; but—

" It has been found that communications were always given in the spelling and phraseology of the person through whose agency they came.—Jones's mediumship was not successful in the presence of persons who allowed their unbelief to appear."

[3] " From Matter to Spirit, the Result of Ten Years' Experience in Spirit Manifestations, intended as a Guide to Inquirers." By C. D., with a Preface by A.B. London : Longman and Co. 1863.

But there is still another direction of the greatest importance — namely, that

"Those who wish to try experiments must, if they do not desire to be repelled at the outset, preserve a really religious, earnest, and truth-loving spirit."

It is manifest that no little of that faith which can remove mountains is requisite to tip a table. The author admits and attempts to explain, of course by a spiritual hypothesis, the not very remarkable fact, that a large proportion of powerful mediums are at present among the uninformed and uncultivated classes; and confesses "it will be found that anything they may write by spiritual dictation never exceeds the ability of the writer to attain and comprehend;" but finds no difficulty in asserting, with all the emphasis that can be given by italics, that the source from whence the revelations of the medium flows is an unseen and intelligent being, asserting itself to be a spirit which has quitted this material earthly form. That these spirits have learnt nothing and forgotten nothing, arouses no suspicion in the mind of so credulous a votary as the writer of this very laborious and silly book. The strange peculiarity that the revelations of ghosts always coincide with the preconceptions of those who see them arouses no suspicion, but rather is made the basis of an elaborate theory of spiritual correspondences. Writers like the author seem never to have heard of the suggestive power of association, and would repel as something approaching to impiety any natural explanation which would clip the wings of their imagination, and reduce them to the common inlets of knowledge to which other mortals are restricted.

The *evidence* brought forward by the author is introduced to the public by A.B., who has received a brief to abuse modern science, and who appears to enjoy the joke. An attack upon the commonly received grounds of belief affords a pretty tilting-ground to any logical gladiator; but the argument *ab ignorantiâ* is but a commonplace, which is as useful to those who maintain that the moon is made of green cheese, as to the modern spiritualist. The whole thing was better done by Glanville, two hundred years ago, in his "Sadducismus Triumphatus," but without producing any very marked effect upon the sane portion of the community then or since.

Mr. Herbert Spencer has published a second series of Essays[4] collected from his contributions to various quarterly Reviews. The author's reputation as one of the most original writers of the day is now so thoroughly established, and his readers know so well what they have to expect at his hands, whatever may be the subject he puts them to, that a simple announcement that he has gathered together some of his scattered works is sufficient for them. It is to be regretted that certain peculiarities of his style will always diminish the value by lessening the popularity of his writings. His endeavour after a scientific exactness of language is encumbered by a kind of circumlocutory precision which is very fatiguing to many who would otherwise be

---

[4] "Essays, Scientific, Political, and Speculative. Second Series." By Herbert Spencer. London : Williams and Norgate. 1863.

attracted by them; while his inordinate fondness for a philosophical terminology, which after all is but the scaffolding of true knowledge, renders them almost inaccessible to those who have not made some considerable advance in the study of the subjects of which he treats. It is to be regretted that the fruits of so much labour and thought are by these peculiarities made comparatively inaccessible. Mr. Spencer is substantially a man of one idea; but like the man of one book, he is more intimately acquainted with it than others. What cannot be treated in the light of the principles of development, evolution, or modification by external circumstances has no interest for him, but how fruitful this idea can become in the hands of a consecutive thinker and earnest inquirer is abundantly manifest in every page of this valuable volume. More than one-half of its contents have first appeared in this Review, and we do our readers a service in calling their attention to the Essays here reprinted from other sources, on the Theories of Modern Geology, on Mr. Bain's book on the Emotions and the Will, which is full of acute remarks and genuine insight into the true philosophical method required for such investigations. In these, and in another paper on Prison Discipline, Mr. Spencer extracts from his favourite principle the most satisfactory results.

On its first anonymous appearance we called attention to a very able exposition of the "Theory of the Foreign Exchanges."[5] A second edition has just been published, to which Mr. Göschen, the member for the City, has now added his name. The volume has been revised and enlarged by a very interesting disquisition on the striking phenomena lately displayed by the American Exchanges. The clear manner in which the author, starting from the fundamental fact of a balance of international indebtedness, proceeds to the consideration of every circumstance which can affect the mode of its ultimate and necessary liquidation, leaves nothing to be desired. A subject usually imagined abstruse and recondite is reduced to its elements, and rendered intelligible to any one who will give Mr. Göschen's treatise the small amount of attention which, from its lucidity, it demands. A slight tendency to overestimate the power of the so-called correctives of the Foreign Exchanges, on which we formerly remarked, is no longer apparent in the volume, which is now firmly based on those bullionist theories which alone can be safely relied upon in all questions connected with its subject.

The second volume of the "Law of Nations," by Dr. Travers Twiss,[6] which treats of the rights and duties of political communities in time of war, is very opportune in the time of its publication. The matters with which it is concerned fill at the present day a large amount of public attention, and no method could be more judicious than that adopted by the author. There is no word of theoretical construction in

---

[5] "The Theory of the Foreign Exchanges." By G. J. Göschen, M.P. 2nd Edition. London: G. Wilson. 1863.

[6] "The Law of Nations, considered as Independent Communities (on the Rights and Duties of Nations in Time of War)." By Travers Twiss, D.C.L. Oxford: Clarendon Press. London: Longmans and Co. 1863.

the whole volume ; the special divisions of the subject are treated in
an historical manner, and the occasion and grounds given of every limitation to absolute freedom which from time to time have been agreed
upon among contending nations.   The gradual and slow progress, not
always a continuous one, by which the uncompromising exercise of the
power given by victory has been brought into harmony with the
softening manners of an advancing civilization, is brought before the
reader in the most complete manner.   The utilitarian standard, to
which alone international morality can appeal, is shown by this history
in conflict with the most powerful antagonistic forces, and its adequacy
illustrated by the constant progress made in spite of them by force of
that appeal.   The moral law of nations, as it cannot concern itself with
anything but a criticism of the nature of the acts which it denounces,
is free from many of the ambiguities which constantly surround
questions of personal duty; and its study is, if possible, even more
interesting, from the collateral light it thus throws upon the foundation of general ethics, than on account of the important practical questions with which it is concerned.   The present volume is written with
remarkable clearness, and is encumbered with no professional language
that would render it inaccessible to the general public ;   a subject
generally considered dry and uninviting is treated in it with a fulness
of information and collateral illustration which render it positively
attractive.   One of the most interesting chapters is that which treats
of the Rights of Belligerents on the High Seas, as it illustrates the
great difficulty which even the logical doctrines of the Consolato del
Mare had to maintain themselves in the face of a state of civilization
of which they were in advance, and shows how impossible it is to give
stability to the best doctrines among a community of nations which is
not prepared to receive them.   The chapter, however, on the Rights
and Duties of Neutrals will be most read at the present moment, and
in it will be found a full summary of existing practice.

An admirable volume on the limits within which the executive
power of the State should be restrained has just been published by M.
Edouard Laboulaye.[7]   After a rapid review of those ancient principles
of political government which absorbed all individual rights into the
notion of citizenship, and which admitted no rivalship, he shows the
great significance and strong bearing on the system of ancient society
which was contained in that saying of Jesus—" Render unto Cæsar the
things which are Cæsar's, and unto God the things which are God's."
The overwhelming and authoritative demands of the ancient States
were here met by a claim as penetrating and extensive, and human
liberty had its first foundations laid for it.   The divided duty, which
henceforth was the chief characteristic of the Christian in ancient
times, lay at the root of all the persecution he underwent.   The membership of the Civitas Dei was incomprehensible to those who considered their Roman citizenship entitled to their undivided allegiance.   The various fortunes of these two opposing ideas are

<hr/>

[7] " L'Etat et ses Limites, suivi d'Essais Politiques." Par E. Laboulaye,
Membre de l'Institut, &c.   Paris : Charpentier.   London : D. Nutt. 1863.

rapidly but fully followed out by M. Laboulaye. That Cæsar has still too great pretensions, is the thesis of this book. The grounds and limits of his authority are drawn from Humboldt's *Grenzen der Wirksamkeit des Staats* and Mr. Mill's essay on Liberty. The doctrines of these two important books are advocated with a warmth and ability which leaves nothing to desire. How important such doctrines are in the present position of France, it is needless to point out. In the ardour of their assertion of the paramount importance of freedom for individual self-development, M. Laboulaye is inclined to think that there is danger lest the power of the State should be too much weakened within its legitimate limits, and calls attention to those considerations which have been brought forward by Baron Eotvös in his book *De l'Influence des Idées regnantes au dix-neuvième Siècle sur l'Etat*, in which he contends that nothing should be allowed to weaken the legitimate powers of the State. In the standard by which he tests the legitimacy of those powers, he does not, however, depart from the principles laid down by Humboldt and Mill, but merely states the case of the executive power from the point of view of one who wields it. To this important essay, M. Laboulaye adds a review of the life and works of Alexis de Tocqueville, which will be read with great interest; and we could wish that a short summary which he gives of the reasons why the Northern States of America *cannot* accept a separation from the South were as clearly seen and advocated in this country as by the Liberal portion of the French press. The considerations of origin, geographical conformation, and what the Americans in their large way call manifest destiny, are here brought together in a most able and convincing manner.

From the same author we have a most pregnant discussion of the existing Administrative System in France, in an Essay which he calls the programme of the Liberal party.[8] Nothing will strike an English reader more than the evident consciousness on the part of the author, that he has to contend, not only with the government, but with a national bias, which is, if possible, more averse to his doctrines; and yet in this country the doctrines are so triumphant that they seem truisms. That the only firm foundation of liberty is to be laid in the liberties of the subject, is a theory that has hitherto found but little favour with our neighbours. M. Laboulaye's volume is nothing less than the trial of the whole system of French government by this test. It is, in fact, the practical application of the doctrines of the work just noticed to the daily routine of French political life in the most extended sense of the expression. On this account it cannot fail to be of the greatest interest to all who wish for a clear insight into the present working of French institutions. Nor can we imagine a more accomplished or intelligent guide than the author.

The question of Capital Punishment has been most exhaustively

---

[8] "Le Parti Libéral: son Programme et son Avenir." Par E. Laboulaye. Paris: Charpentier. London: D. Nutt. 1864.

treated in a small volume by Dr. Mittermaier.[9] There is no point of
view from which the subject can be judged that is not acknowledged
and criticised by this accomplished jurist. While he looks forward to a
possible future when this last argument of offended society may be dispensed with, he fully acknowledges that it is quite as much a question
of general civilization as of special legislation, which can only be satisfactorily answered by a complete consideration of all the circumstances
of the community in which it is raised.   This little treatise is not only
admirable for the thorough treatment of its subject, but is also incidentally valuable for the abundant references it contains to the works
of every practical or speculative legist who has at any time, or in any
country, taken it in hand.   It thus not only furnishes a body of excellent doctrine, but is a manual of the literature connected with its
subject, which cannot fail to be most serviceable to all who are engaged
in its study.

From the Mechanics' Institute at Ballaarat we have received two
lectures, one on Stumps and Rags, and the other on Œdematology or
the Science of Swells.[10]   Their humour consists in a scientific classification of popular political cries, a venal press, and of such tumours in
the body politic as are represented by pompous pretence of any kind
whatever.   The author is not above practising some of the arts he
denounces, and fully advertises himself as a well-informed man ; while
a few of the typical characters he draws of 'the talking swell or political adventurer, are too distinctly from the life to escape from the
charge of personality he brings against a large portion of the Victorian
press. Though somewhat pedantic in form, these lectures contain many
a fair hit, and are as applicable to the home market as they could
possibly be to the one for which they were at first intended.   A plea
for straightforwardness and plain dealing, whether it assume the guise
of satire of their opposites or not, cannot but be welcome to all real
admirers of those virtues so much more lauded than practised.

Miss Le Hardy's " Home Nurse,"[11] contains the results of a manifestly large experience in the sick-room.   It is full of practical details,
and abounds in judicious remarks on the general treatment of invalids.
With great good sense she never fails to suggest, where it is possible
to do so, some cheap substitute for many of the more expensive luxuries which are often so bitterly missed at the bedside of the comparatively poor.   It is, however, to be regretted that the good things in
her book are only to be had at the cost of perusing an amount of
moralising and feeble satire of the weaknesses and errors of fashion that
is somewhat provoking.   The objects of her satire are, it is true, fair
marks for ridicule and reprobation, but her resources for the improvement of the moral health of the world bear no proportion to those she
undoubtedly possesses for meeting the difficulties which surround the

[9] " Die Todesstrafe." Geprüft von Dr. C. J. Mittermaier, Geheimerath und
Professor, Heidelberg. Mohr : 1862. London : D. Nutt.
[10] " Stumps and Rags, and Œdematology." Two Lectures, delivered by J. H.
Pope, at the Mechanics' Institute, Ballaarat. Ballaarat: Chas. Boyd, Printer. 1863.
[11] " The Home Nurse and Manual for the Sick Room." By Esther Le Hardy.
London : J. Churchill and Sons. 1863.

treatment of physical disease. If it were not for these digressions beyond the proper limits of her subject, there are few books which treat it with so much judgment and good sense.

It were greatly to be wished that every account of missionary enterprise were characterized by the good sense and moderation of Miss Whately's description of "Ragged Life in Egypt."[12] There would then be much less need for the judicious remarks she makes on the qualities of mind and heart which alone can fit the missionary for his task. Nothing but the most absolute and entire conviction can support him amidst the difficulties which surround his path in a Mahometan country; the slightest taint of secondary motive disqualifies a man otherwise to all appearance the most fitted for his work. A very small share of prudence will suffice to protect him from danger or persecution, but it is impossible to exaggerate the absolute faith in his mission which is needed to contend against ignorance and prejudice which are impregnable by anything short of the most complete self-devotion. The most interesting features of Miss Whately's book are to be found in the personal histories of those Egyptian and Coptic girls with whom she came in direct contact, and in the rare union of a strong sense of duty with the clearest insight into the small progress that can be candidly claimed as an external reward for its energetic discharge.

An English combatant in the army of the Confederate insurrectionists gives us an account of the feats of his companions in arms.[13] His residence in the South has thoroughly denationalised him; neither in his sentiments nor his language are there left many traces of his origin. Southern morals and Southern opinions—for it would be a profanation of the term to call them principles—possess him wholly; yet in the absence of direct information on the condition of the Confederate armies, his book will be read for want of a better. Its subject is notoriously one of the most difficult: what can a subordinate tell of a battle that is not summarised in the old description which declares it to be but as a confused noise and garments rolled in blood? He successfully disputes with the North the supremacy which its ill-wishers have accorded to it in bragging. In his pages the Confederates are never beaten. His sketches of the chiefs under whom he serves are mostly undisguised panegyrics, and are valuable only for the biographical particulars they contain. Of the discipline in the Southern forces his account is perfectly astounding. On one occasion a private in the ranks, taking offence at the tone of his commanding officer, warned him to be more polite, and on finding that the implied threat was not attended to, threw down his musket, stepped out of the ranks, and stabbed his officer to death on the spot with his bowie knife. The court-martial (save the word) which was held on the offence, pronounced it an *affair of honour*, and he was allowed to go free. On another occasion a regiment, in position under fire, thought their

[12] "More about Ragged Life in Egypt." By M. L. Whately. London: Seeley and Co. 1863.
[13] "The Battle Fields of the South, from Bull's Run to Fredericksburg, with Sketches of Confederate Commanders, and Gossip of the Camp." By an English Combatant. 2 vols. London: Smith, Elder, and Co. 1863.

mounted officer too exposed, and after repeated remonstrances from
the ranks, he at last *took the advice* thus offered him and dismounted.
The usual arguments of the South in support of their institution, of
course abound in these pages. The high morality which consists in
the worship of the great principle, " Let the weakest go to the wall,"
is accepted as unanswerable. In this camp, at any rate, there is no
delusion about the base treachery of the members of the Buchanan
ministry, by which the North was, as far as possible, disarmed before
the concerted outbreak ; it is simply boasted of as a master stroke of
policy, and no disguise affected in a matter of which none but
Southerners could be proud.

Another Southern book, more valuable and able, but equally entangled in the toil of making the worse appear the better reason, is Mr.
McHenry's account of the Cotton Trade.[14] The title, in which we hear
for the first time of the American Republics, indicates the argument.
In Europe we have been accustomed to suppose that there was but
one American Republic, and that it bought nearly all the land now
occupied by the Secessionists of Napoleon in 1804 for seventy-five
million dollars, or of Spain in 1820 for twenty-five, with Union funds ;
to which sum the South can hardly pretend to have furnished one-
third. The special possessions of the South rest upon a basis that is
inseparable from Union, if there were no higher arguments which condemn their effort to engross their ownership. The vogue which their
arguments have so long enjoyed was founded on the too general ignorance of American politics in Europe : there are abundant signs that
better knowledge is gradually becoming fatal to those who were but too
glad to seize upon an apparently simple issue. The advocates of the
South are manifestly preparing to execute a strategic movement but
too similar to many they have ridiculed. Mr. McHenry's
pages which are devoted to the cotton trade are full of statistical returns on its growth and magnitude, and are substantially the old note of homage to King Cotton, a king whose
kingdom is departing from him. It is somewhat symptomatic that
the stress of the argument is made to rest on the qualities of the Sea
Island descriptions, and no longer reposes on the sole possession of the
market which was once so confidently relied on. The negro question
is treated as though it were to be definitively settled on physiological
principles. The inferiority of the race, their inability, when free, to
cope, without education, with the comparatively instructed white—are
accepted as a full and unanswerable indication that they are born for
the state from which every means of exit is shut out. The evils of
slavery are thus made to furnish a ground for its continuance, and
wrong unblushingly defended by a parade of its own consequences. An
effort is made in this volume to escape from the reproach of repudiation
on the part of the South, which substantially amounts to this, that

---

[14] " The Cotton Trade : its Bearing upon the Prosperity of Great Britain and
Commerce of the American Republics, considered in Connexion with the System of
Negro Slavery in the Confederate States." By G. McHenry. London : Saunders,
Otley, and Co. 1863.

the repudiating States would not be bound by the acts of their agents and hold themselves absolved from cheating others, when they can make it appear that they have been cheated themselves.

A very careful and copious account of the Cotton Cultivation in the South of India has been brought together by Mr. Wheeler.[15]   For all practical purposes it must be most valuable to the grower.   Its ultimate conclusions are, that the quality of the native sorts, though susceptible of great improvement from careful cultivation, can never be brought to equal the finest New Orleans descriptions ; and that the American plant degenerates in an Indian climate.   This permanent inferiority in staple must ever give American cotton the command of the market, and to a certain extent renders the Indian cultivation dependent upon political contingencies.   Peace in America and the maintenance of the old servile basis of southern society, would necessarily restore to the slave states a great part of their old predominance in the European market.   But peace on these terms becomes with every year less and less probable, and on none other can negroes who have been studiously educated to care for nothing but their simplest animal wants, be expected to work at all more energetically than will suffice to supply them.   The effects of our own emancipatory measures are too palpable to be ignored even by those who are blind to the necessary consequences of a sudden freedom conferred on men who for generations have, both in mind and body, been confirmed in habits which incapacitate them for its exercise.   There seems, then, every chance that political circumstances will long compensate India for the natural inferiority of its conditions of cotton cultivation.

In the summer of 1861 the Canadian Government determined on sending an expedition up the River Moisie, which falls into the Gulf of St. Lawrence, to explore its course to the watershed which divides its course from the streams that flow into the Atlantic at Hamilton Inlet.   The enterprise could not have fallen into better hands than those of Mr. Hind,[16] already well known from his accounts of the Red River Exploration of 1859, and the Assinniboine Expedition of 1858.   We do not remember to have ever read a book of travels which so completely brings the country before the reader's eyes.   The author's natural susceptibility to the savage beauties of the country is seconded by powers of description of the rarest sort ; whilst his knowledge of, and sympathy for, the Indian character, kept his mind constantly open to every trait which could throw light upon their customs and superstitions.   It is a sad story of a ruined country and a perishing population.   The elevated plateau of which the Peninsula consists, was once well wooded and full of game, on which the Indians lived in vastly greater numbers and comparative plenty.   But that which was of old sufficient for their simple wants is now almost exhausted by the demands of their trade

---

[15] "Hand-book to the Cotton Cultivation in the Madras Presidency." By J. T. Wheeler.   London : Virtue Brothers.   1863.

[16] "Excursions in the Interior of the Labrador Peninsula, the Country of the Montagnais and Nasquapee Indians."   By H. G. Hind, M.A., F.R.G.S.   2 vols. London : Longman and Co.   1863.

with Europeans. They must now wage a dreadful war with constantly
impending famine; and the demoralization which is induced by this
hopeless life, has greatly increased the natural thoughtlessness of their
savage character. More frequent fires have devastated the forests
they inhabit, and almost exterminated the remnants of animals on
which they lived. There is a plaintive and melancholy tone about all
their tales which is most touching, in spite of the stoical firmness with
which they repress all signs of feeling before strangers. The great
majority of them have given up their primitive worship of a good and
evil spirit and become converts to Roman Catholicism, owing to the
self-denying character of the Jesuit Missionaries. But they have
changed in little else than in the worship of Maria in the place of
Manitou. Their new religion, too, calls them to the coast for the sacraments of their church, and the dampness of the seaboard afflicts them
with every variety of pulmonic disease, from which they never suffer in
the dry highland they inhabit, in spite of exposure to a prolonged
winter which lasts for half the year. If a company of twelve come down
in the summer, it is rare if six return to their native hunting-grounds.
The efforts which have been made to induce them to relinquish the
wild freedom of their lives as hunters, and to appreciate the more reliable results of an agricultural life, have proved so fruitless, that the
French missionaries have frankly declared that it is useless to teach
them anything more than religion. The consequence has been that
the only change produced is one of dogma leaving but small traces
upon their general character.

The Moravians in the northern parts of the peninsula have, from their
method of instructing their converts in useful trades, been somewhat more successful; but their exertions have chiefly been among the
Esquimaux of the coast — a much milder and more stationary people.
It is, however, impossible in this place to touch upon the multitude of
interesting questions connected with the race of Indians whose remnants
at present people this almost desert land; but hardly any page of Mr.
Hind's journal is devoid of some feature of their life which shows how
hard is that first step in civilization which lies between the hunter and
the husbandman. The mere physical difficulties encountered by the
expedition were by no means contemptible, as may be imagined from
the fact that the river they were ascending in some places fell as much
as 506 feet in 2¼ miles. The ascent could, consequently, only be made
in native birch bark canoes, which could be carried round the rapids
and cascades that constantly interrupted its progress. These paths,
or portages as they are locally called, were often of extreme difficulty,
frequently involving the ascent and descent of rocky barriers of 500 or
600 feet. The beauty of the pine woods and moss and lichen-covered
rocks among which they grew, fully recompensed the toil of such of
the party as could appreciate them, and has found an enthusiastic and
most adequate describer in Mr. Hind. These lovely and many-coloured
lichens, which first break the surface of the hardest rocks and render
other vegetation possible, are succeeded by mosses as varied as themselves, but after, by a thousand years' growth and decay, they have yielded
earth enough to support a pine forest, they are the means in a dry

summer, by carrying the sparks of a hunter's ill-extinguished fire before the slightest breeze, of destroying all this patient work of nature over an extent that has sometimes consumed hundreds of square miles in one conflagration.

The rivers and lakes of this region abound in salmon and trout. Fish of 60 lbs. weight have been taken under the falls which occur so frequently in their course. The moose, rein-deer, and the beaver, the wolf, marten, and rabbit were once abundant, but are fast disappearing, and with them must, at no very remote period, the Indian population also vanish.

The second volume of this excellent book is filled with the fullest particulars of the coast, and every question connected with its geography. The important fishing trade carried on in the Gulf of St. Lawrence and on the eastern shore of Labrador, is treated in the fullest manner, both from an economical and political point of view. Our treaty obligations with the French and Americans on the subject of these important fisheries are treated, it is true, from an exclusively Canadian point of view; but with a temper, insight, and judgment, which fairly raises the question—whether the mother country has not, on these points, been somewhat too facile in assuming them; they are not, however, so easily escaped from as incurred, and the remedy, though not an easy one—for it calls for a capital not at present at their disposal—is in the hands of the Canadians. They would do well, however, to compare the melancholy appeal, given in this volume, which is made to them in the petition of the native Indians of Labrador, in which they hopelessly beg for a restitution of their right of fishing in their rivers, which has been leased to Americans and enterprising Canadians by the Colonial Government, with their own to the Home Government for the exclusive possession of their ocean fisheries. A more striking parallel could not be found, or one more calculated to moderate any exaggerated complaints in the mouth of a Canadian.

" Wanderings in West Africa," by a F.R.G.S.,[17] though but a description of one voyage on board the African Steam Ship Company's vessel the *Blackland*, and professing to give the impressions of a day at Teneriffe, a day at Bathurst, six hours at Cape Palmas, &c., is really the work of one very well acquainted not only with the general questions connected with the " Dark Continent," but also with all the geographical literature connected with his subject. Although the book is in the last degree desultory, and the author's opinions by no means universally acceptable, there exists no fitter companion for the voyager or trader to these coasts, our constantly increasing trade with which makes any well-written manual highly desirable. The great insalubrity of the stations on this coast is attributed by the author to the ill-chosen situations in which they are placed; but as a more healthy site is only attainable by removal some miles into the interior, a healthy port seems hardly consistent with the necessary conditions of the trade.

---

[17] "Wanderings in West Africa: from Liverpool to Fernando Po." By a F.R.G.S. London: Tinsley Brothers. 1863.

On the question of slavery the author holds very strong opinions, and is not far from accusing the advocates of emancipation of a sentimental ignorance of the subject. In this he falls into the common error of supposing that if he can prove the condition of the blacks more miserable and immoral in their native countries than on an American plantation, he has sufficiently answered those who differ from him in disapproving of such a means of civilization. This is only to look at one side of the question, and to carry the Darwinian argument which he puts in the promise to adopt emancipation views when the black rat shall get the better of the grey one, to an ultimate result which completely shuts out all moral considerations. On that side of the question which regards the influence of slavery on the master and on the social condition of the community which accepts it as its basis, he is judiciously silent. This book contains a great deal of valuable information on the character and habits of the different tribes of Africans on the Sierra Leone Coast and on those of the two Bights of Benin and Biafra. He gives a very full account of the condition of the Gold Coast, and is of opinion that extended trade will ultimately open a wider field than that of California. He grounds this opinion chiefly on the rude methods employed by the natives in gathering the gold which is now exported from the coast; but it has always been the case that gold has yielded more to such simple methods than to the improved processes which attack it on its native sites, rather than in those diluvial deposits which are accessible by the simplest means, and in which nature has on a great scale done all the preparatory work for the gold-seeker. There can, however, be but little doubt that this branch of African export will share in that advance which is daily made by palm oil, nuts, and the other staple productions of the country. There seems also to be no doubt of the capabilities of this country to supply cotton to almost any extent, were the condition of the native communities more favourable to any such protracted industry. The slow progress of the artificial wants which they must contract by the continuance of European trade will ultimately bring about a civilizing change in their manners and habits; as their desires increase, their faculties will advance with them, and new necessities are the bitter root from which alone improvement can be expected.

A slight account of three weeks' tour in Majorca[18] may be recommended as indicating a new ground to those in search of an unhackneyed district for a summer holiday. The Valley of Soller, on the west side of the island, seems to promise an excellent situation for invalids who stand in need of a southern winter. The determination to be interested and pleased, with which the author meets the most insignificant incidents, though it makes his book as pleasant to his readers as no doubt it made his trip to himself, is yet carried to so great an extent, that those who may be inclined to follow him should not forget what excellent travelling companions they are, nor attribute to him any disappointment they may meet with among the genial and simple inhabitants.

---

[18] "Three Weeks in Majorca." By W. Dodd, A.M. London: Chapman and Hall. 1863.

Dr. Abraham Roth, editor of the Swiss journal the *Bund*, has published an account of an ascent of two hitherto unscaled summits in the Bernese Oberland of the Doldenhorn and the Weisse Frau.[19] The Alpine Club has made the public familiar with every feature of adventure attendant on these exploits ; but we have seen nothing which can compare with the admirable illustrations with which Dr. Roth has adorned his little volume. These are so good that the fullest idea of such snow-covered heights is conveyed to the most uninitiated. The care with which some natural object is always introduced is especially to be praised, as it at once conveys, what is so often wanting in similar pictures, an immediate appreciation of the enormous extent of the snow fields, and fully suggests the perilous heights attacked by the hardy tourists. We have seldom seen colour-printing so successfully applied to landscapes. The author does not disdain any mountain legend which came in his way, and thus gives an agreeable relief to the somewhat monotonous details of Alpine climbing. Perhaps nothing is so difficult to convey to those who have not experienced it as the enjoyment and exhilaration attendant on those otherwise somewhat purposeless feats.

The votaries, however, of these exploits will be glad of the collection of Journeys just published by Melchior Ulrich,[20] which gives the necessary directions, so far as books can give them, for more than twenty different passes through the Alps of Valais, and Switzerland. Two of these, it is true, are taken from the publications of the Alpine Club, but many are new, and those in the district of the Bernina are especially interesting and beautiful.

In a very handsome volume Mr. Gould gives us an account of a trip to Iceland,[21] which he and some friends made, apparently in 1862, for the purpose of collecting the legends of the country and filling a portfolio with water-colour sketches; these last are excellent, and give a truer idea of that land of volcanic rocks and stone marshes than can easily be got from any other sources. Those views which he gives in colour are beautiful and poetical landscapes, and show how fine an effect may be produced by very simple means in the hands of a competent artist. It is to be regretted that the woodcuts do not do equal justice to the originals, which are always interesting in subject and often picturesque in the highest degree. The author, there can be no doubt, succeeded in filling his portfolio with a most interesting series of drawings, full of the delicate beauty of northern skies and the savage grandeur of the country. The greater part of the volume is filled with translations of local legends, which have great simplicity of feeling and strong national peculiarities. We are not, however, of the author's

---

[19] "The Doldenhorn and Weisse Frau, ascended for the First Time by Abraham Roth and Edmund Von Fellenberg." Coblenz: Karl Baedeker. London : Williams and Norgate.

[20] "Berge und Gletscher Fahrten in den Hochalpen der Schweiz." Von G. Studer M. Ulrich, J. J. Weilenmann, H. Zeller. Zurich: F. Schultess. London : D. Nutt. 1863.

[21] "Iceland: its Scenes and Sagas." By Sabine Baring Gould, M.A., Fellow of St. Nicolas College, Lancing, &c. London : Smith, Elder, and Co. 1863.

opinion, that the translations are improved by the introduction of
antiquated and provincial words where they happen to resemble the
Icelandic ones. Byre, a farm; bonder, a farmer; to busk, to make
ready, and the like, are no ornaments where they occur in the midst of
the most familiar vernacular; nor does he restrict himself to their use
in the legends, but *busks* himself every morning for his day's journey
with an amusing complacency. The travellers landed at Reykjavick
as usual, but made a much longer tour than is customary, traversing
the whole of the eastern side of the island and visiting the Eyja Fjord,
and the remarkable falls at Dettifoss; on their return south, the Geysir
was of course examined and described. The tone of the book is that
of a cheerful well-enjoyed holiday; indeed, the high spirits of the party
sometimes took strange shapes. On one occasion they went solemnly
through the old joke of teaching their hostess to make stone soup. As
she had nothing to give them, they proposed she should boil a piece of
lava, and by the judicious addition of certain ingredients from packages
bought at Fortnum and Mason's they astonished her with a very palat-
able result. Another time, being forced to talk Latin to the clergyman
of village near the Geysir, and finding his colloquial accomplishments in
that language run rather short, one of the party treated him to a
galimatias out of Henry's First Latin Book—a kind of joke that would
send the lowest form into a roar, but was hardly consistent with the
courtesy due either to the person or character of his interlocutor. One
of the most useful features of the book is the minute particularity of
each day's journey, and of the means of accomplishing it; this makes
the volume, in spite of its bulk, a most desirable guide-book to any
one who may wish to devote a two months' summer holiday to a visit
to one of the most interesting spots in Europe. It is also furnished
with very full appendices on the natural history and geology of the
country.

Those who wish for more detailed information on the characteristic
forms and geographical distribution of the crystalline rocks of the
island would do well to consult the work of Herr Winkler[22], who has
made them the object of a special study.

SCIENCE.

IN the "Correspondence of Alexander von Humboldt with Heinrich
Berghaus,"[1] we were in hopes of obtaining, if not any important
scientific information, at least some interesting particulars of the life
and works of one of the greatest philosophers of our day. In this
respect, however, we think, the readers of the three volumes just pub-

---

[22] "Island der Bau seiner Gebirge und dessen geologische Bedeutung." Von
Gustav G. Winkler. München: E. H. Gummi. London: D. Nutt.
[1] "Briefwechsel Alexander von Humboldt's mit Heinrich Berghaus, aus den
Jahren 1825 bis 1858." Leipzig: Costenoble. 1863. 3 vols. 8vo, pp. 348, 308,
and 336.

lished will be somewhat disappointed; except as manifesting the constant activity of his mind, and his incessant watchfulness of everything tending to throw light upon those subjects so admirably treated in his "Cosmos," they give us but little insight into the inner mind of Humboldt, and will be of more value to the biographer of Heinrich Berghaus than to those who desire to investigate the life and doings of his great friend. Indeed, a very considerable portion of the third volume—and this is by no means the least amusing part of the collection—is devoted to the correspondence between Berghaus, Humboldt, Dr. Hooker, and Mr. B. H. Hodgson, of Darjeeling, and to the full development of a grievance which the first-named *savant* considers that he possesses against the two Englishmen. Professor Berghaus, it appears, undertook the preparation of an elementary physical geography, to be translated by Mr. Hodgson into the Hindu vernacular, for the use of young natives in our Indian schools, and having completed half his task, and received half the stipulated remuneration, hesitated a little about the remainder in consequence of his finding that there was some little difficulty in the way of Mr. Hodgson getting his book patronized effectually by the Indian Government. After much correspondence he proceeded with his work, with an express stipulation that the remainder of the manuscript should be paid for on its completion and delivery; but finding, as many a literary man and philosopher has done before him, that it would be very convenient to draw a little money on account, he sent off a portion of manuscript to Dr. Hooker, who was to be his paymaster in England, as agent for Mr. Hodgson, with a request for an immediate remittance. To this request Dr. Hooker demurred, and ultimately, Professor Berghaus refusing to proceed without the advance, the whole business was dropped. This grievance Professor Berghaus parades *in extenso;* the letters, conversations, and statements relating to it occupying a very considerable part of 170 pages in the third volume, and including the most curious lamentations about postage, and his having been charged no less than 4 thaler 23 silbergroschen by the Berlin bankers on the payment of his first remittance. He nevertheless evidently considers it very odd and decidedly shabby on the part of Dr. Hooker, to complain of being put to about the same expense in postage in connexion with the advance of money which the latter declined sending. The whole affair has its melancholy side, from its showing that even such men as Humboldt and Berghaus were not superior to the ordinary Continental practice of getting as much advantage as possible out of John Bull; whilst their simultaneous reflections on the money-loving mania and business habits characteristic of that individual, even when he disguises his ordinary shopkeeping character under the garb of a *savant*, are exceedingly ludicrous. In other respects these letters, as we have already said, give us but little insight into the character of Humboldt, except that they display that genial and often sportive habit of mind which is generally attributed to him by those who knew him. Of anecdotic matter we find scarcely any, although there is one capital story of Humboldt's meeting with a young man who professed to have ascended Chimborazo in his company, and to have actually reached the summit, when the great traveller was left panting some distance below. To make his story consistent with his own age, this veracious individual shifted the time of the ascent twenty years forward; he fled precipitately, however, when he discovered that the person to whom he was talking was no other than Humboldt himself. The letters, extending over a period of thirty-three years, from 1825 to 1858, contain, as might be expected, much that will prove interesting to the student of the history of geographical discovery; indeed, from the care with which Humboldt watched for everything bearing upon physical geography, and the constancy of his communications upon such matters with Berghaus, the foundation of a history of the modern progress of geographical science might almost be derived from these letters alone. They contain numerous criticisms upon the results obtained and published by various travellers, and through them are scattered many original remarks and hints which will prove of interest to the geographer. Professor Berghaus publishes with the correspondence a considerable number of articles furnished to the geographical journals edited by him for many years (the "Hertha" and "Zeitschrift für Erdkunde"), either by Humboldt himself or by his friends, and also several to which Humboldt refers in the correspondence. In this respect the worthy Professor has done rather more than was necessary—as, for example, in reprinting the whole of the Treaty between Mexico and the United States, by which the Californian and other territory was ceded to the latter; but to make up for this, he has added several papers mentioned and quoted by Humboldt, but which had not previously appeared in print.

Out of three astronomical works which we have to notice, two are intended for the demolition of the Newtonian philosophy. In one of them, bearing the proud title of "Victoria toto Cœlo; or, Modern Astronomy recast,"[2] the author, a Mr. James Reddie, endeavours to show that, as we now believe that the sun, with all his attendant planets, is moving through space at an awful rate, the laws formerly supposed to govern the revolutions of the planets can no longer apply. According to the author's notion, the earth in following the sun, and the moon in following the earth, would describe *in space* neither circles nor ellipses, but a series of either looped or semi-elliptical curves, the latter united by pretty sharp angles, at each of which he assumes that there would be a sort of jerking stop of the planetary body very disagreeable to any inhabitants which it might possess. That this might be the optical expression of the phenomena to an eye capable of grasping the whole series of movements at once, and placed outside that portion of space which is assumed to be moving along with our planetary system, cannot be denied; but this, if demonstrated, cannot invalidate Newton's sixth corollary of his first proposition (Book I.), which refers only to the motions of bodies relatively to the centres round which they revolve. If Mr. Reddie will take the

---

[2] "Victoria toto Cœlo; or, Modern Astronomy recast." By James Reddie, F.A.S.L. London: Hardwicke. 1863. 8vo, pp. 64.

trouble to read carefully over "this extraordinary corollary," as he calls it, he will find that he has somewhat mistaken its meaning. Again, if he will examine the second corollary of the second proposition (Book I.), in which the possible existence of a resisting medium is alluded to, he will find that he is in error in regarding the resisting medium as the supposed cause of the acceleration of the description of areas, and in fact that he has entirely missed the sense of that corollary. Mr. Reddie's notion, that instead of an orbital motion, the course of planetary bodies accompanying a centre moving in a given direction would consist, according to received opinions, of a series of curves in which the planet would either remain stationary for a moment, or become retrograde at its passage from one curve to another, constitutes the foundation of his argument against modern astronomers. Of this we can only say that its absurdity may be practically demonstrated by any one who will study the revolutions of a coachwheel, or of a stone or other body swung round at the end of a string by a person running.

Dr. Pratt, the second of our anti-Newtonians, does not commit himself, in his work "On Orbital Motion,"[3] in the same way as his *collaborateur*, Mr. Reddie, of whose writings, however, he speaks in terms of praise, although their views upon some important points differ widely. Dr. Pratt's general theory of astronomy seems to be as follows. At the centre of the space occupied by all the celestial bodies visible to us is a central body, occupying the *celestial polar centre*, round which our sun and all other celestial bodies are revolving in vast orbits. The plane of revolution of the sun is said to be perpendicular to that of the solar system. The *mean orbits* of all the celestial bodies are circular, but owing to the oscillatory revolution of the central body of each system round the orbital centre of the latter, the actual orbits oscillate spirally on either side of the mean orbits. We cannot follow Dr. Pratt through all the details of his system of astronomy, but we believe that the above is a fair statement of his general views as to the interpretation of the phenomena observed in the heavens. It is in his theory that he makes his direct attack upon the Newtonian philosophy; and here he strikes at the very foundation. He says that the *vis inertiæ* is not, as stated by Newton, a tendency on the part of bodies to persevere in their present state, whether that state be one of rest or motion, but a constant tendency to a state of rest. *Vis inertiæ* thus, in the author's view, becomes equivalent to gravity, as indeed he admits; and thus it is evident that Newton and he speak of very different things under the same name. Having thus disposed of the *vis inertiæ*, Dr. Pratt has to find two forces, equivalent to the so-called centripetal and centrifugal forces by which his orbital motion might be effected, and these he describes under the names of the centric and eccentric forces. The former is the attractive force exerted by the central body upon those which revolve round it; the latter is said to be a typical expression for "the sustaining power of God!" It does not

3 "On Orbital Motion: the Outlines of a System of Physical Astronomy." By Henry F. A. Pratt, M.D. London: Churchill and Sons. 1863. 8vo, pp. 196.

appear why centric force is left to its own devices, and the direct interposition of the Deity is called in to account for the force acting in opposition to it; we can see no positive reason why the terms "centric"
and "eccentric" are to be preferred to their predecessors, nor can we
understand why the character of infidelity should be fastened upon the
Newtonian theory, because it supposes the Deity to act throughout by
laws impressed upon matter, and not by law in one instance and by
direct interposition in another.　Until the appearance of some more
powerful arguments than those of either Dr. Pratt or Mr. Reddie,
we shall venture still to believe in the truth of the Newtonian
philosophy.

Two unpretending little books now before us may be regarded as, to
a certain extent, constituting an antidote to the ill effects which the
crude speculations of the authors just referred to may produce in some
minds.　One of these is the "Introduction to Astronomy" of Mr.
Hind,[4] which has now reached its third edition, and in its present form
furnishes a good elementary account of the chief results of practical
astronomy, with indications of so much of the theories upon which
physical astronomy is founded as will suffice to give the beginner a
notion of the general bearings of astronomical science.　The descriptions of celestial phenomena are very clear, and the student's comprehension of the subject will be greatly facilitated by the "Astronomical
Vocabulary," originally an independent work, which is incorporated
with this edition, and made to serve as an index.

"The First Principles of Natural Philosophy," by Mr. W. T.
Lynn,[5] is the title of the second little manual which we should recommend to those who are in any danger of being led astray by such
writers as Dr. Pratt and Mr. Reddie.　In its section on Dynamics
they will find a most intelligible exposition of the laws of motion, after
reading which, if they fall into error, they will at least have the satisfaction of doing so with their eyes open.　This work is divided into
five sections, treating of Statics, Dynamics, Hydrostatics and Hydro-
dynamics, Pneumatics and Optics respectively, and we have never seen
the principles of those branches of science so clearly and concisely explained as in its pages.　In the first two sections the author has given
sufficient indications of the working of the more important mechanical
problems, and the whole is most admirably adapted for an educational
book, the purpose for which it is intended.

Whilst some of Newton's countrymen have been making a dead
set at his theory of universal gravitation, certain German philosophers
appear to have been engaged in an equally violent effort to destroy his
theory of colour, and to set up in its place that of their countryman,
Goethe, apparently on the principle so clearly enunciated by Tristram
Shandy, that by demolishing your opponent's hypothesis, you at the

[4] "An Introduction to Astronomy, to which is added an Astronomical Voca-
bulary containing an Explanation of Terms in use at the present day."　By J. R.
Hind, F.R.A.S., &c.　Third Edition, revised and greatly enlarged.　London:
H. G. Bohn.　1863.　Small 8vo, pp. 216.

[5] "First Principles of Natural Philosophy."　By William Thynne Lynn, B.A.,
&c.　London: Van Voorst.　1863.　Small 8vo, pp. 100.

same time establish your own. In opposition to these "Göthe-nianer," Dr. Karl Neumann has published his "Discourse upon the most essential errors of Goethe's Theory of Colour,"[6] in which he has pretty clearly shown that his opponents know very little of the subject on which they have ventured to write. As Dr. Neumann's pamphlet consists entirely of a review of two works by a Dr. Bähr and a Herr Pössnecker, it will be unnecessary to follow him through all his arguments, but the reader will form a tolerable notion of the calibre of the anti-Newtonians from the following example of what one of them regards as a "strong case" in opposition to the theory of the different refrangibility of colours. "Objects of different colours at the same distance," says Dr. Bähr, "such as a green tree, a red roof, or gay clothing, could only produce confused pictures in our eyes, if the colours of these objects possessed a different refrangibility. The painter would be unable to represent the human form correctly in its outlines, whenever its clothing consisted of different colours." We can fully concur with Dr. Neumann in asking, "whether any one could have believed such nonsense possible," and also in thinking that a little rough handling will be very good for men who, like his present adversaries, venture to write upon the nature of colour with so little notion of the meaning of refraction, as to attribute to a mind like Newton's the origination of a theory, according to which, as our author says, we ought to see the collar of a letter-carrier going about quite distinct from his coat, and "indeed the whole man, sweeping through the air, as if broken up into separate pieces!"

The prizes of fifty pounds and twenty pounds offered by the North-wich Salt Chamber of Commerce for the best essays on "The Use of Salt in Agriculture,"[7] have produced two memoirs which that body has considered worth publication. These are by Mr. Robert Falk and Dr. T. L. Phipson, the former having obtained the first and the latter the second of the above prizes. Mr. Falk has devoted his attention especially to the subject set before him; Dr. Phipson, with a more discursive pen, runs through the general uses of salt, including its application to agricultural purposes. The evidence in connexion with the latter seems to show that the advantage of the use of salt alone as a manure is very doubtful, but that when added to nitrogenous manures it generally proves of the greatest service. This appears to be partly due to its own direct action when absorbed, partly to its influence on those materials of the soil which are required for the proper nutrition of the plants, and lastly, in part to its rendering more equable the action upon the plants of the nitrogenous manures associated with it. There is no novelty in the views set forth in these essays, but their authors will have done some service to agricul-

---

[6] "Vortrag über die wesentlichsten Irrthümer in Göthe's Farbenlehre; gehalten in Dresden, von Dr. Carl Neumann. Dresden: Ernst und Portèger. 1868. 8vo, pp. 52.

[7] "The Use of Salt in Agriculture." By Robert Falk, and Dr. T. L. Phipson, F.C.S., &c. Prize Essays published by the Salt Chamber of Commerce at Northwich. Liverpool: G. J. Poore. London: Simpkins. 1868. 8vo, pp. 56.

ture, by calling the attention of farmers to what is at least a cheap mode of greatly increasing the efficacy of their ordinary manures.

Mr. Jukes's "School Manual of Geology,"[8] intended not merely as a class-book, but also as a means of exciting, and to a certain extent fulfilling, in the minds of young people, a desire to obtain some knowledge of the marvellous phenomena revealed by geology, appears to us to be admirably adapted for these purposes. In the earlier chapters, starting from the theory of an incandescent and fluid central nucleus, he explains the means by which rock masses have been produced; and in his second section describes the changes of position and physical condition brought about in these rocks, after their deposition, by various causes. The third section includes the discussion of the sequence of the rocks as indicated by their superposition and contained fossils. The whole arrangement and treatment of the subject is very clear, and such as to render many points, which often appear to be surrounded with difficulties, comparatively easy of comprehension to the beginner. We may remark, however, that in his etymological translations of the names of fossils the author is frequently not very fortunate, and sometimes wrong.

Karl von Hauer's report "On the more important Iron-Ores of the Austrian Monarchy,"[9] possesses but little general scientific interest; its chief value consisting in the details which it will furnish to the mineralogist as to the character and distribution of the iron-ores of the large portion of eastern Europe subject to Austrian rule. The ores appear to be scattered through nearly all the states of which that incongruous monarchy is composed, and to differ about equally in their geological position, mode of deposition, and mineralogical nature. Their amount of iron varies, according to the analyses made in the laboratory of the Imperial Geological Institute, from 7 to nearly 64 per cent. The number of blast-furnaces at work in 1861 in the Austrian empire was 234, and the total amount of iron turned out by them rather more than 5,600,000 hundredweights.

An excellent popular summary of the modern theory of physiology is furnished by Mr. Savory in his Lectures "On Life and Death;"[10] which, as now given to the public, form a well-written and most interesting little treatise on matters, a knowledge of which must be of importance to every one. Life, according to Mr. Savory, is "essentially a state of dynamical equilibrium, consisting in a definite relation between destruction and renewal—in a regulated adjustment between waste and repair, whereby the condition is maintained notwithstanding constant change." Waste is caused by action, repair takes place during repose, assimilation is necessary for repair; life, therefore,

[8] "The School Manual of Geology." By J. Beete Jukes, M.A., F.R.S., &c. Edinburgh: Black. 1863. 12mo, pp. 362.

[9] "Die wichtigeren Eisenerz vorkommen in der Österreichischen Monarchie und ihr Metallgehalt." Von Karl Ritter von Hauer. Vienna: Braumüller. 1863. 8vo, pp. 187.

[10] "On Life and Death: Four Lectures delivered at the Royal Institution of Great Britain." By William S. Savory, F.R.S. London: Smith, Elder, and Co. 1863. Small 8vo, pp. 203.

" may be said to present essentially two phases—one of assimilation, and one of function. Assimilation is a source of force ; function causes its expenditure." In the development of these principles, in their application to the varied phenomena of life, and in the indication of the influence of external forces upon the organism, the author has been, it seems to us, particularly happy ; and his pages contain some remarks upon such subjects as metamorphosis, the nature and possible effect of rudimentary organs and type of organization, which will prove highly interesting to the naturalist. Of death in general, the completion of the great mystery of life, (for it must be observed that, whatever we may say about the correlation of vital force with the other manifestations of physical force, we do not approach one step nearer to the solution of the question of the nature and origin of life,) the author can say little more than that it is the cessation of those processes which constitute vital actions. But upon the relations between molecular death and the general life and death of the organism, and upon the different means by which death is brought about, the reader will find much to interest and instruct him in Mr. Savory's lectures.

The little " Manual of Zoology" of Milne-Edwards,[11] of which the English translation by Dr. Knox has now reached a second edition, is certainly one of the best works that we possess for effecting the purpose for which it was intended—namely, furnishing the general reader with an elementary notion of the structure, functions, and classification of animals. The introductory section, which treats of the general structure and physiology of animals, and explains the general principles of classification, is admirably clear ; and the succeeding portion, giving the details of the system, with illustrative examples of the different groups, is also excellent as regards the vertebrata and the higher articulata ; but the treatment of the lower divisions (mollusca and zoophytes) is very imperfect, and passes by, wholly without notice, many of the most interesting and important results of modern zoological research. Dr. Knox, who was engaged in revising the proofs in the last days of his life, has added several notes in different parts of the book ; these are generally of value, but sometimes appear to be introduced without much reason. The little volume is beautifully printed, and the illustrations, many of which are peculiar to the English edition, are generally of great beauty. We notice that the names appended to the illustrations, which were very imperfectly translated in the first edition, are much better in this, although there is still room for improvement.

Under the long-winded title of " Not Like Man, Bimanous and Biped, nor yet Quadrumanous, but Cheiropodous,"[12] we have received

---

[11] " A Manual of Zoology." By M. Milne-Edwards. Translated from the last French edition by R. Knox, M.D., F.R.S.E. Second Edition. Edited by C. Carter Blake, F.G.S., &c. London : Renshaw. 1863. 12mo, pp. 564.

[12] " Not Like Man," &c. By George Britton Halford, M.D., Professor of Anatomy, Physiology, and Pathology in the University of Melbourne. Melbourne : Millar. 1863. 8vo, pp. 16.

a small contribution to the controversy as to the position of man in nature. It is a voice reaching us from the Antipodes, its author being Dr. Halford, Professor of Anatomy, &c., in the University of Melbourne. The statements contained in this pamphlet are founded on the dissection of two Macaque monkeys. As regards the characters of the brain, the author entirely confirms the observations of Professor Huxley; but he is at variance with him with respect to the agreement in structure between the foot of man and the posterior extremity in the monkey. He founds his opposition to Huxley's view chiefly on the arrangement of the muscles of the fourth layer in the foot of the Macaque, which he shows to agree precisely with those present in the hand of the same animal and in that of man, but to differ entirely from the corresponding layer of muscles in the human foot. When we look into the functions of these muscles, however, we find them to be connected with the general grasping power of the foot, and especially with the opposability of the great toe; and as Professor Huxley certainly does not deny this, it will not surprise him to learn (if he does not know it already), that the undoubted functions of the member are thus expressed in its musculature. Professor Huxley's argument as to the identity of the inferior limb in man and the apes is drawn from the consideration of the general arrangement of the bones and muscles entering into the composition of the respective members, and certainly is not affected by the details put forward by Dr. Halford.

Under the title of "New Materials for the History of Man,"[13] Mr. R. G. Haliburton has sent us impressions of two essays communicated by him to the Nova Scotian Institute of Natural Science. Mr. Haliburton has long occupied himself with investigations into the unity of those singular superstitious practices which are so widely spread amongst the most various tribes of mankind, in the hope thereby of obtaining evidence of the unity of origin of the human species. His first essay is devoted to the discussion of the almost universal attribution of a more or less ominous character to the act of sneezing, and his second treats of the very general prevalence of the custom of holding "festivals of the dead" at the beginning of the month of November. This practice the author finds prevailing in the Southern hemisphere in connexion with the rising of the Pleiades, which marks the beginning of the year, and he hence supposes that the custom took its rise south of the equator in the form of a New Year's commemoration of departed friends and relatives. In support of this hypothesis, involving, as it does, migration northwards of the ancestors of those European and Asiatic peoples amongst whom a similar custom is to be traced, Mr. Haliburton adduces many curious and interesting facts.

In medical literature we have an interesting volume by Mr. Hilton, on "The Influence of Mechanical and Physiological Rest in the Treatment

---

[13] "New Materials for a History of Man, derived from a Comparison of the Customs and Superstitions of Nations." By R. G. Haliburton, F.S.A. Halifax, Nova Scotia. 1863. 8vo.

of Accidents and Disease, and the Diagnostic Value of Pain."[14] After an accurate exposition of the means adopted by nature to secure a state of quiescence of the various viscera, illustrated by a reference to the anatomical arrangements by which the brain and spinal cord are protected from injury and from the effects of shocks to other parts of the body, the author discusses the points of interest in the phenomena accompanying concussion of these organs; for the proper treatment of which he urges strongly the necessity for long-continued rest, both mechanical and physiological. Passing from the consideration of these special cases, the author, by details of numerous instances of injury and disease coming under his own observation, and by much judicious criticism of the phenomena presented, points out the value of rest in the restoration of injured parts, and shows how the main object of the surgeon ought to be, by every means at his disposal, to secure the most perfect quietude of structures suffering from injury or disease, in order that nature may not be disturbed in her efforts to repair the mischief.

In many surgical diseases the author shows how the removal of some cause of irritation, as a foreign body, stone in the bladder, &c., leads to the recovery of the patient by securing the rest of the organ. Our space will not permit us to follow the author through all the numerous illustrations he gives of the value of rest, both physiological and mechanical, in the cure of disease; suffice it to say, they are as instructive as they are varied.

In considering the question of the diagnostic value of pain, the author justly lays great stress on the necessity there is for an intimate acquaintance with the origin and distribution of the nerves, to enable the practitioner rightly to appreciate the value of pain as a symptom of disease or injury in any given case. The importance of this knowledge, and its value in assisting our diagnosis, is more especially shown in reference to diseases affecting parts remote from the seat of pain, as is the case in some affections of the spine and of internal organs, pain at the peripheral extremities of nerves being frequently due to disease or irritation in some remote part of their course. Under this head the author makes some judicious observations, and gives examples in illustration, showing the indication as to the seat of disease afforded by pain affecting the body symmetrically and otherwise. The author shows how much may be done in clearing up many doubtful cases by an accurate knowledge of the nervous distribution in the parts affected.

Although the work before us contains but little that is new as regards fact, yet the author places the facts so forcibly before the reader, and so clearly indicates their value in the diagnosis and treatment of disease, and moreover, suggests so much that is important in

---

[14] "On the Influence of Mechanical and Physiological Rest in the Treatment of Accidents and Surgical Diseases, and the Diagnostic Value of Pain. A Course of Lectures delivered at the Royal College of Surgeons of England in the Years 1860, 1861, and 1862." By J. Hilton, F.R.S., F.R.C.S., &c. London : Bell & Daldy. 1863. 8vo, pp. 499.

the investigations of morbid conditions of the system, that we venture to predict the profession will regard Mr. Hilton's work as one of the most useful of recent contributions to practical medicine.

A third edition of Dr. F. Winslow's work, " On Obscure Diseases of the Brain and Mind,"[15] is little more than a reprint, in a more compact form, of the preceding editions of this work. The author discusses at considerable length the various phenomena which present themselves in the earlier stages of structural disease of the nervous centres and of insanity, that border land between health and disease, between sanity and insanity, where the first warnings of the coming storm must be detected if we wish to give our patient the full benefit of that treatment which experience indicates. The various indications afforded by alterations in the functional activity of different parts of the nervous system, and the value of those trifling changes in the manifestation of the mental faculties which so frequently, if not invariably, precede more serious diseases, are clearly pointed out, and the necessity for and importance of their early recognition forcibly illustrated. Throughout the volume the author strongly insists on the necessity for the early recognition and treatment not only of insanity, but of the structural changes in the brain, which ultimately give rise to apoplexy and paralysis, and shows how much may be done towards maintaining the health and vigour of the mind by attention to those early threatenings which a careful investigation will in most cases detect. In a series of elegantly written chapters, the author discusses the questions of interest to the physician arising out of the various morbid phenomena affecting the different faculties of the mind. Like the preceding volume by Mr. Hilton, the work of Dr. Winslow is perhaps quite as valuable for the methods of inquiry and observation it suggests, as for the facts it contains—its careful perusal cannot fail to render the practitioner more alive to the early indications of disordered intelligence, and therefore more successful in warding off attacks of disease which, when once established, are but too frequently beyond the reach of remedial measures. To the psychological physician the work is a valuable repository of facts and suggestions in his particular department, and well sustains the reputation of its author.

A little volume of Lectures by Mr. Beale,[16] contains, in a popular style, a brief exposition of the principal features of interest in the physiology of digestion, and the influence of the stomach and its functions on the mental and moral health; they display not only an intimate knowledge of the subject, but also the power of imparting that knowledge to the non-professional reader. There is much sound advice in these lectures, without a shade of quackery.

In a pamphlet of considerable importance, Dr. Chapman indicates a new method of treatment in certain forms of disease hitherto found

---

[15] "Obscure Diseases of the Brain and Mind." By Forbes Winslow, M.D., D.C.L., &c. &c., Oxon. Third Edition, revised. London: R. Hardwicke. 1863. pp. 618.

[16] "The Stomach Medically and Morally Considered." Lecture delivered at the St. Martin's Library Reading Room. By L. J. Beale, M.R.C.S., &c. London: Harrison. 1863. pp. 104.

difficult to control, and in which the application of remedies has not hitherto led to any certain or satisfactory results.[17]   A paper published in the *Medical Times and Gazette* for July, 1863, and printed in the Appendix, contains an exposition of the principles of treatment which the author suggests.   He says :—

"It has long been known that the sympathetic nerve, called by Bichat the nervous system of organic life, presides over those processes by which the body is developed and sustained.   It stimulates and controls the action of the heart, alimentary canal, genito-urinary organs, and all those processes of growth, repair, and removal of *effete* materials, on which the continuous vitality and health of the animal organism depend."

After referring to the researches of Brown-Séquard and others, as to the influence of the sympathetic in controlling the action of blood-vessels, or what have been termed its vaso-motor functions, he says :—

" But as the sympathetic and cerebro-spinal nervous systems are intimately related, and indeed, in some parts, inextricably and indistinguishably blended both in structure and function, the nervous influence, whether healthy or not, which is exerted over the several organs of the body, is twofold; hence, when that influence becomes abnormal, either in kind or degree, the most potent method of restoring it to its healthy condition, would be by a direct action at once on the sympathetic and cerebro-spinal nervous systems.   The physician who acquires the power of directly controlling these great controllers of the organic functions, would immediately obtain the mastery over a large number of diseases.   I have discovered that a controlling power over the circulation of the blood in the brain, in the spinal cord, in the ganglia of the sympathetic nervous system, and through the agency of the nervous centres, also in every other organ of the body, can be exercised by means of cold and heat applied to different parts of the back.   In this manner the reflex excitability or excito-motor power of the spinal cord, and the contractile force of the arteries in all parts of the body, can be immediately modified."

Having examined this theory by the test of experiment, the author finds that cold applied to the back exercises an important influence in raising and sustaining the force of the heart's action; whilst heat, similarly applied, exerts a contrary influence. Herein lies the importance of the discovery: given a power by which we can modify, and, when so modified, maintain the circulation in a certain condition, and we have an agency which cannot fail to exert a potent influence on all those structural and functional diseases which arise from deficient or irregular supply of blood.   On referring to the cases quoted by the author, we find that these are precisely the class of cases in which the author has found the greatest benefit from the treatment suggested—viz., epilepsy, disordered uterine functions, cold extremities, certain forms of paralysis, and diabetes.   The whole theory is so calmly and temperately stated, and the illustrative cases so numerous and well-selected, that we feel

---

[17] " Functional Diseases of Women : Cases illustrative of a New Method of treating them through the Agency of the Nervous System by means of Cold and Heat; also an Appendix, containing Cases illustrative of a New Method of treating Epilepsy, Paralysis, and Diabetes." By John Chapman, M.D., &c. London : Trübner & Co. 1863. pp. 74.

no hesitation in saying that the author's method deserves the attentive and impartial consideration of the profession. The theory is based on sound physiological principles; and in the hands not only of the author, but of others, to whom he has submitted his views, it has borne the test of experiment.

The work just noticed indicates how, in the present state of our knowledge of physiology, the influence of physical agents in the treatment of disease is daily becoming a matter of more importance; but although many practitioners are in the constant habit of resorting to physical remedies in their treatment of particular cases, there is but little information to be obtained from books upon this department of therapeutics. Under these circumstances the " Text-book of Physical Remedies," of Dr. Oppenheimer,[18] will be a welcome addition to the libraries of most medical men, treating as it does fully and well upon the application of physical agents in the practice of medicine. The physical remedies described by the author are—1. Movements of the air and sound; 2. Light; 3. Electricity; 4. Heat; and 5. Climate. The first of these sections might, we think, have been omitted altogether without any great injury to the book—air-douches can hardly be regarded as physical agents, and notwithstanding the case of Saul, the remedial power of music is not of very general application. The greater part of the section on light, also, is occupied by a description of various kinds of spectacles and optical instruments, which are scarcely to be regarded as therapeutical agents. These two sections, however, form but a small portion of the whole book; and the sections relating to the application of electricity in its various forms, and of heat and cold to the treatment of disease, are copious and satisfactory.

According to Dr. E. Leyden,[19] the principal cause of those forms of disease commonly included under the name of *Tabes dorsalis*, including the *Ataxie locomotrice progressive* of French authors, is to be found in the " gray degeneration of the posterior columns of the spinal cord." The general course of the symptoms indicative of this organic lesion is described by the author as being somewhat as follows :—Neuralgic pains in the lower extremities first set in, and, after affecting the patient intermittently for a longer or shorter period, are succeeded by uncertainty in the movements of the limbs, usually accompanied by an incontinence of the urine and fæces. The latter symptoms gradually increase, until the patient becomes completely helpless, and at the same time the anterior members become similarly affected to a greater or less extent, whilst strabismus and defective sight are gradually established. Keeping pace with these changes, interruptions of other functions of the organism usually occur, and it is to these that the fatal termination of such cases is to be ascribed. The course of the

---

[18] " Lehrbuch der physikalischen Heilmittel, für Aerzte und Studirende der Medizin, von Dr. Z. Oppenheimer. Würzburg : Stabel. 1864. 8vo, pp. 431.
[19] " Die graue Degeneration der hinteren Rückenmarksstränge, klinisch bearbeitet," von Dr. E. Leyden. Berlin : Hirschwald. 1863. 8vo, pp. 280, and three plates.

disease is divided by the author into three stages—1. The prodromal or neuralgic stage ; 2. The ataxial stage ; and 3. The paraplegic stage, in which disturbances of the function of nutrition always occur. Each of these stages may vary greatly in duration ; they sometimes follow each other very quickly, in other cases they will last for years. The author cites thirty-two cases (twenty-three from other authors, and nine from his own observations), in which these and other correlated symptoms led at length to death, and the autopsy revealed gray degeneration of the posterior columns of the spinal cord. As regards the cause of the disease, the author considers that the generally received notion that *Tabes dorsalis* is directly caused by excessive sexual indulgence, is unfounded ; according to him, the chief cause of the degenerative process is chill, especially of the feet. The anatomical characters presented by the altered spinal column, and the physiological effects consequent upon the alteration, are fully described by Dr. Leyden ; but neither the nature of the process by which the changes are brought about, nor the proper treatment of the disease, are known with any certainty.

A valuable series of cases illustrative of " The Diseases of Old Age" has been published by Dr. Mettenheimer,[20] of Schwerin. Feeling that actual cases of death by old age are very rare, and that although comparatively few diseases are peculiar to that period of life, the characters of the complaints affecting old people are often so greatly modified as to lead to serious mistakes on the part of medical attendants, the author has brought together a series of upwards of sixty cases observed by himself, chiefly as medical officer of the Lunatic Asylum at Frankfort on the Maine. As the accounts of these cases are very full, and accompanied by descriptions of the appearances presented on the *postmortem* examination, they will prove an important contribution towards our knowledge of the diseases of advanced life.

HISTORY AND BIOGRAPHY.

WE will introduce our notice of Mr. Froude's " History of the Reign of Elizabeth," [1] with an admirable sentence from the first volume—a sentence which, with obvious alterations, will serve as well to characterize the bankruptcy of the established faith in our own day, as it does that of the superseded creed of the old Tudor times. " However men might argue and wrangle, however they might persuade themselves that they believed what they did not believe,

---

[20] " Nosologische und Anatomische Beiträge zu der Lehre von den Greisenkrankheiten." Eine Sammlung von Krankengeschichten und Nekroskopien eigner Beobachtung herausgegeben von Dr. C. Mettenheimer. Leipzig : Teubner. 1863. 8vo, pp. 356.
[1] " History of England, from the Fall of Wolsey to the Death of Elizabeth." By James Anthony Froude, M.A., late Fellow of Exeter College, Oxford. Reign of Elizabeth. Vols. 1 and 2. London : Longman, Green, Longman, Roberts, and Green. 1863.

Catholicism had ceased to be the expression of the true conviction of sensible men on the relation between themselves and heaven. Credible to the student in the cloister, credible to those whose thoughts were but echoes of tradition, it was not credible any more to men of active and original vigour of understanding. Credible to the uneducated, the eccentric, the imaginative, the superstitious; credible to those who reasoned by sentiment, and made syllogisms of their passions, it was incredible then and evermore to the sane and healthy intelligence which in the long run commands the mind of the world." Besides the "liberal application" which this sentence suggests, it contains, in its closing words, an intimation of the spirit in which the subject of the *earlier* English Reformation is treated. The value of that great reform Mr. Froude conceives to lie rather in its moral than in its dogmatic phase: it was produced by the action of "the sane and healthy intelligence which in the long run commands the mind of the world." Our ancestors cared something for dogma, but it was not so much a Genevan or an Anglican system of belief that they desired, as a good work-a-day religion: a religion which, without minute examination into this or that doctrine, included what was found generally credible in the interest of common sense, and excluded theological sophism and sacerdotal practice in the interest of common honesty. But against this popular conception of religious reform, ambiguity of religious position strongly militated. For the sake of comprehension a studied equivocation was introduced into the liturgy. This, however, was not the case with the Articles. They were then symbols which distinguished the orthodox Protestant from the concealed Catholic, by whom they could not be subscribed without peril to his soul; though "strained and cracked by three centuries of evasive ingenuity, they scarcely embarrass now the feeblest of consciences." Indeed, "the clergyman of the nineteenth century subscribes them with such a smile as might have been worn by Samson when his Philistine mistress bound his arms with the cords and withes." If, owing to the "purposed ambiguity" of the liturgy, the ecclesiastical establishment of Elizabeth was still in some sort a compromise, allowance must be made for the extreme difficulties of a position in which Calvinistic tyranny, popular profanity, and royal affectation of Catholic usage, were the opposing elements that had to be conciliated. If Mr. Froude be right, the anarchical state of the English Church in 1565 is not attributable only to the Puritans. If the reformers themselves "were aggressive and tyrannical;" if "prebends' wives melted the cathedral organ-pipes into dish-covers, and cut the frames into bedsteads," so as to afford an argument for clerical celibacy, the Queen's attachment to a semi-demi mystical Catholicism, her insulting attitude to the bishops, and her enforcement of uniformity, contributed to the general ecclesiastical misrule and inefficiency. We should be glad if no other accusation could be brought against this really great Sovereign; but if our historian read our annals rightly, and we can find nothing to object to his interpretation, Elizabeth, in her first years of government, committed grave errors. It is not, however, her general *policy* to which exception should be taken; it is her *conduct* of that policy which is so reprehensible. Let us look at the three or four principal questions which required to be disposed of, — the settlement of Ireland, the Scotch war, her own marriage, the marriage of Mary Stuart. Mr. Froude's graphic and humorous account of the state of Ireland, shows us, in the intestine quarrels, the strife with England, the frightful savagery of the people, the cardinal difficulties that had to be met. Elizabeth *did* meet them, and ultimately, under Sir Henry Sidney, re-attached Ireland to her crown. But whereas Sidney at first found only "suspicion and hard words," Lord Sussex, who stooped to treachery and proposed the assassination of Shan O'Neil, "continued a trusted and favoured councillor of Elizabeth." Again, in 1560, "the conspiracy of the Guises and the necessity of defending her throne, forced Elizabeth into the Scotch war." Here a firm, consistent, and decisive action was required. But Elizabeth, after first inciting rebellion, abandoned the nobles, broke her word, and told a deliberate falsehood. Then, again, with regard to her marriage, she coquetted, procrastinated, vacillated, retaining the equivocal Dudley near her, till her fair fame was whispered about, if not actually compromised. Nor was this all. Forbearing to marry Leicester herself, out of fear of her subjects' resentment, she proposed him as a husband to the Queen of Scots, and she did so after having offered her the choice of any English nobleman. On the other hand, there are considerations which ought to incline us to construe charitably part at least of this misbehaviour, and Mr. Froude does not fail to point them out. Surrounded by difficulties, the young Queen acted with the caprice and vacillation which belonged to a perplexed cause. If "her conduct in its details were alike unprincipled and unwise, the broader bearings of her policy were intelligible and commendable." Mr. Froude's readers —those at least of them who ardently admire this great Queen—may be disappointed at our historian's estimate of her early career. Unfortunately, the verdict seems warranted by the evidence. Elizabeth, it should be remembered, was but twenty-five years of age when she became the inheritor of a troubled throne, with an unruly Protestantism to manage, and a menacing Catholicism to repress. Her infatuation for Dudley increased the complexities of her position ; and culpable as she was, through all her errors she was essentially true to the noble policy of England for the English, no popery, no priestcraft, no foreign domination. The next principal actor, at least the most conspicuous in the historical drama, is the ill-fated Queen Mary of Scotland, Elizabeth's rival. The portrait of this high-spirited and accomplished woman is drawn by Mr. Froude with a powerful and truthful pencil. Her splendid physical and intellectual qualities are made strikingly prominent, and you feel the fascination attaching to her witchlike presence as you contemplate the picture. The vexed question of her participation in the Darnley murder is decided in her disfavour. It is rather implied in the simple, pathetic, but carefully-wrought narrative which records the tragedy than formally discussed. Taking the "Casket Letters," as many very competent judges do, for genuine, Mr. Froude infers from their evidence and the evidence of facts, the complicity of this magnificent sinner in her husband's murder. Truly, if she was not guilty she must have been preternaturally unlucky. The death of Amy Robsart is another of the standing historical puzzles. Dr. Mottley considers Amy's death to have been accidental. He says that the jury (including Appleyard and Arthur Robsart, brother-in-law and brother of the lady) impanelled to investigate the occurrence, and rather hostile to Leicester than otherwise, were unable to find any other verdict than that she was killed by a fall downstairs. Mr. Froude, however, quotes an angry expression, followed by an explanatory statement, of Appleby's, which, while tending to acquit Leicester himself of the murder, accused him of want of zeal in prosecuting the inquiry. The value of Appleyard's testimony (seven years after) may be questioned. Certainty here is not to be had. But Mr. Froude inclines to the opinion that although Dudley was innocent of direct participation in the crime, the unhappy lady was sacrificed to his ambition, and that the investigation at Cumnor was inadequately conducted. Leicester, however, if we accept the correspondence between him and Sir Thomas Blount, must be allowed, at the time of the inquest, to have urged vigorous and minute inquiry, so that it is not easy to arrive at an undoubted conclusion. The period of Elizabeth's reign which is traversed in the two volumes now before us comprises something more than eight years. The leading topics have been already indicated. There was war with France, there was fighting in Scotland, there was military success in Ireland, there was negotiation with Philip, Elizabeth's early friend and supporter. The social condition of the country, the state of the clergy, the reform of the currency, the first expansion of the English navy, are among the subjects reviewed by the historian. The concluding chapter of the second volume, which traces the rise of England's sea-sovereignty, is at once an animated narrative and a philosophical essay. In the general break-up of the old European order, " the primitive tendencies of human nature" showed themselves for a time in the privateering ventures of English gentlemen, whose condition " had many analogies with that of the Grecian chiefs " who roved the seas and took what the gods sent them, or of " the true believer, Israelite or Mahometan," who remorselessly plundered the heathen. "English Protestants, it was too evident, regarded the property of Papists as lawful prize wherever they could lay hands on it ; and Protestantism, stimulated by these inducements to conversion, was especially strong in the seaport towns." Bad as this was, the Elizabethan Calvinists had " the sanction of religious conviction for their worst deeds," even negro-capture. The first Englishman who engaged in this atrocious traffic was John Lok, who. discovering that the blacks of the African coast were living without God, law, religion, or commonwealth, "gave some of them an opportunity of a lift in creation, and carried off five as slaves." His example was followed by Hawkins, of Plymouth. Lord Pembroke made sixty per cent. on his investment in this great sea-attorney's slave fleet of October, 1564 ; so did the other contributors, and probably the Queen herself, who had placed at Hawkins's disposal one of her best ships. " Cecil alone—ever honourable, ever loathing cruelty and unrighteousness—though pressed to join with the rest, refused, having no liking for such proceedings." This wise statesman has a noble prominence in the history of Elizabeth. Mr. Froude regards him as a master mind for whom nothing was too small and nothing too great, ever busy in the settlement of Church and State, employing his indefatigable pen in the Queen's cabinet or in his own, fighting the great duel with Rome, urging the war with Scotland, counselling or restraining his vacillating and imperious mistress, devising plans of popular improvement, or caring " for the terraces and orange-groves of Burleigh." In the new volumes of Mr. Froude's history we see every evidence of the desire to write a true, honest, unvarnished narrative of the reign of Elizabeth. The excesses of Protestantism and the evils of superstition are in general fairly stated ; the duplicity and irresolution of the Queen herself are forcibly exposed. The vindicators of her Scottish rival, if they reject the historian's sentence, cannot complain that his tale is not truly told. On the value of De Quadra's correspondence opinions may differ. It is not easy to say on the one hand *when* a notorious liar speaks truth, though on the other it cannot be affirmed that he *always* speaks falsehood. Truth, gossip, and invention, conscious or unconscious, are the materials of which we might expect his letters to be composed. Referring to the paper published some time since in *Fraser's Magazine*, Mr. Froude maintains that he has nothing to retract " from the essential part of what he then wrote," but he admits that he " misread the notes " which relate to the proceedings in council after Amy Robsart's death. In the composition of his book the author has received valuable assistance from the Marquis of Salisbury, who has allowed him to examine Lord Burleigh's private papers at Hatfield ; from Don Manuel Gonzales, who has the care of the archives at Simancas ; from Count de Laborde, who holds a similar position at Paris ; from Messrs. Hardy, Brewer, and Gairdner, in the English Record Office, and from the late Mr. Turnbull, to whose ability and integrity Mr. Froude bears emphatic witness. For the accommodation of readers who may not care to possess the earlier portion of the Tudor history, the present publication is made, as it were, the commencement of a second work, comprising the seventh and eighth volumes of the entire history.

The Calendar of State Papers on the Reign of Elizabeth has a right to honourable mention here.[2] It promises, indeed, to be a most valuable work, but the records which the first volume contains scarcely extend over a whole year—the accession year—so that it only invites the research of the minute historian. Mr. Stevenson, in his biographical preface, sketches the early life of the Sovereign who is the central

---

[2] " Calendar of State Papers, Foreign Series, of the Reign of Elizabeth, 1558—1559, preserved in the State Department of Her Majesty's Public Record Office." Edited by the Rev. Joseph Stevenson, M.A., of University College, Dublin. Under the direction of the Master of the Rolls, and with the sanction of Her Majesty's Secretary of State for the Home Department. London : Longman, Green, & Co. 1863.

point of half a century of English History. In describing the studies of the young princess, is it Roger Ascham or his reporter who says that Elizabeth read select portions of *Socrates?* There was an ecclesiastical historian of that name, but we presume that it is the snub-nosed sage of Athens, whose authorship was confined to the versification of some of Æsop's fables, portions of whose works Elizabeth is here somewhat strangely affirmed to have read.

The concluding instalment of Dr. Vaughan's useful and meritorious, if not very original, work on English History[3] commences with a delineation of the character and government of Elizabeth's successor. We do not know that there is any fresh discovery brought to light in it, but the introductory essay, on the Decline of Royalism, shows the points of connexion between the kingcraft of James I. and the un-kinged estate of Charles I. amply and clearly. Dr. Vaughan's view of the civil war is very nearly, if not quite, the same as that held by Mr. Forster. He defends the Parliamentary procedure, in the main, vindicates the attainder of Strafford, but does not vindicate, though he does not condemn, the sentence pronounced on the unhappy Charles. The Protectorate is regarded with favour. The greatness of Cromwell, whether he was culpable or not, is so generally allowed now, that Dr. Vaughan's appreciation will surprise no one. This appreciation, how-ever, is, he contends, strictly his own, and was published long before Mr. Carlyle had written on the subject, and "when the notions of that gifted writer concerning the leaders in the Long Parliament were not what they now are." Among the facts which, if not absolutely new, are not generally known, in these volumes, are the part taken by Oliver Cromwell in the Huntingdon municipal reform transaction, and his resistance to the "knighthood fine," ultimately paid either by himself or his royalist uncle. Our author further points out that the law of Edward VI. which required the evidence of two witnesses in cases of treason, had never been allowed in favour of persons so accused, and that the only precedent for granting counsel *at all* in cases like Strafford's was that of Middlesex, in 1624. From the recently-published "Fairfax Correspondence," Dr. Vaughan also discovers the alleged circumstances under which Strafford lost his first wife. "It appears that, coming into her ladyship's chamber from the garden, she saw a strange fly on his breast, and on her attempting quickly to wipe it off, the insect opened a pair of large wings, which so alarmed her that she fell backwards, and her fatal sickness followed." If Lady Strafford really died of this fly-fright she was easily killed. The Restoration and the reaction which succeeded the Republic, the policy of Charles II., and the arbitrary measures of James, are described in the third of the three main divisions of Dr. Vaughan's new volume, while the fourth contains a sketch of the national progress since 1668, closing with a glance at the corresponding social life.

On the 24th June, 1497, Sebastian Cabot caught the first glimpse of

[3] " Revolutions in English History." By Robert Vaughan, D.D. Vol. III. London : Longman, Green, & Co. 1863.

Terra Nova, either Newfoundland proper or part of the neighbouring coast of Labrador.[4] The cod fishery did not fail in due time to attract adventurers. In 1623 Sir George Calvert obtained a grant of an immense tract of country which he called the Province of Avalon, into which he introduced English colonists. These colonists, as well as those brought to Conception Bay under the auspices of the London Company, were probably respectable persons enough. It proved a refuge, however, for men of a different order—men perplexed with the double encumbrance of family obligations and pecuniary liabilities. Hence the society of the new island was not very select. A history of such a people, after every addition and improvement, is not attractive. In truth, however, there is little to tell. In October, 1839, Newfoundland, together with Bermudas, was constituted a separate see : in 1855 it began to share the advantages of responsible government, and in 1860 it was visited by his Royal Highness the Prince of Wales. A great fire, a tremendous tempest, a popular disturbance, severe military flogging, and some tyranny on the part of the ruling powers, are among the incidents or characteristics of this rather parochial history. Perhaps not much was to be made of so impracticable a subject : but might not Mr. Pedley have told us the little that was worth telling in half the number of pages ?

Before we return to the Old World we will go further, and, reversing the alphabetical sequence, take Mexico after Newfoundland.[5] In July, 1861, the Mexican Government, being very " hard up," issued a decree for the suspension of all payments assigned to foreign creditors, British, French, and Spanish. To enforce just claims and exact reparation for wrongs, the three interested countries entered into a convention on the 31st October of the same year, it beinge specially stipulated that the high contracting Powers were "not to exercise in the internal affairs of Mexico any influence of a nature to prejudice the right of the Mexican nation to choose and constitute freely the form of its government." An expedition sailed, the English share in which was small. The French demands were regarded by the English representatives as preposterous, and a general disaccord soon prevented all co-operation. The separate action of the French Commissioners being an infraction of the Convention of London, the English and Spanish forces were withdrawn, and the alliance ended. It remained with the French flag alone, says M. Félix Ribeyre, in his history of the war that ensued, to defend the national honour on Mexican soil. Affirming this flag to be that of right, justice, civilization and liberty, the historian displays, with sufficient amplitude, the course of the campaign of the heroic soldiers of France, describes the battle of Combrès, the march on Puebla, the check and retreat under General Lorencez, the

---

[4] "The History of Newfoundland, from the Earliest Times to the Year 1860." By the Rev. Charles Pedley, of St. John's, Newfoundland. London : Longman and Co. 1863.
[5] "Histoire de la Guerre du Mexique." Par Félix Ribeyre, Redacteur du *Constitutionnel*. Illustré d'un Portrait de l'Empereur Napoleon III., &c. Paris : Eugene Pick. London : David Nutt. 1863.

subsequent reinforcement, the achievements at Chapulco, San José, the second attack on Puebla and the capture of Mexico, and concludes with the establishment of the compulsory freedom by which a republic was converted into a kingdom. The volume, which is interesting and meritorious enough, contains, in addition to the main narrative, notices of the lives of the principal personages engaged in the war, as Forey, Lorencez, Mirandol, de la Gravière, Prim, Miramon, and the rest. Various orders, proclamations, and other illustrative documents are interspersed, and with some allowance for French prepossession, the volume may be accepted as, at any rate, a proximately correct account of the last imperial *do*.

Quitting the American Continent, we return to Europe in the company of Sir Archibald Alison. It is not necessary to characterize so well-known a work as his "Continuation of the History of Europe."[*] The first volume of a double-columned edition, which is not stated to be either revised or enlarged, begins with the Peace of Paris in 1815 and ends with the Spanish and Italian Revolution of 1820. From the "general sketch of the whole period from the fall of Napoleon to the accession of Louis Napoleon," we quote two striking and contrasting, though not contradictory statements. "Great have been the efforts made both by the Protestant and Roman Catholic Churches, especially of late years, to diffuse the tenets of their respective faiths in heathen lands: but with the exception of some of the Catholic missions in South America, without the success that was, in the outset at least, anticipated. Sectarian zeal has united with Christian philanthropy in forwarding the great undertaking: the British and Foreign Bible Society has rivalled in activity the Propaganda of Rome; and the expenditure of 100,000*l.* annually on the enlightening of foreign lands has afforded a magnificent proof of devout zeal and British liberality. But no lasting or decisive effects have as yet followed these efforts. No new nations have been converted to Christianity: the conversion of a few tribes, of which much has been said, appears to be little more than nominal; and the durable spread of the Gospel has been everywhere co-extensive only with that of the European race." So that if the people of Asia or Africa have no affinity for the tenets of the spiritual faith, the influence of Christianity is, it would seem, obviously increasing in all the nations of Europe, and nowhere more so than in France. In France "Louis Napoleon has secured supreme power: but he secured it by the aid of the clergy. His first step was a solemn service in Nôtre Dame, the theatre of the orgies of the Goddess of Reason; his last, the coronation by the hands of the Church. The votes of seven millions of Frenchmen demonstrated that the vast majority of the people coincided with his sentiments. In England, the influence of religious opinion has increased to such a degree as to become in some measure alarming: it begets in the thoughtful mind,

[*] "History of Europe from the Fall of Napoleon, in 1815, to the Accession of Louis Napoleon," in 1852. By Sir Archibald Alison, Bart., D.C.L., Author of the "History of Europe, &c. Vol. I. Eighth thousand. Edinburgh and London: William Blackwood and Sons. 1864.

the dread of a reaction. Christianity in Russia is the mainspring both of government and national action : the Cross is inscribed on its banners : it is as the representative of the Almighty that the Czar is omnipotent." These observations, recorded in 1852, are worth pondering, as well for what they assert, as for what they suggest.

The sway of the clergy who aided the third Napoleon in his seizure of power is stigmatized by a lively and piquant writer as " incompatible with any constitutional government, with anything but a military tyranny." Imperialism itself he describes as, at present, a convertible term for the permanency of brute force. As to Christianity, it seems to have a complete sinecure in Paris, if not in France. Mr. Kirwan at least says that the social system in France is rotten, corrupted, and putrified to the very core—in the towns the people are sensualist and materialist, in the country, superstitious, ignorant, and stupid ; the public men are utterly selfish and unprincipled, and there is little regard for oaths and promises. In France there is no liberty of thought, no liberty of discussion. Literature is degraded almost to its lowest level, no new talent appears : the press is fettered ; the suffrage manipulated ; voting papers altered and destroyed. In one commune the 5000 votes obtained by Thiers were counted as only 4000 : "at Libourne 800 electors were prevented from voting." In the reckless extravagance of the present *régime* lies, however, the final break-up of the system. There is hope, too, in the courageous opposition of the leading members of the bar, and in the recent election of about five-and-thirty independent men. These opinions, expressed in clear, sharp, cutting language will be found expanded and illustrated in " Modern France," a series of articles on its Literature, Journalism, and Society, reprinted from the *British Quarterly Review, Fraser's Magazine,* &c.[7] Mr. Kirwan's opposition to Napoleonism is uncompromising and indiscriminating : but his bitter philippic is not altogether undeserved. Of the collected papers, that on Journalism in France from 1635 to 1846, and again that on Journalism and Literature, from 1848 to 1863, contains some curious information ; that on the Bourse is short and sharp ; the paper on Paris, the Emperor and Empress, is personal and amusing ; that on the Military System of France will interest and inform. In writing of the French literary celebrities we are glad to see Mr. Kirwan's warm vindication of Lamartine against "a malignant slanderer in the English press," and his glowing eulogy of Béranger. Among other notabilities, he describes the famous Père Lacordaire.

An estimate of the character and career of this eloquent ecclesiastic by Count de Montalembert, may be consulted by all who care to know what the former was or what he did, and what the latter thinks of him. As the book is not, strictly speaking, a biography, we will take from Mr. Kirwan's pages a sketch of his external life. Lacordaire, the son of a doctor, was born in 1802, at the village of Recy-sur-

---

[7] " Modern France," &c. By A. V. Kirwan, Esq., of the Middle Temple, Barrister-at-Law. London : Jackson, Walford, and Hodder. 1863.
" Le Père Lacordaire." Par le Comte de Montalembert, l'un des quarante de l'Académie Française. Deuxième Edition. Revue et Augmentée. London. D. Nutt. 1862.

Ource, five leagues from Chatillon-sur-Seine. From 1810 to 1819 he studied at the Lycée of Dijon. About 1822 he commenced his legal career in Paris, and soon after began to plead with considerable success. In 1824 he renounced the bar and entered at St. Sulpice. Five or six years after we find him engaged with Lamennais and Montalembert in the *Avenir*, and when the question raised by this journal was before the Chamber of Peers, he made a ready and vigorous reply to the remarks of the Attorney-General. It was in the " conférences" which he preached at the Collége Stanislas, in 1834, that he first became known as a preacher. He continued his sermons for two years at Nôtre Dame, acquiring no little influence over the student class, when suddenly he left for Rome, and assumed the habit of a Dominican, which he has worn ever since 1841 without any loss of popularity. Lacordaire's three celebrated funeral orations are those on O'Connell, the Bishop of Nancy, and General Druot. The last Ste. Beuve pronounces a masterpiece among modern productions. In 1848, Lacordaire occupied a seat in the National Assembly, but after the invasion of that Assembly, he resigned, confining himself to his duties as a preacher. In 1854 he terminated his twenty years' career as a pulpit-orator, and dedicated the rest of his life to the regeneration of the great school of Sorèze. Lacordaire was at once favourable to liberty and favourable to the Papacy. He sympathized with the Italians in their desire for independence, but he disbelieved in the unity of Italy, and he disapproved of "the anti-social and anti-Christian policy" of Cavour. This disbelief and disapprobation of course win the applause of his friendly appreciator. Happily the unity of Italy has proved something more than a Utopia ; while the social character of the great statesman's policy is attested by the growing prosperity of his regenerated country.

At a moment when Poland—in which France has ever shown some interest—is struggling for an independence, which, without imperial intervention she seems very little likely to obtain, the republication of de Rulhière's classical " Révolution de Pologne,"[8] is opportune. Printed in small but clear type, the three volumes already issued bring us down from the earliest period of Polish history to the first partition of 1772. The literary merit of this work has been recognised by Guizot, Villemain, and other competent judges, and in its now revised and completed form, it has reached a fourth edition. Before his death in 1791, Rulhière appears to have had several copies deposited in different quarters. Hitherto no unmutilated copy of this posthumous work has been found, but Christian Ostrowski, the new editor, claims to have given to the world a more complete text than Daunou, by the discovery of the two halves of the twelfth and thirteenth books, which had escaped the notice of the latter : a discovery the reality of which, French criticism will readily investigate. Rulhière's predilections are in favour of Polish nationality. His con-

---

[8] "Révolutions de Pologne. Par Claude Carloman de Rulhière, de l'Académie Française. Quatrième édition. Revue sur le Texte et complétée. Par Christian Ostrowski. Vol. 1, 2, 3. London : D. Nutt.

tinuator, Ferrand, whose history it is intended to publish on the completion of the present work, agrees with Rulhière in reprobating the partition of Poland, and in his estimate of its disastrous consequences, though the two men were of essentially different schools.

The student may compare with their version of the history of Poland the German narrative of Dr. Jacob Caro.[9] Of this version, the first instalment brings us down to the end of the fourteenth century; the purely historical portion concluding with the baptism, marriage, and coronation of Jagiello (Yaguellon) the pagan Grand Duke of Lithuania. In the two remaining chapters the social and commercial relations of the people are discussed; a glance is given to what we must call the literary or intellectual element, and some few pages are dedicated to a statement of the position of the Jews in Poland. Dr. Caro's work forms part of the "History of European States," published by Heeren and Ukert.

Ascending the stream of time, we encounter, about two centuries before the union of Lithuania and Poland, by the marriage of Yaguellon and Hedwig, the Polish queen, the grand mediæval figure of Frederick II. Schirrmacher's history of this renowned emperor has been noticed in a previous number of the *Westminster Review.* With this work Dr. Winkelmann—who admits the surpassing excellence of some portions of it—does not pretend that his own can compete.[10] His object has been to elucidate certain passages in Frederick's life and career, and especially to investigate the sources whence he derived his extraordinary culture. His inquiries, contemporaneous with, but independent of Schirrmacher's, and carefully conducted through a period of many years, he offers as supplementary to his countryman's greater work. Dr. Winkelmann's book has every appearance of being the result of learned and genuine examination.

Returning once more to France, we are present at the birth or rather the baptism of Matthieu Marais (11 October, 1665), who subsequently becomes advocate to the Parliament of Paris, and the intimate friend of the redoubtable Bayle. The "Dictionary" of this eminent thinker gave the young lawyer a charming peep into the tempting region of Doubt. He corresponded with the author, drew up papers which Bayle himself says shed lustre on his work, wrote the life of the philosopher of Rotterdam, and associated himself with Madame de Mérigniac in the defence of the memory of their common master and the conservation of his posthumous works. Marais died on 21st of June, 1737; and notwithstanding the charming prospect "so dear to sceptics," he died, says the editor of his Journal and Memoirs, in an attractive biographical introduction, not only *simplement, doucement, modestement,* but *chretiennement, comme il avait vécu.* The volume of his literary productions, now published for the first time from the manuscript in the Imperial Library, besides the

---

[9] "Geschichte Polens." Von Dr. Jacob Caro. Zweiter theil. London: D. Nutt. 1863.

[10] "Geschichte Kaiser Friedrichs des Zweiten und seiner Reiche 1212—1235." Von Dr. Eduard Winkelmann. Oberlehrer an der Ritter- und Domschule zu Reval. London: David Nutt. 1863.

" life " and correspondence with Madame de Mérigniac " the man-minded offset " of M. d'Ostrel, a Fleming, contains five Journals by Marais, extending over a period of about as many years from 1715 to 1720.[11] M. de Lescure describes the clever author as an excellent type of the parliamentary chroniclers, who, while writing in an off-hand way, sometimes give us what comes very near real history and real literature.

The mother of Napoleon III. would have been more appropriately mentioned in an earlier part of this section.[12] Hortense, the future queen of Holland, was the daughter of Vicomte de Beauharnais and Mademoiselle Tascher de la Pagerie, the unhappy Josephine. The mother and daughter were equally ill-fated in their matri-monial life. Josephine and Beauharnais married for love and lived as the cat and dog of proverbial infelicity. Hortense was in-tended by Napoleon to be the bride of his favourite aide-de-camp Duroc, to whom the graceful and accomplished young girl was really attached. Josephine, however, for purposes of her own, opposed the arrangement. To retain her position with her husband, she endea-voured to bring about a marriage between Hortense, loving Duroc, and Louis Napoleon, loving Louise-Emilie, her own niece—a very pretty Midsummer Night's Dream, for the cross-complications of the project. Josephine's efforts were crowned with success. Louis, in love with somebody else, was compelled to marry Hortense, also in love with somebody else. Louise-Emilie, who, it should be said, did not return his passion, fell to the share of Lavalette, and turned out a model wife of European renown. Hortense and Louis seem to have been no worse than the rest of the imperial family ; but she did not like him, and he returned her antipathy. She had two children, Charles Napoleon, who died young, and Louis Napoleon, "whom we know." Separated from his wife since his flight from Holland, Louis resided in Styria and Switzerland under the title of the Count de St. Leu, settling at Florence in 1826, where he died, about twenty years after Hortense found her eventual resting place at Arenemberg, within sight of the lake of Constance, though making an occasional residence at Rome. Poor Queen Hortense ! Flying in her babyhood from Black insurrection and incendiarism in Martinique, she was sacrificed, in her beautiful girlhood to State policy. The step-daughter of " Napoleon le Grand," and the mother of " Napoleon le Petit," she holds rather a conspicuous place in history. Her musical talent lives in her world-renowned song, " Partant pour la Syrie." Her life has been written by M. Ch. Bernard-Derosne in a vivacious novelesque fashion, not without a seasoning of claptrap. Hortense died—or, as her biographer presses it—" En 1837, Hortense s'eteignit. Fatiguée d'une vie de

<hr>

[11] " Journal et Memoires de Matthieu Marais, Avocat au Parlement de Paris. Sur la Regence et le Regne de Louis XV., &c. Avec une Introduction et des Notes." Par M. de Lescure. Tome premier. London : Williams and Norgate. 1863.

[12] " Mémoires sur la Reine Hortense, Mère de Napoléon III." Par Ch. Bernard-Derosne. London : David Nutt. 1863.

malheurs et d'exil, après avoir longtemps langui, elle courbe la tête et alla rejoindre dans un monde meilleur Napoléon et Joséphine." The notion of rejoining Napoleon in a better world is as good a joke as we ever heard. Southey, who was on intimate terms with the prince of darkness, and knew all the secrets of his prison-house, places the disturber of Europe in a very different region. We quote from memory :

> " But there is a place that he must go to,
> Where the skies are so red and the fields are so blue,
> Morbleu ! Parbleu !
> He'll find it hotter than Moscow."

We fear we are less interested in Maurice[13] and Eugénie[14] de Guérin than we ought to be. It is not hard indeed to sympathize with genius and grace, with goodness of heart and beauty of soul under all forms and disguises, and thus, in some sense and in some degree, we can admire the gifted and sensitive brother, and his high-minded and saintly sister. In Maurice—a sort of embryo French Keats and Wordsworth in one—an exquisite delicacy of descriptive power is easily recognisable. Eugénie's letters and journals will charm and edify all who share the pious belief and aspirations of this "beautiful soul." To those, on the other hand, whose leanings are *from* and not *to* the faith she held, who look not to feeling or imagination, but to calm thought and growing insight into the "orderly mystery" un-folding itself before us for an explanation "of all this unintelligible" world, her book will have little more than an historical, psychological, or artistic interest. A human soul there certainly is in it ; and the grace, energy, variety, and simplicity which her editor claims for Eugénie's prose will scarcely be disallowed. Unwilling to publish, Eugénie would yet have consented to give to the world her written thoughts, if she could only have been convinced that they would have had the effect of inspiring others with her faith in God, and her admiration for her brother. This brother she loved with a most self-denying devotion. To secure his glory was the great wish of her heart. After his death, Maurice's literary remains—the publication of which she so earnestly desired—found their way into print, being introduced to the reading world by Ste. Beuve, in a critique in the *Moniteur Universel*, which M. Trebutien has been permitted to insert in the volume before us. From this paper we learn that Georges-Maurice de Guérin was born on the 4th of August, 1810, of a poor but ancient family, educated at Toulouse and Paris, and in 1832 found an agreeable retreat at La Chenaie, an oasis in the centre of the steppes of Brittany. Here he became acquainted with the noble and energetic La Mennais, valued him, and was influenced by him, though

---

[13] " Maurice de Guérin. Journals, Lettres, et Poëmes." Publiés avec l'assenti-ment de sa Famille", par G. S. Trebutien, et précédés d'une étude biographique et littéraire. Par M. Sainte-Beuve, de l'Académie Française. Quatrième édition. London : D.Nutt. 1863.
[14] " Eugénie de Guérin. Journal et Lettres." Publiés avec l'assentiment de sa Famille, par G. S. Trebutien. Ouvrage couronné par l'Académie Française. Cinquième édition. London : D. Nutt. 1863.

he afterwards threw off the Abbé's influence, refused to be any man's disciple, and re-embraced the religion which he had discarded.	At length he stood on the very threshold of fame.	Happy in his recent union with a beautiful Creole lady, he saw the years with their glittering hopes rise brightly before him, when the latent seeds of decay began to develop, and hardly had he been carried to the warm skies of his native South when he died in the summer of 1839.	Eugénie de Guérin, who was five years older than her brother, outlived him by nearly nine years.	She drew her last breath in her beloved solitude of Cayla, on 31st May, 1848.	Maurice's most celebrated composition is the "Centaur," a prose poem.	The Centaur represents a humanlike, untameable animal power, a primitive redundant vitality, gifted with intelligence, and having the whole domain of a wild luxuriant nature for its field of exercise.	It is certainly fine.	The fabled creature's fancy, when he first sees a man that he is looking on "la moitié de ' son' être," " un centaur renversé par les dieux," has a Swift-like verisimilitude about it.	The recorded admiration of George Sand, Ste. Beuve, and Matthew Arnold, is a guarantee that this young French poet was a man of no common promise.	To make amends for our own shortcomings, we advise our readers to study his journals, letters, and poems, of which a fourth edition has just appeared.	The collected writings of his sister, whom an eminent critic thinks his equal if not superior " en talent et en âme," have already reached a fifth edition, and challenge further examination from all independent and reflective minds.

We will associate music with poetry, and say a passing word on the biographical portrait drawn by Max Maria von Weber, of the distinguished musician, his father.	The admirers of the author of *Der Freischütz* will find in it a complete and, as we presume, carefully-written " Life" of their hero.[15]	The volume only of the work before us terminated with the year 1817, leaving the incidents of nine years (for Weber did not die till 1826) to form the materials of a second instalment.	The family on whose name he had conferred such brilliant distinction derives its origin from John Baptista Weber, a doctor of law, and a loyal servant of more than one Emperor of Germany, born about 1550.	A descendant of John Baptista chose, as his second wife, Geneveva von Brenner.	Their son, Karl Maria von Weber, was born on the 18th or 19th of November, or possibly December, 1786, at Eutin, in Holstein, where his father was the state-musician. Young Karl seems to have made but a poor fiddler when he first began his musical education.	His step-brother, Fridolin, chafing at the boy-pupil's clumsiness, one day exclaimed, " Karl ! you may be anything else you like, but you'll never be a musician."	At Salzburg Karl was placed under the tuition of Michael Haydn, brother of the famous Joseph, whom he afterwards knew.	His first composition, consisting of six fughetti, was published before he had quite attained his twelfth year, and was favourably noticed by Nochlitz, in the

---

[15] " Carl Maria von Weber."	Ein Lebensbild von Max Maria von Weber. Erster band.	Mit Portrait.	London : David Nutt.	1864.

Musical Gazette. An Opera, entitled *The Power of Love and Wine*, was composed in the following year, 1849, but *durch Feuersbrunst vernichtet.* The boy seems now to have been greatly attracted by the newly-discovered art of lithography, and not only to have executed lithographs, but to have introduced certain improvements in the process or in the press itself. Resuming his musical studies, after a short diversion, he composed *Das Waldmädchen*, at Munich, in 1800, and the year following, *Peter Schmoll und seine Nachbarn*, both operas. The opera of *Abu Hassan* was written at Darmstadt in 1810. In 1804 we find him employed as Director at Breslau; and, two years later as Musical Intendant at the Court of Carlsruhe, by Prince Eugene of Würtemberg, who treated him as a friend. In 1807 he appears at Stuttgart, as the secretary to Duke Louis, and, subsequently, as teacher of music to his children. In 1818 he accepted the directorship of the Opera at Prague; which, after an effective service of some years, he resigned, at the close of 1816. The narrative concludes with his betrothal to Caroline Brandt, and his appointment to the office of Chapel-master to the King of Saxony. An excellent survey of the musical compositions, with dates of place, and time, and brief annotations will be found at the end of the volume.

The "Life of Blücher"[16] by Dr. Scherr is written with the same kind of minuteness as that of Weber by his son. The third volume—the only one we have seen of the work—brings us to the end of the story of the great fighting hero of the Germany of our own time. In estimating his character our author lays great stress on Blücher's sympathy with the real and practical. This military anti-idealist, he tells us, took men as he found them; understood human interests and human passions. It is doubtful whether he ever read a book through, or even turned over its leaves; but of life, which to so many learned men is a seven-sealed volume,' he was an early and diligent student. Dr. Scherr's version of Blucher's career may be compared with the more rapid sketch of it given by Keller, a brief notice of which will be found in a recent number of the *Westminster Review.*

Herr W. Rüstow, whose leading political principle is *national freedom in opposition to all state oppression,* has written the annals of the Kingdom of Italy in the period 1861-1863.[17] The first book of these annals is occupied with the ministry of Cavour. Rüstow, looking to the complications and perplexities arising out of "the new diplomatic era," and believing that an alliance with Germany and England, in order to be in a position to wage war with Austria and even France, was the eventual policy for Italy, is of opinion that the great statesman died in a happy hour for his fair fame, so escaping the imprecations which fell so heavily on the doomed head of his successor.

---

[16] "Blucher: seine Zeit und seine Leben. Zwölf Bücher in drei Bänder." Von Dr. Johannes Scherr, Professor der Geschichte am eidgenössischen Polytechnicum in Zürich. Dritter Band, 1813—1819. London: Williams and Norgate. 1863.

[17] "Annalin des Königreichs Italien, 1861 bis 1863." Von W. Rüstow, Oberst-Brigadier, Ritter des Militärischen Ordens von Savoyen. Erstes Buch das Ministerium Cavour. London: David Nutt. 1864.

"It was in Italy that opera came into being; from thence she travelled, first into France, next into England, and lastly into Germany." Accordingly the Queens of Song, whom Mrs. Clayton has celebrated in her pleasing volumes,[18] have reigned on the lyric stage, some with all, some with more than all, few with less than all, the grasp of empire here indicated. Of these melodious sovereigns there are about fifty, who have swayed the sceptre of their wide dominion from the earliest days of the opera to the present time. Among the best and most devoted of them was Anastasia Robinson, the Countess of Peterborough. Among the worst and wildest was the duellist, La Maupin. The wittiest seems to have been Sophie Arnould. It was this lady who, hearing one day that a Capuchin had been devoured by wolves, compassionately observed: "Poor beasts! hunger must be a dreadful thing." The earliest celebrities noticed in the work before us are Catherine Tofts and Margarita l'Epine; the latest are Marietta Piccolomini, Louisa Pyne, and Teresa Tietjens. The lives of the heroines are rather sketchy, but contain perhaps in general all that we need know of them. The work is "embellished" with six portraits, and is got up handsomely enough to serve as a New Year's present.

The history of "The Marine" of all nations, by M. A. Du Sein, professor at the Imperial Naval School, seems a somewhat ambitious undertaking.[19] The first volume begins with an account of Noah's Ark, in which the writer proves, to his own satisfaction, that that gallant ship was large enough to contain all the different species of animals and all the provisions requisite for their support, during the year of the deluge. It strikes us that M. Du Sein does not know what he is talking about, but we will leave him to try conclusions with the learned Kalisch and the calculating Colenso. Following the primitive marine which succeeded the deluge, we have the Egyptian, Phœnician, Jewish, Assyrian, Persian, Greek, Macedonian, Carthaginian, and Roman marine. Then comes that of the Emperors of the East, then the Venetian, and then the Genoese marine. The work is intended principally for young persons. It is a narrative of expeditions, voyages, and sea-fights; not a scientific account of ship-architecture, or a philosophical explanation of naval affairs. It contains, however, descriptions with wood-cut illustrations of ancient and mediæval vessels.

Theodore Mommsen's "Roman Researches" consists of articles contributed to German periodicals in 1859-1861, and is calculated to interest only the scholar, the antiquarian, or the minute student of history.[20] The first of these articles relates to the original form and later modification of the prænomen; it also treats of the cognomen

[18] "Queens of Song: being Memoirs of some of the most Celebrated Vocalists, &c. To which is added a Chronological List of all the Operas that have been Performed in Europe." By Ellen Greathorne Clayton. In 2 vols. With six Portraits. London: Smith, Elder, and Co. 1863.

[19] "Histoire de la Marine de tous les Peuples depuis les Temps de plus reculés jusqu'à nos Jours." Par A. Du Sein, Professeur à l'Ecole Navale Impériale. Tome premier. London. 1863.

[20] "Römische Forschungen." Von Th. Mommsen. Erster Band. London and Edinburgh: Williams and Norgate. 1863.

and its development, and includes a survey of the Patrician families, especially of the fifth, sixth, and seventh centuries of the commonwealth. The second discusses the patricio-plebeian or mixed comitia of the Republic, maintaining the non-existence of separate Patrician assemblies in the republican period, and describing the separate assemblies of the Plebs, the Patrician and the mixed Senate of the Republic; and the third article deals with the Patrician Claudia gens, the Roman right of hospitality, and the Roman clientela.

The Rev. Joseph Stevenson has edited from MSS. in the Imperial Library at Paris, two narratives of the Expulsion of the English from Normandy, and an account of the Conferences between the Ambassadors of France and England.[21] Robert Blondel, the author of the valuable work entitled "De Reductione Normanniæ," was born about the year 1300, held an appointment in the household of Queen Yolande of Sicily, and " lived to record the triumph of the national independence in 1449." The incidents which occurred in Normandy, Britanny, and France from the capture of Fougéres to the final dislodgment of the English from Cherbourg, are narrated by the patriotic member of a family who refused to acknowledge the claims of the conquering invader Henry V. The second narrative, "Le Recouvrement de Normandie," by Jacques le Bouvier, surnamed Berry, the first king of arms of Charles VII., appears to complete and illustrate that of Blondel. Blondel's Latin text is not translated; the antique French of Bevry, as well as that of the compiler of the *Conférences*, is rendered into English, and the volume has an index and an introduction, from which last we have derived our brief notice of the work.

Another publication illustrative of mediæval life and usage, "The History and Cartulary of the Monastery of St. Peter at Gloucester," edited and prefaced by Mr. W. H. Hart, merits the attention of the archæological student. In a second volume the editor proposes to offer certain remarks on the cartulary, the first part only of which is now published.[22]

The Land of the Permauls, or " (Foreign) Governours," is used by Mr. Francis Day, as a fancy name for the State of Cochin, on the western coast of Hindustan.[23] After a rapid review of the legendary origin of Malabar, the settlement of the Portuguese and Dutch in Cochin, the policy of both these peoples, and the cession of Malabar to the English, the religion, ethnology, zoology, botany, the manners

---

[21] " Narratives of the Expulsion of the English from Normandy, 1449—1450, &c." Edited from Manuscripts in the Imperial Library at Paris. By the Rev. Joseph Stevenson, M.A., of University College, Dublin. Published by the Authority of the Lords Commissioners of Her Majesty's Treasury, under the Direction of the Master of the Rolls. London: Longman, Green and Co. 1863.

[22] " Historia et Cartularium Monasterii Sancti Petri Gloucestriæ." Vol. I. Edited by William Henry Hart, of the Public Record Office, &c. Published by the Authority of the Lords Commissioners, &c. London: Longman, Green and Co. 1863.

[23] " The Land of the Permauls, or Cochin : its Past and its Present." By Francis Day, Esq., F.L.S., H.M. Madras Medical Service, Civil Surgeon British Cochin, and Medical Officer to the Government of His Highness the Rajah of Cochin. Madras : Printed by Gantz Brothers, at the Adelphi Press. 1863.

and customs, and the trade of the country, are investigated or described with sufficient detail to satisfy the inquisitive reader.

It seems unnecessary to comment on the English translation of the Memoirs of the Empress Catherine II., as we have already noticed the original work in a previous number of the *Westminster*.[24] A similar remark applies to the second edition of "The Life of Sir James Graham."[25]

"Tools and the Man," according to the dictum of Mr. Carlyle, being the true epic of our time, the author of the "Lives of Engineers," has attempted, not indeed to sing, but to say it. In this attempt he has, in our opinion, been very successful. Of moving incident, it must be owned that there is little in the compact volume of "Industrial Biography" which Mr. Smiles has produced; but the curious consecutive history of the iron and of the iron-workers of Great Britain, affords at once entertainment and instruction.[26] Something of monotony there must inevitably be in the treatment of such a subject; yet, taken as a whole, Mr. Smiles' essay at a prose-epic of tools is not wanting in variety, any more than in other elements of interest. From the Roman iron-smelters in Wales and the Forest of Dean to the war-smiths of Anglo-Saxon times, from the monkish iron-workers of the middle ages to the iron-making and iron-importing under Queen Elizabeth; from Dud Dudley, the royalist, and Andrew Yarranton the Parliamentary iron-manufacturer, to the last inventors and improvers of our own time, the story travels down with a unity of subject and purpose, and a clearness of style and illustration, that entitle it to respectful commendation. How, in one of its phases at least, England's greatness rests on the solid basis of plain iron, how the "hard hands and skilled heads" of our great master-workmen have built up English life and civilization, and created English commerce and English wealth, is told by Mr. Smiles, briefly, unpretendingly, but not without due emphasis. We gather, among other things, from his useful and agreeable pages, that there has been a school of craftsmen in England connected by a common or successional discipleship. Thus Maudsley and Clement worked with Bramah; Clement, Nasmyth, Roberts, and Whitworth with Maudslay, Whitworth working also with Clement.

Of Mr. Smiles's portraits of heroes of the iron age, those that have pleased us most are the sketch of Bramah's life, of Henry Maudsley's, William Fairbairn's, and James Nasmyth's. The strength and versatility of Mr. Nasmyth's genius, and the picturesque material available for biographical portraiture, make his life a most attractive bit of reading. By a rare natural combination of gifts, Mr. Nasmyth, is known as

---

[24] "Memoirs of the Empress Catherine II." Written by Herself, with a Preface by A. Herzen. Translated from the French. New issue. London: Trübner and Co. 1863.

[25] "The Life and Times of the Right Honourable Sir James R. G. Graham, Bart., G.C.B., M.P." By W. T. McCullagh Torrens, late M.P., Author of the "Industrial History of Free Nations," "Life of Sheil," &c. In 2 volumes. Vol. I. Second Edition. London: Saunders, Otley and Co. 1863.

[26] "Industrial Biography: Iron-workers and Tool-makers." By Samuel Smiles, Author of the "Lives of Engineers." London: John Murray. 1863.

a mechanician, an artist, and a scientific discoverer. As an artist, indeed, he takes no high rank, but Mr. Smiles thinks that his works display both fertility of imagination and great skill in drawing. As the inventor of the steam hammer he has won himself an imperishable name: while, if Sir John Herschel be right, in his discovery of the leaf-like organisms which traverse the sun, he has detected *the immediate sources of the solar light and heat.* Had Mr. Nasmyth lived two hundred years ago, he would, as his biography suggests, have had a far better right with that " very fine telescope of his own making," to the fiery honours of the stake, than his remote relative Jean Smith of Hamilton, who was burnt for a witch about that time— being "one of the last martyrs to ignorance and superstition in Scotland—because she read her Bible with two pairs of spectacles."

A class-book on Scripture History by the Rev. Robert Demaus seems to be very fairly drawn up, from the writer's own point of view —that of an uncritical orthodoxy.[27]

We, who know nothing of " Arionic science," who are unable to " hidrymatize masonic co-ordinates," and who if told that "ecpyrosis set in at the eighth cubit of cataclysmal time," are none the wiser for the information, must content ourselves with drawing the attention of the learned world to Hekekyan Bey's " Treatise on the Chronology of Siriadic Monuments," which has for its object to demonstrate "that the Egyptian dynasties of Manetho are records of Astro-geological Nile observations which have been continued to the present time."[28] With one statement in it which we feel pretty certain we do understand, we as certainly disagree. The key to the Hebrew chronological system, we are told, is the Chronological Revelation made to Abram in Mamre, and the Zootomic formula preceding the Revelation. The *Zootomic formula* is a figment manufactured out of Genesis xv. 9, 10, which specifies the sacrificial offering of the patriarch—namely, a heifer of three years old, and a she-goat of three years old, and a ram of three years old, and a turtle-dove and a young pigeon. By an arithmetical process that would have puzzled the famous Mr Cocker, "the addition of the collective ages in years, of the heifer, the she-goat and the ram, and the two birds, to the number of the animals produces the number sixteen. Halving the carcases of the three quadrupeds the number becomes twenty-two; and the addition of the two birds and their collective ages, which, in the third stage of the masonic formula would not amount to two years, the pigeon being designated 'young,' the number twenty-six, less by the fraction of that year is obtained." These three complementary numbers are then employed in three rather hard sums, the elements of which are furnished by the three versions of the Patriarchal chronologies—the Samaritan,

---

[27] "'A Class-Book of Scripture History." By Rev. Robert Demaus, M.A., Author of " Class-Book of English Prose," &c. Edinburgh: Adam and Charles Black. 1863.

[28] " A Treatise on the Chronology of Siriadic Monuments, &c." By Hekekyan Bey, C.E., of Constantinople, formerly in the Egyptian Service. For Private Circulation. London. 1863.

Septuagint, and Hebrew—to aid in effecting " the description of the scale of Sothis periods based on or in terms of the Egyptian astrogeological Nile records," which is as clear as mud. In happy contrast to this pseudo-erudition stands the recent decipherment of the Hieratic papyri of the time of king Ammenenos I. B.C. 2400, by Mr. Goodwin and M. Chabas, the substantial agreement of whose mutually independent interpretation of a coherent and tolerably lengthy narrative is calculated to revive our languishing faith in the reality of Egyptological science, and affords some promise of its confirmation and development in the future—unless, indeed, it can be shown that a fallacy is involved in the application of a common hermeneutic process.

The life of George Beattie of Montrose, a poet and humorist of local reputation, is the last work in our quarterly list.[29]

BELLES LETTRES.

A NEW edition of the " History of Spanish Literature,"[1] carefully revised and containing much new matter, has rendered this valuable book yet more complete, and further secured its already well established reputation as a standard work, worthy of an honoured place in that brilliant series of which America may well be proud. The venerable author dwells with affectionate interest on the work which has occupied so many years of his life, the result of researches commenced in Spain nearly half a century ago, and which he now sends forth again probably " for the last time" (to use his own words); enriched by all that the studious prosecution of a favourite study has added to his knowledge since its first publication in 1849. During this interval it has been translated into German by Dr. Julius of Hamburg, and into Spanish by Don Pascual de Gayangos, to whose notes and annotations Mr. Ticknor professes himself largely indebted. His own notes are copious and highly interesting, abounding in curious information, gathered in many instances from unpublished sources.

The literature of Spain, like the fauna of Australia, belongs to a period which other countries have done with and forgotten, and from which they are separated by centuries of progress and change. Equal to the foremost European nations in old romance and dramatic literature; unrivalled in the ballad poetry and the quaint proverbial wisdom, which bespeak a deeply-rooted and widely-spread principle of national and intellectual life, Spain has presented for more than three centuries the deplorable spectacle of a nation once renowned, forbidden

---

[29] " George Beattie of Montrose : a Poet, a Humorist, and a Man of Genius.' By H. S. M. Cyrus, M.A. Second Edition. Edinburgh: William P. Nimmo. London : Simpkin, Marshall, and Co.

[1] " History of Spanish Literature." By George Ticknor. Third Edition. London : Trübner and Co. 1863.

to think, to change, or to improve, and condemned to see every attempt to kindle within her the new life and light which dawned in the sixteenth century, extinguished in blood. How far her sudden retrogression and decay were the effects of national character, and how far they were caused by the triumph of kingly and clerical despotism, is a question which Mr. Ticknor only incidentally discusses; but he is inclined to attribute the latter to a "misdirection of the old religious faith and loyalty," which in earlier times and under different circumstances had carried the country to its highest pitch of greatness. However difficult to assign an adequate cause, the fact is indubitable that during four centuries the history of Spanish literature was one of abundant promise, and that it has ever since been a record of stagnation and decline. It is thus that Mr. Ticknor sums up its condition and prospects in the sixteenth and seventeenth centuries :—

"As we proceed we shall find, in the full developement of the Spanish character and literature, seeming contradictions, which can be reconciled only by looking back to the foundations on which they both rest. We shall find the inquisition at the height of its power, and a free and immoral drama at the height of its popularity,—Philip the Second and his two immediate successors governing the country with the severest and most jealous despotism, while Quevedo was writing his witty and dangerous satires, and Cervantes his bold and wise Don Quixote. But the more carefully we consider such a state of things, the more we shall see that there are moral contradictions which draw after them grave moral mischiefs. The Spanish nation, and the men of genius who illustrated its best days, might be light-hearted because they did not perceive the limits within which they were confined, or did not, for a time, feel the restraints that were imposed upon them. What they gave up might be given up with cheerful hearts, and not with a sense of discouragement and degradation; it might be done in the spirit of loyalty and with the fervour of religious zeal; but it is not at all the less true that the hard limits were there, and that great sacrifices of the best elements of the national character must follow the constraint and subjection they implied. Of this, time gave abundant proof. Only a little more than a century elapsed before the Government that had threatened the world with a universal Empire was hardly able to repel invasion from abroad, or maintain the allegiance of its own subjects at home. Life—the vigorous, poetical life, which had been kindled through the country in its ages of trial and adversity—was evidently passing out of the whole Spanish character. As a people, they sank away from being a first-rate power in Europe, till they became one of altogether inferior importance and consideration; and then drawing back haughtily behind their mountains, rejected all equal intercourse with the rest of the world, in a spirit almost as exclusive and intolerant as that in which they had formerly refused intercourse with their Arab conquerors. The crude and gross wealth poured in from their American possessions, sustained, indeed, for yet another century, the forms of a miserable political existence in their Government; but the earnest faith, the loyalty, the dignity of the Spanish people, were gone; and little remained in their place but a weak subserviency to the unworthy masters of the State, and a low timid bigotry in whatever related to religion. The old enthusiasm, rarely directed by wisdom from the first, and often misdirected afterwards, faded away; and the poetry of the country, which had always depended more on the state of the popular feeling than any other poetry of modern times, faded and failed with it."—vol. i., p. 432.

A work of this nature necessarily includes small writers as well as great, and Mr. Ticknor's conscientious industry has dragged from their natural obscurity an innumerable host whose names are as unknown as their works are of little value;—a circumstance little surprising when we remember the sure fate that awaited any loftier spirit that dared to rise above the prescribed level of mediocrity. The great writers of Spain are few, and her great thinkers fewer, but of these it is hard to mention one, Cervantes excepted, whom the Inquisition did not surround with its toils, and the genius must have been irresistible indeed that could force itself to surmount such obstacles as were arrayed against it. Philip II. ordained the punishment *of death* in 1558 to whomsoever should sell, buy, or keep any book prohibited by the Index Expurgatorius promulgated by the Supreme Council of the Inquisition ; the physical and exact sciences were excluded from the universities; the existence of the mathematical sciences became known to Diego de Torres by accident, when he had been five years at Salamanca ; this was in the early part of the last century ; but fifty years later Blanco White would have left the university of Seville equally ignorant of modern literature if a chance acquaintance had not introduced him to the subject of Spanish poetry. But Mr. Ticknor looks forward hopefully to a brighter future, and no one can be more competent to judge of the genius of the Spanish nation than the author of these learned and most instructive volumes.

So calm and dispassionate a tone as that of Mr. Ticknor is hardly to be expected of any one, least of all a Frenchman, in criticising the literary achievements of his own country, but " Les Harangues de l'Exil"[2] of Mr. Bancel show a hardihood in the use of superlatives which even his countrymen do not often attain to. His work consists of thirteen discourses selected from lectures which he has delivered during the last six years at the University of Brussels, upon French literature in the seventeenth and eighteenth centuries. He is an eloquent declaimer rather than a judicious teacher, and is so often carried away by his feelings into that region of fanciful paradox and grandiloquent apostrophe in which Frenchmen delight, that the effort to keep up with his soaring flight through three volumes becomes somewhat fatiguing. The great dramatists are the subjects of nine discourses ; the " sublimes tirades" of Corneille (so designated by Mde. de Sevigné), are amply commented upon ; Racine is elaborately analysed and Athalie pronounced, though with some hesitation, to fall short of the Hebrew Psalms and perhaps of the Greek tragedians ; but Molière is exalted above both,— his life is compared to that of Shakspeare *moins les orgies*, and he is set upon a lofty pedestal before which M. Bancel falls down and worships. Pascal, Bossuet, and Bayle are handled with more discrimination, and the lectures on Montesquieu are both able and just ; but the author's faculty of ecstatic admiration bursts forth with increased strength when he comes to Voltaire, the apostle of tolerance, to the encyclopedists who reared " the citadel and the temple of modern philosophy," and to Rousseau, the author of a moral revolution,

---

[2] "Études Historiques et Littéraires: Les Harangues de l'Exil." Par F. D. Bancel. Paris : Lacroix et Cie. London : Nutt. 1868.

namely, "*il mit l'amour maternal à la mode.*" M. Bancel's point of
view is that of a political exile of the most extreme liberal sentiments,
and he writes of liberty and the struggle between authority and
opinion with a fervour that is pathetically expressive of personal
experience.

On the subject of Rousseau, M. Arsène Houssaye publishes a new
edition of a strange volume.[3] He informs his readers that he made a
pilgrimage to Les Charmettes during a deep snow in January, and that
having searched Chambery in vain for a copy of the Confessions, he
telegraphed to Paris for one, which duly arrived on the day following.
He has availed himself largely of its contents, and has filled nearly a
third of his book with Rousseau's own history of his life with Mde.
de Warens. The remainder is made up of fragments, letters, imaginary
conversations, the Pensées of Madame de Warens, and descriptions of
the present aspect of the abode from which successive pilgrims have
carried off, bit by bit, nearly the whole of what was once Rousseau's
bed.

M. Victor Fournel publishes the first volume[4] of a work which, when
completed, will be a collection of all scarce, unedited, and little known
comedies played from 1650 to 1650, with notes, criticisms, and short
biographical memoirs of the authors. The undertaking promises to be
useful in rescuing from the oblivion of the unedited compositions
which, although belonging to the second and third class of plays, have
nevertheless certain merits, and throw light on many points of contemporary life and manners. The author has spared no pains in
hunting out these neglected trifles, and his book contains a good deal
of gossiping information. It will consist of four or five volumes, in
which the pieces produced at the various theatres will be given in
order. The present volume is devoted to the most ancient, the
theatre of the Hôtel de Bourgoyne, which was granted by letters
patent of Francis I. to the Confrères de la Passion, actors of the old
mysteries and moralities, and whose privileges were afterwards confirmed by the Parliament of 1548, on condition that they should
renounce their sacred plays and restrict themselves to subjects
"honnêtes, licites, et profanes." Thus began the modern comic drama
of France. With but few exceptions all the specimens given are in
verse, often witty, always gay, and the characters always Frenchmen
and women, whatever may be the historical or foreign personage nominally represented. One amusing little piece, by Raymond Poisson,
entitled " Le Baron de la Crosse," gives a lively picture of the contempt of the Parisians for the provincial aristocracy. The baron
detests the Court, but his loyalty impels him to desire greatly to see the
King, for which purpose he undertakes a journey to Fontainbleau.
There he is treated with great indignity; and having rashly set himself close to a door which stood ajar in order to listen to what is going

---

[3] "Les Charmettes: Jean-Jacques Rousseau et Madame de Warens." Par
Arsène Houssaye. Paris: Didier. London: Williams and Norgate. 1864.
[4] "Les Contemporains de Molière." Par Victor Fournel. Tome premier.
Paris: Firmin Didot Fréres. London: Nutt. 1863.

forward, the door is suddenly shut to, and closes tight upon his long, undressed hair. He only escapes from the jeers and laughter of the attendants, who cannot get over the fact of his wearing no perruque, by severing himself from his imprisoned locks, which he leaves behind him, and makes his escape, vowing never to undertake so profitless an expedition again. In another one act comedy, by Montfleury, "Les Bestes Raisonnables," a polite, facetious Ulysses intercedes with Circe to restore to their human form four personages whom she has changed into different animals. They all bitterly reproach him for doing them so ill a turn, until one, a courtier, is assured that he will find a terrestrial paradise in place of the corrupt court which he had left; and the piece winds up, like *Tartufe*, in extravagant adulation of Louis le Grand. But there is much similarity of plot in all these little plays; the rival lovers, the stratagems and disguises of their mistresses; and Philippin, the inevitable valet, always ready to out-trick the deepest and wiliest schemes.

The short introductory memoir with which Mr. Blanchard Jerrold prefaces the new edition of his father's works,[6] tells the story of a life of strenuous labour for daily bread in that which might seem to the uninitiated to be the brightest and most flower-strewn path in the wide field of literature, but which has too often been the dreariest and the most stony. Unlike Charles Lamb and Thomas Hood, with both of whom he had some affinity of temperament, Douglas Jerrold lived to taste the sweets of prosperity and success; and the last twelve years of his life were spent in comparative sunshine, after forty of unceasing toil. "Self-helped and self-guided," to use his own words, "I began the world at an age when, as a general rule, boys have not laid down their primers; the cock-pit of a man-of-war was at thirteen exchanged for the struggle of London." While still a boy, he had resolved to live by his pen; and before he was three-and-twenty there was a wife and family to share the slender maintenance. He wrote incessantly whatever editors and managers would pay for, and turned his naval experience to account in his first successful drama, "Black-eyed Susan." "All this time," writes his son, "he was educating himself. He would have his fire laid overnight, and rise by candlelight on winter's mornings to read his Latin and French, and to make ready for his Italian master (he still lives in Boulogne to tell the story), who was to come presently. He read all the old dramatists and poets; and he was not content until he could enjoy Rabelais easily in the original. He was a diligent student of Jeremy Taylor, and an enthusiastic Shakspearian." Besides his dramatic compositions, he wrote theatrical criticisms and leaders for the *Morning Herald*; stories and articles for the annuals; magazine papers for Blackwood, &c. He edited and contributed largely to *The Heads of the People;* and from the time that *Punch* was started, in 1841, he was its most constant contributor. The present volume contains besides "St. Giles's and St. James's," *Punch's* Letters to his Son, clever, caustic, and witty satires written in that

---

[6] "The Works of Douglas Jerrold." Vol. I. London: Bradbury and Evans. 1863.

peculiar style of quaint make-belief gravity in which he excelled. Whether the enthusiastic admiration of contemporaries for one whose personal character was singularly amiable and winning, will be ratified by the cooler judgment of their children, remains to be proved; but there can be no question that the graver writings of Douglas Jerrold have had their share in healing the "feud of rich and poor," and in proclaiming the rights of the latter and the responsibilities of the former, and this will be his better and more enduring monument than even the Caudle Lectures, though we are informed that their "wild popularity travelled over Europe;" and Mr. B. Jerrold possesses a translation of them in Dutch.

If Mr. Trollope's last novel[5] falls short of some of its predecessors in variety of character and incident, it is inferior to none of them in many of the special qualities which have been their chief attraction, and must be read with pleasure by all who can appreciate a good design correctly drawn and coloured, though the subject may be homely and prosaic. There is not absolutely a single figure in the whole story fitted to play a great, a startling, or an intricate part; scarcely one that rises above the ordinary level of humdrum humanity; none that sink very deeply below it; but out of these common-place materials Mr. Trollope's practised hand has produced two pleasant, entertaining volumes, and a story which secures the reader the luxury of seeing his neighbours' follies and weaknesses in a thoroughly ridiculous light, without any tinge of malice. The female characters are, as usual, those upon which the author has bestowed most pains, and in which he is most successful. Rarely has a more charming picture of simple maidenhood, unconsciously awakening to the troubled joy of first love, been more delicately drawn, than in the story of Rachel Ray's acquaintance with Luke Rowan; and equally good is the description of the utter consternation produced by it upon the minds of her strong ascetic sister and her gentle doubtful-minded mother. The sister, a young widow of stern Dorcas-meeting principles, thus communicates the terrible news :—

"She had heard tidings of—a young man! Such tidings, to her ears, were tidings of iniquity, of vanity, of terrible sin; they were tidings which hardly admitted of being discussed with decency, and which had to be spoken of below the breath. A young man! could it be that such disgrace had fallen upon her sister. She had not as yet mentioned the subject to Rachel, but she had given a dark hint to their afflicted mother. 'No, I didn't see it myself, but I heard it from Miss Pucker.' 'She that was to have been married to William White-coat, the baker's son, only he went away to Torquay and picked up with some-body else. People said he did it because she does squint so dreadfully.' 'Mother!'—and Dorothea spoke very sternly as she answered—'what does it matter to us about William Whitecoat, or Miss Pucker's squint? She is a woman eager in doing good.' 'It's only since he left Baslehurst, my dear.' 'Mother! does that matter to Rachel? Will that save her if she be in danger? I tell you that Miss Pucker saw her walking with that young man from the brewery!' Though Mrs. Ray hated Miss Pucker—at this special moment—

---

[5] "Rachel Ray: A Novel." By Anthony Trollope. London: Chapman and Hall. 1863.

she could not deny, even to herself, that a terrible state of things had arrived if it were really true that Rachel had been seen walking with a young man. She was not bitter on the subject as was Dorothea and poor Miss Pucker, but she was filled full of indefinite horror with regard to young men in general. They were all regarded by her as wolves—as wolves, either with or without sheep's clothing. I doubt whether she ever brought it home to herself that those whom she now recognised as the established and well-credited lords of the creation had ever been young men themselves. When she heard of a wedding—when she heard that some struggling son of Adam had taken to himself a wife, and had settled himself down to the sober work of the world, she rejoiced greatly; but whenever it was whispered that any young man was looking after a young woman—that he was taking the only step by which he could hope to find a wife for himself, she was instantly shocked at the wickedness of the world, and prayed inwardly that the girl at least might be saved like a brand from the burning. When young Butler Cornbury came to Cawston after pretty Patty Comfort, Mrs. Ray had thought it all right, because it had been presented to her mind as all right by the rector; but had she heard of Patty's dancings without the assistance of a few hints from Mr. Comfort, her mind would have worked in a different way. . . . For ten minutes the mother sat herself down, thinking of the condition of her youngest daughter, and trying to think what words she would use. . . . When the ten minutes were over she had made up her mind to nothing, and then she also took up her candle and went to her room. When she first entered she did not see Rachel. 'Mamma,' she said, 'put down the candle that I may speak to you.' Whereupon Mrs. Ray put down the candle, and Rachel took hold of both her arms. 'Mamma, you do not believe ill of me, do you? You do not think of me the things that Dorothea says? Say that you do not, or I shall die.' 'My darling, I have never thought anything bad of you before.' 'And you do think bad of me now? Look at me, mamma. What have I ever done that you should think me to be such as she says?' 'I do not think that you have done anything; but you are very young, Rachel.' 'Young, mamma! I am older than you were when you were married, and older than Dolly was. I am old enough to know what is wrong. Shall I tell you what happened this evening? He came and met us all in the fields. Had I not believed that he was in Exeter I should not have gone. I think I should not have gone.' 'Then you are afraid of him?' 'No, mamma; I am not afraid of him. But he says such strange things to me; and I would not purposely have gone out to meet him. As I went through the churchyard he came there too, and then the sun was setting, and he stopped me to look at it; I did stop with him—for a few minutes, and I felt ashamed of myself; but how was I to help it? Mamma, if I could remember them, I would tell you every word he said to me, and every look of his face. He asked me to be his friend. Mamma, if you will believe in me, I will tell you everything. I will never deceive you.' She was still holding her mother's arms while she spoke. Now she held her very close, and nestled in against her bosom, and gradually got her cheek against her mother's cheek, and her lips against her mother's neck. . . . Mrs. Ray was vanquished, and put her arm round her girl and embraced her. She spoke soft words, and told Rachel that she was her dear, dearest darling. She was still awed and dismayed by the tidings she had heard of the young man; she still thought that there was some terrible danger against which it behoved them all to be on their guard. But she no longer felt divided from her child. 'You will believe me?' said Rachel. 'You will not think that I am making up stories to deceive you?' Then the mother assured the daughter with many kisses that she would believe her."—vol. i. p. 78.

But although the chief interest is centred in Rachel's love story, and some readers will complain that we are told too much about it,

there are subordinate interests and persons free from any taint of sentiment described with the author's customary cleverness and point. He
is not afraid to introduce the hackneyed subject of a contested election,
and descends to the particulars of an election dinner, concluding as
follows :—

> "I venture to assert that each liberal elector there would have got a better
> dinner at home, and would have been served with greater comfort ; but a public
> dinner at an inn is the recognised relaxation of a middle-class Englishman in
> the provinces. Did he not attend such banquets his neighbours would conceive
> him to be constrained by domestic tyranny. Others go to them, and therefore
> he goes also. He is bored frightfully by every speech to which he listens. He
> is driven to the lowest depths of dismay by every speech which he is called
> upon to make. He is thoroughly disgusted when he is called on to make no
> speech. He has no point of sympathy with the neighbours between whom he
> sits. The wine is bad. The hot water is brought to him cold. His seat is
> hard and crowded. No attempt is made at the pleasures of conversation. He
> is continually called upon to stand up that he may pretend to drink a toast in
> honour of some person or institution for which he cares nothing ; for the hero
> of the evening, as to whom he is probably indifferent ; for the church, which
> perhaps he never enters ; the army, which he regards as a hotbed of aristocratic
> insolence ; or for the Queen, whom he reveres and loves by reason of his nature
> as an Englishman, but against whose fulsome praises as repeated to him *ad
> nauseam* in the chairman's speech his very soul unconsciously revolts. It is all
> a bore, trouble, ennui, nastiness, and discomfort. But yet he goes again and
> again, because it is the relaxation natural to an Englishman. The Frenchman
> who sits for three hours tilted on the hind legs of a little chair, with his back
> against the window-sill of the café, with first a cup of coffee before him and
> then a glass of sugar-and-water, is perhaps as much to be pitied as regards his
> immediate misery ; but the liquids which he imbibes are not so injurious to
> him."—Vol. ii. p. 248.

"Leo,"[7] a new work by Mr. Dutton Cook, possesses in unusual
measure the requisites of a successful novel. It is throughout amusing, the story is good, and is well and dramatically told. Besides
these merits, it has some which are less common and which distinguish
it from many of its school. Though it deals with people of all classes,
noblemen and adventurers, the toiling actress and the tenderly-nurtured
beauty, it never enlists a false sympathy on the side of weakness or
wickedness ; it paints human nature fairly, and throws no veil over its
frailties, but it never confounds virtue with vice ; and from the beginning to the end there is no trace of that moral confusion which seeks
to banish the terms of good and bad, and loves to point to the fine
grapes and admirable figs produced from thorns and thistles. The
hero being well intentioned, but careless, falls an easy prey to an ill-
intentioned scheming brother-in-law, and the beautiful little heroine,
being more winning than firm, yields to persuasion and accepts one
lover though her heart is given to another—a step which has to be re-
traced at no slight cost to the feelings of the poor simple-hearted Lord
Dolly, whose character is one of the happiest sketches in the book.
We trace throughout the influence of the Great Disenchanter,—the

---

[7] "Leo." By Dutton Cook. London : Smith and Elder. 1863.

innocent-minded, who lived before Vanity Fair, never read such a postscript as this:—

"Who presumes to express interest in the background figures of the tragedy? Who would dare to summon the author of 'Hamlet' to give us detailed histories of his minor personages? 'Take up the bodies,' says Fortinbras. "Go bid the soldiers shoot!' And so a dead march; a bearing off of the corpses; a peal of ordnance shot off—and an end. We may know no more. What became of Horatio? Did he marry the player-lady, who had increased in stature by the altitude of a chopine? In what manner did Osric conduct himself in his after life? Were his last days anything like Brummell's? Did those twin snobs Rosencrantz, and Guildenstern, fall out prior to their execution, or manifest any change in that surprising unanimity which distinguished them during the play? Did the actors recover from the disastrous failure of their performance at Elsinore? Did the second clown improve at all in the guessing of riddles?"

But this is not the tone which comes most naturally to Mr. Cooke, and he writes best when he drops it. His strong sense of humour leads him sometimes to burlesque, as in his description of the Misses Biggs and their seminary for young ladies, which is conducted on the system of Do-the-Boys Hall, the terms being 150*l*. per annum. This is simple caricature, but the book abounds in scenes and characters drawn with the same power and keenness without any obtrusive exaggeration. This is especially true of the portraits of Mr. and Mrs. Lomax, which, although by no means the best in the collection, will suffer less from being detached than would be the case with some more telling portions of this well-compacted performance:—

"As far as I can make out, the height of official ambition is to sit in a room furnished with a Turkey carpet—after that there seems only the Premiership, or perhaps an Archbishopric worthy of aspiration. . . . Mr. Lomax of the Wafer Stamp-office was a Turkey-carpet man. In age he was about forty, he might even have been a little more, for he was a carefully-dressing man, and carefully-dressing men, I find, are always rather older than they seem. A handsome man, with a sharp, thin, aquiline nose, large light-blue eyes, the pupil a mere speck, that never dilated or lent new light or colour to the rather stony-looking irids, and beautifully arched eye-brows—(he had a habit of smoothing these out with his little finger, perhaps to show his superb diamond ring)—it was these, possibly aided by his small, lipless, pinched mouth, that gave to his face a certain supercilious expression, which many of his friends accounted very aristocratic. He was tall, slight, stooped a little as he walked, from constant bending over his desk, as he explained. . . . Winter or summer, he wore light-coloured gloves and carried a neat slim green-silk umbrella. He was carefully shaven, only a slight fragment of whisker, the shape of a pine on an Indian shawl, was left on his cheeks; his well-formed chin was decorated with a dimple, and his hair, thinning very much over his white forehead, was yet adroitly arranged so as to conceal as much as possible this little deficiency. . . . He was a man who, it was evident, had set a high value upon himself, and somehow it happened in most cases that he succeeded in bringing round to an almost identical opinion, everybody with whom he came in contact. . . . The claims of Mrs. Lomax to be ranked as a beauty, perhaps could be no longer fairly substantiated. Her features were not less perfectly proportioned and regular, but an unpleasant rigidity had seized upon them; her once delicate and transparent complexion had faded now into a uniform dull waxen tint; the rich flaxen tresses had thinned, receding from her forehead, always inclined to be over prominent, and under conditions of greater exposure looking disagreeably hard and bony. People talked of her more as a 'charming woman' and less as a beauty. For she was decidedly clever, adroit in manner, with that social requisite (the comfort of which has been a little overrated) a flow of conversation. She was certainly accomplished, understood dress thoroughly, and before her marriage could play Thalberg's fantasias upon the piano-forte, and produce really creditable imitations of Prout in water-colours. She had written stanzas to her sleeping children, and a poem, only a very limited number of copies printed, strictly for private circulation, and called 'Como Revisited.' By-and-bye, as she left her youth still further behind her, and her artificial manner of thought, speech, and action, grew upon her, she became more and more self-possessed and self-venerative, with an inclination to languor of spirits and an indolent, almost insolent, disdain of effort or of interest on behalf of anything. Society now began to speak of her as 'an elegant woman.' She complained of her nerves, was fond of the sofa in her boudoir, and of 'putting her feet up,' and shrank at the slightest noise. In fact, she was a good deal like many other 'elegant women' who, as a rule, I find are generally nearing middle-age, and not over-pleased with the fact, rejoicing in weak nerves and very delicate health, inclined to be, to use a harsh word, scraggy, and leading their handmaidens very desperate lives indeed. She was suffering from what she called, as though she were the original inventor and vested with patent rights in regard to it, and what was consequently known throughout the household as, 'one of her headaches.' She looked especially old and cross, and plain, on days when she was thus afflicted. . . . But there was something 'elegant' about her invalid condition, which perhaps made Mrs. Lomax rather nurse her headaches, treasuring them as evidences of birth, and breeding, and culture, as other people cherish pedigrees, diplomas, and examiner's certificates. . . . She had a considerable affection for her brother, though she had been a good deal in the habit of plastering over her feelings with sham sentiment very dangerous to their vitality; just as other ladies are prone to spoil the beauty of their complexions by injurious coatings of rouge and pearl-powder." —vol. iii. p. 90.

One of the most remarkable and original novels of the season is a new story of American Life by Mr. Bayard Taylor.[8] It is the high prerogative of genius to give the impulse to thought and to determine its current and direction, and this has been one great service that Mr. Hawthorne has done for American fiction. Since the appearance of "The Scarlet Letter," the tendency of the best writers has been to work the rich unexplored vein of romance that lay hidden under the stubborn unpoetical forms of New England life, and to enter faithfully into its spirit, undismayed by its anomalies and peculiarities which are an offence to the established traditions of the Old World. In "Hannah Thurston" everything is essentially American, and if, as the author avers, "that in it which most resembles caricature is often the transcript of actual fact," it is a picture as valuable as it is curious, and its interest rests less upon its merits as a story than "on the fidelity with which it represents certain types of character and phases of society." Regarded as a work of art, these qualities, in a certain degree, constitute its imperfection, and it is undoubtedly true, that the impression cannot always be resisted of the characters being purely re-

---

[8] "Hannah Thurston: a Story of American Life." By Bayard Taylor. London: Sampson Low and Co. 1863.

presentative—studies for a moral purpose rather than creations for an artistic one—and yet there is no lack of art or of imagination in their treatment, nor does the action of the story flag, though it is made subordinate to the development of special and minute shades of feeling in the actors. We are shown the outer modes of a very singular phase of society with great pictorial effect, but the author's strong bias towards mental and emotional dissection is apparent through the whole. In the hero, Maxwell Woodbury, he has drawn a character of almost ideal perfection and refinement, and it is through his eyes that we see the inner social economy of Ptolemy, the small provincial town near to which he has purchased an estate, after making a fortune in India, and being twice shipwrecked in love. Before he has had time to look round him, he is visited by Mr. Hamilton Bue, agent of the "Saratoga Mutual," and the Honorable Zeno Harder, member of the Legislature for Atauga County, who think he may find his first evening " a little lonesome," and from whom he learns the state of opinion of the community of which he will soon be a member. But the scene must be given in the author's words :—

"The member was a coarse, obese man, with heavy chaps, thick, flat lips, small eyes, bald crown, and a voice which had been made harsh and aggressive in its tone by much vigorous oratory in the open air. The lines of his figure were rounded, it is true, but it was the lumpy roundness of a potato, rather than the swelling opulent curves of well-padded muscle. Mr. Hamilton Bue, in contrast to him, seemed to be made of angles. His face and hands had that lean dryness which suggests a body similarly constructed, and makes us thankful for the invention of clothing. . . . Neither of these gentlemen possessed a particle of that grapy bloom of ripe manhood, which tells of generous blood in either cell of the double heart. In one the juice was dried up ; in the other it had become thick and slightly rancid. . . . The Hon. Zeno, taking a cigar, elevated his feet upon the lower moulding of the wooden mantel-piece, spat in the fire, and remarked—' You find Ptolemy changed, I dare say. Let me see—when were you here last—in '32 ? I must have been studying law in Tiberius at that time. Oh, it's scarcely the same place. So many went West after the smash in '37, and new people have come in—new people and new ideas I may say.'—' What are the new ideas you mentioned, Mr. Harder ?' ' Well, sir, I can't exactly say that Hunkerism is a new thing in politics. I'm a Barnburner, you must know, and since the split it seems like new parties, though *we* hold on to the same principles. Then there's the Temperance Reform swep' everything before it, at first, but slacking off just now. The Abolitionists it's hardly worth while to count—there's so few of them—but they make a mighty noise. Go for Non-Resistance, Women's Rights, and all other isms. So, you see, compared to the old times, when 'twas only Whig and Democrat, the deestrict is pretty well stirred up.' . . . As for Women's Rights it's the biggest humbug of all. A pretty mess we should be in, if it could be carried out ! Think of my wife taking the stump against Mrs. Blackford, and me and him doing the washing and cooking !' ' Who was the abolitionist with whom you were talking last evening at Mr. Bue's ?' Woodbury asked. ' Wattles, a tailor in Ptolemy—one of the worst fanatics among 'em !' the irate Zeno replied. ' Believes in all the isms, and thinks himself a great Reformer. It's disgusting to hear a man talk about women's rights as he does. I don't mind it so much in Hannah Thurston ; but the fact is, she's more of a man than the most of 'em. . . . Between ourselves, I'll admit that she's a first-rate speaker—that is, for a woman. I was tempted to have a round with her at the last meeting they held; but then, you know, a woman always has you at a disadvantage. You daren't give it back to them as sharp as you get it.' 'Do you really mean that she makes public harangues?' exclaimed Woodbury, who, in his long absence from home, had lost sight of many new developments in American society. 'Yes, and not bad ones either when you consider the subject. Her mother used to preach in Quaker meetings, so it doesn't seem quite so strange as it might. Besides, she isn't married, and one can make some allowance. But when Sarah Merryfield gets up and talks of the tyranny of man, it's a little too much for me. I'd like to know, now, exactly what her meek lout of a husband thinks about it. . . . 'Our ladies are now very earnest in the work of assisting the Jutnapore Mission,' said Mr. Bue. 'I think Miss Eliza Clancy would have gone herself if she had been called in time. You know it requires a double call.' 'Excuse me if I do not quite understand you.' 'Why, of course, they must first be called to the *work ;* and then, as they can't go alone among the heathen, they must afterwards depend on a personal call from some unmarried missionary. Now Miss Clancy is rather too old for that.' Woodbury could not repress a smile at this naïve statement, although it was made with entire gravity. . . . 'Absalom Merryfield was really a fine, promising fellow,' said the member, 'but they spoiled him with their isms. They were Gershamites for a year or two—lived on bran-bread and turnips, boiled wheat and dried apples. Absalom took up that and the water-cure, and wanted to become a patent first-class reformer. He had a spell of pleurisy one winter, and doctored himself for it ; he went off the very next fall.' . . . 'You will attend church, I presume, Mr. Woodbury?' said Mr. Bue. 'Of course you have convictions?' 'Certainly,' Woodbury answered, without a clear idea of what was meant by the word, 'very strong ones.' 'Of course ; it could not be otherwise. I shall be very glad if you will now and then accept a seat in my pew. Mr. Styles is a great authority on Galatians, and I am sure you will derive spiritual refreshment from his sermons.' "—vol. i. p. 80.

Speedily, and as by a subtle magnetism, Woodbury is drawn towards the pale young Quakeress, whose opinions shock every conviction of his mind, but whose exquisitely pure and womanly nature satisfies every craving of his heart. With great power, delicacy, and an almost feminine acuteness of perception, Mr. Taylor has traced the growth and course of the mutual feeling which springs up between the strong, experienced, world-worn man, and the fervent, saintly-minded apostle of Female Emancipation. Very true and very beautiful is the character of Hannah Thurston, and the seriousness with which justice is done to her advocacy of Woman's Rights is perhaps a strong evidence of the unrecognised but salutary effect of a movement which could never have existed without some real cause, and which, in spite of much deserved ridicule, had a germ of truth under its fallacious doctrines. In fact, Mr. Taylor's book owes its chief interest to the earnest, reverential spirit in which he has treated a question which has more deeply agitated his country than our own. His mode of solving the difficulty is simple. Miss Thurston has an eager disciple in a pretty, coquettish little seamstress, Carrie Dilworth, who talks about moral and intellectual beauty, believes that *beau-ideal* means an ideal beau, and to whom the unnatural assumption of the equal-rights theory is as " a helmet of Pallas, which not only covered her brow, but fell forward over her saucy *retroussée* nose, and weighed her slender body half-way to the earth." Her lover falls ill of a brain fever, and it becomes her duty to nurse him, which she does with unwearied devotion, marries him as soon as he recovers, and in the happiness of a new home-sphere, and the support of a strong man's arm, soon forgets all about rights or wrongs.   But the case of the heroine is less easy.   She has devoted the whole energy of a lofty and ardent nature to a cause in which she entirely believed, and it is only through terrible struggles and self-contempt that she allows her heart to listen to what she has forced her reason to despise; but, of course, love triumphs, and the intellectual spell is broken.   The result is brought about very happily, and the conclusion resembles that of Tennyson's "Princess:" but it is still poetry and not argument; and while we are under conditions which, as has been well remarked by De Quincey, tend to encourage celibacy among women, and especially among the highest order of women, the claim for a more equal participation in the world's work must and will be asserted.   For those who have studied this difficult question, Helen Thurston will have a peculiar interest.   Mr. Taylor writes the ornate style which his countrymen so much affect, and sometimes falls into flowery affectation, as, for instance, when he says, "a sweet, serious smile betraying that breath of dried roses which greets us as we open some forgotten volume of the past;" but it is for the most part pure and elegant, and in the description of natural scenery he greatly excels.

Captain Meadows Taylor has attempted a very difficult, if not impossible task in "Tara,"[9] and if he cannot be said to have accomplished it with success, the cause is to be traced more to the nature of his subject than to his mode of treating it, and something also to his having written in a style the very opposite of that which is now most in vogue.   Had it appeared forty years ago, it would probably have met with a warmer reception than it is likely to receive from our own impatient, excitement-loving generation, for its smooth elegance of style would have recommended it to the fastidious, and the curious would have been attracted by the novelty of the scenes and events it describes.   Great knowledge of the country and considerable powers of narration are apparent at every page, and the plot of the story is not wanting either in conception or detail; but were these merits infinitely more conspicuous than they are, they would not compensate for the want of that which is the *sine quâ non* of modern fiction—sharply-marked individuality, more of passion, and less of incident. Another and very serious disadvantage is the unusual length of the story.   The author has lived so long in the East that he has learnt to see no tedium in prolixity, and appears to be quite unconscious that a novel in three closely-printed volumes, describing events and people with which the English reader can have little or no sympathy, makes too heavy a demand upon the time and patience of a "sensation"-loving public.   The rise of the Mahratta power in the middle of the seventeenth century, and the romantic career of Sivaji Rajah, still the hero of popular songs and legends, are the historical events upon which

9 "Tara: a Mahratta Tale."   By Capt. Meadows Taylor.   London and Edinburgh: Blackwood. 1863.

the story is founded, and with them is also interwoven the confused web of plot, treachery, and intrigue by which the Mogul Emperors of Delhi were seeking the subjugation of Beejapoor, at that time a great and important state, its capital, now in ruins, the richest and most magnificent city of the Deccan. Here are materials enough for a telling background to the picture of Tara, the beautiful heroine, whose history embraces every element of Eastern romance—the child-widow, the inspired priestess, the victim snatched from voluntary suttee, and wedded at last, in spite of creed, to the gallant young Mahommedan chief, Fazil Khan. But the want of coherence in the plot, the interminable conversations, the over-minuteness of detail, and the unartistic tameness of treatment, produce an effect of oppressive monotony which is only relieved by occasional passages of graphic and picturesque writing. Among these, the scene in which Tara is rescued from her intended self-immolation, surrounded by all the dread accessories of a great religious ceremonial, is one of the best. It is a painful addition to the toil of perusing this conscientious book, that it is overlaid with native terms, which are explained in foot-notes it is true, but a novel should not require foot-notes.

"Janet's Home"[10] has little to distinguish it from many other domestic chronicles in two volumes, in which a feminine minuteness of detail is allied to considerable literary accomplishment, and the practical good sense which comes of a clean heart and a right mind. Stories of this class are so admirably true to life that they almost oppress the reader by making him a participator in the confused activity and tread-mill monotony in which many daughters of struggling professional men live. The home is a type of many English firesides; the father bravely earning the daily bread as head-master of a school, and giving professorial lectures besides; the mother, fond, careworn, and a little tiresome, living only in and for her children. She can never forget that she was well born, the rightful heiress to a large Welsh property when she gave her hand to Mr. Scott, a poor tutor, and has taught her children to think of their mother's early history as of a dream of fairy land. The characters of the four children of which the family consists are well drawn, and that of Janet, the narrator, is made to unfold itself gradually and naturally amidst the cares, distractions, and sorrows of her home. A great calamity, the failing sight and ultimate blindness of her father, calls forth the latent strength of her dreamy, imaginative nature, which excites a deeper interest than that of her softer and beautiful sister. The character of Lady Helen Carr, the disappointed, false-hearted woman of the world, is well drawn, and also that of her clever son, who, while yet in his early youth, has discovered that "naught is everything, and everything is naught," and has written a poem which is only intelligible to readers under twenty. They are both set before the reader as they would have presented themselves to the eyes and understanding of an observant and inexperienced girl. If it be the work of an unpractised writer— which the want of finish in the working out of the story seems to

[10] "Janet's Home." London and Cambridge: Macmillan. 1863.

indicate—"Janet's Home" contains the promise of still better things from an author whose powers of observation and description are of no mean order.

A new edition of "The Moors and the Fens"[11] condenses into one closely-printed volume a story which, though not wanting in power, yet deals so much with the gloomy and the repulsive that the general effect is dark and painful, in spite of the attractive colours in which the heroine, Mina Frazer, is painted, and the occasional gleams of brighter light that fall upon her. The story is made dismal and oppressive by the shadow of the gloomy place in the Lincolnshire fens where lives an old miser, Sir Ernest Ivraine, with his horrible miserly sister, indulging his greed for gold, and making his sons as unhappy as possible. Such a character has always been a favourite in fiction, and the author has treated it in the usual manner, including the unexpected will and the host of disappointed relations; but there is a touch of originality in the closing scene between the miserable old man and his lawyer, after the will has been duly attested, and he lies back waiting for the last stern creditor, Death :—

"Mr. Medill gazed around the dreary, carpetless apartment, at the tattered draperies, at the flickering candle, and a horror came over the attorney's soul —albeit he was neither a particularly religious nor timid man. He knew the miser was thinking, not of another world, but of this; he knew just as well as if he had seen his heart what was dwelling there—regret, not for having abused the great gifts entrusted to his keeping, but because he could not carry his estates and guineas, and title-deeds and mortgages with him; sorrow, not for having cursed his children's lives, but for being at last compelled to relinquish all to the son of one of them. At length the old man, as if struck by some sudden thought, made a feeble sign for Mr. Medill to bend his head close to him; and hoping that some better desire had occurred, even at the eleventh hour, to the baronet, the solicitor inclined his ear to the white trembling lips. 'There is no use in wasting the candle,' gasped his client; 'blow it out.' For a moment Mr. Medill felt too much astonished to obey; and then, ere he had time to comply with the request, born of 'the ruling passion strong in death,' a chill blast from the boundless gulf of eternity came sweeping through the room, and extinguished for ever the faint mortal light that flickered within the old miser's attenuated frame."—p. 331.

An historical romance from the productive pen of Louise Mühlbach[12] carries the reader on through every sort of improbability and extravagance, and compels him to peruse to the end its stirring and spirited pages. Prince Eugene first shows his natural genius as a military commander in repelling an attack of the Parisian mob, headed by the son of Louvois, upon the palace of his mother, the famous Duchesse de Soissons, and in the character of a lover he shows himself equally daring, but the lady is suddenly married to some one else, disappears wholly from the story, and the whole of the third volume is devoted to the prince's campaigns, and the historical events relating to them.

---

[11] "The Moors and the Fens." By F. G. Trafford, Author of "Too Much Alone," &c. With Illustrations. London: Smith, Elder, and Co. 1863.
[12] "Prinz Eugen und Seine Zeit." Von L. Mühlbach. Berlin: Otto Janke. London: Nutt. 1864.

A new novel[13] by the author of "Sylvan Holt's Daughter," fails to satisfy the expectations which the writer has hitherto justified. "Annis Warleigh" is not wanting in cleverness, nor in a certain freshness of tone and philosophic amiability which characterized its predecessors, but there is an absence of clearness in the plot which greatly mars the effect, and an indistinctness of outline about some of the most prominent characters, as of figures seen in a fog. The ostensible heroine, Miss Rachel Withers, is a very excellent uninteresting woman, who, after one unsuccessful attempt at matrimony, settles down into a patient, cheerful spinster; and Annis, the real heroine, does not appear on the stage until nearly the end of the first volume. There is a strange attempt to infuse an element of weird mystery in the person of an awful old Lady Fowlis, who lives in dark seclusion and plays ghostly music at night upon the organ, but who dies eventually at the age of ninety-eight, without, as far as we can discover, having been in the least degree wanted; nor is the secret of her very extraordinary manner of life more than obscurely hinted at. The writer excels in the portraiture of old ladies: the two charming old sisters who adopt Annis are very well drawn in their piety, simplicity, and godly fear of all the snares of the world outside their own Arcadian home; and better still is the character of Mrs. Sara Grandage, familiarly known as Bittersweet, who thus sums up the fruits of her own very different experience:—

"Bittersweet clung to her old books of philosophy to the end, but she heard her Bible read too—some people fancied she never opened it; she left them in their delusion, but Rachel knew better. 'It is the soundest philosophy of all, my dear, and stick to it,' said the old lady, towards the last. 'I stuck to it when it was no more clear to me than High Dutch, but light has glimmered out since —enough to see by. Good people are not very different at bottom, only they fight so over their dogmas, that they seem really to hate each other for the love of God. Never mind religious *ideas*, Dumpling, and don't worry youself with so-called good books; they reason all round the compass if you read enough of them, and if you do not you only get the views of a party. I do not think myself there are any parties where I am going. Do your best and trust God, my dear; there is nothing else for it; I hope I have not done you harm. Delia thinks me a scoffing old woman; but that was my rule, and it has answered. I had some sharp trials in my youth, and it alone withheld me from being a discontented, utterly miserable, perhaps wicked woman. I was married at sixteen to a man older than my father, and if I were to say that I was married in payment of one of my father's debts of honour, I should probably be as near the truth as ever we can get in such transactions. He was excellent company, my husband, to everybody but his wife; I was too young and simple to amuse him long, and I was only on the verge of becoming wise enough for the duty when he died. He was very charitable and serious in his later years, and the world always gave him a good word in every one of his phases. In his early and middle life he was a great rake; but he reformed when he grew weary of sinning and turned saint, proposing me to himself as a devotee—but I thought his last estate worse than his first. I used to try to provoke him by showing my lack of faith in the genuineness of his conversion, and he bore with me very philosophically. Cousin Delia would say he had got a changed heart—I don't know; it always gave me an uncomfortable feeling to see him trying to circum-

---

[13] "Annis Warleigh's Fortunes." By Holme Lee. London: Smith, Elder, and Co. 1863.

vent his old master. Rachel, am I growing profane? Ah, my dear, I was much worse at twenty—Heaven forgive me! Draw the curtains—now I'll go to sleep.' "—vol. ii. p. 217.

There are the materials for an excellent story in this book, but they are badly focused and not made the most of, in consequence of which the general result is, to use a favourite word of the author, a little " weariful."

A story for children by the same hand,[14] is a much more successful performance, and one of the best and prettiest of the season, worthy of as universal popularity as the veracious history of " Puss and the Captain." To the same juvenile public we commend for the amusement of the Christmas holidays, a pretty little volume of Miscellaneous Tales,[15] and a tempting selection from Grimm's " Fairy Tales."[16] Gammer Grethel, the supposed narrator, was a real personage—a certain Frau Viehmännin, the wife of a peasant in the neighbourhood of Hesse-Cassel, from whose mouth the Grimms wrote down a great portion of the stories. Her family suffered severely in the French war, and she herself died soon after the Messrs. Grimm published their first collection. A large illustrated volume, containing a history of Eastern adventures and marvels,[17] also deserves to find favour with young readers.

Mr. Bohn publishes a new edition—the thirtieth—of John Foster's well-known Essays[18] on—I. A Man's Writing Memoirs of Himself; II. On Decision of Character; III. On the Application of the Epithet Romantic; IV. On some of the Causes by which Evangelical Religion has been rendered less Acceptable to Persons of Cultivated Taste.—It would be difficult to account for the persistent popularity of this book. Rigid in style, austere in sentiment, there seems to be little in it calculated to attract the many who only care to read what they can understand at once and without effort, while readers of a different stamp would be likely to be repelled by the somewhat sectarian narrowness of tone which chills and cramps the clear and just thoughts with which it abounds.

The first volume of a philosophical work by M. Moriz Carriere[19] attempts what the author truly says has never yet been done—namely, to trace the history of the human mind in every age and country. The present volume is devoted to the consideration of the peculiar intellectual characteristics of Oriental nations as shown in their religion, poetry, and art, and includes Egypt, China, the Hebrew nation, India, and Persia. The introductory chapters on language and myth explain the broad principles by which the author has been guided in his

[14] " The True, Pathetic History of Poor Match." By Holme Lee. London: Smith, Elder, and Co. 1863.

[15] " Tales of Many Lands." By M. Fraser Tytler. London: Virtue.

[16] " German Fairy Tales and Popular Stories, as told by Gammer Grethel." Translated by Edgar Taylor. London: Bohn. 1863.

[17] " Adventures of Alfan ; or, the Magic Amulet." By Holme Burrow, B.A. London : Smith, Elder, and Co. 1863.

[18] " Essays, in a Series of Letters." By John Foster. London: Bohn. 1863.

[19] " Die Kunst im Zusammenhang der Culturentwickelung und die Ideale der Menschheit." Von Moriz Carriere. Leipzig: Brockhaus. 1863.

attempted survey of universal history; and in the rapid summary he gives of the moral and religious tendencies which are expressed with more or less distinctness in the artistic forms of every race and people, he has brought together the results of the latest research; but they embrace so wide a field and include the investigation of so many weighty problems, that it is only possible here to indicate the nature and scope of an undertaking which, whatever may be its ultimate success, has been entered upon in a wise and enlightened spirit.

In the same province of inquiry we have a volume of Essays[20] by M. Maury. In those on the religions of India and Persia he takes a general survey of the theology of the Rig Véda, from which he quotes largely, and which he pronounces to be "a conception of God as he is revealed in nature where Divine action is manifested but cannot be handled; a worship based upon the subordination of men to the gods; a system of morals interwoven with this worship, and owning, as its chief principle, the love and fear of celestial beings, the desire of obtaining benefits from them, and the fear of their chastisements. Of images and idols the Aryans knew nothing, but if anthropomorphism did not outwardly prevail, it is to be found abundantly in their language and figures of speech, and it needed but the birth of art to give it expression in idols." In a paper contributed to the memoirs of the French Antiquarian Society in 1849, entitled "Camulus et Grannus," the author gives the results of his researches respecting these two ancient Celtic divinities, and identifies them with those to whom Cæsar gave the names of Apollo and Mars. The title "Camulus deus sanctissimus" occurs in many inscriptions discovered at Nîmes, Narbonne, and elsewhere. Grannus, the Gallic Apollo, seems to have been the tutelar deity of thermal springs; hence the ancient name of Aixla-Chapelle, *Aquæ Granni*, and the name *Granus thurm* still borne by an ancient tower there.

Another contribution to philology[21] brings within the reach of English readers a series of papers by one whose learning was gigantic. Their author, Ludwig Preller, a short sketch of whose life has been published by his friend Dr. Stichling, was librarian at Weimar, and the greater part of his enormous erudition was contributed to different archæological journals, and to those vast monuments of industry, the Encyclopædias, in which Germany is infinitely richer than we are. The contents of this volume are very miscellaneous, touching upon numerous subjects of classical lore. One long paper discusses the various theories held in Greece upon the origin of man; another seeks to rescue from oblivion the Alexandrian author Mnaseas of Patara, known only by a few fragments; a very instructive paper is devoted to the examination of the uses and value of archæological studies; and the volume concludes with "the stray thoughts of

---

[20] "Croyances et Légendes de l'Antiquité." Par L. F. Alfred Maury. Paris: Didier. London: Nutt. 1863.

[21] "Ausgewählte Aufsätze aus dem Gebiete der classischen Alterthums wissenschaft." Von Ludwig Preller, Herausgegeben von Reinhold Köhler. Berlin: Weidmann. London: Nutt. 1864.

a librarian," in which for a moment the author lays aside his learning and becomes almost playful.

A lecture by Mr. Campbell,[22] Greek professor of St. Andrew's, sets forth in strong and eloquent words the importance and value of studies which, now more than ever, are needed to counteract the confusions and complexities of modern thought. The professor briefly sketches the growth of Greek literature in the classic period, and points out with much earnestness and ability how it is at once a chapter and an epitome of the human mind.

The learned Essay by Friedrich Diez,[23] on the Romance Languages, appears in a very good English translation, and recommends itself to all students of comparative grammar. It examines the "jurisdiction" of the six languages which are not derived from the pure Latin of classical literature, as was formerly believed, but from a popular Roman language which the later grammarians had begun to complain was creeping in and corrupting the written language. A large admixture of other elements was inevitable under the circumstances in which these dialects grew into languages; thus more than nine hundred German words are given in the "Etymologisches Wörterbuch" of Diez as existing in the Romance language, of which the greatest number are in the French, and the smallest in the Wallachian, which, on the other hand, represents the Greek element more largely than any of the sister-languages, the Italian not excepted, and contains besides, a mixture of Slavonic, Albanian, Hungarian, Turkish, and other roots, which tell the tale of conquest, foreign irruptions, and colonization to which Dacia was subjected since it was subdued by Trajan.

"The Chart of the History of Architecture," which accompanies Mr. Huggins' little book[24] is an ingenious attempt to depict the origin of the various styles, to show their mutual relations, and to record their chronological development. At the top of the map is a grey cloud whence flow one green and two blue streams; the green represents Assyria and Persia, the blue Egypt and Greece, and later, Rome. The intermingling of these various elements to produce the Byzantine and Saracenic styles, is indicated by numerous shades of yellow and orange, while the Teutonic influences upon the Romanesque are shown by a tinge of red in the blue, brightening at last into pure vermilion for complete pointed Gothic. A well-arranged synoptical table in the book further elucidates the chart, and explains the leading principle of construction in each style, and a short sketch is given of its history and growth. The author is no believer in the possibility or the necessity of a new English style; but while admitting the difficulties which beset the cultivation of any art of which the master pieces belong to countries where the chief object of all buildings was to admit

---

[22] "The Study of Greek. An Inaugural Lecture." By the Rev. Lewis Campbell, M.A. London and Edinburgh: Blackwood. 1863.

[23] "Introduction to the Grammar of the Romance Languages." By Friedrich Diez. Translated by C. B. Cayley, B.A. London: Williams and Norgate. 1863.

[24] "The Course and Current of Architecture." By Samuel Huggins, Architect. Designed as a Companion to his "Chart of the History of Architecture." London: John Weale. 1863.

air or exclude heat, he believes that the Italian style, properly studied and applied, would meet all the requirements of our climate, and satisfy our highest conceptions of architectural beauty. Mr. Huggins considers the study of architecture to be a necessary part of a liberal education, and his treatise is well adapted to popularize knowledge upon a subject in which the taste of this country is grievously wanting in some clearly recognised principles.

In ancient times sculpture and architecture were usually combined, of which the Life of Scopas[25] is an illustration. Very little is known of his life, but his works were as numerous as they were celebrated: his name is associated with the Mausoleum of Halicarnasseus and the Temple of Diana at Ephesus, of each of which renowned structures, Herr Urlichs gives minute and elaborate accounts, drawing largely on Mr. Newton's work, but not referring to that of Mr. Faulkner. His book is a dry collection of citations, and the references to authorities, which all come in the text, do not make it more readable.

A thin brochure from the Hague[26] gives minute information upon the subject of the birth and parentage of Rembrandt, and a sort of catalogue raisonné of the works of his predecessors and contemporaries, with remarks upon the conflict between the Italian influences and the native Dutch School in the sixteenth century.

Two books, with little apparent resemblance, serve to throw considerable light on the nature of the mental sustenance of the French poor. The first[27] is a collection of street songs—a species of composition in which Paris has always been peculiarly fertile ever since the days of the Fronde. The specimens here given have all appeared since 1848, during which period more than thirty thousand have been printed. The most popular subject is the glory of Napoleon III., and next to it ridicule and abuse of marriage. The demolition and reconstruction of Paris also furnish themes for the ballad-singers. The songs are not left to speak for themselves, but are interspersed with remarks and elucidations which are often curious. The other volume[28] to which we refer, is a new edition of a work which appeared seven years ago, entitled "Physiologie de l'Imprimerie," and which contains, besides many revelations of matters connected with printing and printers, a good deal of miscellaneous information on the subject of periodical literature and minor authors, and points out the notable deterioration in the small cheap papers which are rapidly driving the *roman-feuilleton* out of the field.

Of translations, we have to notice a blank verse rendering of

[25] "Skopas Leben und Wirke." Von Ludwig Urlichs. Greifswald: Koch. London: Nutt. 1863.
[26] "Rembrandt Harmens van Rijn: ses Précurseurs et ses Années d'Apprentissage." Par C. Vosmaer. La Haye: Nijhoff. London: Nutt. 1863.
[27] "La Muse Pariétaire et la Muse Foraine, ou les Chansons des Rues." Par C. N. Paris: Gay. London: Nutt. 1863.
[28] "Typographes et Gens de Lettres." Décembre Alonnier. Paris: Michel Lévy. London: D. Nutt. 1864.

Virgil[29]—a posthumous publication; and a volume, by the Chevalier de Chatelain,[30] of translations from the English, several of which are remarkably well done, especially Goldsmith's " Deserted Village," and Mrs. Hemans's " The Graves of a Household."

---

[29] " Æneid of Virgil. In English Blank Verse." By John Miller. London and Cambridge: Macmillan and Co. 1863.

[30] " Rayons et Reflets." Par le Chevalier de Chatelain. Londres: Rolandi. 1863.

THE

WESTMINSTER

AND

FOREIGN QUARTERLY

REVIEW.

APRIL 1, 1864.

ART. I.—THE BASIN OF THE UPPER NILE AND ITS INHABITANTS.

1. *Journal of the Discovery of the Source of the Nile.* By JOHN HANNING SPEKE, Captain H.M. Indian Army, &c. London, 1863.
2. *A Lecture on the Sources of the Nile, and on the Means requisite for their Final Determination. Delivered in the Theatre of the London Institution on the 20th January,* 1864 By CHARLES T. BEKE, Ph. D., F.S.A., &c. [Not Published.
3. *Address to the Geographical Society of Berlin, on the 6th June,* 1863. (Vortrag, &c.) By Dr. HEINRICH BARTH, C.B.
4. *On the Origin of the Gallas.* By Dr. BEKE. From the " Report of the British Association for the Advancement of Science," for 1847.

THE opinion that the source of the Nile was discovered by the celebrated traveller Bruce nearly a century ago, is one which we have reason to believe is still entertained by many persons, who therefore cannot but be surprised at hearing that the discovery has only recently been made by Captains Speke and Grant.

It is not at all times easy to free the public mind from a popular error. Still, with the knowledge which we at present possess of the Upper Nile, it will, we think, be no difficult task to show, not only that its source was not discovered by Bruce, but that it still remains undiscovered ; notwithstanding the claim made by Captain Speke to have worked out the great geographical problem which has hitherto defied solution.

In justice to the gallant and adventurous traveller whose work stands at the head of the present article, we hasten to explain that we have no idea of gainsaying any of the facts narrated in that work.* It is to his inferences from those facts, or his opinions formed, as we conceive, on insufficient data, that we demur; and we do not hesitate to assert that on many of these points we shall have to differ very materially.

Before, however, proceeding to the consideration of these matters, we will, with a view to render the subject generally intelligible to our readers, first take a general survey of the Nile and its head-streams, as they were known to us before Captain Speke's return from his last journey; for which purpose we shall avail ourselves chiefly of Dr. Beke's lecture, which stands likewise at the head of the present article.

The Nile is in every respect a most remarkable river. For a distance of more than 1300 geographical miles from the Mediterranean, into which it discharges its waters by several mouths, this mighty river, the largest of the African continent, and probably unsurpassed in length by any in the world, is a single stream. Fed by the copious rains of the tropics, collected by its innumerable head-streams and its immense lakes in the south, it is thus able to contend with the burning sun and the scarcely less burning sands of Nubia and Egypt, throughout this extent of country, without the aid of a single tributary,—a phenomenon presented by no other river.

Another peculiarity of the Nile scarcely less singular is, that for upwards of six hundred geographical miles above the point just indicated, or in all full 2000 miles from its mouths, the river receives no affluent whatever on its left or western side. On its eastern side, however, within the same limits, it receives three large tributaries—the Atbara or Bahr-el-Aswad (Black River), the Bahr-el-Azrek (Blue River), and the Sobat or Telfi; all having their origin in the elevated table-land of Abyssinia.

The Atbara (the *Astaboras* of Ptolemy) is called the Black River, from the quantity of black mud brought down by it during the rains, which is so great as to affect the colour of the main stream. This branch of the Nile is most important, because it contributes the largest portion of the slime which manures and fertilizes Egypt. It is not less important, perhaps, for the reason that by means of a "branch of the Astaboras," its waters with their fertilizing mud might be directed from the Nile, and poured down into the Red Sea near Sawakin; in which case "the whole of Egypt and Syria, whose subsistence depends on that river, would perish with hunger." Such are the words of a Greek writer of the fifteenth century. At the present day, we may add,

---

* There is, however, an eclipse of the moon said, in page 243, to have occurred on the 5th or 6th of January, 1862, which requires explanation.

such a calamity (which Theodore, the present King of Abyssinia, actually threatens to inflict,) would prove scarcely less fatal to *our* manufacturers, by depriving them of the timely supply of cotton, which has begun to be received from Egypt.

The Bahr-el-Azrek or Blue River (the *Astapus* of Ptolemy), known in Abyssinia as the Abai, is that branch of the Nile with which we are best acquainted, from its having been supposed to be the main stream, first by the Portuguese missionaries in Abyssinia in the beginning of the seventeenth century, and after them by our countryman Bruce. Whatever reasons there may have been at that time for imagining the Blue River to be the Nile, they have now become invalid; since the diminutive size of this stream, as compared with the immense masses of water from the regions lying hundreds, nay thousands, of miles to the south, which are carried down past it by the main stream, proves it to be only a tributary like the Atbara.

The main stream or true Nile (the *Nilus* of Ptolemy), usually called the Bahr-el-Abyad or White River, was a quarter of a century ago unknown above the junction of the Blue River at Khartum, with the exception of a small portion of its course explored by M. Linant in 1827. Between the years 1839 and 1842, however, three expeditions were fitted out by the late Mohammed Ali, Pasha of Egypt, and despatched from Khartum up the White River, with the object of exploring the Nile to its uttermost sources. The results of these expeditions, especially the second of them, were most important. In the ninth parallel of north latitude they reached and passed through the lakes or marshes, at which, eighteen centuries before them, the two centurions of the Emperor Nero had turned back; and after discovering three large streams flowing through extensive plains, where geographers had taught them to look for the river's sources in the Mountains of the Moon,—a chain supposed to traverse the continent of Africa from east to west,—they proceeded up the middle stream of the three, and succeeded in penetrating southwards to within five degrees of the equator; and though nothing positive was determined on any of these expeditions with respect to the position of the sources of the Nile or the Mountains of the Moon, it clearly resulted that both of these had been entirely misplaced in our maps.

As far as the ninth parallel of north latitude, there can be no doubt that the Bahr-el-Abyad, or White River, is the Nile. Above that parallel, where the three great arms of the river meet, it yet remains to be decided which of those three arms is the upper course of the Nile.

The middle one, which was selected by the Egyptian exploratory expeditions, is generally regarded as the main stream. But it may be questioned whether the western arm, called Bahr-el-Ghazal, is not in reality the Nile of Herodotus and all other writers of antiquity before the time of Claudius Ptolemy of Pelusium, the renowned astronomer and mathematician, who flourished in the second century of the Christian era; and also whether the Sobat, which joins the Bahr-el-Abyad from the south-east by means of three streams forming a delta of considerable size, may not be one of the two arms of which Ptolemy made the Nile to consist, the other being the Bahr-el-Abyad itself; the sources of both arms being placed by that geographer in the Mountains of the Moon.   In the existing state of our knowledge of the Upper Nile, we may, however, be content to follow the example of the officers of the Egyptian expeditions, and regard the river which they denominated the Bahr-el-Abyad, or White River, as the Nile.   This river was ascended by the second of those expeditions to the neighbourhood of Gondókoro, in 4° 54′ north latitude; and numerous Egyptians and Europeans have since then penetrated about one degree further to the south.

Before quitting this part of our subject, we may suggest to our geographers and map-makers that they would do well to discontinue the terms "Blue Nile" and "White Nile," as only tending to mislead.   So long as the White River was but partially explored, and there remained room for contending that Bruce's "Nile" was the true Nile, a compromise was not unreasonably effected between the two rivals by regarding them *ex æquo* as the White and Blue "Niles."   But now that Bruce's river is demonstrated to be no Nile at all, but merely the *Astapus* of Ptolemy (as the learned D'Anville contended a century ago), it would be absurd to continue to apply to it the name of "Nile" in any shape.

We will briefly recapitulate the conclusions come to by Dr. Beke.   The Atbara, Black River, or Takkazie, is the *Astaboras* of Ptolemy; the Blue River, or Abai (now called the Blue "Nile" for the last time), is the *Astapus* of Ptolemy; and the White River as far as 9° north latitude, is the *Nilus* of ancient history; whilst to the south of that parallel the Sobat and the upper course of the White River are apparently the eastern and western arms of the Nile of Ptolemy; the Nile of Herodotus and all historians and geographers anterior to Ptolemy, being the Bahr-el-Ghazal, of which the upper course has been but partially explored, but of which a large branch, named Djour, running parallel to the Bahr-el-Abyad, has been traced as far as about the parallel of Gondókoro.   Trusting that we have thus cleared the ground, or we might rather say the water, sufficiently to see our way, we now proceed to the consideration of the alleged discovery by Captain Speke of the source of the Bahr-el-Abyad or White

River, declared by him, without any qualification, to be *the Nile.*

The expedition of which the results are given in this traveller's Journal, was undertaken by him and Captain Grant in the year 1860, with a view to complete what had been left undone on the previous expedition of 1856, on which the former officer accompanied Captain Burton.

The main object of the first expedition had been to visit and explore an immense lake, named Nyassa, or the "Lake of Unyamwezi," said to extend from the equator to the twelfth parallel of south latitude, and so laid down in a map—known as the "Mombas Mission Map"—published by the Royal Geographical Society in the first volume of their Proceedings; for which purpose Captain Burton was directed by the Society to proceed to Kilwa (Quiloa) on the east coast of Africa, in about 11° south latitude; and after surveying the lake and completing his labours in that quarter, he was instructed "to proceed towards the range of mountains marked upon our maps as containing the probable sources of the Bahr-el-Abyad, which (it was stated) it will be your next great object to discover."

As that portion of Africa in about 8° north latitude, where this "range of mountains" is "marked upon our maps," had been traversed by the Egyptian expeditions fourteen or fifteen years previously, without a trace of any mountains having been met with; and as this imaginary range of mountains had long previously been expunged from all continental maps of Africa, as well as from such English maps as made any pretensions to tolerable accuracy; it certainly does not say much for the knowledge of the interior of Africa possessed by the Royal Geographical Society, that they should have given such antiquated instructions to Captain Burton.

But, if behind the age as regards the sources of the Nile, they were not less so with respect to the enormous lake Nyassa; for Captain Burton, on his arrival at Zanzibar, soon "heard sufficient to convince him that the Nyassa or Kilwa Lake is of unimportant dimensions, and altogether distinct from the Sea of Ujiji"—now best known as Lake Tanganyika; adding the significant remark that "though these two waters had been run into one by European geographers, no Arab of Zanzibar ever yet confounded them;" and he further stated that "this consideration mainly determined his entrance into Africa by the great western line of road leading through Unyamwezi," instead of entering at Kilwa, in accordance with the instructions of the Royal Geographical Society.

It is certainly surprising that Captain Burton should have received such instructions, when the existence of two lakes (at the least), instead of one, had been long known; and only a few months before he and his companion, Captain Speke, left England, Dr. Beke, who was then in Mauritius, published in the *Athenæum*[*] some very precise information respecting these lakes, which were not only asserted to be distinct and separate, but " the roads to them were likewise quite distinct and in different directions; that to the Nyassa Lake starting from Kilwa and proceeding to the southward of west, whilst that to the Nyamwezi Lake leads either from Buromayi or from the mouth of the river Pangani in a direction to the north of west :" the former of these roads being the one Captain Burton was directed to take, and the latter that which he eventually adopted.

The particulars of the expedition of Burton and Speke have been long before the public ; so that it is unnecessary to dwell on them here, further than to state that, at a distance of nearly six hundred geographical miles from the coast, they reached the main object of their journey, Lake Tanganyika, which they navigated and partly explored. The elevation of this lake is 1844 feet above the ocean, and its waters are fresh ; which leads to the inference that it must have an outlet either to the north or to the south. Unfortunately, the travellers did not visit either extremity, so that they were unable to decide anything positive on the subject. In the opinion of both Burton and Speke, the outlet is towards the south ; in accordance with the suggestion of Earl De Grey and Ripon, when President of the Royal Geographical Society in 1859, that it may yet be found to be connected with Lake Nyassa. The evidence collected by Dr. Beke tends, on the contrary, to show that the outlet is towards the north, in which case Tanganyika would be connected with the Bahr-el-Ghazal, and would, in fact, be the upper course of the Nile. Upon this point it would be premature to express any decided opinion ; but the following recorded evidence is certainly deserving of consideration :—

" Many years ago Mr. Macqueen received from a native of U-Nyamwezi, named Lief-bin-Said, some valuable information. . . . . After describing the lake with remarkable accuracy, he added—' It is well known by all the people there, that the river which goes through Egypt takes its source and origin from the lake.' In confirmation of this assertion of Lief-bin-Said, Capt. Speke himself, on his return from his first journey, recorded the following statement made by Sheikh Hamed, a respectable Arab merchant: ' A large river called Marungu supplies the lake at its southern extremity ; but, except that and the Malagarazi river on the eastern shore, none of any considerable size pour their waters into the lake. But on a visit to the northern end, *I saw one* which was very much larger than either of them, and *which I am certain flowed out of the lake ;* for, although I did not venture on it

. . . . . *I went so near its outlet that I could see and feel the outward drift of the water.*' And in his present 'Journal' (p. 90), the same traveller thus expresses himself:—' Ever perplexed about the Tanganyika being a still lake, I inquired of Mohinna and other old friends, what they thought about the Marungu river [at its southern extremity]: did it run into or out of the lake? And they all adhered to its running *into* the lake.' "—*Lecture*, p. 80.

Captain Burton being laid up by severe illness, the travellers were prevented from carrying out the instructions given them to proceed home northwards : but on their return from Tanganyika to the coast, Captain Speke made an excursion from Kaze, the chief trading station of U-Nyamwezi—the " Country of the Moon," as it has been fancifully rendered—to the northern lake, Nyanza, respecting which Burton had obtained intelligence, and which Speke considered to be larger than Tanganyika and to be connected with the Nile.

On his return to England in 1859, Captain Speke lost no time in making arrangements for a second expedition, being that which he undertook in 1860, accompanied by Captain Grant, and from which they both returned to England last year by descending the Nile to Egypt. Notwithstanding the time employed on this adventurous journey through the heart of Eastern-Intertropical Africa,—a journey which must always occupy a conspicuous place in the annals of African Discovery,—its main points may be soon related. Proceeding from Zanzibar to Kaze in U-Nyamwezi, the central point of the former expedition, the travellers thence turned northwards; but instead of directing their steps towards the southern extremity of Lake Nyanza, as Captain Speke had done on the former occasion, they took a course to the westward of north, passing between Nyanza and the northern portion of Tanganyika, and traversing the countries of U-Zinza and Karague ; after which they entered the kingdom of U-Ganda, and skirting the western end of Nyanza, arrived at the residence of the king, Mtesa, on the shores of the lake, which they here reached for the first time.

Here they were detained several months by the arbitrary and capricious monarch ; and when at length they obtained leave to depart, instead of being allowed (as they had desired) to navigate the lake and proceed down the river issuing from it, " the fleet admiral put a veto on this," and ruled that—

" The better plan would be to deposit our property at the Urondogani station, and walk by land up the river, if a sight of the falls at the mouth of the lake was of such material consequence to us."—p. 449.

Accordingly, the travellers left the shore of the lake and proceeded northward on their way to Urondogani ; but on reaching

Kari, about twenty miles from that place, Captain Speke states that—

"As it appeared all-important to communicate quickly with Petherick, and as Grant's leg was considered too weak for travelling fast, we took counsel together, and altered our plans. I arranged that Grant should go to Kamrasi's direct with the property, cattle, and women, taking my letters and a map for immediate despatch to Petherick at Gani, whilst I should go up the river to its source or exit from the lake, and come down again navigating as far as practicable."—p. 458.

This one-sided arrangement resembles that of the "two pretty men" of the nursery rhyme,—

"You go before with the bottle and bag,
And I'll follow after on little jack-nag."

Its effect was to deprive Captain Grant of the gratification of participating in what was manifestly the realization of the grand object of their long and perilous journey. Captain Speke reached the "Nile" alone, and he thus describes the impression which the scene made on him :—

"Here at last I stood on the brink of the Nile; most beautiful was the scene, nothing could surpass it! It was the very perfection of the kind of effect aimed at in a highly-kept park; with a magnificent stream from six hundred to seven hundred yards wide, dotted with islets and rocks, the former occupied by fishermen's huts, the latter by sterns and crocodiles basking in the sun,—flowing between fine high grassy banks, with rich trees and plantains in the background, where herds of the nsunnū and hartebeest could be seen grazing, while the hippopotami were snorting in the water, and florikan and guinea-fowl rising at our feet."—p. 459.

From this point Captain Speke, still alone, ascended the left bank of the river, till he—

"arrived at the extreme end of the journey, the furthest point ever visited *by the expedition* on the same parallel as King Mtésa's place, and just forty miles east of it. We [?] were well rewarded; for the 'stones,' as the Wa-Huma call the falls, was by far the most interesting sight I had seen in Africa. . . . . Though beautiful, the scene was not exactly what I expected; for the broad surface of the lake was shut out from view by a spur of the hill, and the falls, about twelve feet deep and four hundred to five hundred feet broad, were broken by rocks. Still it was a sight that attracted one to it for hours."—p. 466.

The author adds :—

"The expedition had now performed its functions. I saw that old father Nile without any doubt rises in the Victoria Nyanza, and, as I had foretold, that lake is the great source of the holy river which cradled the first expounder of our religious belief."—p. 467.

If there be anything to console Captain Grant for not having formed part of "the expedition" on this memorable occasion, it must be the knowledge that Captain Speke is mistaken in his idea that he saw here the source of the holy river. The poet's words,—

> "Arcanum natura caput non prodidit ulli,
> Nec licuit populis *parvum* te, Nile, videre,"

have not yet lost their force. All that Captain Speke has really done is to see the river *Kivira*, which he assumes to be the Nile, issue from Nyanza, which he incorrectly calls its source :—or hardly this, since, when he was at the Ripon Falls, he says he did not see the river's exit from the lake.

Captain Speke now descended the river Kivira again to Urondogani, and thence proceeded to Chaguzi, the residence of Kamrasi, the King of U-Nyoro ; having on the road fallen in with Captain Grant, who, in spite of his "weak leg," had walked back a considerable distance to meet him.

On his way both to and from the Ripon Falls, Captain Speke crossed two large watercourses, or "rush-drains" as he calls them, named Luajerri and Kafu, both of which are described as conveying the waters of Nyanza into the Kivira, thus making the lake to have three outlets.

This phenomenon has given rise to much discussion, based, of course, on the assumption that there is but one great lake,—the "Victoria Nyanza," as it is styled,—to which these three outlets belong. It may, however, be worthy of consideration whether it is not possible for Captain Speke to be mistaken in his assumption :—whether, in fact, his "Victoria Nyanza" may not be a repetition, on a smaller scale, of the "Lake of Unyamwezi" of the Mombas Mission map.

Let us see what evidence there is to prove that this expanse of water—of which the area is at least 25,000 square geographical miles—is a single lake. On his first journey, in 1858, Captain Speke merely visited the southern extremity of the lake in about 2° 30' south latitude. On his second journey he and Captain Grant, though they skirted the north-eastern side of the lake, did not reach it except at the Murchison Creek, in 0° 21' 19" north latitude, and 32° 44' 30" east longitude. When the travellers quitted the lake at this place, they went northwards to Kari, whence (as already related) Captain Speke proceeded alone to the Ripon Falls, in about the same latitude as the Murchison Creek, but forty-five geographical miles further to the east, though here he did not succeed in again seeing "the broad surface of the lake" (p. 466) ;—so that, in point of fact, the Nyanza was actually visited at only two points, the one at the north and the other at the south end. And it must be remarked that the coloured route-line, shown on Captain Speke's map as extending along the northern end of the lake from the Murchison Creek to the Ripon Falls, is wrongly inserted ; for such a route was. never taken by either of the travellers. Everything then, beyond what has been stated above, was derived by Captain Speke from native oral information. How easy it is at all times for such information, even if correct, to be misunderstood, is well known, and in this particular instance it is proved by the admissions of the author himself.

When at Mtesa's capital on the Murchison Creek, he heard that the king was going " with his women on a pilgrimage to the Nyanza ;" and on his wishing to be of the party, he was told this might not be, as no one was ever permitted to see the women.

" Well, said I, if I cannot go to the Nyanza with him (thinking only of the great lake, *whereas they probably meant a pond in the palace enclosures*, where Mtesa constantly frolics with his women), I wish to go to Usoga and Amara, as far as the Masai ; for I have no companions here but crows and vultures."—p. 324.

From this it is manifest that the author was already at cross-purposes with respect to Nyanza. Indeed it could not be otherwise, when he himself is under the necessity of explaining, with reference to another occasion, when the king " had started for the Nyanza and wished him to follow without delay," that—

"*Nyanza*, as I have mentioned, *merely means a piece of water*, whether a pond, river, or lake ; and *as no one knew which Nyanza he meant*, or what project was on foot, I started off in a hurry," &c.—p. 389.

Such being the indiscriminate use of the term by the natives, we cannot be surprised at the author's employing it as indefinitely. In page 279, when speaking of the Mwérango river, " a broad rush-drain of 300 yards' span," which lower down its course is called by him the Kafu, he, on not very certain or conclusive evidence, declares it to be " one of the branches of the Nile's exit from the Nyanza ;" whilst at the top of the next page he describes this river as going " to Kamrasi's palace in U-Nyoro, where it joined the Nyanza, *meaning the Nile*."

On such insufficient and inconclusive evidence, what certainty have we then as to this great " Victoria Nyanza ?" As far as we can see, it may be a single lake, or it may be two separate lakes, or indeed even a larger number. It will doubtless be urged that the author surely must have possessed the means of obtaining correct information of what he was so near to. But the same, or even more, might be said in favour of the missionaries Erhardt and Rebmann ; and yet, notwithstanding their many years' residence at Mombas, and their intercourse with the natives and knowledge of their language, they fell into the error of confounding the lakes

Nyassa, Tanganyika, and Nyanza, and blending them all three into the slug-shaped "Lake of Unyamwezi," which is shown in the margin of Captain Speke's map ; and if (as it would appear) the author was mostly "thinking only of the great lake," the existence of which was with him a foregone conclusion, his error would be far less inconceivable than that of the missionaries, who had no preconceived ideas on the subject.

After a considerable detention at Chaguzi, the travellers proceeded on the last stage of their journey, following the course of the river downwards for about fifty miles, as far as the Karuma Falls, in 2° 15′ north lat. Here the Kivira, running to the west, was quitted a second time ; and Captains Speke and Grant continued their journey northward, as far as Faloro, in 3° 10′ 33″ north lat., where they fell in with the persons who had been engaged to meet them by Consul Petherick. After leaving the river at the Karuma Falls, they appear to have quite lost all traces of it ; and as the people whom Captain Speke met "would or could not tell him where the stream had gone to," the heads of the villages were called together—

"To give me (he says) all the information I sought for, and went with me to the top of a high rock, from which we could see the hills I first viewed at Chopi, sweeping round from south by east to north, which demarked the line of the Asua river. The Nile at that moment was, I believed, not very far off ; yet, do or say what I would, everybody said it was fifteen marches off, and could not be visited under a month."—p. 585.

On this Captain Speke coolly remarks, "*I knew in my mind all these reports were false*," which they most undoubtedly must have been, if he himself is not wrong in his assumption as to the "Nile :" for the very first march from Faloro brought him to "Paira, a collection of villages *within sight of the Nile!!*" "It was truly ridiculous," he exclaims ;—

"Here had we been at Faloro so long, and yet could not make out what had become of the Nile. In appearance it was a noble stream, flowing on a flat bed from west to east, and immediately beyond it was the Jbl (hills) Kūkū, rising up to a height of 2000 feet above the river."—p. 591.

A short way below this they reached Apuddo, in 3° 34′ 33″ north lat., where they were shown the tree said to have been marked by Signor Miani two years previously as his "furthest." Here they remained several days, occupying themselves with sporting, and seemingly quite indifferent as to the Nile ; but on the sixth day, when following a herd of buffaloes, Captain Speke relates that—

"After walking up a long sloping hill for three miles towards the east, I found myself at once in view of the Nile on the one hand, and the long-heard-of Asua river on the other, backed by hills even higher than the Jbl Kūkū.   The bed of the Asua seemed very large, but, being far off, was not very distinct, nor did I care to go and see it then ; for at that moment, straight in front of me, five buffaloes, five giraffes, two eland, and sundry other antelopes, were too strong a temptation."—p. 593.

Nothing more is said of the " Nile" till several days afterwards, when they " went ahead again," and—

" In a little while we struck on the Nile, where it was running *like a fine Highland stream* between the gneiss and mica-schist hills of Kūkū, and followed it down to near where the Asua river joined it.   For a while we sat here watching the water, which was greatly discoloured, and floating down rushes.   The river was not as full as it was when we crossed it at the Karuma Falls, yet, according to Dr. Knoblecher's account, it ought to have been flooding just at this time : *if so, we had beaten the stream.*   Here we left it again as it arched round by the west, and forded the Asua river, a stiff rocky stream, deep enough to reach the breast when waded, but not very broad.   It did not appear to me as if connected with the Victoria Nyanza, as the waters were falling, and not much discoloured ; whereas, judging from the Nile's condition, it ought to have been rising.   No vessel ever could have gone up it, and it bore no comparison with the Nile itself."—p. 598.

This is all we are told about the " Nile," and certainly it does not leave a satisfactory impression on our minds, as we shall proceed to show.

But before doing so, we may remark that the difficult and disagreeable part of the journey was here at an end ; for the descent of the Nile to Egypt can only be regarded as a pleasure excursion, on account of the upper portion of the river—we speak not of the lower, which is now almost as common as the Rhine, —having of late years been visited by so many Europeans.

However positively Captain Speke may express himself as to the identity of the Kivira with the Tubiri—that is to say, the river he quitted above, with the one he fell in with below,—he evidently had misgivings on the subject ; for he says—

" Since returning to England, Dr. Murie, who was with me at Gondókoro, has also come home ; and he, judging from my account of the way in which we got ahead of the flooding of the Nile between the Karuma Falls and Gondókoro, is of opinion that the Little Lūta Nzigé must be a great backwater to the Nile, which the waters of the Nile must have been occupied in filling during my residence in Madi ; and then about the same time that I set out from Madi, the Little Lūta Nzigé having been surcharged with water, the surplus began its march northwards just about the time when we started in the same direction. For myself, I believe in this opinion, as he no sooner asked me how I could account for the phenomenon I have already mentioned of the river appearing to decrease in bulk as we descended it, than I instinctively advanced his own theory. Moreover, the same hypothesis will answer for the sluggish flooding of the Nile down to Egypt."—p. 611.

To this conclusion a ready assent cannot be given. The distance along the assumed course of the river between the Karuma Falls and Madi is about one hundred and sixty geographical miles, and the time that elapsed between their arrival at the junction of the Kafu with the Kivira—(p. 560)—on the 10th November, 1861, and their departure from Madi on the 6th February, 1862, was eighty-eight days; so that the river must have flooded at the rate of about two miles in twenty-four hours. With a fall of upwards of 1000 feet known to exist between the two extremes, the current would surely have been more rapid. A far more likely supposition is, that, instead of having beaten the river, Captain Speke *missed* it. For it is hardly conceivable that what he compares to "a fine Highland stream" should be the channel of the waters from a lake larger than the whole of Scotland; and we should rather be disposed to regard it as a separate river, having its sources in the Jebel Kūkū, apparently a considerable range, possessing an elevation of 2000 feet. That there is ample room for such a stream is unquestionable, when we take into account the author's description, in page 283, of the Moga (or river) Myanza, which, though rising in "the hills to the southward" of his route along the north-west end of the lake—"not in the lake, as the Mwérango did,"—and consequently having its entire basin limited to the narrow strip between that river and the lake itself, "was of much greater width even than the Mwérango, and so deep" that, to cross it, the author "had to take off his trousers and tuck his clothes under his arms."

When we reflect, then, on Captain Speke's own misgivings, which prompted him to consult Dr. Murie, who was not an eyewitness, and adopt his solution of the difficulty, it certainly is most strange that he did not, when on the spot, take the natural and simple course of examining the river himself. Though he may have been unable to descend the stream which he left at the Karuma Falls, there was surely nothing to prevent his ascending the one which he saw at Paira. Often when persons fear the worst, they not unnaturally prefer remaining in a state of suspense, and we cannot but suspect this to have been Captain Speke's case. He had *assumed* that the "Nile" was close at hand; he was assured by all the natives that it was not so; but he "*knew in his mind* all those reports were false;" and so, when he saw the "fine Highland stream," he decided "in his mind" that it must be and should be the mighty Nile. Further investigation could not make it more than he wished and believed it to be. Why, then, run the risk of finding himself to have been deceived ?

If we are right in our conjecture, the river which Capt. Speke left at the Karuma Falls flowing towards the west, will, in fact, the upper course be of the Djour or some other river joining the Bahr-el-Ghazal to the west of the Tubiri or White River ; this latter stream being restricted to the lower course of the Asúa. Should this prove to be the case, then the Asúa issuing from Lake Baringo, and the Kivira from Lake Nyanza (and not the Sobat and Tubiri, as Dr. Beke conjectured) would be Ptolemy's two arms of the Nile, and Captain Speke may yet be right, though not in the way that he intended, in making Lake Nyanza to be the " top-head of the Nile."

But the " top-head " of a river is not necessarily its source, as Captain Speke insists on its being. As was first pointed out by Dr. Petermann in the *Cologne Gazette*, and as is shown in the instructive comparative map in his " Mittheilungen," the Lake of Geneva is the top-head of the Rhone, that is to say, the portion furthest distant *in a direct line* from its mouth ; yet it is not, and never was imagined to be, the source of that river. What we have to look for, are the sources of the principal feeders of the lake, which will consequently be the sources of the river which the lake feeds in its turn ; and having discovered these sources, we shall then be able to decide which among them is entitled to be regarded as the principal source of the main stream. The choice may even be arbitrary ; but, in whatever manner it may be made, it is unquestionable that the source of one of the principal feeders of the lake will eventually acquire the proud title of *the* Source of the Nile,—with this proviso always, that the Nyanza is really the " top-head" of the Nile. This, however, is, for the present, merely an assumption ; for the extensive country of the Masai and other tribes situate to the east and south-east of Nyanza and larger than the whole of England and Wales, is still unexplored ; besides which it is not yet proved that Tanganyika is not connected with the Nile; and lastly, we do not at all know what there may be to the west of Tanganyika. Such are the difficulties with which the problem of the discovery of the Source of the Nile is still surrounded !

If the hydrographical system of the regions visited by Capt. Speke remains so unsettled, their orography, as assumed by him, is yet more unsatisfactory. " The continent of Africa," he asserts—

" is something like a dish turned upside down, having a high and flat central plateau, with a higher rim of hills surrounding it ; from below which, exterially, it suddenly slopes down to the flat strip of land bordering on the sea. A dish, however, is generally uniform in shape—Africa is not. For instance, we find in its centre a high group of hills surrounding the head of the Tanganyika Lake, composed chiefly of argillaceous sandstones, which I suppose to be the *Lunæ Montes* of Ptolemy, or the *Soma Giri* of the ancient Hindus. Further, instead of a rim at the northern end, the country shelves down from the equator to the Mediterranean Sea ; and on the general surface of the interior plateau there are basins full of water (lakes), from which, when rains overflow them, rivers are formed, that, cutting through the flanking rim of hills, find their way to the sea."—pp. xiv., xv.

Now, this is simply a series of assumptions so perfectly unfounded, that it would really not be worth while to show their fallacy, were it not that Capt. Speke, as the explorer of an extensive tract of the African continent, and the author of a goodly volume describing his travels, has a *primâ facie* claim to the confidence of the general reader, who can only look to persons in his position for instruction on subjects with which he himself cannot be expected to have more than a superficial acquaintance.

Captain Speke has travelled from the east coast near Zanzibar as far as Tanganyika, over rather more than one-third of the width of the continent on that parallel, and a section of the country traversed by him is given in the map accompanying his work. From that section it will be seen that from the Robeho Pass, in about 36° E. long., at an elevation of 5148 feet, the land slopes generally towards the interior as far as it has been explored, Lake Tanganyika being no more than 1844 feet above the ocean. Further, the elevation of Lake Lūta Nzigé (though not marked in his present map) was reported by Captain Speke to be estimated at 2200 feet ; and we know that between the Karuma Falls and Madi there is a fall of more than 1000 feet ; so that it is demonstrated that the fall of the land throughout the valley of the Nile (including therein Lake Tanganyika) is altogether towards the west. So far, then, as we may generalize from the facts already before us, we are warranted in entertaining the opinion that the eastern side of the continent of Africa from 30° N. lat. as far as 8° or 9° S. lat.—being about three-fifths of the whole length of the continent from north to south—consists of a mountain-range running in a general direction parallel to the sea-coast, and falling westwards to about the 30th meridian of east longitude, where the greatest depression of this portion of the continent exists ; and that this depression forms the bed of the Nile, of which river the fall from south to north is so very small, that its course appears to be almost stagnant except during

the rains, and, as Dr. Beke described it in 1846,[*] to " consist in
the dry season of a succession of lakes and swamps rather than to
be the channel of a running stream,"—or as Captain Speke himself now expresses it (p. 623) to be " more like a long pond than
a river."

What the country on the western side of this depression may
be there are no data for enabling us to do more than cautiously
speculate ; but most probably it does not possess the same
strongly-marked features as the eastern side, where we find a
massive and elevated mountain-range, with summits rising to ten,
fifteen, and even twenty thousand feet, towering above the limits
of perpetual snow.

The alleged " high group of hills surrounding the head of the
Tanganyika Lake, ... supposed to be the *Lunæ Montes* of Ptolemy or the *Soma Giri* of the ancient Hindus," is an unfortunate
affair altogether.   On the map published by Capt. Speke in
Blackwood's Magazine for 1849, shortly after his return from
the first expedition with Captain Burton, these mountains were
introduced, their elevation being marked as " 6000 to 8000 feet"
above the ocean.   Captain Burton, however, in his "Lake
Regions of Central Africa" (pp. 90, 91), unequivocally denied
the existence of any such range, which he stigmatized as " wholly
hypothetical or rather inventive ;" and in the original map of
Captain Speke himself, sent from Egypt to the Royal Geographical Society, after his return from his second journey,—which
map contains a note signed "J. H. Speke, Captain, Feb. 26,
1863," declaring that "nothing remains to *perfect* the map, but
to shift the longitudinal lines, if required,"—this moon-shaped
range of mountains is not laid down, but the name is transferred
to two parallel ranges, represented as flanking the northern portion of Tanganyika, at least two degrees to the south of the position attributed to the " Mountains of the Moon" in the author's
present map.[†]   And his own " view of Mount Mfumbiro and
drainage system of the Lunæ Montes," given in page 214 of his
work, though it may be regarded as a fair representation of what
the mountains marked in his original map of Feb. 26, 1863, may
be supposed to be, is certainly quite inapplicable to the immense
and distant range laid down in the map accompanying that work.
It is for Mr. Keith Johnston, who constructed the latter map, to
satisfy the scientific world as to the authority upon which he has
introduced these mountains into it, in lieu of those laid down in
Captain Speke's original manuscript map.

---

[*] " Journal of the Royal Geographical Society," vol. xvii. p. 80.
[†] See Dr. Beke in the *Athenæum*, Jan. 2, 1864.

According to the recent observations of Baron Carl von der Decken, the line of perpetual snow at or near the equator is at the height of about 17,000 feet above the sea ; consequently, as Dr. Barth justly remarks, " the assumption that the mountains at the northern end of Tanganyika, the loftiest of which, Mount Mfumbiro, is no more than 10,000 feet high, are the representatives of Ptolemy's Mountains of the Moon, of which the exclusive characteristic is their snowy summits, is opposed to every principle of true criticism (widerspricht jeder richtigen Kritik)."

Before discussing the subject of the true position of the Mountains of the Moon, we must first dispose of the "*Soma Giri* of the ancient Hindus." These mountains are shown in a map accompanying a paper by Lieut. (afterwards Colonel) Wilford, published in the third volume of the "Asiatic Researches ;" the authority of which paper is so implicitly relied on by Captain Speke, that, besides giving in his work a *fac-simile* of this map, he does not scruple to express himself in the following terms :—

"I came, at the same time, to the conclusion that all our previous information concerning the hydrography of these regions, as well as the Mountains of the Moon, originated with the ancient Hindus, who told it to the priests of the Nile : and that all those busy Egyptian geographers, who disseminated *their* knowledge with a view to be famous for *their* long-sightedness in solving the deep-seated mystery which enshrouded the source of their holy river, were so many hypothetical humbugs."—p. 264.

The most fitting rebuke to such unsuitable language is the fact pointed out in the *Athenæum** by Mr. Cooley, that Lieut. Wilford's paper (as he himself subsequently acknowledged in a communication to the Asiatic Society, printed in the eighth volume of the "Asiatic Researches"), was based on false information furnished to him by his Brahmin pundit, by whom the names of "Egypt" and "the Nile," among others, were fraudulently introduced to meet the inquiries of his employer, who fancied to himself an early connexion between India and Egypt, and who, not being able to read the Puranas himself, sought the assistance of a clever but unscrupulous native, who took advantage of his foible. As full particulars of this imposition are given under the head "Wilford" in works of such general reference as the "Penny Cyclopædia," and the "English Cyclopædia" (Biographical Division), it certainly is surprising, not perhaps that Capt. Speke himself, but that those about him who might have known better, should have fallen into the trap.

We come now to the consideration of the true position of the

Mountains of the Moon, on which subject we may again follow Dr. Beke, who remarks that—

"The Mountains of the Moon are an established feature of African geography. All writers, whether Arabian or European, mention them; all travellers in Central Africa hear of them; and yet so indefinite, so varied, so contradictory are the statements respecting these mountains, that no satisfactory conclusion has been arrived at as to their magnitude, extent, or even their locality."

It may, however, be confidently asserted, that all that has been written and said on the subject of the Mountains of the Moon, and of their containing the Sources of the Nile, is founded on the well-known passage in the "Geography" of Claudius Ptolemy,* on the exposition of which Dr. Beke has occupied himself during so many years. This passage is to the following effect:—

"Around the Barbarian Gulf (in which is the Island of Menuthias, or Zanzibar) dwell the man-eating Ethiopians, from the west of whom extend the Mountains of the Moon, from which the lakes of the Nile receive the snows."

It has been argued by Mr. Cooley, with no little ingenuity,† that this passage is an interpolation of as late a date as the thirteenth or fourteenth century; but this notion is now completely disproved by Dr. Beke's reference to a passage in the "Meadows of Gold and Mines of Gems" of El Masudi, the earliest of the Arabian historians, who flourished about the middle of the *tenth* century, and who, after quoting largely from Ptolemy's work, makes this explicit declaration:—

"I saw in the *Jighrafia* (جغرافيا Γεωγραφία), a drawing of the Nile, as it comes forth from the Jebel-el-Kamar (جبل ال قمر), rising from twelve sources."

This statement, besides establishing the authenticity of the corresponding passage in the body of Ptolemy's work already cited, likewise conclusively proves the Arabic name *Jebel-el-Kamar* to have been derived from the Greek; though the later Arabian geographers, in their ignorance of Greek, sought to make the name significant in their own language.

Ptolemy plainly intimates that his knowledge of the sources of the Nile was derived from the reports of persons who had visited the east coast of Africa and there obtained information respecting the interior, much in the same way as the Portuguese did in the

---

* Book iv. ch. 9.
† "Claudius Ptolemy and the Nile." London: 1856.

fifteenth and subsequent centuries, and as other Europeans have done within the last few years ; and in constructing his map from such insufficient information, the great geographer fell into the fundamental error with respect to the position and direction of the Mountains of the Moon, which Dr. Beke corrects by making those mountains to be a meridional, instead of an equatorial range —to run along the east coast of Africa to the west of the Barbarian Gulf, instead of crossing the continent from east to west.

This theory that the principal mountain system of the continent of Africa extends from north to south, on the eastern side adjacent to the Red Sea and the Indian Ocean, resembling in its rough parallelism to the coast and principal meridional direction the Andes of South America, and the western ghauts of India, is further corroborated by the similar meridional extension of the mountain system of the eastern portion of Arabia, which has been pointed out by Mr. Palgrave in a paper read before the Royal Geographical Society, on the 23rd of February last.

The difficulty of mapping general and vague information respecting countries otherwise unknown, is well understood by geographers ; and that nothing could be more natural than that Ptolemy should have regarded the Mountains of the Moon as an equatorial range, is proved by the fact that the idea of such a range, running from east to west across the continent, has always prevailed among geographers, as the ordinary maps of Africa plainly show. In that of the Irish Education Commissioners, used in all the National Schools, the Mountains of the Moon are prominently marked in the position thus indicated ; and as this direction of the principal mountain range of Africa is dogmatically maintained by the Royal Geographical Society, it is only natural that it should be adopted without question by most travellers in remote parts of Africa. Accordingly we find Captain Burton stating that " from the fifth parallel of south latitude to the equator an elevated mass of granite and sandstone formation crosses from the shores of the Indian Ocean to the centre of Tropical Africa," and probably extends even to the west side of the continent, there to " inosculate with the ridge which is . . . . . popularly known, according to Denham and Clapperton, as el Gibel Gumhr —Jebel Kamar—or Mons Lunæ ;"* and M. Du Chaillu, from the other side of the continent, expresses himself in his work on " Equatorial Africa" as follows :—

" Judging, therefore, from my own examination and from the most careful inquiries among people of the far interior, I think there is good reason to believe that an important mountain-range divides the con-

---

* " The Lake Regions of Central Africa," pp. 40-1.

tinent of Africa nearly along the line of the equator, starting from the west from the range which runs along the coast north and south, and ending in the east, probably in the country south of the mountains of Abyssinia, or perhaps terminating to the north of the lake Tanganyika of Captains Burton and Speke."—*Preface*, p. vii.

Geographers in Germany and France, and some also in England, are, however, not of the same mind. When Sir Roderick Murchison, in his anniversary address on the 25th May, 1863, communicated to the Royal Geographical Society the first report received from Captain Speke, he explicitly announced that that traveller had established the fact that "the hypothetical chain of mountains which had been called the Mountains of the Moon, and which Ptolemy spoke of as traversing the equatorial regions of Africa from east to west, have no such range as theoretically inferred by Dr. Beke;"—meaning, of course, that their having no such range had been theoretically inferred (as it had been repeatedly asserted) by that geographer; and that Captain Speke had from actual observation confirmed Dr. Beke's inference. This announcement made Dr. Barth, in his Address at Berlin, on the 6th of June following, exclaim, "I was quite right, then, in rejecting as untrue the equatorial mountain-range which has been smuggled (eingeschwärzt) back again into African geography by Du Chaillu."

Nevertheless, Captain Speke, since his arrival in England, appears to have been unable to withstand home influences. In his published work he makes no allusion whatever to his vaunted discovery of the non-existence of this equatorial range of mountains, but on the contrary, he reproduces "the high group of hills surrounding the head of the Tanganyika Lake," which he had abandoned in his manuscript map of February 26, 1863; and he makes "these highly saturated Mountains of the Moon to give birth to the Congo, as well as to the Nile, and also to the Shiré branch of the Zambeze,"—(p. 264)—in which he merely adopts the speculative views expressed by Earl De Grey in his anniversary address of 1859.

On the other hand, Sir Roderick Murchison, in a letter inserted in the *Times* of the 11th June, 1863, authoritatively declares that "All the waters occupying the position [from 4 deg. to 11 deg. south latitude], including the Lake Tanganyika of Burton and Speke, are known to flow southwards; the watershed between North and South Africa in that meridian having been happily defined."

We are, however, bound to assert, with all due respect for the accomplished President of the Royal Geographical Society, that for the statement just cited there is no real authority; for who can possibly have "defined" the physical character of a region which no European has ever yet visited?

There is far more reason for the belief that Lake Tanganyika is within the hydrographical system of the Nile, and that its deep-sunk bed is the termination of the great meridional depression of Eastern Africa. If so, it will not be till after we have passed its southernmost extremity, that we shall come to "the watershed between North and South Africa,"—the parting between the head-streams of the Nile and those of the two great rivers of Southern Africa, the Congo and the Zambezi. Where this central point of division between the waters flowing to the Mediterranean, to the Atlantic, and to the Indian Ocean—the great *hydrophylacium* of Africa, as it is styled by the recondite Jesuit, Athanasius Kircher,*—actually exists, our still insufficient knowledge of the interior of the continent does not enable us to determine. But Dr. Beke suggests that "if it were allowable to attempt to be definite in a matter which is necessarily indefinite, it might be placed in 9° south latitude and 27° east longitude."

But a subject of infinitely greater interest than the discovery of the sources of the Nile, is the history of the races of mankind inhabiting the upper basin of that river, or the determination of any question of physical geography. This subject is dilated on by Captain Speke in the course of his work, but instead of being elucidated, it is only rendered more confused and unintelligible.

A fact recognised by all ethnologists is, that, throughout the whole of the southern portion of the continent of Africa, the languages spoken among the native races belong to what is denominated the Caffre or Kafir family or class. Without entering into any critical examination of these languages, which have all a close affinity with one another, we will content ourselves with citing some remarks made by Mr. Edwin Norris, in his valuable edition of Dr. Prichard's "Natural History of Man," as sufficient to give our readers a comprehensive idea of the languages, and at the same time to render intelligible certain compound terms employed by Captain Speke throughout his work, which to the ordinary reader must be not a little perplexing. Mr. Norris says,—

"The fact is, that all the Kafir tongues have certain particles distinguishing singulars from plurals (and sometimes duals), adjectives from substantives, and one kind of substantive from another. Dr. Krapf, in the narrative of his journeys into Sambara in 1852, speaks of the Kisambara language, spoken by the Wasambara, who live in

---

* See "Journal of the Royal Geographical Society," vol. xvii. p. 82.

Usambara; and now and then mentions a Masambara, one of a Kisambara family. Different dialects have different particles : in the language which the editor would wish to call Chuana, a native of the country is a Mochuana, two are Buchuana, the people generally are the Bichuana, and the language is Sichuana ; and the latter words have become current in England, to the puzzlement of readers of African intelligence. Wherever the Kafir prefix has not become part and parcel of the English appellation, the editor omits it."

Captain Speke remarks to the like effect :—

"There is one peculiarity, however, to which I would direct the attention of the reader most particularly, which is, that *Wa* prefixed to the essential word of a country, means men or people ; *M* prefixed, means man or individual ; *U*, in the same way, means place or locality ; and *Ki* prefixed, indicates the language. Example :—Wagogo, is the people of Gogo ; Mgogo, is a Gogo man ; Ugogo, is the country of Gogo ; and Kigogo, the language of Gogo."—p. xxxi.

There cannot be a question that if, after this explanation, the author had dropped all these prefixes and continued to speak of the people and the language of the country of *Gogo*, he would have simplified the matter very much, and rendered the perusal of his work a far less laborious and disagreeable task than we fear it is at present to the generality of his readers, who cannot be expected to bear in mind these verbal minutiæ. In order to remedy the evil as far as lies in our power, and in the hope that Mr. Norris's rule will eventually be adopted, and the prefixes of the Kafir languages dropped altogether by English writers (as we believe they are by Bishop Colenso, among others), we have taken on ourselves, even in quotations from Captain Speke's work, to separate the prefixes from the roots ; for we cannot but think it more euphonious, and certainly more intelligible, to style Mtesa (for instance), king of the country of Ganda, and to speak of a native or natives of Ganda, and of the Ganda language, than to be constantly ringing the changes on Uganda, Mganda, Waganda, and Kiganda.

Captain Speke is, however, not content to follow even his own rule ; for he says (p. 16), "U-za-Ramo, which may mean the country of Ramo," though he admits that he "never found any natives who could enlighten him on the derivation of this *obviously* (?) *triple word.*" We should say it is U-Zarámo, the country of Zarámo, of which the natives are called by Captain Speke himself (p. 17) Wa-Zarámo. So, too, he speaks of "U-Sagára, or as it might be interpreted, U-sa-Gara—country of Gara" (p. 33) ; whereas we should say, U-Sagára ; and Captain Speke himself uses Wa-Sagára (p. 34).

The same objection applies yet more forcibly to the important word Unyamwezi, which Captain Speke splits up into " U-n-ya-

Mwezi — Country of Moon" (p. 84) ; whereas, according to his own rule and his own practice in speaking of the Wa-Nyamwezi and Ki-Nyamwezi, it ought clearly to be U-Nyamwezi ; a single native of which country, by an excess of inconsistency, is called by him Myamwezi (p. 85), a form which was never met with before. It ought to be M-Nyamwezi — or "Monomoezi," as the name used formerly to be written, in its application to the country not less than to a native of it or to the people generally.

Leaving these minor points, we return to the consideration of the general subject of the South African family of languages, respecting which we have to remark, that, whilst the limits within which these languages are spoken have been ascertained to extend from the mouths of the Congo in the Atlantic to those of the Zambezi in the Indian Ocean, and southwards to the Hottentots, their limits towards the north remain undetermined ; though Dr. Krapf states in his "Vocabularies of East African Languages," that on the eastern side of the continent they extend northwards to the equator, or thereabouts. In Captain Speke's original map the northern limit of these languages, between the 30th and 35th meridians of East longitude, is marked as being in about 2° N. lat. ; and though this limit is not indicated in the map accompanying his present work, we may take it to be substantially correct ; for in speaking of a native of Amara, a country marked on the map as situated at the northeastern extremity of Nyanza, the author says :—

"I took down many words of his language, and found they corresponded with the North African dialects, as spoken by the people of Kidi, Gani, and Madi [all beyond 2° north lat.]. The southerners, speaking of these, would call them Wa-Kidi, Wa-Gani, and Wa-Madi ; but among themselves the syllable *Wa* is not prefixed, as in the southern dialects, to signify people."—p. 234.

Unfortunately no vocabularies of these "North African dialects" are given ; so that we are left in the dark as to what class the languages of Kidi, Gani, and Madi belong. The numerous languages and dialects collected in Dr. Koelle's "Polyglotta Africana," show what a mass of distinct tongues— many of which appear to be radically distinct—exist in Africa ; and in the vocabularies of East African languages collected by Dr. Beke and printed in the second volume of the "Proceedings of the Philological Society," there are several which are not included in Dr. Koelle's collection nor in that of Dr. Krapf, and which, from their being spoken in the countries lying to the south of Abyssinia, in the direction of those visited by Captain Speke, are not unlikely to have some affinity to the latter's "North

African dialects." From Captain Speke's silence, we are not only unable to class these languages of Kidi, Madi, and Gani, but we cannot even decide whether they are in any way allied to that of the Wa-Huma, the most remarkable people met with by Capt. Speke, and respecting whom he furnishes some most interesting information.

In passing out of U-Nyamwezi in about 3° south lat., Captain Speke came into U-Zinza ; which country, he says—

"Is ruled by two Wa-Huma chieftains of foreign blood, descended from the Abyssinian stock, of whom we saw specimens scattered all over U-Nyamwezi, and who extended even down south as far as Fipa." —p. 124.

In order to keep pace with our author and to render his meaning intelligible, we have to explain, that precisely in the same way that he starts with the *assumption* that the river Kivira, which he saw at the Ripon Falls, is the Nile, the whole Nile, and nothing but the Nile, so he broadly *assumes* that these strangers, the Wa-Huma, are the descendants of the Abyssinians. His system of ethnology is of the simplest and at the same time most comprehensive character. In the introduction to his work, under the head " Fauna," he thus expresses himself :—

"In treating of this branch of natural history, we will first take man—the true curly-headed, flat-nosed, pouch-mouthed negro—not the Wa-Huma."—p. xvii.

He then enters into a lengthened description of the manners and customs of these " negroes," but says not a word more respecting their physical characters, except that " the hair of the negro will not grow." From this we might have been led to infer that in this peculiarity the " South Africans " were distinct from the Wa-Huma, were it not for the description given of the great King Kamrasi, the despot of the U-Nyora, who (we are told) looked—

"Enshrouded in his mbūgū dress, for all the world like a pope in state—calm and actionless. One bracelet of fine-twisted brass wire adorned his left wrist, and his hair, half an inch long, was worked up into small peppercorn-like knobs, by rubbing the hands circularly over the crown of the head. His eyes were long, face narrow, and nose prominent, after the true fashion of his breed ; and though a finely-made man, considerably above six feet high, he was not so large as Rumanika."— p. 511.

Rumanika himself and his brother Nnanaji had been previously described as " men of noble appearance and size," and as being—

" as unlike as they could be to the common order of the natives of the surrounding districts. They had fine oval faces, large eyes, and high noses, denoting the best blood of Abyssinia."—p. 203.

He further describes a M-Huma woman in the following terms :—

"She was a beautiful woman, with gazelle eyes, oval face, high thin nose, and fine lips, and would have made a good match for Saim, who had a good deal of Arab blood in him, and was, therefore, in my opinion, much of the same mixed Shem-Hamitic breed."—p. 161.

The fact appears to be, that in the construction of his extraordinary theory respecting these Wa-Huma, the author was led entirely by the nose. This theory is summed up by him in these words :—

"I propose to state my theory of the ethnology of that part of Africa inhabited by the people collectively styled Wa-Huma—otherwise Gallas or Abyssinians. My theory is founded on the traditions of the several nations, as checked by my own observation of what I saw when passing through them. It appears impossible to believe, judging from the physical appearance of the Wa-Huma, that they can be of any other race than the semi-Shem-Hamitic of Ethiopia. The traditions of the imperial government of Abyssinia go as far back as the scriptural age of King David, from whom the late reigning king of Abyssinia, Sahéla Selassié, traced his descent.

"Most people appear to regard the Abyssinians as a different race from the Gallas, but, I believe, without foundation. Both alike are Christians of the greatest antiquity. It is true that, while the aboriginal Abyssinians in Abyssinia proper are more commonly agriculturists, the Gallas are chiefly a pastoral people; but I conceive that the two may have had the same relations with each other, which I found the Wa-Huma kings and Wa-Huma herdsmen holding with the agricultural Wa-Zinza in U-Zinza, the Wa-Nyambo in Karagué, the Wa-Ganda in U-Ganda, and the Wa-Nyoro in U-Nyoro.

"In these countries the government is in the hands of foreigners, who had invaded and taken possession of them, leaving the agricultural aborigines to till the ground, whilst the junior members of the usurping clans herded cattle—just as in Abyssinia, or wherever the Abyssinians or Gallas have shown themselves. There a pastoral clan from the Asiatic side took the government of Abyssinia from its people, and have ruled over them ever since, changing, by intermarriage with the Africans, the texture of their hair and colour to a certain extent, but still maintaining a high stamp of Asiatic feature, of which a marked characteristic is a bridged instead of a bridgeless nose.

"It may be presumed that there once existed a foreign but compact government in Abyssinia, which, becoming great and powerful, sent out armies on all sides of it, especially to the south, south-east, and west, slave-hunting and devastating wherever they went, and in process of time becoming too great for one ruler to control. Junior members of the royal family then, pushing their fortunes, dismembered themselves from the parent stock, created separate governments, and, for reasons which cannot be traced, changed their names. In this manner we may suppose that the Gallas separated from the Abyssinians, and located themselves to the south of their native land."—p. 247.

Notwithstanding the author's unqualified assertion that this theory is "founded on the traditions of the several nations, as checked by his own observations of what he saw when passing through them," we do not find in his work a trace of any tradition among the Wa-Huma, that they came from Abyssinia; and as to the traditions of the Gallas, and the written history of the Abyssinians themselves, they are directly opposed to the author's theory; for which, as far as we can see, the only foundation is that the Wa-Huma are a foreign. race, whose characteristic distinction from the native races is (in the author's eyes) " a bridged instead of a bridgeless nose," in which however they resemble not only the Gallas and the Abyssinians, but also the natives of many other countries, with whom it would be simply absurd to connect them.

So engrossed, however, does Captain Speke seem to have been with his own "theory," that instead of caring to acquire information from the natives, as to what they really knew or believed respecting their extraction, his grand endeavour was to instil his own notions into their minds. Thus he began by saying to King Rumanika—

" If he would give me one or two of his children, I would have them instructed in England ; for I admired his race, and *believed them to have sprung from our old friends the Abyssinians*, whose king, Sahela Selassie, had received rich presents from our Queen. They were Christians like ourselves, and had the Wa-Huma not lost their knowledge of God, they would be so also."—p. 208.

This last assertion would apply to many other people besides the Wa-Huma ; but it does not make them to be of the same stock as the Abyssinians ; of whom, by the bye, Sahela Selassie never was, and never pretended to be, the king. His title in the treaty which he entered into with Major Harris as the representative of Her Britannic Majesty, was " King of Shoa, Efat, and the Gallas ;" and though he ruled as an independent sovereign, he never absolutely repudiated the supremacy of the " King of the Kings of Ethiopia," who since Sahela Selassie's death has hurled his son from the throne of Shoa, and appointed an ordinary provincial governor in his stead.

But Captain Speke is determined that the Wa-Huma shall be not only Abyssinians, but Christians. For he relates that—

" Rumanika, on hearing that it was our custom to celebrate the birth of our Saviour with a good feast of beef, sent us an ox. I immediately paid him a visit to offer the compliments of the season, and at the same time regretted, much to his amusement, that *he, as one of the old stock of Abyssinians, who are the oldest Christians on record, should have forgotten this rite ;* but I hoped the time would come when, by making it known that his tribe had lapsed into a state of heathenism, white teachers would be induced to set it all to rights again."— p. 238.

If it be assumed that the end justifies the means, it was no doubt quite proper to tell the king that he was a descendant of the Abyssinians, and that these latter were the oldest Christians on record, the one assertion being just as true as the other. But let us see how it operated :—

" Ever proud of his history *since I had traced his descent from Abyssinia and King David, whose hair was as straight as my own,* Rumanika dwelt on my theological disclosures with the greatest delight, and wished to know what difference existed between the Arabs and ourselves ; to which Baraka replied, as the best means of making him understand, that whilst the Arabs had only one Book we had two ; to which I added, ' Yes, that is true in a sense ; but the real merits lie in the fact that we have got the better *book,* as may be inferred from the obvious fact that we are more prosperous, and their superiors in all things.' "—p. 240.

This is all very lamentable. The only hope is that the fables which Captain Speke and his spokesman, Baraka, palmed on the ignorant Africans were forgotten as soon as they were heard.

King Kamrasi, to whom the same childish stories were told, was, however, a match for Captain Speke in ethnological knowledge, as the following conversation will prove. Being summoned to the Kafu palace, the latter says :—

" After arriving there, and going through the usual salutations, Kamrasi asked us from what stock of people we came, explaining his meaning by saying ' As we, Rumanika, Mtesa, and the rest of us (enumerating the kings) are Wa-Witu (or princes), U-Witu (or the country of princes) being to the east.' This interesting announcement made me quite forget to answer his question, and induced me to say, ' Omwita, indeed, was the ancient name for Mombas : *if you came from that place, I know all about your race for two thousand years or more.* Omwita, *you mean,* was the last country you resided in before you came here ; but originally you came from Abyssinia, the sultan of which, our great friend, is Sahela Selassie.'

" He pronounced this name laughing, and said, ' Formerly our stock was half-white and half-black, with one side of our heads covered with straight hair, and the other side frizzly : *you certainly do know everything.*' "—p. 536.

If Kamrasi believed what Speke told him about his descent, it is manifest that the latter was convinced he had derived some valuable information from the former.   For, a few days afterwards he says—

"Taking a Bible to explain *all I fancied I knew* of the origin and present condition of the Wa-Huma branch of the Ethiopians, *beginning with Adam, to show how it was that the king had heard by tradition that at one time the people of his race were half white and half black*.   Then, proceeding with the Flood, I pointed out that the Europeans remained white, retaining Japhet's blood ; whilst the Arabs are tawny, after Shem, and the Africans black, after Ham."—p. 546.

Finally, to prove the greatness of Kamrasi's " half white and half black " ancestors, the learned expounder of the Bible " read the 14th Chapter of 2nd Chronicles, in which it is written how Zerah, the Ethiopian, with a host of a thousand thousand, met the Jew Asa ;" and finished his lecture with the statement that " at a much later date, we find the Ethiopians battling with the Arabs in the Somali country, and with the Arabs and Portuguese at Omwita (Mombas) ;"—the whole of this farrago having been ground out of the casual resemblance between the two words " Omwita " and " U-Witu."

That in this exposition of Bible history, the seed fell on stony ground, may be inferred from what is related of the termination of the interview.

"Kamrasi then began counting the leaves of the Bible, an amusement that every negro that gets hold of a book indulges in ; and concluding in his mind that each page or leaf represented one year of time since the beginning of creation, continued his labour till one quarter of the way through the book, and then only shut it up on being told, if he desired to ascertain the number more closely, he had better count the words."—p. 547.

Captain Speke would make but a bad teacher if he were thus to snub his poor childish scholars for counting the leaves of their books instead of studying their contents,—a practice which we fear is not peculiar to Africans alone.   But why call Kamrasi a " nigger ?"   His " nose, prominent after the true fashion of his breed," ought to have saved him from this indignity.

At a later period, the author was told by the Governor of Madi that—

"Tradition recorded that the Wa-Huma were once half-black and half-white, with half the hair straight and other half curly ; and how was this to be accounted for, unless the country formerly belonged to white men with straight hair, but was subsequently taken by black men ?"—p. 569.

Instead of seeking into the origin of this curious tradition,

Captain Speke imposes on the poor ignorant man his own crudities ; saying—

" We relieved his apprehensions by telling him his ancestors were formerly all white, with straight hair, and lived in a country beyond the salt sea, till they crossed that sea, took possession of Abyssinia, and are now generally known by the name of Hubshies and Gallas ; but neither of these names were known to him."—p. 570.

We should think not, were it for no other reason than that those names are, neither of them, native names, but are attributed by strangers to people of very different races, possessing only a general resemblance of complexion and physiognomy. These designations are, in fact, as indefinite as the Oriental term " Frank " as applied to Europeans generally, or our own term " Indian" as applied indiscriminately to the various races of the Indian Peninsula, however widely distinct in origin and even in appearance.   We learn from Dr. Beke, whose opinions on African ethnology are certainly somewhat different from those of Captain Speke, that—

" The slaves of Kaffa and the neighbouring countries of Southern Abyssinia, when taken to the market of Baso in Godjam, are by the Galla slave-dealers called Sidamas, this being the general denomination for Christians, which many of those poor creatures are ; but, in the transit across Abyssinia, they become ' Gallas ;' and when carried from the latter country into Arabia, Egypt, or Persia, they are known as ' Hubshees,' or Abyssinians."—*The Sources of the Nile*, p. 65.

The Gallas themselves proudly declare that they are *Ilm'Orma* —" the sons of men," and their language *Afan'Orma* — " the tongue of men ;" and they no more recognise the appellation of Galla than the Abyssinians do that of " Hubshee," which is the Arabic designation of all East Africans who are not negroes.

Had Captain Speke taken pains to record, without admixture, the traditions of these Wa-Huma, to collect vocabularies of their language and particulars of their manners and customs, as contradistinguished from those of the negro nations whom they have subjugated, he might have supplied us with most desirable and valuable information respecting this really remarkable and interesting people.   But so far was he from thinking of doing this, that, even when an opportunity fell in his way, he thrust it aside to make room for his own fancies.   Among his band of servants was one Saidi, " formerly a slave captured in Walamo, on the borders of Abyssinia," whom he introduced to King Rumanika, in order—

" to show him, by his similarity to the Wa-Huma, how it was I had come to the conclusion that he was of the same race.   Saidi told him his tribe kept cattle with the same stupendous horns as those of the

Wa-Huma ; and also that, in the same manner, they all mixed blood with milk for their dinners, which, to his mind, confirmed my statement."—p. 243.

Had Captain Speke been acquainted with Dr. Beke's vocabularies, to which we have already alluded, he would have seen that the language of Saidi's country, Walamo, Wolamo, or Wolaitza, is cognate with those of the neighbouring countries of Kaffa, Waratta, and Yangaro, forming a class, to which, in the " Report on the Languages of Africa," made by Dr. Latham in 1847 to the British Association for the Advancement of Science, is attributed the distinguishing appellation of "Gonga;" such being the name of a people formerly widely spread over the countries lying to the south of Abyssinia, which countries were overrun, and their inhabitants in great part destroyed, by Galla tribes, who advanced into them from the south, before penetrating into Abyssinia Proper, about the middle of the sixteenth century, as is recorded by many travellers in Abyssinia. It would be unnecessary to repeat—were it not for the purpose of warning the general reader against adopting the notion that these people have anything in common, beyond the general outward physical condition resulting from their being the inhabitants of countries possessing the same climate and other physical characters,—that the Gonga class of languages (to which that of Walamo belongs) is as distinct from the Galla, as this latter is from the Abyssinian, whether it be the primitive native Agau or Falasha tongue, or the Ethiopic, to which latter alone an Arabian origin may reasonably be attributed.

As regards the true origin of these rude invaders of Abyssinia, there can in truth be no question. Nearly a century ago it was observed by Bruce, that—

" The Galla are a very numerous nation of shepherds, who probably lived under or beyond the Line. What the cause of their emigration was we do not pretend to say with certainty ; but *they have, for many years, been in an uniform progress northward.* They were at first all infantry, and said that the country they came from would not permit horses to breed in it, as is the case in 18° north of the Line round Sennaar. Upon coming northward, and conquering the Abyssinian provinces, and the small Mahometan districts bordering on them, they have acquired a breed of horses, which they have multiplied so industriously that they are become a nation of cavalry, and now hold their infantry in very little esteem."—*Travels*, vol. ii. p. 216.

From these historical facts, which are beyond measure more authoritative than any mere tradition delivered down orally from one generation to another, it is undeniable that the Galla invaders of Abyssinia came from regions far to the south of that kingdom. The position of their original country is lost to them ; but some very curious traditions respecting it have been collected by Dr. Beke, in the paper "On the Origin of the Gallas" which stands at the head of the present article ; one of which has been specially referred to by Dr. Barth, in his "Address to the Geographical Society of Berlin," and is deserving of being reproduced here. It is as follows :—

" According to several individuals with whom I spoke on the subject, their forefathers came from *Tulu* (Tullo) *Wolál*, which, as *Tulu* signifies 'mountain,' I at first understood to mean some particular mountain called ' Mount Wolál.' "—p. 6.

Dr. Beke then gives the statements of various persons respecting the position of this mountain, all disagreeing, more or less, with one another; and remarks—

" When, however, the signification of the term *Wolál* comes to be investigated, it will be seen that no dependence can be placed on these attempts to fix the position of the locality which this expression is intended to designate. For the verb *wálala* or *wólala* in the Galla language signifies ' to lose one's way,' ' to forget,' ' to know no more.' So that *Tulu Wolál*, instead of being a proper name, resolves itself into ' Mount *Unknown*,' that is to say, some mountain or mountainous country whose situation is lost, forgotten, and no longer known.

" From the name thus given by the Gallas to the country of their ancestors, and from the various directions in which it is said to lie, it may be concluded that they are in fact ignorant of its real position. Still, this very name *Tulu Wolál*, or the unknown *mountains*, may seemingly be regarded as a proof that the primitive Gallas were the inhabitants, not of the low plain country bordering on the Indian Ocean, where they are known to have been settled for upwards of two centuries, but rather of some high and *mountainous* one. And this conclusion is corroborated by the fact, that, as a people, their complexion is fairer than that even of the Abyssinians, whose colour as a *red* race results from their country generally being of much greater elevation than that of the negroes inhabiting the valleys of the Nile and its tributaries towards the west, or than that of the dark but not negro nomadic tribes skirting Abyssinia to the east."—p. 7.

Dr. Beke further records the following curious particulars :—

" On the table-land of Eastern Africa and bordering on the country of Mono-Moezi [U-Nyamwezi] to the north, dwells the nation of the Meremongáo, whose country, according to information obtained by Mr. Cooley, is about two months' journey inland from Mombas, behind the Wanyika. The Meremongáo are known to the merchants on the coast as the great smiths and cutlers of Eastern Africa, and as the principal consumers of brass wire, which they wear twisted tightly round their arms. These customs of the Meremongáo, coupled with the position of their country, lead to the opinion that they are Gallas.

For, in Southern Abyssinia it is the Gallas who are noted as the most skilful cutlers and workers in iron ; and in Shoa, the inhabitants of which kingdom are essentially of Galla extraction, the custom prevails of wearing a number of brass rings, sometimes covering almost the entire fore-arm from the wrist to the elbow, which rings or bracelets are not removable at pleasure, but like the ' brass wire ' of the Meremongáo, are tightly and permanently fixed on the arm by a smith."—p. 7.

And he sums up the whole in the following words :—

"So far, then, as our information will allow us to offer an opinion, the country of the Meremongáo, as a mountainous region, situate far to the south of Abyssinia, and lying in the vicinity of a large river (the Nile), presents strong claims to be considered as the place whence the Galla tribes of Eastern Africa issued eastwards to the shores of the Indian Ocean, and northwards into the countries intervening between them and Abyssinia, and subsequently into Abyssinia itself. Nevertheless, in the present insufficient state of our knowledge on the subject, it would be wrong to regard this as anything more than a first approximation."—*Ibid.*

The publication of Captain Speke's "Journal" has imparted to the foregoing interesting particulars a significance which they could not be imagined to possess at the time when they were recorded; and it now enables us to add that these "Meremongáo" likewise issued from their mountains westwards into the regions beyond Lake Nyanza, where they are known as Wa-Huma.

Dr. Barth, in adopting the general conclusions of the author we have just cited, expresses his decided opinion that the Galla, Orma, or Wa-Huma tribes met with by Captain Speke did not emigrate from the north or north-east, but from the east or south-east, and in fact from the mountainous country surrounding the snowy summits of Kenia and Kilimandjaro, where at the present day we find the warlike tribes of the Wa-Kuaki and Masai. For, he remarks—

"That these tribes are the aborigines of the regions they inhabit, and not an exotic race, is incontrovertibly proved by the fact of their religious veneration of one at least of those two mountains, namely, Kenia, which appears to be the more considerable of the two, and to which even at the present day they undertake pilgrimages and bring offerings."—p. 445.

With the knowledge of these facts, we may now also attach a meaning to some particulars of information picked up and recorded by Captain Speke, quite unconsciously of their real value.

While in Karague, he had some conversation with one of King Kamrasi's servants, a man of Amara, which he cites as throwing "some light upon certain statements made by Mr. Leon"—meaning Father Leon des Avranches—" of the people of Amara being Christians." This conversation we value, not for the futile attempt made to prove a set of wild pagans to be Christians, but for the fact asserted by this man that—

" Associated with the countries Masau or Masai and U-Sambūrū, which he knew, *there was a large mountain, the exact position of which he could not describe.*"—(p. 234.)

Which mountain is evidently Kenia, to the natives of Amara as much a *Tulu Wolál* or "Unknown Mountain," as it is to the Gallas of Guderu. In addition to this we have the tradition repeated by King Kamrasi, that U-Witu, "the country of princes," lay *to the east;* as likewise the assertion of the Governor of Madi, that—

" *On the east,* beyond Kidi, he only knew of one clan of Wa-Huma, a people who subsist entirely on meat and milk."—p. 570.

This peculiarity of living entirely on meat and milk is especially noticed by Father Jerome Lobo, as being that of the Gallas who, in the sixteenth century, invaded Abyssinia from the south.

" Ils ne sement ni ne cultivent les terres qu'ils occupent ; *ils vivent de chair et de lait ;* ils n'ont aucune demeure fixe, et campent comme font les Arabes."—*Voyage d'Abissinie,* p. 66.

The feeding on milk appears to be carried to an extraordinary extent among the Wa-Huma ; and Captain Speke gives us some amusing examples of the custom and its consequences.

When in Karague, having heard that " the wives of the kings and princes were fattened to such an extent that they could not stand upright," he paid a visit to the king's eldest brother, " with the hope of being able to see for himself the truth of the story ;" and he relates that—

" On entering the hut I found the old man and his chief wife sitting side by side on a bench of earth strewed over with grass, and partitioned like stalls for sleeping apartments, whilst in front of them were placed numerous wooden pots of milk. . . . I was struck with no small surprise at the way he received me, as well as with the extraordinary dimensions, yet pleasing beauty, of the immoderately fat fair one his wife. She could not rise ; and so large were her arms that, between the joints, the flesh hung down like large loose-stuffed puddings."—p. 209.

On his inquiring what they did with so many milk-pots, the prince—

" pointing to his wife, said, 'This is all the product of those pots : from early youth upwards we keep those pots to their mouths, as it is the fashion at court to have very fat wives.' "—p. 210.

The effects of this " high feeding" are thus more minutely— though not very delicately—recorded :—

" After a long and amusing conversation with Rumanika in the morning, I called on one of his sisters-in-law, married to an elder brother who was born before Dagara ascended the throne. She was another of those wonders of obesity, unable to stand excepting on all fours. I was desirous to obtain a good view of her, and actually to measure her, and induced her to give me facilities for doing so, by offering in return to show her a bit of my naked legs and arms. The bait took as I wished it, and after getting her to sidle and wriggle into the middle of the hut, I did as I promised, and then took her dimensions, as noted below.* All of these are exact except the height, and I believe I could have obtained this more accurately if I could have had her laid on the floor. Not knowing what difficulties I should have to contend with in such a piece of engineering, I tried to get her height by raising her up. This, after infinite exertions on the part of us both, was accomplished, when she sank down again, fainting, for her blood had rushed into her head. Meanwhile, the daughter, a lass of sixteen, sat stark naked before us, sucking at a milk-pot, on which the father kept her at work by holding a rod in his hand, for as fattening is the first duty of fashionable female life, it must be duly enforced, by the rod if necessary. I got up a bit of flirtation with missy, and induced her to rise and shake hands with me. Her features were lovely, but her body was as round as a ball."—p. 231.

We are not aware that this custom of increasing the *embonpoint* of the ladies prevails among the Gallas of Abyssinia ; but they are still extensive herdsmen, and the Galla *sanga,* or cattle with enormous horns, which are figured by Mr. Salt, have been introduced by them into that country from the south.

And this fact leads us to remark, that, if it were necessary to adduce further evidence to prove the total groundlessness of Captain Speke's notion that the Wa-Huma of U-Zinza, Karague, U-Ganda, and other countries visited by him, are descended from the native Abyssinians, or even from the Galla invaders of Abyssinia, we should find it in the fact that the latter people, at the time of their advance from the south, were essentially a pastoral nation possessing large herds, on whose milk and flesh they subsisted, but not having among them any horses ; whereas, after their invasion of Abyssinia, a country which from time immemorial has possessed horses, procured originally from Arabia on the opposite coast of the Red Sea, the Gallas became a nation of horsemen. When the same pastoral people, under the name of Wa-Huma, advanced from the east into the countries situate to the west and north of Nyanza, they in like manner had no horses ; and those animals are to this day as unknown in these latter regions as they are in the native country of the Wa-Huma. But had it been, as Captain Speke assumes, the Gallas *of Abyssinia* who invaded these southern negro countries, they

---

* Round arm, 1 ft. 11 in. ; chest, 4 ft. 4 in.; thigh, 2 ft. 7 in. ; calf, 1 ft. 8 in.; height, 5 ft. 8 in.

would have come as horsemen, and horses would consequently be found in these countries;—which is not the case.

We have an impression of having read somewhere that the Gallas, when they first entered into Abyssinia, rode on cows; but we are unable, just now, to refer to any authority. We find, however, in Bruce's description of the visit paid by Guangoul, the savage chief of the Gallas of Angot, to the King of Abyssinia, the following statement :—

" In his country it seems, when he appears in state, *the beast he rides upon is a cow*. He was then in full dress and ceremony, and mounted upon one, not of the largest sort, but which had monstrous horns. He had no saddle on his cow."—*Travels*, iv. p. 99.

Be this as it may, there is manifestly a great resemblance between the habits of the Wa-Huma princes and those of Sahela Selassie, King of Shoa, as recorded in the works of travellers who have visited the latter country. The treatment which Captain Speke received from the chief Kasoro, when he went to visit the Ripon Falls (p. 469), is just like that to which Europeans were subjected in Shoa, where they were under constant surveillance, and not allowed to move about without the king's permission. On his expressing the wish to go where he might obtain a magnificent view of the lake, he was told " there were orders given only to see the stones." He next asked for boats, to shoot hippopotami, " but boating had never been ordered." Then bring fish. " No, that had not been ordered." The statement of his complaints made by King Kamrasi to Captain Speke (p. 251), is, in like manner, almost similar to those of King Sahela Selassie to Major Harris ; whilst in the practice of " conducting all business himself, awarding punishments and seeing them carried out," the resemblance between the two princes is most striking.

In their disregard of human life, the Wa-Huma appear, however, to go far beyond the Gallas of the north, who, though a warlike and even ferocious race, are, like the native Abyssinians generally, not coolly bloodthirsty (the reigning king, Theodore, who is a native of Kwara, being a singular exception); and we cannot but think that the brutal acts recorded by Captain Speke arise from the fact, that the pure blood of the Wa-Huma race has been sadly mixed with that of the negroes whom they have conquered. We will cite a few instances of their barbarism :—

" No one dare stand before the king whilst he is either standing still or sitting, but must approach him with downcast eyes and bended knees, and kneel or sit when arrived. To touch the king's throne or clothes, even by accident, or to look upon his women, is certain death."—p. 256.

" An officer observed to salute informally is ordered for execution, when everybody near him rises in an instant, the drums beat, drowning

A A 2

his cries, and the victim of carelessness is dragged off, bound by cords, by a dozen men at once. Another man, perhaps, exposes an inch of naked leg whilst squatting, or has his mbûgû tied contrary to regulations, and is condemned to the same fate."—p. 258.

These "court customs," which are equalled only by those of Dahomey, are described by the author in the coolest manner imaginable. Thus he says—

"Nearly every day since I changed my residence, incredible as it may appear to be, I have seen one, two, or three of the wretched palace women led away to execution, tied by the hand, and dragged along by one of the body guard, crying out, as she went to premature death, ' Hai Minangé !' (O my Lord !) ' Kbakka !' (My King !) ' Hai N'yawo !' (My mother !) at the top of her voice, in the utmost despair and lamentation ; and yet there was not a soul who dared lift a hand to save any of them, though many might be heard privately commenting on their beauty."—p. 359.

And at a later date he relates that—

—" During this one day we heard the sad voices of no less than four women dragged from the palace to the slaughter-house."—p. 365.

These wretched women appear to have been made away with in the most heartless manner. Here is another instance :—

"On the way home, one of the king's favourite women overtook us, walking, with her hands clasped at the back of her head, to execution, crying, ' N'yawo !' in the most pitiful manner. A man was preceding her, but did not touch her ; for she loved to obey the orders of her king voluntarily, and, in consequence of previous attachment, was permitted, as a mark of distinction, to walk free. Wondrous world ! It was not ten minutes since we parted from the king, yet he had found time to transact this bloody piece of business."—p. 450.

On one occasion, after Captain Speke had been shooting some cows for Mtesa's amusement, he relates that—

"'The king now loaded one of the carbines I had given him with my own hands, and gave it full-cock to a page, told him to go out and shoot a man in the outer court ; which was no sooner accomplished than the little urchin returned to announce his success, with a look of glee such as one would see in the face of a boy who had robbed a bird's nest, caught a trout, or done any other boyish trick. The king said to him, ' And did you do it well ?' ' Oh yes, capitally.' He spoke the truth, no doubt, for he dared not have trifled with the king ; but the affair created hardly any interest. I never heard, and there appeared no curiosity to know, what individual human being the urchin had deprived of life."—p. 298.

Another time he says :—

"I found the king dressed in red, with his Wakungu in front, and women behind, travelling along in the confused manner of a pack of hounds, occasionally firing his rifle that I might know his whereabouts.

He had just, it seems, mingled a little business with pleasure; for noticing, as he passed, a woman tied by the hands to be punished for some offence, the nature of which I did not learn, he took the executioner's duty on himself, fired at her, and killed her outright."— p. 389.

On one occasion the author boldly interfered, and by so doing, saved the life of one of Mtesa's wretched wives. One day, it appears, they went on an excursion on the lake, when, after landing and picnicking,—

"The whole party took a walk, winding through the trees, and picking fruit, enjoying themselves amazingly, till, by some unlucky chance, one of the royal wives, a most charming creature, and truly one of the best of the lot, plucked a fruit and offered it to the king, thinking, doubtless, to please him greatly; but he, like a madman, flew into a towering passion, said it was the first time a woman ever had the impudence to offer him anything, and ordered the pages to seize, bind, and lead her off to execution.

"These words were no sooner uttered by the king than the whole bevy of pages slipped their cord turbans from their heads, and rushed like a pack of cupid beagles upon the fairy queen, who, indignant at the little urchins daring to touch her majesty, remonstrated with the king, and tried to beat them off like flies, but was soon captured, overcome, and dragged away, crying, in the names of the Kamraviona and Mzungu (myself), for help and protection; whilst Lūbūga, the pet sister, and all the other women, clasped the king by his legs, and, kneeling, implored forgiveness for their sister. The more they craved for mercy, the more brutal he became, till at last he took a heavy stick, and began to belabour the poor victim on the head.

"Hitherto I had been extremely careful not to interfere with any of the king's acts of arbitrary cruelty, knowing that such interference, at an early stage, would produce more harm than good. This last act of barbarism, however, was too much for my English blood to stand; and as I heard my name, Mzungu, imploringly pronounced, I rushed at the king, and, staying his uplifted arm, demanded from him the woman's life. Of course I ran imminent risk of losing my own in thus thwarting the capricious tyrant; but his caprice proved the friend of both. The novelty of interference even made him smile, and the woman was instantly released."—p. 395.

That Captain Speke did not more frequently interfere arose not, most unquestionably, from any want of courage; for on very many occasions his conduct was such as to have endangered his personal safety. Indeed we really do not understand how any educated European could go into a foreign country and behave in the reckless way he did, according to his own showing; and it is highly to the credit of his hosts that he should have acted as he did with impunity.

King Kamrasi, like Sahela Selassie and all other African potentates, was most eager for presents; and on one occasion, having paid Captain Speke a visit, and not having received a parting gift, as he had looked for, and as would seem to be the custom of the country, he said, " I never visited any big man's house without taking home some trifle to show my wife and children." To which Speke insultingly replied—

"'Indeed, great King! then you did not come to visit us, but to beg, eh? You shall have nothing, positively nothing; for we will not have it said the king did not come to see us, but to beg.' Kamrasi's face changed colour; he angrily said, 'Irokh togend' (Let us rise and go), and forthwith walked straight out of the hut."—p. 522.

Not satisfied with thus insulting the king to his face, the author exultingly relates how he followed up this most unbecoming conduct :—

" To save us from this kind of incessant annoyance, I now thought it would be our best policy to mount the high horse, and bully him. Accordingly, we tied up a bag of the commonest mixed beads, added the king's chronometer, and sent them to Kamrasi, with a violent message that we were thoroughly disgusted with all that had happened; the beads were for the poor beggar who came to our house yesterday, not to see us, but to beg; and as we did not desire the acquaintance of beggars, we had made up our minds never to call again, nor receive any more bread or wine from the king.

" This appeared to be a hit. Kamrasi, evidently taken aback, said, if he thought he should have offended us by begging, he would not have begged. He was not a poor man, for he had many cows, but he was a beggar, of course, when beads were in the question; and, having unwittingly offended, as he desired our friendship, he trusted his offence would be forgiven."—p. 524.

And on another occasion when Speke "sent a threatening message, to see what effect that would have,"—

" Kamrasi, in answer, begged I would not be afraid; there was no occasion for alarm; Bombay would be here shortly. *I had promised to wait patiently for his return*, and as soon as he did return, I would be sent off without one day's delay, *for I was not his slave, that he should use violence upon me.*"—p. 546.

There can be no doubt that Kamrasi showed himself to be the better gentleman of the two.

This overbearing manner of treating the "natives" of East Africa would seem to have been copied from that of Major Harris on his mission to the Court of Shoa, where he was often induced to " mount the high horse and bully" our "old friend Sahela Selassie." The latter, like Kamrasi, did not forget the laws of hospitality so far as to subject his guest to personal injury or indignity, but he adopted the most effectual means of preventing the recurrence of such treatment ; for as soon as he had got rid of his troublesome visitor, who took with him a " Treaty of Amity and Commerce" which stipulated for the free ingress, egress, and regress of British subjects, he shut the door upon them for the future, and forbad the Dankali merchants to allow any more Englishmen to accompany their caravans to Shoa. We should not be in the least surprised if future travellers in the countries of these Wa-Huma sovereigns were made to suffer for Captain Speke's ill-judged, and (as far as we can see) uncalled-for, conduct towards them. The principle of *Civis Romanus sum* may be carried out too far.

We do not believe, however, that Captain Speke's behaviour to those African potentates arose so much from a desire to maintain the superiority of his nation, as from personal vanity. In fact, the besetting sin of his entire narrative is vanity and self-glorification. "I" and "me" are oftener repeated perhaps than any other words; and any one who does not please the author or agree with him in opinion is set down as a "humbug." The "hypothetical humbug," Claudius Ptolemy, has already been adverted to. We may now notice (among many others) Maula, the queen's favourite, who is described as "a clever humbug and exceeding rogue" (p. 333); King Kamrasi "humbugged" them (p. 497); the Kidi visitors gave the king "a lot of humbug and affectation" (p. 504); and Mahamed, Debono's vakil, is called a "humbugging scoundrel" (p. 583), just after Captain Speke had been complimenting—we would not for the world say "humbugging"—him, on the efficiency of his "ragamuffin" corps.

Some of the instances of this failing are most characteristic. On the author's arrival at the Court of U-Ganda, "on being shown into a lot of dirty huts, which they said were built expressly for all the king's vistiors," he was highly indignant, saying—

"At first I stuck out on my claims as a foreign prince, whose royal blood could not stand such an indignity. The palace was my sphere, and unless I could get a hut there, I would return without seeing the king."—p. 284.

He then proceeds to describe how Nyamgundu, an old friend of Usui, in a terrible fright at his blustering, fell at his feet and implored him not to be hasty; and how at length he "gave way to this good man's appeal." The manner in which this good man had managed to obtain such influence is thus naïvely explained :—

"Nyamgundu delighted me much : *treating me as a king*, he always fell down on his knees to address me, and made all his 'children' look after my comfort in camp."—p. 272.

It is scarcely necessary to add that Nyamgundu is nowhere called a "humbug."

At their first audience of the King of U-Nyoro, that monarch—
"asked Bombay, 'Who governs England?' 'A woman.' 'Has she any children?' 'Yes,' said Bombay, with ready impudence, '*these are two of them* (pointing to Grant and myself). That settled, Kamrasi wished to know if we had any speckled cows, or any cows of peculiar colour, and would we like to change four large cows for four small ones, as he coveted some of ours. This was a staggerer. *We had totally failed, then, in conveying to this stupid king the impression that we were not mere traders,* ready to bargain with him."—p. 513.

So King Kamrasi is called stupid for not believing the assertion made by Bombay " with ready impudence," and " settled"—
—that is to say, adopted—by Captain Speke, that he and Captain Grant were two of Queen Victoria's own children.

Such being the author's assumed character, it certainly was quite out of keeping—to say nothing else of it—that when the " foreign prince" met Mr. Baker at Gondókoro, and from him first heard of the death of H.R.H. the Prince Consort, the intelligence should have made him " reflect,"—not on the loss of the bereaved Queen or of the British nation,—not even on the instability of human life,—but, as he complacently records it, the news of the Prince's decease—

" made me reflect on the inspiring words he made use of, *in compliment to myself,* when I was introduced to him by Sir Roderick Murchison, a short while before leaving England."—p. 602.

Self being, then, the engrossing object of Captain Speke's thoughts, we cannot be astonished at his want of consideration for every one but himself. We have already commented on the fact that Captain Grant, though sharing in all the dangers and privations of the journey, was not allowed to accompany Captain Speke on his visit to the " Nile" and the Ripon Falls; so that his first sight of the grand object of the expedition was obtained at Chaguzi, the residence of King Kamrasi, more than a hundred miles away from Lake Nyanza. Indeed the manner in which Grant is placed altogether in the background, is the subject of general animadversion. Captain Speke himself was not treated in this ungenerous manner by Captain Burton on the first expedition, as he takes care to boast in page 2 of his work, when turning the former's words against himself. But Grant will have little to regret and Burton will be more than avenged, should Tanganyika, and not Nyanza, eventually prove to be the head of the Nile.

The author's language respecting Consul Petherick is likewise anything but proper. That he was disappointed in not being met by him is quite natural; but we have yet to learn from Mr. Petherick the reason for this apparent breach of his engagement.

And it has at the same time to be seen whether Captain Speke, on his side, duly performed his part of the agreement.   If Petherick was not at his post when Speke came down the Tubiri, had he been there at the time appointed ?   And should it happen to turn out that the Kivira is not the upper course of the Tubiri, but of a more westerly arm of the Nile, then the fact so bitterly complained of that he was " actually trading at Nyambara, seventy miles due west" of Gondókoro, might, perhaps, after all, be only a proof that Petherick was in the right and Speke in the wrong ; for had the latter followed down the course of the river, instead of quitting it at the Karuma Falls, and cutting across the desert between the Kivira and the Asua, he would probably have fallen in with Petherick instead of Baker.   Whatever may be the facts of the case, an explanation is unquestionably due from Mr. Petherick, not so much to Captain Speke as to the Royal Geographical Society and the friends, from whom the latter states a subscription of 1000*l.* was raised, and to whom his work is dedicated.

But let the result be what it may, it is indisputable that the steps taken by Mr. Petherick (whatever may have been his shortcomings) were of essential service to Captain Speke. Throughout his work we have evidence of the moral support afforded to him at the courts of the several native princes by the knowledge that a party of Europeans were expected from the north to meet him.   Nothing can be more certain than this. As early as the beginning of 1862, when he was in Karague, he says :—

" The new year was ushered in by the most exciting intelligence, which drove us half wild with delight ; for we fully believed Mr. Petherick was indeed on his road up the Nile, endeavouring to meet us. . . . Rumanika enjoyed this news as much as myself, especially when I told him of Petherick's promise to meet us, just as these men said he was trying to do ; and more especially so, when I told him that if he would assist me in trying to communicate with Petherick, the latter would either come here himself, or send one of his men, conveying a suitable present, whilst I was away in U-Ganda ; and then in the end we would all go off to Kamrasi's together."—p. 242.

Indeed Kamrasi appears to have been in actual communication with Petherick ; for Captain Speke relates that when, to avoid the king's importunities, he advised his using ivory as money, and purchasing what he wanted at Gani, the suggestion brought out—

" the interesting fact, the truth of which we had never reached before, that *when Petherick's servant brought him one necklace of beads, and asked after us,* he gave in return fourteen ivories, thirteen women, and seven mbúgú cloths.   One of his men accompanied the visitors back to the boats, and *saw Petherick,* who took the ivory and rejected the women."—p. 537.

There can likewise be no doubt that the return of Bombay from his visit to Petherick's outpost (see page 549) was not without its effect in accelerating Speke's departure from King Kamrasi's Court.

Into the question between the author and Dr. Beke we need not enter further than to express our regret, that the former should have made so great a mistake as to arrogate to himself a merit, which a mere reference to recorded facts and dates could not but prove not to belong to him.

Passing now to the general consideration of Captain Speke's work, we should have been glad, differing from him as we do on so many points, had it been in our power to say that he had written an entertaining and instructive, even if not a learned work; but this satisfaction is denied to us.

As regards the extent of the unknown regions traversed for the first time, the journey is inferior to those of Denham and Clapperton, of Barth, and of Livingstone, and even to the former expedition in which Speke accompanied Burton;—for from Kaze, the point of departure from the line of the first journey, to where Speke and Grant met Petherick's party, is a distance of little more than eight degrees of latitude, or about 500 geographical miles. Still, had the new ground been even less, the special object of the expedition and the peculiar character of the countries visited and of their inhabitants, afforded the richest materials for a work of the highest order. The author tells us in page 2 of his Journal that, "in addition to the journey to the source of the river, he also proposed spending three years in the country, looking up tributaries, inspecting watersheds, navigating the lake, and making collections in all branches of natural history." These splendid promises have not been fulfilled beyond the spending of three years in the interior of Africa, and by Captain Grant's making a tolerably large and interesting botanical collection, and also contributing the far larger portion of the illustrations with which the pages of the work are profusely studded, and without which it would hardly have been more attractive than a "Blue Book" to the general reader. We lament this the more, because an admirable work might have been written, if not by the author himself, at all events by some good book-maker for him, out of the almost endless materials of his really important and interesting journey.

Art. II.—Strikes and Industrial Co-operation.

1. *The Co-operator: 'a Record of Co-operative Progress.* By Working Men. Edited by Henry Pitman. Manchester: 1860-1863.
2. *Self-Help by the People—History of Co-operation in Rochdale.* By G. J. Holyoake. London: 1858.
3. *Companion to the Almanac; or, Year Book of General Information for* 1862. London.
4. *Manual of Political Economy.* By Henry Fawcett, M.A. London: 1863.

AMONG the dangers which the political economist, while watching, as in duty bound, the signs of the times, and sweeping the social horizon with the perspective glass of his philosophy, may descry, or fancy he descries, looming in the distance, not the least serious is the apparent tendency of advancing civilization to establish among us a serfdom less coarse and brutalizing, but scarcely less stringent, than the feudal bondage which the same civilization has destroyed. The saving obtainable, when business is conducted on an extensive scale, from the command of costly machinery, from the division of labour, and the comparative cheapness of superintendence, gives to great capitalists an advantage over men of inferior pecuniary means, against which the latter find it difficult to contend, and before which they are gradually retiring. In husbandry, in handicrafts, in trade, large undertakings are continually taking the place of smaller ones. Hedgerows and homesteads are thrown down to allow of the formation of fields of fifty, and farms of five hundred acres each; spinning-wheels and hand-looms have been driven out of sight by spinning-jennies and power-looms; and worsted-weavers and lace-makers, instead of being scattered, as they used to be, over the length and breadth of the Midland Counties, are now for the most part congregated in factories in the towns of Yorkshire, Lancashire, and Nottinghamshire. Even retail trade has now begun to assume wholesale proportions: drapers, mercers, ironmongers, and grocers, occupy shops stretching along half a street, and many of the gentlemen and all the gents of London are fitted out by some dozen or so of colossal tailoring establishments, presided over by Hebrew or other unchristian taskmasters. It would be unfair to deny that in all this there is good as well as evil. Commodities of many kinds are certainly supplied much more cheaply than they could be if the various businesses concerned with their production and distribution were less concentrated ; and except in the districts which are suffering from the temporary scarcity of cotton, it is probable that the wages proper of hired labourers were never higher in the United Kingdom than at present. In truth, what is to be apprehended is not so much a deterioration of the condition of the individual as the overgrowth of the class. The danger is, that the time may come when, in the unequal competition between large and small capitals, the latter may entirely disappear, and when the industrial community may, in consequence, become separated into two strongly marked divisions, the one consisting of some hundreds of millionaire employers, the other of many millions of employés of various grades from the manager or secretary, with his three or four thousand a-year, to the operative with his twenty or thirty shillings, and the ploughman, with his ten or twelve shillings a-week, but all alike mainly dependent for a livelihood on their periodical earnings, and all alike dependent, too, on the will of an employer for permission to earn a livelihood.

The prospect is not a pleasing one, but the clouds that darken it are not without their silver lining. The remedial power of nature, which seldom allows the germs of evil to attain complete development, has, in this instance also, placed the antidote close beside the bane. Those very multitudinous assemblages of workpeople, by which capital most remarkably displays, and most efficaciously exercises its authority over labour, afford also to labour a means of emancipating itself from the thraldom of capital. Men are seldom collected together in large masses without discovering that union is strength, and the design of this article is to consider how the strength, of which the working classes have thus become sensible, has hitherto been expended, and in what manner it may, for their own purposes, be better employed henceforward. We propose to inquire whether, in any circumstances, and to any extent, it is possible for strikes to promote the interests of those engaged in them,, and whether, by a judicious application of what is styled the co-operative principle, may not be made the nearest practicable approach to a satisfactory solution of some of the most momentous as well as embarrassing of social questions.

In entering upon the first branch of the inquiry we shall be careful to steer clear of the exaggerations by which the subject is on both sides beset. Every period of national existence has its own distinguishing characteristics, and in almost every period of progress, the *laudatores temporis acti* are apt to take offence and alarm at disagreeable changes in the language and demeanour of their social inferiors, and in the new and startling forms assumed by popular agitation. About such novelties there is, indeed, almost always a good deal that is very reprehensible, as well as exceedingly unpleasant; but how repulsive soever their aspect may be, they always deserve the closest attention, as betokening the existence of some new cause of discontent, or some newly awakened desire or aspiration. The nature of the craving may, perhaps, be very imperfectly apprehended, even by those who experience it. They may scarcely know what it is they want, and in endeavouring to obtain it they may be guilty of all sorts of disorders as well as mistakes, but it is not the less certain that the thing they are in search of has, from some cause or other, become a necessity to them, and that the longing for it is not to be appeased by expostulation or denunciation, but must be substantially satisfied before the tranquillity which it has disturbed can be restored. At such a time it is useless to attempt to turn back the tide of popular feeling. The utmost that is practicable is to moderate its violence by removing any artificial obstructions against which it may be fretting, and by correcting the irregularities of its course, and leading it more smoothly towards its appropriate outlet. We must bear these considerations in mind in our investigation of strikes. Those outbreaks are of comparatively recent date, and outrageous and suicidal as they too commonly are, it is still at least possible that they may be protests against some recent grievance; and, before condemning them as altogether groundless and irrational, it behoves us to inquire whether the suspected grievance may not be a reality, and whether the protest must needs be altogether unavailing.

It will not be necessary to detain the reader with any of the stock arguments for or against strikes, with which he is doubtless familiar, and by which he may be presumed to have been convinced. It will be taken for granted that a workman has as much right to refuse to sell his labour as a tradesman has to refuse to sell his wares at less than a certain price, and that just as all the bakers or butchers in a town might, if they pleased, agree together at what price they would sell their loaves or joints, so all the operatives in a factory may arrange among themselves at what wages they will consent to continue to work. On the other hand, it will be assumed to be admitted that, although workmen have a perfect right to strike, and to combine for the purpose of striking, they have no right to assault or otherwise maltreat such of their companions as may not choose to join in the combination. If any one is content to accept for a day's work fewer halfpence than would content his fellows, that can certainly be no reason why the latter should insist on making up to him the deficiency in kicks.

It will also be taken for granted that a strike cannot for more

than a very short time raise wages in any employment, unless
the strikers are able to limit the number of labourers in that employment, which they obviously cannot do without inflicting two
very serious injuries on other people : one, on the labourers,
whom they shut out of a highly paid occupation, and force into
other occupations, in which wages, low perhaps already, are reduced still lower by the extraordinary influx of fresh competitors
for employment ; and the other on the community at large, who,
in proportion to the rise of wages which the strikers have obtained, will have to pay more dearly for the goods which the
strikers produce.   They will have to pay more dearly, that is,
if the rise of wages be lasting, and if the ultimate effect of the
strike be not, as is generally the case, to drive the business in
which it has taken place, from its ancient seats, to some other
situations, in which it will not be subjected to the same restrictions.
    These propositions are too well established to require further
elucidation here.   The conclusion to which they point is, that
strikes, although almost always to be regarded as national calamities, are usually peculiarly injurious to that portion of the
community with whom alone they are in favour, and whom alone
they have ever been supposed capable of benefiting.   What
misery they cause when unsuccessful to all who take part in them,
has been shown over and over again by direful experience ; but
even when most successful and when the end they have in view
is most perfectly attained, any permanent good which they may
do to one section of the working class is invariably more than
counterbalanced by the harm done to other sections of the same
class.   If wages rise in any business owing to an artificial limitation of the number of persons employed in it, they must infallibly fall in corresponding degree in every open business, and the
recipients of the reduced wages will have moreover to pay more
dearly for all articles produced by the recipients of the
increased wages.   The enhanced price of such articles will,
of course, affect every one who purchases them ; but the fall of
wages which a permanently successful strike (involving, as it
necessarily must, the closure of an employment previously open)
occasions in every employment still remaining open, affects
members of the working class alone.   By no class of persons
therefore, it appears, ought strikes to be in general so earnestly
deprecated as by the working class, since even when they are
most successful, whatever permanent advantage is gained from
them by one section of that class, must needs be gained altogether at the expense of other sections of the same class.
    So much is probably sufficiently clear, but what is perhaps less
obvious, though scarcely less important, is that, even if it were
possible for a strike to raise wages permanently in one branch of

industry without depressing them in others, and without raising the price of the produce of the particular branch in which wages had risen, still those who benefited by the strike would even then be appropriating something to which they were not entitled, and which belonged of right to others. To explain this it must be premised that there are always certain rates both of wages and profits which and which alone can for the time being be denominated fair and equitable rates. It will readily be perceived that there are two extreme points, one above which wages cannot possibly be permanently maintained, and the other below which they cannot possibly be permanently depressed, for employers will never knowingly consent to pay wages so high as to trench upon the profit requisite to make it worth their while to continue their business, and labourers cannot live and keep up their numbers, unless wages be at least high enough to procure for them a sufficiency of the necessaries of life. The rate of wages, however, seldom or never touches either extreme, but fluctuates between the two, and the intermediate point at which it may at any time rest for a while, depends upon the proportion between the demand for and the supply of labour ; that is to say, between the utmost amount which the whole body of employers would pay for the labour they require, rather than not obtain it, and the quantity of labour just then seeking for employment. The rate thus determined is the fair rate of wages—the fair price of labour. It bears no definite relation to the intrinsic value of labour, for which, precisely as for every other commodity, a purchaser pays, not at all according to its utility to himself, but simply what he can get it for.

Bread is the staff of life, and for bread or some adequate substitute it would be worth a man's while to pay its weight in gold if he could not otherwise procure it. But in practice there are generally plenty of people willing to supply it for less than its weight in copper, and accordingly pence not pounds, are given in exchange for the quartern loaf. It is just the same with respect to labour. Operatives in a cotton mill, observing how much the material they manipulate, which without such assistance as theirs would be almost worthless to its owner, is raised in price by their skill and toil, are apt to regard as a very inadequate recompense the comparatively small portion of the increased price which falls to their lot, while the lion's share is appropriated by one who seems to have little else to do but to look on and grow rich. They are apt to think themselves defrauded because they receive so much less for their labour than it is worth to their employer. But, if the latter pay the full price for which similar labourers would be willing to place their services at his disposal, he pays the utmost that can justly be demanded of him. The circumstance of the

labour being of especial utility to him is no reason why he should
pay more than the market price for it, any more than it would be
incumbent on a half-famished day labourer, who should have the
good luck to pick up a sovereign, to give the whole of it for a
penny roll, because in his starving state the roll might do him a
sovereign's worth of good.　　What labourers are really entitled to
as the fair price of labour is neither more nor less than the price
it would fetch in an open and uncontrolled market, and the employer who pays that price is equally entitled to take as profit the
whole difference between the cost to him and the sale price of
the article which his labourers produce.　The whole of that difference, whatever be its amount, belongs of right to him ; it constitutes his fair profit ; and labourers have no more right to encroach
on the fair rate of profit, than masters on the fair rate of wages.

But if this be true, the converse of the proposition must be at
least equally true : and masters would have no reason to complain
if an attempt on their part to reduce wages below the market rate
were met by a strike on the part of the men.　Now, there will be
no difficulty in showing that circumstances do occasionally arise,
in which large employers, in their dealings with their men, might,
if the latter were quiescent, be able to act somewhat in opposition
to the natural laws that ought to govern their procedure.

Let it be supposed that in any business, as, for instance, in the
cotton manufacture, the average rate of profit had for some time
been ten per cent., and that, owing to the opening of new markets
or to any other cause, the rate were suddenly raised to fifteen or
twenty per cent.　The millowners would naturally be desirous of
extending to the utmost a business which had suddenly become
so extraordinarily profitable.　But this they could not do without
engaging more hands ; and if, in order to obtain them, they should
enter the market unconnectedly and bid against each other, a
very little reflection will show that wages would, by their competition, be raised so high as to bring down profits to the original
rate.　When this had been done, whatever advantage still continued to arise from enhanced prices would be monopolized by the
operatives, though the millowners also might be greatly benefited
by the extension of their trade.　The high rate of wages would,
however, be continually attracting fresh hands, and would be continually declining in consequence, while production would be
simultaneously increasing and causing a corresponding decline
of prices, until, as a final result, wages, profits, and prices would
all return to their original level, and the only alteration from the
previous state of things would be that the millowners would be
doing more business and would be employing more men.　Both
masters and men would, however, each in their turn have been
in receipt of a considerable bonus derived from enhanced prices,

and the masters, although eventually obtaining no more than the original rate of profit, would be receiving that rate on greatly extended sales.

This is what would take place if it were true, as is commonly supposed, that the labour market is a field of free and uncontrolled competition, and that the price of labour is invariably regulated by the proportion between supply and demand. But this is very far from being the fact. Large employers in any one extensive department of industry are not at all in the habit of competing with each other for labour. On the contrary, their custom is to deliberate together from time to time, in order to determine what wages it may, in existing circumstances, be advisable for them to offer, and some uniform rate is agreed to accordingly. The rate so fixed could not indeed in ordinary times be maintained, if it were lower than that which would result from competition, but, in an extraordinary juncture like that described, when trade, receiving a sudden impulse, creates as suddenly an increased demand for labour, it is often within the power of employers, by combining among themselves, to prevent wages from rising so high as they otherwise would. It is, of course, indispensable that they should raise wages sufficiently to attract labourers from other occupations, but, provided they do so much, it is quite possible for them to secure to themselves all the additional labour immediately procurable, and yet arbitrarily to fix wages at a point below that which they would reach if the laws of barter were allowed free play. It is demonstrable, however, that in so doing they withhold from the labourer part of his due; they do not pay him in full the fair price of his labour, the price which it would fetch in an uncontrolled market. Such a proceeding on their part is naturally regarded by their men as an injustice, and in opposing to the combination from which it emanates a counter combination of their own, they are simply obeying a primary instinct of our nature. A strike, in such exceptional circumstances, ceases to be aggressive, and becomes a legitimate act of self-defence. The only questions with regard to it are whether it is likely to be effectual for its purpose, and whether the end proposed is worth the means, and both questions might plausibly be answered in the affirmative. One main reason, as Mr. Fawcett has pointed out, why strikes so seldom succeed, is that they most frequently take place when trade is dull and profits declining, and when, as labour has temporarily lost something of its value, the moment is peculiarly inopportune for an attempt to raise its price. This is one reason why trades' unions so seldom attain their ends, but another not less important is the habitual extravagance of their pretensions. They are in truth constantly meditating the very same offence, the occasional commission of which is their only just ground of complaint against the masters. They are continually seeking to adjust wages, according to some arbitrary standard of their own, instead of simply insisting that they should be left to adjust themselves in conformity with the operation of natural laws. If their demand were limited to this, their undoubted right, and if this were pressed only when disputed, which it practically never is, except when trade is flourishing, prices rising and labour in extraordinary demand, unanimous action on the part of the workmen could not fail to obtain for them every reasonable concession. The masters, being eagerly on the look out for additional labour, would certainly, rather than lose what they already had, pay for it any price which would permit them still to obtain the rate of profit which prevailed before their branch of trade had received its recent stimulus ;—such a price, and nothing less than such a price, being, in the circumstances supposed, coincident with the fair market price. If strikes were undertaken only in the circumstances and with the views thus indicated, they would be pretty sure to succeed, and that without subjecting those engaged in them to any prolonged trial of endurance. It would be difficult, too, not to wish them success, though it is probable that all necessity for resorting to them would then speedily cease. When the masters had discovered that the men possessed the power of enforcing payment in full of the market price of labour, they would not waste time by offering less than the market price, and if there were any doubt as to what that price would be, the question might be amicably settled without appeal to force. A tribunal analogous to the French " Conseils de Prud' Hommes " might perhaps be constituted, or a sort of conference of peers and commons might take place between the representatives, on the one side, of cotton lords, iron masters, or other commercial magnates, and, on the other, of those of the particular body of operatives concerned in the dispute. At such a meeting, in the presence of all who chose to listen, and where both parties were sincerely seeking to ascertain the limits of their respective and mutually consistent rights, it need not be doubted that justice would be permitted to hold the scales.

In the foregoing observations will be found, as we believe, the utmost that can be said in excuse of strikes. They may not be deserving of unqualified reprobation. Unwarrantable, extravagant, and mischievous as they too frequently are, they are nevertheless expressions of a power of combination on the part of workmen, which though exceedingly liable to abuse, is yet a salutary counterpoise to the corresponding power of the masters. The warmest apologist of strikes, however, will scarcely contend that they can at best be more than temporary expedients calculated to serve a temporary purpose. They may sometimes be legitimately employed to resist an arbitrary depression of wages, but they cannot, unless very partially and ephemerally, nor without resorting to violence and injustice, raise wages above the current market rate; and if that rate be, as it unfortunately very often is, unequal to the due remuneration of labour, they are quite powerless to supply the deficiency. Neither in any other respect can they avail to produce a lasting change in the mutual relations of employers and employed, or to modify the conditions of their interdependence. So far as labour is the vassal of capital, there is but one way of effecting its enfranchisement. Labourers must themselves become, or must have opportunities of becoming, capitalists; and we shall now proceed to consider how far it is possible for industrial co-operation to assist in thus elevating them in the social scale.

The story of the rise and progress of co-operation in England affords a good example of " what mighty compounds spring from trivial things." Twenty years ago twenty-eight flannel weavers of Rochdale, disgusted, as they well might be, with the villanous quality and outrageous prices of the provisions and groceries procurable from the petty tradespeople with whom they were in the habit of dealing, conceived the idea of becoming their own purveyors. That such a notion should have occurred to them shows that they must have been superior specimens of their class, and must have already exercised resolution enough to emancipate themselves from the despotism of the "tally shops," in which, in those days, the great majority of their order always had credit— that is to say, were always in debt. Having prepared themselves by getting rid of this encumbrance the weavers clubbed together, and subscribing each his twopence or threepence a week, until they had made up amongst them the sum of twenty-eight pounds, they were enabled to obtain from Manchester at wholesale prices single barrels of flour, sugar, butter and oatmeal. From this common stock they supplied their wants, every one paying for what he took in ready money, and at the prices current in the shops of the neighbourhood, and when the barrels were emptied, and the sale proceeds of their contents were divided rateably among the party, every one experienced a glad surprise on finding himself in receipt of a considerable addition to the amount of his original venture. Of course a speculation which had turned out so well was presently repeated. More flour, sugar, butter and oatmeal were sent for to Manchester, and this time, it seems, in larger quantities than on the former occasion, when the embryo association had been jeeringly told that their whole stock in trade would not fill a respectable wheelbarrow. An entire room was considered to be necessary for the stowage of the new consignment, and one was accordingly taken for three years, at an

annual rent of 10*l.*, on the ground-floor of a house in a narrow
bye street, whose name by successive stages had become corrupted
from " The Old " into T'old, T'owd, and, finally, into Toad Lane.
Here it was arranged that one of the members, dignified with the
title of salesman, should attend for a few hours in the evening
twice a week.   But though the weavers had now got a place for
a shop, they were half ashamed to open it.   When the day and
hour for commencing business arrived, the little party assembled
within to take part in the preliminary ceremony, were abashed at
the largeness of the crowd waiting without to witness it.   Some
delay took place before any one could muster up courage to take
down the shutters, and when at last the " store" and its contents
were exposed to public view, all Toad Lane was in a roar.   Loud
and long were the shouts of derision that rose from a host of
" doffers" (a species of street-boy peculiar to the clothing districts), who, set on by persons who ought to have known better,
stared through the windows or blocked up the doorway, evincing
their characteristically precocious sense of the ridiculous by the
nature of their comments on the modest display of the " owd
weavers' shop."*

Those may laugh that win.   Co-operative stores, though
designed primarily for the use of the shareholders, are free to all
comers ; and of the present generation of Rochdale " doffers,"
one and all are most likely regular customers at the flourishing
mart into which that same " owd weavers' shop" has now been
metamorphosed.   In 1845, the second year of their occupancy,
its tenants, already increased in number from twenty-eight to
seventy-four, with a capital of 181*l.*, made a net profit of 32*l.*
In the two following years they divided 80*l.* and 72*l.*, and they
have gone on prospering ever since with almost the celerity of
geometrical progression, extending, too, their operations in proportion as they received fresh accessions of members and capital, and
as a growing consciousness of utility encouraged them to embark
in new branches of trade.   In 1847, linen and woollen drapery
was grafted on to the original grocery and chandlery business ;
in 1850, a butcher's shop was set up, and soon afterwards a
slaughter-house, and in 1852, shoemaking, clogmaking, and
tailoring were commenced.   In August of last year the number
of members had risen to 3630, and their capital, or assets, to
42,349*l.*   The cash received for goods sold during the previous
quarter was 37,884*l.* and of this 4677*l.* was profit.   The
head-quarters of the society are still in Toad Lane, where they
possess four houses, but the draper's shop is in another street,

---

* " Self-Help by the People" (p. 13) : a little history, full of good sense,
and with occasional dashes of humour.

and the slaughter-house in a third. In this last, the number of animals of all kinds—oxen, sheep, pigs, lambs and calves—killed in the first six months of 1861 was 1196, and the weight of meat sold 287,531lbs., and when we lately visited the place, the most tempting sausages we ever saw were being made by steam machinery. There are also branch stores in different parts of the town for the convenience of persons living at a distance from the central premises. All the stores are now open every day, except Sunday, and all day long, but the busiest time is Saturday night, when the scene presented by Toad Lane is worth a long journey to Rochdale to see. Operatives, and others having then just received their wages, come in swarms to the stores, either in person or by deputy, and cluster like bees at favourite counters. The grocery and general store is as full as it will hold of members and their wives and children laying in next week's stock of flour, potatoes, rice, sugar, and butter, while others are chatting outside, waiting their turn to go in. In the draper's shop there are seldom less than nine or ten women selecting what they require, and in the butcher's, three assistants have as much as they can do to attend to the constant succession of applicants for the chief material of next day's dinner. The newsroom and library are crowded with men and youths reading the papers and magazines, or exchanging and renewing books; and by eleven o'clock, when the premises are closed, between four and five hundred pounds will have been taken during the day in exchange for goods, and the librarian will have given out about two hundred volumes.*

"Equitable Pioneers" is the title which, with something of prophetic instinct, was assumed on first starting by the Rochdale Association. After they had cleared the way, others were not slow to follow, and similar societies are now to be counted by hundreds, scattered over all parts of the kingdom. Some of them are in immediate connexion with the original Pioneers, having, indeed, been founded by detachments from that body. Such are the Rochdale Flour Mill Society, the Rochdale Co-operative Manufacturing Company, and the Rochdale Co-operative Land and Building Company (limited). The first-named of these occupy a strongly built five-storied brick edifice, of which they have purchased the freehold, and in which a steam-engine of thirty-five horse power keeps constantly at work fourteen stones, grinding annually flour and meal enough to sell for more than 130,000*l.*, at a profit of more than 10,000*l.*† Of the Manufacturing Society we shall speak hereafter. Not less noticeable than these offshoots from the parent stem is the

---

* "Self-Help by the People," p. 38.
† The average weekly deliveries in 1862 were 989 sacks of flour and 127 loads of meal, each sack containing 280 lbs., and each load 240 lbs.

Leeds Co-operative Flour and Provision Society, which, set on foot in 1847 by some hundreds of working-men subscribing first their 20s. and afterwards their 50s. each, had in a few months accumulated funds enough to embolden them to purchase suitable premises for conversion into a flour mill, at a cost of 4000*l.*, though it was not till 1853 that they were able to pay off the debt incurred in consequence. By that time, however, their capital had increased to nearly 10,000*l.*, with which they were doing business to the extent of nearly 60,000*l.*, and obtaining nearly 5000*l.* profit. These examples may suffice to show the general character of establishments which, as we have said, are already to be found in every part of Great Britain, not merely in the towns of Lancashire and Yorkshire, but in places so remote from each other as Aberdeen and Truro.

At the close of 1862 the aggregate number of so-called Co-operative Societies in England and Wales alone (registered under the Industrial and Provident Societies Act) was 336, comprising 90,458 members, with a share capital of 429,315*l.* The amount of business done by them in the year was 2,331,650*l.*, and the profit realized, 165,770*l.* The nature of their transactions is very varied. Almost all are grocers, and most of them are in addition drapers or provision dealers, or tailors or hatters, or shoe or clogmakers, or butchers or bakers, and many combine several, and some all of these trades. Seven are corn millers only, and two bakers only. By one coal only is sold, and by another only tobacco and snuff. There is one store at which beer is sold, and co-operators of the stricter sort shake their heads when they speak of it, though what ought rather to be regretted is that there should be only one place affording so much security that the liquor to be had there will be good. In one case farming is combined with other occupations, and in four the members confine themselves to some manufacture or handicraft. Some of the societies are doing much better than others, but as the average rate of profit of all taken together was, last year, more than thirty-four per cent., it is needless to say that very few of them are doing at all badly.

The secret of their success is to be found in their mode of doing business, which, in the cases of such as adopt (as most of them do, more or less) the pattern of the Rochdale Pioneers, possesses some very decided advantages. Making all their purchases with ready money, they obtain a discount on all they buy. Never selling on credit, they have no bad debts. Never permitting any article to be removed from their shops without being replaced by cash, they are able to turn over their money five or six times in the course of a twelvemonth, and thus to do with it as much as would be possible with many times the amount under the usual system of slower returns. Possessing in their own shareholders a large body of regular customers, they have no necessity for any of the heavy expense which ordinary tradesmen are often obliged to incur to make themselves and their pretensious known ; nevertheless, in order to attract outsiders, they employ a device far more efficacious than claptrap advertisements or showy shop fronts. At the Rochdale, Leeds, and many other stores, whenever any one, whether a member or not, makes a purchase, he receives one or more tin tickets denoting the sum he has paid. At the end of every quarter, when profits are declared, a deduction is first made sufficient to pay interest, at the rate of five per cent. per annum, on capital ; two and a-half per cent. of the remainder is next appropriated to a separate fund, to which we shall have occasion to advert more particularly hereafter, and the surplus is then divided among the holders of the tin tickets, whether members or non-members, some favour being, however, generally shown to the former, who, at Rochdale for instance, in the last two quarters reported, got back half-a-crown in the pound of what they had spent, while non-members received only twentypence. Now, as nearly everything that a working-man wants for the daily use of himself or his family may be obtained at a co-operative store—as he may buy there his bread, meat, cheese, butter, tea and sugar ; coats and trousers, boots and shoes, for himself; and dresses, bonnets, and shawls, parasols, and pattens, for his wife and daughters, the sum represented by his tickets is often something considerable, amounting to 60*l.* or more in the course of a year, and the drawback is proportionate. Thus, to take an example, verified by Mr. Plummer,* by personal examination of the Rochdale Pioneers' books, a member who, in 1850, began by subscribing 1s. 3d., and afterwards paid in four successive quarterly instalments of 3s. 3d., making 14s. 3d. in all, was then able to stop paying in cash, for the drawbacks which meantime had been entered to his credit had raised his subscription to the prescribed minimum of 5*l.* Leaving this untouched, he drew out between January, 1851, and December, 1860, a sum in all of 41*l.*, to which he had become entitled in the quality, not of shareholder, but of customer. A story, too, is told of a woman who, being advised to draw out her money from the store which, she was assured, was going to break, replied, " Well, let " it break ; if it does it will break with its own. I have only paid

---

* Mr. Plummer is himself a member of the working class. His paper on "Co-operation in Lancashire and Yorkshire," in the " Companion to the Almanac for 1862," would be worth reading, if only for the purpose of showing to those who require to be informed, how well some members of that class can write.

"one shilling in, and I have fifty pounds there now." Another case worth mentioning is that of a man who, having paid in fifteen shillings, gained 18*l.* in two years. In all these instances the persons spoken of were members ; but if they had been simply customers the bonuses received by them as such would still have been very substantial. The man who gained 18*l.* in two years must have spent at the stores in one year at least 70*l.*, the drawback on which, even at the non-member's rate of twenty-pence in the pound, would have been very nearly 6*l.* Customers are not likely to be wanting in shops in which, besides being sure that everything is good of its kind, they are so munificently rewarded for their good sense in coming.

In our opinion, the drawbacks allowed by the Equitable Pioneers are unnecessarily large. Buyers cannot reasonably expect to be supplied at prices below those which will permit sellers to make the average profits of trade, and shareholders in a store might safely, therefore, deduct ten per cent. profit instead of five per cent. interest before dividing the surplus of their net receipts among purchasers. They might do this without any risk of being undersold by the small shopkeepers who are their principal rivals, for the latter require much more than the average rate of profit to enable them to live, and they are compelled to charge proportionate prices. Their entire profits are generally swallowed up in the salaries which they are obliged to allow themselves, whereas, in co-operative stores, the cost of superintendence is a very small percentage indeed on the net receipts. The latter, too, are commonly so large, that after deduction of a sum equal to ten per cent. on the share capital, there would still be an ample balance. The present annual profit of the Rochdale Pioneers cannot be stated at less than 20,000*l.*, which is equal to 50 per cent. on the aggregate amount of their shares. Ten per cent. on that amount would be 4,000*l.*, and if that were deducted, there would remain 16,000*l.* for distribution among customers, suf-ficient to allow of an average of one-and-ninepence in the pound being returned upon the 160,000*l.* or so received in exchange for goods. If, however, in the matter of bonuses, any mistake be made by the Equitable Pioneers and their imitators, it is at least well that the mistake should be on the generous side.

The same politic liberality, which though carried perhaps somewhat farther than necessary for that particular purpose, certainly has the effect of securing abundance of custom to indus-trial trading societies, might apparently be so applied as to repair the only serious defect in their constitution. For there is one respect in which they seem to stand at some disadvantage, as compared with individual tradesmen. The latter are pretty sure, for their own sakes, to attend closely to their own business, whereas the superintendence of a co-operative store must be entrusted to salaried officers without selfish motives for greater activity than may appear just sufficient to ensure a continuance and to procure a possible augmentation of their salaries. Apathetic management is indeed the one single element of uncertainty in the conduct of a co-operative store, the success of which—assured beforehand of its market and free from all the risk involved in giving and taking credit—might otherwise, as Mr. Fawcett remarks, be absolutely guaranteed. No doubt the uncertainty is diminished by the fact that associated working men are likely to be well acquainted with each other's character, and are able to select for the management of their affairs such of themselves as are best fitted for the duty by probity and disinterestedness as well as by intelligence and activity. No doubt, too, the members selected will have a strong fellow feeling for their constituents, and will be anxious to show themselves worthy of the confidence reposed in them. Still it may be a question whether it is wise to rely exclusively on personal earnestness and on *esprit de corps*, and whether it might not be prudent to enlist something of self-interest on the same side, as might easily be done, by making the remuneration of managing officers rise and fall with the amount of business transacted or of profit realized. The expedient has not, however, been adopted at Rochdale, nor, so far as we are aware, anywhere else ; and there may seem to be no great reason for resorting to it as long as things continue to go on without it as well as they have done hitherto.

The rapid progress of Co-operative Stores affords matter for unqualified congratulation, for nothing but unalloyed good can proceed from them. In the first place, they offer to all who are in a position to avail themselves of it, a means of obtaining most of the necesaries and many of the conveniences of life of the best procurable quality and at the lowest possible price. On this point, the author of " Self-Help by the People" warms into justifiable enthusiasm.

" The whole atmosphere of a store," says he, " is honest. In that market there is no distrust and no deception, no adulteration and no second prices. Buyer and seller meet as friends : there is no overreaching on the one side and no suspicion on the other. Those who serve neither hurry, finesse, nor flatter. They have no interest in chicanery. Their sole duty is to give fair measure, full weight, and pure quality, to men who never knew before what it was to have a wholesome meal, whose shoes let in water a month too soon, whose waistcoats shone with devils' dust, and whose wives wore calico that would not wash. These men now buy in the market like millionaires, and, as far as pureness of food goes, live like lords. They weave their own stuffs, make their own shoes, sew their own garments, and grind their own corn. They buy the purest sugar and the best tea, and grind their own coffee. They slaughter their own cattle, and the finest beasts of the land waddle down the streets of Rochdale for the consumption of flannel weavers and cobblers."*

When a child, he adds, is sent to a shop, it is usual (as children can be put off with anything) to caution him to go to some particular man, as, for instance, the one with grey whiskers and black hair, and to be sure and ask him for the best butter. But in a store, all the men seem to have grey whiskers and black hair; a child cannot go to the wrong man, and the best butter is sure to be given without being asked for, for the simple reason that no bad is kept. Nor is the beneficial influence of co-operative stores in this particular likely to be confined to those who deal with them, for just as the building of model lodging-houses often causes all the lodging-houses in a neighbourhood to be more or less remodelled, so may the general establishment of stores—the contents of which, having been provided primarily for the use of the storekeepers themselves, are sure to be unadulterated—eventually leave no choice to other retailers of similar goods, but either to cease adulterating or to shut up shop. Thus may not impossibly be closed one prolific source of disease and physical deterioration against which neither legislative denunciation nor the strenuous exertions of Dr. Hassall and his colleagues in the *Lancet* Commission, have hitherto proved of any sensible avail. Nor would the moral result in such an event be of less moment than the sanitary. When it is considered how almost universal among tradespeople is the practice of adulteration, and how conventional is most people's standard of morality, few persons questioning the propriety of anything which they see their fellows continually doing—how apt, too, is the habitual commission of any one species of dishonesty to prepare the way for kindred transgressions,—it will readily be understood how great a moral advance might be expected to follow a general cessation of the customs of sanding sugar and watering milk, of whitening bread with alum and colouring tea with copperas.

A second recommendation of co-operative stores is the effect they are likely to have in superseding the hucksters' shops, from which the bulk of the manufacturing population are fed and clothed. The excessive number of such shops would of itself be a sufficient reason for wishing that some of them should be got rid of, for, as has been lately remarked by the highest authority on all questions of economics—

"It is the enormous multiplication of mere distributors who are not producers that really eats up the produce of labour, much more than the mere profits of capital, which in the great majority of cases are not

---

* "Self-Help," pp. 38, 39.

more than a reasonable equivalent for the industry which created the capital and the frugality which prevents it from being squandered. The direction in which the greatest improvement in social economy is to be looked for is in the suppression of the multitude of middlemen, who share among themselves so large a proportion of the produce of the country, while the services they render, although indispensable, might be better performed by a tenth part of their number,"*

—by a central store with its half-dozen branches, for instance, rather than by an additional hundred of the small provision and clothing stalls, which, in a town like Rochdale, still meet the eye at every turn. But irrespectively of their excessive multiplication, "tally"-shops (which most of the shops in question are) have long been one of the curses of the manufacturing districts. Those who deal regularly with them are furnished with " strap-books" in which their purchases are entered, and which are balanced weekly or fortnightly, according to the period at which wages are paid in the neighbourhood, a balance being always suffered to remain on the wrong side of the account, in order that the shopkeepers may retain a hold upon their customers. Thus the latter are always in debt, and, as a natural consequence, are careless and wasteful, since for them to be sparing would be more immediately for their creditors' benefit than for their own. Co-operative stores are, however, gradually putting an end to all this. They are drawing to themselves the supporters of the "tally"-shops, and they are doing so by previously encouraging in them the growth of forethought and thrift. They offer for sale, instead of poisonous trash and flimsy frippery, good wholesome food and good stout clothing, and they offer too a handsome premium to buyers; but none are permitted to buy who do not come with money in their hands, which none can habitually do without first getting, and afterwards keeping out of debt. This rigid enforcement of cash payments is just the sort of discipline required by those to whom it applies. Many a man with thirty or forty pounds in a store is ready to acknowledge that, before joining, he was for years together always in debt, and that what made him begin to economize was the desire of gaining access to the store. When persons, originally so circumstanced, have once saved enough to enable them to pay off their shop debts and to become regular dealers at a co-operative store, material for further saving is supplied to them without any effort of their own. At the end of every quarter, if they have been pretty good customers, a present of perhaps twenty shillings is made in consideration of their having—not produced but consumed; and as, moreover, the largest consumers are those with the largest families, those who need most are also those who receive most: in Lancashire phrase, " The more they

---

* Mr. J. S. Mill in the " Co-operator" for September, 1863.

eaten, the more they geten."[*] By leaving untouched the first instalments of the money which thus comes to them, as it were, spontaneously, and letting them accumulate until they reach the sum of five pounds, they may in a year or two literally eat their way up to the rank of shareholder, when the donations made to them quarterly will, in consequence, be increased by one-third. If by that time a confirmed habit of saving has not been acquired, at any rate the necessity for forethought and thrift will be as strong as ever. No one without ready money can participate in the benefits of a store, and no one can have ready money at his disposal without living within his means.

We have thus indicated what appear to us to be the chief merits of co-operative stores. Another of their recommendations is, no doubt, the investment afforded by them for the sums which they may be the means of inducing working-men to save, but their possible as well as actual utility in that particular is, in our opinion, somewhat apt to be exaggerated. An advantageous field for small investments is, in truth, one of the greatest wants of our working classes, but it is one which co-operative stores can only very imperfectly supply. If "husbandry" be not more " an English virtue" in these days than it was a century and a half ago, when Defoe[†] remarked that whereas an Englishman could but "just live" on twenty shillings a week, a Dutchman with nine shillings would have everything "handsome about him, and leave his children in very good condition," the deficiency may be accounted for without supposing any extraordinary propensity to self-indulgence to be inherent in our poorer countrymen. If the latter spend, in comparison with foreigners, an enormous portion of their earnings at the publichouse, they may not unwarrantably plead in excuse that they have less inducement to practise self-denial. Even though they should absolutely abjure beer and skittles, their petty earnings could not for a great length of time yield them any appreciable increase of income, and it could rarely be till towards the close of a life of privation that they would find themselves in possession of a hundred pounds. And what could they then do with that, for them, almost unattainable sum ? The acquisition of a bit of land, the great object of a continental labourer's ambition and economies, would in their case be next to an impossibility, and a solitary hundred pounds would have little chance in trade amidst the crowd of colossal capitals which are daily more and more completely monopolizing the domain of commerce. If placed in a savings bank, which until lately would have been its best depository, the fifty

---

[*] Mr. Pitman, in " Co-operator" for November last.
[†] " Giving Alms no Charity."

shillings of annual interest allowed upon it would be but a poor compensation for the previous long years of lenten abstinence. So paltry an annuity might not improbably be absolutely useless to its recipient. Instead of serving in any degree as a provision for his old age, its most likely effect would simply be to induce the parish officers to deduct just so much from the allowance which they would otherwise have made to him. The result of all his saving might to him be precisely the same as if he had never saved at all. No wonder that, perceiving these things, English labourers should not have been much in the habit of saving, but should have preferred enjoying themselves after their own fashion to the extent of their means, to stinting themselves for no other end than that of keeping down the poor-rates. That they should have made this choice is the reverse of a sign of improvidence, for a calm calculation of consequences might very naturally have led to it.

Now, though co-operative stores are on the whole vast improvements upon savings banks, the difference between the two in the one respect which we are now considering is not very material. The store might allow twice as much interest as the bank, but in the first place five per cent. is no very magnificent reward for the extraordinary industry and frugality which a working man must have practised in order to amass the principal; and, in the second, even that rate is allowed only upon a limited sum. As a general rule, five shares of one pound each is the minimum number which a member of an industrial trading society is required; and a hundred the maximum number which he is permitted, to hold—and five per cent. on five shares is only five shillings. It is true that in addition to such interest, a member may get perhaps twenty times as much under the name of bonus or drawback on purchases; but this he obtains not as shareholder, but as customer, and its amount is not at all affected by the value of his shares, which it does not therefore give him any motive to increase. If the aggregate capital (429,315*l.*) of all the co-operative stores in England and Wales be divided by 90,458, the number of partners, it will be found that the average proportion belonging to each of the latter is rather under 5*l.*, showing that it is not usual for one individual to hold much more than the prescribed minimum number of shares. The instances alluded to above of persons holding as many as forty or fifty shares can be only exceptional. The majority of members evidently only leave their dividends to accumulate up to five pounds, and thenceforward draw them out as they accrue. Interest at five per cent. it seems is of itself scarcely a sufficient inducement to invest in a store, nor, even though it were, could it have more than a limited

effect, since no one is permitted to invest more than a hundred
pounds.*

It may, perhaps, be thought that the limitations to investment
in co-operative stores are artificial and removable at pleasure ; that
there is no reason why profits should be restricted to five per cent.,
or why new shares should not at any time be created in numbers
sufficient to enable any member to hold as many as he pleased, or
why the holder of the maximum number in one store should not
acquire shares in another also. But this view of the question is
only partially correct. We have ourselves suggested that the
rate of profit should be not merely raised but doubled ; but the
field for investment opened by co-operative stores has its bounds,
and will not admit all who may be naturally desirous of entering,
unless they be limited as to the amount of capital they bring with
them. The quantity of business which any working men's store
can do cannot well exceed the demand for provisions, clothing,
and other articles, of the industrial population within the sphere
of its operation. If all the working men of the neighbourhood
were partners in the store, the sellers would be equally numerous
and identical with the buyers ; each of them would as it were be
dealing with himself, and no one could hold more than the very
limited amount of stock required for that purpose, without preventing some of his associates from holding even so much. If then
the majority of working men are to become, as it is most desirable
they should, partners in co-operative stores, it can only be on
condition that no one shall be permitted to invest more than
others, nor consequently even so much as the maximum at present allowed. Whatever, therefore, be the utility of stores in
other respects, and no one can rate it more highly than ourselves, they can assist little in bringing about that intimate
alliance with capital which has been assumed to be the grand
desideratum of labour. Resort must, it is evident, be had to some
other machinery before any material progress can be made in converting labourers into capitalists.

For the credit of co-operation, we must no longer delay to
point out that " Co-operative Stores" is in so far a misnomer, that
what are so designated have no connexion whatever with the
most important of co-operative principles. Co-operation implies
working together ; but partners in a working men's store do not
work—they only trade together. The circumstances of their
having combined to form a store, and of their permitting purchasers to participate in profits, do not constitute co-operation.
The same things in effect are done by those insurance companies

---

* That is to say, by the rules of Co-operative Societies : the limit assigned
by law is 200*l.*

which give bonuses to policy-holders, but which are, nevertheless, in the strictest sense of the word, joint-stock companies. Such, likewise, and as strictly, are industrial trading associations, which differ in no respect from other joint-stock companies, unless it be in the class of persons from which their members are drawn, and in the more than ordinary precautions with which their business is conducted. To constitute industrial co-operation—if by that newly-adopted term be indicated something possessing a new and distinctive feature—it is indispensable that labourers working together in concert shall either themselves have provided the capital that maintains them at work, or, at least, that besides wages they shall receive also a share in the profits. Now the comparatively small number of employés in a co-operative, or, as we should prefer calling it, an associative store, may very possibly have provided no portion whatever of the capital, and cannot possibly have provided more than a very small portion; and whatever may be paid to them in addition to wages, is received by them, not as labourers, but as shareholders or customers. It is only in what, for distinction's sake, may be denominated co-operative workshops or factories, that the essential conditions of co-operation are really fulfilled; and even of factories, there are many to which the distinguishing epithet has been incorrectly applied. In the corn-mill of the Rochdale Industrial Association, for instance, the labourers, as such, get nothing but ordinary wages; and the case is the same in the cotton-mill of the Bacup Manufacturing Society; and it has lately become so likewise in that of the corresponding Society at Rochdale. Still there are in this country some, and on the Continent several, industrial associations that have adopted the true co-operative system, the peculiarities of which will well repay investigation. The theory on which it is based is, that labourers may, by being permitted to participate in profits, be stimulated to such extra diligence and carefulness as will add more to profits than the share assigned to themselves will take away. If this hypothesis be correct, consequences are deducible from it of so beneficial a character, that co-operative factories by which those consequences should be brought about, would deserve to take rank above even associative stores. But whereas the excellence of the latter has already been placed beyond dispute by short but conclusive experience, the former are still on trial, and arguments and evidence concerning them must be carefully weighed before a verdict can be pronounced in their favour.

At first sight, indeed, established as they are primarily for the sake of pecuniary profit, they might seem to be singularly ill-adapted to accomplish their object. Partners in a co-operative factory resemble those in an associative store in constituting, like them ,a joint-stock company of working-men, but they have none of their peculiar advantages. They may, if they please, decline to take credit, but they cannot refuse to give it, if they wish either wholesale or retail dealers to take their goods: they do not possess in their own shareholders an adequate number of customers, but must compete for custom with active rivals, and cannot therefore afford to dispense with any of the usual arts of competition ; and no method which they can adopt of remunerating superintendents and managers can ensure, on the part of those officers, all the desirable qualifications. In this last respect, a large manufacturing association appears to more than usual disadvantage as compared with individual enterprise : for manufacturing is not like banking, or insurance, or mining, or railway management, or any other of the businesses to which joint-stock companies, for the most part, judiciously confine themselves. It partakes less of the character of routine, and is less susceptible of being carried on in accordance with fixed regulations. It requires that the state and prospects of the market should be carefully watched with a view to the timely contraction or expansion of business. To accommodate it to frequent changes of circumstances requires not only practised sagacity, but singleness of purpose, and promptitude of decision and of action, from those who have the direction of affairs : above all, when operations are on an extensive scale, unremitting vigilance is necessary to prevent the numerous hands engaged in toilsome or tedious tasks from shirking or slurring over their work. A master's mind and a master's eye may supply these requisites, but nothing short of the affection which a man feels for concerns exclusively his own can be expected to keep attention constantly on the alert ; and unity of counsel is scarcely to be looked for in a multitudinous assemblage of equals, all of whom have a right to take part in all deliberations. Accordingly, in some important particulars, co-operative working associations will always be found more or less wanting ; and to compensate for their deficiencies, the only special advantage belonging to them is the direct interest which every member takes in the general prosperity. This solitary set-off appears, however, to be amply sufficient. The interest of any one co-operator cannot, indeed, be anything like that of a solitary employer, but the conjunction of many units produces an aggregate of superintending power more efficacious than that of any single master. Every member knows that the amount of profit to be shared between himself and his companions will depend on the manner in which he and they do their work ; and even though this should not induce him to do his best himself, it will at least make him anxious that all the others should do theirs. Thus every one is watched by every one else. Every one has upon him not one, but some hundreds of pairs of eyes. Not that such Argus-like supervision is likely to be really required. Those who would have no scruple in defrauding a master with whom they have little community of feeling, and who would neglect his work as much as they dared, may yet be honest in their dealings with each other. Among men aiming at a common object, emulation and the desire of self-approval are generally more powerful than the love of idleness; and he must be a very mean-spirited fellow indeed who tries to escape from contributing his proper quota of exertion. At any rate, whether it be owing to the influence of selfish or of unselfish motives, the fact certainly seems to be that when profits are shared in judicious proportion with labourers, the increase in the efficiency and productiveness of labour is likely to be fully proportionate to the extra remuneration which the labourers receive. The most decisive proofs of this are those afforded by some of the "associations ouvrières" of Paris; but before speaking more particularly of these, we wish to cite some of the evidence, notwithstanding its somewhat less satisfactory character, obtainable nearer at hand.

In Bridge-street, Manchester, is a house rented and occupied conjointly by two little communities,—one of six tailors, the other of nine hatters—distinct in their organization, but residing side by side in brotherly harmony. Our information regarding the former is only fragmentary, but it enables us to state that in the first half of last year, their capital being then 173*l*., their sales amounted to 495*l*., the wages divided amongst them to 169*l*., and their net profit to something less than 16*l*. Taken by themselves, these figures might suggest too favourable a notion of the state of affairs, for the tailors have not work enough to keep them fully employed, and the most that can be said of them is that they have kept their heads well above water. Their average annual earnings are not much short of 50*l*. per head, but as yet they have never received any dividend beyond bare wages, whatever profit they may have made having apparently been applied to the augmentation of their capital. The hatters, although they also have reason to complain of want of patronage, are doing better. Their capital, which when they started in 1851 was only 38*l*., is now (including the reserve fund) more than 600*l*., the difference having been made up entirely by appropriations from profits, which, in one instance within the last three years, were 67*l*., and in another 30*l*., in six months. During the twelvemonth ending with June last, however, in consequence of rates having doubled, and the price of raw materials having greatly risen, net profits were only 20*l*.; but more than 300*l*. were distributed as wages among the four members, who alone are regularly engaged in the business, and the three or four extra hands who are occasionally taken on. All those employed, whether members or not, share rateably in proportion to their wages in any surplus profits remaining after payment of interest at five per cent. on capital. What keeps back both hatters and tailors is want of custom, owing probably to the fact of their existence not being sufficiently known, but, as was observed to us by the foreman hatter,—a man evidently of no ordinary intelligence—they are well content to bide their time, in full assurance that what they require, though slow in coming, will come at last. If all the members of the Manchester co-operative stores would resolve to get their hats and coats from their brother co-operators in Bridge-street, the twin establishments then would soon assume an appearance which, besides being satisfactory in itself, might have an excellent effect in encouraging, by its example, the growth of the higher branch of co-operation.

No more encouraging example, if it had but lasted, could be desired than that which was for a time afforded by the Rochdale co-operative cotton manufacturers. This society, one of the colonies thrown off by the Equitable Pioneers, started in 1854, with funds too limited to allow of their hiring more than a single room, in which of course mechanical appliances could be only very partially used. An incentive was, however, applied to labour which more than made up for the deficiency of material aids. The operatives were given to understand that from the net profits realized, interest at five per cent. should first be paid on capital, and that the remainder should be divided rateably between capital and labour, the portion assigned to the latter being distributed among the workpeople in proportion to the wages they had severally earned. They consequently set to work with a will only to be expected from men working for themselves, and the interest they took in their business and the skill and care displayed by them, produced in the very first season an abundant net return. This attracted many new members, by whose subscriptions the capital was raised to 5000*l*. Part of an old mill was then hired and stocked with looms, and by the end of another year or two the accession of fresh subscribers and the accumulation of profits were such as to enable the society to purchase a site for a new mill, and to place upon it, at a cost of 50,000*l*., a factory better built, better looking, and better arranged than any other in the town, and fitted up with steam-engines of 120-horse power, and with other machinery of the very best description. The co-operators were their own architects, purchased all the materials, and contracted for the building at so much a foot, and paid for everything in cash. Here, before the American civil war broke out, 800 operatives were employed, making, as we were informed on the spot, a profit of at least twenty per cent. per annum, nor has the mill ever since been closed, even when the dearth of cotton was most severe. It was the last in Rochdale to resort to half-time, and the first to return to full time, and when we went over it a few months ago, we found all hands completely occupied, though no longer on the same system, nor with such results as formerly.

It is strange that anything should have induced the shareholders to swerve from the course taken by them when they first set out, after it had so clearly proved itself to be the right one. A majority of them, however, after a while began to regard the extra payments made to the operatives under the name of bonuses on wages as a needless waste of money. They did not perceive that the fund from which those extra payments had been made would not have existed but for the extra efficiency to which industry had been stimulated by the prospect of obtaining them, and that the same fund, beside providing for the bonuses, provided also a surplus wherewith to swell the dividends on capital. It need not be supposed that it was mere greed of gain which blinded them to these considerations. The explanation given to us by some members of the dissentient minority was that the society were injured by excess of prosperity. The large profits made by them at first attracted an accession of capital for which profitable employment could not immediately be found, but which nevertheless became entitled to a share of the profit produced by funds more advantageously invested. The consequence was a decrease in the rate of dividend, which it was hoped might be obviated by dividing only among shareholders. We are further inclined to think, however, that the shareholders having begun by being too liberal, afterwards rushed into the opposite extreme. They had committed a mistake in deducting only interest at five per cent. before sharing profits with their workpeople. Their object in entering into business may be presumed to have been to obtain the ordinary rate of profit, and supposing that ordinary rate to be ten per cent., they might in justice to themselves have begun by deducting that percentage. Unless co-operation could secure to them so much, there was little use in their becoming co-operators. As to any surplus, however, beyond ten per cent., it was clearly for their interest to agree that a considerable part, or even if needs were, the whole should be distributed as bonuses among the mill hands, who without some such incentive could not be expected to exhibit the extra diligence and attention requisite to counterbalance the inherent defects of a joint-stock manufacturing company, and to enable it to make even the ordinary rate of profit. But other counsels prevailed. After a somewhat prolonged struggle with a more far-seeing minority, a resolution that thenceforward all profits should belong exclusively to capital, was carried by a sufficient majority of votes. By this enactment the society ceased to be co-operative except in name. It has now descended to the condition of an ordinary joint-stock company, and is as such endeavouring, with what result remains to be seen, to carry on a branch of business for which such a company is peculiarly unfit.

If this narrative suffices, as we think it does, to show that the co-operative principle is intrinsically sound and full of vigour, it must be admitted to show also that there are some serious obstacles to the proper application of the principle. It is to be hoped that the Rochdale Manufacturing Society may ere long discover that they have been killing the goose for the sake of the golden eggs, and may set about hatching a new bird before it is too late; but even though the expediency of sharing profits with labourers were admitted in the abstract, there would still be great difficulty in determining to what extent the participation should be carried. If, indeed, all the shareholders and none others were employed as workers, there would be no difficulty in the matter. If ten per cent., or whatever else were the ordinary rate of profit, were first deducted from the net returns, and the remainder were divided rateably among the members in proportion to their several earnings, there could be little room for dissatisfaction. Capital, having received its established due, would then be less disposed to grudge to labour extra recompense for extra service, and capitalists and labourers, being the same individuals, would perceive that whatever were sacrificed by them in the one capacity might be recovered in the other. But of the supposed conditions one could not be enforced at all, nor the other without materially contracting the scope and usefulness of the undertaking. The funds of an association of working men cannot possibly at the outset be sufficient to afford full occupation to all the members; yet provided individual members be permitted to increase their investments *ad libitum*, the capital may eventually become so large as to require for its profitable employment many more hands than the association can supply, and if non-members cannot then be taken on, part of the capital must remain idle, and the extension of business must be arrested. Since then it is practically impossible that in a flourishing society the two bodies of employers and employed should continue identical, a partition of profits between the two will seem to require some sacrifice from the former, and to demonstrate to their satisfaction how much the sacrifice should be must always be a matter of some difficulty. The question, however, would be greatly simplified if profit on capital at the ordinary rate were deducted before the partition was made, for the owners of the capital would then have obtained that for which they entered into business, and that, too, which they probably could not have obtained without offering some extraordinary encouragement to the workpeople. To ensure a continuance of profit at the ordinary rate, it would evidently, if necessary, be well worth their while to make over to the workers all profits in excess of the ordinary rate. Whether it would be necessary to give up so much would depend upon the amount of the surplus, and on whether less than the whole might not serve as a sufficient stimulus to industry; but these are points which would vary with circumstances, and would require corresponding changes of arrangements. There need be no fear that means of making liberal arrangements would often be wanting. We have before us a paper, prepared with much care, by Mr. Max Kyllmann, a German gentleman resident at Manchester, who has made co-operative societies his study, and is intimately acquainted with their working both here and abroad. It exhibits in a tabular form a number of interesting particulars relative to fourteen "associations ouvrières" of Paris. Most of these have been several years in existence, one dating from 1834, and all the rest, except one founded in 1858, having been established in or before 1850. Their occupations are severally those of jewellers, chair makers, masons, tanners, turners, filemakers, last makers, spectacle makers, locksmiths, carriage-frame makers, and house painters. At the end of 1862 the total number of members was 340, and the number of hired workmen employed by and working with them 618. In eight of the fourteen societies wages are paid by the piece : in the others by the day according to capacity, the earnings of individuals ranging apparently from 48*l.* or 50*l.* to 60*l.* per annum. In all, in addition to wages, the workmen get a larger or smaller share of the profits. In some cases all the profits are divided amongst them in the ratio of their wages, and in others three-sevenths or six or nine-tenths are similarly distributed. Three societies divide equally among the workers without reference to wages ; one divides in proportion to capital and wages added together ; and one, in which none but members are employed, on capital only. The aggregate amount of capital of all the fourteen is 36,122*l.*, with which the amount of business done in the last year recorded was 106,678*l.*, and on which the profit realized during the same period was 8298*l.*; or very nearly 23 per cent. If from this last amount 3612*l.* had been taken as profit at ten per cent. on share capital, there would still have remained 4686*l.* available for distribution among labourers. With funds like these at their disposal, there would be little hesitation on the part of co-operative societies in granting corresponding bonuses on wages if the theory of co-operation were generally understood by co-operators themselves. The latter may be pretty sure that whatever profits are realized by them in excess of the ordinary rate are mainly due to the extra efficiency to which labour has been stimulated by the prospect of extra remuneration. They can well afford, therefore, to expend a considerable portion of their extra profits in maintaining unabated the extra care and industry that have created them.

But it is not only by shortsighted parsimony on the part of the owners of capital that the progress of co-operation may be impeded. Other obstructions may be apprehended from jealousies and dissensions among the workpeople, causes for which may easily arise. By what method, for instance, can the proportion of profits assigned to labour be so divided that no one shall receive either more or less than his due? Apparently, the fairest plan would be the one actually in use., viz., that of dividing in the ratio of wages; but may not this tend to aggravate the discontent natural to those in receipt of the lower rates of wages? Hired servants of a master, supreme within his own sphere, must accept, without murmuring, the tasks he assigns to them, for they can scarcely dispute his right to judge for himself how his work shall be distributed. But members of an association which all have joined on equal terms, may not be so submissive to the decrees of one of their own peers, and will be very apt to accuse the manager of favouritism, and to take themselves off in disgust, if a worse-paid description of work be allotted to them than to others whom they consider no abler than themselves. Possibly, there may always be some little risk of this kind, but there are two reasons why there is never likely to be much. For, firstly, as the manager's incomings, like those of every other member, depend upon the productiveness of the labour under his direction, he is interested in selecting for every man the kind of work for which that man is best fitted; and, secondly, the members collectively are interested in seeing that he does so. In general, he will honestly try to put the right men in the right places, and if, by mistake or otherwise, he should fail in this part of his duty, the parties aggrieved will certainly not fail to appeal to their fellows, who, being well acquainted with each other's characters and abilities, will be able to decide at once whether any one has been unjustly treated, and if so, will, for their own sakes as well as his, insist on his having redress. If, on the other hand, a complainant cannot persuade his companions to accept his estimate of himself, he may be induced to suspect that he has overrated his value, and to acquiesce in a sentence confirmed by the general voice.

Still, it must be owned that, to be able to submit in this manner implies a strong sense of the necessity for subordination, and, in truth, there can be no hope of permanence for co-operative associations without the exhibition, by the members generally, of an amount of submission and modesty in self-assertion, as well as of rectitude and zeal, which, it has been objected, "although "not, perhaps, rarer among the working classes than among "other ranks, is rare everywhere."* To us, however, the very fact that co-operative societies cannot endure, except on this condition, instead of an objection, appears to be a special recommendation—instead of a cause of weakness, we regard it as a source of strength. For the law concerning the adaptation of supply to demand holds good in morals as well as in economics, to this extent, at least, that when an object, which large bodies of men have greatly at heart, cannot be accomplished without the presence of certain virtues, those virtues will generally be forthcoming. If there is honour even among thieves, because, unless rogues were true to each other, there could be little successful roguery, there will surely be no lack among co-operators of the loyalty and mutual faith, without which the ends of co-operation cannot be attained. If, indeed, co-operation preached a doctrine of extraordinary self-devotion ; if its votaries were required habitually to forego their own wants and wishes for the general good, some radical change in human nature might also be requisite to allow of its continuing long in vogue. But its precepts are really no such self-denying ordinances. For every sacrifice exacted by it, abundant requital is promised. If co-operators are exhorted to exercise patience and diligence, to subordinate their separate opinions to the general will, and to do their duty in the stations allotted to them, the inducement held out to each individual is not so much the good of others in common with himself, as his own exclusive advantage. His indolence and negligence might scarcely, of themselves, very perceptibly affect the association's aggregate gains, but they may very materially diminish his share of them, for every man's share is in proportion to the wages he receives ; and in a society in which every man's eye is upon every man, all work must partake of the nature of piece-work, and no one would be permitted to continue in the receipt of wages which he was seen not to be fairly earning.

As then co-operators have a direct interest in showing themselves modest, just, and honest in their dealings with each other, and as, indeed, they can scarcely continue co-operators except upon that condition, it may be hoped that they will, by dint of practice, if not otherwise, acquire habits of the virtues so essential to their existence ; and virtue can scarcely have a better foster-mother than habit. Moreover, whatever vice is found to be inconsistent with the well-being of any community is sure to be

* "Essays on Political and Social Science." By W. R. Greg. Vol. i. p. 578.

held by it in peculiar detestation, while the opposite excellence is held in corresponding honour, and the feelings thus engendered will not be confined to the intercourse of members with each other, but will affect, likewise, their commerce with the external world. Conscientiousness, then, in the most comprehensive sense of the word, may be expected to obtain a high place in the estimation of co-operators, while unconscionableness of every sort incurs their especial odium. As co-operation spreads, it may be expected to introduce, in continually increasing quantities among the working classes, a moral leaven, which, diffusing itself upward and downward and all around, may ultimately leaven the whole lump. Already the good work has been perceptibly begun by Co-operative Stores, and Co-operative Factories are admirably adapted to further its progress.

But we are anticipating. The subject before us is one in which economical considerations may fairly take precedence even of moral, and we ought perhaps to have begun by inquiring how co-operation can elevate the social position, rather than how it can improve the characters of working men. What the latter are most apt to find fault with in existing social arrangements is, their frequent inability to obtain what they call a fair day's wage for a fair day's work—the excessive difference which, in the division of the produce of labour, is often observable between the shares of the employers and the employed. Their notion of fairness is, no doubt, a little exaggerated ; for, as we have endeavoured to show, it is only in very exceptional circumstances that they fail to obtain in exchange for their labour quite as much as it is commercially worth, and quite as much, therefore, as they are really entitled to. Still, it is not the less to be regretted that they should sometimes be entitled to and should obtain so little ; and the peculiar praise of genuine co-operation is that, so far as it extends, it removes all ground and pretext for dissatisfaction on that score. As a rule, individual co-operators engaged in the service of their association do actually receive for their own use nearly the whole net proceeds of their industry, and, provided they have contributed their full numerical proportion of capital, they may obtain the whole without abatement. Whoever, therefore, can scrape together the sum required to procure him employment by a co-operative working society, may receive in profits and wages together much more than it would otherwise be possible for him to obtain. He will possess, too, a means of profitably employing whatever further sum he may at any time thereafter be able to save, for in the facilities which it affords for that purpose, a co-operative factory has a marked superiority over a co-operative store. The field for investment opened by the latter cannot be much more than commensurate with the demand

for food and other articles by the poorer classes of the neighbourhood; but there are practically no bounds to the extension of
which a co-operative manufacturing business is susceptible.
Provided it can once make good its footing by the side of
individual enterprise, there is no reason why it should ever be
distanced in the race of competition, or should not keep pace with
its rival in every subsequent advance. As population and capital
increase, and as the augmented wants of the one afford additional
scope for the advantageous employment of the other, conglo-
merates, composed of a number of small capitals, will be quite as
well able to avail themselves of the new opportunities as masses
of more uniform consistence. Any one who can carry to a
co-operative factory funds sufficient for the occupation of one
additional labourer, may, if he pleases, become a full participator
in co-operative advantages, and these are so inviting that even
the best paid servants of individual masters may think that they
would gain by taking corresponding service under a co-operative
society, and may only consent to remain where they are until
they have saved money enough to enable them to make the
change. Thus the workshops and factories of individual proprietors might become, as it were, preparatory schools for candidates seeking to qualify themselves for better occupation elsewhere,
unless, indeed, individual employers, in order to prevent the
desertion of their best men, should so far adopt the co-operative
principle as to agree to distribute among their workpeople a
certain proportion of all profit in excess of a certain rate. This
experiment has been tried with notable results in the well-known
case of M. Leclaire, the house painter of Paris, whose workmen
appear, on an average, to have received, in consequence, about
12*l.* yearly per head in addition to wages, but whose willing
testimony we nevertheless have that, whereas previously to adopting the system of participation, he could never get out of his
men more than two-thirds of the work they were capable of, the subsequent increase in the produce of their labour more than made
up to him for the extra recompense he allowed them. If M.
Leclaire's example should ever be generally imitated—if the
success of co-operation within its own more immediate sphere
should ever be so complete as to lead to this further modification of the mutual relations of employers and employed, a new
era will have commenced, in which, to use the words of Mr. Mill,
will be effected the " nearest approach to social justice, and
the most beneficial ordering of industrial affairs for the general
good which it is possible to foresee." An alliance on something
like equal terms will then everywhere exist between labour and
capital. A certain proportion of labourers will be their own
masters, occupying a position to which the rest may look up with

hope, while the larger proportion, who will doubtless always be found in the service of others, instead of regarding their employers as natural antagonists, will be united with them in a common cause by identity of interest. Masters, as well as men, would find their account in such a state of things. Even pecuniarily they would derive some gain, since as analogous experience shows, the increased amount and value of the work done for them would more than compensate for the increased price paid for it; but a gain which the better class of masters would more highly appreciate would be the improvement of feeling between themselves and their men—an improvement, too, arising from a cause which would render strikes almost impossible.

To the labourers the most palpable advantage would be the general augmentation of their earnings. But whence, it may be asked, could this augmentation be derived? How can those who have the disposal of the wages fund give out of it to some persons more than before, without being obliged to give less to others? By what possible means can the average of wages be raised above the point determined by the ratio between population and capital? The best answer to these questions will be a simple restatement of the first postulate of co-operation—viz., that labour may be stimulated to increased efficiency by the prospect of a proportionate reward. Co-operators are warned beforehand that if they desire to obtain bonuses in addition to ordinary wages, they must make an addition to the previous wages fund. If this be duly considered, it will be seen that there is no ground for the apprehension expressed by Mr. Plummer, that the more the number of co-operative manufacturing associations increases, the greater will be the competition between them, and the more severely will the system of bonuses increase the cost of production.[*] Associations founded on the true co-operative principle cannot give bonuses to labour except from a fund created by the extra exertions of the labourers. Their undue multiplication, therefore, would have the effect of diminishing—not of increasing—the rate of bonus, and thus the evil would correct itself.

On the truth or fallacy of the postulate just referred to mainly depends the future of co-operation. If this fundamental proposition be unsound, the whole theory must fall to the ground. If, on the other hand, it be just, there are no obstacles to the fullest realization of the brilliant anticipations founded upon it which need be regarded as insuperable, none which the growth of good feeling and intelligence among the working classes may not eventually overcome. But not the smallest among the many merits of industrial associations is their value as educational agents, and

---

[*] " Companion to the Almanac for 1862," pp. 78, 79.

the more they are examined under that aspect, the better fitted will they appear to promote that very progress, moral and intellectual, which, always on the supposition that their basis is sound, is the one other thing needful for their indefinite development.

In our account of the Equitable Pioneers, mention was made of a separate fund, consisting of two and a half per cent. of the entire net profits. This money is appropriated chiefly to the maintenance of a library and a reading-room in the upper story of the society's principal warehouse, the one containing about six thousand volumes in all departments of literature, and also a pair of large globes and a telescope and microscope, and the other kept constantly supplied with metropolitan and provincial newspapers, and with most of the best magazines and reviews. Here may frequently be seen as many as fifty readers at a time chuckling over Thackeray or Dickens, musing over Wordsworth or Tennyson, intent on the glowing pictures of Macaulay or the quaint fascinations of Carlyle, or deep in the study of "Some of the Applications of Political Economy to Social Philosophy" of John Stuart Mill and his disciples. Here, too, the members are in the habit of congregating after working hours for friendly chat, and here are still held some of their more formal meetings, although, when a general assembly is convened, the Public Hall of Rochdale is now usually hired for the occasion, no one of the Society's own apartments any longer sufficing for a constituency increased in number to between three and four thousand. At these gatherings it is ordained, in the words of a memorable and time-honoured resolution, that "every member shall have full liberty to speak his sentiments on all subjects, if brought forward at a proper time and in a proper manner," all subjects being further declared to be "legitimate when properly proposed." Accordingly, whatever is uppermost in men's thoughts is freely brought forward, and specially the state and prospects of their own affairs, questions connected with the past and future management of which often give rise to animated, though never to acrimonious debate. Observations and reflections are compared, lessons learnt from books are illustrated and tested by the results of experience, and opiniative angularities and crudities are rubbed and moulded into shape by mutual friction. There used to be also, and, we believe, is still, an annual dinner, and there are occasional tea-parties, at which temperate feasting is combined with reasoning, and flowing cups help to open the heart as well as to invigorate the brain. Nor are these usages confined to Rochdale. Industrial Associations all over the kingdom, taking pattern from the Pioneers, hold deliberative and legislative assemblies, and, as soon as they can

afford it, establish libraries and reading-rooms, and indulge in
modest periodical festivities. How much all this tends to cherish
good fellowship and to elicit public spirit may be estimated from
the fact that, although the Rochdale pioneers have always had
arbitrators appointed to settle disputes between members, no
single case has ever, in the course of twenty years, been brought
before their tribunal ; and whoever wishes to know how much it
has tended, also, to diffuse juster views on those speculative
points on which the working classes are most liable to error,
cannot do better than look into some of the more recent numbers
of the " Co-operator," a penny monthly paper, designed to record
and promote the progress of Industrial Associations, and of which
the contents are, for the most part, contributions by working men.
Perfect freedom of discussion is permitted in its pages, in which
many sufficiently wild doctrines have at times been broached;
but if the manifesto of the Trades' Unionist, or even of the
Communist—

> of him who has yearnings
> For equal division of unequal earnings,

may be found there occasionally, there, too, close beside, or
following hard upon, will commonly be seen a well-considered
counter argument, calmly and judiciously discriminating between
the natural rights of labour and its not unnatural cravings.
The temper in which this and cognate subjects are now discussed
by the literary representatives of the élite of the industrial community, indicates a very remarkable advance on the part of a
large section of the latter in that department of political science
with which they and their brethren are most immediately concerned. The lessons they have learnt are all the more deeply
impressed for having been, to a great extent, self-taught. Personal experience has been their best instructor. Having themselves become capitalists, and having set up in business, though
but in a fractional capacity, for themselves, they have not failed
to discover that capital has its rights as well as its duties ; that
the rate of wages cannot be arbitrarily settled in conformity with
any abstract notions of the fitness of things ; and that as hands
are of little use without heads, the few by whom manual operations are directed may possibly be entitled to a higher rate of
remuneration than the many by whom they are actually performed.
    If our deduction from these data be just, most of the ninety
thousand persons who, according to the last return, are at present
partners in Associative Stores, may be assumed to be receiving
the practical training requisite to qualify them to take a new step
in social dynamics, and to advance from the comparative
quiescence of simple Association to the earnest activity of genuine

Co-operation. In proportion as they become qualified, many of them will doubtless enter upon a course holding out so fair a prospect of extraordinary advantage. Many formidable obstacles will be met with on the way, and probably, too, many disheartening disappointments and temporary failures ; but if, as we have endeavoured, and we trust not altogether unsuccessfully, to prove, the co-operative principle be intrinsically sound, it will not lead its persevering followers finally astray. Well-wishers of the working classes must, however, be content to leave them to apply the principle in their own way. It is because, in the matter of association, they have hitherto been left pretty much to themselves, that they have already done so well. It was because they expected no help from others, that they were led to help themselves, and that the self-control and force of character were developed in them, without which it would have been impossible for them to reach or to maintain a position of independence. What has happened once will, in corresponding circumstances, happen again. The same necessity which has already called forth to a certain extent the moral prerequisites of successful co-operation, will, no doubt, as demand for them increases, cause them to be supplied in increasing quantities. Nor for those prerequisites can any extraneous substitute be found. If the condition of working men is to be generally and permanently raised, they must themselves provide the means of their own elevation. The utmost that the Legislature or any other outsiders can do to assist them is to remove from their path any artificial barrier which bad legislation may have placed there, and to offer, as we have ventured to do, a few hints as to precautions to be taken, and dangers to be avoided.

Our object has been less to sketch the history than to exhibit the principles of co-operation, and for such statements of facts as appeared necessary to illustrate our views, we have generally preferred drawing on English experience. We should have been glad, however, if space had permitted, to give some account of the remarkable progress which co-operation has made and is making in Germany under the able guidance of M. Schulze-Delitzch. A report on the subject by Professor Huber of Berlin will be found in the Social Science Papers of 1862, and another very interesting paper regarding it, by Mr. Kyllmann, was read at the recent Social Science Congress at Edinburgh.

Art. III.—The Abolition of Religious Tests.

A Plea for the Abolition of Tests in the University of Oxford.
By Goldwin Smith.   Oxford: 1864.

WE shall make no apology for shortly discussing the advisability of removing those religious tests at Oxford which virtually exclude all but members of the Church of England from the full enjoyment of the many privileges of the University. The subject is becoming one of national importance, and will doubtless, before long, attract to itself a considerable share of national attention. The mere abolition of tests no doubt only forms a part—not, perhaps, the most essential part—of a much larger measure of academical reform, the outlines of which are already rising into view.* But, besides the fact that no large measure of reform can be conceived at all without the abolition of tests as an integral part of it, there is this further difference between the part and the whole, that a general reform cannot be expected to come without a long, ample, perhaps tedious, discussion of rival schemes—a protracted, painful inquiry as to the feasibility of various methods—for reform means here reconstruction in great part—with the difficulties of the whole subject aggravated tenfold by the heats of party and religious animosity. Now the abolition of tests is simply a measure of relief. It is only unloosing a galling chain. This ground alone would determine us to limit ourselves to the smaller inquiry.

The law at present requires that all persons proceeding to the degree of Master of Arts shall subscribe to the Thirty-nine

---

* With reference to University Reform, we cannot help calling attention to an able letter which appeared in the *Spectator*, Feb. 6, signed "Academicus." The writer considers that the evils of the present system may be divided under three heads—College Monopoly, Religious Monopoly, and the practical Monopoly of Classical Studies, inasmuch as they receive an altogether disproportionate share of the student's attention. These monopolies well abolished, he "would increase the influence of the University, and diminish that of the Colleges;" he would create a sub-professoriate of able men, who, by reason of adequate remuneration, with no restriction as regards marriage, would select the University, and public instruction in it, as their sphere for life. The sinecure Headships at present absorb 30,000*l.* a-year. These "Academicus" would abolish, and apply the funds to some useful purpose, *e.g.*, endowing the sub-professorships.

Articles, and the Three Articles of the Thirty-Sixth Canon. The test is usually offered in the following form :—

" I do willingly and from my heart subscribe to the Thirty-nine Articles of Religion of the United Church of England and Ireland, and to the Three Articles of the Thirty-sixth Canon, and to all things that are contained in them."

The Three Articles of the Thirty-sixth Canon are—

" 1. That the Queen's Majesty, under God, is the only Supreme Governor of this Realm, and of all other Her Highness's dominions and countries, as well in all spiritual or ecclesiastical things or causes as temporal : and that no foreign prince, prelate, state, or potentate hath, or ought to have, any jurisdiction, power, superiority, pre-eminence, or authority, ecclesiastical or spiritual, within Her Majesty's said realms, dominions, and countries.

" 2. That the Book of Common Prayer and of ordering of Bishops, Priests, and Deacons, containeth in it nothing contrary to the Word of God, and that it may lawfully so be used, and that he himself will use the form in the said book prescribed in public prayer and adminis-tration of the Sacraments, and none other.

" 3. That he alloweth the book of Articles of Religion agreed upon by the Archbishops and Bishops of both Provinces and the whole Clergy in the Convocation holden at London, in the year of our Lord 1562, and that he acknowledgeth all and every the Articles therein contained, being in number Thirty-nine, besides the ratification, to be agreeable to the Word of God."

If any man, from conscientious grounds, refuse to take this test, the consequences are as follows :—

1. He cannot hold a Fellowship.

2. He is excluded from Convocation, that is, the governing body of the University.

3. He cannot open a private hall for the reception of students.

Against a system that inflicts these disabilities for conscience' sake, its opponents allege that—

1. It is immoral.

2. It is useless.

3. It is injurious to the University and to the country at large.

It is immoral, because it tempts men, by the offer of worldly advantage—*e.g.*, Fellowships, Headships—to neglect or stifle the voice of conscience. It is useless, because it has utterly failed in the effect it was intended to produce—viz., unanimity. Unanimity in the Church or the University is not nearer, but farther off than ever it was, after three hundred years of tests. It is injurious, because it excludes conscientious Dissenters from the University; but admits them if they be not conscientious. It excludes the thoughtful and scrupulous, if they do not happen to think the Articles and Prayer-Book the perfection of truth and wisdom; but it admits the careless and lax, even though they never thought about them at all.

Such are the evils—most inadequately here set forth—which attend the infliction of these tests on persons taking the degree of M.A. They afflict individuals, and they injure the University; and even then they do not effect what their contrivers intended —viz., unanimity in religious faith. But their sinister influence does not stop even here. They are the means—the visible, the tangible means—by which Oxford is kept in a perpetual state of bitterness and strife. They are at once fuel and bellows to the *odium Theologicum.* They are the armoury from which either of the two great parties in the Church takes its missiles wherewith to assail opponents. Each party in turn has the dismal glee of placing its adversaries on this Procrustean bed and of admiringly contemplating their agonies. It would almost seem that the pleasure of vexing enemies were more than an equivalent for personal sufferings. During the controversy of the "Tracts for the Times," the High Churchman was on the orthodox gridiron. Carefully and tenderly was he turned on the heated bars, till in several instances he could endure it no longer, and preferred to jump right into the fire of Popery. But during the Gorham controversy his sufferings were avenged, or, rather, his compensating joys had come; and it was not his fault if his Low Church tormentor did not get a new insight into the value of "the Formularies." And now these secular foes, scathed and scored as they are by reciprocal injuries, have coalesced with spasmodic energy to thrust their Broad Church brother "into the place of torment." Yet we are told that these are articles of peace. Can any one, not blinded by faction, suppose for a moment that the result is otherwise than most injurious to the interests of true religion and sound learning. It will not do to say that a holy zeal for Divine truth cannot stop to consider the maxims of cold, worldly prudence; that we are told that offences shall come, but woe to them by whom they come. It must be impressed on the puny persecutors of the present age that persecution is nothing unless it be thorough. That to vex, vilify, and irritate opponents will never convert them, will never extinguish them. If you have power to burn the bodies of all whose opinions you dislike, your denunciation of their tenets will doubtlessly have a practical effect of no common kind. If you are able to inflict social ostracism or infamy as a penalty for holding certain views, you will—as, in fact, English society has done till quite lately— suppress at least ostensible opposition to you. But when parties are not unfairly matched, as they have been at Oxford, to keep up a perpetual wrangle without a hope of ultimate success, to continue pelting adversaries with abuse whom you cannot expect to conquer or kill, is not only a most unprofitable waste of time, but is a course tending to nourish and propagate some of the very worst passions in human nature. And for enticing men into this course, and, consequently, for the exhibition of very evil passions, the subscription of tests is not a little, but very greatly to blame.

When the formularies were imposed on the nation by Queen Elizabeth and her Ministers, these tests had a meaning. The object of the Government being Conformity, the tests were one means among many of discovering Nonconformity. When Nonconformity was manifest, the Tudor sovereigns had never any difficulty in knowing what to do with it. Fines, imprisonment, death, were resorted to with unflinching consistency. It was a glorious time, doubtless, for those who happened to be on the right side. But in these modern days tests have lost the sting as of scorpions which once lurked in them. They can only irritate like gnats, or even less noble insects. It is always competent to the opponents of a clerical member of the University suspected of heterodoxy, to call down upon him one, at least, of the plagues of Egypt. Is this such a boon that it cannot be given up? Will the Church really be undone if the power of inflicting minute, but constant pain be abolished? Will the Gospel of Peace perceptibly lose its attractive beauty when a fertile source of ill-will has ceased? Will that "new commandment, to love one another," be more often neglected or infringed when a potent instrument to plague one another shall be broken? Most deliberately, we reply in the negative to these questions.

We would wish to recur for a moment to the three charges stated above as brought against tests. And first, that they are immoral. Professor Goldwin Smith has put the matter with a force and clearness which cannot be excelled. He says :—

"In truth, who can look the present system fairly in the face without seeing at once that it is immoral? A man presents himself to receive the final reward of his industry as a student, a reward in which the friends who have supported him at the University have an interest as well as himself, and the renunciation of which involves not merely the direct loss of the degree or fellowship, but the fatal stamp of social nonconformity and of an eccentric mind. You contemplate the possibility of his being unwilling to subscribe to such a mass of doctrine as the Thirty-nine Articles, either from a doubt as to its being unmixed truth, or simply because he feels it his duty to God to keep his conscience free : otherwise there would be no need of tests at all. Yet you call upon him to subscribe as the condition of his receiving the reward. Do you not hereby wilfully and deliberately tempt him, by the bribe of worldly advantages, and the threat of worldly degradation, to lie

to God and to his own soul ?   Such a system may serve the political
interests of an Establishment, but is it possible that it can serve the
spiritual interests of the Christian Church ?   Can it long stand before
the awakened moral sense of mankind ?   If we were not made callous
by official custom and party casuistry, should we fail to perceive that
no imaginable sin against the God of Truth can be greater or more
deadly than that of deliberately corrupting the spirit of truth in a
young heart ?"

Unless human nature be perfect, the temptation here described
must often take effect and defeat conscience.   The result must
be, both to those who succumb to the temptation and to those
who witness the fall, demoralizing in no slight degree.   At a
critical period of life when the character is forming and acquiring
the mould it will ever afterwards retain, young men see bribes to
slight conscience offered and accepted.   It is of no avail to say
that such as yield to this would yield to any other seduction that
offered, that such a want of principle cannot be guarded against,
that no temptation is intended, and that if young men neglect
the voice of conscience it is very lamentable but cannot be helped.
You have no right to multiply stumbling-blocks for men's
weakness ; you have no right to put a strain on the virtue of men
which you have reason to know will be too much for them, still
less have you a right to do this with young men ; least of all have
you a right to do this with young men committed to you as
teachers and masters.   What would be said of an instructor who
should permit temptations to profligacy or gambling to be constantly and persuasively paraded before the eyes of his pupils ?
Would it be accepted as a sufficient answer for him to say, " Ah !
if they are so weak as to yield to these allurements, they are sure
to fall sooner or later ; such weakness is very deplorable.   It is
as far as possible from my wish.   If my pupils go astray, it grieves
me ; but I cannot help it."   Would he not be told—" It is your
business to see that they do not go astray.   What else are you
there for ?"   But this supposed case does not do justice to the
actual one of the University.   It is Alma Mater herself who is
the seducer ;   it is she who displays the glittering prize of
weakness and sin ; it is she who says to her little ones, " Stick
to conscience, if you are such fools ; but see what I have
got for you if you have too much sense to strain at a gnat or
two."

It is certainly a fact worthy of notice, that hundreds of
honourable, worthy men are now ready to take tests and
subscribe to Articles in which their belief is infinitesimally
small.   Had the same tests been offered to their fathers a couple
of hundred years ago, most assuredly they would rather have walked
to the stake or the gibbet than take them if they had believed

them as little as many do now. Why is this? Are modern men unblushing perjurers as compared with their ancestors? We do not think that is the explanation. The matter stands thus, we apprehend. These tests, these barriers, these drawbridges, to stop and challenge men on life's journey, are only respected and taken into account when all agree to consider them of importance —when the ideas and doctrines contained in them are the subjects of enthusiastic hatred or veneration. It is evident to all that these ideas and doctrines have lost not a little of their importance with the world at large, whether as objects of love or hatred. Those who believe them do not assert them as their fathers once did ; those who do not believe them are apt to forget almost their existence. Still, they are there—the old toll-gate is still on the highway—still has to be passed through, if you do not wish to strike across country. But the world is less particular than it used to be, or rather, is particular on different points. Going through the gate does not mean what it once did. See, hundreds are going through, and they hardly seem aware of it. But what use is the toll-gate then? It is difficult to say.

That these reflections are constantly made is manifest. Dean Stanley says, "The subscription required is probably not construed literally by any single person who makes or receives it. A large number of those who make it look upon it as an act of humiliation, only to be justified by what they regard as sophistical casuistry. If it does not exclude more, this is because it is regarded as a mere form which ought not to exclude any one."* This is a true statement, beyond all question. During the long lethargy of the national mind with regard to religion and philosophy, such a state of things could easily exist. But is it so likely to continue, now that the public conscience is beginning to stir itself? Is it not probable men will say, " We refuse to be humiliated ; we will not resort to sophistical casuistry merely to please certain solemn personages, for whom, on the whole, our respect is moderate?" The solemn personages plead their own tender consciences and "the interests of the Church of England" as difficulties. The men of England are likely to hint that the Church of England would be wise not to put herself too much in the way.

As regards the second point, viz., the uselessness of tests, we again quote Professor Goldwin Smith :—

" Is it to secure unanimity of opinion on religious subjects in the Universities that the Legislature imposes these tests ? If so, we have an argument against the continuance of the system, the validity of which statesmen never fail to recognise. Decisive experience

---

* "Letter to the Bishop of London on Subscription," p. 30.

has shown that it entirely fails to secure the object for which it was instituted. There is not unanimity, but the greatest diversity of opinion, in the Universities ; and this diversity extends, the advocates of the present system themselves being witnesses, not merely to secondary questions, but to the fundamental principles of faith. The division is not kept secret, but is displayed in fierce controversies and mutual persecutions. Nor is it only of to-day or yesterday. It appeared with equal violence in the times when the Arminians, headed by Laud, were contending with the Puritans for the possession of Oxford. It has appeared alike at every period when intellect has been active and conscience has been awake. It has slumbered only in seasons when intellectual torpor and spiritual indifference prevailed in the University, in the Church, and in the nation at large."

The third charge in this indictment against tests, the injury they cause to the University and nation at large, Professor Goldwin Smith has treated positively rather than negatively ; he has preferred dwelling on the reasons which counsel, and the benefit which would accrue from, the opening of the University to Nonconformists, to a simple critique of the evils of the present system. And doubtless he has chosen the higher and more philosophic course. Gladly would we give a notion of his broad and comprehensive argument. We have space for only a most meagre outline. He addresses himself particularly to establishing the following points :—

Firstly, that the modern maintainers of tests stand in a very different position from the original imposers of them. Queen Elizabeth and her ministers really hoped to get the better of Nonconformity. They did not regard it as a permanent social element, which must be endured as it could not be cured. They considered it rather in the light of a very deplorable but still a transitory phenomenon, which a judicious state-craft would be able to remedy. It is well known that the Reformed churches adopted liberty of conscience in practice, but spurned it in theory. They were at liberty to revolt from Rome, but no one was at liberty to revolt from them. The Church of England carried this inconsistency to greater lengths than any of her sisters, simply because she was more powerful than any of them. Her union with the State doubled the evil, and religious bigotry gave a welcome hand to political despotism. Nonconformity was made a sin before God and a crime against the king, which must be rooted out. With light hearts and serene consciences, the bishops and politicians of that day proceeded to their work, full of hope as to the result. Fines and thumbscrews, the pillory and the dungeon were the arguments on which they relied, for it was absolutely necessary that England should conform ; frightful evils would overtake her if she did not. God's wrath would be kindled against her, if men prayed to Him otherwise than was ordered by Act of Parliament. Marvellous delusion! comparable in magnitude to any in the history of man. But deluded and benighted as were the Tudor and Stuart statesmen in this particular, they had the excuse that they had no doubt, sooner or later, of carrying their point. A little more "rigour" they thought would be sure to give them what they wanted. A little more rigour was granted them, and they, instead of their victims, mounted the scaffold. From that time it became clear to discerning men that the Nonconformist difficulty was not to be settled in that way.

The long period of toleration which followed was essentially one of passive persecution. It treated the Nonconformist, as Professor Goldwin Smith says, half as a criminal and half as a citizen. It was a toleration founded not on principle, but on compromise, doubtless a great boon in its day; but the question is, whether its day be not past. Has any one reason to be satisfied with it? Has Nonconformity been extinguished by it? Will it be? Has religious equality still to plead for itself at the bar of public opinion? We cannot avail ourselves of the excuse which, to some extent, may be allowed to the Tudor legislators. We know the results of attempting to coerce men for religious opinions, results which have recurred not here only, but wherever the attempt has been vigorously made. We know what half ruined France, and what precipitated Spain from the summit of national glory to the most abject degradation. With these facts before us, we have to deal with Nonconformity as a social fact, now evidently *not* a transitory one. Shall we repeat the past as far as we can? Shall we persecute dissent—or, failing power to persecute, shall we sullenly and spitefully continue to exclude it from those national privileges which are still denied to it? Supposing, for argument's sake, dissent to be an error, shall we make it an angry and venomous error, or shall we allow it to become a harmless and passive one? Shall we, in a word, refuse to be taught by failure, scorn experience, and court fresh disaster, or shall we frankly adopt new methods suited to the new time? Of these alternatives, the maintainers of tests would choose the former; those who seek their abolition would prefer the latter.

Professor Goldwin Smith next combats at considerable length the notion " that the Universities belong not to the Nation but to the Anglican church." He says that this, if not expressly stated, is constantly suggested or implied in the reasonings of the clerical party.

"Legally, the Universities are lay corporations. They are represented by Burgesses in the National Legislature. They are visited by the Crown in the Court of Queen's Bench. Their Chancellors may be, and in modern times always have been, laymen. Holy Orders are not required as a qualification for admission to their governing bodies, or for any office in them, excepting those the holders of which must have taken Theological degrees."—pp. 30, 31.

From history he deduces the same result.   But—

"Even supposing that the Universities were legally and historically the property of the national Church, the property of the national Church, as distinguished from its spiritual organisation and attributes, is the property of the nation ; and the Legislature is not only entitled, but bound to deal with it, and every part of it, for the good of the whole community.   But, if the foregoing view of the facts is correct, no real change of destination is required ; no appropriation having taken place but by accident, and accident that carries with it nothing legally, historically, or morally entitled to any respect whatever."— p. 37.

And, lastly, as to the evils of the present religious monopoly. A large portion of our countrymen is cut off from the benefit of the high education which the University affords.   It cannot be supposed that such deprivation inflicted on a large class is without injurious effects on the body politic. The Dissenters are rich, numerous, and have full political power ; but a mental training proportionate to these has always been denied them.   This policy is essentially a revolutionary policy.   You allow them to thwart you or assist you in making the laws ; but the intellectual preparation to fit them for the task, as far as in you lies, you withhold from them.   You let their votes and voices colour the statute-book ; but you do all you can to prevent their votes and voices from being wise and weighty.   And this you call Conservatism, and the "good old paths."   You will not meet these men at the University, where angles might be rubbed off, mutual esteem acquired, a community of intellectual tastes and habits imparted.   You cannot forget you have to meet them at the hustings and in Parliament, fierce, angry, and prejudiced from mutual estrangement, and from the consciousness of a wrong done and received.   You dislike these men, and dread their hostility to much that you hold dear.   You sometimes dwell complacently on their "narrow bigotry," and impracticable turn of mind.   Do you expect to disarm their hostility by exclusiveness and injustice ?   Do you think their narrowness will be removed by depriving them of classical and philosophical training ?   Do you suppose their crotchets will disappear by compelling them to herd in coteries by themselves, and only to leave them when they come forth to oppose you ?   Is it not one of your arguments for withholding the franchise from the masses, that it is not safe to entrust political power to men intellectually unprepared to use it wisely ?   Is intellectual preparation, then, less necessary to members of Parliament and religious teachers than it is to voters ?

Have you never had reason to think that an able, energetic, but essentially uncultivated ·demagogue may be a dangerous kind of person ? Are fanatical preachers altogether to your liking, or do you think education has no effect on fanaticism ?

" Whatever may be thought by the High Church clergy, to whom the extirpation of Dissent always seems not only desirable but near, a statesman, looking to the fact that the teachers and guides of large masses of the people are, and to all appearances must long continue to be, Nonconformists, will think it an object that those who exercise such an influence in the community should be trained, by a superior education and an enlarged intellectual intercourse, to exercise it, as far as possible, in an enlightened and liberal way. A high Anglican journal, and one not only very able, but very moderate and charitable in its general tone, reviewing the other day a book by an eminent Nonconformist, acknowledged the substantial merits of the work, but concluded by remarking, as a curious fact, that ' no Dissenter could write like a gentleman.' Few things are more irritating than to hear those who maintain an oppressive system in their own interest taunting the oppressed with defects which are the consequences of the oppression. The Irish peasant, to complete ⸱the wretchedness of his lot, is complacently pronounced a being of degraded nature, by those whose ruthless misgovernment and wicked laws have been almost the sole cause of his degradation. The Dissenter is held up to derision for his want of cultivation by those who are all the time engaging the holders of political power by the bribe of Church support, to exclude him, as a social Pariah, from the institutions where alone the highest cultivation can be obtained. The remark, however, though made by those who ought to be somewhat ashamed to make it, is not without foundation. The writings and preachings of the Nonconformists have been the channels of spiritual life to great masses of the English people : they have even been almost the sole support of religion in England at times when, as during a great part of the last century, the Establishment, lethargic from over-endowment, filled with unworthy ministers by family patronage, and enslaved to the purposes of worldly politicians, lay inert and helpless in face of spreading scepticism and dominant vice. But, generally speaking, they unquestionably show, by defects of style which their Anglican critic rather severely describes as an inability to write like a gentleman, and perhaps by some defects deeper than those of style, that the system of academical exclusion has not failed to produce its natural effects ; and that emancipation would be a great and certain benefit to the State, inasmuch as it would be productive of intellectual improvement among a body of men who, as was before said, must be expected long to remain the guides and teachers of a great part of the people."—pp. 40—42.

The concluding portion of Professor Goldwin Smith's pamphlet is devoted to remarks on a question which cannot long be absent from any thoughtful or observing mind at the present day. We mean the prevalence of religious doubt. These remarks are too long to quote, and too good to abridge ; but they are well worth the attentive consideration of any one who takes an interest in by far the most important question of our time.

We do not think this last expression too strong. The crumbling decay and eventual downfall of a wide-spread faith and cultus which have existed for centuries, is not only an important event in the epoch which witnesses it, but is memorable and important to all time. For what does it signify and portend ? Even this—that the world for the time being has lost its loadstar, that the ideals which for ages have borne up the weak and strengthened the strong, have fallen from the empyrean into the mire of earth. Of all that can happen to man and his outward fortunes, what can compare with this silent internal phenomenon ? The ideals turn out to be no ideals ; what were considered fixed stars are found to be Chinese lanterns, with the candle inside very low in the socket ; and this discovery gradually taking place in every mind, in the wise and the foolish, the learned and the simple, till every man can see the doubt and the scorn in his neighbour's eyes. Meanwhile, the streets are full of prophets, each assuring you with vehement affirmation that the new loadstar has been found—has been found, and he has seen it, and would show it you at this very moment, only that the weather is thick and the chimney-pots are in the way. Truly, when creeds get worn out and have to be changed, it is a very serious business to all concerned. Yet it must be gone through with. Man must either advance or retrograde. If he advances, he must accept the difficulties of progress as part of his task, part of his glory, and not fall to whimpering as soon as the road becomes rough and the outlook gloomy. The question which the present age has to decide is this—Is man's moral nature subject to the same law of progress as the rest of his faculties ? Have we reason to suppose that his notions of God, of right, of wrong, of holiness, of sin, form a strange exception to the general rule of his being, and are exempted from those conditions of slow but constant change which influence his other ideas and emotions ? Has man, once for all, been provided in any of the traditional creeds of Christendom with something invariable and indestructible, which no progress can throw out of date, no discovery permanently injure, no change of circumstance render unsuited to society ? These questions are now fairly put before the world, and must be answered one way or the other. They can no longer be evaded and put aside till a more convenient season. They stand in every man's path, and stop his progress till he has given his reply, which sends him to the right or to the left.

On the Continent, as it is well known, these questions are a hundred years old and more ; and among the cultivated classes at least they have been answered in a way which is also well known; but England differs from the Continent in many respects, and in nothing more than in the relation she has hitherto held towards religion. Fifty years after Voltaire had done his best or his worst, English gentlemen, statesmen, and scholars were still Christians as authentic and as believing as St. Louis himself, while the analogous classes on the Continent were—well, it is hard to say what they were, except that they were not Christians. England had become a moral fossil in Europe, and the mixture of wonder and contempt which the vulgar Frenchman or German felt always called upon to manifest with regard to the "hypocrisy" of the English, became quite offensive in certain portions of their literature. It would lead us too far to inquire into the causes of this marked difference between our countrymen and foreigners; but we may say this much, that the immense development of political and commercial activity in this country has contributed not a little to the withdrawal of public attention from high speculative topics of all sorts, religion included. The average Englishman hates first principles as a rule, and is apt to consider pure reason as only a fine name for pure moonshine. Working like a slave in business or the public service, he does not consider that it fell within his province to meddle with the grounds of faith, or to weigh or repel infidel objections. That was work which belonged to bishops and deans, and he was always quite willing to accept the assertion of his friend the clergyman, that all was right; that the objectors were a most shallow set of persons, who had been utterly crushed by the orthodox apologists. Thus infidel opinions, though frequently promulgated by individuals, some of them in the highest ranks of society and literature, never extended to any depth in England. The public mind was at best passive with regard to them, generally hostile. Witness the explosion which greeted Gibbon's first volume. Yet this was at a period when Voltaire and French opinions were supposed to have their greatest vogue here. Time, however, was doing its work. Science was noiselessly undermining the old fabric of Orthodoxy. It began to be known that German commentators were arriving at new and strange results, and a few of the bolder sort among us, not without a certain tremor, read them. Historical criticism was slowly emerging, and gaining disciples; still the champions of orthodoxy were defiant, and full of mettle. They boldly carried the war into the enemy's territory, and laughed pitifully over the "infidel's credulity," for being taken in by such "paltry cavils."

And now it seems as if a great change were at hand. It cannot be said now that sceptical opinions fall inert on the public mind. Rather, they fall like sparks on tinder. They pervade literature and society like an atmosphere or a gas which no doors or windows will exclude. They have reached the Universities; they may even be heard from the pulpit. All men seem to say—"The Old, the solemn, venerable Old, was good, but we must have a New and a better. The old Jewish garments are no longer suited to us; they impede our movements, they half strangle us at our work. We must get them off at all risks."

"No!" say the clergy; "you shall not take them off if we can help it. You shall wear them, and all generations of men till the end of time shall do the same." The present attitude of the clergy is calculated to excite alarm even in the most phlegmatic mind. They seem determined to force on a conflict with the spirit of the age: they seem utterly ignorant of the entire feebleness of their position: they denounce and scold and "rebuke" the world, and do not perceive all the while that the world is only politely and mercifully waiting for them to say something pertinent and to the point, if they have got anything to say. There is absolutely no hostility to them as a body; on the contrary, their social virtues have ensured for them the esteem of all classes. Let them beware how they forfeit that esteem: let them observe and reflect on the position of the priesthood among our French neighbours: let them notice the mixed loathing and contempt in which the *parti prêtre* is universally held. And why? Because that priesthood has for generations placed itself in standing opposition to the intellect of the country. Their influence for good is gone: they can only plot and intrigue, and strike bargains with despots to keep them in their seats, they agreeing to return the favour. Is *that* a position which high-minded clergymen of the English Church admire or envy? Yet can they doubt that they are losing day by day their hold on the intelligent laity? If they do doubt, we, as laymen, and better placed for observation than they are, can tell them it is so; that their proceedings are watched now with a curious interest, soon to be replaced by an angry one. Angry, we say, not because laymen cannot endure difference of opinion from themselves, but because it is only human to be incensed at contemptuous scorn of reason, and vociferous clamour poured forth without pause or modesty in behalf of an evil cause. *Absit omen;* but unless the clergy unexpectedly become wise in their generation to a degree now apparently hopeless, they are preparing for us a Voltairean epoch of persiflage and cynicism; for themselves, isolation and contempt in the midst of a hostile nation.

In truth, the attitude maintained towards science is getting to be hard indeed to bear. Rubrics, Canons, Creeds, these we must revere, these we must accept, or, "without doubt, we shall perish everlastingly." But the laws which the Eternal has given to his creation may or may not be important. If they agree with our rubric, well and good; if they square with our Articles, they are not beneath notice. But if they do not agree—if they suggest doubts as to the rubric !—" Here, then, is the mode of rightly striving against doubt. Treat it as a temptation of the enemy. . . . . Watch against it, work against it, pray against it. . . . . Fling it from you as a loaded shell shot into the fortress of your soul."* *Ipse dixit.* Change, growth, development, may be allowed to pervade the universe of things from insects to solar systems ; the very floor of heaven itself, bright with those serene orbs which give us our deepest and sublimest ideas of infinity and eternity, is moving, is passing away, and shall wax old as doth a garment ; but the notions of a Council, of a Church, the propositions agreed upon after a faction fight at Nicæa, at Chalcedon, the dogmas which arose in the powerful but gloomy mind of Calvin—these, forsooth, are to last for ever ! Louder and louder rises the scream from the clerical party—" The Bible and science can't disagree, shan't disagree. If you say they do, you are a very wicked, most likely a very licentious person." And this is said when the youth of England have before them specimens more than one, of men who do say and think that Genesis and Geology are not in accord, and whose lives are one long anthem in praise of holy simplicity and truth.

Our conclusion, then, is that neither the physical nor moral mechanism of the world is likely to stop at present ; that the stream which has flowed from the great primeval dawn of existence is not probably going to be frozen into an ice-pack of Orthodoxy. We believe that the world is going onward, but not therefore going to perdition. We have all history to lead us to think that such periods of growth as the present are not periods of decrepitude or decay, but turning-points in the history of man, which are looked back to with admiration and thankfulness by succeeding generations ; and in all confidence we expect a future, not darker, but brighter than the past.

---

* Sermons of the Bishop of Oxford. Serm. xiv., " Doubts as to the Revelation."

ART. IV.—THE PREROGATIVE OF PARDON AND THE PUNISHMENT OF DEATH.

1. *Jeremy Bentham, to his Fellow Citizens of France.* On *Death Punishment.* December 17, 1830.
2. *On Capital Punishment for Murder. An Essay.* By Lord HOBART. London: 1861.
3. *Capital Punishment in England viewed as operating in the present day.* By SHELDON AMOS, M.A., Barrister-at-Law. London: 1864.
4. *Suggestions for the Amendment of the Laws of Appeal in Criminal Cases.* By HARRY G. PALMER, Barrister-at-Law. Read before the Law Amendment Society. 1864.

THE history of great rulers teaches us that of the arts of government in which they have excelled, the rarest and most valuable has been that of knowing when they ought to yield. Yet it is scarcely less difficult and important for a free Legislature to be able to see when the time has come for the practical application of reforms whose necessity has been theoretically demonstrated. In this respect it has often been our boast as Englishmen that we have succeeded better than other nations. In aiming at that happy mean between haste and tardiness wherein lies the essence of practical wisdom, we have certainly very seldom erred on the side of precipitancy. We are not apt to be too ready to surrender at the bidding of theorists any of those relics of the past which, in the growth of ages, have become imbedded in the fabric of our institutions. The process of removal of anomalies of this kind has been tolerably uniform. Their existence has first been exposed and condemned by some philosophical thinker, who has pointed out the evil consequences which, sooner or later, must make themselves felt from their maintenance. His conclusions have been gradually accepted by all competent and independent inquirers. Then, when the general intelligence has become thoroughly imbued with the conviction of the theoretical indefensibility of the existing system, there comes some striking example which shows the immediate necessity for reform. The evil now first recognised is no new result. It must often have followed before. Nothing is changed but the aspect in which men view it. The old apologies for its existence having lost their efficacy, and the practical inconvenience being urgent, the advocated change takes place at once, almost without opposition. Men even soon come to wonder how an institution or a system whose foundations are seen to have been so long undermined could have stood so long. Yet the influences by which it was preserved may have been in themselves by no means inconsiderable. Originally framed perhaps to remedy the defects of ancient laws and administration, it was guarded from attack by its traditional association with benefits which it once was the means of conferring. Statesmen, too, in hereditary dislike to innovation, often attempt, with more or less success, to adapt such antique machinery to the altered requirements of modern times. Lastly, the fanciful virtues which had been attributed to it by the panegyrists of the obsolete system to which it belonged still adhere to it in the popular imagination. Thus it comes to pass that those who, in the spirit of practical philosophy, endeavour to bring these virtues to the definite and easy test of general utility are often stigmatized as mere theorists by the very men whose whole defence of the whole system rests upon an imaginary symmetry in its arrangements, which, if it ever was more than an ideal conception of its admirers, has certainly long been marred by the innovations of time.

Of this general description has been the law of progress illustrated by the history of the Crown Prerogative of Pardon, to the nature of which attention has been drawn by recent examples of interference with the extreme sentence of the law. These examples it is not intended to discuss here; but the practical defects of the existing system have by them been brought home to many minds which would never have been affected by any merely theoretical objections. The moment, therefore, is opportune, for examining more fully the anomalies which were long ago pointed out by the theory of scientific jurisprudence, and at the same time for considering whether some remedy cannot be found for them. It is just one hundred years since Beccaria, in his immortal work on " Crimes and Punishments," laid it down as a principle of penal law, that the right of pardon (*i.e.*, of remitting a lawful sentence on a convicted offender) should be regarded as an abuse which would be excluded from a perfect system of justice, where clemency would be the prerogative of the law and not of the magistrate. And the objection to any such arbitrary power of reversing judicial sentences is forcibly put by the founder of the only school of scientific jurisprudence which has existed in this country. " If the laws are too severe," says Bentham, (" Theory of Legislation," P. II., chap. 10), " the power of pardoning is a necessary corrective, but that corrective is itself an evil. Make good laws, and there will be no need for a magic wand which has the power to annul them. If the punishment is necessary, it ought not to be remitted; if it is not necessary, no convict should be sentenced to undergo it."

This argument, which admits of no increase of force by expansion, though it obviously does not apply to pardons granted on account of discovery of the innocence of the convict, yet condemns all others, not only free and unconditional pardons granted by favour of the Crown, but also all extra-judicial commutations of sentences fixed by law.

What is there, then, which can be alleged on the other side of the question?   The most tenable form in which the defenders of the prerogative can put their case is this: human laws are imperfect, and it is therefore necessary to provide some means by which in individual instances their sentences may be reversed when erroneous, commuted when unduly severe, and remitted when their execution would be injurious to the interests of the community.

The apologies for each of the different branches of the prerogative here enumerated rest on distinct grounds.   But by none of them is any excuse suggested for the arbitrary interference of the Sovereign on the ground of pity or favour.   Yet it is in support of this very unconditional mode of exercising the prerogative that the most popular arguments, founded on its antiquity and the lustre which it confers on the Crown, have been repeatedly urged.   Such pleas are evidently purely sentimental, and can have no weight now with the scientific jurist.   Happily, too, the likelihood of the power vested in the Crown being thus abused is at the present day very small; yet they deserve some notice as a curious exemplification of that scholastic and metaphysical habit of thought which naturally pervaded the writings of the feudal jurists, and the influence of which is so plainly traceable in all their successors down to the very recent time when a more rational method was introduced into our study of legal science. And in this particular instance even the sentimental sanction which is given to the prerogative by the idea that its immemorial possession by the Crown has always been undisputed, is by no means warranted by an investigation of the facts.   No one who considers how every crime was regarded by our early criminal law as an offence against the peace of the king, will be surprised that he reserved to himself, in all cases where the inquisition brought offenders to light, the option of abstaining, at his own pleasure, either from the further proceedings against them, or from the execution of the legal sentence pronounced by himself, or the judges who represented him.   But this right did not reside in the Crown alone.   Its origin was clearly seignorial, and long after the criminal procedure had assumed its present form, and a uniform system had been introduced throughout England, we find the right of pardon shared (in theory, at any rate,) by all those vassals of the Crown who, within the limits of their own fiefs, enjoyed sovereign rights either by prescription or grant. Though probably rarely exercised by these inferior lords, it was not till the most absolute period of the monarchy that the right of pardon was declared (by 27 Henry VIII. c. 24) to be vested in the Crown alone. Its exercise indeed by the Sovereign himself appears always to have been looked upon with considerable jealousy by the other branches of the Legislature. For, besides several other statutes limiting it by various conditions, it was enacted in the thirteenth year of Richard II. (by a law soon after repealed, but which is evidence of the temper of Parliament) that it should be a penal offence to solicit pardon from the Crown, and that such pardons should be held null and void without warrant of the Privy Seal. And in the reign of Henry VII. Parliament again petitioned that no pardon might be granted except by advice of the Privy Council. The jealousy thus evinced was no doubt immediately traceable to the fear lest the Sovereign might abuse this prerogative in protection of the favourites or Ministers whom he had employed as instruments of oppression or illegality; but it must have been in some measure founded on the sense of the general insecurity which must be caused by the multiplication of such arbitrary interferences with the course of justice. Indeed, the right was rarely, if ever, exercised by the Crown in favour of offenders convicted of the more heinous descriptions of felony, and Lord Coke expressly says that " he never saw any pardon of murder by express name." It was, however, decided by Chief Justice Holt, in an important case of murder (King *v.* Parsons : 1 Showers, p. 283) that the right of pardoning (there expressly contested) extended to all offences, and was an inseparable incident in the Crown and its royal power ; and that right does not appear to have been since disputed. A considerable change, however, has taken place in the mode of its exercise. Until a recent statute (6th Geo. IV. c. 23) all pardons were granted under the Great Seal, and those given under the Sign-manual were only warrants to the justices to bail the prisoner. Before that Act, the commutation of sentences (then so general in consequence of the growing antagonism between public feeling and the bloody statutes of that age) was almost always ordered, as now, in compliance with the recommendation of the judge presiding at the trial. His recommendation was laid before the Privy Council, and the king in person was in the habit of taking part in the discussions of that body as to the proper objects for mercy. For some time, however, previous to the Act of George IV. the exercise of that prerogative, together with other ministerial functions, had come to be vested almost exclusively in the Secretary of State, and the sanction of the Privy Council was therefore a mere form ; so that the change by which pardons under the Sign-manual have now the legal effect of those under the Great Seal, was one of little practical importance.

From this slight historical sketch it will be seen that the Crown prerogative of pardon, as at present exercised, is, on the score of antiquity and inherence in the Sovereign's person, by no means worthy of the veneration which is sometimes expressed for it. It has not, however, been difficult for the legal theorists, who are such blind apologists of monarchical institutions, to throw a halo of reverence round its other virtues. And not entirely without justice. Doubtless it often has served to mitigate the injustice or harshness of a barbarous code or a rude administration. And "this brightest jewel in a monarch's crown" it was which, more than any other, would become endeared by exercise to the best feelings of his nature, and which secured him most readily the favour of the common people, in ages when the weak had often too much cause to regard the law as an instrument employed by their immediate superiors for oppression or wrong, from which the only refuge lay in the hope of the Sovereign's mercy. But this glory, too, has now departed from the prerogative. It is not the Sovereign, but the Home Secretary, who now pardons. In our days, too, no such false bond of union is needed between Sovereign and people. It is rather as the Fountain of that justice which is the right of all, than as the arbitrary Dispenser of a mercy which none but the vicious ever hope to require, that reverence is now paid to the Supreme Magistrate.

These observations (however self-evident when stated) were not unnecessary, in order to expose the real value of arguments which are still adduced in favour of the existence of a power of unconditional pardon—a power now so rarely exercised, and yet so open to abuse, that its abrogation would be attended with no difficulty whatever.

The three other descriptions of pardon—by reversal on account of error, by remission on account of public convenience, and by commutation on account of undue severity—must be treated separately. Of the first, more will be said presently. The second class of pardons by remission need not detain us long. It is undeniable that instances may occur where this kind of pardon may be advisable on one of two grounds—either from the number of criminals, or from the services which, if spared, they may render by evidence or otherwise. But the cases which could properly come under the first head are so uncommon, and must always be so closely connected with political events properly so called, that it would, generally on other grounds, be desirable to provide for them as they arise, by special legislation, or at any rate by an application for an indemnity on the part of the executive to the Legislature. As to the more normal cases, in which the offer of pardon may be necessary in order to procure the evidence of accomplices, it is not clear why this object cannot be secured (in the few instances in which such an evident failure of justice would be desirable), merely by abstaining from the indictment of the approver. This is, indeed, virtually an exercise of the prerogative of pardon ; but it is one which is shared by every private person who refuses to prosecute for an offence committed against himself.

It is as to the other description of pardon, that in commutation of a sentence, that the warmest controversy has been maintained. The circumstances of individual crimes, and the amount of guilt which they imply, are (it is plausibly argued,) so various, that no legislation can foresee them all. Cases must perpetually be happening in which no hand but that of one who can weigh all the special circumstances can exactly balance the scale of justice. This duty, therefore, must be left to some supreme authority, and none is so proper as the Crown acting by its constitutional advisers. To this reasoning two answers may be given. In the first place, the apologist who is so ready to admit the shortcomings of the law, appears to forget that the Minister who exercises (in this instance alone without any legal or parliamentary responsibility) the delicate function of correcting its sentence, is still more liable to be misled by his own feelings, or the representations of others. And secondly, even if we admit that redress may here or there be thus obtained, yet it must not be forgotten that the benefit of the remedy may be more than counterbalanced, if any appearance of uncertainty is thus given to the operation of the law. For it cannot be too strongly insisted on that the general effect of a penal enactment on the community is always to be considered before the individual interests either of the person injured or of the criminal. This axiom appears self-evident. Yet many of the difficulties with which the late discussions on the subject of punishment have been perplexed owe their origin to its being forgotten. And recent experience has undoubtedly shown that it is impossible for this prerogative of pardon to be exercised, even by the ablest and most conscientious Minister, without sanction being given to some theory in justification or extenuation of the crime, which, if true, should be recognised by the normal action of the law. Thus serious injury is inflicted on Justice in her most vital attribute—her character for certainty. The framers of the Code Pénal attempted to provide for this want of a revising authority by the power given to the jury of finding extenuating circumstances in their verdict. It is very doubtful, however, whether this is a function which it is well to entrust to those who should be judges of the fact rather than interpreters of the law. It is, indeed, open to far less objection than our own system of revision by the Home Secretary would be, if it were in practice what it is in theory—a personal act of clemency on the part of the Sovereign ; for such clemency is, in reality (what Bentham describes it to be), " an act of treason against the community, of which the most pardonable sources are feebleness and folly." But, in fact, the opinion of the judge is generally the chief element in the consideration of each case by the Minister. Why not, then, vest in the person thus confessed to be best qualified to weigh all the circumstances, the only power of commutation which is really necessary ? For the very gravest offences the punishment should be absolutely fixed by the law, and the sentence, once passed, incommutable and irreversible, except by a Court of Appeal. In other cases, the penalties should be as at present, variable within fixed limits at the discretion of the judge. And in order to secure the secondary end of reformation, the sentence of the judge might itself also be variable within fixed limits, according to the industry and conduct of the convict. The minimum of punishment fixed by the sentence should always be irreversible ; but the criminal might by this means still be offered the hope of diminution in that fluctuating margin which would lie between the maximum and the minimum of suffering. Thus, while the full penalty of the law was reserved for the worst and most hardened offenders, no inducement to crime would be offered by the uncertainty which operates so fatally under the present system.

The remaining class of pardons, those exercised in correction of the error of the law, evidently stand on a very different footing from the two others. If, on the grounds here stated, it be thought advisable to supersede in other cases the present power of pardon, it will still be necessary to find some tribunal more appropriate than the Minister's private room in the Home Office for the revision of the only sentences which would still require investigation after the verdict of the jury had been pronounced— those, namely, in which the conviction was bad, either from an error in law or from fresh evidence as to material facts. In the former event, of a conviction bad in law, there are two remedial courses at present open, according to the nature of the error. If a question of law has arisen at the trial as to the legal offence proved by the evidence, or as to the admissibility of the evidence by which the conviction has been procured, the judge has the discretion of reserving the point, which is then decided by the Court for Crown Cases Reserved, who have the power to quash the conviction and discharge the prisoner. If, on the other hand, any substantial informality has taken place in the procedure of the trial, the prisoner has the right of entering it specially on the record of the court, and obtaining a writ of error in the Court of

Queen's Bench. This Court of Error, which can either reverse the sentence or direct a new trial, was established by an Act of this reign (12 Vic. c. 78), and preceded by two proposals of a much more extensive reform; one made by Sir F. Kelly, in 1844, and the other by Mr. Ewart, in 1848. By both of these proposals the right of appeal in criminal cases would have been very nearly assimilated to that in civil suits. By Sir F. Kelly's Bill the appeal to the Superior Courts of Westminster to grant a new trial, either on ground of technical defect or of new material fact, was to be matter of right, and to extend to all offences. The only restriction on it was to be in the discretion of the judge presiding at the trial, who might refuse to allow it when in his opinion the grounds were frivolous or vexatious. But even this restriction was to be removed in the case of capital sentences, in all of which the right of appeal was to be absolute. By both of these measures it would seem that it was contemplated to merge the two modes of reversing a wrong verdict at present existing into one. The Court of Criminal Appeal would assume the functions both of that for Crown Cases Reserved and the Queen's Bench in writs of error; it would either reverse the sentence where the verdict was contrary to law, or direct a new trial where the informality was only unsubstantial or new facts material to the issue were put in evidence. The chief objections urged at that time against these proposals (and which are still advanced against all similar measures), were on the ground of the delay which the appeal would involve, and of the expense entailed by the creation of the new Court of Appeal, to which it was expected that resort would on conviction be the rule rather than the exception. We are now in a position to judge how far these dangers are real. The right of obtaining a writ of error, granted by Lord Campbell's Act, has been fifteen years in existence, and the number of cases brought before the Court of Queen's Bench has never been such as to increase materially the labour of the judges, and it has been very seldom used for merely dilatory purposes. The cause why this Court has not been as much resorted to as was expected, is to be found in the discretionary power reposed in the judge, of refusing the appeal where the point raised is obviously unimportant. By giving him a similar power where the new trial is moved for on the ground of fresh evidence, it would be easy to check the abuse of the privilege of appeal. It would be neither necessary nor desirable to allow the right of appeal in any cases, except where the verdict was either bad in law or insufficient from the absence of material evidence; therefore the objection sometimes made, that the verdict of the second trial would be no more satisfactory than that of the first, has no value whatever. And as little weight is to be attached to the idea that the jury's sense of responsibility would be seriously lessened, since they would know that their decision on the evidence before them was more final than it is now, when liable to be reversed by the Home Office.

There would, indeed, be one class of sentences in which (as long as the punishment of death is retained) it might fairly be expected that every possible device would be exhausted in order to delay execution. But the evil here is in the nature of that punishment, and not in the system of appeal. Expunge that punishment from the Statute-book, and the only valid objection to the establishment of a Court of Criminal Appeal disappears with it. There would be no great inducement, in the case of any other sentence, for any but those who could show a *primâ facie* case for appeal, to submit themselves to a new trial. The objection on the ground of delay has, indeed, most force where the penalty is death. For though the old maxim —" *Nulla unquam de morte hominis cunctatio longa est* "—is a very salutary safeguard against the hasty execution of an irreversible sentence, yet in no case is the benefit (if there be any) of example so completely neutralized by any lengthened interval between the crime and the punishment. On the other hand, where the criminal himself, so long as he survives, is a continual warning of the severity of the penal code, the short delay which would sometimes intervene, in order to give every security to the innocent, would be productive of very little advantage to the guilty, and could not perceptibly diminish the impressiveness of the example of the punishment.

As to the argument that the prosecutor ought to have a right of appeal in cases of wrong acquittals, this is, no doubt, theoretically true, and it would be very desirable to secure this end, if practicable. Though, in fact, the ancient principle that no man should be vexed twice in the same cause, appears to us too deeply rooted in popular feeling to be thus violated. And we ought not to forget that a criminal trial is not a mere litigation between two parties, in which each has a claim to equal advantages ; but a solemn inquiry, only the immediate object of which is the discovery of the guilt or innocence of the accused ; while its final purpose is to secure the life and property of the whole community, of which the accused himself is an integral unit.

If the objections here urged against the prerogative of pardon in all the forms in which it is now exercised are well founded, it would appear unnecessary to examine in detail the vices peculiar to the machinery at present employed in this country. Yet, as such vices undoubtedly do exist, it may not be amiss to enumerate them. First, then, the general defect of uncertainty is here greatly aggravated, as the decision in each particular case brought before the Home Secretary must vary with the temperament or theories of the Minister, the influence of the friends of the convict, or even the accidental direction of public sympathy at the particular moment. The effect of variation in this last particular may be traced in the influence which the fate of the two criminals, Townley and Wright, threatened to exercise (if they did not actually exercise) on each other. Secondly, there appears to be this peculiar disadvantage attached to the pseudo-judicial mode of procedure in the Home Office, which is in one way more injurious to the interests of justice than the merest caprice could be. For where all is known to depend only on the arbitrary will of one man, no precedent, either of undeserved leniency or undue severity, can be established ; whereas, under the existing system, comparison is perpetually made by the public of cases in which different courses have been pursued, while the specific grounds for the difference are unknown to any but the officials immediately concerned. Other objections of a more technical character are summed up in the paper read by Mr. H. Palmer before the Law Amendment Society.

" The Home Office, which was originally only a medium of inquiry for the information of the Sovereign, has now grown into a Court of Review, without rules of procedure or well-defined powers. Its investigations are secret. Statements which would be rejected in a court of justice, on the ground of not being evidence, are received, and no opportunity is afforded to contradict or explain them. The inquiry is conducted by some person or persons who have no public responsibility. It is doubtful whether there is any jurisdiction to administer an oath on making an affidavit to be submitted to the Home Office. False statements may be made, and are in point of fact made, with impunity ; and lastly, the whole investigation is *ex parte*, no notice of the application being ever given to the prosecutor. Statements are frequently sent to the Home Office relating to facts which are alleged to have occurred after the trial, which, if true, seem to change the whole complexion of the case. The truth of such statements is tested in a flimsy and imperfect manner, and yet upon these very statements the deliberate verdict of a jury may be cancelled. Instances have occurred where persons have been in court during a trial who have not ventured to give their evidence, and yet have afterward made affidavits of facts which ought to have been properly inquired into in public court."

The preceding review of the whole question of the prerogative of pardon appears to prove conclusively that, with one important exception, it may, in all the necessary functions which it so inadequately discharges, be satisfactorily replaced by the regular action of the law. That one exception is in its application to the punishment of death. Here it is impossible to deny that the immediate intervention of some supreme authority is often necessary to preserve the law from being the instrument of irreparable injustice. We are therefore forced to inquire,—what is there in that particular form of punishment to recommend its maintenance, in spite of its apparent incompatibility in this respect with the true theory (by which, of course, is only meant the *rationale* of the most beneficial practice) of punishment? There are, no doubt, some who will be ready to maintain that this very incompatibility is conclusive in favour of the prerogative which has been here assailed. According to these reasoners, the punishment of death is so indispensable, and has so great a sanction from usage and authority, that no scheme of justice which dispensed with or repudiated it could be allowed to have anything more than a mere speculative value. However this may be, it is, at all events, consolatory to those who have arrived at an opposite conclusion to remember how confidently the same assertion was repeated, as every fresh attempt was made to modify the Draconian Code which, but a generation ago, prevailed in England. As the event has completely falsified the predictions of the increase of crime which was to follow each successive mitigation of the cruelty of that code, it would be quite useless in this place to recapitulate the progress of public opinion and legislation on the subject of capital punishment in this country and abroad. By a series of reforms, from 1827 to 1841, the law has gradually been brought to the point at which it now stands, at which death is retained as a penalty for murder alone. The honour of having advocated and carried out these changes will always add lustre to the names of Bentham, Romilly, and Mackintosh. Their conclusions were originally founded on experience as well as on reason, and they now command immediate and universal approval as applied to all those crimes which were once punishable with death; and there are probably few, if any, whose opinion deserves the least respect, who would now wish to reimpose that penalty for any of those offences. The arguments on either side must now be confined to the single crime of deliberate and wilful murder.

Though the theological arguments of an Inglis or a Drummond have long ceased to have any authority either in Parliament or out of it, yet, unfortunately, the question is still sometimes encumbered with similar difficulties by the counter-theories of the advocates of the abolition of the punishment of death. It was argued by Beccaria, and has often since been repeated by others, that as no man possesses a right over his own life, and cannot therefore delegate to others a right which he does not possess himself, the State, which exercises its authority only in virtue of such a delegation on the part of individual citizens, cannot have a right to take away life. It is hardly necessary now-a-days to examine very closely this argument. Neither premiss would now pass without question. The fallacy of an original contract on which it is ultimately based has long been exploded, and it is only necessary to observe here that the right which is here denied to the State is really founded not on any surrender of individual rights, but on the principle of the supremacy of the general over particular interests. Indeed, the right (in the only sense of that term admissible in jurisprudence) is already given to the State by the law as it now stands. What the objectors must be understood to mean is, that the act of taking away life is contrary either to divine laws or to general expediency. But it is certainly recognised by the only divine law which is acknowledged by the objector, and to deny it the sanction of general utility is merely to beg the whole question at issue. It appears, therefore, impossible to maintain *à priori*, that the State has not the right to put to death any political offender (such as a pretender or a rebel) whose existence may be dangerous to the public peace or security. At any rate, if this be so, then by parity of reasoning war, which is nothing but the infliction of death in the interest of the community, would be equally indefensible. Happily, however, we may hope that the time for such a necessity in England is gone by never to return. Should it, however, become at any time advisable to inflict the punishment of death for high treason, the plea of the danger of keeping the criminal alive may be admitted in justification of its retention. Is there, however, any other class of crimes for which the same penalty is on the same grounds necessary? Should the murderer be placed in this category? Surely society is quite strong enough to restrain the small number of criminals of this description. There must evidently be other grounds for visiting murder with death. Why, then, has the tide of legislation, which swept away this penalty for all other offences now for twenty-five years, stood still at this point in its beneficent course? To explain this fully it will be necessary to examine the advantages which have been supposed to justify the maintenance of death punishment for this particular offence. If our examination shall show that these advantages are either imaginary or overbalanced by the evils attendant on the practice, nothing but the proposal of a satisfactory substitute will be wanting in order to warrant our pronouncing a sentence of condemnation on the whole system of death-punishment.

Dismissing, then, the theological and metaphysical theories which are urged with equal confidence on either side, we shall find that the best arguments which have been advanced for the retention of death-punishment for murder may be resolved into this: That it is necessary for society to have some punishment more deterrent than any other in reserve for the most dangerous offence; that death is the most deterrent punishment, and murder the most dangerous offence. For if there be any other offence equally dangerous, it ought to be repressed by an equally deterrent punishment, and if there be any other punishment equally deterrent, then it may be substituted for that of death. The tacit assumption implied in this argument, that the chief object of all punishment is to deter, will not here be disputed. But it may be observed, that as the secondary object of punishment cannot be at all served by this particular form of it, there will be the greater necessity that its superiority in the main point should be clearly demonstrated. It has been very forcibly maintained by Beccaria and others that the duration of the suffering inflicted by imprisonment for life more than compensates as to deterrent influences for any deficiency in point of intensity. What is of importance, it is justly urged, is the effect, not on the convict, but on the beholder, whose mind takes in at one glance and as one whole an amount of suffering which is rendered tolerable to the sufferer only by its division into infinitesimal parts. By these thinkers, who do not attempt to disguise the fact that most men while under sentence of death would hail with delight the tidings of its commutation to perpetual imprisonment, it is further observed that this by no means proves that the general deterrent influence of the one punishment would be less than that of the other. The condemned man (say they) alone can adequately realize the terrors of an immediate death, but the prolonged misery of a life imprisonment may be as well, if not better, measured by the imagination of him who is free. Yet, however just this distinction may be, we cannot deny that there exists in the mind of almost every man a fear of death which is all the more felt because it is in most cases very ill-defined. The words which the great master of the human heart most appropriately puts into the mouth of a condemned criminal are indeed true in some degree of us all—

> " The weariest, most loathèd worldly life
> That age, ache, penury, and imprisonment
> Can lay on Nature, is a Paradise
> To what we fear of death."

It is a conviction of this supreme terror that has always caused death to be fixed as the penalty for offences which legislators were most anxious to repress, and which has therefore retained it in our code as the punishment of murder. The other arguments in its favour, such as its " characteristicalness " (to use Bentham's expression for the analogy between the crime and the penalty), and its complete and uncostly removal of the criminal, can only be admitted as subsidiary to this main plea. Still, while admitting that the threat of death is in general the most powerful deterrent which can be presented to the mind of man, we must guard against the fallacy of concluding that by this admission the expediency of retaining this most terrible of penalties is by any means established. If this were so, we might argue from the same premisses that the old code of burning, boiling, torture, annihilation, with all its machinery for graduating the horrors of death, ought never to have been altered. Under the supposed code of Draco, if it were not intended to level the distinction of all crimes, torture must have been an indispensable accompaniment of death. The real point—and this is what is oftenest forgotten by reasoners on both sides of the question—is neither whether death is the most terrible punishment, nor what punishment is a just recompense for the crime of murder (a question often asked, but for answering which in any definite terms there can never be any materials), but whether no other punishment can be found which would sufficiently answer the end of deterring offenders, and which is free from the defects inseparable from death-punishment. And there can be no question that, considered as a mere deterrent, the merits of this punishment are often exaggerated, because sufficient attention is not paid to the different classes of persons who would come under its influence. By far the most numerous and dangerous class of murders are those which are committed under the excitement of some strong passion, such as revenge, jealousy, or avarice, which so completely seizes possession of the criminal that the penalty attached to the gratification is entirely lost sight of at the moment of perpetration. Fear is here, as in other cases, strong only where the other passions are weak. And during the whole dread interval of preparation for the deed, the idea of discovery is by a familiar process of self-deception thrust aside. For this whole class of offenders, then, no punishment, however terrible, would be an adequate deterrent ; and the slightest diminution in the certainty of punishment (and it will presently appear that the diminution is considerable) would far outweigh, as an influencing motive, the calculable gain from any increase of severity. As for the other class of murders which are the acts of habitual criminals (such as burglars, &c.,) in the exercise of their criminal profession, judging from the demeanour, not only of those who suffer the sentence of the law, but of their associates and followers who form the principal constituents of an execution-mob, we should doubt very much whether even over these persons the influence of the terror of death is as great or as lasting as is often asserted. True, this influence would be measured best by the number whom it eventually holds back from taking the last step on the ladder of crime. But this calculation being evidently out of our power, we must satisfy ourselves with such an estimate of the deterrent value of public executions as can be drawn from their immediate effect. What this is will be considered more appropriately under the next head.

These considerations diminish much the apparent advantages

of death-punishment even as a mere deterrent.   But when we turn to the examination of its other positive attributes (omitting altogether the negative attribute of total deficiency in all the secondary good qualities of reformation) we discover that the evils with which it is attended are far more than enough to outweigh even a far heavier list of virtues.   First among these positive evils (because it is the best known, and not because it is most weighty in itself) may be placed that which has been depicted in all its deformity by our greatest moralists and observers of human nature—the demoralizing example afforded by public executions. We have on this point a concurrence of testimony, against which the anonymous assertions of those who write only to bolster up preconceived conclusions, can have no weight whatever.   The sympathy of the assembled multitude even at the very moment of execution takes the form either of savage exultation (a very fit expression of that doctrine of vengeance which those who ought to know better often put forward in justification of death-punishment !) or of equally misplaced sympathy with the criminal ; while their contempt is invariably reserved for the person who ought only to attract respect—the minister of the law.   And what profit is derived from the example of the sufferer ?   The more heinous the guilt expiated, the more obdurate and unflinching is often the bearing of the criminal.   Where, to use the coarse phrase suitably coined for the occasion, the convict " dies game," that is, with brutal indifference or assumed bravado, the lesson of terror is entirely lost, and his spurious courage excites the admiration of his associates who are sure to be there to applaud it ; whereas, if his demeanour be that of a penitent submitting to his punishment, the natural sympathy for his fate excites in those who might be disposed to profit by the warning a compassion or a compunction which of itself shows how contrary the punishment is to the better instincts of our nature.   For many hours before the execution there are protracted orgies of vice and ribaldry ; and after it men separate with feelings deadened by that involuntary reaction which follows all such morbid excitements.   As to this point, what can be more significant than the fact testified by the Chaplain of Newgate, that he never knew a condemned criminal who had not been at an execution ? or the statement of the Rev. J. Roberts, of Bristol, that out of 167 persons whom he visited after sentence of death, 164 had attended (mark the expression) a public hanging.

It is sometimes proposed to avoid such scenes by private executions in the gaol, before a specified number of witnesses.   By this course, however, the advocates of capital punishment abandon their stronghold, which certainly lies in the alleged deterring power of the punishment.   By this change, the whole force of the apology on the ground of the deterrent effect on habitual criminals would be greatly lessened, if not altogether annulled. Whatever may be thought of the true value of that apology, it is on this that opponents must chiefly, if not solely, rely. For it is almost certain that the fate of a criminal quietly put out of the way before a few witnesses, within the precincts of a prison, would be far less impressive on the minds of the criminal population, than that of one who was known, if not seen, to be detained there in life-long hardship and confinement. Thus, in attempting to escape the evils consequent on public executions, we surrender entirely the problematical advantages which have been supposed to justify them. It may, indeed, be safely predicted that, whenever executions are made private, they will soon cease altogether.

The evil which has just been pointed out is one which may be considered, perhaps, as an accident (however inseparable) of death-punishment; but there is another which is involved in its very idea. The punishment is of necessity irremissible, a property which, in a perfect system of justice, would be no disadvantage. But, that from the sentence of a fallible tribunal there should be no escape for the condemned man, in case of detected error, is a circumstance in itself so disastrous, that the bare possibility of its occurrence seems sufficient to condemn the system which involves it. And the danger in the case of death-punishment is by no means a mere imaginary one. Every lawyer can remember instances in which persons have been convicted of notorious murders on evidence which failed to satisfy not only those engaged in the trial, but many others who had carefully watched the whole case. And who can say what further circumstances might be brought to light, if the accused still survived to give the clue to the investigations of his family's legal adviser? It was argued by Sir J. Romilly in the House of Commons, in 1848, that murder differed from all other offences, in that here the crime most completely destroyed the evidence of guilt. This is true; but we may add that death-punishment also differs from all others in that it too often destroys the only proof of innocence. If the reader has any suspicion that this fearful danger is in the present day merely fanciful, let him not only recal to his own mind instances in which juries have with the greatest hesitation acquitted men whose innocence has afterwards been undoubted; but let him consult the numerous cases of wrong convictions in capital cases, cited in detail by Mr. Commissioner Phillips in his work entitled " Vacation Thoughts on Capital Punishment." And let it be remembered that the writer's experience as a criminal lawyer adds great authority to his testimony.

A kindred fault to that of irremissibility, and equally of the essence of death-punishment, is that of invariability. In this respect the old law which discriminated between different modes of death, however abhorrent to our feelings, was certainly more just. The effect of this invariability on the public mind also should be noticed. This was seen plainly in the recent agitation respecting the fate of the convict Wright, where comparison was naturally suggested to men's mind between the criminality of different murders. And while we write, a similar and still more flagrant instance is occurring of the injustice of inflicting the same punishment on every man who commits murder. It is not too much to say that if Wright was not hanged because Townley was pardoned, certainly Hall might have been pardoned if Wright had not been hanged.*

These last two defects of irremissibility and invariability are closely connected with another which is the heaviest accusation which can be brought against any system of justice. This is, uncertainty. Whenever it is found that from any combination of circumstances a punishment has become so unpopular, or so difficult of application, that its infliction in any particular case is rendered uncertain, then that punishment may be condemned as offering a positive immunity to crime. Death-punishment is every day becoming more open to this fatal objection. The introduction of the comparatively new difficulty as to the sanity of the accused, together with the greater sensitiveness of juries, on the ground of the irreversible consequences of their verdict, now render it a matter of speculation in almost every case, whether justice will not be defeated altogether. The very rarity of executions makes men feel more seriously the sacredness of life. It is, indeed, better that many guilty should escape than that one innocent man should suffer, but in this instance we may truly say, " Lex (if not ' judex') damnatur cum nocens absolvitur," as it is the direct effect of the law, as it now stands, to put obstacles in the way of justice. On this branch of our subject we gladly avail ourselves of the words of the able and succinct pamphlet of Mr. Amos: " This increased uncertainty of conviction in the present day is of the very essence of capital punishment. Jurors are, after all, but men. Like their friends and neighbours they have their sympathies, their desires, their feelings of compunction and tender indulgence. They cannot set out of sight—as they are told to do, and perhaps even themselves believe that they are doing—the consequences of their verdict. They naturally incline in a capital charge to pay more deference to each iota of the defence, than to the crushing weight of evidence adduced by the

---

* Since the above was written, the reprieve of Hall, wrung with difficulty from the Home Secretary at the eleventh hour, affords another exemplification of the truth of our argument.

Crown. They fondly fan into a flame the minutest sparks of extenuation alleged in favour of the prisoner. To much relevant matter on the side of the prosecution they unconsciously close their eyes and ears. Where the probabilities are at all nearly balanced, their feelings and not their judgments start the scale. Any one familiar with the scenes exhibited in courts of justice, on trials for murder, will recognise this description as not ideal or imaginary, but a mere transcript of daily experience. It is peculiar to capital charges, and it does not mend the matter to declaim against the ignorance and cowardice of uneducated jurymen. Where life and death are concerned, this will continue to be so, and not otherwise. And it is appalling to think that, inasmuch as the most atrocious murders are those which are plotted with the most artful sagacity, it is just these which secure the largest immunity from a cautious and scrupulous jury, and are most likely to pass unavenged. If this be so, the prospect for the future is not the diminution, but the fearful encouragement of crime."

In strict accordance with this powerful statement, are the opinions expressed by Sir F. Kelly in the House of Commons; by Sir J. Romilly in his evidence before the Commissioners on Criminal Law, in 1836, and by Sir R. Phillips, who, as Sheriff of London and Middlesex, brought both study and observation to the subject. And these opinions are verified by the statistics quoted by Lord Hobart, which show that in years 1857-9 the proportion of committals to convictions in cases of murder was as four to one, while the general average in other crimes was only four to three. That is, on the part of a person committed for trial, the degree of expectation of acquittal on a charge of murder is to the degree of expectation of acquittal on other charges as three to one.

Mr. Amos's conclusion is, we fear, only too true. Yet it affords the best ground for hope of reform. Public opinion has now reached that point where all that is needed to turn the scale in favour of the abolition of death-punishment, is that the question should be dispassionately reviewed. The feelings of men are already enlisted in the cause which we advocate, and they only wait for evidence to justify their judgment in following under the same banner.

There is, however, one other consideration which recent circumstances press home to our attention with all the weight of experience. It seems almost certain, that except death-punishment be speedily abolished, a great danger threatens the very foundation of our judicial institutions. Within the last few years we have had a series of cases (besides the names of McLachlan, Townley, Wright, and Hall, it is only necessary to recal that of Smethurst, as presenting all the worst consequences of the present system in the most glaring light), in which discredit has been thrown upon the administration of the law by extensive popular agitation respecting the fate of individual convicts. This agitation has more than once, to all appearance, overridden the sentence of justice. This is a danger which from its very nature is rapidly progressive. Let it be arrested at once in its commencement. Law should be the guide and exponent, not the slave of popular feeling. That complete independence which is essential to the administration of justice can only be preserved by the sacrifice of this last remnant of a barbarous code—a custom which has long been condemned at the impartial bar of reason, and whose sentence can now no longer be delayed by the pleas of popular favour or temporary expediency. Let our statesmen consider the real force of this last argument, which cannot be charged either with sentimentalism or theoretical sophistry.

Our task is drawing to a close ; it only remains to consider one point. What substitute can be found which will replace death-punishment without its inevitable drawbacks ? This is a question which can be answered best by an appeal to facts. It is obvious that the conclusions drawn from the experience of the abolition of capital punishment for other crimes in other countries and at other periods can only be evidence of the probable effects of the abolition of this penalty for murder now in this country. The determining causes are too numerous and complicated to admit of the effects being stated with the precision of a law. But the results of such experience are very valuable, when not strained beyond their true purpose. The most satisfactory way of applying the test would be a comparison of the effects of the abolition of death-punishment for murder in other countries. If we assume that the causes of the crime are pretty nearly the same everywhere, and that no abnormal change in social feeling has taken place in either of the countries compared, it will follow that the effects must be similar likewise. Unfortunately the full statistics on these points are too voluminous to be inserted here. But one fact may be stated, which is in itself very strong *primâ facie* evidence of the wholesome effects of abolition. In none of those countries where the experiment has been tried has any return been made to the punishment of death, with one exception, which will be examined presently. The states in which the total abolition of capital punishment has been, and is in operation, are Tuscany, seven states of America (Alabama, Michigan, Illinois, Rhode Island, Wisconsin, Louisiana, and Columbia), and two cantons of Switzerland (Friburg and Neufchâtel). It was also tried with signal success by Sir James Mackintosh in Bombay, and by Lord Metcalfe at Delhi. Nothing can be more varied than the races, religions, and climates included in these countries, yet in all it has been found, to use the words of a commission recently appointed in Friburg, that " neither crimes in general, nor special crimes against life and safety, have been in any way relatively more numerous in the period (in this case fifteen years) following the abolition of capital punishment." The history of Tuscan legislation is peculiarly interesting. This was the first European state in which the reform was carried out by the enlightened Leopold, the friend of Beccaria. After an experience of more than twenty years, he formally congratulated his subjects on the success of the change. His reign was marked by a most extraordinary diminution in the number of murders, so great, that in Tuscany (which was formerly about on a par with Rome in this respect) only five murders were committed in twenty years ; while in Rome, where death-punishment was inflicted with great pomp and parade, sixty murders were committed in only five months. After Leopold's death, during the long period of Austrian domination, the punishment of death was re-enacted, in order, as it was hoped, to repress the political agitation which was the consequence of foreign tyranny. By what success that plan was followed, we all know. In 1847 the reigning grand-duke again abolished capital punishment, and with most satisfactory results. It was, however, once more reimposed in 1852, in the terror of the reaction from 1848, and for the same purpose of political terrorism. But no sooner was the Tuscan legislature free, and enabled to act independently by its union with the kingdom of Italy, than in 1859 they returned to the system so happily inaugurated by Leopold. And this return is expressly confirmed by a decree issued in 1860, and now in force. Nothing can well be stronger than the argument this instance furnishes of the probable effects of substituting some other punishment for that of death. We may here observe that in a comparison of statistics on this question, it will always be desirable to take as wide a range of time as possible ; because it may be shown that on the first substitution of a lighter for a heavier penalty the crime has often a tendency to an immediate increase, but that after a time the increased certainty more than compensates for the difference in severity. It would appear as if the standard of terror necessary to be kept up varied directly with the severity of the punishment. And this would of course apply equally to any increase in severity. No one would now expect permanently to reduce the limit of the crime of murder by adding torture to hanging ; or by substituting any of those obsolete forms of cruelty with which that crime was once visited.

There is another more imperfect test by which we may try the probable effect of the abolition of death-punishment for murder.

This would be by comparing the consequences of the substitution of lesser penalties for that of death in the case of other offences. Here we should expect to see that the operation of the increase of certainty of conviction (from the strong objections which formerly juries had to convict, prosecutors to come forward, and witnesses to give evidence) would be so perceptible as to disturb the calculations altogether. Yet in spite of the distinction between the ten periods compared, the figures are most encouraging. The following return was made to the House of Commons in 1846 :—

Number of Persons Committed and Executed for each of the following Offences :—

OFFENCES.	During the five years ending with an execution.*		During the five years immediately following.	Year of last Execution.
	Committed.	Executed.	Committed.	
Cattle stealing	144	3	119	1820
Sheep stealing	1231	11	1320	1831
Horse stealing	990	37	966	1829
Stealing in a dwelling-house	834	9	875	1831
Forgery	296	17	331	1829
Coining	44	8	16	1828
Returning from transportation	52	—	50	1835
Letter stealing	14	1	27	1832
Sacrilege	33	2	33	1819
Robbery	1829	17	1579	1836
Arson, and other wilful burning	391	42	183	1836
Piracy	52	2	4	1830
Attempts to murder unattended with bodily injuries, shooting at, stabbing, wounding, &c.	687	8	1111	1841
Rape, &c.	278	14	319	1836
Riot and Felony	215	6	68	1837
Unnatural crimes	105	11	118	1835
High Treason	81	8	1	1837
Total	7276	196	7120	

A few remarks on this table may make its true import clearer. It will be observed that the offences in which the most rapid increase appears to have followed the abolition of capital punishment are those comprised under the head, Attempts to Murder—

* *i.e.*, during the five years preceding the last execution for each specified offence.

which are in intention quite indistinguishable from murder itself. This increase, therefore, may confidently be cited as a proof of the inefficacy of the fear of death as a deterrent. Hardly one of the criminals convicted of an attempt to murder could tell that he might not render himself liable to the extreme penalty. We are therefore justified in classing these offences with murders. And if we compare the rate of increase in the two classes of crime taken together during the periods over which the table above given extends, we shall find the results even more unfavourable to the advocates of capital punishment. The numbers are these—

Committals for Murder, or Attempts to Murder, during each of the Five Years ending

1826	1831	1836	1841	1846
661	770	1023	1221	1459

And yet the fearfully rapid growth of this class of crime was ignored entirely by those who contended that the abolition of death-punishment for lighter offences was followed by increase of crime. As to the other crimes in which a very much smaller increase is observable, they are of such a special nature that, no doubt, the removal of the objection to prosecute for the capital offence would more than account for the increase in committals.

These figures appear, then, to show conclusively that, so far from there being any probability that the abolition of death-punishment would be followed by a permanent increase in the number of murders, the direct contrary result may reasonably be expected. And if the comparison of the effects of commutation of sentences as compared with executions were drawn out, the same result would follow.

In all these cases the substitute for death (and it is the only possible one) has been some form of imprisonment, a punishment which is capable of almost as many modifications of severity as the crime of murder is of degrees of criminality. But one precaution will always be necessary. The scale of severity fixed by the law must be absolutely irremissible on any consideration of clemency. The only limits of variation must be laid down by the judge in his sentence. Due provision will thus be made for the exclusion of that element of uncertainty which is the greatest vice of the present system. Death-punishment is defensible only on the same grounds as war, where it is inflicted by society in strict self-defence. And as the dangers of war have hardly any calculable effect when opposed to those passions which are generally weakest in the human breast, because the fate of those who engage in it is proverbially uncertain, so it is with all punishments. Where can so remarkable a proof of this be found as in the inefficacy of the popular belief in the penalty of everlasting misery to restrain those who think they hold it most firmly? because here, too, he who breaks the law, in his inmost heart only half believes that the penalty will ever be enforced. Could a penal code be made as certain in its operation as the laws of Nature, self-caused misery would no more be banished from the State than it is from the physical world; but at any rate men would know what to expect when they offended against it, and he who incurred its penalties would be regarded by himself and others as a suicide, and not as a victim. This end can never be perfectly attained; but two important steps towards it would be secured by the removal of the kindred anomalies of arbitrary pardon and irremissible punishment.

ART. V.—NEW ZEALAND.

1. *New Zealand in* 1842. By T. M. D. MARTIN, M.D., President of the New Zealand Aborigines' Protection Association, and lately a Magistrate of the Colony. Auckland.

2. *New Zealand and its Aborigines.* By WILLIAM BROWN, lately a Member of the Legislative Council of New Zealand. Smith, Elder, and Co. 1845.

3. *Plain Facts relative to the late War in the Northern District of New Zealand.* Auckland. 1847.

4. *The New Zealand Question and the Rights of Aborigines.* By LOUIS ALEXIS CHAMEROVZOU. London: J. C. Newby. 1848.

5. *A Speech delivered in the Provincial Council of Auckland, exhibiting a Picture of Misgovernment and Oppression in the British Colony of New Zealand; preceded by a Letter to his Grace the Duke of Newcastle, Her Majesty's Principal Secretary of State for the Colonial Department.* By JAMES BUSBY, Esq. Auckland. 1853.

6. *A Page from the History of New Zealand.* By MÉROUXΟΣ. Auckland. 1854.

7. *The First Settlers in New Zealand; being a Speech delivered at the Table of the House of Representatives, August* 1st,

1856. Revised and enlarged. By JAMES BUSBY, Esq. Auckland. 1856.

8. *A Letter to his Excellency Colonel Thomas Gore Browne, C.B., Governor of New Zealand, on " Responsible Government" and " The Governmental Institutions of New Zealand."* By JAMES BUSBY, Esq. Auckland. 1857.

9. *Observations on the State of the Aboriginal Inhabitants of New Zealand.* By F. D. FENTON, the Compiler of the Statistical Tables of the Native Population. Auckland. 1857.

10. *The Right of a British Colonist to the Protection of the Queen and Parliament of England against the Illegal and Unjust Acts of a Colonial Legislature or Government. A Letter to his Grace the Duke of Newcastle, Her Majesty's Principal Secretary of State for the Colonies.* By JAMES BUSBY, Esq. Auckland. 1860.

11. *Illustrations of the System called " Responsible Government;" in a Letter to his Excellency Colonel Gore Browne, C.B.* By JAMES BUSBY, Esq. Auckland. 1860.

12. *The Maori King Movement in New Zealand ; with a full Report of the Native Meetings held at Waikato, April and May,* 1860. By the Rev. THOMAS BUDDLE. Auckland, 1860.

13. *The Taranaki Question.* By Sir W. MARTIN, D.C.L., late Chief Justice of New Zealand. Auckland. 1860.

14. *Remarks upon a Pamphlet entitled " The Taranaki Question," by Sir W. Martin.* By JAMES BUSBY, Esq., formerly H.M. Resident in New Zealand. Auckland. 1860.

15. *Remarks upon a Pamphlet by James Busby, Esq., commenting upon a Pamphlet entitled " The Taranaki Question," by Sir William Martin.* By GEORGE CLARKE, late Chief Protector of Aborigines. Printed for private circulation only. Auckland. 1861.

16. *Notes on Sir William Martin's Pamphlet.* Published by authority of the General Government. Auckland.

17. *Memorandum.* By Mr. RICHMOND. Auckland.

18. *Remarks on Notes published for the New Zealand Government, and on Mr. Richmond's Memorandum.* By Sir WILLIAM MARTIN, D.C.L. Auckland. 1861.

19. *The Land Question of Taranaki.* By F. A. CARRINGTON. [Unpublished.] Taranaki.

20. *New Zealand Memorial to his Grace the Secretary of State for the Colonies ; together with a Memorandum on New Zealand Affairs.* London.

21. *The War in New Zealand.* By WILLIAM FOX, Member of the House of Representatives. Auckland.

22. *One of England's Little Wars: A Letter to the Duke of Newcastle, Secretary of State for the Colonies.* By OCTAVIUS HADFIELD, Archdeacon of Kapiti, New Zealand.

23. *New Zealand and the War.* By WILLIAM SWAINSON, Esq., formerly Attorney-General for New Zealand. London: Smith, Elder, and Co.

24. *The War in Taranaki during the Years* 1860-61. By W. J. GRAYLING, of the Volunteer Rifles. New Plymouth. 1862.

25. *Letter to the Right Honourable the Lord Lyttelton, on the Relations of Great Britain with the Colonists and Aborigines of New Zealand.* By CROSBIE WARD, a Member of the Government and of the House of Representatives of the Colony. London: Edward Stanford. 1863.

OF England's fifty colonies, not one has excited so much interest, has been the subject of so many experiments, or has given so much trouble to the Colonial Office, as New Zealand. Never before did a colony present so many tangled questions for solution, or become a prey to so many conflicting interests; yet never was there a country which might have been more easy to govern, or a case in which the interminable difficulties which have arisen were more indisputably of our own creation.

New Zealand has certainly no cause to complain of neglect by the Home Government. On the contrary, she has been the victim of good intentions, of harassing watchfulness and needless interference; in fact, of over-nursing. The Benjamin of colonies, the youngest and the best-beloved, she risked the fate of the apeling that was smothered with hugging by its dam. Nostrum after nostrum was tried upon her, though all that was needed to ensure a hardy growth was to have turned her loose to shift for herself. The lesson has now been learned, and acted up to; but at no trifling cost, and somewhat late in the day. Experience has at least been gained, and a subject for an instructive book (should any one be minded to take such a work in hand), which might be entitled "Errors of Colonization;" drawing examples from the case before us, and showing how all might have been avoided by simply placing a little confidence in the right-mindedness and practical good sense of the colonists themselves. "The Comedy of Errors," we should rather have suggested as a title, were it not for the tragic issue—an internecine war, an enormous expenditure, and, by way of anti-climax, a hot dispute as to who shall pay the bill.

Like those of Tristram Shandy, the misfortunes of the colony began before its birth. Begotten of a quarrel between the Colonial Office and a land-trading company, that state of conflict which, in one form or another, has been throughout its normal condition, was ready prepared for the child at entry into the world. We have seen party feeling — that bane of the country from first to last—engendered at the very outset among the colonists, being the inevitable consequence of the formation of rival settlements, north and south, by the Home Government and the New Zealand Company respectively. Contentions of almost unparalleled bitterness between the colonists and their governors; each side incessantly striving to make good its own case at the Colonial Office, and neither side, unfortunately, abstaining altogether from misrepresentation. We have seen governors, when Maori sympathy was fashionable in England, ostentatiously parading themselves as the protectors of the natives against the greed and violence of the settlers (a charge only in one instance handsomely retracted—by Colonel Gore Browne, whose well-known, "Si possint, recte, si non, quocumque modo," was unsaid for him by a friend, in the Assembly); advertising themselves as "the real original Maori sympathizers," and manifesting extreme jealousy whenever the settlers attempted to exert themselves in behalf of their red fellow-subjects—an interference which seemed to be treated as poaching on the Government manor; and even going so far, in one instance, as to accuse the old settlers, including the Church Missionaries, of having provoked the war in the north.

We have seen the colonists, on the other hand, indignantly rejecting the imputation; casting it back upon an incompetent Government; protesting against the timid procrastinations and temporizing system of native management; styling it the "flour-and-sugar policy," degrading to both races alike; and maintaining that the sole object of governors was to make political capital out of the Maori — to keep all quiet by palliatives during their respective terms of office, but never venturing upon any effective measures for their permanent benefit; each in turn looking to the time when he should escape from the colony, bequeathing his difficulties to his successor. We have seen that even when recrimination between the governors and the governed was put an end to, by concession of representative institutions and of parliamentary government, this normal conflict was not yet at an end, for it broke out afresh between the races, and remains undetermined still.

The colonial history is known only to those who have taken a part in making it. It has still to be written, and ought to be, while yet the tradition of it lives; for the earlier actors, upon whom, and not upon blue-books or despatches, dependence must be mainly placed, are fast disappearing from the scene. Our present object is to redeem a portion of it from oblivion.

In any account professing to be at once complete and intelligible, three subjects, which might be likened to the three strands of one rope, would have to be carefully distinguished, while collaterally treated ;—namely, the political history of the Europeans ; the policy adopted towards the natives ; and the land question. In the limited space at our disposal, such an arrangement is out of the question ; we must therefore confine ourselves to the last. But events happen of themselves to grow up around it so naturally, that we still hope to give a tolerably continuous account. For it may be said that the history of the land question, that *fons et origo malorum,* is substantially the history of the colony.

We have said that there was never a country more easy to govern. Those who are content to derive their information from official sources, and who forget that the temptation to exaggerate difficulties in order to enhance the credit of overcoming them is not invariably resisted, will remain of a different opinion. But some of these difficulties are imaginary ; others are overdrawn, and the rest are of the very creation of those who complain—who have set up their own windmills, in order to run a tilt against them.

Government was an easy task, because the character, both of the settlers and of the natives, was such as to make it so. Of the first we need say little, save that in social station, education, and intellectual ability, they ranked far above the ordinary average of colonial pioneers. Since the days of the cavaliers of Virginia, there has been nothing to equal, in this respect, the original body of emigrants to New Zealand. The novelty of systematic colonization, as yet an experiment, had taken the fancy of the moment in England, and recruiting had been active among the better classes of society. All that was needed, to ensure quiet and happiness, was to have allowed such men to take care of themselves, and, as the sequel proves, of the natives also ; to have reposed that confidence in them from the first which it has been found necessary to accord at last. For it stands upon record that they saw their way forward more clearly than did the successive officers appointed by the Home Government ; the principles enunciated by the leaders of public opinion among them having made their way, one by one, and being at the present moment in practical operation. These same men, as many as are left, can now point to the frank admission made by the present Secretary of State for the Colonies, that "he could not disguise from himself that the endeavours to keep the management of the natives under the control of the Home Government had failed ;" and to their own refusal, in the session of 1862, to take upon themselves the responsibility of governing the native tribes until the troubles induced by neglect of their advice should be allayed.

The mistake in regard to the colonists was the supposed necessity of keeping them *in statu pupillari ;* of " preparing them gradually"—the accredited phrase of the time—for representative institutions, in forgetfulness of the great truth that, the longer Englishmen are debarred from the exercise of English rights, the more unfit do they become for the performance of English duties. The mistake in regard to the natives was of a similar nature. They were considered, not as men of like passions with ourselves, equally self-confident as ourselves, acting from the same motives, and subject to the same errors ; but as children. The Government forthwith proceeded to pamper the child, and the attempt, far from winning confidence, was resented. It was perfectly understood and appreciated. Yet, in our belief, there does not exist among uncivilized nations a more manly people, or more easy of reasonable guidance,—a people whose qualities, good and bad alike, afford a stronger leverage by which to move them. Docile, because endowed with high powers of reasoning ; equable in temper, making it a point of honour to abstain at least from the outward manifestation of anger ; imperturbable, and therefore patient under provocation, affording ample time to justify or make amends ; but dogged in resistance to force, and inexorable, even to barbarity, when satisfied that the action is " correct,"— that is to say, according to precedent. For the Maori is at once democratic and conservative in temperament ; paying to his chief—whose rule, if not altogether based upon opinion, must at least not run counter to opinion—very much less deference than is usual among the islanders of the tropical Pacific ; but a slave to custom and to etiquette, which are, to him, the unwritten law —the wisdom of his forefathers. Faithful to engagements at any sacrifice, until taught by us to break them, being accustomed to treat a *bargain* with something like religious reverence, and to consider that which is formally done as irrevocable. Even should the bargain prove a bad one, a Maori casts it off his mind, neither indulging in regret, nor giving himself the least further trouble about the matter. Apparently covetous to the extreme, because unrestrained by conventional notions of delicacy from asking, and because wanting in those finer feelings, only developed among long civilized races, by which covetousness is sometimes overborne ; deficient, though not wholly so, in gratitude, because not accustomed to give or to exact more than is due. Where a native gift is not virtually an exchange, ostentation is generally the motive; and in that case it is thought of the giver, that " he has his reward." Teeming with vanity —the less offensive because coupled with perfect self-reliance; full-blown with pride, which nevertheless will not hinder a great chief—a *tino rangatira*—from begging the smallest trifle; and not wanting in a certain chivalry of feeling, after his own fashion, though that be not always identical in outward form with ours.*

We reserve for more especial notice the chief characteristic feature of the native mind, by acting upon which the Maori might have been moulded like clay under the potter's hands,—his keen, appreciative sense of justice. Not that the Maori idea of justice is absolutely co-extensive with our own; for the word is used by us, conventionally, in a restricted sense. The abstract form of justice is the perception of equality; the desire to equalize unequal quantities—to balance and weigh. With civilized justice must be included " wild justice," which is, revenge. The Maori is a metaphysician born, with an instinctive perception of the law of compensation. The ruling passion—the mainspring of his conduct, is to " come off quits;" to be even with every man, whether friend or foe. For everything but hospitality he must have an equivalent: blood for blood; service for service; rights for cession of rights. And with an equivalent, though not indisposed to try for more, he is certain, ultimately, to rest content. That upon which everything rests in Maoridom, the dominant institution, is Utu,† generally translated payment, ransom, reward; but which,

---

* Sometimes it is. Lieutenant Brookes, who was killed at Puketakauere, bravely defending himself while entangled in a swamp, was to have been spared by the party with whom he was actually engaged, on account of their admiration of the courage he displayed. He lowered his sword at last, in token of surrender; the assailants, supposing this to be a feint, were considering among themselves how to take him, when he was shot by one who came up at the last, and had not held council with the rest. Such at least is the native account, which may be probably relied on.

At the time of the war in the North, the natives considered it " incorrect " to hinder the bringing up of ammunition or supplies; for the want of them might spoil a fair fight. When joked about it by some officers, rather indiscreetly, after the making of peace, they answered, significantly, " We shall know better next time."

† The following characteristic story is related by Mr. Brown:—"An acquaintance of mine who has been settled for some time among them, had on one occasion a dispute about the payment of some timber which the tribe had been dragging out of the bush for him; and as he showed no symptoms of acceding to their unreasonable demands, one of the chiefs, in their usual braggadocio style, advanced towards him, flourishing his arms, yelling, and looking as if he would annihilate him. This was more than John Bull could stand, and he struck the chief a blow with his fist which sent him reeling away. The chief at first got more furious than ever, but soon calmed down again, as his friends thought he was to blame, and did not interfere in the quarrel. Next day the same chief came privately to the settler, and begged of him to give

taken in conjunction with its congener, *uto*, may rather be described as "measure for measure." This appears to be the real clue to most of the seeming anomalies in the Maori mind. It is this, for instance, which causes kindness, offered from simple impulse, to be so dimly appreciated by a native. For, not understanding why he should receive more than he is commercially entitled to, he seeks a motive, too often imputing an ignoble one—fear, or the hope of gain. Such a temperament is ungracious, but the advantage derived from it by the ruling powers is inestimable. No need for favour, of which there has been too much, in judicial decisions between the white man and the red; none for gifts or for cajolery; nothing required of them but to fulfil their own engagements, and, among a nation of hard bargainers, faithfully keep the bargain driven by the Crown at Waitangi.

After all, allowing for a few national peculiarities, they are in character much the same as the rest of us. There is no mystery about Maori matters, as the *periti—*

> With purpose to be dressed in an opinion
> Of wisdom, gravity, profound conceit,

would have had others believe. Manners and customs must of course be studied there as they must elsewhere; but they are easy to learn, for secrecy is unknown to the race. And it is only fair to bear in mind that if their virtues are less conspicuous than ours it is because the possessors do not take the trouble to parade them; while their faults are more so, because uncloaked. The Maori do not care to whiten their sepulchres.

The story of the New Zealand troubles would be one mass of confusion, utterly bewildering to all but those who have been

---

him half-a-crown, in order that he might show it to his friends, and tell them that it had been paid as a satisfaction for the insult which had been offered to him. In this case it was clearly his vanity that had been wounded; not the slightest degree of resentment was retained, nor was there the least consciousness of loss of dignity, either in the original insult, or the still more degrading subterfuge to which he had resorted to wipe it away."

Under certain circumstances, governed by Maori etiquette, perfectly comprehensible to them, though hardly so to us, the victors would give *utu* to the vanquished, as payment for losses, in order to end the war upon fair terms. This was the case at Kororareka in the year 1837, when the Ngapuhi, from Whangaroa, Matauri, and the Bay of Islands, made an attack upon Kawiti and Pomare, at Kororareka. Hengi, a superior chief, fell; and though the assailants were repulsed, Kororareka, together with a large portion of land as far as Cape Brett, was ceded to them.

The perpetrators of the massacre at Wairau were suprised at our not claiming the land in dispute immediately afterwards, as *utu* for the death of the white chiefs. We could have had it for the asking; for the demand would have been "correct." Far from attributing our conduct to forbearance, they only looked down upon us as "unenlightened Britishers."

locally acquainted with the progress of events, were it not that our difficulties, apparently so diverse in character, have a common origin ; being all traceable, with care, to the same source. In one form or another, the contention has been, from first to last, about the LAND. There were millions of acres to be fought for, and of fighting there has been no stint. Where the prey is, there the eagles are gathered together. A long period of desultory warfare, sometimes between governors, and settlers sometimes between governors and natives, now waged on paper, and now with lead, has closed in a struggle between the races for supremacy.

We pass over the details of the dispute between the Home Government and the New Zealand Company in 1839, which for a long while so seriously affected the fortunes of the colony, with the simple observation that the cause of it was land. The object of the Company was to buy land cheap, and sell it dear. In order to create a market, they undertook colonizing operations. They succeeded, as they supposed, in purchasing from the natives many large tracts of land, defined by degrees of latitude and longitude ; but, owing to haste and ignorance combined, obtained but a very questionable title to a small portion, and to the rest no title at all. But they had no difficulty in effecting sales in England. It being clear that such irregular settlement of a colony could not be allowed, the Home Government, with some reluctance, determined to found a colony, and also to undertake colonizing operations. For this purpose, they prepared to form a rival establishment at the other end of the Northern Island, where the Government also would be able to deal in land, without clashing with the Company. This may seem a very bare and downright statement of the case ; but, setting aside benevolent intentions towards the aborigines, and eliminating a sufficient amount of Blue Book verbiage, nothing else remains. Disguise it as they may, the Home Government joined in the land-jobbing race. The only real distinction was, that the expected profits realized at one end of the island were to go to the Company's share'holders ; while those at the other end were to go towards defraying the expenses of the Government establishment.

The first step to be taken was to acquire the sovereignty of the country. And here let us give all due credit to the English Government for the spirit in which they commenced the enterprise, and the ends which they proposed to attain, notwithstanding the woful falling off in execution. They undertook to acquire the country, without violence and without fraud, to civilize and preserve a barbarous race ; to bring them peaceably into subjection to the law ; assuring to them at the same time the full privileges of subjects of the Crown. But the land lay between the projectors and their object.

To obtain a peaceful cession, the expedient of treaty was resorted to. This did not accord with the views of the Company, and was considered by a select committee of the House of Commons in 1844 to have been " an injudicious proceeding." With this opinion we agree, but not upon the same grounds. It appears to us that a treaty was more than enough for the purpose: it encumbered us with difficulties that were never contemplated at the time, and was subsequently wrested to the disadvantage of those whose interests it was intended to guard. All that was substantially required, was a solemn declaration that certain native rights should be preserved intact: not a treaty, but a guarantee. By adopting the *form* of treaty, meaning thereby a compact between two independent nations, we subjected ourselves to all the incidents of treaty, hampering ourselves with the dogmas of international law. It involved us in a strange dilemma; for the right of interpretation either belongs to the natives, equally with ourselves, or else to the Crown alone; the first conclusion rendering all government impossible; the second, endowing the Government with the powers of a despot.* But the most practical objection is, that there was no Maori nation with which to treat; no recognised head or confederation of chiefs having power to bind those who withheld consent. Consequently, when, a few years afterwards, a prisoner of war who had not signed was hanged as a rebel, there was not wanting high authority for pronouncing the execution illegal, or, as some did not hesitate to say, a murder.

The first signatures were obtained at Waitangi—the Runnimede of native New Zealand. Not, however, without some difficulty. The main anxiety of the natives was then, as it has been ever

* Here is the main proposition on which Mr. Richmond (native minister in 1861) relies : " In law, as well as in fact, their territorial rights and obligations are not subject to the interpretation of our courts. These rights stand upon treaties, of which the Crown itself is, rightfully, the sole interpreter." The practical consequence is drawn in par. 121 : " If the Governor had jurisdiction, he was justified in asserting it in the only practicable mode, viz. by force ; in other words, the Governor being of right the sole judge of questions respecting native territorial rights, is justified in enforcing his jurisdiction in the only practicable mode, viz by military occupation." . . . Mr. Richmond has entirely overlooked the consequences of his theory, namely, that if the treaty of Waitangi be (as his argument assumes it to be) a treaty in the ordinary sense, then the right of interpreting and enforcing the treaty must belong, not to one party, but to both equally ; that the natives are at liberty to resort to force in support of their view, as much as the Governor in support of his ; and that they cannot be charged with rebellion if they do so.— *Remarks, &c., by Sir William Martin*, p. 42.

since, about the land. Accordingly, the "entire chieftainship" [rangatiratanga] of their lands, of their kaingas, and of all their property, was guaranteed. Of this chieftainship, it must be observed, no mention is made in the English version of the treaty; and it was for the exercise of this by Wiremu Kingi in 1860, that war was declared against him at Waitara. They, on the other hand, according to the English version, were required to yield to the Queen " the exclusive right of pre-emption over such lands as the proprietors thereof may be disposed to alienate."

The meaning of this the natives assuredly did not understand; nor would they ever have agreed to it had they perceived all the bearings of the demand. The stipulation was for the exclusive right of buying all the land ; and in effect, though not in words, at *whatever price* the Government chose to give, and at *whatever time* they found it convenient to purchase. No such consequence could be drawn from the corresponding words in the Maori version of the treaty, which, literally translated, are, " shall surrender to the Queen the purchase of those portions of ground as agreeable to any person being the proprietor of such land." They were led to believe that the Crown was to have the option of purchase; in their own language, the "HOKONGA;"* not that they should be debarred from selling at all, if the Government, as actually happened, was short of funds to buy with ; or that the Crown, being sole bidder, should have power to fix the price, and be thus enabled to acquire extensive tracts at the rate of a mite an acre, to be presently retailed at from 1*l.* to 1600*l.*†

From this point of our intercourse with the natives commences that distrust of the Government, which in the end ripened into open dislike and rebellion. The present war is traceable, step by step, up to this unfortunate reservation of power, which at once placed the Governor, theoretically supposed to be the chief protector of native interests, in the position of chief bargainer for the much coveted land, buying cheap and selling dear. After two-and-twenty years of unintermitted attack upon what was called " the Government brokerage," the exclusive right of pre-emption was abrogated by law, to the great triumph of those who were mainly interested in the welfare of the native race, and notwith-

---

* We may here take occasion to observe, that the native interpretation of the pre-emption clause was supported by Dr. Phillimore and Mr. Shirley Woolmer, to whom the question was referred, for a legal opinion, by the Society for the Protection of Aborigines.

† For all their good intentions, the Government, to borrow an illustration from *Measure for Measure*, " concluded like the sanctimonious pirate, that went to sea with the ten commandments, but scraped one out of the table." They meant well when they assumed the tutorship, but razed the prohibition to make a profit out of the ward.

standing the protest of those who considered the tax which had been so long wrung from the aboriginal landowners as a legitinate addition to the provincial revenues. But the evil had been consummated, for the ill-will of the natives had been almost irretrievably aroused. It was but idle talk assuring them that the profit derived from the retailing of the land was indirectly carried to their account through the expenditure upon public works, and the increased value given thereby to the lands which remained in their hands for sale; for they perfectly well knew that value would be no more than ideal where there was not a market price for the commodity; nd they learned by experience that the promises thrown in by Government as make-weights to the price were not fulfilled. Our readers may be surprised when we inform them that the whole of the land commencing at Kaiapoi, in the Middle Island, and extending south to Molyneaux, amounting to about 22 million of acres, was acquired from the natives by a payment of 2000*l.*, with an assurance given by the Commissioner, on behalf of the Government, that they must not regard the 2000*l.* as the principal payment, but must allow for the benefits they would gain from schools erected for their education, from medical attendance, and the general hospitable care of the Government. These lands, said the Commissioner himself (at that time Native Minister) in the House of Representatives, had passed to the Government; but the promise had never been properly fulfilled.

It would be unfair, however, to leave entirely without notice, the alleged motive for the pre-emptive reservation; good in itself, though based on an assumption which was soon discovered to be groundless. It was said, and believed by those unacquainted with the country, that Europeans, if allowed to purchase directly from the natives, would take advantage of their inexperience, and succeed in despoiling them of their possessions for a nominal consideration. The plea fell into disuse; for it was soon discovered that a native could hold his own in a bargain against the smartest European. All he needed was an open market, in which to get the best price he could for himself; but this was the very advantage denied him by the Government.

Only the northern island was acquired by treaty; the middle and southern islands were at once taken possession of by proclamation. We dispensed with formality, being apprehensive that the French might be beforehand with us. But having thus secured the acquisition, we went through the process of acquiring the middle island over again, by virtue of a treaty with certain natives residing at Cloudy Bay. There is something not quite satisfactory in the exemplification of an over-worldly maxim, that " it is well to have two strings to one's bow;" and this, coupled with the fact of Governor Hobson having brought down of Government officers with him from Sydney, though necessarily uncertain whether or not the treaty would be agreed to, seems to indicate that the annexation of New Zealand to the empire was a foregone conclusion. It is, moreover, remarkable that no stipulation for the abolition of slavery should have been inserted in the treaty. Some of our transatlantic cousins would be not ill-pleased to learn that the "peculiar institution" existed for years unnoticed in a remote nook of the Queen's dominions. The only emancipation on an extensive scale that has ever taken place, was at the instance of the missionaries; and even their efforts were crowned with only partial success.

Such was the arrangement under which we obtained the sovereignty of the country, and secured to the Government a monopoly in the trade for Maori lands. In return we engaged to impart to the aborigines all the rights and privileges of British subjects. The advantages we made the most of; the duties we forgot. The fruit of it was not long in ripening. The very first purchase effected by the Government was the cause of bloodshed. The facts must be disposed of in a few words.

In June, 1840, when Mr. Shortland, the Colonial Secretary, was at Monganui, obtaining the consent of the natives in that quarter to the treaty of cession, he met with a chief named Noble, who represented himself as the rightful owner of the lands in that quarter, while the occupiers claimed in right of conquest, some thirty years before. Taking advantage of the dispute about title, Mr. Shortland concluded a purchase; the inevitable result was a fight; about thirty were slain, the Monganui party being the victors. This was but the first instance out of many, distributed over a period of twenty years, and finally leading to the war in which we are now engaged.

The conduct of the Government towards the colonists was as vexatious as it was unjust towards the natives. Having founded Auckland, as a rival to Wellington, and attracted a large number of settlers by declaring it the capital of New Zealand, it then proceeded to extract the uttermost farthing from them by a very questionable expedient. The Company were offering for 100*l.* one hundred acres of country land, with a town acre given in. The Government, in order to give artificial value to their own land, brought into the market not nearly so much as was required to meet the demand, and thus succeeded in obtaining for town allotments from 300*l.* to 1600*l.* per acre; much to the surprise and dissatisfaction of the original native owners. But a still greater mistake was committed. The land-fund, instead of being set apart, and strictly reserved for its legitimate purposes—namely, immigration, roads, and the making further purchases of native lands—was treated as ordinary revenue; not as capital to be made reproductive, but as income, to be swallowed up by salaries and departmental expenses. It will presently be shown that the colonists themselves, when they obtained the power to amend, only perpetuated the error.

The Government, apparently deeming that the monopoly of land sales was not sufficiently secured to them by the exclusive right of pre-emption, now proceeded to declare war against the old settlers, who had purchased land from the natives before the annexation of New Zealand to the Empire, and who, if left undisturbed, might become rival vendors. To borrow an expression from Dr. Martin, "they attempted to found a new colony on the ruins of the old;" decrying land speculators in order to monopolize their trade; even the Government officers; with the Colonial Secretary at the head of them, taking advantage of their official position to job, and in a manner so irregular as to draw a rebuke from the Secretary of State for the Colonies. The feudal doctrine that all title to land derives from the Crown, was brought to bear against the landowners. This, in itself not quite an incontrovertible proposition,* at all events did not apply to the purchases in question. The position in law of those who had bought from the independent Maori before 1840, corresponded exactly with that of an Englishman who might have acquired an estate from a French Canadian before the annexation of Canada, or from a Dutchman before that of the Cape. In the three cases alike, private rights of property existing at the time of the cession of the country would remain intact. Nevertheless, an ordinance was made by the Legislative Council of the colony (composed of the Governor, three officials, and three nominees) confiscating the greater portion of these acquisitions, and empowering the Governor to give Crown grants for the remainder. Hence arose an acrimonious controversy, varied by occasional litigation, which for years made bitter the position of successive Governors, and entailed ruin upon the greater number of the aggrieved. It was alleged, in extenuation of so high-handed a measure, that estates had been bought for "a hatchet, or a blanket;" and that the property which had been acquired, was upon a scale prejudicial to the latent interests of the community. Pains were taken to give colour to the allegation by carefully confusing the *bonâ fide* land claims† about

---

* *Vide* Allen on Prerogative.

† This is one of the most curious features in the story of the claims. It appears that payments to the value of upwards of ninety-five thousand pounds were made by Europeans to natives for the purchase of land. Yet this sum, though it includes all that can be ascertained with tolerable certainty, by no means represents the whole amount which was paid away.—*Mr. Commissioner Bell's Report, July,* 1862.

No claim *acknowledged and maintained* by the natives was of such an extent

which alone was there any serious question, and which were of moderate extent, with certain imaginary purchases, mainly by Sydney speculators, defined after the fashion of the New Zealand Company, by degrees of latitude and longitude, or perhaps by the expression, " as far as a cannon-shot can reach."

The extent, however, of these acquisitions appears to be immaterial ; the simple question being whether a native tribe could convey a valid title to land fairly purchased from them during the period of their independence. It appears to us that nothing less than an act of the Imperial Parliament could destroy titles thus obtained ; and that Governor Hobson's ordinance was void, on the ground of repugnancy. But it was none the less effective; for Chief Justice Martin, in a judicial decision, stated that— " As a British subject could not be allowed to plead the invalidity of British law in a British court of justice, so a colonial subject of the Crown could not be allowed to plead the invalidity of colonial law in a colonial court." Without impugning a dictum from such high authority, we may observe that such is not the ordinary opinion of jurists ; and that there is at least one instance of the validity of a law having been successfully impeached in a colonial court.

The ordinance limited the claimants, as it was thought proper to term the owners, to a maximum (save in exceptional cases) of two thousand five hundred and sixty acres. The question remained, what was to become of the surplus, where the estate was larger in extent. Whereupon a curious doctrine was broached, namely, that the native by selling the land, had divested himself of his own title, but that the European buyer could not acquire that title ; *argal*, the land became demesne of the Crown ;* a somewhat startling extension of the rule that a felon can acquire property for the Crown, but not for himself.

The Government, whilst inveighing against greed, showed its own disinterestedness by absorbing the balance. But a dangerous effect was produced on the minds of the natives. Unable to ap-

---

as to justify the Government in disallowing it, on the ground of its extent or value making its recognition " prejudicial to the latent interests of the community." It appears from an official return, that five persons laid claim to 26 tracts of land, estimated, in the aggregate, at 7,950,000 acres ; but that of these five persons, four never made any attempt to substantiate their claims, and that the fifth does not appear to have made good his claim to a single acre. On the other hand, it is officially reported that out of 750 claims which had been examined by the Commissioners, only four or five had been disputed.

* Lord Stanley's authority has been adduced in support of this doctrine. If the despatch in question be referred to, it will be found that he reasons hypothetically, being careful to restrict himself to the terms of the case drawn up for him by the New Zealand Government.

preciate the subleties of legal distinctions, they regarded with a jealous eye the expropriation of those to whom they had sold land in favour of a new authority which had never purchased. They could see nothing in it but an arbitrary act of violence. " If the Queen," said they, " treats her own children so, how will she treat us?" They sided with their old friends, and determinately resisted the first attempt of the Government to occupy.* In return for this, for the good offices were mutual, the claimants, who would much rather that the surplus went back to the natives than to the Government, were careful to open their eyes to another view of the case, namely, as argued by Mr. Terry :—

" That the land must be the property either of the buyer or the seller; it cannot belong to a third party. If a claim is altogether invalid, surely the land will remain the property of the Aborigines; so ought whatever portion is disallowed by the Commissioners to revert to them by the same rule of equity,"—

an argument which was deemed unanswerable by the sellers.

Bloodshed was spared, in this instance, through timely concession; but shortly after occurred the fatal massacre at Wairau, proceeding from a dispute about land, claimed by the Company, but of which no valid purchase had been effected. The natives, under their chiefs, Rauparaha and Rangihaeta, finding the surveyors on the ground, requested them to desist. No regard being paid to the demand, they carefully removed all property out of the huts, carried it into the surveyors' tents, and then set fire to the huts, observing that they had a right to do as they pleased with their own. The surveyors returned to Nelson, and procured from the police magistrate a warrant against the chiefs for arson. The Government brig was then in port; the magistrate himself, with Captain Wakefield, the Company's agent, several of the principal gentlemen of the settlement, and about forty labourers, all armed, proceeded in her to the Wairau to execute the warrant. A collision ensued; Rangihaeta's wife was shot in the *mêlée;* the Europeans were over-matched, but the gentlemen stood their ground, were taken prisoners, and tomahawked in revenge.

Governor Hobson died in office, and Captain Fitzroy was appointed in his stead. He reached New Zealand at an unfortunate time for himself, for troubles were fast gathering around. His administration has been much decried, mainly by those connected with the Company, and he was ultimately recalled. Nevertheless, upon a dispassionate view of his career, with the advantage of the experience that has since been gained, it remains to be shown how, upon the whole, he could have acted better, under the circum-

---

* Terry's case.

stances. His issue of paper money, the one unpardonable sin at the Colonial Office, was unavoidable.

He was more sinned against than sinning ; and none will deny him the credit of unselfishness : of having sacrificed himself to what he believed to have been his duty to the colony. It is now perceived that he saw farther into the future than others ; he was in advance of the time, and shared the general fate of those who do not chime in with the dominant ideas of the period.

The colony had already lapsed into a state of extreme financial embarrassment. The new Governor was left without the means to fulfil the obligation incurred at Waitangi, of purchasing the land offered for sale : the northern natives were clamorous with disappointment. In want of money, troops, and military stores, he followed the only course left open, that of waiving the Crown's right of pre-emption, on payment of a small fee to the Government. Lord Stanley, Secretary of State for the Colonies, showed a generous appreciation of the difficulties with which the Governor was beset, and sanctioned the arrangement. The natives were so far content ; as well they might be, in again obtaining, as before the treaty, a market price. For the lands favourably situated, near to Auckland, about 1*l.* per acre may be taken as an average. As much as 5*l.* an acre was in one instance refused ; but that was for land which they chose to keep. Explicit instructions had been given to the agents of Government, during the administration of Mr. Shortland, not to pay more than 3d. per acre.

Further difficulties were awaiting Governor Fitzroy in another part of the colony—at Taranaki, where the conflicting interests of Maories and Europeans have been throughout most glaringly opposed. The Company had effected what they called a purchase. The deed was drawn out in English, and the boundaries defined by latitude and longitude, embracing a space of country belonging to thousands of natives who never saw the Company's agent. One Richard Barrett, a Pakeha Maori, acted as interpreter. Colonel Wakefield himself acknowledged that his object in so loose a transaction was " to secure the land from Sydney speculators." This title was inquired into by Mr. Commissioner Spain, who recommended a Crown grant for 60,000 acres, on the assumption that certain of the Ngatiawa tribe had, by their captivity or absence, lost all claim to the land. This was not good Maori law, and the greatest excitement prevailed.

A large meeting of Europeans and natives was assembled at New Plymouth, to hear the final decision of the Governor. The Governor refused to confirm the award, and allowed in all their integrity the claims of those of the Ngatiawa tribe who were not parties to the sale in 1840. In consideration of a further payment, the natives gave up all claim to the site upon which the town was built, and to the adjacent land, 3500 acres in all. The governor publicly and officially recognised the right of the ancient owners to resume the rest of the district, including the Waitara, the block for the possession of which the present war was entered on.

Governor Fitzroy was not equally successful in hindering an outbreak at the north. The point from which the hostile movement had its rise, was a belief, fostered by various ill-disposed persons, that the Treaty of Waitangi was violated, that the land was to be seized, that the people were to be made slaves, and that the Government only waited for an opportunity to carry these intentions into effect. Yet the natives were desirous to avoid bloodshed. When Heke commenced his " war with the flagstaff at Maiki," as he termed his opposition to the Government, he declared constantly that he fought " not against man, but against *he rakau, i. e.,* the wood of the flagstaff, which had no blood. His quarrel was not with the settlers, but with the emblem of the Queen's authority.

The disturbance out of which the war immediately arose commenced in April, 1844, in the seizure of two American whalers in the Bay of Islands, fined 300*l.* for non-compliance with the Customs regulations. The agent for these ships was reported by the natives at the time to have informed them that mischief would befal them in consequence of the flagstaff and Custom House ; that no American ship would visit the Bay on account of these seizures ; that he would proceed to America to fetch men-of-war to rectify these evils, and remove the flagstaff and Custom House. In a few days after the delivery of this speech, he sailed from the Bay, leaving the natives under the impression that he had departed for the purpose of putting his threat into execution. This part of the account we do not remember to have seen in print ; but it is authentic.

The disaffection increased rapidly ; Heke twice cut down the flagstaff ; the third time it was defended, and in the fight which ensued the town was burned, though not by design. The attacking party even assisted the settlers, with whom they had no quarrel, in carrying their goods down to the beach. Hostilities were then commenced in earnest, but, owing to the rashness of the officer commanding the forces, with ill success on our part. The Home Government, for various causes, became dissatisfied, and Governor Fitzroy was superseded by Governor Grey.

The natives professed to have no cause of quarrel against us, so long as the flagstaff was down ; and we, on our part, did not risk the setting it up again. But they were still quite willing to fight when attacked. At this time only the embers of war were left.   Governor Grey, deeming it advisable to gain some success to redeem the disaster at Ohaeawai, renewed it.   Kawiti's Pah, Ruapekapeka, was invested by a mixed force of regulars, volunteers, and native allies ; and one fine Sunday morning, while the defenders were outside at prayers, our natives crept in, and we followed, without the loss of a man.   The others, in the endeavour to retake the Pah, inflicted some loss on us, but suffered more themselves.   Governor Grey, considering that enough had been done to save our credit, accepted overtures of peace ; nominally, with the advantage on our side ; in reality, on theirs ; for the flagstaff still lay prostrate.   Nor was it raised until the time of his successor.

The policy of Grey was diametrically opposite to that of Fitzroy, as Fitzroy's had been to that of Hobson, and as that of Gore Browne was, in its turn, to Grey's.   The Company, who had been jealous of the favour shown to the landholders in the North, and had exerted themselves to the utmost to procure Fitzroy's recal, had no reason to be dissatisfied with the views of his successor. He retracted the waiver of pre-emption, and attacked certain of the grants already made to the original settlers ; but unfortunately, in a " secret and confidential" despatch, immediately made public by the Secretary of State, he also committed himself to the assertion that the grantees, including Church Missionaries, had caused the war.   The charge was resented and disproved ; but the Governor steadily refused either to substantiate or retract. A period of bitter controversy ensued, the damaging effects of which endured until his departure from the colony.   He probably wrote under a hasty impression, misled by imperfect or one-sided information ; but his main error was in making no amends when the refutation, by proof unanswerable, was made good.   A reputation for infallibility is dearly earned at such a price.

We touch upon these matters as lightly as fairness to the colonists will permit ; for the most prominent supporters whom Governor Grey has now in the colony are those who were most strongly opposed to him during his former administration.   Being of those who have defended native rights throughout, they cordially support him in his present endeavours to save the race, even while vigorously prosecuting a war which has become a necessity ; and bury all former causes of grief under this—the one essential consideration.

The pre-emption land claimants were obliged to accept such terms as were offered by the Government.   Their legal position was unsound, and their only reliance was on the good faith of the transaction between themselves and the Crown.   The grantees and the old land claimants offered a sturdy resistance.   In the Supreme Court, judgment was given in favour of one of Fitzroy's augmented grants. This led to a partial settlement of the claims, although the decision was reversed on appeal to the Judicial Committee of the Privy Council, who, while not questioning the Governor's power to make the grants, discovered an informality in his mode of doing it. So obstinate was the resistance, that the Government was driven to very questionable shifts to obtain possession of the confiscated lands.

One of these consisted in a pretended extinction of the native title. The process was to offer money to the original owners of the land, tempting them to sell it a second time, in order that the Government, upon the strength of the native conveyance thus acquired, might take possession. If the natives refused the bribe, alleging that the land had been fairly bought from them before, it was pressed upon them until their virtue failed ; thus breaking down in the native mind that punctilious respect for agreements by which they had been once so honourably distinguished. The following example is quoted from a speech delivered by Mr. Busby, formerly British resident in New Zealand, at the table of the House of Representatives. Whether the native actually used the strong expressions towards the Governor which he mentions in his narration, we cannot undertake to say ; but the account of the interview is accurately rendered from the Maori recital. Nor is it likely that the native should have coined so gratuitous an untruth.

" His parting remembrance to me was to send for a native of Wangarei, and tell him that he was to go to Mr. Johnston, who was going to Wangarei to purchase the land which was mine. The native came to me, and gave me the following account of the interview :—' I was led,' said he, ' into the presence of the Governor, who told me I was to go with Mr. Johnston, who was going to Wangarei to purchase the land. I said to him, " O Governor, the men of Wangarei will not sell that land to you, for they sold it many years ago to Mr. Busby.' He said he intended to pay you for the land in proportion as you had paid for it—if much, much ; if little, little. I then replied, ' The men of Wangarei will not allow any white man to live on that land without the leave of their father (meaning myself.)' The Governor then said, ' Are you a gentleman ?' O Mr. Busby, great was my boldness in the presence of the Governor when he asked me if I were a gentleman ; and I said to him—' Amongst my own people I am a gentleman, although I may appear a slave in your sight. But if you stood in the presence of my people divested of your Governor's clothes, perhaps you would appear as little a gentleman there as I do here.' He then said I was a child ; the elders would listen to Mr. Johnston : and I replied, ' O Governor, I now perceive you are a robber of land !' . . . . . .

" The first person who received money from the Government for my land no sooner reached Wangarei, than he was forced by the other natives to bring it back to the Government. He was again prevailed upon to take the money (200*l*.), and he was then deprived of the whole of it by the rest of the natives. Though his signature was to my title-deed, he was a very inconsiderable person amongst them who sold me the land. At this time I wrote to the Government, entreating them not to corrupt the natives, who had already divested themselves in my favour of all title to the land, and who could not convey to the Government a title they had ceased to possess, but to try the legal question between the Government and myself in the Supreme Court.

"The Government declined this proposition: I then offered to convey my title—which had never been disputed by any one—to the Government, on their agreeing to refer to the decision of the Chief Justice what amount of money would be an equitable compensation, under all the circumstances, for my having procured the tract of land in question, and having conveyed it to the Government. This proposition was also met by a refusal. The Government continued their efforts to corrupt the natives, of whose integrity it is a remarkable proof, that it was eighteen months after the principal chief first told the commissioner that the land was mine, and refused to treat with him respecting it, that that chief told me that he 'had then, for the first time, consented to take money for my land.' These were the words he used, and here capitulated at length the arguments by which his conscientious objections had been overcome.

"The Government in this way worse than wasted between 3000*l*. and 4000*l*. of the public money. One is lost in astonishment at the fatuity of men in such a position as that of the principal officers of Government, in supposing that men could convey a second time rights of which they had previously divested themselves; and that they could procure for the Government a title, by forcing money upon men who told them the title was not theirs to convey. The waste of money was but one part of the evil. A large assemblage of armed natives took place soon after at Kororareka, headed by one of the most troublesome of those who commenced the war on the first occasion. Their object was to obtain from the settlers there a second payment for the land, to which they said they were as well entitled as the people of Wangarei. Nothing prevented a second outbreak but the influence of Pene Taui, the most influential chief of Heke's party, who had been gained over to the Government by having been employed, with his people, to make a road from the harbour to his village."

We must restrict ourselves to one more instance, which created a great sensation at the time, and which has at last been decided in favour of the person aggrieved. A man named Meurant had married a native woman, by whom he had a family. Certain chiefs transferred to her by native deed thirty acres of land, " as a marriage portion and for the support of her children." This land being within two miles of Auckland was considered valuable. The Government seized it; retained twenty acres, and gave the *husband* a Crown grant for the remainder—this grant containing a false recital. A petition was presented to the Legislative

Council by the husband on behalf of his wife. In this it was shown that the confiscation of the land, under such circumstances, was in fact a premium upon concubinage ; for that if the woman had lived unmarried with Meurant, no power in New Zealand could have touched her land. It was also shown that this case had a direct bearing upon the political status of half-castes—whether they had English rights, Maori rights, or no rights at all ; a question which the Legislature had been careful never to decide, because of its obviously awkward bearing upon the Government doctrine concerning land. The case was stifled in Council, on the plea that the petitioner had told an untruth, *i. e.*, had made a misstatement ; which, however, was afterwards traced to the Colonial Secretary himself, petitioner having merely copied it. The Government attempted to make a title by purchasing the land from the donors, but the money was rejected by all but one. The land was twice put up for sale by public auction. The first time no one could be found to bid, the case having excited strong public feeling ; subsequently, the Colonial Secretary, we believe, made a purchase. The matter was brought again and again before the Secretary of State for the Colonies, who declined to interfere, and would not even allow the correspondence to appear in the New Zealand Blue Book, though specially requested to do so. Had it not been for the watchfulness of the Society for the Protection of Aborigines, the case would entirely have escaped notice in England. The story may appear incredible ; but can be substantiated, in every particular, from the papers concerning it in the Colonial Office.

We must now make mention, in the fewest possible words, of the war in the south, which began at the Hutt, near Wellington, spreading to Porirua and Wanganui. The Company had made one of their usual loose purchases, and the natives objected to the occupation of a piece of land, on the ground that some of the owners remained unsatisfied. The Company's agents stated that the land had been paid for three times over. This may or may not have been ; but the question still remained, whether the money had been paid to the right men, and to all of them. The Company, who bought in a hurry, were not aware of the extreme care required in making purchases. The punctilious fidelity of natives to their land bargains is remarkable ; but the extinction of title must be absolute and complete. The Company should have taken a lesson from the warier and more experienced purchasers in the north. The primary rule with them was to institute the most searching inquiry for all the owners, and never to make sure of complete success. Those who were to receive the larger portion of the purchase-money would come forward readily enough ; but it was always possible that two or three of those whose share

was inconsiderable would keep in the background, for the purpose
of raising a difficulty at some convenient time, and being bought
off on good terms. The sum originally agreed upon being paid,
the buyer would hear nothing more about the matter, possibly
for years, until entering into *actual occupation.* Then, after a
while, a native would stalk into his *whare,* sit down for half a day
without a word; but intimate at last that he had not yet been
settled with. No surprise would be manifested, for some such
visit had been expected. The fellow might demand—say, a cask
of tobacco; he would be quietly talked down (the great secret
with natives) perhaps to a single fig of it, value threepence; would
walk away perfectly content, never to reappear: for the "correct"
thing had been done. But this same man would have died on
the land, sooner than abandon his claim. He would, if he could,
have said, with Hotspur:—

> "I do not care: I'll give thrice so much land
> To any well-deserving friend:
> But in the way of bargain, mark ye me,
> I'll cavil on the ninth part of a hair."

The troops were ordered up to the ground in dispute, where
they burned a small chapel; an accident that was made the most
of by Rangihaeta, though himself a heathen. A murder—the
almost invariable native preliminary to war—was committed.
During the consequent hostilities, Martin Luther, a prisoner of
war, was hanged as a rebel. He was a Wanganui native; and this
execution appears to have been the cause of the outbreak at
Wanganui, which was only hastened by the accidental discharge
of a pistol in the hands of a midshipman. This war came to a
conclusion in a most indefinite manner. The last authentic fact
discoverable is, that the natives, after inviting the soldiers to
come out of their stockade and fight, took themselves off,
politely informing us that they were going to plant their potatoes,
but would willingly come back again when wanted.

Let us now give a few words to the New Zealand Charter of
1846, and its accompanying Letter of Instruction. Earl Grey,
the author of it, had come into office with views differing much
from those entertained by Lord Stanley. He favoured the Company, and proceeded to dispose of the land question on a new
principle.

The political merits or demerits of this short-lived constitution
are beside the present purpose; we have to deal with it only as it
affects the land. It met with no favour in New Zealand, either
from colonists or Governor, being far too complicated and fanciful
for use. With the exception of the thirteenth chapter of the
Letter of Instruction, it was laughed at; but that exception

caused consternation among all those who understood the natives, and were aware of the tenacity with which they would maintain their rights over even a single rood of land. Lord Stanley had administered a severe rebuke to the Company for desiring to set aside the treaty, after obtaining the advantages derived from it, even though it might " be treated by lawyers as a praiseworthy device for amusing and pacifying savages for the moment." But Earl Grey's Instructions do most clearly violate that treaty. It is true, that in the accompanying despatch, he accepts the treaty as *un fait accompli;* guarding himself, in words, from being supposed to entertain the intention of disturbing it; he also, in a subsequent despatch, defending himself from the imputation, reminds Bishop Selwyn that his observations concerning the treaty were only theoretical. But the fact remains, that by the Instructions, which are definite and precise, he over-rode it. He probably did not himself perceive the effect of them; but about that effect not a shadow of doubt can exist.

The question had been often asked in New Zealand—" What are the demesne lands of the Crown?" There was no land in the country without an owner; the natives had been guaranteed possession of their own; the land acquired from them by the Government had been purchased with the money of the colonists; and there was none other left but the surplus land, *i.e.* the land confiscated from the estates of the original settlers. Lord Grey introduced a very short and effective mode of creating " demesne lands of the Crown." By the fifth and sixth clauses of the chapter in question, it will be seen that, in the first place, an officer appointed at the pleasure of the Government, is called upon to find out claims; to register provisionally, and within a given period, the land of the aborigines within his province: in default thereof—within a time not specified—all lands not claimed, or thus registered, are to be escheated to the Crown. But there is no guarantee to the natives that the officer will be able, or willing, or competent to fulfil the conditions of these clauses. The rights which had been secured to the natives are now made to depend upon the fallibility, or even the wilful neglect, of an individual.

Land courts, whose decision is final, are also constituted, to which the natives are compelled to submit their claims. The court is appointed by the Crown, presided over by an officer of the Crown, and limited in its judgment of the validity of claims by rules laid down by a functionary of the Crown. The injustice of such an appeal is flagrant, and would never have been submitted to.

The rules laid down by this functionary, had he been left unrestricted, might have been fair, and so far not repugnant to the treaty. But the Instructions proceed, on the theory of labour alone constituting right of property in land, to define the rules by which the Land Court shall be guided in the adjudication of such claims as are referred to its arbitrary decision.

"IX. No claim shall be admitted in the said Land Courts on behalf of the aboriginal inhabitants of New Zealand, to any lands situate within the said islands, unless it shall be established to the satisfaction of such Court, that either by some act of the Executive Government of New Zealand, as hitherto constituted, or by the adjudication of some court of competent jurisdiction within New Zealand, the right of such aboriginal inhabitants to such lands has been acknowledged and ascertained, or that the claimants or their progenitors, or those from whom they derived title, have actually had the occupation of the lands so claimed, and have been accustomed to use and enjoy the same either as places of abode, or for tillage, or for the growth of crops, or for the depasturing of cattle, or otherwise for the convenience and sustentation of life by means of labour expended thereupon."

Setting aside the fact that the land which has *not* been subdued is of the greater value to the natives; that they abandon the land which has been worn out by use, not practising the four course system of farming, or understanding the mysteries of guano, but working progressively forward into the heart of the forest, upon virgin soil; to say nothing of the casting the *onus probandi* on the native owners; of the expenses attendant on proof; of the certainty that they would refuse, as many of the colonists had already refused, submission to an *ex post facto* law; it is enough to observe that the treaty recognised the native title unconditionally, even guaranteeing the chieftainship over the lands. The thirteenth chapter of Instructions is simply a scheme of confiscation under colour of law.

The Governor could not be brought to admit that a breach of treaty was committed; but he appears to have stood alone in his opinion—at least in the North: for among the Company's settlers many held the Company's views. The receipt of the Instructions was followed by a period of extraordinary excitement, both among Maori and Europeans. Nothing hindered the natives from rising but the strenuous exertions of Bishop Selwyn and the missionaries, by whose influence they were induced to give time for a reference to the Queen.

The judgment passed upon the Instructions by the Northern settlers was, we believe, unanimous. Public meetings were held; memorials drawn up; the local press laboured to the utmost, but while protesting against Chapter 13, refrained for a while from giving it publicity, in order that the natives should *not* learn precisely what was intended for them. The Chief Justice put forth a pamphlet, in which he proved, unanswerably, the breach of treaty;

the Bishop addressed a protest to the Governor, which caused some very sharp correspondence, in which the two parties went so far as to come to issue about a matter of fact. But we must avoid reviving old griefs ; for, though Mr. Labouchere asserted in the House that " he did not believe that there really existed, on the subject of waste lands, any difference of opinion between Governor Grey and Earl Grey," the former appears to be entitled to the credit of having obtained an abnegation of intent, with which the natives were satisfied. The Governor also procured a suspension of a portion of the Charter and Instructions on grounds less disagreeable to the Secretary of State ; but it is remarkable that the objectionable clauses were suffered to remain nominally in force, though never acted on.

We pass lightly over the break-up of the New Zealand Company, and the interminable complications connected therewith, as being a mere money matter, not directly affecting the government of the colony, and interesting only to political antiquarians. It is enough to say, that Earl Grey admitted what his predecessors did not, that the Company had been aggrieved by the Home Government, and granted it terms of extraordinary favour. Now the whole point in dispute between the Company and the Government was, whether they had fairly extinguished the native title to the twenty millions of acres claimed in right of purchase at the rate, it has been calculated, of a halfpenny an acre. The great and ultimate grief, to which all the rest are merely incidental, had been the refusal of the Government to recognise the title of the Company without proof of equitable purchase. On the assumption that the natives had no right to any more land than they cultivated, the Company had a good grievance. On the assumption that the treaty, guaranteeing to the natives the whole of the soil of their country, was based on principles of justice and equity, the Company was as clearly out of court.

An Act, intituled the New Zealand Company's Colonization Act, was passed, by which, firstly, all the demesne lands of the Crown in the Province of New Munster—that is to say, all New Zealand except the northern half of the northern island—were vested in the Company in trust for certain purposes. Secondly, power was given to the Treasury to advance to the Company, by way of loan, 136,000*l.* in addition to 100,000*l.* authorized under a former Act. Thirdly, the Company was enabled to relinquish the undertaking, at a given time, should it prove unprofitable ; and fourthly, by Section 20, which well merits an attentive perusal, all claim to either of the said loans was remitted, upon reversion to the Crown of the lands belonging to the Company, and the sum of 263,370*l.* was to be paid to the Company out of the proceeds of all future sales of the demesne lands of the Crown in

New Zealand, being after the rate of five shillings for each acre of certain lands to which the Company were entitled.

It can cause no surprise that the Company, taking advantage of terms so favourable for winding up, should have relinquished the undertaking at the appointed time. But how such an Act could have got through the House, it is less easy to understand. The views expressed by Earl Grey concerning the treaty explain the bringing in of the Bill; but we must fall back upon the immense parliamentary influence possessed by the Company—at one period strong enough to shake the ministry of Sir Robert Peel—to account for its being passed. It would be idle to waste a word upon what appears on the face of the Act; but there is more behind. When the management of the waste lands of the Crown was entrusted to the colonists, it was made a condition that they should take upon themselves the reduced debt of 200,000*l.*, against the Company's estate, which was given up to them. They found that, after satisfying the liabilities contracted by the Company, the estate would not nearly meet the charge, at the rate per acre named in the Act. They were then informed that even if not a single acre were left, they would still be liable for the whole debt. And, indeed, upon close examination of Section 20, it will be found that the first impression conveyed by it is not the right one. Again, the debt was charged against the whole colony, including the Auckland settlement, which was unconnected with the Company, and had only been injured by it. Much to the credit of the southern provinces, they agreed to relieve the Auckland province from the share imposed.

We now reach the Constitution Act of 1852, under which the colonists at last came into their estate; being invested with a trust the most important that could be confided to a subordinate authority—that is, the administration of the public lands. Notwithstanding what we have said in reproof of the suspicion with which the colonists had been previously regarded, we must admit that it would have been better had the estate been more closely tied up.

But the Act itself, at least as appears to us, deals with the Land Fund upon an erroneous principle. By Section 66, it is provided that all the revenue arising from taxes, duties, rates, and imposts, and *from the disposal of the waste lands of the Crown,* shall be subject to be appropriated [to the purposes of the entire colony] by act of the Assembly; and the surplus which shall not be so appropriated shall be divided among the several provinces, to be subject to the appropriation of the Provincial Councils. In other words, the provinces are empowered to spend their shares of the Land Fund in salaries or any purpose they may think fit.

By this, it will be observed, customs and land revenue are treated alike as income; whereas the land revenue, so called, is in fact merely an encroachment upon capital. Year by year, the custom duties increase in amount; while year by year there is less land remaining for sale. This is clearly bad husbandry: every farmer knows that what he takes from the soil he must put into it again, under pain of reducing his acres to sterility. In like manner, ought the Land Fund to be reserved for purposes immediately connected with the land—for the improvement of the face of the country itself, by roads, bridges, and such-like public works. So would the remainder quantity, like the Sibyls' books, gain value in inverse ratio to its diminution. But the framers of the Imperial Act, without sufficient forethought, fused the two sources of revenue together, setting an example which the colonists were not slow to follow, bettering the instruction.

The manner in which the Assembly acquitted themselves of the trust is remarkable. Without any power of delegation, they transferred it to the provincial authorities; each province to make the best of its own share. Though a subordinate Legislature, with derivative authority strictly defined by the Act of Parliament which gave it existence, they undertook to confer powers upon themselves, making "An Act to authorize the General Assembly to empower the provincial Councils to enact laws for regulating the rate, letting, disposal, and occupation of the waste lands of the Crown." This Act, since admitted to have been illegal, was carelessly passed by the law officers of the Crown, who little know what trouble and confusion might be avoided did they only exercise a more vigilant censorship, and resolutely disallow every colonial statute that is in any way repugnant to English law.

The evils of thus handing over the lands soon became apparent. By this transfer of power the provinces were invited to compete with each other for immigration,—to outvie each other in the apparent favourableness of the terms offered to emigrants, which brought in shoals of helpless adventurers before the country was prepared for them; in some cases even before the lands on which they were to be settled had been surveyed. But worse than this accrued. The colonists, who when in bondage had so eloquently inveighed—and with just cause—against the unscrupulousness of the governing powers, were themselves found wanting. The provincial land-regulations, made and changed not only according to the fancy of those several provinces, but also according to that of the successive governments of those provinces, were too often prostituted to party purposes. Rival candidates for provincial honours soon found that the most effective move in vote-catching was to promise extraordinary

advantages in the acquirement of freeholds to the poorer class
of voters; and, as the New Zealand suffrage may be practically
termed universal, such appeals were not always made in vain.
And if there be instances in which the expected harvest of
suffrages has not been gathered, the credit is rather due to the
honesty of the people than to the political morality of some of
their leaders.

Many matters of interest have now to be passed over as not
directly bearing upon the question to which we must confine
ourselves—that of the land. We therefore step forward, from
the introduction of representative institutions, to the establishment of Parliamentary or "responsible" Government. Colonel
Gore Browne arrived in 1855 with instructions to concede to the
colonies complete local self-government. In the Session of 1856
the Crown officials were replaced by gentlemen possessing the
confidence of the Legislature. From this time began the division
of the Government into two branches, one for the administration
of European, the other of Maori affairs. In the mode of creating
and carrying out this distinction lie the main facts connected
with the question which has arisen between the colonists and the
Home Government,—the question whether we are at this moment
in New Zealand waging an imperial or a settlers' war.

The sole condition imposed by the Home authorities upon the
concession of Parliamentary Government was the making provision for the Crown officials who were about to be displaced.
Either they had forgotten the natives, or they considered that
certain restrictive clauses in the Constitution Act were a sufficient
safeguard to native interests. But Governor Browne took upon
himself to impose a further condition. He coupled the concession by which the powers of the Governor were to be handed over
to a Parliamentary majority with the very proper stipulation that
matters affecting imperial interests should be reserved for his
own consideration. But, unfortunately, as shown by subsequent
events, he included among imperial subjects "all dealings with
the native tribes, more especially in the negotiation of purchases
of land." In this reservation he was supported by the greater
number of those whom he thought proper to consult upon the
subject; by nearly the whole body of the clergy (Archdeacon
Hadfield being the only one, as far as we are aware, who openly
advocated the putting faith in colonial management), and by
those connected with the Native office; also by many of the
members of the House of Representatives. The Auckland members were unanimous; for although confident enough in their own
ability to undertake the care of the natives, among whom they
had lived and whom they thoroughly understood, they looked
forward to the possibility of a purely southern ministry coming

into office, who, through an assumed want of experience in native matters, might mismanage them. Others were unwilling to begin by opposing the Governor, who had already acquired much personal influence by his straightforwardness and prepossessing manner. Eventually, the reservation was quietly agreed to. But it may be questioned whether, if it had been stoutly opposed, the Governor could have risked, in the face of his instructions, a fracas with the Assembly. All parties acted conscientiously, all for the best; but those who induced the Governor to stipulate for the uncontrolled power of declaring war are indirectly responsible for the unhappy result. For it may be safely assumed, putting the question in its lowest form, that no responsible ministry would have been suffered by the House to advise a war, the whole expense of which must in that case have indubitably fallen upon the colony.

The argument mainly relied on by those who thought it unsafe to entrust native affairs to a parliamentary majority, was, that the instability of ministries, changed at the caprice of party, must entail a corresponding instability in what is somewhat ostentatiously termed "the native policy." To this it was replied, that the argument would equally apply to a change of governors. For a Governor, newly arrived, must be destitute of the information which could enable him to judge for himself, and it was mere matter of chance what hands he might fall into. It will presently be shown that Governor Browne fell into the wrong hands, committing himself to incompetent advisers, under whose guidance he was led to introduce a new policy, worse than the old one, which finally threw the colony into a state of almost inextricable confusion.

The Governor's assumption of exclusive responsibility in native affairs was approved by the Home authorities ; for it does not seem to have been perceived in England, any more than it was in the colony, at the time, that the double government must inevitably break down. For the reservation of such power to the Governor was, in point of fact, reservation to the native office, generally composed of officials whose main qualification was fluency in speaking the Maori language ; but who (to borrow an expression current in the colony) worshipped Diana of the Ephesians, treating Maori matters as a mystery, understood only by themselves ; who could not look forward with complacency to an abrogation of their craft, or to a fusion of duties which would take away exclusive powers from themselves ; and who might be expected to resent any attempt by the colonists to amend the administration of native affairs as an intrusion upon their prerogative. It was moreover soon discovered that the limits of jurisdiction, easily enough traced on paper, were practically indefinable ; that European and native questions must frequently overlap, and that each government, apart from all jealousies and misunderstandings, must find itself from time to time encroaching on the other.

The first collision was unavoidable, being in regard to laws for the benefit of the native race, which only the Assembly had power to enact. As soon as the first party ferment had subsided, the responsible ministers addressed themselves to the task of making good the engagements of the Crown at Waitangi,—of atoning for the *laches* of previous governments. This, owing to the partial inapplicability of English law to Maori conditions, could be effected only by legislation. The natives had been guaranteed " the full, exclusive, and undisturbed possession of their lands and estates," together with " all the rights and privileges of British subjects." But it became evident—and for this there is the authority of the Law Officers of the Crown, that the possession of the land did not involve the possession of the territorial rights which by English law are inseparable from the land. " Suppose," say the Law Officers of the Crown, " in a district of native land lying within the limits of an Electoral District, that one native by consent of the rest is permitted to have exclusive possession of a piece of land, in which he builds a native hut for his habitation, but is afterwards turned out or trespassed on by another native ; could he bring an action of ejectment or trespass in the Queen's Court in New Zealand ? Does the Queen's Court ever exercise any jurisdiction over real property in a native district ? We presume," they say, " this question must be answered in the negative ; and it must of necessity, therefore, follow that the subjects of householding, occupancy and tenements, and their value in native districts, are not matters capable of being recognised, ascertained, or regulated by English law."

It was our plain duty, if there be a shadow of value in a pledge, to have enacted, with the least possible delay after the signing of the treaty, fitting laws for the determination of questions relating to territorial rights ; to have established a competent tribunal for the hearing, not only of intertribal questions, but of questions between the natives and the Government,—a tribunal, in the words of Sir William Martin, perfectly independent of the Government ; wielding the full powers of a court of justice, and subject to the same checks and safeguards. There is but one cause to be assigned for the neglect :—that we feared throughout to do whatever had a tendency to confirm the native title, which it was convenient, for reasons already given, to leave, like the rights of half-castes, undefined. And the colonists found, when they were enabled, by the establishment of responsible Government, to undertake the duty for themselves, that nothing worth mentioning had been done for the native race, beyond the appointment of some resident magistrates, whose principal employment was in settling small debts, and in the subsidizing some missionary schools, useful so far as they went, but whose teaching did not reach the masses.

The ministerial scheme of native government, when matured, was embodied in five Acts of the Assembly :—for the constitution and regulation of native districts—for the administration of justice in those districts—for the support and management of native schools—for the colonization of mixed settlements—and for the recognition of aboriginal title to land in such a manner as to give to individual natives, under conditions, the rights incident to landed property, including, though to a limited extent, that of selling to the best bidder; thus at last sanctioning what had been so long urged upon the Government by the northern colonists—the principle of "direct purchase," or, as it was preferably termed, "the enfranchisement of native lands." To all of these, but the last, the Governor was a consenting party. But the Territorial Rights Bill, as the last was termed, contained provisions to which he could not agree. Among other objections, the chief of all was this,—that not the Governor, but the "Governor in Council," was empowered to act. The Council consisted of the colonial responsible advisers. This limitation of power was resisted by the Governor, who thought it an infringement of the compact made when Parliamentary Government was inaugurated. The representatives of the colonists insisted that they had been most careful not to trespass in the slightest degree upon the powers retained by the Governor; that he had them still, but that if additional powers were to be given by the Assembly, the Governor must be content to exercise those, but those only, under the advice of his ministers ; otherwise, they would leave him where he was before. Both parties thought themselves right; but not the slightest irritation was manifested on either side. The Governor did not veto the Act, but sent it home with reasons why it should be disallowed by the Queen ; and it was disallowed accordingly.

Now these five Acts were intimately connected, being, in reality, several portions of a whole. The Territorial Rights Act was the very keystone to the arch. When this was disallowed, the others became little better than dead letters : the attempt of the colonists to provide effectual government for the Maori was baulked ; and the native office reigned supreme.

But the state of native affairs was becoming more and more critical. There was evidently a great upheaving of the Maori mind. The people were fast awakening to the hollowness of our promises—to a sense of their true position, which was that of the fabled bat, between the birds and the beasts. British subjects only in subjection; called upon to pay allegiance without enjoyment of the corresponding privileges; their own nationality lost, and even such influence as their chiefs had once possessed for the maintenance of something like order, melting away. Hitherto we had ruled them on the principle of *divide ut imperes;* they now, for the first time, turned their thoughts to unity of action. The Government were warned, through the public press, of the serious nature of the movement, but the native office turned a deaf ear. *Laissez-faire* was the order of the day. The idea of combination was scouted by the old school of "Maori doctors," who in all their experience had never heard of such a thing. The colonists recognised the signs of the times, but the native office slept.

The land again was the cause of the revolution. The time had been when the natives were dissatisfied because the Government could not buy. Now, after having parted with more than half the country, they began to be chary of offer. Dislike to a Government which appeared to them a mere bargainer for their property, joined to a deep-rooted jealousy of further European advance into their territory, caused many to oppose any further cession of territory. Yet more land was really wanted in the northern portions of the colony, on account of the influx of settlers, who certainly were not slow to complain. In order to meet the pressure, the "ground-bait" system, so called in the Assembly, and severely commented upon, was introduced. It is impossible for us to say precisely when, or by whom, it was invented; it is enough to say that it was in common use.

It is scarcely necessary to mention that Maori lands are held, not in severalty, but in common; and that they cannot be alienated unless by consent of the tribe. "Ground-bait" was the clandestine purchase, from individuals, of their part interest in the block—the scattering of small sums of money among those of the tribe who might be found accessible to temptation. Mr. Commissioner, without entering into further negotiations, would then retire from the scene of operations, leaving the mischief to work. "Tahae whenua" (land-stealing) was the expression applied to the system by the natives. The certain result would be dissention within the tribe; and at last the objectors, wearied out with strife, would sometimes consent to the formal public sale, for the sake of quiet. Sometimes the land would be kept, and the money too; but it is to be presumed that the manœuvre was, upon the whole, found profitable, for otherwise it would have been abandoned. This, together with the advantage we had undoubtedly taken of the frequent intertribal feuds, even while honestly deploring them and the consequent bloodshed, begat the fixed idea that our main endeavours were bent towards obtaining undisturbed possession of the country, by causing them to consume each other.

The one strong feeling in the Maori is that of independence. From the first, they had never lost sight of their nationality. They had never intended to coalesce with the Pakeha, though willing and pleased to pay common allegiance to the Queen, whom they regarded with trust and affection ; to whom they were always ready to appeal against any invasion of their privileges ; against the Instructions of 1846, and against the occupation of the Waitara. Governors they cared little about, though ready to sign any number of complimentary addresses ; "for what," they would say, "is the value of a piece of paper?" The Governor was to them not so much the Queen's representative,* as the man who carried the bag. When there was a Lieutenant-Governor, who had no power over the public purse, they nicknamed him "Hikepene" (sixpence). For the white Runanga (the Assembly) —they cared still less, not even troubling themselves, save in exceptional instances, to register their votes ; for which, we believe, many might legally have qualified as householders, though not, under their custom of common tenure, as freeholders. They were content to keep amicable company with us—to enjoy the benefit of the same laws ; but not to amalgamate. The fusion of races was what they mainly feared. "Salt water and fresh," they said, "do not mix well together."

The Maori were as well aware as we are of the political importance which the possession of landed property confers. They had already parted with nearly the whole of the Middle Island, and with seven millions of acres in the Northern Island. It is true that they had yet far more than they could ever expect to use ; but if alienation were to go on at the same rate, it would not take long to reduce them all to pauperism. They did not take example from the Roman epicure, who slew himself for fear of starvation when reduced to a fortune of not more than eighty thousand pounds ; but took effective means of securing what was left. A number of influential tribes combined in the formation of a Land League.

We pass over, as comparatively unimportant, the Taranaki Land League, so called ; making mention of it only because it

---

* The Governor is commonly, but erroneously, regarded as the "representative" of the Crown. "Not in fact," says Lord Brougham ; "he does not even represent the Sovereign *generally*, having only the functions delegated to him by his commission, and being only the officer to execute the special powers with which the commission clothes him." And the Maories have always been taught by authority to regard the Queen personally as their ruler and governor, who, though far away, is ever mindful of their interests, and to whom, if wronged, they are to appeal as one ever willing to listen to their words.— Swainson's "New Zealand."

has been assiduously confused, for political purposes, with the true one. It was originated on the western coast, in 1849, on account of the sale by Ngatiapa of a piece of land lying between Whanganui and Otaki ; the price paid for which was deemed unsatisfactory. This movement appears to have been merely of a local nature, to hinder further alienation of a specific tract of country, and differing in so far from the Land League κατ' ἐξοχην, subsequently formed at Waikato, which was based on the principle that no lands whatever ought to be thenceforward alienated. The Waikato league was a serious affair, for the more northern settlers were much cramped in their farming operations. It was also needless ; for the Government, with all their shortcomings, were far from desiring to denude the Maori to a really injurious extent. But the absolute right of league was undeniable. " Unwise as it may be," observes the late Attorney-General, " this compact, so long as it is confined in its operation to those who are parties to it, is no more an offence against the law than an ' eight hours' movement,' or a ' temperance league.' "

Not so the King movement, which, in a technical point of view, was treasonable. Not that the promoters of it intended treason, any more than did that unlucky publican who was condemned and hanged for having said that he would make his son heir to the Crown. They seem, so far as they thought at all about the matter, to have deemed it not inconsistent with allegiance ; and had they chosen to confer upon Potatau the First a different title—had they called him Patriarch, or Superintendent, it would have been difficult to prove any contravention of the forms of law. So little, indeed, did the Government object to the word, that they left the King in receipt of his pension, and paid for his coffin furniture.

It is dangerous to speak precisely, either in regard to motive or time, of what was long in assuming a definite form, and which in its origin was no larger than a grain of mustard-seed. We are inclined to believe, however, that the main object of the King movement was, the consolidation of the land league. As might be expected, when it waxed strong, its purposes were extended. A characteristic story is told of an occurrence which took place at one of the earlier deliberative meetings, at Taupo, in 1856. Many proposals had been made to adopt extreme measures ; the more violent party advocated a clear sweep of all the pakehas, Governor, missionaries, pakeha Maories, and all. At one of the evening meetings, which was held in a large house lighted up for the occasion, one of the advocates for a general clearing out was very eloquently pressing his views upon his audience, when Tarahawaiki of Ngaruawahia walked quietly round, and, one after the other, put out the lights, till the place was in total darkness, and the speaker in possession of the house was brought to a full stop. "Don't you think you had better light up the candles again?" he said. "Most certainly," replied Tarahawaiki, "it was very foolish to extinguish them!" The meeting at once apprehended the meaning of this symbolical act, and the orator sat down amid roars of laughter, enjoyed at the expense of the exterminator.

The motives by which the King party were actuated are succinctly given in the following extracts from a despatch written by Governor Grey to the Secretary of State for the Colonies, contained among the papers laid on the table of the New Zealand House of Representatives, just now received from the colony:

"The natives allege, in reference to their disputes before the war, that these arose from a native assessor of the Crown, whilst trying to meet the wishes of the Government in obtaining land for the Europeans, having, with some of his people, been treacherously slain by some natives. They go on to state, that in this and similar instances, especially of land disputes, they in vain besought the Government to take some steps for establishing law and order in the country, and for affording protection to life and property amongst the native race. That their appeals were treated with indifference. That at last many of them arrived at the settled conviction that the Government intended to let them destroy one another, either to get rid of them or to obtain their lands. That it was their anxiety to save themselves from such calamities that at length induced many of their leading men, as a last resource, to join in the attempt to set up a national government, which might afford them that protection from the violent of their own race which they had in vain sought from the Queen's Government; and that if the settlers suffered, together with the natives, from such a state of anarchy as Ministers describe, that the settlers, as well as the natives, should refer their miseries to the true cause—the apathy and indifference, or the weakness, of the Government."

* * * * * *

"It is further to be observed, that the natives declare that they did not take up arms to prohibit the alienation of territory to the Crown, or to maintain any seignorial rights. They rest their justification for entering into the general conspiracy, which was undoubtedly formed throughout the island, by declaring that it was a struggle for house and home. Especially on the east coasts the natives have stated this to the Governor; adding, that various similar incomplete purchases of land had been made in their district, from natives who had only a qualified claim to such lands; and that the almost universal belief of the native race was, that a new system of taking lands was to be established, and that if they did not succeed, by a general and combined resistance, in preventing their houses and lands being taken by the Government from the natives of the Waitara, they would have been each in their turn despoiled in detail of their lands."

We now reach the eventful period of the land quarrel at the

Waitara; in considering which, it is necessary to set aside both the land-league and the King movement, with neither of which was it in any way connected; though strenuous endeavours were made, at a time when the proceedings of the Government were being severely scrutinized, to confuse it with them. Indeed, it is only of late that the main question has become somewhat cleared of the enormous masses of rubbish with which it has been purposely overlaid. It is enough to say that Te Rangitake, better known as William King, the chief of Waitara, had refused to receive Potatau's flag when it was sent down to Taranaki. It is true that after his forcible ejectment and the declaration of martial law, he and his tribe did place their lands under charge of the land leaguers, and join the King, for the sake of the Waikato alliance. But this, of course, in no way affects the prior question, namely, whether we were or were not justified in taking military occupation of the Waitara.

It is not our purpose, in this article, either to offer a history of the war, or to argue the question of its origin; for the latter has been already settled, in the most practical and decisive manner, by the restoration of the land to the Ngatiawa tribe. The task which we have prescribed to ourselves is simply to show the unhappy result of that great original error in colonization—the Government monopoly of the land-trade, by which "native policy" was reduced to a scheme for buying cheap and selling dear; and the Governor, who should have been looked up to by both races as mediator in disputes, lowered to the position of head of a firm. Still, it may be useful to indicate some leading points which may save labour to those who desire to learn more, enabling them to cast aside what is irrelevant in the huge pile of correspondence, despatches, and "able memoranda," which has been accumulated. Having ourselves been obliged to master them, we can only liken the work to forcing a passage through the Sargasso of the Atlantic—the sea of weeds.

"The Waitara," (we copy Swainson's description) "a fertile, open district, watered by a small river, ten miles to the north of the town, and navigable at high water by small coasting craft, was the locality which, in the first instance, was fixed upon for the site of the settlement; and it was represented by the surveyor to the New Plymouth Company, by whom the settlement was originally founded, that if they were deprived of that river, they would lose the only harbour in the neighbourhood, and the most valuable district for agriculture. But this much-coveted spot was not to be obtained from its native owners; so the Company were compelled, with great reluctance, to lay out the town upon a much less eligible site; and for nearly twenty years the open land at the Waitara has, with the Taranaki settlers, been an object of almost passionate desire."

As Taranaki is the garden of New Zealand, so is Waitara the garden of Taranaki. The natives had a deep-rooted regard for the spot. The father of the present chief, on his death-bed, had exacted a promise from his son never to sell the land. The feeling about it was much the same as would be that of an English proprietor of ancestral acres, whose pleasure-grounds were invaded by a railway company. But Naboth's vineyard, as the Maori called it, was fated never to remain long unsought. The New Plymouth settlers, "cabined, cribbed, confined" within the limits of a few thousand acres, certainly did put pressure on the Governor, though not, by his own account, of a very stringent nature; for he reports that "although the greater part, and all the most respectable settlers, have abstained from expressing discontent, individuals have from time to time, by letters in the newspapers and otherwise, shown a strong desire to expel the natives and take possession of the lands, to which they consider themselves entitled, in right of the original New Zealand Company's purchase."

We are unable to say whether the opinion of the Taranaki Provincial Council is to be taken as a fair representation of the opinion of the province, for that in New Zealand is far from being a matter of course; but they laid themselves fairly open to the reproof which they received from the Governor. It being supposed that some individual members of the tribe, having a special interest in particular portions of the land, might be induced to sell, the Council memorialized the General Assembly, urging the expediency of setting aside the tribal right; expressing their opinion that such of the natives as were willing to dispose of their proportion of any common land to the Government should be permitted to do so; and that the Government should compel an equitable division of such common land amongst the respective claimants, on the petition of a certain proportion of them. And they added their opinion that "no danger of a war between the Government and the natives need be apprehended from the prosecution of a vigorous policy, inasmuch as a large proportion of the natives themselves would cordially support it, and the remainder would, from the smallness of their number, be incapable of offering an effectual resistance." But the suggestion received no countenance at that time, either from the Government or the Assembly: on the contrary, " I will never," wrote the Governor, " permit land to be taken without the consent of those to whom it belongs; nor will I interfere to compel an equitable division of common land amongst the respective claimants. This decision

is not less one of expediency than of justice, for the whole of the
Maori race maintain the right of the minority to prevent the sale
of land held in common, with the utmost jealousy. Wi Kingi
has no sort of influence with me or the Colonial Government.
We believe him to be an infamous character; but I will not permit
the purchase of land over which he has any right without his
consent."

It is scarcely worth while to notice the Governor's mistaken
impression in regard to William King—who in former times had
saved the town of Wellington from Rangihaeta, and had been
throughout a loyal subject of the Queen—excepting in so far
as it enhances the value of the declaration, which was in good
policy, and was also good Maori law.

The Governor's comments upon the memorial were written in
1858. Early in the following year he visited Taranaki. By this
time he had adopted a " new policy;" that of recognising no right
in the tribe, or in the chiefs, and of allowing no claim but that
of the individual holders. It must be presumed that there was
some connecting link in his own mind between the old practice
and the new; but the nature of it cannot be clearly ascertained
from official papers. We believe, however (although this does
not quite supply the missing link), that he believed the rights
and powers of Maori chieftainship to have devolved upon the
Governor, when sovereignty was assumed by treaty in 1840;
and that consequently, in any dispute about the ownership of
land, he had authority to decide between the rival claimants.
There being no court of law with jurisdiction in such matters,
and no wrong without a remedy, it would follow that right must be
done by the Crown. It is possible that this doctrine, though
involving some confusion of ideas, might be implied from the
English version of the treaty; but in the Maori version it is expressly provided against.* Nor must it be forgotten that the

---

* The following is a literal translation of the original Maori document, made
expressly for us, and subjected to the scrutiny of some of the best Maori
scholarship in the colony:—

" Victoria, the Queen of England, in her kindly regard towards the chiefs
and tribes of New Zealand, in her desire also to guarantee to them their rank
as chiefs and their land, that peace may be sure to them and quiet possession,
she has thought it desirable to send a chief to regulate affairs with the aborigines of New Zealand. Let the sovereignty of the Queen be consented to by
the native chiefs over all parts of this country and the islands, because great
numbers of her people have established themselves in this country, and are still
arriving.

"The Queen is desirous that the sovereignty should be adjusted, that no
evil should befall the aborigines and the Europeans who are residing without
law.

"The Queen is desirous that T. W. Hobson, a captain in the Royal Navy,

Governor, being at the same time head of the Land-purchase Department, would in his own court, as Mr. Clarke observes, " hold the anomalous position of prosecutor, judge, jury, and executioner."

" Women and land," say the natives, " are the destroyers of men ;" and never was the proverb more signally exemplified than in the present instance. There had been a long-standing grudge between William King, the chief of Waitara, and another of the same *hapu*, Te Teira (Taylor) by name. Te Teira took advantage of a meeting at which the Governor was present to offer a piece of land for sale, declaring himself and friends to be the owners. The Governor having agreed to buy, conditionally, on proof of ownership, Te Teira placed a *parawai* (bordered mat) at the Governor's feet. There is something about this theatrical demonstration which we are unable to understand. The ceremony, according to official statements, placed Te Teira's land in the hands of the Governor. We doubt the existence of any such custom, and know that it has been inquired for without success. Yet stress was afterwards laid upon King's neglect to take away the mat. He simply told the Governor that Waitara was in his hands ; that he would not let it go ; and abruptly left the meeting. There has been much wordy warfare, in print and in debate, about the nature of the *mana* (influence) of a chief, in virtue of which it has been alleged that King vetoed the sale. Infinite pains have been taken to prove that the chief could not exercise any " manorial right" over the common land. The labour is lost,

---

should reside as Governor over all those parts of New Zealand surrendered this day and hereafter to the Queen. She says [or proclaims] to the Chiefs of the Assembly of the tribes of New Zealand, and all other chiefs, these decrees now set forth :—

" First, the Chiefs of the Assembly and also all Chiefs who have not met in that Assembly surrender to the Queen of England for ever the entire sovereignty over their country.

" Secondly, the Queen of England guarantees and consents to the chiefs, to the tribes, to all men of New Zealand, the *entire chieftainship of their lands*, of their kaingas, of their property. But the Chiefs of the Assembly, and all other chiefs, shall surrender to the Queen the purchase of those portions of ground as agreeable to any person, being the proprietor of such land, according to the payment which shall be agreed upon between them, and the person nominated by the Queen to negotiate on her behalf.

" Thirdly, this is guaranteed in consideration of the surrender to the sovereignty of the Queen : The Queen of England will protect all the Aborigines of New Zealand. All the privileges in common with the people of England shall be granted to them.

(Signed) " WILLIAM HOBSON,
" Consul and Lieut.-Governor.

" We, the Chiefs of the Assembly of the tribes of New Zealand now assembled, &c. &c. &c."

for King did not pretend to do so. He spoke as the mouthpiece
of the community, as the guardian of those who had not consented
to the rule—residents and absentees.

The opposition was steadfastly maintained ; so was the
Governor's purpose. After the lapse of some months the District Commissioner called a meeting to witness the payment of
the first instalment upon the purchase-money. Out of the proceedings of this meeting arose a fatal misconception, to which
much of the strong feeling manifested by the war-party is to be
attributed, and, not impossibly, the very war itself. King was
present. The Commissioner reported to the Government that he
had put the question to him : " Does the land belong to Teira
and party ?" that King had replied, " Yes : the land is theirs, but
I will not let them sell it." This was too much for the temper
of the colonists, and caused some to side with the Governor, who
afterwards, on maturer consideration, had to withdraw their support. For the expression, even as reported, would not mean that
the land was theirs in fee simple—there being no such title
known—but that as cultivators they had an usufructuary right.
Some while afterwards, however, it became known, though too
late to be of use, that no such admission had been made at all.
Important words, giving an opposite character to the phrase, had
been omitted. The land is theirs, *and ours*, said King: *no
matou katoa hoki.*

The Governor consulted his executive. The Executive Council
in New Zealand differs essentially from the Cabinet (the ministers
responsible to the House), though the two are identical in personality. The Council, constituted by law, dates from the
foundation of the colony. The Governor is bound to consult his
executive, but not necessarily to follow their counsel. They, on
their part, are bound by oath to give it. The Cabinet advises—that
is to say, directs the Governor, in virtue of what is no more than
an honourable understanding, entered into when Parliamentary
Government was conceded. But the Governor had been left
supreme in native matters ; the Cabinet could not interfere ; and
a curious casuistical question remained, whether the Council,
composed of the same officers, had not been freed, by the terms
of the arrangement, from the duty of offering an opinion. It
was a question of conscience : the ministry thought that the
executive function remained imperative, and that it would be
" unchivalrous " to desert the Governor. Also they themselves
were willing to co-operate. A survey of the debateable land was
resolved upon ; the Governor was recommended to protect the
surveying party by military force ; to empower the commanding
officer to proclaim martial law, and to instruct him to maintain
possession. The survey was accordingly attempted, but without

success. The manner of its hindrance was characteristic. The chiefs, keeping a body of men concealed in reserve, directed the old women to kiss the surveyors and theodolites off the ground. Half-stifled with the warmth of welcome, the men of chains were fain to beat an inglorious retreat. Thereupon was martial law proclaimed; a manifesto published, declaring that Te Teira's title had been investigated and found good; that it was not disputed by anyone; that payment for the land (600*l.*) had been received by Te Teira; all of which statements were subsequently found incorrect; and that the land now belonged to the Queen. The troops or their native allies destroyed the homesteads of King and his people, burning their pah, driving away the occupants, and killing the cattle.

The manifesto, as we have already observed, was replete with misstatement. Yet only *per incuriam;* for Governor Browne was the last man to have knowingly sanctioned the slightest deviation from fact. He was unlucky in his choice of agents; took too much upon trust, and was too reserved to go among the natives and learn for himself. Neither can he be justly held responsible for more than one of the errors connected with the declaration of martial law. But this notable document was made the subject of unsparing criticism in the House. For it had been proclaimed in the absence of the Governor, having been left, by a virtual delegation of power, in discretionary charge of the military officer in command at New Plymouth, and was wrong-dated besides. These, however, were questions of form, of small moment in comparison with two material errors in the Maori translation, which declared it to be in force, not as against Ngatiawa, but against the Taranakis, a tribe with whom we were then at peace. It also informed the Taranakis that "the law of fighting was proclaimed;"* to which the Maori response would naturally be—"Very good : let us have it out."

In these and the subsequent proceedings, the ministry had given to the Governor their cordial support; and, in the opinion of many, had involved themselves far more than was advisable. For war is an expensive pleasure; and some of the more far-sighted of the colonists were already considering the payment of the bill. For a dim perception was beginning to arise, that the Home Government, when hard-pressed in Committee of Supply, might dispute the conclusion which had been so confidently arrived at in New Zealand—that a land-quarrel was an Imperial war, unless it could be most clearly shown that the Colonial

---

* A New Zealander would understand it thus :—" Arm yourselves for battle, and we will fight it out." It is, in fact, an invitation to take up arms.— CLARKE, Remarks, &c. p. 17.

Government were in no wise implicated. Not that the Governor had ever shown the slightest disposition to shift any portion of the responsibility, a proceeding which would have been utterly foreign to his known character; but the ministry were supposed to have been meddlesome over-much, and to have afforded a plea for raising a financial question against the colony. Awkward facts were, moreover, beginning to emerge. Few of the settlers had been at first well-informed as to the merits of the case; and some, who had come to a hasty conclusion on the strength of statements published by authority, were already showing signs of recantation. For there were many who had but a single object—that right should be done, wherever right might lie.

The Assembly met. It soon became apparent that the war party were predominant; strong in the Legislative Council; comparatively weak in the House of Representatives, but very determined, and, as colonial majorities are wont to be, somewhat tyrannical. But the composition of it is remarkable, as affording a complete and decisive answer to the supposition—entirely gratuitous—that the settlers had put pressure on the Governor, driving him into a war, in order that contractors might profit by commissariat expenditure. The great majority of those members whose constituents might have profited by increased expenditure in the Northern Island, were opposed to the Governor's policy; while the members for the other island, where not an additional shilling was to be made, supported that policy, though conscious that they were loading their own provinces with a heavy weight of debt.

At the very commencement of the session, a select committee of inquiry was moved for. At first the ministry offered no opposition; on the contrary, they were profuse of assertion that they courted inquiry. But during the course of the debate, in which much more came to light than had been expected, they seem to have felt doubtful about the result. Unable, after the expressions they had used, to meet the question by a direct negative, they suggested a very strange compromise—that only two persons, both selected by the Government, should be summoned to give evidence; one on each side of the question. The proposal being rejected, it was formally moved by way of amendment, and carried. It would have been better for the ministry, having a clear though small majority at their back, to have simply negatived the original motion, on the ground that inquiry would be, in their opinion, prejudicial to the public service; for the evasion of it was so much resented that ultimately it cost them office. They managed, however, to weather that session, defeating a vote of want of confidence by a majority of one. In the following session, the first of a new Parliament, they were in their turn similarly defeated, though only by a combination; for the peace party were still in the minority. It is a curious fact, that every ministerial crisis in the colony has been decided by a majority of one ; so evenly have parties been divided throughout.

The war was carried on with varying fortune, until receipt of a despatch informing the Governor that the Secretary of State for the Colonies—while thinking it indispensable that severe punishment should be exacted on account of the unprovoked murders committed by the tribes south of New Plymouth [Ngatiruanui and Taranaki]—would learn with satisfaction that William King had been induced to make such submission as would enable the Governor to accommodate his quarrel with him without danger to the British supremacy. Accordingly, the head of the Native Land Purchase Department was sent to hear what terms the insurgents had to offer. He had a meeting with the chief of Ngatihaua, William Thompson Tarapipipi, the king-maker, who had come down from Waikato as a mediator. But no conclusive understanding was arrived at. An interview, however, took place between Thompson and King, in presence of the Waitara natives, and the leading men of the Waikato and Ngatiruanui, at which it was agreed that the subject of dispute—the land at Waitara, and the question of peace or war, should be left to the decision of Thompson. At once, with Spartan brevity, he gave his orders :
Waikato, return home.
Te Atiawa ! Te Ngatihaua.
Ngatiruanui ! Home.
Let the soldiers return to New Plymouth.
As for the Waitara, leave it for the LAW to protect.
The command was forthwith obeyed.

Shortly afterwards, the Governor arrived. King, indisposed to meet him, retired inland with a number of his people. The Governor's terms were accepted by the remnant who remained ; the first article being as follows :—" The investigation of the title, and the survey of the land at Waitara, to be continued without interruption." It is worthy of notice, that when the report of the investigation, so far as it should have been at that period carried out, was moved for in the House, the Government were unable to produce it.

Thus did the war come apparently to an end, as usual in New Zealand, without any decided advantage on either side. It was not peace, but a cessation of hostilities ; and in the opinion of many of even those who had been prominent in native advocacy, the greatest mistake of all.

The peace party, repudiating the title of " peace at any price," had come into power. They, in their turn, defeated a motion of want of confidence, by a majority of one. Shortly afterwards, the Assembly being still in session, a telegram from England reached the colony, which was read—"Governor re-appointed." But when the regular mail came in, it was found that two letters—a *G* and a *y*—had been accidentally omitted. Governor Browne received a despatch highly complimentary, but informing him that Her Majesty's Government were about to avail themselves of the peculiar qualifications and experience of Sir George Grey, then at the Cape of Good Hope. Governor Browne left New Zealand, bearing with him the respect and good wishes of opponents and supporters alike.

Governor Grey had a harder task before him than was anticipated in England. It had been expected that the personal influence which he was supposed to have acquired over the natives would enable him to bring them to reasonable terms; and he seemed at first to be himself of the same opinion. But he was warned at the outset that he would find an essential change in the native mind—that they would stop their ears to the voice of the charmer—that his "mana" was gone. The Maori had made a greater stride in knowledge than in civilization, bringing them up to the most dangerous stage for any people—that of unregulated progress. They had become thoroughly intractable; knowing that our promises had not been kept—that nothing of a substantial nature had ever yet been done for them by the Government, they had resolved to put no further trust in Europeans, but to think and act for themselves. It soon became clear that Governor Grey could do no more than any other clever and prudent man could do in his place. But no more was expected by the colonists, who showed themselves almost unanimously ready to give him willing support. For it happened that those among them who had the most strenuously opposed him during his former term of office, belonged (we think with only one exception) to the peace party; and with one accord subordinated all past grievances to the common object. For it was already no secret that the "new policy" was to be reversed.

Governor Grey forthwith proceeded to inquire for himself, and was not long in discovering that the statements on which the minority in the House had based their demand for inquiry were substantially correct. Once satisfied as to that, one course of action only remained—to restore the Waitara, to place himself *rectus in curiâ*, and then to deal with the remaining questions according to the exigencies of the moment. In this he was eventually supported by the responsible Government, among whom were two who had strongly advocated the military occupation of the disputed block.

The grounds of the Governor's decision are thus summarized in a despatch written by the Secretary of State for the Colonies:

"1st. That William King's residence, on the disputed land upon the south bank of the Waitara, was not merely, as had been always represented by the sellers, by permission of the Teira's father, but in virtue of an arrangement made by all that section of the Ngatiawa tribe for the sake of defence against the Waikatos.

"2. That a large number of natives, between 200 and 300, were living upon the block at the time when it was offered for sale, whose dwellings and cultivations were destroyed when possession was taken by the military.

"3. That Teira, as he now asserts, never intended to sell the pahs, one of which was in his own occupation, and did intend to except from sale a reserve of 200 acres, although no such reserve was named in the deed of sale, as ought to have been done."

The ministry base their acquiescence on the ground of having been previously unacquainted with these facts. For this, deriving our information on this part of the question from papers laid on the table of the House, we are unable to account. The first of the three points had been most distinctly affirmed by the peace party; so had the second, except with regard to the numbers, which were not known to have been so large. We cannot multiply quotations; but the following extract from Wi Tompson's letter to Governor Browne is conclusive against the supposition of the fact being a new discovery:—

"War was made on William King, and he fled from his Pah. The Pah was burnt with fire; the place of worship was burnt, and a box containing Testaments; all was consumed in the fire; goods, clothes, blankets, shirts, trousers, gowns, all were consumed.

"The cattle were eaten by the soldiers, and the horses, one hundred in number, were sold by auction by the soldiers.

"It was this that disquieted the heart of William King, his church being burnt by fire. Had the Governor given word not to burn his church, and to leave his goods and animals alone, he would have thought also to spare the property of the Pakeha. This was the cause of the Pakeha's property being lost (destroyed). When William King was reduced to nakedness through the work of the Governor, he said that the Governor was the cause of all these doings. They first commenced that road, and he (William King) merely followed upon it."

The third point is based upon a late admission by Teira himself; but the question of the reserves was mooted in the House, as also that of the boundaries; though the attempt to elicit accurate information from the Government was unsuccessful. It appears, indeed, by the reports lately received, that these various statements have been controverted in the House; but the Governor, on learning the state of opinion, sent down a fair challenge as to fact by message. It must be remembered that the war party were from the first a hard-hearted majority, as may be supposed from their having gone so far, in 1861, as to negative a motion for attaching Sir William Martin's rejoinder to the severe attacks—all duly printed among the Parliamentary papers—which had been directed by the Government, by Mr. Richmond, and by Mr. Busby, against his inquiry into "The Taranaki Question." We are not yet in possession of the final proceedings of the session, but expect to receive, before the completion of this article, intelligence from the colony, which will enable us to offer a more specific opinion on the subject of the question between the Governor and the Assembly.

So far everything pointed to a peaceful solution. But the expectation was premature. A few lines must be spared in explanation of the cause which led to the renewal of hostilities. The Waitara, native territory, is on the northern boundary of the province of Taranaki. To the south of the province is a block called the Tataraimaka, occupied by English settlers under Crown grant. When we drove King from Waitara, the natives drove us from Tataraimaka, and claimed it by right of conquest, as we held Waitara. During the suspension of hostilities, it was distinctly announced by the natives, and especially by the Waikatos, that any attempt to repossess ourselves of Tataraimaka would be treated by them as a fresh declaration of war; for they held it as an equivalent to Waitara. Consequently, Tataraimaka was Governor Grey's chief difficulty. Of course, however well disposed he might have been to temporize with the natives, and to let the sense of injury wear out, it was unendurable that English settlers should remain ousted from their allotments, which had been granted by the Crown. All were agreed that they must be reinstated at any cost. But Governor Grey had made up his mind to restore the Waitara, and had only to proclaim the restoration. What would seem, upon the face of it, to have been a great error in judgment, was now committed. The troops were marched into Tataraimaka before the issue of the proclamation. The consequence was, that the natives kept their word, and renewed the war after their native fashion, by a terrible and shocking murder.

It appears from the papers presented to the Assembly, that the issue of the proclamation declaring the abandonment of the Waitara purchase had been delayed on account of the difficulty which the responsible ministry found in making up their minds about the matter; though what they had to do with a purely native matter is not quite clear. Governor Grey, in his account of the affair, says, fairly enough:—" I take great blame to myself for having spent so long a time in trying to get my responsible advisers to agree in some general plan of proceeding. I think, seeing the urgency of the case, I ought perhaps to have acted at once, without, or even against, their advice ; but I hoped, from day to day to receive their decision,—and I was anxious, in a question which concerned the future of both races, to carry ·as much support with me as I could ; indeed, I could not derive the full advantage from what I proposed to do unless I did so." The admission does credit to the writer ; but it appears to us that a fallacy—the *ignoratio elenchi,* lurks in the reasoning. The argument, as we understand it, is—that if the Ministers had agreed sooner, the proclamation would have preceded the military occupation of Tataraimaka. This is true, yet seemingly beside the question, which is—Why were the troops moved at all before Ministers had made up their minds? The natives had held Tataraimaka so long, that there could have been no great loss of national honour in suffering them to hold it unmolested a short while longer.

Almost immediately afterwards, the Waikatoes, who are supposed to have instigated and directed the murders, rose in arms. This time, the natives placed themselves entirely in the wrong, and a severe lesson has to be administered. There is no longer a peace party in New Zealand. Yet should justice be tempered with mercy. Let it be not forgotten that the present war is but a continuation of the former one, originally provoked by ourselves.

We must now turn back to the session of 1862, which was signalized by two remarkable events—the rejection of the Duke of Newcastle's offer to commit the management of the natives to the colonists ; and the abrogation by act of the Assembly, of the Government monopoly of land sales.

As to the offer, it was mistimed. The conduct of native affairs, refused while easy, was pressed upon the colonists in a time of difficulty. They had moreover been angered by imputations cast upon them, almost from the foundation of the colony ; to which colour might be given should they fail, as was not unlikely, to extricate the colony from the difficulties into which it had been plunged ; they had heard the war called "a settlers' war," and were therefore unwilling to do anything that might tend to confuse their duties with those of the Governor, which it was now more than ever necessary to keep distinct ; and they suspected—justly or unjustly—the motives which prompted the offer. For they supposed it to be preparatory to a claim upon the Colonial Treasury for the expenses of an Imperial war. "Settle first the difficulties in which you have yourselves involved us," was virtually the reply of the colonists ; "start us fair, and we will undertake to govern the natives, defraying every stiver of the cost of quarrels of our own raising, should we so far mismanage what we undertake. But we respectfully decline, at present, to implicate ourselves with that for which we were not allowed to become responsible." The refusal seems to have caused much disappointment at the Colonial Office; for Governor Grey had somewhat prematurely informed the Secretary of State, "that he had arranged to consult his responsible Ministers in relation to native affairs, in the same manner as upon all other subjects."

By the Native Lands Act, a great act of justice was done to the Maori by the colonists, who, it is only right to say, were stoutly supported by Governor Grey. After twenty years' agitation of the question by the northern settlers, a measure was introduced, having for its object the unqualified recognition of the native title over all land not ceded to the Crown, and of the natives' right to deal with their land as they pleased, after the owners, according to native custom, had been ascertained. The promise implied in the Maori version of the treaty of Waitangi —that natives of New Zealand should be allowed to have as good a title to their lands as Europeans, and that they should in the event of their selling or leasing, be allowed to obtain the value of such lands, has been fulfilled. The New Zealand land question is ended.

———

The foregoing pages were already in type when the latest intelligence from the colony reached this country. Concerning this we are unable to speak with that positive knowledge which thus far we have brought to bear upon the subject; being henceforth obliged to rely on the papers presented to the Assembly, on newspaper articles, and the reports of the debates. The first are probably trustworthy; the second must be received with caution, colonial newspapers being mostly characterized by strong party spirit, and much employed in contradicting each other. The debates are not very well reported, unless when the speeches are supplied or revised by those who delivered them.

Another session of the New Zealand Parliament has been held. In the previous session the colonists had declined to accept the management of native affairs until immediate difficulties should have been overcome. This time, however, grateful for the prompt and efficient aid rendered by the Home Government, they consented to undertake the task, thus doing away at last with that system of double government which ought never to have existed, and which had proved so fertile of imbroglio. A change had, moreover, taken place in the circumstances under which the previous refusal had been made. The main points of the question had now been brought into prominent relief; much misconception had been removed, and the colonists could now venture to accept without fear of incurring responsibility for previous events. They had no longer to guard against the possibility of the rebellion being considered as a " settlers' war." The Waitara incumbrance had also been cleared away by the Governor, to whom, in our opinion, the whole credit is due. For it is doubtful, to say the least, whether any responsible Ministry could have ventured on a measure so distasteful to the majority in the House.

In this matter Governor Grey seems to have been not very fairly used. He had laid before the Assembly the facts and evidence on which he had based his restoration of the Waitara. In consequence of the manifest hesitation to accept them, he offered a fair challenge, inviting the distrustful to join issue on the question of fact. The challenge was only productive of the two following resolutions, which do not meet the case :—

" 1. That this House, having supported the measure taken by his Excellency the late Governor of New Zealand, to repress the armed interference of W. King at Waitara ; because as set forth in its Resolution of August 16, 1860, in the opinion of the House, such measures were ' indispensable for the due maintenance of her Majesty's authority' —considers that the renewed and definitive recognition by his Grace the Duke of Newcastle, in his despatch of the 25th August, 1863, ' of the justice of exerting military force against W. King and his allies,' has happily rendered it unnecessary for this House to controvert or supplement statements made by his Excellency Sir George Grey, in his despatches on the Waitara question.

" 2. That, in the opinion of this House, the good faith of the Crown and the interests of both races of Her Majesty's subjects in this colony, demand that the chief Teira and his people should be protected from possible illegal aggression ; and that in justice to him, and in compliance with the request contained in his petition to this House, the investigation into the title to the Waitara block promised by Governor Gore Browne and by Governor Sir G. Grey should be completed at the earliest practicable period."

Much is implied, but little is expressed. Surely such is not the manner in which a public question should be dealt with. It is deemed " unnecessary to controvert or to supplement statements made by his Excellency Sir George Grey, in his despatches on the Waitara question." The time has been when his despatches, during his former tenure of office, were treated with merciless severity : but then they were tangibly and downrightly impugned. The controverted statements were specified ; the counter assertions and disproofs set down with minute precision ; opportunity for vindication was freely offered. Now the Duke of Newcastle's authority is resorted to, apparently for shelter ; but how his Grace's " recognition," in England, should settle questions of fact in New Zealand it is not easy to understand.

The second resolution is a mystification. It is clear that Teira, and all other of Her Majesty's native subjects, ought to be protected from possible aggression. But such has not hitherto been our practice in New Zealand. For our own ease and quietness, we have allowed them to maintain their feuds at pleasure. If the resolution implies no more than a change in our previous policy, it is a step in the right direction. But it seems to hint at more. In regard to the concluding observation—that the investigation of the title to the Waitara should be completed at the earliest possible period—it is gratifying to observe that in this matter, all are now of one accord. But it is remarkable that the mover of this resolution should have been one of those who opposed investigation in the session of 1860.

A bill entituled "The New Zealand Settlements Act" was passed, which we trust will receive careful attention from the law officers of the Crown. Divested of technical phraseology, it is in reality an Act empowering the Governor to confiscate land on suspicion of treason, giving subsequent compensation to such of the owners as shall be able to prove their innocence. While regretting with the Governor that it should have been "found necessary to pass laws conferring temporarily on the Government powers which, under the British rule, are only granted by the Legislature in times of great public danger," we freely admit that some such enactment is required. It is clear that the lands of the rebel natives must be charged, so far as they suffice, with the cost of the war. It is also manifest that, owing to the complication of tribal tenure, nothing short of arbitrary power could deal effectively with the variety of cases that must arise. Nor is there any likelihood that the power will be abused. But a very serious question still remains behind,—whether the Act be within the powers of a Colonial Parliament. What if the Assembly were to go one step farther, and pass bills of attainder? While carefully avoiding anything bearing even the semblance of a legal argument, we take occasion to observe that the New Zealand Constitution Act prohibits the enactment of any law repugnant to the laws of England; not only to statute law, but also (a prohibition too often lost sight of) to the common law, which nothing but an Act of the Imperial Parliament can override. There is no desire in the New Zealand Assembly to transgress their legitimate powers, but there is much difference of opinion as to the extent of those powers. If the law officers of the Crown should deliberately affirm that the Act in question is not *ultra vires*, there is an end to all further dispute. Should they feel themselves obliged, on technical grounds, to advise its disallowance by the Crown, all practical inconvenience might be avoided by substituting an Act of the Imperial Parliament. In any case, such procedure would be advantageous. Such an Act would obviate, among the natives, much heart-burning, jealousy, and suspicion of interested motives. It might even be cheerfully acquiesced in. For although they look down upon the " White Runanga," they pay willing allegiance to the Queen, by whose authority they would suppose such a law to have been made.

The signal success of General Cameron, who assaulted and carried, after a desperate resistance, the entrenched position of the Waikatos at Rangiriri, is supposed to have brought the war " virtually to an end." We refrain from anticipating the future ; but believe the announcement to be premature. Should the natives change their tactics, and avoid making a stand in force, hostilities may yet be prolonged for an indefinite time. They are perfectly well aware that we cannot follow them (away from the water) any faster than we can make roads ; and that while their commissariat costs them nothing, we are expending at the rate of so many pounds an hour. The question of war or peace depends solely upon the present temper of the natives engaged ; upon which no one in this country can pretend to offer an opinion. It must also be borne in mind, that when we shall have done with Waikato, Ngatiruanui and Taranaki, whose atrocities cannot be condoned, have still to be disposed of.

Be this, however, as it may, an intricate and troublesome ques- tion still remains between the colonies and the mother country— that of the apportionment of the expenses of the war. We incline to believe, that if difficulty arises, it will be only on questions of account. The colonists, while steadily maintaining that neither technically nor morally are they *specially* responsible for the cost of an Imperial war, are far from being unmindful of the efforts of the mother country in their behalf. They are willing to con- tribute as far as the limited resources of the colony will allow. There are no symptoms of a niggardly spirit among the thinking men, by whom, and not by those who pander to the passions of the hour for the sake of a few stray votes at an election, the feelings of a country must fairly be judged. Close interpellation must be expected in committee of ways and means, concerning that additional penny in the pound of income tax which the colony is accused of having inflicted on the tax-payers at home. But it does not appear that the ultimate charge, after subtracting the ordinary expenses of the troops, who have to be supported in one part of the world or another, will be nearly so heavy. As a matter of course, the land confiscated on account of rebellion, in' theory escheats to the Crown ; in practice, the colony will have to account for the market value, whatever that may be. It appears indeed to be supposed in New Zealand, that these lands will be found capable of bearing the whole of the burden.' We are not so. sanguine, but have no misgivings about the feeling with which the question will be entertained on either side. It will be liberal and becoming to both. Yet it is high time that some definite arrangement should be come to about the cost of "England's little wars." The colonies, when once allowed the management of their own affairs, have no right to depend upon the mother country for defence, either from rebellion from within, or against aggression from without, so long as they contribute nothing, by way of taxation, to the maintenance of the Imperial armaments. It is easy to raise the well-worn cry of "no taxation without representation;" but it is as easy to raise a counter cry against taxing one portion of the empire for the exclusive advantage of another. All alike are bound in fairness to share the burdens of the empire together with the benefits; and until this be agreed to, it will be difficult to withstand the arguments of those economists who maintain that it would be better for the mother country to sever the connexion, turning her colonies adrift. The equitable arrangement would be, for all alike to contribute, on the principle of mutual insurance, the British Government in return rendering assistance whenever it might be needed, free of additional charge; and this, if insisted on, might be reached with less difficulty than experience would lead us to suppose. For the tables have been turned. In the old times, whenever a colony felt herself aggrieved, her first resource was to threaten to "cut the painter." Now, on the contrary, that the value of the connexion is better understood, and that all real causes of complaint have disappeared, England could bring any one of her dependencies to order, by simply retorting the threat; provided only that she could succeed in inducing belief that she would act up to her expressed intention.

Art. VI.—Taine's History of English Literature.

1. *Histoire de la Littérature Anglaise.* Par H. Taine. Trois Tomes. Paris: Hachette et Cie. 1863.
2. *The Afternoon Lectures on English Literature.* London: Bell and Daldy.
3. *English Writers. The Writers before Chaucer; with an Introductory Sketch of the four Periods of English Literature.* By Henry Morley. London: Chapman and Hall. 1864.

IT is neither difficult nor meritorious to swell the chorus of praise chanted in honour of him who, by his literary prowess, has ascended to the pinnacle of fame. The real duty of a critic consists in forestalling the universal verdict, by decreeing to him whose name is comparatively obscure, and whose works, though of striking excellence, are not already popular, the laurel crown which the general public will afterwards consider to be his proper and well-earned guerdon. About three years ago, when discharging that duty, we introduced to our readers a young French author, of whose abilities we had formed a very high estimate, and whose writings thoroughly merited, as we thought, to be studied and appreciated in this country.* Moreover, we believed that M. H. Taine was destined to render still greater service to literature, and attain a loftier rank among its most distinguished cultivators, than he had then done or achieved. The work by him which heads this article, fully confirms the correctness of our anticipations. It will be strange indeed should his name continue unfamiliar to lettered Englishmen! M. Taine has a title to their notice and respect which it would be ungracious to overlook; for he has produced the most elaborate and valuable history that now exists of the copious and splendid literature of England.

In order to do full justice to the result of M. Taine's labours, we must pass with brief mention two valuable works in which the same subject is treated by native writers. "The Afternoon Lectures on English Literature" are entitled to a careful perusal. Each of the topics is handled with marked discrimination and uncommon

---

* See an article on the "Critical Theory and Writings of H. Taine," in the *Westminster Review* for July, 1861. It is a curious coincidence that another writer, in an article similar in tone and scope to the foregoing one, introduced M. Taine to the American public through the medium of the *North American Review* for July, 1861.

freshness, that on "National Character" displaying, in addition, both subtlety and depth of thought. "The Writers before Chaucer" is the first instalment of a larger work, in which Mr. Morley proposes to traverse the whole field of our literature. The plan is a vast one. If the succeeding volumes shall be as carefully and skilfully composed as the first, Mr. Morley will have succeeded in worthily doing what he says in the preface it is his object to do, that is, "to tell, with something of the sustained interest of national biography, the story of the English mind." The work will be indispensable both for reference and study.

When writing the history of our literature, M. Taine inculcates and supports a theory of criticism and a theory of history. On a former occasion we explained his theory of criticism, and expressed our dissent from the author's view that, by means of his theory, it would be possible to give to the results of criticism the certainty of scientific demonstrations. We still think, as we formerly thought, that in M. Taine's hands his theory leads to important conclusions; but we attribute this far more to the talent of the writer than to the use of his theory. We shall again state what that theory is, without entering into a discussion as to its value: we shall next state M. Taine's views as to how history ought to be written, and then give a sketch of the history of our literature from his point of view, and endeavour to make that sketch reflect with fidelity M. Taine's particular sentiments and opinions.

According to him every writer is governed by a dominant principle. All his writings bear the impress of a master-thought, and if this master-thought be grasped, the nature and quality of his genius can be estimated and disclosed. External circumstances influence a man's genius and modify its development. Like the plant which if left to itself will become a stately tree, but which if tortured and twisted by the elements, or human devices, will remain dwarfed, or assume an unnatural shape; so will the growth of a writer's genius terminate in abnormal or capricious results, if banefully affected by his position in life and the circumstances of his era. In order, then, to ascertain with correctness in what a writer's characteristics consist, it is necessary to determine both what he was by nature and to what extent his natural bent was influenced by external circumstances. What is true of an individual, is equally true of the nation of which he forms a part. A nation's literature is chiefly useful in representing the innate character and acquired bias of those who compose it. When writing the history of national literature, these three questions must be posed and answered:—First, from what *race* does the nation spring? Second, what *position* did it occupy when the various sections of its literature were produced? Third, at what *period* were these sections begun and ended? By *race* is meant the innate and hereditary dispositions implanted in man at birth, and with which are usually associated marked peculiarities in frame and temperament. By *position* is meant the particular part of the earth whereon man lives, and the various accidents of politics and social status by which he is affected. Besides the first impulse and the given condition, there is the velocity acquired, and this constitutes the *period*. When national character and surrounding circumstances are in full play, they do not operate on a blank page, but on one where a distinct impress is already perceptible. According as the page be regarded at one time or another the impression will appear different, and the operation proceeding under changed conditions will suffice to alter the final result.

In truth, history is a psychological problem. "The only distinction between problems in morals and in physics is, that the direction and amount of the forces cannot be determined and weighed in the former as in the latter. If necessities or faculties are quantities having degrees like pressure or weight, these quantities are not measurable like those of pressure or weight. We cannot clothe them in a correct, or approximately correct, formula; we can but have and give with regard to them a literary impression; we are reduced to note and cite the salient facts wherein they are manifested, and which roughly indicate about what part of the scale we must class them." In both cases, however, the final result is produced after the same rule. It is great or small, in proportion to the smallness or magnitude of the fundamental forces, and as the effects of *race*, of *position*, and *period*, combine to add something to each of these forces or to nullify each other. Hence it is that long barren epochs, and epochs of striking success, appear at irregular intervals and without apparent reason in the life of a people. The cause of these appearances is internal contrariety or concord. It was the concord of the creative forces which produced the finished politeness, the regular and noble literature, of the age of Louis XIV. and of Bossuet; the grandiose metaphysical systems and the all-embracing critical spirit of Hegel and Goethe. Discordance between these forces produced the imperfect literature, the scandalous comedy, and abortive drama of Dryden and Wycherley.

The problem which history ought to solve is—" Given, a literature, a system of philosophy, a society, an art or a class of arts, what are the moral states in which they are produced, and what conditions of race, position, and period are best fitted to induce these moral states? There is a distinct moral state suitable for each of their formations and their offshoots; there is one for art in general and for every description of art, for architecture, painting, sculpture, and music; each of them has its special germ in the wide field of human psychology, each its law of virtue by which we see it flourish, as if by chance, and isolated among surrounding failures, like painting in Flanders and Holland during the seventeenth century, like poetry in England during the sixteenth century, like music in Germany during the eighteenth century." The rule of human growth is what history must find ; the appropriate psychology of each formation is what it must frame ; the complete picture of these essential conditions it must strive to produce. Behind the smeared page should be sought and disclosed the peculiar sentiments, the ferment of ideas, the frame of mind which prevailed when the document was written. In this respect, a great poem, a novel, or the confessions of a man of genius, are infinitely more instructive than a pile of histories and a crowd of historians. "I would give fifty volumes of charters and one hundred volumes of diplomatic documents for the Memoirs of Cellini, the Epistles of St. Paul, Luther's Table-talk, or the Comedies of Aristophanes." The study of different literatures is the best preparation for composing an ethical history and advancing towards the knowledge of those psychological laws upon which events depend. It is the special feature of English civilization, " that, over and above its spontaneous development, it presents a compulsory deviation, that it underwent the last and most influential of conquests, and that the three conditions whence it proceeded, race, climate, and the Norman invasion, may be regarded in its monuments with perfect distinctness ; so well, indeed, that we may study in its history the two most important sources of human transformation, I mean nature and restraint, and they may be studied, too, without pause or uncertainty, in an authentic and complete series of monuments. I have striven to define the original motive-springs, to show their gradual effects, to explain how they have resulted in bringing to light great works in politics, religion, and literature, and to unveil the mechanism whereby the barbarous Saxon has become the Englishman of the present day."

The element of race which has influenced and determined the course and character alike of English history and of English literature, is Saxon. The idea of duty, in other words, self-denial exercised for a noble end, was the ruling principle of that race. The Saxons were continent, and faithful to their marriage vows. They produced no love songs, because they regarded love as a serious thing and the reverse of a frivolous pastime. In their social as in their conjugal relations they were grave and sober ; in Saxon England as in Germany, " amidst the gloom of the melancholy temperament and the savagery of a barbarous life, we see the tragic faculties of man alone dominant and active, the strong power of love and the strong power of will." Hence it is, the heroes of the Anglo-Saxon and the Germanic poems are truly heroic.   Of this, the poem of "Beowulf" is a striking example and conclusive proof.   The Anglo-Saxon poets crowded their thoughts into short verses ornamented with three words beginning with the same letter.   Their supreme efforts were directed towards condensing to the utmost their thoughts and expressions, giving to both the greatest conciseness, and thereby making them produce the greatest possible effect.   The traits which distinguish Anglo-Saxon poetry also distinguish that which will one day succeed it.

By their sadness, their aversion for a sensual and an expansive existence, they were admirably prepared to embrace the Christian faith, and to produce biblical poems like those of Caedmon ; but when they wrote in Latin, they displayed a natural incapacity to adopt the Latin spirit.   Unable to think or reason, the profoundest of them "re-wrote the dead doctrines of dead authors." The national literature expired when its cultivators ceased to employ their native language.   Yet the peculiar genius of the race was too innate and permanent to decay or be destroyed by any external influence, and if the Anglo-Saxon genius vanished after the Conquest, "it was as a river which sinks into and runs under the soil.   It will issue forth after the lapse of five hundred years."

The Normans who subjugated the Anglo-Saxons were of Scandinavian origin.   They had first settled on French soil, had intermarried with the natives, and their offspring had become imbued with the ideas and had acquired the national characteristics of Frenchmen.   They formed the French language so completely that Frenchmen even now understand their codes and their poems. A century and a half of residence in France had refined their manners and polished their ideas to such a degree as to make them consider the Anglo-Saxons illiterate and barbarous.   The Anglo-Saxon was by nature prone to meditation, and found in his meditations motives and incentives to action.   The Norman's natural tendency was to "*conceive an event or an object*," and to do this speedily and clearly ; he was no visionary, and did not possess high imaginative powers.   "His emotion was skin deep ; he was not impressed by an object in its complexity or totality, but piecemeal, in a discursive and superficial manner.   Hence, no European race was less poetical."   Norman poets sought facts, strung them logically and harmoniously together ; never adorning them with warm colours, or embodying them in splendid pictures.   They were too fluent and too clear, while the Anglo-Saxon poets were too brief and too obscure.   "How to co-ordinate ideas is what the French have taught Europe ; what ideas are most pleasing they have shown to Europe, and these are the things which the French of the eleventh century, first with the soldier's lance, then with the master's rod, and lastly with the schoolmaster's birch, were occupied during five hundred years in teaching and exhibiting to their Saxons."

All the efforts of the Normans to impose their manners and language on the conquered race wholly miscarried. That race was too inert and stolid to be materially affected by the influences brought to bear upon it. The mass of the people clung to old habits and the old language with wonderful courage and tenacity, the result being that the habits and speech of the mass dominated those of the few. The Norman had to learn the language in order to command his Anglo-Saxon dependents, or to converse with his Anglo-Saxon wife. His children were taught Anglo-Saxon by their mothers and nurses. At length a new language was formed, having for foundation and idiom the old Saxon, containing several Norman words and phrases, and being the tongue spoken and understood by the whole body of the nation. While this transformation was in progress, several literary works were produced, but these had little value. They were imitations, translations, and unskilful copies; mere repetitions of French works without their merits and with greater faults. The only literature of which England could be proud was her ballad-poetry; poetry produced by uneducated men to express the feelings of their class, heartily relished by those for whom it was composed; admirable because of the genuineness of the sentiments expressed, and the vigour and truth of its tone.

Chaucer was the first great writer of the new language, as well as the founder of a new literature. Although impregnated with the notions of his time, yet in one respect he far outstripped his contemporaries. He was the first who studied and noted differences of character, who essayed to image forth living personages, personages whose past history could be read, whose future actions could be divined, and who, after the lapse of four hundred years, stand forth before our eyes as individuals and as types, and occupy places in our memories like the creations of Shakespeare. If, in some of his works, Chaucer wrote only to amuse others and himself, in others, because he had studied and reflected, he wrote with the gravity of a thinker and the solicitude of a great artist. His "Canterbury Tales," instead of being a simple string of incidents like other contemporary poems, is a carefully arranged and completed whole. Because so perfect as a whole it is so noteworthy. Preceding poets, whether barbarians or semi-barbarians, warriors of the heptarchy or knights of the Middle Age, expressed their sentiments in the manner most natural and congenial to them, but without heeding form of expression or method of arrangement. In Chaucer we see for the first time the presiding spirit which, at the moment of conception, sits in judgment on the thing conceived, and says, "Erase that sentence, it is a repetition of the preceding one; unite these two ideas, they do not hang together; re-write that description, it is spun out." When a writer acts thus he is, where Chaucer was, "on the brink of independent thought and fruitful discovery." "Although five hundred years apart from them, yet he approaches the Elizabethan poets by his gallery of pictures, and the reformers of the sixteenth century by his portrait of the good priest." He approaches them, but no more. He did wholly emancipate himself from the bondage of the Middle Age. "To-day he composes the 'Canterbury Tales,' yesterday he translated the 'Romance of the Rose.' To-day he studies the complicated mechanism of the heart, discovers the consequences of the primitive training and dominant habits, and invents the comedy of manners; to-morrow he will take delight only in strange events, pleasing allegories, in amorous dissertations imitated from the French, in learned moralities copied from the ancients. He is in turn a minstrel and an observer; instead of taking, as he ought, a full pace, he advanced a half pace only." What checked him as well as others was the scholastic philosophy.

That philosophy taught men not to look around them and observe, not to meditate and record the result, but to consult authorities in place of experience, to cull the thoughts of others instead of cultivating their own minds. That philosophy was as dogmatic as it was unfruitful. Whoever ventured to differ from it, ran the risk of meeting the fate of Roscelin and Abélard, of being excommunicated, imprisoned, or exiled. The majority of the authors of this period wrote without having anything to say. Among poets the "moral Gower" was little better than a pedant. Lydgate displayed talent and imagination, especially in his descriptions; being unable to address the mind, he tried to dazzle the eyes. Hawe's "Temple of Glass" is a copy of Chaucer's "Palace of Fame," and his "Passetyme of Pleasure" an imitation of the "Romance of the Rose." If originality of tone can be anywhere procured, it is in Barclay's translation of the "Shippe of Foules," and Lydgate's translation of the "Danse of Death." In Skelton's satires we see an entire disregard of style, metre, rhyme, language, and art. Yet there is life in his verse, though of an ignoble and contemptible kind. "It is a kind of life, however, possessing two great features soon to be made manifest, the hatred of the ecclesiastical hierarchy which constitutes the Reformation, the return to sense and natural life which constitutes the Revival."

During the Middle Age man has been degraded into a mannikin, capable only of repeating the catechism and singing hymns. To this period of depression and inanity succeeded an age of discovery and action. New worlds and new sciences were discovered, property became more secure and life more comfortable, wealth increased, and with its increase came new desires, tastes, and habits, a new ideal of life, and a new literature. The Revival was at once Pagan and Saxon in character. "A Latin race cannot invent save when expressing Latin ideas; a Saxon race cannot invent save when expressing Saxon ideas; and we shall find among the master minds of the new civilization and poetry, the descendants of old Caedmon, of Adhelm, of Piers Plowman, and of Robin Hood."

Chief among the poets of the new literature are Surrey and Sir Philip Sidney, the former more mindful of his masters than of his feelings, the latter a genuine and brilliant poet. But Sidney was one of a large band, little inferior to him in talent, and the authors of works which rank hardly below his own. There is one form which towers above all the others. Chief among the poems of that period "is one which is truly divine, so divine that the reasoners of succeeding ages have found it wearisome, which even now it is with difficulty that any one can comprehend —the Faërie Queene by Spenser."

Spenser is a creator and a dreamer of the most natural and instinctive kind. Among modern poets he most closely resembles Homer. He is at all times simple and clear, never abrupt; he never omits any argument, never employs words except in their primitive and common significations, and always ranks ideas in their natural order. Like Homer, he, too, is redundant and infantine, keeps nothing back, abounds in obvious reflexions, incessantly repeats striking ornamental epithets. We feel that he perceived all objects under a uniformly beautiful aspect. He painted them with all their details, without haste or hesitation; and, without fearing the departure of the enchanting vision, he carefully noted all its outlines. Indeed, he is too diffuse and too much disposed to forget both himself and his audience. His thoughts are spread forth in vast and redoubled comparisons, like those of the old Ionian bard.

Everywhere he proves himself to be both a colourist and an architect. His great poem differs from all similar productions of the Middle Age in being a work of art. From the manner in which it is composed we are compelled to sympathize with its author. In it are depicted not objects merely, but himself also. His dominant thought is apparent in the great work of which it was the product and which it directed. "Spenser is superior to his subject, embraces it in its entirety, shapes it to his purpose, and thereby imprints on it the distinctive mark of his mind and of his genius. Each narrative is arranged in concert with another, and all in view of a certain effect which is produced; hence it is that a certain beauty springs from this combination, that which is in the poet's heart and which his entire work contributes to render palpable; a noble and yet charming beauty, composed of moral elevation and of external attractions, English in sentiment, Italian in its externals, chivalric in substance, modern in its perfection, and rendering manifest a unique and admirable period when Paganism appeared in a Christian race and the worship of form in a northern imagination."

This period was a short one. From the beginning of the seventeenth century men's manners and minds had been deteriorating. The court of James the First was a scene of vulgar debauchery. Literature changed its character. The best poets, such as Carew, Suckling, and Herrick, cultivated the pretty instead of the beautiful. The general aspects of things did not impress them, nor did they care to depict the essence of things. They had none of the large conceptions, the involuntary penetration, which distinguished the great Elizabethan writers, by means of which men become parts of the objects they behold, and acquire a capacity for creating them anew. They were mere court favourites, who made a parade of imagination and style. Their love songs were not inspired by any genuine sentiment. Instead of the divine shapes, the virgin and passionate expressions we meet with in the works of the old writers, we find in their works only pleasing trifles embodied in pleasing verses.

Another sign of decadence was the prevalence of affectation. A studied style always degenerates into jargon. The first masters of an art discover the idea, and being imbued with it, give themselves up to produce it in its own natural form. The imitators, who succeed them, purposely reproduce that form, and alter by exaggerating it. Some of the affected writers possessed talent, among them Quarles, Herbert, Habington, and Donne. The latter displayed great force, as well as great coarseness, in his satires. But he wilfully spoilt his natural gifts, and succeeded, after intense exertion, in fabricating absurdities. For example, when addressing his mistress, he says, in order to prove the intensity of his passion for her—

> "O do not die, for I shall hate
> All women so, when thou art gone,
> That thee I shall not celebrate,
> When I remember thou wast one."

Be it remarked, that at this time the grave Malherbe, in his "Tears of St. Peter," wrote things nearly as absurd as anything penned by Donne, and that the sonneteers of Italy and Spain were guilty of the like follies. Hence we may conclude that an age of poetry was about to terminate throughout Europe.

On the frontier line of the old and the new literature stands Abraham Cowley. Like Pope, having a better acquaintance with books than with human passions, he cared more for words than things. Although capable of saying what he pleased, yet, unfortunately, he had nothing to express. Excepting in some descriptive pieces, and a few tender effusions, he gives no signs of feeling. His poetry sprang from his brains, and not from his heart. His amorous poems serve only to show the extent of his scientific attainments and his knowledge of books—" that he is acquainted with geography, is versed in anatomy, has a tincture of medicine and astronomy, and is able to discover parallels and allusions fitted to split a reader's head." Yet he possessed a description of talent unknown to the old masters, indicating a different kind of culture, requiring for its development different manners, and betokening a new state of society. In truth, Cowley was a prose writer, and was the first Englishman worthy of that name. " His prose *is* as easy and sensible as his poetry is perverted and irrational." The writers of a succeeding age took his prose for a model. He was the progenitor of the dignified and admirable race of essayists perpetuated by Temple and ending in Addison.

Towards the close of the Pagan Revival, men still looked upon Nature, not to admire and embody their admiration in poetry, but in order to study and comprehend her laws. Artists and learned men were all impressed with the notion that Nature has an independent existence, that every being contains within itself the mainspring of its action, that the causes of events are laws inherent in things ; " an all-powerful idea, whence sprang modern civilization, and which at this period in England and Italy, as formerly in Greece, gave birth to true science alongside of perfected art ; producing, after Leonardo da Vinci and Michael Angelo, the school of anatomists, mathematicians, and naturalists which culminated in Galileo, and, after Spenser, Ben Jonson, and Shakespeare, the school of thinkers encompassing Bacon and preparing the way for Harvey." " A prodigious influx of facts, America discovered, antiquity revivified, philology restored, arts invented, industry developed, human curiosity traversing the far past and the whole earth, contributed to furnish materials, and prose writing began." From the universal ferment arose many striking thoughts, but few beautifully written books. There were wanting both that analytic power which is the art of following step by step the natural order of ideas, and that conversational talent which is the art of refraining from wearying or shocking others. Style was so ornate that the sense was eclipsed by the ornaments. Prose was very unequal in quality, being either too poetical or too dull. But the writers thought for themselves and believed what they said. A new spirit emerged from the superabundant mass, the spirit of scientific inquiry.

Robert Burton was imbued with this spirit. His "Anatomy of Melancholy" is composed with the regularity of a treatise, by Thomas Aquinas. The torrent of erudition contained in it is guided throughout into correctly-cut channels. There is too vast a mass of ideas, and an absence of selection, yet the result was a more valuable product than had been known before. Sir Thomas Browne was equally imbued with the same spirit; but he was a poet as well as a pedant. "No other thinker better represented the restless and prolific curiosity of the age. No other writer has ever manifested in equal measure the splendid and sombre imagination of the North." He carried his poetical gifts into his scientific investigations. In the presence of Nature he was like an artist. Before a living visage, he was an observer "who noted every trait, every movement of the physiognomy, in order to divine the passions and inner character, incessantly correcting and cancelling his interpretations, and altogether impressed with the notion of invisible forces acting beneath the outward covering." He posed questions, suggested explanations, withheld his reply. Though he did no more, yet this was sufficient. Whoever shall seek truth as earnestly and in so many ways as he did, with an equal scrupulousness in making sure of the prize, will approach it as closely as he.

Among the band of learned men, of dreamers, and of seekers after truth, Francis Bacon stands conspicuous : he was the most comprehensive, rational, and innovating spirit of the age. Like his forerunners, he was naturally prone to clothe his ideas in magnificent apparel. In that age, a thought did not seem completely expressed unless it had been endowed with shape and colour. What distinguished him in this respect was that the image concentrated the thought. "His style is admirable for its richness, gravity, and vigour, being at one time solemn and symmetrical, at another condensed and incisive, always laboured and coloured. Nothing in English prose is superior to his diction." He was pre-eminent for a practical turn of mind such as we observe in Bentham, and which circumstances combine every day to render the predominant trait of Englishmen. For pure speculation he had little taste : it was the application which delighted him. His philosophy is merely an instrument; indeed, each science, and science as a whole, were regarded by him as tools. How to enable man to accomplish whatever his capacity fits him for, and extend his empire over Nature, were the objects he had at heart. " Whence came this great and just idea?" It could not have germinated and flourished during a period of discouragement and decay, when the end of the world was expected, when the Christian mysticism of the earlier ages, when the ecclesiastical tyranny of the fourteenth century, demonstrated man's helplessness by perverting his inventive faculties or in restraining his freedom of will. That idea was the offspring of the age. In order that man should aspire to be master of things and should labour to better his condition, it is indispensable that everywhere there should be amelioration in progress, industry thriving around him, knowledge increasing, the fine arts spreading, that an incalculable weight of evidence should be constantly proclaiming the reality of his power and the assurance of his improvement. The age in which Bacon lived co-operated in doing his work. His great merit lay in foreseeing what science and industry would one day accomplish. He taught man what route to take, but did not follow it himself; he taught them how to discover natural laws, but he never discovered a law of nature. Although the first to announce the promised land, yet he refraind from entering it.

The most original fruit of the Revival in England was the drama. Its peculiar trait is naturalness. No other drama is more complex, because at no other period was man so complete. It is as unique in history as the period during which it arose, being " the work and picture of a young society as natural, as unbridled, and also as tragic as itself." The originators of a new and national drama are always thoroughly imbued with the sentiments they express. They reflect popular feelings better than other men, because those feelings actuate them more powerfully than others. With the exception of Beaumont and Fletcher, the Elizabethan dramatists were all sons of the people, though poor, they were educated, their poverty contrasting strongly with their attainments. Ben Jonson was the son of a bricklayer, and a bricklayer himself; Marlowe was the son of a shoemaker, Shakespeare of a woolstapler, Massinger of a nobleman's servant. They lived as they best could, wrote for bread, went on the stage. Peel, Lodge, Marlowe, Jonson, and Shakespeare were actors. Most of them lived hard, and died like dogs. They were the willing slaves of their passions, and wrote plays representing characters who indulged every passion to excess. The actions of these personages appear strained and exaggerated to us : but they are really true to nature as it was then understood. " At the present day we no longer know what nature is ; we still entertain the benevolent prejudices of the eighteenth century concerning nature ; we behold it humanized by two centuries of culture, and accept its acquired tranquillity for innate moderation. At bottom the natural man is blindly impelled by irresistible impulses, passions, appetites, and lusts," as are the personages in Marlowe's plays. In the closing scenes of his " Dr. Faustus" we see the " living, acting, natural, individual man ; not the philosophical symbol created by Goethe, but the primitive and genuine man, an impassioned and excited being, the slave of his passions and sport of his dreams, altogether absorbed in the present, filled with lusts, contradictions, and absurdities, and who, shouting and shuddering, with cries of joy and of anguish, wittingly and willingly rolls over the edge and down the side of his precipice. The whole English drama is concentrated there, like a plant in its germ, and Marlowe is to Shakespeare what Perugino is to Raphael."

Marlowe was succeeded by others who constructed their plays with greater regard to the rules of art ; the result of their labours being the most life-like and extraordinary drama ever produced. The new art which they practised was great, because it was natural : it was Germanic and fundamentally opposed to classical art. It disregarded the usual laws of proportion, the logical laws of connexion. Those who practised it did not regard man as possessing any one passion, but an innate character; did not view the hero in his heroic aspect only, but as an individual endowed with specific habits and displaying personal traits. While the men of this drama are more manly, the women are more feminine than elsewhere. Both bear the stamp of their origin. No other than a Germanic race could furnish heroines like those of Shakespeare, or like those of Ford, Greene, Webster, Beaumont, and Fletcher. The abnegation, patience, and inexhaustible affection displayed by those heroines, are qualities unknown to the women of Latin race, and, above all, are unknown in France.

When a new kind of civilization gives rise to a new kind of art, several men of talent give a partial expression to the prevailing sentiment, and one or two men of genius express it perfectly.. Ford, Marlowe, Massinger, Webster, Beaumont, and Fletcher were those men of talent. In their plays we find detached scenes, passages, and particular characters, which could not be surpassed ; but we also find numerous scenes, passages, and personages which are gross failures and egregious caricatures. Where they failed, the men of genius succeeded. Among Elizabethan dramatists the two men of commanding genius were Ben Jonson and Shakespeare.

Ben Jonson studied the authors of antiquity till he became thoroughly imbued with their ideas ; but so great were his natural powers, that the pressure of his acquired knowledge did not impede their free exercise. He possessed the classical gift of arranging and developing ideas in the most effective manner, according to the rules of rhetoric and eloquence. If other poets deserve to be called visionaries, he might be styled a logician. Herein lay his talent and his defect. Although he wrote more correctly and planned his plays far better than his predecessors, yet, unlike them, he could not breathe life into his personages. He was too observant of rule and method. He chose some quality or vice,

K K 2

made of it a personage, and gave it a distinguishing name. When endeavouring to create characters, he was contented with a surface glance, ignored the fundamental springs of human nature, and created nothing which lives in the memory of mankind. In his works, we see for the first time a settled and carefully worked-out plan, an intrigue having a beginning, middle, and end; in short, an art similar to that taught and practised by Molière and Racine. Besides this, he had the prominent characteristics of his age and race, a sense of what is natural and life-like, an exact knowledge of minute details, the ability of openly describing strong passions in vigorous terms. The men of his day never shrank from literal truthfulness of expression.

His satirical comedies were attempts to work a new vein. There is little that is charming in them, but they are works of great power and of genuine humour. Unlike Molière, Ben Jonson had nothing of the philosopher in him; hence, instead of seizing and fixing the leading traits of human life, the predominant features of his country and time, he selected as subjects for his comedies evanescent follies and too universal vices.

That he was a true poet is proved by his "Masques," which over-flow with the splendour and the imagination which characterized the works of the great writers of the English Revival. In his love-songs, his poetical genius is still more apparent. Each of them resembles an antique idyl in grace, voluptuousness, and charm. It was when stricken in years, oppressed by poverty, and confined to his room by disease, that his poetical gifts were most lavishly displayed. " A halo of poesy shone around the paralysed old man. He may well encumber himself with science, and burden himself with theories, become a critic on the stage, and a censor of mankind, the heavenly visions have never departed from him; he is the brother of Shakespeare."

To Shakespeare, the dominating spirit of that age, we now come. Resounding phrases and formal eulogy are wasted when applied to him. He does not require to be praised, but to be comprehended, and in order to comprehend him we must call science to our aid.

Properly speaking, man is by nature irrational as his body is naturally prone to disease; both reason and health are exceptional states and happy accidents. If we ignore this, it is because our inward promptings have grown into partial harmony with the courses of things. Yet the primitive forces are latent beneath an apparent regularity, and burst forth in their might in times of danger and revolution. Our ideas do not naturally range them-selves in consecutive order, but press each other in undisciplined crowds. Hence, man possesses no distinct and independent power of action: he is composed of a series of impulses and teeming fancies, which have been subdued but not destroyed by civilization ; these may remain for a time in partial equilibrium ; man's true life, however, is that of a lunatic, who at intervals simulates sanity, but who is really of "the stuff that dreams are made of." Such is man as conceived by Shakespeare. Than he, no other writer has pierced so profoundly beneath the outer crust of good sense and logic which covers the human machine, for the purpose of discovering the brute forces which constitute its substance and its spring.

Shakespeare accomplished this because he was endowed with "imagination all compact."* When ordinary men think out a subject they do so in detail, perceiving an isolated side of it, perhaps one or two sides together ; their mental vision cannot reach farther, an infinite chain of intertwined and multiplied properties escapes them altogether ; they have a suspicion of something beyond their ken, and this suspicion is the sole part of their idea which represents to them what they cannot know. Shakespeare, on the other hand, instantly conceived an object as a whole, with all its connecting links and outlying dependencies ; all its parts and properties being instantaneously mirrored in his imagination, and, conceiving in this fashion, he was capable of reproducing his conceptions in the same way that Nature creates. " The other artists of his time could do likewise ; they had the same cast of mind and the same idea of life : in Shakespeare we discern similar faculties of larger growth, and an identical idea in bolder relief."

When we survey and analyse Shakespeare's plays and countless creations, we perceive in all of them the special imprint of that wondrous imagination which constitutes his genius. All his personages have a trait characteristic of himself; in the background of the vast crowd we recognise the poet's figure.

His imagination was impressed far more strongly and by minuter objects than ours. Because of this, his style is so overladen with imagery and extraordinary metaphors ; it being the product of a mind that at the slightest touch produced too much and rebounded too violently. Because endowed with his peculiar imagination, he was capable of exercising such marvellous penetration, as to grasp in an instant all the results of a situation, all the details of a character, make them manifest in every action of a personage, and endue his figures with the hues and sharpness of reality. That imaginative faculty which he possessed renders him so fascinating to us. Hence, regarding him as Desdemona did Othello, we love him because he loved much and suffered much.†

* The following are M. Taine's own words : " Il avait *l'imagination complète ;* tout son génie est dans ce seul mot."—Vol. ii. p. 67.
† The section devoted to Shakespeare is the most elaborate one in M. Taine's work. It would require more pages than we have lines at our command to give an adequate outline of it. Hence we have contented ourselves with giving a bare abstract of M. Taine's opinions regarding Shakespeare's genius.

The Christian succeeded the Pagan Revival. Although the English Reformation was brought about indirectly, yet when five millions of men abandon one faith for another, whatever be the circumstances which lead to this, it is unquestionable that five millions of men are desirous of conversion. Both the new faith, the English Bible and the Prayer-book, were adapted to the English race ; they appealed to innate predispositions, and opened out to their imaginations a prospect which had special attractions for men of that race, the prospect of a better life than what they led here, of an existence beyond the grave happier than an earthly one. Unlike the Roman Catholicism it superseded. Protestantism was not antagonistic to science, poetry, or free inquiry. Bishops, and clergymen of lower grade, wrote poetry; for example, Hall, Corbet, Wither, and Donne. Theologians like Hooker, John Hales, Jeremy Taylor, and Chillingworth called reason and philosophy to aid them when discussing religious tenets. "Then arose a new literature, elevated and original, eloquent and measured ; armed both against the Puritans who sacrificed liberty of judgment to the tyranny of the text, and also against the Catholics who sacrificed free inquiry to the tyranny of tradition, battling alike against the slavery of literal interpretation, and the slavery of a fixed interpretation."

Foremost among the authors of the new literature appears Hooker, at once the mildest and most conciliatory of men, the soundest and most convincing of logicians, capable of taking comprehensive views of human nature, and worthy of respect in the double capacity of a father of the church and one of the founders of English prose. John Hales and Chillingworth ably laboured in the same field and with not less success. In Jeremy Taylor we recognise a writer of genius, a prose poet, endowed with the imagination of Spenser or Shakespeare. His imagination was so complete as to enable him to grasp the real even in the mire, and the ideal in its highest heaven.

Between the new faith as embraced and expounded by men of position and education and men of low estate and no learning, an opposition speedily arose. Men who interpreted the Bible literally were dissatisfied with the church as established by law. Events concurred to give those men supreme power for a period, when they essayed to establish the kingdom of heaven upon earth. The view which they took of life was fatal to literature. They had no admiration for the beautiful in art or letters, and a literature devoid of the sentiment of beauty is an abortion. They held in abhorrence the natural promptings of the heart, and a literature in which these promptings are not depicted is worthless. The drama, and poetry, eloquence, and ornate writing were stigmatized by them as abominations. Some of Prynne's pamphlets are vigorous productions, but the histories of that time are for the most part dull and insipid. The memoirs, even those of Ludlow and Mrs. Hutchinson, are spun out and wearisome : the authors of them, as Guizot has remarked, " appear forgetful of themselves and wholly concerned for the destiny of their cause.'' Many works of piety were produced, plenty of solid and convincing sermons like those of Baxter, Barclay, and Calamy, of personal narratives like those of Baxter, Fox, and Bunyan. The artist, however, is absorbed in the Puritan. If we find a Milton among them it is because he was superior to his sect. The Puritans had but one poet, one who attained the beautiful in seeking the useful, and who by accident proved himself a great artist.

The foundation of English Protestantism is salvation by faith, and in rendering that doctrine popular no artist has rivalled John Bunyan. He had the kind of imagination best adapted for creating and describing supernatural impressions ; an imagination which acted independently of his volition, and governed him like a master spirit. Allegory, the most artificial of all kinds of composition, was natural to him. " His allegories are hallucinations as sharply defined, as complete, and as healthy as ordinary perceptions. No one, excepting Spenser, is so lucid." Bunyan has the flow, the naturalness, the ease and the clearness of Homer, and approaches the singer of heroes and creator of deities as nearly as an Anabaptist tinker can do. " I am wrong ; he approaches him still closer. Inequalities of rank disappear before the sentiment of sublimity. Grandeur of emotion elevates to the same height the peasant and the poet. And here allegory aids the peasant. It alone, in the absence of inspiration, can paint heaven ; for it does not profess to paint it : by displaying heaven in a figure, it declares it invisible, like the burning sun which we cannot gaze on, but can behold the reflection in a mirror or a rivulet. Thus the unseen world remains shrouded in mystery; warmed by allegory, we can imagine, beyond the splendours we see, and can feel, behind the beauties disclosed to us, the infinity which remains concealed, and the ideal city vanishing as soon as seen, ceases to resemble that lumbering Whitehall which Milton built for Jehovah."

Milton was not gifted with the imaginative powers of the Elizabethan poets : his impulses and passions were under his control ; his logical power was great, and his erudition boundless ; he was thoroughly qualified to compose odes, but not to create souls.

As a prose writer, while deficient in elegance and amenity, he displays unsurpassed vigour. " It is doubtful if Voltaire's cutting sentences would prove more mortal than the blow of such an iron mace as this. 'If in less noble and almost mechanick arts he is not esteemed to deserve the name of a compleat architect, an excellent painter, or the like, that bears not a generous mind above the peasantly regard of wages and hire, much more must we think him a most imperfect and incompleat divine, who is so far from being a contemner of filthy lucre, that his whole divinity is moulded and bred up in the beggarly and brutish hopes of a fat prebendary, deanery, or bishoprick.' Were Michael Angelo's prophets to speak, it would be in this style ; and while regarding the writer we repeatedly perceive the sculptor." The powerful logic which lengthened his periods, buoyed up his images. Sustained metaphors like his acquire an exceptional amplitude, pomp, and majesty. They are spread out without interfering with each other, and resemble the ample folds of a scarlet mantle, bathed in light and fringed with gold. Every literature will be ransacked in vain to discover any poetry which can match Milton's prose.

As a poet Milton differed widely from his masters, the great Elizabethan poets. He wrote not from impulse but after reflection, and aided by his books, : he conceived objects through the medium of books as much as in themselves. It was the sublime and not life which moved him. He wrote incomparable poems, but none of them have that warmth of colouring and vividness of outline which distinguish works proceeding direct from the imagination and untinctured with reflection.

The subject which he chose for his great epic was far better suited for a lyrical drama in the style of the " Prometheus" of Æschylus. The supernatural can only be successfully treated in a style which makes us forget reality. We should expect Adam and Eve to act and feel in conformity with their primitive natures ; Satan and the Messiah in conformity with their superhuman natures. To have accomplished this might have baffled Shakespeare. Milton, a logician and reasoner, failed in the attempt.

Adam and Eve, in the " Paradise Lost," resemble an English couple of Milton's time ; for example, Colonel Hutchinson and his wife. They reason so correctly, and give so many proofs of culture, that we should have expected them at least to have invented clothing. Adam's discourse is so edifying, and his morals are so correct, that he must have passed through England on his way to Paradise. " He is the true head of a family, an elector, a member of parliament, a graduate of Oxford ; he is consulted on occasion by his wife, and gives scientific answers to her queries." When an angel visits them, Eve prepares a repast with the alacrity and skill of a practised housekeeper. Happily, as the meats are uncooked, there is " no fear lest dinner cool." At dessert Eve leaves the table and goes into the garden. Desiring to alter its arrangement, and requiring Adam's aid, he compliments her in this fashion :—

"Nothing lovelier can be found
In woman, as to study household good,
And good works in her husband to promote."

The description of heaven reminds us of earth as much as the picture of our first parents. Milton's Jehovah strongly resembles Charles I., and his celestial dwelling is modelled upon Whitehall. How very different is the God of Goethe in the second part of "Faust!" If any one wish to know how far Milton has fallen short of his subject, and would measure the depth of his fall, let him peruse that genuine Christian poem the Apocalypse.

But if he failed in some things, he has wondrously succeeded in others. In the "Paradise Lost," the finest part is the description of hell; the true hero of the poem is Satan. Spenser has created as striking figures, but he had not the tragic force requisite to depict hell to a Protestant. Nothing more sublime was ever penned than the spectacle which Satan witnessed when issuing from his den.

Born with noble instincts, which were strengthened by solitary meditation, by learning, and by logic, Milton became master of a store of maxims and beliefs which no temptation could sap, which no reverse could overthrow. His grandiose imagination illumined his prose writings with an unexampled affluence of imagery, and enabled him to attain in his odes and lyrical pieces to an unsurpassable pitch of sublimity. During the first part of his career the spirit of pagan antiquity; during the second, that of modern Christianity, inspired him and tinctured his writings. The odes and choruses produced during that first period are almost perfect. Fettered and constrained during the second period by his theological opinions and bent of mind, he filled his epic poem with cold dissertations; he degraded God and man into vulgar mouthpieces for his opinions, and only displayed his genius in imbuing Satan with his own haughty republican spirit, in producing magnificent descriptions of scenery, in creating colossal spectres, and in consecrating his poetical gifts to the eulogy of religion and of duty.

The England of two different periods is reflected in Milton's writings. We see the England animated with the sentiments and tastes which are represented in the works of Sidney, Spenser, Shakespeare, and the brilliant band of poets that for half a century adorned her soil and illustrated her genius. We also see the England of the Puritans, in which a practical religion had taken root, in which measured common sense and narrow views prevailed, yet which attained to the highest possible eminence in power, prosperity, and freedom. "From this point of view Milton's style and ideas are historical monuments; they concentrate, recall, or forestall the past and the future, and withint he compass of a single·work we can study the events and sentiments of several ages and of one nation."

"When we turn over the works of the court painters during the reigns of Charles I. and Charles II., and leave Vandyke's noble portraits for Lely's figures, the descent is sudden and profound; we seem to have left a palace and entered a brothel." The restoration of Charles II. was followed by the triumph of licentiousness. Virtue was decried as puritanical; duty was considered synonymous with fanaticism; man's better nature was swept away in the vicious torrent; the mere animal survived, who sated his lusts without regard for modesty or for justice.

One of the first literary products of the new state of society was Butler's "Hudibras." This poem "contains neither action nor naturalness; is filled with abortive satires and gross caricatures; is devoid of art, measure, and taste; is written in a puritanical style transformed into an absurd gibberish, its envenomed rancour missing the mark by its very excess, and disfiguring the portrait it essays to trace." One of the leaders of fashion and an admired poet of this time was Rochester, who wrote of love in the style and language of a cold-blooded and jaded libertine.

Hobbes was the philosopher of this society. In direct contrast to the Puritans, the courtiers had degraded human existence into an occasion for animal gratification. Hobbes taught that the mere animal part constituted human nature. The courtiers were atheists and brutes in conduct; he was the same in speculation. They had erased from their hearts every fine and generous sentiment; he erased every fine and noble sentiment from the human heart. His theories were modelled on their manners; his system was a manual for their guidance. In him, as in Descartes, was manifested for the first time a mode of philosophizing which soon became general throughout Europe. It consisted "in granting perfect independence to reason, which, disregarding tradition, and misapplying the results of experience, recognised its sovereign in logic, in mathematics its model, its organ in speech, and its audience in polite society; which busied itself with minor truths, found material for speculation in man in the abstract, its formula in ideology, in the French Revolution its glory and condemnation, its triumph and its end."

The new society had no taste for the dramatic works which had been the delight of a bygone age. Shakespeare's plays were re-cast, yet even then did not attract so well as the productions of playwrights of the day. From the theatre where the new plays were acted, "even Charles II. and Rochester could depart more firmly convinced than ever that virtue was only a pretence, the pretence of cunning rogues who wished to sell themselves dearly."

Dryden, Crowne, Shadwell, Afra Behn, Etherege, and others composed the new school of dramatists. By far the most conspicuous and successful of that school was Wycherley. He is, without exception, the filthiest writer that ever sullied the drama. He appears to have laboured as earnestly to disgust as to deprave his audience. "Whatever he composes or states, whether he creates or copies, blames or praises, his plays calumniate mankind, repel when they attract, and harden as well as corrupt." However, he possessed, in common with his countrymen, the gift of vigour.

The change which gradually took place in the mode of life during the seventeenth century, directly affected literature. Men grew more polished in manner, passed their time in paying visits and turning compliments : they endeavoured to amuse their neighbours, and expected to be amused in return. To shine in conversation was accounted a merit. To write as men conversed was considered a duty ; hence, writers grew solicitous about style and language, the structure of periods and choice of epithets, and were prompted to express clever things in a neat manner as much by vanity as good taste. One of the leading writers of this class was Sir William Temple. His learning was superficial, his acquaintance with affairs considerable, his love of ease was only equalled by his desire to be envied for an amount of knowledge which he did not possess. Sir John Denham, in his poem entitled " Cooper's Hill," displayed a finished rhetorical style. With respect to style, as well as other matters, France exercised a direct influence over England at this period. " Bossuet was consulted, Corneille translated, Molière imitated, and Boileau's authority respected." This influence is distinctly traceable in the comedies of Wycherley, Congreve, Vanbrugh, and Farquhar. The first of them was a gross writer, the others displayed more urbanity than libertinage. Yet both the art and the philosophy of Molière were absent from their productions. They were clever men, but no thinkers. Their works had a striking, but short-lived success, and are not now regarded among the most praiseworthy monuments of English literature. " Essays, romances, pamphlets, and dissertations superseded the drama, and the English classical art, withdrawn from departments of literature repugnant to it, was employed upon works better fitted to express and perpetuate it."

While the English drama was declining, and before it has become extinct, some noteworthy comedies were produced ; for instance, " The Beggar's Opera" of Gay, and " She Stoops to Conquer" of Goldsmith. More striking and brilliant were Sheridan's works. Although they always glitter, yet the metal of which they are composed is not always of first-rate alloy. Each of them resembles an exquisitely engraved phial, into which the author has distilled all his wit, and all the results of his reflection and reading. "The School for Scandal" is composed of two of Fielding's heroes, Blifil and Tom Jones, and personages borrowed from Molière's "Misanthrope" and "Tartffue." The result is the most dazzling spectacle of literary fireworks ever witnessed. If Sheridan's productions are less solid than the stronger meats of the earlier dramatists, they furnish an admirable dessert to the literary banquet. The dessert over, we leave the table. Sheridan was the last writer of English comedies. After him, comedy gave place to farce. At the present day, no other dramatic literature is so barren as that of England. The explanation is, whereas formerly literary men could find but a scanty audience unless they wrote for the stage, they can now address a larger and more intelligent audience through the medium of books. In England, novels have superseded plays.

In tracing the progress and fall of the modern English comic drama, we have passed over the most conspicuous English writer of the seventeenth century, and the founder of the classical literature of England. John Dryden was formed by nature and circumstances to be a great writer rather than a great poet, being more akin to Corneille than to Shakespeare. He was too good a theorist to be a great artist; too clever a critic to produce great poems. In composing heroic plays on the model of French tragedies and intended to rank with them as compositions, he failed in his object; "because literary style blunts dramatic truth, dramatic truth corrupts literary style, because his works were neither sufficiently life-like nor sufficiently well written, because he was neither a great poet nor a great orator, and was destitute alike of the passion and imagination of Shakespeare, of the urbanity and art of Racine." His only notable poetical success was his famous ode, but even it is addressed to the senses rather than the heart. Dryden succeeded best in those branches of literature for which his nature and talents qualified him; in producing finely versified pamphlets and dissertations, biting satires, faithful translations, and clever imitations, and in writing clear, idiomatic, and excellent prose.

After the Revolution of 1688, it would seem as if nothing had been gained by the final establishment of constitutional government in England. At no other period were the people more lawless, or statesmen more corrupt. The populace drank ardent spirits to excess. Members of Parliament took bribes without shame. Many of the peers plotted to overturn the constitution and restore the exiled dynasty. Vile intrigue and brutal debauchery were the occupations and amusements of men holding high position, and who plumed themselves on setting the fashion. Even the grave and polished Lord Chesterfield inculcated on his son to be gallant to women, and cringe to men in power, citing as noteworthy examples of successful men the two greatest profligates of the age, Lord Bolingbroke and the Duke of Marlborough.

However, the bad lay on the surface; the nation was still sound at the core. Polite society did not give the tone to the body of the English people, as was the case in France at the same period. The mass of Englishmen retained a sense of morality, and was still subject to the law of duty. The race was too religious by instinct to be rendered permanently irreligious by circumstances. When Wesley and Whitfield began to preach, it was evident that their listeners were naturally predisposed to religious impression.

Sermons formed a large portion of English classical literature. Tillotson was so famed for his style, that Dryden called him his master in the art of writing. To a Frenchman his style seems heavy and insufferably wearisome. But his sermons were admirably suited for his audience. They desired to be taught, not to be charmed; to be confirmed in their opinions and induced to apply them in practice. Barrow is equally heavy, but his analytic capacity and logical grasp have never been equalled. Without employing any rhetorical artifice, he could explain and demonstrate whatever he undertook, and could carry conviction to the minds of his hearers. South, who was regarded as the wittiest of divines, would be regarded by Frenchmen as coarse beyond measure. Yet the preaching of English divines was far more effective than that of their French contemporaries. "If Barrow be redundant, Tillotson heavy, South trivial, and the others unreadable, they are all convincing; their discourses are not models of eloquence, but instruments of edification. Their glory consists not in their books but in their works. If they wrote badly, they formed men's manners."

It was necessary, however, in addition to forming men's manners, to defend the faith against the assaults of free-thinkers. Bolingbroke, Toland, Tindal, and Mandeville were encountered by far greater men than themselves; the most notable men in science, learning, and letters siding against them. But neither the laity nor the clergy distinguished themselves in philosophical speculations. If Berkeley produced his theory of the non-existence of matter, it was not in the interests of independent philosophy, but with a view to undermine the bases of immoral and materialistic theories. Newton proved himself a great mathematician, but a poor philosopher. Locke studiously avoided lofty inquiries. He wrote his book to settle what objects are within and what are beyond the reach of the human intellect. Having defined these limits he rested satisfied. Hume went further, but in the same path. He endeavoured to explode the highest kind of speculation altogether. According to him we cannot know either substance, cause, or law; when we affirm that one fact is linked to another we do so gratuitously, and cannot prove our assertion. The natural consequence of this sweeping scepticism was a reaction towards established beliefs. Reid became alarmed for the stability of society, and set up common sense as the supreme judge of truth. "If a municipal corporation were to order a system of philosophy, Reid's philosophy of churchwardens would be selected." It was not in the domain of metaphysics but of psychology that the thinkers of that day distinguished themselves. The best fruits of their labours were theories of the moral sentiments. In this field Shaftesbury, Hutcheson, Price, Smith, Ferguson, and even Hume laboured diligently, and reaped original and lasting ideas.

The predominant trait of the English mind at this period was a consciousness of the dignity of personal independence, and a sense of the importance of maintaining individual rights and respecting the rights of others. This conviction inspired those orators who, in the diversity of their talents, the energy of their opinions, the magnificence of their diction, rivalled the most renowned orators of ancient Greece and Rome. The elder Pitt was never more sublime than when asserting the inherent rights of men : a Miltonic and Shakespearian vehemence were displayed in his splendid harangues. The unbridled passion and masculine assertion of right which distinguished political speeches, gave pith and effect to political writings also. When Junius condensed his sentences and chose his epithets, it was not for the sake of improving his style, but that his utterances might wound more deeply and insult more grossly. In his hands, artifices of rhetoric became instruments of torture. "Has any other human writer than Junius, Swift excepted, cherished and concentrated within his heart hatred and venom ? Yet he was not vile, for he believed himself to be acting as the servant of justice." Other more genial temperaments displayed the same characteristics. We discern them even in him who was the favourite of fortune from infancy ; who was hailed as the first of debaters, and selected to lead a great party upon attaining manhood ; whose manners were bland and sociable, whose enemies overlooked his faults, and who was adored by his friends ; who was not wearied by toil, embittered by rivalry, or spoilt by power, and the richness of whose genius was manifested in the persuasive flow, the unadorned beauties, the uniform lucidity of his speeches. Yet on occasion no one could match even Charles James Fox for vehemence of language and virulence of invective. A sort of impassioned exaggeration predominated in the discussions concerning the impeachment of Warren Hastings and the French Revolution. It was manifested alike in the piercing rhetoric and stilted declamation of Sheridan; in the pitiless sarcasm and sententious pomp of William Pitt. The force which distinguished them all was the most prominent trait of the leading spirit of the time, Edmund Burke.

Burke was superior to other men, not alone in the extent of his erudition, but also in the comprehensiveness of his views. He possessed an imagination so fertile and vivid as to be able to conjure up distant countries and strange nations with every particularity of scenery, of costume, of habit, and of physiognomy. To the mental powers which form the man of system, were conjoined in him the qualities of heart which form a fanatic. He nobly combated for noble causes. He opposed the excesses of power in England, the excesses of the people in France, and the tyrannical exercise of authority by individuals in India. "Everywhere he became the champion of a principle or the opponent of a vice, and, equipped with his astounding knowledge, his lofty reason, and splendid style, he rushed to the attack with the unquenchable and intemperate ardour of a moralist and a knight-errant." In common with his neighbours he was wholly deficient in good taste.

The difference between the courtesans of Sir Peter Lely, and the maidens, and mothers surrounded by their children of Sir Joshua Reynolds, indicates what a transformation had taken place in English society. Every walk of life gave evidence of the alteration. Bakewell had improved the breed of sheep; Arthur Young had introduced improvements into agriculture; Howard had improved the prisons; Arkwright and Watt had revolutionized industry; Adam Smith had reformed political economy, and Bentham the penal code; Locke, Hutcheson, Ferguson, Butler, Reid, Stewart, and Price had reformed psychology and ethics. Manners had become refined; the Government was more stable; religion was held in veneration. In one thing only did the nation fall short; it had no capacity for lofty speculations. At this same moment proficiency in this last point constituted the chief glory of France.

When the French Revolution occurred, the English nation was conservative and Christian, while France was a nation of free-thinkers and revolutionists. Neither understood, and each detested the other. Never were differences between the minds and the civilizations of the two countries more strongly marked, and it was Edmund Burke, who, with the superiority of a thinker and the bias of an Englishman, placed the points of difference in the clearest possible light.

While the foregoing changes, which occupied the whole of the eighteenth century, and ended in giving to England a fixed ethical and political character, were still in progress, two men arose who were opposed to each other in politics, who were the antithesis of each other in manners, culture, and intellect, and in whom we can clearly discern the inner characteristics of the foregoing changes: they were Jonathan Swift and Joseph Addison.

The writings of Addison are masterpieces of English urbanity and English sense : all the points of his character and incidents of his career contributed to mature that sense and urbanity.   His poem entitled " The Campaign," which made him so famous, is a model of conventional and classical style.   As he truly said in the *Spectator,* the aim of his prose essays was "to banish vice and ignorance out of the territories of Great Britain."   These writings had an astonishing success, quite equal to that of the most popular modern novels.   This was because they abounded in genuine English sense : both his talent and doctrines harmonized with the requirements of his age and country.   " He taught that time is capital, that occupations are duties, that life is a business and nothing else."   If he regarded life from a loftier than a sensual point of view, he never rose to the contemplation of it from the heights of philosophy.   His system of morality was earthly and practical.   The expectation of a future state never obscured his consideration of the best way to enjoy life.   He founded virtue both on morality and self-interest.   The chief concern, according to him, is "to be easy here, and happy afterwards."   The sum of his philosophy is that "the business of mankind in this life is rather to act than to know."   However meanly we may estimate his views, it was no trifling thing to succeed as he did in making morality fashionable.

Addison's prose is a pure well of classical style.   It is rich in ornament, yet devoid of rhetoric.   It is always lucid, and presents old ideas under new and pleasing aspects.   Its defect is too great monotony.   However perfect it may seem to an Englishman, yet a Frenchman would find grave fault with it.   Compared with the prose of Tillotson, it is charming ; compared with that of Montesquieu, it is but half polished.   If Addison were well qualified for teaching the French rules of conduct, they could show him in return perfect models of conversational style.

Though classical by culture, he had the fondness of his race for nature.   Possessing a lively imagination, he could depict with minuteness all the incidents of a situation or consequences of an action.   He created Sir Roger de Coverley, and proved that he had but another step to make in order to rank with Richardson and Fielding as a novelist.   All his writings indicate that he was a poet.   But there is more poetry in his prose than in his verse:

this is chiefly conspicuous in his " Vision of Mirza." That tale is an epitome of Addison's distinctive talents. In it may be perceived those shades of difference which separate the classical literature of England from that of France. These are, " a more bounded and practical reason, a more poetical and less eloquent urbanity, a fund of wit richer and more copious, less sociable and less delicate."

In striking contrast to the genial Addison stands forth Swift—

" The most unhappy man of genius of the classical era and of history ; English to the backbone, inspired and carried away by the preponderance of his English qualities, possessing that profundity of desire which characterizes the race, that excess of pride which habits of freedom, of command, and of success have imprinted on the nation, that sturdy practical cast of mind which the exercise of affairs has rooted in the land ; who was excluded from the sphere of power and action by his unbridled passions and untractable arrogance ; debarred from poetry and philosophy by his piercing, yet narrow common sense ; deprived of the consolations afforded by a life of contemplation and the occupation furnished by a practical career ; too superior a man to give himself up heart and soul to any one religious sect or political party, too contracted to find a resting-place in the high doctrines which conciliate all beliefs, or to cherish the expansive sympathy which embraces all parties ; condemned by nature and circumstances to fight for, without being attached to a cause, to write without being enamoured of the art, to think without attaining to a dogma, who was a condottiere against all parties, a misanthrope with regard to mankind, a sceptic with regard to beauty and truth. Yet these very circumstances and that very nature which forced him beyond the pale of happiness, of love, of power, and of science, elevated him, in an age of imitation of French models and the practice of classical moderation, to an extraordinary eminence, where, by the puissance of his original and inventive genius, he equals Byron, Milton, and Shakespeare, and manifests in bold relief the characteristics and mind of his nation. Sensibility, a practical mind, and pride, contributed to form his unique style, which is terrible in its force, overpowering in its coolness, practical in its effect ; dipped in scorn, truth, and hatred, a dagger of vengeance and of war, which aroused the shrieks or caused the deaths of his enemies when subjected to its edge or poison. As pamphleteer against both the Opposition and the Government, he rent in pieces or smothered his adversaries by his irony or his judgments, delivered with the tone of a judge, sovereign, and executioner. As man of the world and poet, he may be said to have invented the atrocious pleasantry, funereal mirth, and convulsive gaiety of bitter contrasts, and, even while encumbered with the mythological armour, he created a poetry of his own by depicting the crude details of low life, by indulging in pitiable antics, by unsparingly revealing filthy particulars which others conceal. A philosopher against all philosophy, he created the realistic epic, the solemn parody, resembling a mathematical deduction, as absurd as a dream, as trustworthy as an affidavit, as fascinating as a tale, as debasing as dirty rags wreathed like a crown around the head of a god.

Such was his wretchedness and his strength : we turn away from the spectacle with hearts contracted yet filled with admiration, remarking inwardly that a burning palace is still a beautiful object, to which artists will add, that it is most beautiful when in flames."

The English novels of the classical era were essays in an untrodden literary field. They differed from the Spanish romances of the Middle Age in neither exalting nor engrossing the imagination, and from the French novels of the eighteenth century in neither reproducing nor embellishing the sentiments and language of polite society. The objects of their writers were to depict scenes taken from life, to analyse character, suggest plans of conduct, decide upon motives to action.

Daniel Defoe was the first as well as the most successful cultivator of this new field. His mind was singularly solid, precise, and destitute of ingenuity, enthusiasm, and grace. He had the matter-of-fact imagination of a tradesman. It would seem as if he had himself enacted what his heroes performed, so literally and correctly did he describe every detail of their actions. Before him, no one had been so realistic ; nor have any of his successors equalled him in this respect. The realistic writers of the present day are immeasurably inferior to him : what he did was done naturally ; what they do is the result of choice, calculation, and artifice. He deceived not the eye but the mind. "His very imperfections were servicable to him ; the absence of art had the effect of profound art ; his negligences, repetitions, and diffuseness contributed to produce an illusion : nobody could object that a a certain trivial and unimportant piece of detail would have been invented ; it would be said that an inventor would have omitted it because perfectly useless ; that art selects, adorns, and interests ; that an artist would never have heaped together such a mass of trifling, common-place incidents ; that what Defoe wrote could not be fiction but must be truth."

Two leading ideas govern morals, and have always governed them in England. Either conscience must be acknowledged as sovereign, or instinct must be taken for guide. At one time men have considered themselves the slaves of rule, at another entitled to pursue the bent of their inclinations. These two ideas have alternately had the mastery over Englishmen. "From Shakespeare to the Puritans, from Milton to Wycherley, from Congreve to Defoe, from Sheridan to Burke, from Wilberforce to Lord Byron, we see licence succeeded by constraint, tyranny by revolt, and this contest between rule and nature is depicted in the novels of Fielding and Richardson.

Richardson's "Pamela" was composed with the express object of eulogizing virtue and disparaging vice, and proved so successful that Dr. Sherlock recommended it from the pulpit. However, both it and his other works are too padded with moral lessons. A novelist should insinuate and not preach morality. Richardson's artifice is so transparent that we reject his conclusions, knowing very well that the lot of the virtuous is not so splendid, nor that of the vicious so sad, as he would have us believe. Human nature, when moved by vehement passions, bursts the barriers within which he would confine it. Nature punished him for his deficient love for her, by always concealing her countenance from him.

Nature as she really is, as opposed to Richardson's conception of her, was what Fielding professed to represent. "By nature we mean the secret passions, some baneful, for the most part vulgar, and always blind, which we carry within and which influence us, which are imperfectly concealed beneath the cloak of decorum and reason we throw over them, which we suppose to be under our control, but which govern us, the actions we ascribe to ourselves being caused by them." It was the art and delight of Fielding, as of Molière, to make his personages act rationally, and then exhibit to the reader, through a rent in the outer cloak of decorum and reason, the vanities, follies, lusts, and concealed hates which constituted the mainsprings of their conduct. He, too, is a moralist; but regarding nature as wholly opposed to rule, he makes of virtue an instinct and generosity a primitive inclination. There is a great void in Fielding's representation of nature. "Cervantes, whom he copied, and Shakespeare, of whom he reminds us, showed that delicacy of mind is as truly natural as rude and boisterous vigour: in the large harvest which Fielding reaped, he forgot the flowers." The outbursts of the senses, the surging of the blood, and tender effusions were familiar to him, but with nervous exultation and poetical ravishment he had no sympathy. "Man, as conceived by him, is but a fine buffalo, and this perhaps is the most suitable hero for a nation that glories in the nickname of John Bull."

Smollett copied life with more fidelity: he was less jovial than Fielding, and less straitlaced than Richardson; but his pictures want the illumination of genius. His heroes are all gross and sensual, without having the redeeming quality of goodness which is possessed by those of Fielding. In his hands Fielding's generous wine became transformed into the fiery liquor of a tavern; but his "Humphry Clinker" was an original work, and is interesting as a study of character. The study of human follies was carried to excess by Sterne. He regarded everything through a magnifying glass. He sought for and described whatever was absurd, affected, and scandalous in men. As manners were refined, literature became more polished, the grossness of Smollett and indecency of Sterne were tabooed, and the novel, before reaching the almost prudish hands of Miss Burney, passed through the honest hands of Goldsmith.   When we look upon a picture by a great Flemish artist, we shall probably see a woman making her market, or a burgomaster draining a long glass full of beer, or some other homely incident.   The personages may be of low station, and the incident may be trivial, yet all the personages have such a look of contentment and self-satisfaction, that we feel disposed to envy them.   A similar impression is made on us by a perusal of Goldsmith's " Vicar of Wakefield."

In the centre of a large group of writers we behold one whom Goldsmith adored even when the butt of his caprice, with whom Gibbon, Reynolds, Garrick, Burke, and Sir William Jones delighted to hold converse.   His society was courted by every one ; his decisions were law ; he was the arbiter of style.   We inquire whether it was the liberality of his opinions that attracted all men to him, and are told that he was the Hercules of Toryism, that he hated the Whigs, thought James II. and Charles II. the best of monarchs, and considered Voltaire and Rousseau to be rascals.   We turn to his writings, and find little to charm us. Throughout them all the same solemn tone predominates ; by him classical prose was brought to the perfection that classical poetry was by Pope.   " Art could not be more consummate, or nature more outraged."   We can well understand that a rhetorical generation would take him for master, and accord to him that pre-eminence in eloquence which had been accorded to Pope in poetry.   What astonishes a Frenchman is the kind of ideas that he made popular.   His truths are too indisputable, his maxims we already know by heart.   " He teaches that life is short, and that men ought to improve themselves during the brief space at their disposal ; that a mother should not educate her son in the fashion of a dancing-master ; that men should repent of their sins, yet shun superstition ; that it is always right to be busy but not in a hurry.   We thank him for these sage counsels, at the same time saying inwardly that we could have dispensed with them." However, they pleased those to whom they were addressed, because those who read them loved sermons, and this writer's essays are sermons.   His readers did not desire dainties but solid and wholesome food.   In this respect, these essays are a national aliment.   A Frenchman finds the food insipid and heavy.   But because it pleased their palates, Englishmen regarded with such favour and revered as a philosopher the respectable and unbearable Samuel Johnson.

After viewing the caricatures of Hogarth, it may be remarked that the lessons taught by him seem fitted for the education of barbarians.   It may also be said that there is nothing amiable in the English lay preachers, such as Defoe, Hogarth, Smollett, Johnson, and others.   To this we reply, that moralists are useful under certain circumstances, and that these moralists transformed a society of semi-barbarians into a society of civilized beings.

In all the works produced between the Restoration of the Stuarts and the French Revolution, we perceive over and above genuine English traits, the impress of a classical style. Every writer from Waller to Johnson, from Hobbes and Sir William Temple to Robertson and Hume, aspired after the same ideal. Their efforts had for result the perfection of prose compositions, of all works appertaining to conversation and eloquence; the impoverishment of all poetical works, and the production of historical works written in correct language and agreeable style, but utterly lacking both colour and picturesqueness. The predominance of this special style is manifest in the poets of Queen Anne's reign. Open the first that comes to hand, Parnell or Philips, Addison or Prior, Gay or Tickell, and the same kind of versification and general turn of thought will be perceived. All have the same features; all are cast in the same mould. We seem in the presence of a family of plants : the names differ, the height, size, and colour differ, but they all belong to one class. One plant will manifest the pervading type with greater distinctness than the others. Pope is to his brother poets what that plant is to the family. In him, we have the type of the class.

It is always unfortunate for a poet to be what Pope was, too great a master of versification ; as he is certain to become more of a versifier than a poet. Pope wrote verses in the style of an Italian singer who should make a shake on every note. His style is exceptionally condensed and ornate. Excepting naturalness, it wants nothing. His poetry resembles cookery, an art in which excellence can be attained without the aid of genius, what is essential being a light hand, observant eye, and practised taste. His "Rape of the Lock" and "Dunciad" were universally admired by his contemporaries, and extolled by them as far surpassing the "Lutrin" and "Satires" of Boileau. The eulogy, if deserved, is not excessive, seeing that the larger portion of Boileau's verses resemble those of a clever schoolboy, the smaller portion those of a clever undergraduate. Although the "Rape of the Lock" is on a par with most French poems as respects cleverness, it is far inferior to all French poems in polish. Had Pope dedicated it to a Frenchwoman instead of to an Englishwoman, the dedication copy would have been returned with the advice to go and learn manners, seeing that for one compliment to the fair sex contained in it, there are ten sarcasms against feminine frivolity.

Yet there was true poetical stuff in Pope. To be sensible of this we must read his works in fragments. Thus it is at the close of all literary periods. What is true of Pliny the younger and of Seneca is equally true of Pope.   A paragraph, a sentence, or a couplet by them is a masterpiece.   Pope's descriptive talent was great: the imitative harmony of his verses has never been surpassed.   He was an excellent rhetorician, and could versify precepts and arguments with marvellous skill.   Despite his art, his writings soon weary us.   Stendhal has said that a woman of forty is beautiful in the eyes of those only who have loved her when young.   Unfortunately, Pope's muse is not merely forty, but one hundred and forty years old to us.   We cannot regard it with the eyes of his contemporaries.   To them, nature unadorned was unendurable.   To us nature is all in all, and, in proportion to the intensity of our love for nature must be our distaste for the writings of Pope.

Prior did not attain classical elegance, although employing classical forms.   Gay was an English La Fontaine, which means that he resembled La Fontaine very distantly.   The first who broke through the crust of conventional mannerism was Thomson.   If his style be too emphatic it is truly opulent.   He painted what he saw, and because he loved it.   Thirty years before Rousseau, Thomson   expressed   Rousseau's   sentiments,   and   in   a   very similar style.   After this, Ossian was fabricated by Macpherson, "Ossian, who along with Oscar, Malvina, and the others, went the round of Europe, and ended about 1830 in supplying baptismal names for hair-dressers and milliners."   Gray and Akenside, who skilfully imitated the poetry of ancient Greece, Beattie with the nerves of a young girl and the affectation of an old maid, Goldsmith, Collins, Glover, Watts, Shenstone, Smart,—all occupied themselves with sentimental poetry, were disposed towards melancholy, to indulge in reveries and dissertations, and willingly mounted on stilts in their endeavours to attain the grand style. The most celebrated of them was Young, who having lost his wife and children consoled himself by composing his "Night Thoughts."   There are certainly many flashes of imagination in his poems.   In making Christian philosophy the subject of a poem, he anticipated M. de Chateaubriand and M. de Lamartine. In the odes of Gray and reflections of Akenside are to be found the melancholy sadness, the exquisite art, and beautiful reasoning which compose the one-half of M. de Lamartine's poetry.

History was the only branch of literature in which England was trully original at this time, and classical art prevented history attaining its proper growth.   Gibbon, Robertson, and Hume were imbued with French notions, and wrote with French art. They were liberal, moderate, and impartial in their views and judgments, and were destitute of fanaticism and prejudice; but they dwarfed human nature, and painted revolutions and outbreaks like men who had lived in dusty libraries; they judged fanatics with the coolness of parsons and the smiles of sceptics, effaced the distinguishing traits from human nature, and covered the rough surface of truth with a uniform and brilliant varnish.

As the nineteenth century approached, the classical age finished its work, and a new literary era commenced. Society had grown wealthier and more enlightened, the middle class had become better educated and more powerful, men were thrilled with new desires and aspired after higher standards of excellence. France led the way in the revolution in manners ; Germany in the revolution in ideas. Two currents of thought, the one French the other Germanic, spread over England, and the result was the foundation of modern literature.

Robert Burns, a poor Scottish peasant, was one of the earliest who manifested with striking clearness the altered spirit of the period. Dissatisfaction with the prevailing social inequalities first cradled him into poetry. Like Rousseau, he wrote in the capacity of an oppressed plebeian who had risen in revolt. He detested the official cant of the time, and loved nature with unexampled enthusiasm and constancy. The majority of his poems show an utter disregard for established and acknowledged precedents in style and ideas, being protests against invidious distinctions of class or creed, and demands for position in society on the sole ground of personal merit. His poems were written, not to flatter or please society, but to express his genuine feelings and give vent to his strong passions. After protracted listening to formal and empty declamation, we hear in them the echo of a man's voice ; nay more, we enter into close commune with a human soul. Like other men of natural genius and imperfect culture, he is very unequal. When mimicking the formal epistolary style which had long been fashionable, he excites our compassion: when appearing, as he sometimes did, ashamed of being accounted an untutored peasant and poor villager, he erred as those men usually do who owe everything to merit and nothing to fortune. After all, his shortcomings are trifling, and do not lessen our admiration for his incomparable genius.

William Cowper was another of the innovators in poetry. He wrote for pastime, regardless of popularity. He described the most commonplace incidents, not after the fashion of realists, but in the style of a true poet. He saw matter for poetry in the sparkling of burning logs, in the motion of fingers plying the needle, because—and this is distinctive of a poet—all objects issued from his mind not only better defined than when they entered it, but also purified, ennobled, and coloured, like thick vapours which the effects of distance and light transofrm into satin clouds fringed with purple and gold. He demonstrated the absurdity of seeking poetical subjects in heroic deeds in palaces in Greece or in Rome, when they lie around us, if we but knew it; if we know it not, the blame is ours.　Crabbe did this also; but he handled things in the classical style, and was, as has justly been remarked, a Pope in worsted stockings.　True poetry consists in the sensations with which we regard objects.　Cowper did not strive to render his ideas conspicuous by antithesis or repetition; being a true poet, he contented himself with noting his sensations.

Next appeared the romantic school.　Its founders, Southey, Coleridge, and Wordsworth, were radicals in politics as well as innovators in poetry.　When young they talked about founding a society in America, from which kings and priests were to be excluded; in riper years they were devoted churchmen and staunch Tories.　They wished to dispense with poetical diction, and employ the ordinary speech of ordinary men.　They discarded the conventional forms of verse.　Southey and Coleridge were especially assiduous in making new rhymes and inventing new metres, some of which were as happy and some as bad as those adopted by Victor Hugo.　"It was as if a plebeian, having thrown off a court-dress, and seeking another one, had borrowed one piece from a barbarian; another from a knight, another from a peasant, and another from a journalist, and, without being sensible of the want of congruity, had decked himself in the motley garment, and was contented with it, till at length, after several essays and failures, he became conscious of his real wants and selected suitable apparel."

While these attempts were being made, two ideas gained the ascendancy over men, the one leading to the production of historical, the other of philosophical compositions.　The predominance of the one tendency is visible in Southey and Sir Walter Scott, of the other in Wordsworth and Shelley.　This tendency was not confined to England, but was manifested throughout Europe; in France it influenced Victor Hugo, Lamartine, and Musset; in Germany, in far stronger measure, it influenced Goethe and Schiller, Rückert and Heine.　The first of these ideas was the recognition of the fact that every age and race had a separate ideal; that the barbarians, the men of feudal times, the knights of the Revival, Mussulmans, and Hindoos had each an ideal of the beautiful which was really beautiful.　Recognising this, men began to paint the heroes of a particular clime and race, surrounded by the accessories which accorded with their characters, and endeavoured also to enter into their feelings and sympathize with their views.　Englishmen are disqualified by nature for succeeding in such an undertaking.　"They regard their own form of civilization as the most rational, their own morality as superior to that of any other nation, and every religion, except their own, extravagant.

In order to write an Indian poem, it is necessary to be something of a pantheist at heart, and something of a visionary. In order to write a Greek poem, it is necessary to be a polytheist at heart, pagan at bottom, and naturalist by profession. Hence, Heine has written so well about India, and Goethe so well about Greece. However, after every attempt in this line, it has become generally felt "that it is in the writers of bygone ages, that we must seek for a picture of bygone ages ; that the only real Grecian tragedies are those written by Greeks; that the historical romance must give place to authentic chronicles, like modern to original ballads; in fine, that historical literature of the above sort must pass away or be transformed into criticism and history, that is to say, into an exposition of, and a commentary upon documents."

What, for instance, is the value of the historical sketches of the most notable man of that age, whose reputation was European, who was more popular than Voltaire, and whom some ranked with Shakespeare ? Did Sir Walter Scott really revivify the past in his poems and romances ? No, he stopped short on the threshold, preferring that which would interest to that which was true. Had he painted the past as he knew it to have been, the picture would have shocked the majority of his readers. He dared not draw with fidelity either the voluptuous enthusiasts of the Revival, or the heroic brutes and ferocious beasts of the Middle Ages. His real glory lay in throwing a poetical and unfading halo over his native land, in making Scotland for ever attractive to mankind.

Coleridge and Wordsworth carried into poetical literature the spirit of philosophy. Wordsworth was by nature a thinker and dreamer. He saw a beauty in common things to which others were blind. Being so much of a philosopher, he addressed the heart rather than the senses. In "The Excursion" we forget the absence of scenic decoration in our admiration for the chastity and elevation of the thoughts contained in it. The same philosophical spirit which influenced Wordsworth, the staunch Tory, influenced in equal measure Shelley, the uncompromising socialist, just as formerly the classical style served as an instrument in the hands alike of the genial Addison and of the misanthropical Swift. Shelley was destitute of that knowledge of men which most poets possess : his personages are phantoms. He lived in another world than ours, a world governed by other laws. In his poetry, fancy disported like a happy child with a splendid skein of forms and colours. Has any one since Spenser and Shakspeare had visions so tender and enchanting as he had and described ? Could anything be more exquisite than several of his poems, especially that on the "Sensitive Plant" ? The history of that plant is the history of himself. There was a poetical fitness in his identifying his own life with that of a plant. Assuredly, there is a soul in all things :

underneath the external covering is a secret essence—something, we know not what, of the divine, of which we catch a glimpse at intervals, but never obtain a clear view and full knowledge. This presentiment and aspiration which all modern poets have felt, are expressed sometimes, as by Campbell and Wordsworth, in Christian meditations; sometimes, as by Keats and Shelley, in pagan visions. They all felt the palpitation of the great heart of Nature, and wished to penetrate to its recesses, either by way of Judæa or Greece, by means of consecrated dogmas or proscribed doctrines. The greatest of them died in the attempt. Their poetry was mutilated in scaling the lofty height they aspired to mount. Byron alone reached the summit.

Byron was proud and passionate by nature, and inclined to rebel against all established customs and opinions. Only when attacking somebody or thing were his powers brought into full play. His life and poetry were for the most part those of a Skald transported in to modern times, and who, in a world too well regulated, could find no congenial employment.

Compared with the prodigal splendours of Byron, the writings of Wordsworth and Scott seem dry and poor. Never since Æschylus has more tragic pomp been displayed than in some passages in " Childe Harold." Yet he is no mere phrase-maker or scene-painter; he has lived among the scenes he depicts, he has experienced the emotions he recounts. In " Manfred" we observe the two products which civilization has caused to flourish in England, an imperious will and practical talent. If in " Faust" Goethe has shown himself the poet of the universe, in " Manfred" Byron has shown himself the poet of the individual; and if the genius of Germany has its interpreter in Goethe, the genius of England has its interpreter in Byron.

" Over and above British cant, there is universal hypocrisy; over and above English pedantry, Byron warred against human rascality." This is the true sense of " Don Juan." When he wrote it, experience of life had taught him what man really was: the sublime sentiments of " Childe Harold" had vanished from his mind. He had come to regard man as a being who spends the principal portion of his time in sleeping, eating, and yawning; in working like a horse, and amusing himself like a monkey. After passing the greater part of life in braving public opinion and employing his poetical powers to defend revolt, he finally took delight in composing a poem directed against all human and poetical conventions. Yet even " Don Juan" languished under his hands. The latter portion lacks the fire and spontaneousness of the earlier. In his longing after novelty and excitement, Byron went to lead a life of action in Greece, and just as he had begun his new career he died.

Looking backwards across the ages in which were produced

the literature of which we have written the history, we can now embrace at a glance the whole course of English civilization.

The most important element in it is the principle of race. A body of Angles and Saxons extirpated or subjugated the natives of Britain, effaced all vestiges of Latin culture, and welcomed in the Danish invaders recruits of kindred blood. "This is the aboriginal trunk; from its substance and innate qualities nearly all future vegetation will spring." Beyond a few warlike poems and a few religious hymns and poems, some of them very remarkable on account of the vehemence and splendour of their style, Anglo-Saxon literature was barren. Excepting that the nation has become Christian, it was nearly as barbarous after the lapse of six centuries as at its origin.

"The empire of this world belongs to the mightiest." Hence the rude Anglo-Saxons succumbed before the more cultured Normans, whose mental resources sufficed to quadruple their bodily powers. The Conquest gave an impress to the history and character of the people which has never been obliterated: it imprinted on their character and history that practical and political bias which distinguishes both from those of other Germanic races. Norman organization repressed the energies, but did not eradicate the innate capacities of the Anglo-Saxons. Their position and necessities forced them to band themselves together against their Norman masters, in order to resist oppression, to defend their lives and their properties, to strive to restore their old laws, to obtain or extort charters; and being engaged in this way they gradually acquired those faculties and inclinations by which freedom is won and a nation founded. By a happy accident the Normans were obliged to obtain the aid of their Anglo-Saxon vassals against the encroachments and tyranny of regal power. When the Anglo-Saxon yeomen took their seats in Parliament alongside of the sons of Norman nobles, the social inequality between the two races was at an end. The bulk of the nation had been too much engaged with hard travail to have had any leisure for the cultivation of letters. Hence the prevailing literature was either produced by Norman pens or adapted to Norman tastes. With the exception of ballads, the Anglo-Saxons after the Conquest produced little that is attractive or noteworthy. Only one man towered highly above the rest of his contemporaries—Geoffrey Chaucer. For a second time, we find a civilization of five centuries comparatively sterile, if we except Chaucer's poems, in important literary works.

During the barbaric era a nation of Germans had settled on English soil; the feudal age imposed on that nation habits of resistance and of association, and fostered political and utilitarian tastes. At the period of the European Revival, five great nations started together in the same career. "From all appearance, we should infer that accidents and circumstances controlled their speed, their fall, or their success.   Not so ; on themselves alone will depend the result ; each will prove the founder of his fortune : chance can have no influence over events so vast ; national inclinations and national faculties, overturning or raising up obstacles, will irresistibly conduct each to its destined place, some to the lowest depth of decadence, others to the summit of prosperity. After all, man is his own master and his own slave."   Look at an Englishman of the sixteenth century, and you will perceive in him the powers and aptitudes which during three centuries will govern his progress and shape his constitution.   In the works of Shakespeare, Jonson, and the tragic dramatists, in those of Spenser, Sidney, and the poets, we behold represented with incomparable profundity and splendour all the national traits, as these were moulded and fixed by the events and influences of preceding centuries.   By nature and circumstances the nation was prepared to embrace Protestantism, and to manifest the Protestant spirit, which consists in the determination to obtain the mastery over self, and in acting on the conviction that man is a free moral being, who having conceived for himself and in the sight of God what is the rule of conduct, is bound to apply this rule to himself and to others with unflinching energy.   This spirit disappeared during the debauch of the Restoration, but reappeared afterwards, and obtained the ascendancy it has ever since retained.

Two principles influenced the literature of the eighteenth century, the desire to copy French models, and the disposition to display English traits.   The result was, that such works as essays, pamphlets, parliamentary speeches, political satires, or personal lampoons, were all good in their way, being correctly written, sensible in tone, well adapted either to instruct a friend or pain an adversary.   In all works of a high speculative class and of poetry, that literature is extremely poor, if not wholly deficient.

Wealth, education, and prosperity gradually transformed the nation.   The fount of poesy which welled forth so copiously during the sixteenth century, welled forth again towards the beginning of the nineteenth, and a new literature arose.   The influx of new ideas was perceptible in every branch of this literature.   To introduce continental ideas in science and letters was then, as it is now, the aim of the most distinguished minds.   The men who now labour for this object are patriots as well as innovators : they wish to renew rather than destroy.   They know that England is finally established on a sure basis, and that she is more capable than any other nation of future progress without either forgetting or disregarding the traditions of the past.

Whatever exceptions may be taken to some of M. Taine's

doctrines, it is unquestionable that he has mapped out the epochs of English literature with singular originality and precision, that he has analysed the works of the greatest English writers with acuteness, has stated the results of his investigations with a fulness and grasp of thought which denote an acquaintance with that literature at once minute and comprehensive, and an admiration for whatever is noble in it, as genuine as rare. His doctrines, as stated in our sketch, appear to disadvantage ; they lack those accessories of illustration and argument which in the work itself illumine and enforce them. The doctrine which underlies all his speculations, that of the influence of race, has never yet been applied to our whole literature by any other writer. Of its importance we are fully aware. That even M. Taine has not applied it with perfect success we attribute to the imperfection of his generalization. The Saxon race is undoubtedly the backbone of the English people ; but other races have had an influence on their history and progress. No one who carefully considers the peculiar talents displayed by such very dissimilar yet very national writers as Edmund Burke, Richard Brinsley Sheridan, and Thomas Moore can contend that these men displayed much in common with the Saxon temperament and talent. That Celtic influence has largely modified the Saxon character is rightly, though rather too unreservedly, maintained by Mr. Morley. According to him, "but for early, frequent, and various contact with the race that in its half-barbarous days invented Oisin's dialogues with St. Patrick, and that quickened afterwards the Northmen's blood in France, Germanic England would not have produced a Shakespeare." "It may be said that there is in the unmixed Anglo-Saxon an imagination with deep roots and little flower—solid stem and no luxuriance of foliage. The gay wit of the Celt would pour into the song of a few minutes more phrases of ornament than are to be found in the whole poem of Beowulf." The admission that there has been a Celtic influence at work in English literature would not destroy the value of M. Taine's speculations, it would merely necessitate the reconsideration and enlargement of his doctrine. It is the narrowness, not the tendency, of his doctrine which dissatisfies us.

The absence of a detailed account of the origin, progress, and character of English journalism is a great blemish in a work purporting to be a history of English Literature. This omission may be remedied in a future edition, as well as several trifling errors of detail, which on a careful revisal of the work must become apparent to its author. When reviewing a work so valuable and masterly as this one, we gladly exchange what Chateaubriand styled the paltry and meagre criticism of faults, for the large and prolific criticism of beauties. The beauties predominate. As a piece of historical composition, this history has few equals in our day. As a gallery of pictures, it rivals the matchless work of Macaulay; as a statement of philosophical views, it more than rivals the pregnant disquisitions of the late Mr. Buckle.

No other history of our literature can match M. Taine's in comprehensive grasp of thought, brilliancy of style, and trustworthiness of statement. It deserves a conspicuous place in every library filled with the immortal works of which it narrates the history, explains the character, and magnifies the excellence. English literature now owes the same debt to a French author which that of Italy owes to a Frenchman, that of Germany to an Englishman, and that of Spain to an American. If we would understand the history of Italian literature, we must turn to the work of Ginguené; if we would comprehend the greatest genius that Germany has produced, we must peruse Mr. Lewes's life of Goethe. Whoever desires to become acquainted with the literary talent which Spaniards displayed before their intellectual powers had been repressed by the tyranny of the Inquisition, had been dwarfed and blighted by superstition and religious bigotry, must turn for information to the great work of Mr. Ticknor. Until superseded by a better history than any yet produced, M. Taine's masterly volumes will supply the best and most finished picture that can be found of the noble literature of England.

ART. VII.—THE PHILOSOPHY OF ROGER BACON.

1. *Fratis Rogeri Bacon, Opus Majus, à Samuele Jebb. Londini editum.* 1733.
2. *Fratis Rogeri Bacon: Opus Tertium, Opus Minus, Compendium Philosophiæ.* Edited by J. S. BREWER. London. 1859.
3. *Roger Bacon: sa Vie, ses Ouvrages, ses Doctrines.* Par EMILE CHARLES. Paris. 1861.
4. *Histoire des Sciences Naturelles au Moyen Age.* Par F. A. POUCHET. Paris. 1853.

EDUCATED people are for the most part agreed that social and political revolutions are caused by changes in the state of opinion. Any rational account of events thus becomes an account of the ideas which have governed those events, and the philosophy of history and the history of philosophy are in effect resolved into one. But the substitution of one belief for another is rarely direct and immediate. In individuals generally, and always in societies, there is a transition period, more or less marked both in duration and intensity, of doubt, hesitation, and questioning. It was thus that, in the history of science, the negative method of Zeno divided the abstract physical theories of the Ionic school from the more precise views which Aristotle entertained on the nature of the material world; it was thus that, in the history of morals, a complete body of Ethics was disengaged, by the questioning of Socrates, from the confusion of physical and metaphysical ideas which had previously obscured it; and in a later age, in obedience to the same law, Theology itself entered upon its most dogmatic phase under the hand of Aquinas, after Abélard had shown the difficulties which beset any systematic statement of religious doctrine.

The negative method, as such, has therefore a definite place in the order of speculation, and plays a part, and by no means an unimportant one, in those successive changes of belief from which great events arise. But the degree of its influence and the permanence of its effects vary with the source from which it springs. The suspense produced by a conflict of opinion with opinion in what is called metaphysical science, ends either in a mere balance of judgment, or else refers the inquirer back by some different road to his original point of departure. In either case it is equally and wholly negative. The suspense produced by the conflict of phenomena with opinion in physical science produces, first, distrust, then inquiry, and leads, finally, to proof. It is, then, negative in its inception and positive in its result.

The history of the natural sciences becomes therefore a very important consideration for whoever desires to trace the course of European civilization : for there is no pursuit which so directly tends to keep alive the habit of watchful inquiry as the study of Nature,—none in which it is more necessary that men should be hard of belief and suspicious of any evidence short of the best,— none in which credulity is so immediately punished by error,— none through whose whole course from its simplest to its most complex form, an open and a balanced intellect is more constantly necessary. This habit of mind is the result of the physical method, and is perfectly independent of the positive value of the acquisitions of the particular sciences to which that method is applied. It may be found, and is found, in times when, owing to the absence of some necessary condition, the course of discovery has seemed to be arrested or diverted into a barren channel. But, whenever found, it has not failed to react upon social life by preparing the way for those changes of opinion upon which the structure of society ultimately rests.

It is chiefly from this point of view that the philosophical system of Roger Bacon deserves to be considered at this day.

No additions to our positive knowledge are to be looked for from the labours even of the wisest of the schoolmen. But the class of thinkers of whom Bacon has come down to us as the representative in the thirteenth century, exercised an influence on mediæval history which it is worth while to attempt to understand. In the midst of an almost universal slavery, they kept alive the traditions of liberty; they vindicated the right of free inquiry even in matters in which it is unimportant whether they were right or wrong,—in the barren fields of metaphysics, and in the investigation of mysteries which they could not hope to understand;—and they did this in the face of persecution, in spite of Popes and Bishops and General Ccouncils of the Church. Such men were Roscellinus, Abélard, and Roger Bacon.

The thirteenth century was a period of reconstruction and change throughout the whole of western Europe. It witnessed in France the substitution of an absolute monarchy for a feudal league; in Germany, the establishment of the territorial sovereignty of the princes; in Spain, the emancipation of the people from the dominion of the Moors; and in England, the fusion of the Norman and Anglo-Saxon races into one organic whole. During its course there was seen, both in France, in Germany, and in England, the creation of a national language and the dawn of a national literature. It was then that, by obtaining municipal privileges, the towns first became of account in European States; it was then that the people took rank with the nobles and the king as an acknowledged part of the nation.

These constitutional changes all point to some antecedent change in the state of thought and opinion; and contemporary history makes it clear that, from one cause or another, the intellectual world had been deeply stirred. The revolt of the Albigensian churches, the rise of the Mendicant Orders, the rapid extension of universities throughout the Continent, are only some of the forms in which this movement was manifested. Its main cause we believe to have been the sudden impulse given to speculation by the introduction of the Arabian texts into the studies of western Europe. Nor will this cause seem inadequate to the effect, when it is remembered that it was through the writings of Averroes alone that the schoolmen became first acquainted with the physical works of Aristotle. Under the influence of those writings, of the questions to which they gave rise, and of the methods which they suggested, there grew up a degree of scepticism which had not been seen before, and which the materials in the hands of even the boldest thinkers of preceding ages were not fitted to develope. It is true that those eminent men had made the most of the problems before them. Out of the doubt of Porphyry regarding the nature of genus and species—a question, as M. Cousin well observes,* scarcely worthy to occupy the dreams of philosophers, rose the theory of Nominalism. In Roscellinus culminated the scepticism of that first period. When it had been established that universal terms did not exist at all, that they were mere words, and when the principle of Nominalism had been applied to almost the only Christian doctrine to which it is directly applicable,—the dogma of the Trinity—speculative criticism reached the limit at which, having regard to the materials before it, it was obliged to pause. With a somewhat wider range of subject, by playing the theory of Nominalism against the theory of Realism ; by constructing a method of logical criticism, and using that method in theology ; above all, by the fruitful idea of balancing the evidence for and against a given proposition, Abélard, the pupil of Roscellinus, carried still further the freedom of opinion, and struck the first blow at authority. When we remember what Abélard did, we should not forget with what instruments he did it.

The "Timæus" in the version of Chalcidius, the two introductory treatises of the "Organon" in the translation of Boethius, four logical commentaries by Boethius himself, and the introduction of Porphyry, form the sum of the external aids to speculation in the twelfth century. But in the early part of the thirteenth century a large addition was made to the materials of thought : many original works of Averroes were translated for the first time, and several treatises on natural science, chiefly in the departments of medicine, mathematics, and astronomy—the work of leading Arabic doctors—became known. The "Logics" of Aristotle were completed in a Latin version from the same source ; and to them was added the more suggestive parts of the Peripatetic philosophy, especially the Physics,† the Metaphysics, and the Nicomachean Ethics. At Toledo, and at the Court of the Hohenstaufen, a regular staff of translators was constantly engaged, of whom Herman of Germany and William of Flanders are the best known, and also, if we may trust Bacon, among the worst.‡

---

* Abélard, p. 240.

† "Tempore Michaelis Scoti, qui annis 1230 transactis apparuit deferens librorum Aristotelis partes aliquas de naturalibus et mathematicis, cum expositoribus sapientibus magnificata est Aristotelis philosophia apud Latinos."— Bacon, *Opus Majus*, c. 36. It is probable that, as M. Renan points out, this date indicates the time at which Roger Bacon first became acquainted with the translations of Michael Scot. One of these bears the date 1217, and we know that they were all done about the same time at Toledo.

‡ Herman, like Michael Scot, was in the service of the Hohenstaufen. "Hermannus Alemannus, et translator Manfredi, nuper à D. rege Carolo devicti," says Bacon, *Opus Tertium*, c. 25. He translated the glosses of Alfarabius on the Rhetoric as equivalent to that work, and the abridgment of the Poetics, by Averroes, as equivalent to the Poetics. Aristotle's latter treatise was not

It was to be expected that the introduction of so much new matter would give a fresh impulse to the progress of free thought. Given the " Physics" of Aristotle with which to work, the question could scarcely remain where it had been placed by Abélard, on the basis of his Logics. [Natural science being the subject of all others in which our knowledge first assumes a positive form, it is there that we may hope to find the most strongly-marked indications of that questioning habit of mind which is equally the condition and the result of progress in positive philosophy.] With these motives and advantages, what did the thirteenth century add to the conception handed down to it by the twelfth century ? How far does the doctrine of Bacon supplement and extend that of Abélard ? To give an effective reply to these questions, we should understand clearly to what point critical inquiry had been carried before his time. It had not gone further than to weigh negative instances against positive assertions. Abélard had simply followed the advice given to the youthful Socrates ; he had considered not only what was, but what was not. He formed tables of *antitheta*, something like those in the Sixth Book of the " De Augmentis," and he placed on each side quotations from the Fathers, from the Bible, and from Greek and Roman writers for and against the several propositions. But he expressly refrained from drawing a conclusion, or from pronouncing any opinion on the value of authority as such. Bacon's first efforts were directed to a solution of the problem left thus incomplete. The question he put to himself was this—Within what limits, and within any limits to what extent, are we to be bound by the *dicta* of past and present ages ? Is the statement of Aristotle conclusive on a question of science ? Is the teaching of the Church conclusive on a doctrine of religion ? If so, may we safely rely on the authority of a commentator as expressing the mind of Aristotle, or on a *dictum* of a Father as expounding the opinion of the Church ? On this latter point he gives a decided reply. His advice is in all cases—refer to the original writings to endeavour to ascertain the facts with which you propose to deal. Aristotle, in the shape in which he is presented, is utterly untrustworthy.

" I am sure," cries Bacon, " that it would have been better for the

---

known in the Middle Ages, except by this translation of Averroes' abridgment. "Male translatus est," says Bacon of it, " nec potest sciri, nec adhuc in usu vulgi est quia nuper venit ad Latinos, et cum defectu translationis, et cum squalore." —*Opus Majus*, c. 36. " Hermannus quidem Allemannus—de libris logicæ quibusdam quos habuit transferendos in Arabico, dixit ore rotundo quod nescivit logicam. Nec Arabicum verum scivit, ut confessus est, sed Sarracenos tenuit in Hispania qui fuerunt in suis translationibus principales. Et sic de Michaele; certum est quod Andreas quidam Judæus plus laboravit in his operibus quam ipse."—" Omnes autem alii ignoraverunt linguas et scientias et maxime ille Willelmus Flamingus."—*Compend. Studii*, c. 10.

Latins had the Aristotelian philosophy never been translated, than done so obscurely and perversely, as is proved by those who spend twenty or thirty years upon it, and the harder they work the less they know, and as I have myself proved in the case of all who have closely followed the books of Aristotle."[*]

In theology no less than in philosophy bad translations prevail; the text of the Vulgate is for the most part horribly corrupt— " Textus est pro majori parte corruptus horribiliter," as he idiomatically puts it ;—even the saints blundered in their translations, and if so, adds Bacon, much more those who cared little or nothing about sanctity.[†] St. Jerome is the only writer who can be relied on, but as he stood alone and in opposition to the ancient habit of the Church, he was sometimes afraid to give the proper rendering.[‡] And when he did he incurred no little odium as a tamperer with the letter of Scripture. In vain he pointed out the errors of the Septuagint ; every one stood up for the translation of the Seventy as if their life had depended on it—" Omnes stabant maxime pro translatione LXX. sicut pro vita."[§] Jerome, therefore, lest he should frighten his contemporaries with too much novelty, admits that he allowed many passages to stand which he knew to be wrong.

It is this rooted conviction of the utter worthlessness of all the translations of his day, which makes Bacon place grammar on the threshold of his philosophy. "There are five things," says he, "without which neither Divine nor human subjects can be known ; of which the first is grammar ;"[‖] he then observes on the differences of idiom and the impossibility of preserving the spirit of the original in a translation, and concludes that unless the sciences are read in the language in which they are written, they had better not be read at all. It is, of course, unnecessary to say that Bacon did not confine the term grammar to the restricted meaning it usually bears ; he meant by it the general knowledge of a language, as well as of its structure. Nor did he pause here. He seems to have had an idea of comparative grammar, and of the existence of some laws regulating the forms of universal speech. " Substantially, grammar is the same in all

---

[*] "Certus igitur sum quod melius esset latinis quod sapientia Aristotelis non translata esset, quam tali obscuritate et perversitate tradita, sicut eis qui ponunt ibi triginta vel viginti annos, et quanto plus laboraverunt, tanto minus sciunt, probatur, et sicut ego probavi in omnibus qui libris Aristotelis adhæserunt."—*Compend. Studii.*, c. x.

[†] " Et si sancti erraverunt in suis translationibus multo magis alii qui parum aut nihil de sanctitate curarent."—*Compend. Studii*, c. x.

[‡] " Sed quia solus fuit et contrarius antiquæ consuetudini ecclesiæ non ausus fuit transferre omnino ut oportuit."—*Opus Majus*, p. 34. See *Opus Tertium*, p. 92.

[§] *Opus Majus*, Pars Tertia, c. i. [‖] Ibid., ad init.

languages, although it has accidental variations."* The Schoolmen would have avoided many blunders into which they have
fallen had this hint been acted on.

Philological criticism, however, carried to its utmost point,
only enables us to be sure that we understand the meaning of
the writer before us. Having ascertained his opinion, how far
are we bound by it? The general practice of scholasticism was
decisive on the point. Whatever had been handed down from
antiquity was admitted without inquiry as authoritative; whatever
a father of the Church or a writer of reputation chose to say on
any subject whatever was final; whatever was believed by a man's
superiors, he himself was bound to believe.† You might quote a
poet on a matter of philosophy, you might quote a divine on a
matter of taste—it mattered not; if they were old and if they
were respectable, their opinion was equally binding. In science
as in religion, in what cases soever any one of these three sanctions—the sanction of time, of name, or of position—could be
invoked, the jurisdiction of independent judgment was in effect
ousted.

Bacon's criticism on this standard of belief is substantially as follows:—As to the sanction of age, he observes, sensibly enough, that
the ancients as such are no wiser than the moderns; on the contrary, somewhat less so, since later generations inherit the labours of
their predecessors, and have always made additions and corrections
to what they received.‡ And therefore, while antiquity is to be
respected, it is not necessarily to be followed; the presumption is
against an opinion which is merely old: the past is liable to the
errors of the present, and is without several of those aids which
the present enjoys.

As to the respect due to individual men, this was a matter of
some delicacy, on which his position as the correspondent of the
Pope led to considerable reserve. But he ventures to say that
Aristotle was ignorant on several subjects: he did very well for his
time—*secundum possibilitatem sui temporis*—but was by no means
infallible. Avicenna is sometimes grossly wrong; even Averroes

* " Grammatica una et eadem est secundum substantiam in omnibus linguis,
licet accidentaliter varietur."—*Gram. Græc.* MS. c. i., quoted by M. Charles,
p. 263.

† " Matris exempla sequitur filia, patris filius, domini servus, prælati subditus,
magistri discipulus. Nec discernimus a juventute an exempla seniorum sint
imitanda vel non; sed passim omnia recipimus tanquam salutifera cum tamen
ut in pluribus et frequentius sint pestiferæ tam in studio quam in vita."—
Compen. Studii, c. iii. p. 415. (Ed. Brew.)

‡ " Posteriores successione temporum ingrediuntur labores priorum—nam
semper posteriores addiderunt ad opera priorum et multa correxerunt et plura
mutaverunt, sicut maxime per Aristotelem patet qui omnes sententias præce-
dentium discussit."—*Opus Majus,* c. vi.

is open to criticism. These, however, are all scientific writers: with regard to the saints and fathers his opinion seems to have varied. In the " Opus Majus"* he expressly excludes them from his strictures on authority. " I by no means intend that solid and true authority which is either granted to the Church by the will of God, or which is naturally engendered in the sacred philosophers and prophets through their merit and dignity." But in a later work, the " Compendium of Theology," written after his imprisonment, he allows that the saints are not infallible —that they have often blundered, and advanced much which is open to doubt. In reality, we suspect Bacon felt that there was very little difference between Aristotle and St. Augustin.

As to the claims of living men, of whatever place or condition, to lead opinion, that was a presumption not to be endured. Against those who pretended thus to control thought he pours out, in the most unmeasured language, accusations of vanity and of ignorance. His criticism of the principle of authority cannot be better summed up than in the following remarkable passage : —" Authority is worth nothing unless a reason for it be given ; it makes us believe, but does not make us understand ; we yield to authority, but we are not convinced by it."†

On a careful review of all that Bacon has said on this subject, and making the necessary allowances for the indecisive manner in which he occasionally speaks, his criticism of the grounds of belief is seen to mark a clear advance on that of any former mediæval thinker. He first pointed out the difference between the assent which proceeds from not thinking of a thing, from custom, from hero worship, and that which is grounded on a conscious act of the intelligence ; he first protested against being obliged to receive a statement as true because some one else held it to be so : to the assertion that learned men are to be believed, he first added the limitation, " in the matters in which they are learned ;" and he put the doctrine of the wisdom of the ancients on the footing on which it has ever since remained.

Next to the irrational following of authority, the great defect of the mediæval philosophy was the extreme prominence it gave to the deductive method. That method, as Lord Bacon observes, is no match for the subtilty of nature ; it therefore forces our assent, but has no power over the fact. The weakness here pointed out was as keenly apprehended by Roger Bacon as by the author of the " Novum Organon." Says the former : " There are two modes by which we know, namely, argument and experiment.

---

* " Opus Majus," c. i.
* " Auctoritas non sapit nisi detur ejus ratio nec dat intellectum sed credulitatem ; credimus enim auctoritati, sed non propter eam intelligimus."—*Compend. Studii.* p. 397. (Ed. Brew.)

Argument shuts up the question, and makes us shut it up too; but it gives no proof of it, nor does it remove doubt, and cause the mind to rest in the conscious possession of truth, unless the truth is discovered by the way of experience;" and then he illustrates by examples what he means : " If a man who had never seen fire were to prove, by satisfactory argument, that fire burns, the hearer's mind would not rest contented with this, nor would he avoid the fire, until, by putting his hand or some combustible substance into it, he had proved, by his own experience, the fact which he had been taught by reasoning. And this holds even in mathematics, where demonstration is most powerful ; for let any one have the clearest proof about an equilateral triangle, yet, without experience of it, his mind will never hold to the question, nor will he care for the proof until experience has been given him, but then the man accepts the conclusion in all quietness."[*]

Argument, then, according to Roger Bacon, merely terminates the discussion, but does not prove the fact—" Concludit quæstionem sed non certificat ;" according to Lord Bacon, it binds our assent, but does not coerce things—" Assensum itaque astringit non res."[†] To this faulty instrument of investigation Bacon opposes experience. He does not confine himself to vague praises of the advantages of the experimental method, but lays down a scientific doctrine on the subject, and distinguishes with perfect correctness direct and indirect experience,—experiment and observation.

" There are," he remarks, " two kinds of experience, of which one acts through the external senses, and is that by which, aided with instruments, we have our knowledge of the heavenly bodies. This experience does not satisfy us, inasmuch as it does not give accurate information about bodies, owing to the extreme difficulty of applying it.[‡] The other kind is the one which alone can give us a complete experience of what nature and art can do, and in such a manner that all error is eliminated and truth only remains. This science has three great prerogatives in respect of the other sciences. One is, that it

---

[*] " Duo sunt modi cognoscendi scilicet per argumentum et experimentum. Argumentum concludit et facit nos concludere quæstionem sed non certificat neque removet dubitationem, ut quiescat animus in intuitu veritatis nisi eam inveniat via experientiæ. Si enim aliquis homo qui nunquam vidit ignem probavit per argumenta sufficientia quod ignis comburit—nunquam propter hoc quiesceret animus audientis nec ignem vitaret antequam poneret manum vel rem combustibilem ad ignem ut per experientiam probaret quod argumentum edocebat.—Et hoc habet in mathematicis ubi est potissima demonstratio. Qui vero habet demonstrationem potissimam de triangulo æquilatero sine experientia nunquam adhærebit animus quæstioni nec curabit sed negliget usquequo detur ei experientia,—sed tunc recipit homo conclusionem cum omni quiete."— *Opus Majus,* p. 336. (Venice Ed.)
[†] " Nov. Org.," Aph. 13.
[‡] " De Scientia Experimentali," c. 1.

investigates their conclusions by experience : for the other sciences derive their principles from experience, but draw their conclusions by argument from the principles so established ; but if they wish for a particular and complete verification of their conclusions, they must have recourse to the science of experiment."*

Elsewhere the same idea is expressed in somewhat different language—

"There are three ways by which we can arrive at truth : authority, which only produces assent, and which requires to be justified by reason ; argument, whose most certain conclusions are wanting unless they are verified ; and experience, which is of itself sufficient."†

While reading these passages, we seem to be already breathing the air of the sixteenth century. In the works of no other writer up to that time do we find the procedure of science described with equal force and conviction ; nor has even Lord Bacon related with more precision the conditions and the effects of the process on which the foundations of experimental inquiry are laid.

In contrasting the system above described with the speculations of the most advanced thinkers of the twelfth century, one can scarcely avoid the inference that its great scientific superiority is due to the new direction which had been given to study since their time. A scepticism produced by metaphysics alone might possibly have led to an equally trenchant criticism of the claims of authority to command assent ; but it certainly would not have led to any limitation of syllogistic reasoning, nor could it have supplied a motive for appealing to experience to verify the conclusions which that reasoning supplies. No one whose attention had not been early called to the observation of natural phenomena would have entertained the notion of testing results as well as ascertaining principles. But such a man would soon be convinced that even the apparently strictest inference may be eluded by what Lord Bacon calls the subtilty of nature : he would learn in his practice the necessity of measuring each step by the standard of fact. And among those Franciscans who were constantly engaged in the treatment of disease, some doubts of the value of the syllogistic process, some reliance on observation and experience, would surely spring up. But so far as we know, it was only in the mind of Roger Bacon that these doubts crystallized into a system, and that the interpretation of nature is consciously preferred to the anticipation of it.‡

---

* "Opus Majus," p. 338. † Ibid., ad fin.

‡ "Rationem humanam qua utimur ad naturam, anticipationes Naturæ (quia res temeraria est et præmatura), at illam rationem quæ debitis modis elicitur a rebus, *Interpretationem Naturæ* docendi gratia vocare consuevimus."—*Nov. Org.* 26.

It would be unfair not to own that Bacon's practice was frequently behind his theory. Notwithstanding his forcible language about the prerogatives of experimental science and his bitter invectives against frail and unworthy authority, we find him occasionally resting on authority with childlike faith, and treating his favourite science as if its only prerogative was to provoke a smile. The most striking and valuable part of the " Opus Majus" is the treatise with which it concludes, " On Experimental Science." In this treatise Bacon points out several vulgar errors which have crept in owing to the willingness of the world to accept facts on mere report : he instances the belief that adamant can only be split by goat's blood, that hot water freezes sooner than cold, and many other like cases. Presently he enters upon the consideration of how health may be preserved and old age retarded, and this leads to some examples of the wonderful power of certain herbs and unguents. They are, in truth, sufficiently remarkable. We pass over the man mentioned by Pliny, who put a great deal of oil inside and outside his body, by means of which he was enabled to preserve the vigour of manhood to his hundredth year.[*] Our attention is first arrested by a story told of an old woman in the diocese of Norwich, in Bacon's own time. She had eaten nothing, he assures us, for twenty years : " And yet she was fat and in good condition, as the Bishop proved by a careful examination of her."[†] " Nor," he adds, " was this a miracle, but a work of nature." More notable still is the account of an experiment instituted by a certain philosopher at Paris. This sage observing the longevity of the serpent tribe in general, determined to find out their secret. To this end he caught a snake, and with a most praiseworthy devotion to the method of direct experiment, proceeded to cut it up into small pieces, taking care, however, to leave the skin of the belly entire. What was thus left of the snake crawled as well as it could to a certain herb, on touching which it was immediately made whole. " The experimenter then joyfully gathered the leaves of the plant, which were of an admirable greenness."[‡] The greenness which is most to be admired is not that of the plant.

Hitherto Bacon's teaching has been viewed from its purely logical side. We find him laying down the canons of belief, and distinguishing the functions of the ratiocinative and inductive processes. What were the subjects to which the weapons thus prepared were to be applied ? What was his theory of science

---

[*] " Opus Majus," p. 355.

[†] " Et fuit pinguis et in bono statu, nullam superfluitatem emittens de corpore sicut probavit episcopus per fidelem examinationem."—*Opus Minus*, p. 373. (Ed. Brew.)

[‡] " Opus Majus," p. 534.

as a whole, and in what order or relation did he conceive its parts? In the "Compendium Studii" he addressed himself particularly to this question.

"In everything which we wish to learn we should employ the best possible method, . . . and this method consists in studying those subjects which precede in the order of science, before those which follow in that order; and in learning what is easy before what is difficult, the general before the particular, the less before the greater. We should also choose the most select and useful studies, because life is short."*

These words tempt one to inquire whether Bacon had any idea of arranging the sciences in an order corresponding to the order of their study; whether, in short, he had conceived a classification proceeding from simple to complex, from general to particular. There are passages which might almost lead us to suppose that he did; indeed, the order in which the divisions of philosophy are placed in the "Opus Majus" itself — commencing with mathematics, proceeding to optics, and ending with physiology— favours such a view. But an attentive examination of his writings must satisfy the reader that this arrangement is only accidental, or rather that it was prompted by what Bacon considered to be the practical wants of his time, and not by any theory of the relation of the sciences between themselves. His classification, however, whatever might have been its motive, shows·a marked improvement on that which commonly prevailed. It was at all events original, and not inaccurate. The ordinary classification, when it was anything more than a repetition of the order of the *trivium* and *quadrivium,* was a mere copy of the accidental manner in which Aristotle's works followed one another.

We have already observed on the leading place which grammar holds in Roger Bacon's system. It is the "prima porta sapientiæ,"† the door through which all must pass before they can hope to reach the shrine. It is therefore more strictly an antecedent condition of science in general, than the first of the special sciences. This place belongs to mathematics, and the study of them is insisted upon with all the more earnestness because, notwithstanding their importance, they have been almost wholly neglected.

"Very few are found acquainted with mathematics: it is the devil

---

* "Sed ad omnia scienda modus optimus requiritur. . . . Modus enim est ut priora in ordine doctrinæ sciantur ante posteriora, et faciliora ante difficiliora, et communia ante propria, et minora ante majora, ut manifestum est; et ut in electis et utilibus fiat occupatio studentium, quia vita brevis est."— *Compend. Studii,* p. 379. (Ed. Brew.)

† "Opus Tertium," c. 28, p. 102. (Ed. Brew.)

who has managed this, in order that the roots of human wisdom may not be known. For this science is the alphabet of philosophy, and never can a man learn anything worth knowing unless he is acquainted with its powers."[*]

The neglect into which this pursuit has fallen during the last thirty or forty years has destroyed the whole course of study in Europe.[†] Bacon then traces the outline of the mathematical sciences to the number of eight. Four are speculative—namely, geometry, arithmetic, astronomy, and music, each having its corresponding art or practical division.

It would be a long and not a very profitable task to follow Bacon through the various applications of mathematics set out in the Fourth Part of the " Opus Majus." It is the place which he assigns it in his scheme, and his view of its method and uses, which chiefly arrest our attention. Abandoning any vague and poetic speculations on the properties of numbers and harmony, he concentrates his attention on the qualities of the science as an instrument of proof; and thence proceeds to enlarge on its value in the various operations of life. He finds that under both heads mathematics deserves to be called the key of the sciences.[‡] In every other subject there is room for doubt : in physics nothing is necessarily true : morals have no principles peculiar to themselves : demonstration is found in this science alone. Even logic, the so-called mistress of proof, borrows from mathematics whatever conclusive power it possesses : its *principle* is the theory of the categories, and quantity governs all the other predicaments ; its *mean* is the theory of demonstration, and the only perfect demonstration is in mathematics ; its *end* is persuasion,[§] and rhetoric and poetry are dependent on the laws of harmony—that is to say, on a special department of mathematical science. Turning from the speculative to the practical side, he considers the science of number and quantity in reference to the well-being of man and to the industrial arts generally. Under this head Bacon describes at length the operations to which the relations of quantity may be usefully applied ; such are the construction of houses and towns—of canals, aqueducts, and ships—of machines for flying and propelling vessels without oars. Giving the reins to his imagination, he enumerates various instruments for raising without difficulty the heaviest weights and dragging anything along the surface of the ground at pleasure. In this

---

[*] " Opus Tertium," c. 20, p. 66.
[†] " Opus Majus," Pars Quarta, ad init.
[‡] " Harum scientiarum porta et clavis est mathematica."—*Opus Majus,* p. 43. (Venice Edit.)
[§] By logic Bacon means syllogistic logic, of which he had a very low idea. He did not recognise *proof* as belonging specially to it.

manner, he assures his readers, a single man can pull a thousand others after him.

To produce such effects, Bacon justly thought that several improvements on the instruments in use would be needed. These improvements fall within the range of practical geometry, which is accordingly divided into seven sections, corresponding to as many sciences. The first division embraces the aids and appliances requisite for astronomy and astrology; the second, musical instruments; the third, optical instruments, such as plane, spherical, and concave mirrors; the fourth, the instruments of what is specially called experimental science; the two remaining divisions deal with the instruments of medicine, surgery, and alchemy.

Bacon had a very definite idea of the means by which he proposed to regenerate the arts of life. In the first place, skilled mathematicians would be required. Unfortunately, in his time, there were only four: Peter of Maricourt, John of London, Campana of Navarre, and Master Nicolas. Accordingly, he "notes this part as deficient." Then an almanac and astronomical tables are wanted. He proposes to educate ten or twelve boys, and keep them at work in registering the places of the planets from hour to hour. When this is done, we shall be able to read each day what passes in the heavens, as we read in the calendar the feasts of the saints. Clement's assistance is urgently entreated to aid this part of the work.

The reform of the Calendar, as is well known, was a favourite subject with Bacon. He calls the attention of the Pope to the errors which have grown up from the lack of precision in calculating the length of the year. Its real length, he points out, is less by $\frac{1}{130}$ part of a day than the period actually assigned. Hence, in every one hundred and thirty years a day too much is added. The result is that the feasts of the Church are held on the wrong days: Easter is celebrated out of its time, and the faithful eat meat when they should be fasting. "Horrible and vile errors spring from this neglect; the devil himself has devised this evil against the Church, taking advantage of its ignorance and carelessness."

It is quite clear that Bacon understood the principle on which the Calendar ought to have been corrected, and that he was very near the truth in the actual calculations which he furnished to the Pope. Had they been acted upon, Clement IV. might have robbed his successor of the praise of having carried out the reform which has ever since been associated with the name of Gregory XIII. By what means he calculated so approximately the period of the vernal equinox, which he takes as a point of departure, it is not easy to say. Cuvier thinks that he must have used the telescope ; but, as we shall hereafter show, it is improbable that he was acquainted with the instrument. He *may* have borrowed his views from an Arabian source.

The mechanism of the heavens engaged Bacon's particular attention, not less from the influence which he conceived the stars to exert on terrestrial phenomena than from the confusion he observed in the attempts to explain their motions. He describes and examines the hypothesis of Ptolemy, as well as the explanations of several Arabian astronomers. That which most struck him in the Ptolemaic system was the complication of excentrics and epicycles, against which he protests, adopting in preference the theory of a single movement advanced by Alpetragius. He does not arrive thus far without some hesitation, and it seems a serious matter to oppose an authority so eminent as Ptolemy; but after all, "it is better to preserve the order of nature and to contradict sense, which is often at fault, especially in very distant objects.*" He by no means shared the' opinion of Plato, that there was anything special in the circumstances of heavenly bodies unfitting them to be a subject of human science. But the real facts were to be obtained rather by the aid of abstract reasoning than by reliance on such imperfect means of observation as could be supplied. It was in mathematics alone that he laid the foundations of his astronomy,† and this constitutes at once the strength and the weakness of his method. His reasons, to tell the truth, are on these subjects very inferior to his conclusions. For example, he maintains, in opposition to Aristotle, that the fixed stars do not shine with a reflected light; but then he asserts that the moon does not do so either. The passage offers a fair example of his way of reasoning on these subjects. "The whole crowd of students suppose that the light which comes to us from the moon and stars is the sun's light reflected from their surfaces ; but this is impossible because of the equality of the angles of incidence and reflection. For, as has been shown, if this were so, the angle of incidence and the angle of reflection would necessarily be equal. Therefore, any given ray would only strike a determinate part of the earth's surface, and would not fall everywhere, and so of the whole light which comes from the sun to the surface of the moon. For it may be all treated as one ray falling on the moon at unequal angles, and being reflected in an

---

* "Melius est salvare ordinem naturæ et contradicere sensui, qui multoties deficit et præcipue in magna distantia."

† "His principiis et hujusmodi datis per vias geometriæ potest homo verificare omnem actionem naturæ, quia omnis veritas circa operationem agentis in medium, vel in materiam generabilem, vel in cœlestia, sumit ortum mediate vel immediate ex jam dictis et quibusdam aliis."—*Opus Majus*, p. 57. (Venice edit.)

ascertained direction. Light so coming to the earth could only illuminate a particular part of the horizon. We see, however, that it illumines our whole hemisphere as the sun does. Therefore the light proceeding from the moon and stars is not reflected."* The phenomenon of scintillation excited his keenest curiosity. There is nothing which we see so often, whose reason we less understand :† it is "a philosophical difficulty. Nor is his manner of dealing with it unphilosophical. He begins by stating the facts. The planets are not observed to twinkle; the fixed stars, on the contrary, do. Is this owing merely to their distance? Bacon concludes that other conditions are requisite; for some of the smallest and most distant stars show no signs of scintillation. Various hypotheses are then examined at length: at last, by a rejection of instances not unworthy to be called Baconian, the conclusion is arrived at, that three causes contribute to produce the phenomenon: the effort which the eye makes to observe a very distant object; a sufficient brightness in the body looked at; and a trembling of the medium.‡

Bacon was acquainted with the phenomenon of refraction, and with the fact of the deviation of light passing through the atmosphere: he correctly explains why the sun, moon, and stars, appear larger when near the horizon; and what he says about falling stars is not far from the truth—that they are small bodies, which in their course through the air seem luminous, owing to the rapidity with which they move.§

Bacon's "Physics" are in conception and treatment very inferior to his works on what may be called applied mathematics. They are not easy to understand, and we think ill repay the labour of attempting to understand them. Far more of mere metaphysical speculation enters into them than is found in any of his other treatises; and as readers at this day are naturally impatient of discussions on *essence, substance, nature, power,* and the like, we must confine ourselves to mentioning some of the more valuable theories and facts which are contained in this part of his works.‖ Although the treatise "On the Multiplication of Species," which forms the fifth part of the "Opus Majus," is perhaps more open to the charge of being entangled with what Bacon elsewhere calls "divisions according to Porphyry,"¶ than any other portion of his writings, it almost redeems this defect by the soundness of some

---

* "Opus Majus," p. 58.
† "Nihil tam totiens videmus cujus causam minus sciamus."—*Opus Majus,* p. 249.
‡ Ibid. p. 252. § Ibid. p. 321.
‖ We have made use of M. Charles's excellently-written chapter (pp. 277–295) in describing this part of Bacon's system.
¶ "Divisiones Porphyrianæ."

of its general maxims. There we find an emphatic protest against looking for the cause of a phenomenon in its form : the true way to judge of it is, says the author, by observing the effect, action being the end of every operative force ;[*] there, too, we find frequent mentions of "rules" and "laws," to the ascertainment of which Bacon attaches a high value. This positive habit of mind perpetually exhibits itself even where it would least be expected. The philosophy of Roger Bacon seems always to be tending in the direction of art : on whatever kind of abstract speculation he is engaged, if he sees the slightest opening for doing anything, or still more for making anything, he comes down at once from the clouds, and immediately sets to work. Even some of his chapters in the "Multiplication of Species" are relieved by this happy propensity. There is one which begins in a somewhat formidable manner : "The consideration of the action of natural powers is of the highest importance." Very soon, however, we find ourselves reading the description of a speculum which had been made by an unnamed workman, known to Bacon, for the express purpose of showing some of his experiments. Twelve such glasses, Bacon assures the Pope, would enable the Crusaders, without bloodshed, to defeat the Saracens ; "nor would it be in the least necessary for the King of France to go abroad with his army ; but if he *should* go, and be so lucky as to get the workman in question to go with him, he might dispense with the greater part of his army, not to say the whole." We believe Bacon himself to have been the maker of the speculum which he mentions ; and if so, the way in which he refers to the matter is not without art. For he goes on to say that the artificer was mulct in one hundred Parisian pounds by his labour, besides having to lay aside his studies and other necessary operations : yet so disinterested is he that for one thousand marks he would not have neglected the work, both for the love of science and because his experience will enable him to make better and cheaper glasses in future. "For he is very wise, and nothing is difficult to him, *if only he had money.*"[†]

For the thirteenth century, this is not a bad example of the puff indirect.

The explanation given of the tides deserves notice as an example of what can be effected in spite of wrong principles. The phenomenon is said to be caused by the lunar rays which fall sometimes obliquely, and at other times perpendicularly : when in the former direction, they have but little influence on the water ; but as the moon gets higher in the heavens, and her light shines more

---

[*] "Nam finis et utilitas completa virtutum agentium est actio."—*Opus Tertium*, c. xxxvi. p. 115. (Edit. Brew.)

[†] "Nam sapientissimus est, et nihil ei difficile est, nisi propter defectum expensarum."—*Opus Tertium*, c. xxxvi.

directly, the action of the rays increases, and draws up the water towards the moon. The rise of the tide can be predicted and measured.

It may be expected that a writer who mixes up metaphysics with physics would not be much more scientific when he comes to the more complicated questions of vegetable and animal physiology. It appears, nevertheless, that Bacon had just views of the sexes of plants—that he believed them to possess sensibility, to a certain limited extent ; that he thought them capable of alternations of sleep and wakefulness ; that he knew the part played by the sap, and by some of the liquids they secrete ; that he distinguished the characteristic parts, such as the bark and roots—attempted to determine the part played by the leaf, flower, and fruit, in the economy of vegetable life, and examined whether they have not some essential-organ, which is the seat of their life, and answers the purpose of a heart.*

A great part of the knowledge, such as it was, which Bacon possessed of botany, he had in common with his time. Albert of Cologne is the author of a treatise on the same subject, which is neither better nor worse than that of Bacon, although M. Pouchet will have it that the Dominican was the first to place botany on a true foundation.† But M. Pouchet's views of the basis on which the sciences rest are so strange, that it is doubtful how much this praise is worth. We will allow our readers to judge for themselves :—

" La plus belle gloire d'Albert le Grand est, sans contredit, d'avoir complété et terminé le cercle des connaissances humaines, en comblant son hiatus par le démonstration scientifique des rapports de l'homme et de Dieu !

" Ce grand principe une fois posé, cette vaste intelligence s'est en quelque sorte concentree sur le terre. Pour la première fois, les corps naturels reçoivent une description précise ; et pour la première fois aussi, ils se trouvent rangés d'après leurs analogies, et d'eprès leur degré d'organisation.

" Posées de cette manière, les sciences naturelles apparaissent avec leur caractère fondamental—l'utilité physique et l'utilité théologique !"‡

The real truth of the matter being this—that neither Bacon nor Albert knew anything at first hand about botany. In those days it was the fashion to write encyclopædic works. Therefore Albert, who was a great logician and Aristotelian scholar, but who was assuredly no botanist, notwithstanding the basis of fundamental utility on which he placed the sciences,—borrows as

---

* Charles, p. 284.   † Pouchet, " Histoire des Sciences Naturelles au Moyen Age," p. 308.

‡ Pouchet, 319, 320.

much as he conveniently can from Aristotle and Pliny, and makes up his *De Vegetabilibus et Plantis* in so many pages folio. In like manner Bacon, who did happen to be a man of science, but whose science did not take the direction of vegetable physiology, equally thought it necessary to complete the circle of human knowledge by a treatise on a subject which had been treated by Aristotle. Had he omitted to do so, it would have been tantamount to a confession that he knew nothing about it.* Writers on alchemy have not omitted to inscribe the name of Roger Bacon in the list of the professors of the occult science. If his works on Hermetics, or in particular the tract entitled "The Mirror of Alchemy," justify them in claiming him as a disciple, he was, at any rate, a cautious and rational one. The "Speculum Alchemiæ" contains a definition of the science in which no modern chemist would see anything to complain of—it is merely this: How to compose a preparation which will purify metals. The possibility of purification arises, so says the author, from the fact that Nature constantly tends to produce the most perfect metal, and is only prevented from doing so by accidental causes which disturb her operations. To extract the foreign elements with which the inferior metals are charged is the business of the practical alchemist. When this is done and Nature is left to her unimpeded operations, we shall have gold. The search after the philosopher's stone is a simple operation of metallurgy, in which heat and other purely physical agencies play the chief part. In the experiments of the laboratory, and in the processes which take place in the depths of the earth, there are the same kind of effects produced by the same kind of causes. Bacon observes incidentally on the constancy of temperature which prevails in mines.† If this is alchemy, it is alchemy robbed of its most objectionable features. Bacon fell into many errors, and his belief in the philosopher's stone is not the least of them ; but even there the scientific bias of his mind is felt : there is no recourse to supernatural agents— all is to be done by the imitation by man, on a small scale, of what is done by Nature in a wider field. The power of Bacon's scientific imagination is nowhere more visible than in his definition of alchemy, and in his enumeration of the subjects falling within its scope—it becomes in his hands a true chemistry. We have said that he did not doubt the possibility of transmuting the

---

* "Ille qui fecit se auctorem, de quo superius dixi. nihil novit de hujus scientiæ (perspectiva) potestate, sicut apparet in libris suis quia nec fecit librum de hac scientia, et fecisset si scivisset."—*Opus Tertium*, c. 11. "Leges multiplicationis nondum sunt alibi traditæ adhuc ut apparet in libris istis [*i.e.*, Albertus Magnus], qui nec fecit libros de hac scientia, nec aliquid de philosophia potest sciri sine hac."—*Opus Tertium*, c. 12.

† "In mineralium vero locis invenitur caliditas semper constans."—*Speculum Alchemiæ*, c. 5.

inferior metals to gold—a belief which was also shared by Francis Bacon. He treats this, however, as a mere experiment, and says that it falls within the province of practical alchemy, an art which teaches men to make metals, colours, and many other things better and in a greater quantity than Nature can do. But, he proceeds, there is another science relating to the elementary composition of things, which, being unknown to the mass of students, they cannot but be ignorant of the natural phenomena which depend upon it. Animal and vegetable bodies are made up of elements and humours, and their composition resembles that of inanimate bodies. Hence, and through the ignorance of the many of this department of science, neither natural philosophy nor medicine, speculative or practical, are known. It seems, then, that Roger Bacon believed that by taking advantage of certain laws of composition—*leges, canones,* as he elsewhere calls them,*—men could so far aid the *nisus* of Nature as to make gold at will—just as Francis Bacon did not doubt that the qualities of weight, pliability, and the rest which distinguish gold, could be induced on a given body by any one who knew the causes of those qualities—but he does not forget to remind us that the process by which this is effected has its analogies in the phenomena of the vegetable and animal kingdoms ; the changes which lead to the formation of inorganic bodies are a part of, or to use Bacon's own words, " communicate with "† the changes on which animal life depends ;—both sets of phenomena fall within the same great science—alchemy, without an acquaintance with which the philosophy of nature cannot be thoroughly understood—" propter ignorantiam istius scientiæ non potest sciri naturalis philosophia." If these views are original, we may almost agree with Bacon when he says that his ideas on the principles and applications of chemistry are worth more than the so-called knowledge of all other physicists.

On its highest side, the science of the composition of bodies is thus seen to touch physiology and medicine ; hence, our author is led to treat of the requirements of health, and of the means by which old age is to be averted. This was a favourite subject of Bacon's, and he reverts to it again and again. Men die much sooner than they need. Even Aristotle did not live as long as he might have done ; but instances of extraordinary vitality are not wanting ; as, for example, Astephius, who survived his thousandth year. In the remedies which are proposed, we see evidence of

---

* "Opus Tertinm," p. 37.
  † "Generatio enim hominum et brutorum et vegetabilum est ex elementis et humoribus et communicat cum generatione rerum inanimatanum."—*Opus Tertinm,* c. 12.

the superstition which then, and for some centuries afterwards, encumbered physiology; but notwithstanding his elixirs, his *sperma ceti*, and his miraculous ointments, Bacon had some glimpses of a more rational method of treatment. He recommends particular attention to dietetics, and complains that from the want of it children inherit a bad constitution from their parents.

Such, in brief, is the substance of Roger Bacon's philosophy in the imperfect form in which it has reached us. Regarding it in relation to his age and opportunities, we cannot help seeing in it the marks of a most powerful, original, and prescient mind. The shape in which the "Opus Majus" is cast, although sufficiently repulsive to a modern reader, is not the least of its merits. All the other great writers of that age were either paraphrasts or commentators. Adhering strictly to the subjects and the order prescribed for them by the authority whom they undertook to illustrate, they presented their readers, sometimes with a text enclosed in a vast margin of commentary, and sometimes with an exposition, in which the text and the gloss were indistinguished and indistinguishable. In either case they were bound by the arrangement of their author, and virtually prevented from treating at length any subject on which he had not written. It is for this reason that the titles of Aristotle so long furnished the divisions of physical and mental science. Bacon was the first to break the fetters of this custom: to adopt his own order; to introduce his own subjects; to do away with the never-ending chapters, texts, and paragraphs that perplex and weary the reader, and to produce something distantly approaching what is now meant by a book.

This peculiarity in the form of his writings proceeded chiefly, if not entirely, from the equally original manner in which he regarded science. "All branches of knowledge," he says, more than once, "hold together, and each influences the other—to learn any, we must first learn that which naturally precedes it."[*]

Nor does he leave us ignorant of the order to be adopted in this hierarchy of the sciences. "Let the philosophers of the world know that they will never effect anything in natural science —*in rebus naturalibus*—unless they are acquainted with the power of mathematics." Elsewhere, he calls mathematics the alphabet of philosophy. While we give him credit for the sagacity which led him to perceive the real place of this science in the scheme of education, and to fix on its qualities of certainty and simplicity as the reason for so placing it, we should not forget to add that he was seriously deceived in the estimate he formed of its use and applications. Because all phenomena may be considered

[*] "Opus Tertium," p. 37.

in the relations of number and quantity, he concluded that all formed the legitimate subject of mathematical analysis.

He even carried this principle a step further, so as to make the theory of numbers indirectly, as well as directly, useful. Perspective, or, as we should now call it, optics, was, in Bacon's view, a sub-section of mathematics, drawing its whole value from them. Therefore, said he, wherever optics comes in—in other words, on whatever subjects we rely on observation, the method of mathematical analysis may be applied. It is easy to detect in this principle the influence of the logic of the schools. We thus see in what sense Bacon speaks of the sciences being connected. It is not only that they have, as between themselves, certain relations of affinity and interdependence, but that they are bound together by the universal application of the same processes.

M. Pouchet gives to Albert of Cologne great credit for his investigation into the causes of things; a fertile method, in his opinion, and whose value the learned Dominican was the first to point out to future generations (p. 261). Roger Bacon was nearer the truth when he said, " we must not examine the causes of things;"* and in this he carries away the palm not only from the Bishop of Ratisbon, but from a more illustrious rival. Francis Bacon's definition of science is, "the knowledge of the cause on which the qualities of bodies depend": in the view of Roger Bacon it is, rather the knowledge of the relation between abstract qualities and their effects. We do not pretend that sufficient prominence is given to this maxim to vindicate for it a place among the truths foreseen by its author, but it is to be found in his works. And, in the treatise in which it occurs, mention is made of certain "laws" or "canons" governing the relations in question. It would be hazardous to infer that Bacon distinctly understood the nature of the relation expressed by the ● word "law," or that he looked on the acquaintance with a series of such relations as the final end of science; we believe that he meant both more and less than this; but that he meant something resembling the modern view may be safely conceded.

It has been Bacon's misfortune not only to have been forgotten, but to have been misunderstood. His scientific reputation has been placed on a wrong basis. So far as he is remembered at all, it is as a discoverer. The judgment of learned writers like Dumas, Jourdain, and Cuvier, has united with popular tradition in this belief.† In chemistry, he is said to have been the first who was acquainted with the properties of phosphorus, bismuth,

---

* " Non oportet causas investigare."

† Francis Bacon alludes to him as one of those who, " not caring so much about theory, seek to extend invention by a kind of mechanical subtilty."

and manganese : he is said to have found out the composition of gunpowder ; not only, we are told, did he anticipate the use of steam as a motive power, but he invented diving-bells, suspension bridges, spectacles, the camera obscura, the magic lantern, the telescope, and the mariner's compass. This is an example of the random way in which statements are repeated without any attempt to verify them. If any one of the distinguished men who have helped to father on Bacon this wonderful list of inventions, had referred to his works, they would have easily have satisfied themselves that the credit they have given him is about the last sort of credit to which he is really entitled. He was not a discoverer, but a reformer of scientific method—a discoverer of the means by which discoveries are made. To borrow a favourite simile of Lord Macaulay's, which is equally applicable to both the Bacons, he was the Moses, and not the Joshua, of philosophy ; he pointed out the promised land, but he never entered into it. It can easily be shown that of the things which Bacon is asserted to have invented, several were perfectly well known before his time, and the rest are nowhere described in his works.

First of all, as to the discovery of gunpowder. This is the passage usually relied on to support his claim :—

" We have a proof of the noise and flash which may be made experimentally in the child's game, common in some parts of the world, in which by an instrument not larger than a man's thumb, owing to the violence of the salt called saltpetre, such a terrible noise is made by the bursting of so slight a substance as a piece of parchment, that it exceeds the sound of thunder,* and has a brilliancy greater than lightning."

Elsewhere is found a cabalistic recipe,† by transposing the letters of which the words sulphur, saltpetre, and powdered carbon are said to be obtained. It may, or may not be, that Bacon was acquainted with the art of making gunpowder, but it is pretty certain that this substance had been long known in the East, and that it was introduced into the West by the Arabians in the twelfth century. India is the country to which we should naturally look as its birthplace. It may be observed, too, that Bacon's allusion to the explosive powder which he describes, does not imply either that he claimed to have discovered it, or that it was a novelty : on the contrary, it was so well known, that children were in the habit of playing with it.

The alleged invention of spectacles rests on no better grounds. All that appears is, that he was acquainted with the common optical experiment of placing a portion of a glass sphere

---

* "Opus Majus."

† "Sed tamen salispetræ lu, rac, vo, po, vir, can, utri et sulphuris et sic facies tonitrum et corruscationem, *si scias artificium.*"

on letters or other objects, and so causing them to appear larger. This property of lenses was known centuries before, and it has very little to do with the invention of spectacles.

The nearest approach to a description of the magic lantern is found in a passage of the treatise " De Admirabili Potestate Artis et Naturæ," in which the author says that such a form can be given to a transparent medium, that any one entering a room would see gold, silver, and precious stones, and that all would disappear when he advances nearer. It is difficult to say what Bacon meant by this, but it is not difficult to be very sure that he could not possibly have meant to describe a magic lantern.

There are no passages in Bacon's printed works which can be stretched into a description of the diving-bell, the camera obscura, or the mariner's compass ; although the principle of the diving-bell is explained in Aristotle's problems, and the compass was known in Italy in the thirteenth century.

Scarcely more satisfactory is the evidence on which the invention of the telescope has been ascribed to him. He certainly makes remarks which show that he was acquainted with optics : he says, for example, that the largest objects may be made to appear very small, and conversely, small objects made to appear large ; distant things near, and near things distant : " we may so dispose," he adds, " transparent media in relation to our sight and the object, that the rays may be reflected in any direction we please." But when he comes to describe the results of this arrangement, it is evident that he is not speaking from any experimental knowledge of the matter. He tells us that " an infant will appear a giant ; a man a mountain ; a small army will seem a large one ; although far off it may be made to seem close at hand ; we can make the sun, moon, and stars appear to descend on the heads of our enemies." This is not the language of a man who has ever looked through a telescope ; still less is it the language of a man who has invented one.

Bacon mentions in another place the possibility of constructing instruments which will impel vessels without the aid of oars, and with a single man to guide them, faster than if they were full of rowers ; carriages to roll along with inconceivable rapidity, without anything to draw them ; an instrument only a few inches broad and of equal height, which will lift and lower the greatest weights ; contrivances for swimming and remaining under water ; bridges without buttresses, and other mechanical appliances equally extraordinary.

To infer from such language as this, as has been inferred, that Bacon foresaw the time of railways, suspension bridges, hydraulic machines, and steamboats, is to tax one's credulity rather too far. The fact is this : he had a very strong belief in what he called the powers of Nature, and he rightly thought that there was scarcely any limit to the effects which a combination of art and nature is capable of producing.   Given this idea—by no means a commonplace one for the thirteenth century—and a slight exercise of imagination is sufficient for the kind of prediction which is found in the passages above quoted.   We have only to think of a number of things very difficult or improbable, and then say that the time will come when they will all come about. Many more pretentious prophecies have been constructed on this simple plan.

The obvious similarity between the reform projected by Roger Bacon, and that carried out by Francis Bacon, has given rise to the inquiry whether the author of the "Novum Organon" has not borrowed some of his philosophical views from his predecessor.   Mr. Foster expresses himself very decidedly upon this point: "Friar Bacon was the undoubted though renowned original, whence his great namesake drew the materials of his famous experimental system.   In the 'Opus Majus' in the 'Novum Organon,' we find again and again the fundamental laws of this system announced; uniformly the same in substance—often in the same words."*   Mr. Hallam just hints a doubt on the subject;† but the question has been reopened by the recent editors of Francis Bacon's works.   Mr. Ellis,‡ speaking of the four kinds of idols, says,—

"It has been supposed that this classification is borrowed from Roger Bacon, who in the beginning of the "Opus Majus" speaks of four hindrances whereby men are kept back from the attainment of true knowledge. But this supposition is for several reasons improbable. The "Opus Majus" was not printed until the eighteenth century, and it is unlikely that Francis Bacon would have taken the trouble of reading it, or any part of it, in manuscript.   In the first place, there is no evidence, in any part of his works, of this kind of research; and in the second, he had no high opinion of his namesake, of whom he has spoken with far less respect than he deserves.   The only work of Roger Bacon's which there is any good reason for believing that he was acquainted with, is a tract on the art of prolonging life, which was published at Paris in 1542, and of which au English translation appeared in 1617.   The general resemblance between the spirit in which the two Bacons speak of science and its improvement is, notwithstanding what has sometimes been said, but slight.   Both, no doubt, complain that sufficient attention has not been paid to observation and experiment, but that is all; and these complaints may be found in the writings of many other men, especially in the time of Francis Bacon. Nothing is more clear than that the essential doctrines of his philosophy —among which that of idols is to be reckoned—are, so far as he was

---

* "Mahometanism Unveiled," ii. 312, 313.
† "Mid. Ages," iii. 539.   ‡ "Francis Bacon's Works," i. 89, 90.

aware, altogether his own. There is, moreover, but little analogy between his idols and his namesakes' hindrances to knowledge. The principle of classification is altogether different, and the notion of a real connexion between the two was probably suggested simply by there being the same number of idols as of hindrances."

There are three points raised in this passage :—1. Is the principle of classification on which the *offendicula* of the elder Bacon, and the *idola* of the Chancellor, are founded, the same ? 2. Had Francis Bacon ever read a description of the *offendicula* described in the " Opus Majus" ? 3. Is there any such general resemblance between the spirit in which the two Bacons speak of science, as to lead to the presumption that the one was acquainted with the works of the other ? Notwithstanding the high authority of Mr. Ellis, we think that on two, at least, of these points, there is still considerable room for doubt. It may be admitted at once that the principle of classification of the hindrances to knowledge mentioned by each of the two writers, as those of Roger Bacon are founded an any principle , is entirely different. No reader could arrive at one by the help of the other. Thus far we can quite go with Mr. Ellis. This, however, is a matter of very secondary importance. The al question is, whether Francis Bacon was acquainted with the works of his fellow-labourer : because if he was, it is not easy to resist the inference that he borrowed something from them, and the cursory and slighting way in which he alludes to " the monk in his ould induce us to believe that he desired to conceal his dgments.*

I of all necessary to ascertain whether there is sufficient lance between the philosophies of the two writers to resumption of plagiarism. If, as Lord Bacon's editor irit in which science and its improvement is spoken of by the nor of the " Advancement of Learning," bears only a slight resemblance to Roger Bacon's views on the same subject, a few similarities of thought, of language, or of apparent classification, may be safely disregarded. If, on the contrary, there is a general identity of purpose and of procedure, such points are entitled to weight as corroborative evidence.

Lord Bacon's system, in its outline at least, may be readily described. He conceived that men were busying themselves with wrong subjects—with the logic of the schools, with metaphysics, with Aristotle, with anything but that which alone was really use-

---

* " Accedit et illud, quod Naturalis Philosophia, in iis ipsis viris qui ei incubuerint, vacantem et integrum hominem vix nacta sit ; nisi forte quis monachi alicujus in cellula exemplum adduxerit."—*Nov. Org.* Aph. 80. See also, " Temporis partus Masculus."

ful,—the philosophy of Nature.   Then he considers the causes
which have led to this condition of things, and he finds them,
partly in the frame and constitution of the human mind, and
partly in the reverence for antiquity, in the following of authority,
and in the disposition to be bound by accepted modes of theorizing.
No improvement of these methods would, he was of opinion, be of
any avail—"serum plane rebus perditis hoc adhibetur remedium"
—his only hope lay in reconstructing the whole method of science,
in putting the mind in harness, and in establishing a true induction.

Roger Bacon takes, in like manner, a general survey of the
studies which engaged his cotemporaries.   He finds that they
are altogether vanity.   The sciences which alone are of any
value, mathematics, perspective, and the "mistress art"—experiment—are neglected by the Latins.   And no wonder that they
are neglected.   For in everything which is said or done, authority,
custom, and the practice of the many, are uniformly appealed to.
These are the "pestilent causes" which hold back real knowledge
and cause wrong subjects to be pursued on wrong methods.   So
long as utility is disregarded and facts are drawn from books
instead of from observation and experiment, philosophy, and with
it religion and manners, will inevitably decline.

Both the Bacons have thus the same views as to what constitutes real knowledge ; both place it in the study of phenomena :
but in the words of the one it is " the science of Experiment ;" in
the language of the other it is "Natural Philosophy."   Both in
like manner conceive that its improvement is to be effected by
substantially the same process, only this process is resolved by
Roger Bacon into obtaining facts by observation and experiment
instead of culling them from books ; in the hands of Francis
Bacon it becomes the rejection of syllogism and the substitution
of a true and considered for a false and hasty induction.   This
amount of agreement is quite sufficient to set us upon the inquiry
in what respect their language and general opinions coincide.

The following table of comparison will enable the reader to
judge for himself :*—

POINTS OF AGREEMENT BETWEEN ROGER BACON AND FRANCIS BACON.

1.—*In their Opinion of Antiquity.*

ROGER BACON.	FRANCIS BACON.
"Ad auctorum dicta verorum po-test convenienter addi et corrigi in quampluribus. Et hoc egregie docet Seneca in libro quæstionum natura-	" De antiquitate autem opinio quam homines de ipsa fovent negli-gens omnino est, et vix verbo ipsi congrua. Mundi enim senium et

---

* It has been thought better to retain the original language of the authors
in this table.

ROGER BACON.

ium; quoniam dicit opiniones ve-eres parum exactas esse.—Et ideo licit in prologo majoris voluminis quod nihil est perfectum in humanis nventionibus, et infert *quanto juniores tanto perspicaciores* quia juniores pos-teriores successione temporum ingre-diuntur labores priorum."—*Opus Ma-ius,* c. 6.

FRANCIS BACON.

grandævitas pro antiquitate vere habenda sunt; quæ temporibus nos-tris tribui debent non juniori ætati mundi, qualis apud antiquos fuit."—*Nov. Org.* aph. 84.
" Antiquitas sæculi juventus mun-di."—*De Aug.* 138.

2.—*In their Opinion of Authority, Custom, and Popular Opinion.*

" Semper utimur tribus argumentis pessimis pro omnibus quæ facimus et dicimus; scilicet hoc exemplificatum est, hoc consuetum est, hoc vulgatum est,—ergo faciendum est. Sed oppo-situm conclusionis sequitur ex præ-missis, ut in pluribus, et optime stat cum eis."—*Opus Tertium,* c. 22.
" Et ideo hic accidunt hæc tria mala; scilicet, auctoritas fragilis, et sensus vulgi, et consuetudo."—*Ibid.*
" Auctoritas non sapit nisi detur ejus ratio, nec dat intellectum sed cre-dulitatem; credimus enim auctoritati sed non propter eam intelligimus."—*Compend. Studii,* c. 1.
" Quod pluribus, hoc est vulgo, videtur oportet quod sit falsum."—*De mirabili potestate.*

" Et exemplorum multitudinem de-clinemus, et consuetudinem semper habeamus suspectam, et simus ex paucis et de numero sapientum quantum possumus, et sensum mul-titudinis evitemus. Nam semper a principio mundi sapientes omnes, ut sancti et veri philosophi, se-paraverunt se a sensu vulgi, tam in scientia quam in vita : quia ille ut in pluribus est erroneus, et nun-quam est perfectus."—*Opus Tertium,* c. 22.

" Rursus vero homines a progressu in scientiis detinuit et fere incantavit reverentia antiquitatis et virorum qui in philosophia magni habiti sunt, auctoritas atque deinde consensus."—*Nov. Org.,* aph. 84.

" Illud enim de consensu fallit homines, si acutius rem introspiciant. Verus enim consensus is est, qui ex libertate judicii (re prius explorata) in idem conveniente consistit."—*Ibid.*
" Pessimum enim omnium est augu-rium quod ex consensu capitur in rebus intellectualibus; exceptis divi-nis et politicis in quibus suffragiorum jus est."—*Nov. Org.,* aph. 78.
" Optime traducitur illud Phocionis a moribus ad intellectualia; *ut statim se examinare debeant homines, quid er-raverint aut peccaverint, si multitudo consentiat aut complaudat.*"—*Ibid.*

3.—*In their Opinion of the Value of Experience.*

" Sine experientia nihil sufficienter sciri potest."—*Opus Majus,* p. 336.

" Duo enim sunt modi cognoscendi, scilicet per argumentum et experi-mentum. Argumentum concludit et

" Logica quæ in usu est ad errores stabiliendos et figendos valet, potius quam ad inquisitionem veritatis; itaque spes est una in inductione vera."—*Nov. Org.,* aph. 12, 14.
" Duæ viæ sunt, atque esse possunt, ad inquirendam et inveniendam veri-tatem. Altera a sensu et particulari-

ROGER BACON.

facit nos concludere quæstionem, sed non certificat neque removet dubitationem, ut quiescat animus in intuitu veritatis, nisi eam inveniat via experientiæ."—*Ibid.*

"Et hæc scientia (experimentalis) habet tres magnas prærogativas respectu aliarum scientiarum. Una est quod omnium illarum conclusiones nobiles investigat per experientiam. Scientiæ enim aliæ sciunt sua principia invenire per experimenta, sed conclusiones per argumenta facta ex principiis inventis."—*Opus Majus*, p. 338.

"Si attendamus ad experientias particulares et completas et omnino in propria disciplina certificatas, necessarium est ire per considerationes scientiæ experimentalis."—*Opus Majus*, p. 448.

FRANCIS BACON.

bus advolat ad axiomata maxime generalia, atque ex iis principiis eorumque immota veritate judicat et invenit axiomata media; altera a sensu et particularibus excitat axiomata ascendendo continenter et gradatim, ut ultimo loco perveniatur ad maxime generalia; quæ via vera est sed intentata."—*Nov. Org.*, aph. 19.

4.—*In their Opinion of the Untrustworthiness of the Human Mind.*

"Cogitavi vero quod intellectus humanus habet magnam debilitatem ad se; nam ea quæ sunt maximæ cogitationis secundum se sunt minimæ cogitationis quoad nos, et e converso." —*Opus Tertium*, c. 22.

"Manifestum est quod mens humana non sufficit dare quod necessarium est in omnibus, nec potest in singulis vitare falsum nec malum."—*Opus Majus*, p. 341.

"Intellectus humanus luminis sicci non est; sed recipit infusionem a voluntate et affectibus."—*Nov. Org.*, aph. 49.

"Sensus enim per se res infirma est et aberrans; neque organa ad amplificandos sensus aut acuendos multum valent; sed omnis verior interpretatio naturæ conficitur per instantias, et experimenta idonea; ubi sensus de experimento tantum, experimentum de re ipsa judicat."—*Nov. Org.*, aph. 50.

Each writer attached an extreme and even an exaggerated importance to the value of his method. Roger Bacon frequently maintains that by his own plan the labour of learning would be indefinitely diminished. He promises to teach Greek and Hebrew in three days; geometry in less than a week, and to communicate the result of his forty years' labour in science in three or six months by the aid of a compendium. "Had we competent teachers, I do not doubt that we should learn more within a year than by our present method in twenty years."[*]

Francis Bacon appears to have thought that the facts on which his philosophy was to be based might by proper means be registered in a few years; the space of a generation, if not of a single

---

[*] "Opus Tertium," p. 65.

life, would in his opinion suffice. "My principle of discovery," he observes, "is one which does not leave much to acuteness or strength of intellect; on the contrary, it tends to bring all minds to the same level."*

A mechanical method of procedure, simple, rapid, and easily learned, is of the essence of the discovery which the two Bacons professed to have made.

Mr. Hallam has already pointed out that the quaint word "prerogative," of which Francis Bacon was so fond, is used in the "Opus Majus." We may add that the notion of the other sciences being the handmaidens of natural philosophy is also found in that work.† Further, although the four obstacles to learning, respectively mentioned in the "Novum Organon" and the "Opus Majus" are divided on a different plan, yet they occupy a similar position in each system, and the idea of them is very much the same. To Mr. Ellis's remark, that nothing turns on there being the same number of idols as of hindrances, for that in the earlier form of the doctrine of idols there were only three, —it may be replied that in the later works of Roger Bacon the hindrances are three likewise. Nor is it of any great importance whether Francis Bacon ever saw the "Opus Majus" or not. The "Opus Minus," the "Opus Tertium," or the "Compendium Studii" would equally well have presented the outlines of his predecessor's doctrine. In Cambridge, in Bacon's time, there must have been several manuscripts of some or all of these works. On the whole, we are of opinion that there is sufficient evidence to render it probable that Francis Bacon was acquainted with the scheme of Roger Bacon's doctrine.

In saying this we imply no detraction from the merit or the originality of the great man who first systematized the inductive method. The question is one of literary curiosity alone. There is not much weight in the often-repeated charge of borrowing ideas. Unless a man is capable of thinking for himself, imported thoughts will do him no good. Had Francis Bacon been unable to evolve his system from his own resources, he might have read the "Opus Majus," as hundreds of men read it before him, to little purpose. That he gathered from that work, as we think it probable that he did, here a valuable maxim and there a happy expression, proves only the ripeness of his judgment in matters intellectual; and when all is said, enough remains incontestably his own to justify the admiration in which his name has been so long held.

---

* "Distributio Operis."

† "Mathematica et logica quæ *ancillarum loco* erga physicam se gerere debent" (Bacon's Works, vii. 204.) "Scientia experimentalis imperat aliis scientiis *sicut ancillis suis.*"—*Opus Majus,* p. 476. (Edit. Jebb.)

Nor will any one acquainted with the systems of the two men deny that, even in the points in which they coincide, the merit of superior treatment is with the more modern writer. Roger Bacon, by the necessities of his age and circumstances, had a less precise view of the bearings of the change he advocates than his successor. He was sometimes frightened at his own boldness—he often hesitates; not infrequently he weakens the effect of his theory by the indecision of his practice. There are, we hold, two kinds of reformers : the reformer negative and the reformer positive. The first so far rises above the level of commonplace acquiescence as to see that current theories do not account for facts ; that current beliefs rest on an insufficient basis. He therefore sets to work to destroy ; he pulls down the building in which he dwells, but he has nothing to raise in its stead. The latter proceeds on a different method. He has a definite plan, and his work consists in removing the structure of opinion, not by taking it to pieces, but by building up a better, which must necessarily displace it. Such was the reform of Copernicus, who destroyed the cycles and epicycles of Ptolemy by an explanation of the phenomena more simple and sufficient than his ; such was the reform of Francis Bacon, who substituted formal canons of scientific proof for the defective inductions of the schoolmen ; such was not the reform of the elder Bacon with regard to the science of his day. He saw clearly enough that things were on a wrong footing ; he also pointed out what was wanting to set them right : but when he comes to act, he sometimes hesitates and looks back. His criticism leaves nothing to be desired ; the constructive side of his system is by far the weakest part in it. He protests strongly and always against the error of assuming a thing to be true because the authority of a respectable name can be cited in its favour ; yet he advocates the study of language, for the purpose of enabling men to see what higher authorities have pronounced on the matter. He discredits Peter of Spain and Alexander Hales ; but there are cases in which he would be bound by the opinion of Aristotle or of Averroes. He does not question Cicero's maxim, that a law of nature may be established by a given quantity of affirmative evidence,—he only takes care that the induction shall include certain well-known instances. Hence the practical effect of his protest against authority often comes to no more than this—that authorities should be selected, not that selected authorities should be laid aside ; he merely transfers his allegiance to a worthier object. And so, while with one hand he is destroying an idol of brass, he seems to be setting up with the other, as the object of our intellectual worship, an image of gold.

Bacon's leading idea was undoubtedly a reform of the philosophical systems of the day, to be effected by a recourse to Nature and an observation of her processes. It is no less clear that he considered this as ancillary only to the removal of abuses in the Church and in the State. *Abeunt studia in mores.* False modes of education, vicious systems of theorizing, engender, he thought, depravity of manners and laxity of discipline. He frequently contrasts the life and example of Aristotle, Seneca, Socrates, Cicero,—of the facts of whose lives he probably knew little—with the depravity of the men he saw around him; and that he traced that depravity to ignorance there can be no doubt. Hence, on principle, he was constrained to hold his cotemporaries in slight estimation. This feeling is shared by all reformers in a greater or less degree. Dissatisfaction with the existing structure is naturally a motive with those who modify or reconstruct. But in the highest class of minds it will be found, we suspect, to take the form of a protest against systems rather than of an attack on men; and it is seldom that a thinker of Bacon's stamp arrests himself, as he does, in the course of his argument, in the very flow and current of his thought, to hold up to ridicule a false quantity, an absurd derivation, or a mistranslation.*

There are some men at the mere thought of whom he lashes himself into a kind of fury: they are the " conservative divines;"† " the boy leaders of the two student-orders, as Albert and Thomas, and others;"‡ " the heads of the crowd." These diabolical men, says Bacon, are not ashamed to condemn all learning which they themselves have not got, before prelates, princes, and people. " Hi igitur"—his anger must be left to express itself—" errore et ignorantiæ tenebris velut quodam carcere deterrimo damnati, non habent de jure unde damnent sapientiæ lucem, respectu cujus sunt talpæ cæcæ et vespertiliones lippæ et immundi sues cœno turbido ignorantiæ obducti."§ This is pretty well for a divine and a philosopher.

What passed for divinity, and more especially the sermons of the Dominicans, excited in him, not anger, but a gentle feeling of contempt.

" It is very easy for the members of this Order to talk to people

---

* His style of criticism is not without a certain vigour. He says of the works of Albert :—" Hæc scripta habent peccata quatuor. Unum est vanitas puerilis infinita; secundum est falsitas ineffabilis; tertium est superfluitas voluminis eo quod tota potestas illarum scientiarum posset coarctari utili tractatu et veraci in vicesima parte illorum voluminum; quartum est quod partes philosophiæ magnificæ utilitatis—auctor istorum operum omisit. Et ideo nulla est utilitas in scriptis illis sed maximum sapientiæ detrimentum."—*Opus Tertium,* c. 9.

† " Theologi stationarii."   ‡ " Compend. Studii," c. v. p. 426.
§ Ibid., c. iii. p. 417.

about virtue and vice, heaven and hell, particularly as there are plenty of passages in the sacred texts from which any stupid may quote; but of this I am very certain, that there is a simple brother who never heard a hundred lectures on theology, and who would not have attended to them if he had, who preaches beyond comparison better than the greatest masters of theology."[*]

Thus with the honesty and convictions, Bacon had some of the vulgar faults of a reformer. He was impetuous, intolerant, and frequently unjust. The way in which he praises his own performance cannot but detract from the credit of it. In the opening of one of his works[†] he excuses his delay by saying that neither Albert nor Master William of Shyrwode—a sage, in his opinion, superior to Albert—could have composed in ten years what he had effected, under many disadvantages, in one. "Certainly," he adds, "you will find a hundred passages to which these persons with their present knowledge would never come up to their dying day."

This language and temper every one must regret. It shows that personal feeling came in aid of genuine belief, to give force to the stroke with which Bacon laid about him. Nor can we wonder that this should be so. During a great part of his literary life he was smarting under a sense that he had been cruelly and unjustly dealt with. He saw that the age was out of joint, and he also saw, or thought he saw, the remedy. He had that consciousness of power which irresistibly impels men to be up and doing. In an evil hour he joined a society, by whose rules, and still more by whose rulers, he was fettered and gagged at every turn. He was interdicted from books; he was prohibited from writing; when detected in his favourite pursuits, he was put on bread and water. This was enough to irritate a more temperate man than Brother Roger; and the matter was not mended by the fact that those who so severely repressed learning were not themselves remarkable for possessing it. Bacon, with a vast fund of knowledge of which he was anxious to make the best use, may very well be excused in harbouring bitter feelings against men who sent him from his laboratory to a cloister, who diverted him from the study of Aristotle to the "Book of Sentences," and withal who could scarcely read their missals decently.[‡]

Notwithstanding his frequent attacks on the clergy, Bacon's orthodoxy in essential points cannot be impeached. It would be quite incorrect to represent him as a freethinker of the school of

---

[*] "Compend. Studii," c. v. p. 427, 428.
[†] "Opus Tertium," c. ii.
[‡] " Clerici et sacerdotes rurales recitant officium divinum de quo parum aut nihil intelligunt sicut bruta."—*Compend. Studii*, p. 413.

Averroes. He never attacks the central positions of the Christian belief, violently as he criticizes some of the institutions of the Church herself. So with regard to philosophy. Bold as he was, and with an almost reckless audacity in speculation, there were subjects on which he did not venture to lay his hand. For example, he never entertained the notion—which, is in truth, one of the latest products of modern thought—of the absolute inutility of metaphysics. He would supplement the logic and metaphysic of the schools by sciences of which the schools did not dream, and he would amend the manner in which the sciences in vogue were to be studied.

These defects — and there. are many such in Bacon's writings—should not blind us to the essential merits of his system and the value of the double object which he held constantly in view. This double object—the investigation of nature as a distinct pursuit, and the foundation of natural studies on observation and experiment—constitutes the real aim of his teaching. That a schoolman of the thirteenth century should have seriously set to work to carry out such an idea is not a little remarkable. For it must always be borne in mind that in that age, and indeed, for some century and a quarter afterwards, no science wholly independent of theology was held to exist. The clergy being the sole depositories of learning had subordinated all knowledge to their own special pursuits : they thought that language should be studied, not as a means of informing the mind and refining the taste, but to enable them to read the divines and fathers, and to settle disputed points in the construction of the sacred texts. Astronomy was a means by which they might calculate the times at which the feasts of the Church should be observed : they read the masterpieces of Greek thought—so far as they read them—with the sole object of harmonizing them with Christian theology, and of putting into their own armoury the weapons forged by Aristotle for the use of general science. That a philosophy of nature existed as an object of independent pursuit was not dreamed of ; that there were any other means of arriving at any scientific truth than by comparing what had already been said by the ancients, and grinding their statements down in a logical mill, was an idea which would have been laughed at by an ordinarily educated man then, and which was not generally accepted till some three centuries later.

When Roger Bacon was laid in his grave, the real philosophy was buried with him. The fate of that philosophy is a lasting example of the wisdom of the remark, that Truth is the daughter of Time. Putting circumstances aside, and looking only to the men and to the doctrine, there is no reason why the thirteenth century should not have anticipated the literary and scientific revival of the sixteenth. Grostète was probably as great a scholar as Ascham; Roger Bacon is scarcely inferior to Francis Bacon as a reformer of scientific method. Time, however, and opportunity were on the side of the one and against the other. The seed which Roger Bacon had sowed with so lavish a hand fell on ground as yet unprepared to receive it. A long and dreary winter of scholasticism lay between the promise of the thirteenth century and fulfilment of the Renaissance. For more than two hundred years the most powerful minds of Europe were doomed to contend in vain with the insoluble problem of absolute existence and the chimera of absolute knowledge. At last the change took place. Then it was seen that the truth which had been so long forgotten was not dead but sleeping. It awakened into life at the touch of another Bacon, with the publication of the " Novum Organon."

It has been our fortune to realize all, and more than all, the wild dreams pictured by the heated imagination of the Franciscan;—the " instruments which will enable men to navigate without the aid of oars ;" the " machines by which we can remain under water;" the " rivers crossed by bridges without supports." The man who, six hundred years ago, pointed out the possibility of these results being attained, and who first entered on the course of philosophical speculation by which they have been realized, has some claims on the consideration of the nineteenth century. In saying this, we mean only that he should not be entirely forgotten. To expect any other memorial of him than an occasional place in the thoughts of educated people would be absurd : for he was only the most original thinker which England produced up to the time of Francis Bacon, and, in the deliberate judgment of Humboldt, the profoundest of the schoolmen. He merely anticipated by three centuries one of the most important revolutions which Europe has yet seen, and that to which our present material prosperity is directly due. It would be against all precedent if such a man were to receive those public honours which are reserved for kings, for princes, or for successful generals. But would it be too much to ask that, in the magnificent building which Oxford has lately raised for the cultivation of the physical sciences, the founder of the experimental method should find a place? " Magni animi fuit rerum latebras primitus dimovere, et plurimum ad inveniendum contulit qui speravit posse reperire, et quamvis propter humanam fragilitatem in multis defecit tamen excusandus est."

CONTEMPORARY LITERATURE.

THEOLOGY.

THE judgment of the Judicial Committee of the Privy Council in the " Essays and Reviews" cases completes in a most remarkable manner the judgment of Dr. Lushington in the court below :[1] the two documents dovetail into each other with singular precision, and taken together declare the existence of an amount of liberty in the Church of England which the public generally little dreamt of, and which, though an ancient right and one heretofore partially exercised, it has required no little courage and perseverance on the part of an unpopular minority to establish. Considering merely the numerous issues raised in the two cases of Dr. Williams and Mr. Wilson, it has been a great forensic triumph for them and their counsel in the Arches Court to have defeated their prosecutors on every single point. Not a shred was ultimately left of eleven charges in the one case and of eight in the other. The repulse was complete even as to details of legal practice. Thus the appellants had mutually agreed that Mr. Wilson's case should be first heard before the Privy Council; partly we believe in order to show that the cases were really two and not one " Essays and Reviews" case, and partly to give Mr. Wilson a better opportunity of arguing his case more fully than had been possible in the court below, where judge and counsel were already wearied by the length of time which Dr. Williams's cause had occupied. In order to Mr. Wilson's cause being set down first on the list for hearing, it was necessary that he should press it on with all speed through the formal stages before the Surrogate in the Court of Appeals, Dr. Williams keeping a few weeks behind. Whether the prosecution was really mystified by this proceeding, or whether their object was simply to raise difficulties, a technical objection was raised to Mr. Wilson's proctor appearing for him on the formal admission of his Libel of Appeal. The irregularity, if any, was cured by Mr. Wilson appearing in person; but it is probable the Canon under which this most frivolous objection was taken would not apply to proceedings in the Court of Appeals, only to the Ecclesiastical Court itself. Another objection, as to which the prosecution suffered a most signal defeat, was more formidable in appearance, being founded on the pretence, that the appellants, by reason of not having availed themselves of their option of appeal after the interlocutory judgment of June 25, 1862, were precluded from now being heard before the Privy Council on the merits (See Mr. Wilson's Speech before the Judicial Committee, pp. xx. xxi.). We have before us what the counsel for the respondents called a supplemental case, by which notice was given to the appellants, two or three days only, as we

---

[1] "Judgment of the Judicial Committee of the Privy Council upon the Appeals of Williams v. the Lord Bishop of Salisbury, and Wilson v. Fendall, from the Court of Arches, delivered 8th February, 1864." Official printed Copy.

believe, before the hearing, of this attempt to prevent the discussion of the cases on their merits before the Privy Council.

It would, however, be idle to ignore that other and greater difficulties weighed upon the defendants in these causes. The amount of prejudice against them may be judged of, not so much from the tirades of religious periodicals as from the fact that while doing his duty as interpreter of the law, the judge of the Court of Arches threw out frequent *obiter* observations as to the "fearful consequences" to which some of the doctrines of the essayists might be carried—that the publication of the volume "might be an ecclesiastical offence" in any of the essayists, independently of the authorship, with much of a like kind; and even the calmer heads of the Judicial Committee, while ratifying the opinions of the two essayists to an extent far beyond what was necessary to their mere acquittal, thought it expedient to guard themselves in terms against being supposed to express any opinion as to the general tendency of the volume, or of the whole essays of Dr. Williams and Mr. Wilson. We think that no compositions could have been subjected to a severer test than these two: it is a marvellous result, of which the authors may well be proud, that the ingenuity of lawyers, quickened by the suggestions of the ablest members of the two great ecclesiastical parties, furious with the *odium theologicum*, should not have succeeded in detecting any weak point in their polemical armour. That the Judicial Committee should have thought it advisable to say that they expressed no opinion as to the general tendency of the volume or the effect and aim of the two essays is the more observable, because in the case of Dr. Williams a Charge had been laid concerning the "tendency, object, and design" of the whole essay, and the Court below had decided it to be inadmissible; as throwing on the judge an impossible task; as without precedent; as inconsistent with the requisite precision of pleading. But although these extra-judicial observations may detract very slightly from the dignity of the judgment pronounced by the Privy Council, they rather add to its legal weight. It is evident there was no leaning to the defendants in either Court. They have extorted the decisions in their favour by mere force of law and logic. We apprehend that the extent of this success in the Court below was little appreciated by the general public, so long as it was supposed that the defendants were caught on some of the Charges. For it should be remembered that the Articles of Charge brought into the Arches Court were not counts of indictment laying the same offence under different forms, in which case a conviction upon any one would have been equivalent to a verdict of guilty upon the whole charge. But each Article of Charge laid a separate heresy or offence, and none of these were ultimately brought home: sometimes the prosecutors were found to have forced a meaning into the Formularies which they would not bear; sometimes to have interpreted unfairly the words of the authors; sometimes both. There was however one movement of the prosecution, on the success of which a great part of their case depended, and in which, if they had been successful, clergymen of the Church of England would have been tied down to the merest literalism in the interpretation of the Bible; but as the movement was defeated, the declared liberty of exposition is proportionately great. It was desired to convict Dr. Williams of an ecclesiastical offence by reason of his attempt to indicate beneath some of the Old Testament traditions—as of the sacrifice of Isaac and of the Exodus—some simple fact which would be consistent with human history; and an offence in like manner was to be brought home to Mr. Wilson for suggesting that the miracles of the New Testament might represent ideas rather than facts. Of course there is no commentary authorized by law in the Church of England, nor any exposition anywhere given of the meaning of particular texts and passages of the Bible. But it was sought to cure this defect for the purpose of the prosecution, by charging that inasmuch as the scriptural passages alluded to by the defendants were included in the Epistles, Gospels, and Lessons appointed to be read in the Prayer Book, it was an ecclesiastical offence against the Act of Uniformity which enforces the Prayer Book, to construe them otherwise than in a plain, literal sense. This would have been to constitute the ecclesiastical judge indirectly the interpreter of the whole of the Bible, with the exception of a few chapters, and to set him to reconcile no one knows what difficulties and discrepancies which may be found in it. And this *reductio ad absurdum* was complete when in opposition to some scores of passages from the Bible, produced for the prosecution, which the defendants were alleged to have contradicted, Dr. Deane put in on their part an equal list of texts in support of their views. Thus pelted on both sides, the judge of the Arches saw no safety but in ordering all reference to Scripture embodied in the Prayer Book to be struck out of the Articles of accusation. This at once reduced the case of the prosecution to fragments; but the importance of that part of the decision has been little noticed, either as to the magnitude of the danger which has been escaped, or the extent of liberty which has been affirmed.

Of particular decisions arrived at, the most important have been the entire opening of the interpretation of the prophetical writings, and the admitted lawfulness of eliminating from them all notion of historical prediction of facts. It appears to be open to a clergyman, for instance, to maintain, if he be so convinced, that the 53rd chapter of Isaiah does not contain a prediction of the actual events of the Lord's Passion. The authorship and date of books are also open questions. Daniel may not have been written by Daniel; nor the Second of Peter, by Peter; nor the Epistle to the Hebrews by St. Paul; and even this latter Epistle may be said to *have been post-apostolic.* Thus the way was made perfectly safe for the denial of the Mosaic authorship of the Pentateuch to which Bishop Colenso has been led. The lawfulness of affixing a figurative sense to any part of the Bible has been already mentioned. This liberty both of interpretation and of criticism so amply conceded by the Court below was, however, clogged with an abstract doctrine concerning Inspiration of the Scriptures—for it was no more than that, and one conceived with remarkable clumsiness. Dr. Williams was found to have offended by not having distinguished the operation of the Spirit which suggested the essential parts of the Bible as different *in kind,* and not only *in degree,* from that which moves ordinary men to great and good works. Mr. Wilson was likewise condemned for denying

o o 2

a "special interposition of Almighty power" in the production of the Bible. But in the Privy Council, the distinction between "kind" and "degree" was ignored; and the phrase of the Bible "being the expression of devout reason," was held not to be inconsistent with its being the "Word of God." Moreover it was laid down, that the Bible may well be *denominated* "Holy," and said to be the "Word of God," "God's Word written," although such terms "cannot be predicated of every statement contained in every part of the Old and New Testament;" that it is not a contradiction of the law of the Church, to affirm that some parts of the Scriptures were "not written under the inspiration of the Holy Spirit:" and even as to those parts which were inspired, "nothing has been laid down as to the nature, extent, or limits of that operation of the Holy Spirit." Indeed, it is added, "the framers of the Articles have not used the word inspiration as applied to the Holy Scriptures;" and considering "the caution of the framers of the Articles of Religion," their language must not be taken "as implying more than is expressed," nor conclusions be drawn from it "touching minute and subtle matters of controversy." With respect to other subjects, the Privy Council thought it would be "a severe thing" to make Dr. Williams, as a reviewer or advocate, responsible for everything in Bunsen, "although not in conformity with the doctrines of the Church of England." This point seems to have given no trouble to their lordships, though a great clamour had been raised about Dr. Williams fighting under the shield of Bunsen, and it caused great difficulty to the Court below. Again, the Evangelical party has now been told distinctly that in the 11th Article there is no doctrine "as to the merits of Jesus Christ being transferred to us," ordinarily known as the doctrine of imputation of Christ's merits. Nor will either of the extreme parties be pleased to learn, that to say, with Mr. Wilson, the distinction between covenanted and uncovenanted mercies is a distinction without a difference, is in no contradiction with the doctrine of the Church. Lastly, we may add that the incubus of a fiery Hell, and of endless torment in the world to come, need no longer oppress religious hearts among us as a doctrine necessary to be believed on the authority of the Established Church of the country. We now learn from the highest tribunal that it never has been so since the year 1562, when the Article headed, *All men shall not be saved at the length*, was withdrawn from the standard of doctrine, under sanction of the Parliament and Convocation. Whether the clergy will use their now-ascertained liberty, and whether the laity will encourage and sustain them in doing so, remains to be seen.

The excellent little work of Miss Cobbe's, entitled "Broken Lights," has in the present stage of theological discussion a twofold interest and a double use.[2] It discriminates in the happiest manner the several parties now engaged in the theological arena in this country, and undertakes to show that although the more conservative parties are doomed to inevitable defeat, the essential verities of religion will still

---

[2] "Broken Lights: an Inquiry into the Present Condition and Future Prospects of Religious Faith." By Frances Power Cobbe, author of an "Essay on Intuitive Morals," &c. London: Trübner and Co. 1864.

survive as a ground of faith and a root of spiritual life for the humanity of the future. These essential verities are stated to be, Faith in the existence of a righteous God—faith in the eternal law of morality—faith in an immortal life. Dogmatists, whether of the Sacerdotalist or Evangelical parties, set on the same footing with these essential truths an immense mass of inference, of theory, of ancient history, or tradition. And so effectually have the essentials and non-essentials of religious faith been bound together in the concrete traditional Christianity, that many even of those who perceive some things believed without question by former generations to be doubtful or untenable, are fearful lest the fundamental truths of all religion should now be rendered doubtful with them. After describing the hopeless position of the old parties relatively to advancing inquiries, Miss Cobbe passes in review the more modern schools. What is here called the first Broad Church School, of which Mr. Maurice and Prof. Kingsley may be taken as the representatives, is first criticized. Their signal failure in the attempt to harmonize Church and Bible with modern thought is well traced out. Each point of special difficulty is evaded by them ; and though "the inquirer for bread receives, not an ordinary stone, but a diamond or a ruby," such treatment of the great difficulties of theology must prove unsatisfactory and fatal to the school which adopts it. We need those who will evade and cover up nothing, "who will put the new wine into new bottles." The very basis of the first Broad Church is incredible, for it supposes a special Revelation of Divine Truth and of the Divine Will to have been made *enigmatically*, in language which for many centuries those to whom it was addressed were incapable of comprehending. The contained truth has in successive periods received light, instead of shedding it. The first Broad Church maintains that the Inspiration of the Bible differs in kind as well as degree from that of other books ;.the second Broad Church admits a difference in degree only, and acknowledges fallibility to attach to the human vehicles of Divine Truth. The contrast between these two schools is exceedingly well drawn out by Miss Cobbe. As the two incriminated Essayists have made good the whole of their legal claims, some passages may require modification—especially a very important alteration will be necessary in any future edition in the note at pp. 68-69, concerning the endlessness of future punishment, which it is now decided is *not* a necessary doctrine in the Church of England. The effect of the movement of Bishop Colenso is then described, which will undoubtedly be carried forward into the New Testament. And the inferences which will follow from such investigations as his will be much more fatal to received beliefs than any theoretical or general statements of the second Broad Church School could possibly be. It was politic, no doubt, in the maintainers of the dogma as it is to fight the Bishop at the outworks, upon the numbers and quantities of the narrative of the Exodus. For they very well know that while the numbers of the Israelites at the Exodus would not be essential to be ascertained as a matter of fact in an ordinary historical inquiry, their accuracy and consistency are essential to the credibility of such a narrative purporting to be written by an eye-witness. So, again, the clamour raised at the supposition of Samuel, instead of

Moses, having been the real author of the history of the Exodus, indicates a profound apprehension that little reliance can be placed upon the history if transmitted only by tradition through a period of four hundred years. Would-be conciliators, who speak of its being unimportant whether 600,000 fighting men of Israel came out of Egypt or 600, and unimportant whether Moses or Samuel (who was equally inspired) composed the Pentateuch, do not touch the difficulty as it is secretly felt—that an immense gap will be made in the miraculous history of the Bible, if it shall appear that there is no contemporary evidence to the events of the Exodus as narrated.

The Bampton Lectures of Dr. Hannah present a noteworthy phase of the discussion concerning the Inspiration of the Bible.[3] On one side he may be thought to make very considerable admissions and concessions to the critical spirit ; on the other, to be a strict maintainer of orthodoxy. Indeed, his special object appears to be to show that the human characteristics of the Biblical writings may be largely recognised with safety so long as the critic starts from a supposition that they embody a Revelation, of which the central fact or doctrine is the Incarnation of God the Son. He quotes, for instance, from Dr. Moberly, the observation that, " it makes a wonderful difference in the apparent magnitude and importance of a difficulty, whether it be regarded as the possible entrance to an entire unbelief or an acknowledged perplexity on the fringe or edge of a strong and impregnable faith." And he adds that " setting forth from the firm foundation of such faith, we shall find that disputes on details have a growing tendency to settle themselves and disappear."—p. 140. We ought not to undervalue the candour which leads Dr. Hannah openly to reject the " all or none " and " every jot and tittle" theories of Inspiration, because he carries his concessions only to the point beyond which they would endanger the certitude of doctrines which he assumes to be true. And unless he had secured himself at the very outset against any supposition of weakness as to the received dogma, there are many parts of these lectures which would have excited serious apprehensions in the minds of many of his hearers. His purpose generally is to show the completeness of the divine and human elements in Scripture, but neither so to exalt the divine as to reduce the human author to a mere machine, nor so to insist on the human characteristics as to reduce the divine to the same spiritual influence, which may be said to preside over any great work of human genius. And Dr. Hannah seems to agree with the distinction which Dr. Lushington laid down between the inspiration of the Scriptural authors and that of other great and good men as one of kind and not of degree. The question thus arises in what does this generic difference consist ? Dr. Hannah thinks he answers the question by drawing first a distinction between Reve-

[3] "The Relation between the Divine and Human Elements in Holy Scripture. Eight Lectures preached before the University of Oxford in the year 1863, on the foundation of the late Rev. John Bampton, M.A., Canon of Salisbury." By J. Hannah, D.C.L., Warden of Trinity College, Glenalmond, and Pantonian Professor of Theology; late Fellow of Lincoln College, Oxford. London : John Murray. 1863.

lation and Inspiration, and then between Revelation and other knowledge which comes to man through natural and ordinary channels. Whence, as ordinary literature is to ordinary knowledge in its various degrees, so is inspired Scripture to revealed knowledge. As a framework, indeed, to the Revelation, properly so called, we have a history of thoughts, words, and deeds of men which required no special interposition in order to their observation or record. But a different order of facts could be known only by a miraculous inspiration—such as the commands and warnings of God, and mysterious truths concerning his nature. "And as all this is miraculous, we make no further demand on faith when we add that it was coupled with many other manifestations of miracle—prophecies which none but God could pronounce, direct interpositions of his sovereign will to alter or suspend his ordinary laws."—p. 28. It is, indeed, conceded that it is difficult to draw a line around that which is human history and observation necessary as framework to the record of the Revelation, though not a record of Revelation itself, and as to which consequently the human characteristics may be found to predominate. But the impossibility of drawing this line has not, we think, been sufficiently noticed by the lecturer, nor the important consequence from it, that his argument or exposition is entirely valueless as addressed to those who do not start from the same doctrinal assumptions as he does himself. It is conceded that in matters of science or mere matters of history there may be errors in the Bible, while there can be none in those parts which belong to the Revelation properly so called. And the vehicle of the Revelation is human, while the Revelation itself is divine. Thus in the first chapter of Genesis it is the form or clothing of the doctrine of the creation of the world, and of man as the noblest work of God, which alone is, properly speaking, human, and which may not, therefore, be compatible with scientifically ascertained truth. The lecturer's words are here worth transcribing:—

"If we are asked then, whether we resign the historic reality of the beginning of Genesis, we answer that we resign nothing but a deeply-seated misapprehension, which has confounded records of a different order, and obliterated the distinction between theology and history by transferring the conditions of the one to the other. The first step in what may be technically called the narrative of history is taken at the beginning of the fifth chapter of the Book of Genesis, in the words—'this is the book of the generations of Adam' . . . . With some minor exceptions the first four chapters are rather theological than historical; they belong to the head of pure revelation rather than to that of ordinary narrative. They embody matter which no conjecture could have reached, which no tradition could have furnished. They unfold in such order as God judged to be the fittest, the fundamental truths about God's purpose and God's work in creation, and about the innocence, the sin, and the fall of man. This, then, after all, is the sole residuum of so much 'confident rhetoric,' to which the Mosaic record has been exposed; the assailant has only succeeded in carrying a position which a deeper interpretation makes it needless to defend."—pp. 164–165.

Dr. Hannah must here find himself, we think, on slippery ground. How much is fundamental, how much is vehicle and accessory? Dr. Hannah does not take the descriptive part of the first chapter of

Genesis as fundamental ; nor does he consider the word "day" should be literally pressed, any more than such anthropomorphic expressions as "finger" or "hand" of God. Have we then in the second and third chapters of Genesis a real Eden, real trees of good and evil and of life ; a real apple, a speaking serpent, a historical Adam and Eve ? If not, how elicit Dr. Hannah's doctrine of a moral Fall ?—how elicit it under any supposition ? The doctrine of creation by One God is manifestly conveyed in the first chapter of Genesis, for it is set forth in terms as its very text ; yet it does not follow that a miraculous revelation was employed in making it known. But unless one is predetermined to find in Gen. ii. iii. the " evangelical " doctrine of the " Fall," it appears on the face of it to be nothing more than a supposed account of the origin of certain physical conditions of humanity. The moral difficulties of the Old Testament are dealt with in a still less satisfactory manner. Dr. Hannah seems to solve them, as in the case of Deborah, on the hypothesis that to the divine element of Revelation belongs in such histories the declaration of the contrast between good and evil—true religion and false ; to the human element, the relentless hatred of the Jews towards the foes who were arrayed against the chosen people. And we should remember, says Dr. Hannah, "the real wickedness of the Canaanitish people." But really is there evidence that they were more "wicked" than their invaders ? Nor does Dr. Hannah observe that the difficulty is twofold—partly belonging to what he would call the Revelation—partly to that which he terms Inspiration : partly, that is, that immoral things should be done by God's chosen special instruments—partly that the writers who record the facts, supposing them to have happened, pass no rectifying judgment upon them. Nor, again, does he grapple with the inquiry whether such phrases as "God said," &c., as in the temptation of Abraham—in the command to slaughter the sons of Saul—in the approbation of the treachery of Jehu, are to be understood as implying an immediate divine communication, or a natural though erroneous imagination on the part of the agents, or a formula of the narrator. Do such phrases belong to the divine or to the human element, to the mere 'record of a sin,' or to ' its express approbation ?' (p. 239). Are such phrases, when met with in the Hebrew records, to be interpreted as they would be, if they were met with in "any other book ?" A general statement, that in many respects the Bible differs from any other book, and that so far as it differs the same rules of interpretation are not to be applied to it as to other books, will not solve such a difficulty as this when it arises in detail. On the whole, we cannot think that Dr. Hannah's distinction, as he puts it, between the Revelation and Inspiration of the Bible, its message and vehicle, its matter and form, would prove of any practical utility to an inquirer, though it may be convenient as a temporary shelter against troublesome criticisms to those who take on trust a traditional scheme of doctrine.

Mr. Row's work on Inspiration is likewise directed to preserve the supernatural character of the Christian Revelation, by distinguishing between the divine and human elements in the Biblical writings.[4] With

---

[4] "The Nature and Extent of Divine Inspiration, as stated by the writers and

both authors we have already left behind the platitudes of the Words-worths and the Burgons; but Mr. Row far surpasses Dr. Hannah in intellectual grasp and logical force. The question as to the nature of the inspiration of the New Testament, says Mr. Row, may be con-sidered the great theological question of the day—it must be treated inductively from observation of the facts presented in the New Testa-ment itself, lest we should attribute to the writers an inspiration which they may possibly disclaim, and which may then mislead us in the interpretation of the records. Mr. Row does not recur at all to the Old Testament. The inquiry proceeds indeed on the assumption that the Scriptures of the New Testament contain a Revelation sufficiently attested by miracle. Apart from the question whether the evidence for this attestation is complete or not, there are some good observa-tions on the subject of miracle. The established laws of nature, as they are called, are in fact the mode in which God acts in conformity to His own Will. His energy is ever present and operative in the universe; so that a miracle or suspension of the laws of nature is only God ceasing to act in one way and acting in another (p. 108). There-fore—

"It will be admitted that a miracle is not more a divine act, nor more an exertion of divine power, than the ordinary laws of Providence are divine acts and exertions of divine power. No mistake is more common than to represent that a miracle is an *extraordinary* (*i.e.*, extra great) exertion of a divine power. This error leads to an entire misapprehension of the true end and purpose of a miracle. The performance of a miracle is not intended to display power, but to afford proof of a special intervention of God."

The miracle is an attestation to the reality of the commission of a messenger from God. Mr. Row is of course perfectly justified, for the purpose of a special inquiry, in disentangling himself from an examination into the evidence whether this miraculous attestation has really been given. And his conclusions as to the phenomena actually presented by the New Testament writings, on the supposition of this miraculous attestation, are in many respects the more valuable. Not only because a miraculous attestation is taken for granted, but because the highest possible form of inspiration of which humanity is capable is in-volved in the 'Incarnation,' which every orthodox person would acknow-ledge, it follows that the words and actions of Jesus are the results of the highest possible inspiration. The only object of any inspiration of those who wrote down those words and actions would be to insure an adequate correctness in the report. And whether the writers of the gospels were themselves eye and ear-witnesses, or derived their infor-mation from pre-existing written material, or from oral tradition, the records could only present the results of that highest form of inspira-tion which had manifested itself in the person of Jesus Christ. Any defects attaching to those who were the channels of transmission would be supplemented, it is said, by the prophetic gift bringing all

deduced from the facts of the New Testament." By the Rev. C. A. Row, M.A., of Pembroke College, Oxford, and late Head Master of the Royal Grammar School, Mansfield. London: Longman and Co. 1864.

things necessary to the remembrance of the ultimate compilers according to the Lord's promise. The very remarkable phenomena which the gospels present are exceedingly well described by Mr. Row. On any hypothesis of the origin of the gospels, or of the order in which the Synoptics were written, or however the differences and agreements they present may be attempted to be accounted for, the theory of verbal inspiration is equally excluded. And so it is in a remarkable manner by the fact of the still more striking dissimilarity between the Synoptics generally and the fourth gospel. The author of this last must have conceived it his office to supply an element of divine truth in which the preceding narratives had been deficient. But could he have dared to undertake this, if those other authors had been thought by him to have written under the pure dictation of the Spirit? On this subject one of the facts to which Mr. Row draws especial attention is the greater concurrence of the Synoptics when they narrate the Lord's words than when they report his actions. This is the reverse, he says, of what usually takes place. Witnesses generally agree rather in the report of what they see than of what they hear. And he attributes this peculiar unison to the fulfilment of the divine promise that the Spirit should bring all things to the remembrance of the Apostles, whatsoever their Master had said unto them. We would venture to suggest that the knot may be untied in a natural manner; that the actions were in many cases imagined in order to give occasion for the words. Mr. Row would seem to go, in a certain sense, as far as this, that there is more truth in the words than in the actions. Now this would be accounted for if we suppose that when the real occasions on which the words were used had been forgotten, others were imagined for them, or that the real occasions were embellished with miraculous additions in order to exalt the character of the Master according to the conceptions of the second or third succession of his followers. The book is very full of matter, and there are several other points on which we should have liked to say something—but limits forbid. It is, however, evident from such a work as this, that the two points on which theological discussion will now proximately turn, which are indeed intimately connected, are, the question of miracle and that of the composition of the gospels.

With respect to the order of composition of the gospels, Mr. Kenrick is in accordance with a great consent of modern criticism in giving the priority to Mark over Matthew or Luke.[5] It would be too much, perhaps, to affirm this of Mark as we have it; but that the basis of Mark is anterior to the other two Gospels, or more strictly, stands on an even line with the λόγια, whatever they were, which formed the original of Matthew, does not admit of much dispute. And without doubt there are elements in the Gospels which it is impossible to harmonize both as to the words and actions of the Lord, and also as to the aspect in which his character is presented. All three Essays comprised in this volume show the ripe scholar and careful critic.

<hr>

[5] "Biblical Essays." By the Rev. John Kenrick, M.A., F.S.A. 1. The Gospel of Mark the Protevangelium. 2. The true nature of the Gift of Tongues. 3. St. Paul's designation of the Athenians. London: Longman and Co. 1864.

The Bishop of St. David's, as appears from his recent Charge, is shrewd enough to perceive that the question of Miracle is that which lies at the root of the debate raised by the Essayists.[6] He sees evidence of it not only in the late Professor Powell's Essay, but in Dr. Williams's, and especially in Mr. Wilson's. But he seems to confound a denial of Miracle, or more strictly speaking, a denial of the sufficient proof of Miracle, with a denial of the supernatural, or in fact, with Atheism. For he thinks Professor Powell's language would as aptly express the fundamental doctrine of Spinoza as that of any theist, and that "the argument employed to prove the impossibility of miraculous interposition moves wholly within the circle of a purely materialistic philosophy."—p. 26. Dr. Thirlwall, it is believed, was one of the very first with whom the Originator of the scheme of the Episcopal Manifesto conferred on that subject; and it is not too much to suppose, from the respect which his brethren entertain for his opinion, that if he had declined to co-operate in that design, it would have fallen through. In the present Charge his lordship takes some pains to justify that proceeding; but chiefly in reply to the objection that, before the Essayists were condemned by the bishops, they ought to have been refuted. He urges that they could not have been expected to acknowledge that they *were refuted;* but as the first question really was, under the circumstances of the persons, whether the doctrine of the Essayists was "in harmony with the teaching of the Church," he thinks the bishops might properly declare that in their opinion the contents of the book were repugnant to the doctrine of the Church. *Incidit in Scyllam,* &c. For the bishops personally are not competent to declare officially what is, and what is not, consentaneous to the doctrine of the Church. Their opinion was only that of highly-placed and influential individuals, the expression of which might be seriously damaging to the authors they censured in the event of legal proceedings, and in the like event seriously entangling to some of themselves, who might in the end have to act in a strictly judicial character in a matter whereon they had already committed themselves by an extra-judicial opinion. And, as the event has shown, they must either damage the weight of their judicial opinion if it be in accordance with sentiments expressed out of Court, or damage their own character for consistency, or for understanding the doctrines of their Church, if they acquit in detail what they have condemned in the lump. It may be true, as Bishop Thirlwall says, that the secret history of the volume of "Essays and Reviews" may for some time be known only to a few; still more, we apprehend, may that be said of the secret history of the Manifesto. And Dr. Thirlwall's justification of the Manifesto is unsatisfactory precisely for want of a certain portion of this secret history. Whatever the intentions of some, it may have been the understanding of others, that the issuing the Manifesto would both stop

---

* "A Charge delivered to the Clergy of the Diocese of St. David's." By Connop Thirlwall, D.D., Bishop of St. David's, at his eighth Visitation, October, 1863. Published at the request of the Clergy. Second Edition. London: Rivingtons. 1864.

all agitation for new enactments, and preclude the necessity for legal prosecutions. Apart, however, from these considerations, the Manifesto was substantially justified, the Bishop argues, as directed against doctrines of the Essayists—"not on nice and doubtful questions," but "on such as lie at the root of all revealed religion." It was not indicated in that document itself whereabouts in the volume the objectionable doctrines were to be found. From the Charge of the Bishop, we now learn that they are principally to be met with in Mr. Powell's, Dr. Williams's, and Mr. Wilson's Essays, and that they principally concern the miraculous character of the Christian Revelation; a denial of which, in Dr. Thirlwall's sense, he appears to consider as equivalent to a denial of any supernatural agency at all.—pp. 48-50. There was an observation of Dr. Thirlwall's, in a previous Charge, (which we refer to by memory), to the effect that the recognising the human element in Scripture, or the saying that "the Bible is the voice of the congregation," need not be understood as questioning the divine origin of the Revelation, *but only the mode of its transmission.* Now if this may be said rightly with respect to Inspiration, it is difficult to see why the same may not be said of supernatural agency generally.

We never could understand why, if the authors of the other Essays were to be answerable for Professor Powell's Essay, he should not have the benefit of theirs: why they should be held responsible for his supposed materialism, rather than he have the credit of their obvious theism. But so it has been; and Mr. Kennard[7] shows the true courage of a Christian gentleman in vindicating the Professor's memory from the imputations thrown upon it in the Charge above mentioned. At the same time he claims for the clergy of the Church of England generally, the right to treat the whole question of supernatural agency as an open one. It is a question as to mode of operation in reference to an acknowledged Divine Origin or Source; it is a question as to more or less knowledge on the part of man.

"The solution which has obtained most general acceptance with philosophic divines, is perhaps some modification of that proposed by Bishop Butler, namely—that the distinction popularly drawn between the natural and supernatural, exists only relatively to our partial and most imperfect insight into the nature and extent of that 'wonderful order' established from everlasting by Him who, in the magnificent language of the prophet, 'inhabiteth eternity.' Our notions of what is natural, will be enlarged in proportion to our greater knowledge of the works of God, and the dispensations of His providence."—p. 10.

Mr. Wratislaw is a very straightforward critic, who does not consider the duty of the illustrator of the New Testament writings to be adequately performed by repeating a mass of opinions and leaving difficulties just as they were before.[8] Although himself apparently

---

[7] "The late Professor Powell and Dr. Thirlwall on the Supernatural." A Letter to the Right Reverend the Lord Bishop of St. David's. By the Rev. R. B. Kennard, M.A. Oxon., Rector of Marnhull, Dorset. London: Hardwicke. 1864.

[8] "Notes and Dissertations, principally on Difficulties in the Scriptures of the New Covenant." By A. H. Wratislaw, M.A., Head Master of King Edward the Sixth's Grammar School, Bury St. Edmunds, formerly Fellow and Tutor of Christ's College, Cambridge. London: Bell and Daldy. 1864.

thoroughly orthodox, he is not very complimentary to some orthodox contemporaries. Dr. Wordsworth, he thinks, has "employed himself rather in concealing than in coping with difficulties ;" he cannot call to mind "any instance in which Bishop Ellicott has solved a difficulty which had not previously been solved by others ;" and though Dean Alford has accomplished most in the critical field, he finds in him "many errors and inaccuracies." In one of the best dissertations, for instance, in the volume on Rom. viii. 18, *sqq.*, he is not undeservedly severe on Dr. Alford for his statement, that κτίσις "*never* is used of mankind alone," in the face of Mark xvi. 15. There is a very good dissertation included in this volume upon the *Te Deum*, which, when some interpolations are rejected, would correspond substantially with the amœbæan hymn, recited, according to Pliny, by the primitive Christians in honour of Christ (*carmen dicere secum invicem Christo quasi Deo*).

Religious but thinking persons in England who have become unsettled in many of the dogmas in which they were brought up, yet who are anxious for some definite and positive Christianity in which they may rest, will do well to study M. Réville's "Manual of Religious Instruction."[9] A greater service than the translation of this book could not be rendered to such persons at the present moment. The work is divided into three parts. The first embraces a conspectus of the religious history of man from the earliest ages down to modern times ; the second gives in a few pages the actual teachings of Jesus ; the third, under the title of "Religious Doctrine," has for its object to seek after religious truth. The inquiry here starts from the historical fact that there are and have been in the world many religious systems of unequal value, though proportionate to the spiritual development of those among whom they have arisen. The religious experience of the human race is a necessary element in this investigation, and especially the teachings of the Bible, and especially again, among these, the teachings of Jesus Christ. Religious doctrine concerns God and man, and the moral relation between them. Christianity is the pure religion communicated to man by Jesus Christ. Hence an inquiry into his person and character, the nature of the Church or Society which he has founded, and the influence which he has exercised and continues to exercise upon the human race. We make an extract from the closing chapter concerning "life eternal :"—

"It is an error to consider eternal punishment as an integral part of the evangelical doctrine. The question, in the sense in which we of these days regard it, does not appear to have been present to the mind of the authors of the New Testament. We must not allow ourselves to be misled by the mere sameness of sounds. The adjective which our versions render *eternal* had not in their tongue the definite meaning which it has in our own. It corresponds rather to our words *future, of the other world, of the world to come*. The Jews divided history into two parts ; separated the one from the other by the coming of the Messiah. . . . . And everything which was to take place in the future

9 "A Manual of Religious Instruction." By Albert Réville, D.D., Pastor at Rotterdam, and author of "Critical Studies on the Gospel according to St. Matthew," a work crowned by the Hague Society for the Defence of the Christian Religion. London : Simpkin, Marshall, and Co. 1864.

or Messianic age was designated by that adjective (*aionios*), which doubtless may signify *eternal*, since the Messianic age or world is never to come to an end [but compare 1 Cor. xv. 24, *sq.*], but which may also be applied to temporary things, provided they appertain to that future period, *e.g.*, judgment, Heb. vi. 2. [It is not the idea of time, whether endless or otherwise, that the word *aionios* conveys, so much as the idea of quality, so that *aionios* and Messianic are nearly synonymous; the chief difference is, that Messianic refers to Christ's person, and *aionios* to his spirit, influence, and sway.] Mark ix. 44 indicates the certainty and not the eternity of the suffering. Matth. xii. 32 teaches the certainty of an inevitable punishment, but says nothing of its duration."

The passages in brackets belong throughout to the Translator. We cordially recommend this Manual for its truly religious spirit, clearness, good sense, and practical utility.

The late Dr. Bernard was well known for many years as the authorized teacher of Hebrew in the University of Cambridge, and as the author, in conjunction with his former pupil, the Rev. P. H. Mason, of the only practical grammar enabling the student to learn Hebrew as he would learn any other language.[10] He was of Jewish descent, born at Uman, a small town in Southern Russia (then Poland), in 1785. His father was a banker in wealthy circumstances. In 1825 Hermann came to England, apparently for the purpose of learning the language, but in consequence of his family having met with pecuniary reverses, he never returned to the continent. In 1830 he established himself at Cambridge, where he was soon appointed Hebrew teacher in the University. He retained this office till the time of his death, which took place suddenly, from heart disease, 15th November, 1857. He had become totally blind from cataract since 1850, but his thorough familiarity with the language enabled him to retain his pupils, with some assistance from his friend, Mr. Mason, in correcting their written exercises. The bulk of the present volume, which runs to more than 500 pages, is occupied with a thorough grammatical analysis of the Book of Job, which is followed by a new translation. In the preliminary matter is given, both in Hebrew and English, the Preface of Ben Zev, presenting a good example of the better style of Rabbinical criticism. The learned Rabbi, for instance, discusses the question—"Whether the name of Job was [that of] a really existing man or not?" Various opinions, it is said, have prevailed among the learned men of old, whether Job was a real man, whether the events related actually took place, or whether the book was the creation of a writer who expressed in an allegory or parable the lesson he intended to convey. The objections to the historical character of the book are six. 1. It is unlikely that in real life everything should tally with the sacred numbers—*seven* sons, *seven* thousand sheep, *three* daughters, *three* thousand camels, &c. 2. It is very unlikely that in all the

---

[10] " ‏ספר איוב‏ The Book of Job, as expounded to his Cambridge Pupils." By the late Hermann Hedwig Bernard, Ph. D., M.A., Author of " Creed and Ethics of the Jews," &c. &c. Edited, with a Translation and additional Notes, by Frank Chance, B.A., M. B., late Tyrwhitt's Hebrew Scholar, Fell. Roy. Coll. Phys., &c., &c. Vol. I. (containing the whole of the original work). London: Hamilton, Adams, and Co. 1864.

catastrophes which befell Job's family, there should always be left one man and no more to bring the tidings. 3. How could the writer learn what passed in heaven respecting the sons of men and what Satan answered Jehovah, "except a ladder was set up on earth, and the top of it reached to heaven, and the writer was ascending and descending on it?" 4. How can it be supposed the controversy should be carried on between Job and his friends in lofty poetic language? 5. It would be strange that they should be all bards, all elegant speakers, and all adopt one style. 6. How can the narrator either have been present throughout to set down with pen and ink exactly what was said, or how could his memory have enabled him afterwards to record it? On the other hand—1. The particulars mentioned by the writer must be real, because as they are not essential to the supposed allegory, there would otherwise have been no reason for the mention of them. 2. If Job never lived, how comes Ezekiel to introduce him with Noah and Daniel? (ch. xiv). The learned Rabbi concluded that it was right to take a middle course between the extremes, and to suppose that there had lived a man named Job, celebrated for his dignity and possessions, and remarkable for his righteousness, who was tried with severe misfortune: "this man the writer selected for his subject; and, taking up some of the real facts, he fashioned him with the graving-tool of poetry, and made of him an image according to the likeness and form of the man whom he wished to give life to in his allegory" (p. lv.). The Rabbi mentions also the various opinions concerning the date of the book, some placing it as late as the reign of Ahasuerus; he himself thinks it as ancient as the time of Moses—that it is, in fact, a translation from the Arabic as to the greater part, but that Moses himself wrote the beginning and end of the book; for he observes in those portions the name of the Divine Essence is employed (Jehovah), with which Moses was acquainted, but in the central poem the names of *El, Eloah, Shaddai*—except, indeed, as Mr. Chance notices, in xii. 9— unless perhaps Ben Zev had before him a copy with another reading. Mr. Chance, whose opinions are conservative, and who remarks, sometimes not without effect, upon the hastiness of other critics, guards himself against being supposed to participate even in the moderate latitudinarianism of the learned Ben Zev.

The Essay of Dr. Ginsburg on the Essenes gives in a short compass a complete account of that remarkable sect or modification of Judaism: with the more important ancient authorities, as Philo and Josephus especially, *in extenso:* to which is added a sketch of the modern literature of the subject continued to the latest date.[11] Dr. Ginsburg is sensible and cautious, and while pointing out the Essene element in primitive Christianity, he does not press too far the inferences from a comparison of the maxims of the Essenes with the precepts of Jesus Christ.

The title of Mr. Gurney's pamphlet sufficiently indicates its nature.[12]

---

[11] "The Essenes: their History and Doctrines. An Essay, reprinted from the Transactions of the Literary and Philosophical Society of Liverpool." By Christian D. Ginsburg, LL.D. London: Longman and Co. 1864.

[12] "The Faith against Free Thinkers; or, Modern Rationalism, as exhibited in

It consists principally of papers which originally appeared in the *John Bull* newspaper, and if any of our readers met with them there, they will not be desirous of perusing them again.

Mr. Girdlestone has long been a consistent advocate of liturgical revision as to those matters in which the Prayer Book is distasteful to Evangelical Churchmen.[13] He observes in his present pamphlet that at the successive revisions which the Formularies have hitherto undergone, the alterations made have uniformly been reactionary and in the direction of *quasi* Roman opinions and practices. Strong as the case is which Mr. Girdlestone makes out, we very much doubt whether he and his friends would be able to carry through Convocation as well as Parliament the most moderate reform. But we think it possible that there might be passed through Parliament a permissive or relieving Act confined to a few particulars, and those of omission only. As, for instance, that no clergyman shall be subject to any penalties; 1. For omitting to read the Creed of Athanasius; 2. For substituting a lesson from the Bible for one from the Apocrypha. Mr. Girdlestone would perhaps not agree with us in adding, or of one Biblical lesson for another; but to our minds there are chapters from the Bible appointed to be read in churches quite as unfit for that purpose as *Bel and the Dragon*, or *Susannah and the Elders*; 3. For the omission of the word "regenerate" in the Baptismal Service. We agree with Mr. Girdlestone that it would not answer to leave the omission of words in the Burial Service to the discretion of the minister: that would therefore be a matter for revision properly so called, and could not be embraced in such a short relieving Act as we recommend for a practical beginning. The relaxation also of the declaration of "assent and consent to all and everything," &c. of the Act of Uniformity must wait for a recommendation from the Royal Commission.

The present volume of the late Rev. F. W. Robertson's Sermons completes the series:[14] the discourses contained in it are somewhat more fragmentary than those which have preceded, but will be read with the same interest. It is proposed shortly to publish a volume consisting of skeletons or notes, which will prove no doubt a like aid to some of the present generation of preachers to that which was supplied to the evangelical clergy many years ago by Simeon's skeletons.

The editor of the collected works of the celebrated Edward Irving proposes to select from his mass of material those discourses and treatises which are likely to prove of permanent interest.[15] About one-half of

the writings of Mr. Buckle, Bishop Colenso, M. Renan, and the Essayists." By the Rev. Archer Gurney, author of "Restoration," &c. &c. London: Church Press Company. 1864.

[13] "An Appeal to Evangelical Churchmen in behalf of Liturgical Revision." By Charles Girdlestone, Rector of Kingswinford, Staffordshire, and sometime Fellow of Balliol College, Oxford. London: W. Hunt. 1864.

[14] "Sermons preached at Trinity Chapel, Brighton." By the late F. W. Robertson, M.A., the Incumbent. Fourth Series. London: Smith, Elder, and Co. 1863.

[15] "The Collected Writings of Edward Irving." In Five Volumes. Edited by his nephew, the Rev. G. Carlyle, M.A. Vol. I. London: Alexander Strahan and Co. 1864.

the collection has never hitherto been published. Glancing through a thick volume of more than six hundred pages, we find the discourses now printed to exhibit the great oratorical power pointed with quaintness for which the preacher was famous; there are included also a view of the history of the Church of Scotland previous to the Reformation, together with Irving's Notes on the Standards of the Church of Scotland, showing much independence of thought.

On the Colenso controversy, the feeblest of all the books we have to mention is that of Mr. Kingsley.[16] It may be true, that in a series of sermons to a parochial congregation the author might not be expected to enter very deeply into the questions at issue. But he should not have so insulted any number of English people assembled to hear him give them proofs of the Mosaic authorship of the Pentateuch as to "advise them to believe" that Moses wrote it. Mr. Kingsley seeks in vain to shelter himself under the example of Dr. Stanley. It is true the Dean of Westminster, by the consummate grace of his style and vigour of his descriptions, invites his readers to pay little attention to questions which he thinks would only puzzle them unprofitably; he draws them off from critical inquiries of which he sees no solution; he leads them to trace a providential order in human events, to observe historical analogies (at times, it may be, somewhat far-fetched and fanciful), to learn lessons from narratives wherein the matter-of-fact history cannot be distinguished from its embellishments. He might even say, whether Moses was the author of the Pentateuch, or to what extent, is not a matter of much moment; but, *I advise you to believe* Moses wrote the Pentateuch, we think he never would. Mr. Kingsley has to a great extent mistaken his new master.

Mr. Arnold writes from the point of view of the German reaction, and he thinks Colenso is doomed t) defeat, because Strauss, repulsed in his attack upon the Gospels by the Court-preacher, Hoffmann, "married an actress." His present volume, of less than two hundred pages, consists of three chapters.[17] The first treats of the present crisis and its gravity, acknowledging that the fathers of Protestantism, and it might be said its sons too, "have jeopardized a good cause by a bad theory, which cannot be supported," in their "anxiety to oppose [Roman] infallibility with [Scriptural] infallibility." The second chapter is chiefly occupied with an examination of the Jehovistic and Elohistic theory, which is rejected, yet with the admission, that even Kurtz and Delitzsch recognise a certain double current of authorship, and ultimately "repelling as presumptuous" the inquiry, whether the author of the Pentateuch as we have it, made use of pre-existent material? The third chapter undertakes to show that "the Pentateuch professes to have been written by Moses," and endeavours to explain away the signs of a later authorship; and it is contended, in spite of the

---

[16] "The Gospel of the Pentateuch: A Set of Parish Sermons." By the Rev. Charles Kingsley, F.L.S., F.G.S., Rector of Eversley. With a Preface. Second Edition. London: Macmillan. 1864.

[17] "English Biblical Criticism and the Pentateuch, from a German point of view." By John Mühleisen Arnold, B.D., Hon. Sec. to the Moslem Mission Society. Vol. I. London: Longmans. 1864.

remarkable silence of the subsequent literature, that *the Thorah* in its completeness is recognised throughout the subsequent history.

The "Replies" of Mr. F. Parker[18] turn chiefly upon the form which Bishop Colenso has given to his objections to the historical character of the Pentateuch; that is, in that he has confined himself to the internal inconsistencies of the narrative, without impugning the miraculous portion of it as such. Hence Mr. Parker's solution, that the miracles account for things which might otherwise have been impossibilities or have shown inconsistency. And that miracles were wrought is proved by the institutions of the passover and the Sabbath, which the Pentateuch itself relates, and which were always observed subsequently to their institution.

Mr. Rogers's "Investigation," is the pleasantest written of these answers, but it is very far from being a "full" one.[19] The solution of the chief difficulties is however attained by Mr. Rogers only by appeal to miracle, even when the narrative itself says nothing about it. And it is remarkable, that while it was the favourite resource some time since to suppose a corruption in the numbers of the Israelites, they are found, as Bishop Colenso states, so to run through and through the history that they cannot be torn out. Now, it is obviously no sufficient answer to an objection to the credibility of a narrative to say— it is true that it would be impossible to meet the material necessities of such numbers as are described unless by a continued succession of miracles, and therefore such miracles must have taken place. In other words, where the books mention miracles we appeal to the books as evidence of the miracles; where they do not mention them we assume them, because the history will not stand without them. Everything is tending to re-open the inquiry into the *evidence* for the scriptural miracles.

Belonging to the Renan controversy we have to notice the translation of the "Life of Jesus," published by Messrs. Trübner,[20] which will give the English reader some notion of the extreme beauty of the original, and enable him to understand the various critiques which have appeared upon that important work.

M. de Pressensé criticizes the book from the standing-point of an orthodoxy which many consider very far from orthodox, of a Fall of Man and the Divinity of Jesus in some peculiar sense of his own.[21] His

---

[18] "Replies to the First and Second Parts of the Right Reverend the Bishop of Natal's 'Pentateuch and Book of Joshua critically examined.'" By Franke Parker, M.A., Trinity College, Cambridge, and Rector of Luffingcots, [Devon. London: Bell and Daldy. 1863.

[19] "A Full Investigation of the Difficulties suggested by Dr. Colenso." By Benjamin Bickley Rogers, M.A., of Lincoln's Inn, Barrister-at-Law, and some time Fellow of Wadham College, Oxford. Oxford and London: J. H. and J. Parker. 1863.

[20] "The Life of Jesus." By Ernest Renan, Member of the Institute of France. London: Trübner and Co.

[21] "The Critical School and Jesus Christ: a Reply to M. Renan's 'Life of Jesus.'" By Edmond de Pressensé, Pastor of the French Evangelical Church, and D.D. of the University of Breslau. Author of the "History of the Three First Centuries of the Christian Church." Translated by L. Corkran. London: Elliot Stock. 1864.

recklessness in risking entire Christianity on an alternative may be judged of by the following passage :—

"If he [Jesus] be not the Man-God, his teaching, with the exception of a few ingenious parables and some maxims which were already known, but into which he infused a purer spirit, is nothing but a tissue of tiresome repetitions. If he be not the Way, the Truth, and the Life, the true Vine from which the branches draw the sap, if he be but an ordinary teacher, then there exists no book more absurd and empty than the Gospel."—p. 78.

The pamphlet of M. Réville[22] is reprinted from the "Revue Germanique et Française," and may be taken as expressing the judgment of the liberal Protestant party, of which M. Réville himself, M. Colani, editor of the "Nouvelle Revue de Théologie," and M. Athanase Coquerel fils, lately deprived of his coadjutorship by the intolerance of the Presbyteral Council of Paris, are principal ornaments. While exposing the narrowness of Father Larroque, and the inconsistency of M. de Pressensé, and giving M. Renan full credit for the sincerity of his aim, for the religiousness of his purpose, and the beauty of his construction, he finds much to remark on as unsound in philosophy and criticism, and shocking to the religious instinct. This pamphlet is especially worth reading by those who feel that they cannot accept M. Renan's estimate of the character of Jesus Christ as implied in such words as these: "Jésus dut donc choisir entre ces deux partis, ou renoncer à sa mission, ou devenir thaumaturge."

The sixth volume of Miss Cobbe's edition of "Theodore Parker's Works"[23] contains his discourses on Slavery and on the dangers to the American people from the development of the money-getting spirit ; already, he said, one-eightieth of the people was ruling the rest. The seventh volume comprises discourses on Social Science. Parker did not see any impiety in science, least of all in the science of human nature. Unless the human nature is understood it is impossible to act upon it for its benefit, and that was Parker's great work as a religious teacher. Parker was not a popular man, but he did not expect it, and he has a better reward.

---

[22] "La Vie de Jésus de M. Renan devant les Orthodoxes et devant la Critique." Par M. Albert Réville. London : D. Nutt.

[23] "The Collected Works of Theodore Parker, Minister of the Twenty-eighth Congregational Society at Boston, U.S., containing his Theological, Polemical, and Critical Writings, Sermons, Speeches, and Addresses, and Literary Miscellanies." Edited by Frances Power Cobbe. Vol. VI. Discourses on Slavery. Vol. VII. Discourses of Social Science. London : Trübner and Co. 1864.

POLITICS, SOCIOLOGY, VOYAGES AND TRAVELS.

MR. ROWLAND has presented the public with an enquiry into the foundation of morals,[1] which he supposes himself to have discovered by an induction from the facts of nature, and to have established by their laws; but his conception both of induction and of laws of nature are of the loosest possible description. The latter stand in his mind for much more than formulas of our existing knowledge of nature, and anything which he can deduce from given postulates, he supposes himself to have arrived at by way of induction, as may be seen from the following extract:—

"It seems a reasonable induction from a comparison of man with brutes, that when man was introduced into the world, there was a break in the plan by which life on earth had been previously regulated. The original inhabitants were continued in the state in which from their origin they existed; ruled by instinct but with some intelligence sufficient for their condition, and for the limited intercourse they had with their kind; and free as they ever had been from responsibility to moral law. The new animal was of the same anatomical structure, and physiological organization, but a new system of life was designed for him, by which, through the force of the appetites, under the control of the moral law, and, with the aid of reason, he was destined to rise to a state of social, intellectual, and moral existence, unknown on the earth before. We may feel a rational confidence that the new animal was endowed with these faculties and qualities by the act of his Creator; for brutes could not transmit faculties and qualities which they do not possess, and which do not belong to the race. We may also feel confident that reason and the new system of man's existence on the earth were cotemporary and part of the same design; for when reason was given employment must have been found for it; and the new system of existence could not have been carried on by a creature not possessed of reason."

The whole of the argument suggested by this passage rests upon implied assumptions of the nature of man and the designs of God, which beg the entire question; indeed, this must ever be the case with every theorist who endeavours to hold an intermediate position between the advocates of an innate and immutable morality, and those who content themselves with maintaining that the moral sentiments of mankind are but the result of their experience, and, like everything else human, susceptible of indefinite improvement.

It will be sufficient to enumerate the laws of nature, on which the author supposes the whole fabric of morality to rest. These are—

"The moral law of nature for the protection of labour and the institution of property. The moral law of nature for the institution of marriage, and for the raising and protection of families. And the moral laws of nature for the protection of human life, and for the production of truth."

The supposition that any general regulative laws are implanted by nature in the mind of man is so manifestly contradicted both by his past history and present condition, that we are reduced to a condition

---

[1] "Laws of Nature the Foundation of Morals." By D. Rowland, author of "A Manual of the English Constitution." London: J. Murray. 1863.

of surprise and wonder, when we find the present aspirations of mankind treated as laws implanted from the beginning in the mind of every member of the race. At this rate, a new and fresh theory would be required by every generation; and fresh laws of nature would be required to account for every advance in general morals, and to explain every conquest of mutual forbearance. The enumeration itself of these laws of nature which the author supposes to underlie all moral obligation, is of itself enough to show how inadequate they are to the purpose to which he applies them, if in any proper sense they can be called laws at all. The whole argument of his book is beside the only question which is worth discussion, which is not what is the nature and origin of our moral sentiments, but by what standard shall they be tried? If the nature and purposes of the Deity are introduced into the discussion, the controverted points are only removed one step farther, and gain no new light by the increased distance. Practical morality was summarized more than 1800 years ago in a very short formula, and the only question which has ever been debated is an exclusively speculative one, which has very little direct bearing on man's conduct, but which cannot be overestimated in its importance, when the influence exercised by the answer given to it on the formation of the detailed rules which shall regulate that conduct is taken into consideration.

The interest aroused in the present day by these speculations may be in some degree measured by the appearance of such books as Mr. Rowland's, which may be looked upon as one of the results of the ferment produced by the unquestionable progress of the Utilitarian theory. Another evidence of a like kind will be found in a book just published by Messrs. Longman,[2] in which Mr. Mill's recent treatise on Utilitarianism is subjected to a lengthy criticism, and, in the author's opinion, triumphantly refuted. The method he adopts is to give a new definition of utility, in which he restricts its meaning to material things. "What," says he, "is utility?" and answers, "Every created thing is *a* utility." This occurs so early as page 9, and is a warning to every intelligent reader that he need not trouble himself with the pages that follow it. The Utilitarian theory of morals is not concerned with utilities, but with utility as a standard of conduct. Utilities may, indeed, in this sense, be asserted to result only in convenience and pleasure, and to have no relation to happiness; but, in this sense, the word has never been used except in the technical meaning sometimes given to it in the writings of political economists. As might be supposed, this confusion between utility and utilities leads the author into the most contradictory assertions; at page 11, he says:—"Man never gave anything useful to man. Man can give nothing useful in the true sense of utility;" and at page 29, "in the absence of human efforts there is no utility." It is somewhat surprising that any one who has studied Mr. Mill's treatise can suppose he answers it by such a misrepresentation of its terms. The only

---

[2] "Utilitarianism Explained and Exemplified in Moral and Political Government." London: Longman and Co., 1864.

utility moralists are concerned with is that which is recognisable in certain lines of conduct ; they have nothing whatever to do with the material conditions of that conduct, however necessary they may be, except in so far as it is possible to modify them to the advantage of the utility so recognised. Defining utility as he does, it may easily be imagined what a strange confusion the author introduces into his subject when he has to discuss the differences in the degree and quality of happiness resulting from certain actions. It is, of course, impossible when utility is confined to external things to determine whether porter or port wine be the more desirable drink, except we agree as Mr. Mill does, to be guided by those who are acquainted with both. No amount of ingenious speculation on the quality of the gratification enjoyed by a thirsty cabman will persuade the world at large that the beverage he is accustomed to ought to be preferred to wine. The general judgment of the world must be accepted as proof of the superiority of one taste over another, as, in like manner, it is the sole ground on which one action is pronounced better than another, and the only guide to that judgment, apart from revelation, which has nothing whatever to do with morals, as a science, is the amount of happiness resulting from those actions ; and this is the Utilitarian standard. The absurd outcry that this is a godless doctrine cannot be too severely reprobated. Everything on earth is subject to God's government or nothing is ; and a godly morality is nothing more than a morality deduced from the prevailing notions of the nature of God, which themselves are but the summary of all human knowledge, and a summary most candid when it confesses its limitations. This outcry is nothing less than an appeal to the populace to put down an investigation obnoxious to those who raise it, and it is of itself a confession of incapacity rightly to appreciate the nature of the question under discussion. Speaking of conscience the author says :—

"Thus we have revealed to us by express laws (in the Scriptures), and by those innate feelings, sentiments or emotions, the necessary and sufficient guides and helps for directing our action as to secure the attainment of our ultimate end and object in the greatest possible happiness, quite independent of any question of general utility. We are not committed to the guidance of our slow and fallible reason, but are endowed with feelings which warn us at every step," &c., &c.

This may be very good theology but cannot be allowed any place in a discussion on the scientific grounds of morality ; for it amounts to this, don't talk to me of morals disconnected from religion or strive to found in knowledge what you ought to accept on the firmer basis of faith. A scientific enquiry is not to be set aside by allusions to Moses and the Prophets. Such writers should restrict themselves to improving texts and edifying their hearers by new arguments in support of received moral doctrines; for it is evident that they will never go beyond them, and that the only road open to general progress is irrevocably shut to them. Into the various political speculations and passing questions of the day which the author tacks on to the main purpose of his book, we do not care to follow him, except to remark that the improvement of our criminal law is one of the greatest triumphs of the system he repudiates, and that the standard by which they have been reformed has either been one derived from " human argument," or that higher one to which he appeals was found sadly unequal to the task for many long and weary years.

Very few churchmen will thank Lord Robert Montagu for the plea which he sets up in favour of national churches in his " Four experiments of Church and State."[3] A national Church, as such, should have, in his opinion, no theological or dogmatic basis, but rest solely upon its character as an association for putting down evil *generally.* At this rate there is no difficulty in adhering to a Church which adequately responds to such a calling, but, unfortunately, the question is not to be turned in this facile fashion. There neither is, nor ever has been, any national Church contented with such a restricted sphere; much more than a moral purpose has been set forth by every Christian Church that ever existed; and however true his lordship's rambling account may be of the collateral results of those higher purposes which they have always had in view, the conflicts of centuries have not led churchmen in any way to drop pretensions which they fortify by appeals to a higher sanction than any the world can give. So long as those higher sanctions are believed in the conflict must continue, and the Church of England is as far from resigning the appeal to them as any of her rivals. The last defender of dogmatic belief must die with *finis theologiæ* on his lips before such restricted views of the functions of a national Church can become general; and however this may be the logical result of his lordship's lucubrations, we fancy he would be far from welcoming it. Every form of Church government which he repudiates as degenerating into some form of spiritual despotism, aspires by some shorter cut to the end which he sets up as its only legitimate aspiration. As long as there are differences in the world on dogmatic questions, the conflict of Churches must continue as their only vital expression.

Dr. Edward Reich, of Cassel, has brought together from travellers and historians a very full account of the marriage tie[4] in all times and countries. There is no human institution which, in itself, throws so great a light upon the degree of progress made by any nation or tribe; all the social ideas prevalent among them are reflected in their views of marriage. It is abundantly clear from this review of the different forms which it has put on, that the nature of the tie is absolutely dependent upon the character and direction of those ideas which govern and direct any particular community. Satisfying the most imperious of human passions on the one hand, and lying as it does at the very basis of human society, marriage cannot be expected to display those ideal forms which are dreamt of by the imagination until a greater harmony between the self-regarding and the social feelings is brought about by a general advance of knowledge that cannot reasonably be ex-

---

[3] " The Four Experiments in Church and State and the Conflict of Churches." By Lord Robert Montagu, M.P. London : Longman and Co. 1864.
[4] " Geschichte, Natur und Gesundheitslehre des Ehelichen Lebens." Von E. Reich. Cassel : Theodor Kay. 1864. London : D. Nutt.

pected for many generations. The desires of one generation are the conquest of following ones, and the means of conquest are a full insight into the past. In this respect, Dr. Reich's book is more valuable than in his criticism on the existing practices by which the State endeavours in his own country to regulate, in the interest of the existing community, the circumstances under which it will allow of an increase in the number of its citizens. There is a certain violence of tone in his denunciation of the police regulations, to which marriage is subjected in many of the German States, which is out of harmony with a scientific treatment of the subject; solid conviction is the only basis of progress in this matter. The sacramental character with which marriage was invested in the middle ages, like so many other institutions of that time, was substantially a natural reaction against the lawlessness and violence which could be rendered amenable to no restraint that was not supported by their superstitions. Under the shelter of theological sanctions, men found the opportunity of entering on full possession of their minds and bodies; less terrible ones would have been inefficient, and we are far from believing that their efficiency is exhausted, however great the shock their foundation has received. An indirect proof of this truth may be found in the ˙absence of any practical suggestions on the part of the most ardent satirists of our existing laws on the subject. Into its physiological and pathological details we do not care to follow the author, but this division of his book is as full and well studied as the first and larger historical division. The abundant and careful references to the sources from which the author has gathered his information will be found very valuable to any who wish to pursue the subject from any of the numerous points of view from which it may be taken up.

In two volumes which he calls Caxtoniana[5] Sir E. B. Lytton has collected a mass of those reflections on life, literature, and manners, which, when they occur in his novels, are submitted to as an infliction that must be borne for the sake of the animated action, epigrammatic dialogue, and interesting construction to which they serve as padding. Were it not for the popularity of Tupper we should be utterly at a loss to conceive what public the clever author could have in view in composing this mass of pompous common-place, of poor thoughts in sumptuous raiment, of trite reflections set forth with an air of the profoundest wisdom. It is, perhaps, impossible anywhere to show a more complete misunderstanding than the author displays of his own powers throughout these volumes; an artist in the most thorough sense of the term, in conception, and in talent, he will assume the attitude of a philosopher; quick perception and great facility of expression are set to do the work of patient study and sustained thought. The laborious neatness of verbal construction overwhelms the reader, and he longs with the Danish Queen for more matter and less art. The art, too, in these volumes, is but little more than an intellectual millinery. On every topic the author runs on

---

[5] "Caxtoniana: a Series of Essays on Life, Literature, and Manners." By Sir E. B. Lytton, Bart. London: W. Blackwood and Sons. 1863. 2 vols.

without any restraint, but that which is implied in an artificially balanced period. The frequent moral paradoxes of his novels are far more wholesome than the ethical attitudinizing of these essays for which their writer bespeaks a place beside his other works. Whatever place may be granted to them should be large enough to admit of the immediate neighbourhood of the Proverbial Philosophy.

Mr. Maguire's history of the temperance movement in Ireland, which is associated with the name of Father Mathew,[6] is in many respects the counterpart of the movement itself. The whole subject is handled entirely *ab extra*, and is treated in a tone of indiscriminating wonder and astonishment that partakes largely of the unreasoning enthusiasm by which its short-lived vitality was supported. No sure foundation can be laid for sobriety in a method which attempts to combat intemperance by an excitement greater than itself affords. The passionate allegiance which is given to a venerated name, even when aided by a superstitious reverence for such sacramental symbols as a card or medal, has no roots in itself. As soon as the influence of personal reverence is weakened by time or distance, when the temporary enthusiasm has subsided and old habits knock at the door of the swept and garnished chamber, the symbol exerts no more power than an African fetisch. The movement, the apostle, and their historian, are all thoroughly Irish, and a fire of straw is a fit emblem for all three. Mr. Maguire makes no attempt to account for Father Mathew's success; it is simply heaven-sent, and to be explained only by his vocation; it is not thus that any one can be satisfied who wishes to arrive at reasonable conclusions on what must be admitted to have been a remarkable phenomenon. Its causes must be sought more in the excitable character of the population among which it displayed itself than in the trifling circumstances which attended it. A collection, however large, of more or less amusing anecdotes connected with the subject does but little else than display the singular want of cool reflection with which the movement was animated and maintained. The indiscriminate manner in which the pledge was administered to hasty postulants, and often forced upon unwilling ones, the strange thoughtlessness which often imposed an oath against drinking upon men while yet intoxicated, could not be expected to have any lasting consequences. Sobriety that is not born of self-command is but another kind of slavery; it may be to a master less degrading in a physical sense, but has no firm moral root from which a stable progress or even sure release can be expected. This movement has of late met with its exact parallel in the religious revivals in Ireland, from which no sane man looks for more permanent results. These efforts to draw from excited feeling that which only knowledge and conviction can continuously supply must inevitably share the fate of the seed which fell by the wayside, and be trampled underfoot by the next passing feeling which shall prove as strong as the memory of that which is relied upon. The purity of character and unquestionable self-devotion of the Rev. Theobald

* "Father Mathew: a Biography." By J. F. Maguire, M.P., author of "Rome: its Rulers, and its Institutions." London: Longman and Co. 1863.

Mathew undoubtedly deserved a permanent record, and it may be allowed that a very full insight into his virtues and weaknesses is to be arrived at by the perusal of Mr. Maguire's pages; but the reader has to extract it from a chorus of indiscriminate laudations, and to wade through a mass of sentimental stories given with an exhausting detail that will sorely try the patience of most. A much shorter and simpler account would have far better answered the purpose of reviving the recollection of an amiable and enthusiastic, but not very intelligent nor strong-minded man.

Dr. F. Spiegel has brought together, from various learned periodicals to which he had contributed them, a series of papers on the Iranian peoples between the Indus and Tigris.[7] They form an important addition to our knowledge of this branch of the human race, both in an antiquarian and ethnographical point of view. He enters on a comparison between their sacred writings and those of the ancient Indians, as well as those of the Semitic races. The Zendavesta is placed by him between the Vedas and Genesis; and the modifications which its doctrines have undergone are displayed in a full criticism of the philosophical system of the Parsees, who, in their new homes in Southern India, still struggle to maintain the religion and beliefs of their Persian forefathers. This volume must be welcomed by all who are engaged in those Etymological studies on which its arguments are chiefly based.

Under the title of the Empire in India,[8] Major Bell has published a series of letters from Madras and other places, in which he subjects Lord Dalhousie's policy of annexation to the severest criticism. Though this policy has in many of its features been given up, the same cannot be said of the territorial acquisitions in which it resulted. In reviewing the Carnatic, Sattara, Nagpore, and Jhansi cases, Major Bell, taking his stand upon the letter of treaties concluded with the reigning families, and interpreting their terms in the sense they would convey to Indian conceptions, finds no difficulty in establishing a charge of unjust spoliation against the Supreme Government. It is, however, by no means absolutely certain that the terms of the treaties in question can only be so construed. Where the choice has to be made between two adverse interpretations, the only guide is to be found in principles of general utility; and although Major Bell would himself not shrink from bringing his conclusions to this test, and in the latter part of his volume endeavours to establish them on this very ground, it is to be regretted that, in the separate treatment of the cases just alluded to, he restricts the question to the mere verbal interpretation of treaties; and by his mode of treatment on this narrow ground appears to beg the question. Every one of these cases turns upon the terms of contracts made with a native prince, his heirs, and successors. The whole controversy hinges upon the word heir. In the

---

[7] "Eran, das land zwischen dem Indus und Tigris." Von Dr. F. Spiegel. Berlin : F. Dümmler. London : D. Nutt. 1863.

[8] "The Empire in India : Letters from Madras and other Places." By Major Evans Bell. London : Trübner and Co. 1864.

Hindoo sense a man can never want heirs. Even should he die without children, natural or adopted, his wife has the power, and a religious Hindoo would also feel it her duty, to adopt an heir for him, that those ceremonies might be performed at his interment which are called for by his religion at the hands of a son. We, however, cannot but think that it is an open question whether our treaties with native princes in which the word heir occurs, contemplated one thus made, as it were, to order.

There is no doubt, however, that in another sense the question is also open, and a sense in which it deserves the most serious consideration. After the special argument devoted to each case, Major Bell enters on the consideration of those general motives of policy which are effectively the true standard to which they should be referred. There can be but little doubt in the minds of any at all acquainted with Indian affairs that we hold our dominion in the East by the same means by which it was acquired. An occupancy and growing power of an hundred years has left few traces on the minds of the natives at all commensurate with the extent of our supremacy. Confidence and sympathy are not to be won by the sword, and without either, no sure foundation can be laid either for the continuance of our power or for the best welfare of those subjected to it. Major Bell is a staunch, able, and well-informed advocate for a thorough revision of our mode of governing our possessions in India. A conciliated Hindoo and Mahometan nobility is, in his opinion, the only instrument by which we can hope either to diminish the expense of our government or to secure it from a constant liability to attack. By offering in the fullest manner the highest rewards in our power to able and educated natives, we may, he thinks, make partizans of the class which we must otherwise continue to estrange, and from which most of our dangers are, in future, to be dreaded. Every independent principality which we have gradually enclosed in the area of our dominion, should, in his opinion, have been rather fostered than absorbed, and even where possible new ones should be established.

" I believe," he says, " that the maximum of immediate dominion and direct European agency involves the minimum of European influence : whatever tends to facilitate and promote intercourse and harmony between the higher classes of India and the higher classes of Great Britain, will tend to assimilate their habits and modes of thought, and to diffuse new ideas and new wants among the mass of the population. We must gain the leaders, and the flock will follow."

The native misrule with which we have been disgusted, must be improved by friendly influence, and not abrogated in the interest of the subject; thousands, who cannot comprehend our motives, and give us no credit for anything but what appears to them high-handed injustice to families they have been accustomed to fear and reverence. We relieve them of the fear, but cannot destroy the old-established reverence. If these opinions had been expressed by any home student of our Indian policy, they would be at once disposed of as unpractical, and as betraying a complete ignorance of the impassable gulf which lies between Indian and European ways of thought, but it is impossible to adopt this tone with anyone so manifestly well acquainted as the author with Indian life and character. We have in many points acquired the respect of our Indian subjects; is it not also possible to arrive at their affection? The strong make few allowances for the vices of the weak; and we have been, perhaps, too apt, both for our own happiness and that of the natives, to turn with disgust from features of Indian character which we have rather aggravated than improved. An effort to govern India, for the most part, by the Indians themselves, is one not to be set about in a hurry, and Major Bell is the last man to advocate anything like a precipitate action on the principles he advocates; but he makes out a strong case, and is so thoroughly well-informed, that his arguments can only be met by assertions of their being founded on an ignorance of native character. An assertion of this kind would be very hardy in the face of what he brings forward. In conclusion, we strongly recommend these letters to the attentive consideration of all who are interested in the future of our Indian dependency, assuring them that whether they become converts or not to the views of the author, they cannot but reap valuable information from his pages, or fail to be pleased by the clear and able manner in which he advocates a change of policy in the East which, at least, promises results of the utmost importance. That such a policy would call for the rarest judgment and self-control is unquestionable, but great results are only to be had by corresponding exertions. If this be thought to add to its difficulties, it can hardly be said to contribute to its condemnation, but is rather a fresh recommendation to its attentive consideration.

If it were not for its affectation, Mr. Reade's book on the "Coast of Africa"[9] would be one of the most enjoyable descriptions of a country very little known, and to which, of late, much attention has been devoted. But his unquestionable good sense is dressed out to such an extent that it is almost lost sight of in the smartness of its attire. If he has a good story to tell, he so polishes and completes it that faith breaks down under the accumulated claims he makes upon it. Often humourous and witty, he never counts the cost of the effect he seeks; and if he has a pathetic tale to tell, mostly ends it with a pathos upon an absurd principle of moral relief. These, however, are but faults of exuberance, and may be regarded as passing peculiarities of the author. The worst of the affectations to which he is subject is that of the fine gentleman, because one that is in itself essentially vulgar. Though he has devoted much time and study to the questions connected with the country he describes, and though these questions are neither few nor easily mastered, he everywhere assumes the air of writing for his amusement, and offers what is really the result of much labour, as the relaxation of a young man about town in search of something fresher than Pall-mall; like a gaboon agent who once very opportunely invited him to dinner while ascending the Ncomo, he indirectly apologizes for the best meal he can set before us, and endeavours to impress upon us that under other circumstances he

[9] "Savage Africa." By W. W. Reade, Fellow of the Geographical and Anthropological Societies of London, and Corresponding Member of the Geographical Society of Paris. London: Smith, Elder and Co. 1863.

would have given us champagne. In spite of these peculiarities his book is not only most interesting throughout, but when he has a special subject which calls for careful investigation and serious statement, he lays aside his smartness, and proves that he can be instructive, too, when he cares to be so. His investigations into the natural history of the gorilla are full and complete. He authoritatively sets aside all the fearful features with which M. du Chaillu had endowed this beast, and shows him to be as timid and harmless as the other large apes.

"That which I can attest from my own personal experience (he says) is as follows :—I have seen the nests of gorillas. I cannot positively say whether they are used as beds, or only as lying-in couches. I have repeatedly seen their tracks, and could tell by them that the gorilla goes habitually on all fours. I have never seen the tracks of two gorillas in company. I have seen a young gorilla and a chimpanzee in a domestic state. They were equally docile. I have seen the dung of a gorilla, which resembles that of a man ; and I can say positively that the gorilla *sometimes* runs away from man, for I have been near enough to hear one run away from me. Both the gorilla and the chimpanzee attack by biting. A white man has never yet bagged a gorilla or chimpanzee. The wariness of these animals, the uncertainty of their haunts, and the jealousy of the native hunters will always render ape-shooting a difficult task, and one which offers more interest to the naturalist than to the sportsman. At present we possess only the evidence of native hunters, collected by Messrs. Wilson, Savage, Ford, and myself."

The account he gives of the Fans, among whom he lived for some time, though confirming the accounts of their cannibalism, disproves any special ferocity to attend upon that custom ; indeed, he treats this subject with so much charitable philosophy that we should not be surprised if he has the best reasons for assuring us that man tastes very much like monkey, only is a little fatter and more succulent. His resolute superiority to all prejudices stands him in good stead while reviewing the history of the slave trade, and the efforts we have so long made for its suppression. His last conclusion is that to which almost all acquainted with the subject have now come, viz. :—

"That the export of slaves from Africa can only be prevented by the coasts being walled with civilization ; that the trade is now confined almost entirely to Congo ; and that English settlements in that country would drive it entirely from the west coast."

The whole stretch, however, of this coast is so unhealthy that even the blacks degenerate after a few generations, and sink below the type of their forefathers who descended from the high grounds of the interior. On this subject, and on the continuous migration from the interior to the coast, Mr. Reade has collected many valuable and interesting details. On the general question of the future of Africa, a comparison of our modes of treating the Negro with those of the French in Senegambia, and of the Mohammedans in central Africa is full of indications that are more valuable than likely to be at once accepted as guides in our intercourse with the native tribes. Mr. Reade, after visiting all the Southern stations, passed some time in the French settlements, and loses no opportunity of pointing out those measures which there already promise a success we have long struggled for in vain.

" Some Glimpses into Life in the Far East"[10] is a gossiping account of the external features of society thirty years since, in Penang, Singapore, and the Straits. They are the remembrance of a boy's impressions, and were suggested by the perusal of Captain S. Osborne's " Quedah." Apparently a planter, and consequently in the eyes of Penang officials an interloper, the author fully shares those feelings of exasperation and wounded vanity which the covenanted servants of the East India Company were at that time not slow to provoke. He takes his revenge by highly-coloured portraits of corrupt and incompetent " civil servants," and sets beside them as foils sketches of local celebrities with, it must be confessed, but a qualified success. Although he betrays a strong feeling of opposition to the powers that were, he conveys at the same time a general sense of the truth of his views. His pages abound in stories of Malay pirates, alligators, and wild beasts, some of which are to the full as striking as reliable in all their details. On the general practice of Europeans in these settlements, and in China, of forming connexions with native women he is very condemnatory, and shows how often it brings about the most unhappy results both to the European himself and to those who are subject to his power and influence which are by these connexions often directed rather by the oriental feelings and customs of the Nonia than by those which her master brought with him from Europe. Though slight in construction, and very careless in style, the book has a certain freshness and air of direct experience, which are not without their attractions, and leaves the impression when you lay it down that the couple of hours given to its perusal have not been altogether thrown away.

Very different from the idyllic pictures drawn by the first navigators of those seas are the accounts of recent voyages in the Pacific. Partly this arises from a fuller knowledge, that will not admit of the colouring from Rousseau's philosophy which so greatly influenced the early historians of geographical discovery in these regions. But, most of all is this different picture to be traced to the effects of the tree of European knowledge of good and evil which has borne such strange theological, social, and commercial fruit among the islanders. Our diseases have carried such havoc into their villages, that in several of these islands, after offering libations to their gods at their evening meal, they address any ship seen in the offing with this prayer: " There is ava for you, O sailing gods ! do not come ashore in this place, but be pleased to depart along the ocean to some other land." A very fair report of their present condition will be found in Mr. Hood's account of the cruise of the *Fawn* in 1862,[11] for the purposes of inspection and police, and to collect fines imposed upon the islanders for misconduct in the matter of stranded ships, or boats which visit them for fresh provisions. It is to be feared that the overwhelming power of an English man-of-war is sometimes brought to bear where the case

---

[10] "Some Glimpses into Life in the Far East." London : Richardson and Co. 1864.
[11] "Notes of a Cruise in H.M.S. *Fawn* in the Western Pacific, in the Year 1862." By T. H. Hood. Edinburgh : Edmonston and Douglas. 1863.

has not been judged with that favourable consideration which ought to attend it. The *Fawn* touched at Uvea, or Wallis Island, for the purpose of enforcing payment of a fine of twenty tons of cocoa-nut oil, value about 600*l.*, inflicted by the commander of H.M.S. *Elk* upon the natives for plundering a vessel which got ashore on the reef and for maltreating her crew. This Cornish custom of theirs must certainly be put down, but in this case it would seem from the evidence collected by Mr. Hood, that the vessel was lost through the captain's refusal to take a pilot after he had threatened to flog one of the native chiefs who had offered his services. The queen of the island admitted that some things had been taken when washed ashore, but declared they had been returned as soon as she became aware of it, and that it was quite false that the crew had been maltreated. The claimant's representative had agreed to take half the quantity of oil; but Captain Cator, of course, had no discretion in the matter, and was obliged to enforce payment of the whole amount, though the statements of the queen were confirmed by all the Europeans in the island; and it was found that the complainant had opened a store with the very goods returned by the natives and those left in the vessel, which were brought off for him, and sold them to these people whom he represented as savage robbers. Few, we think, can fail to agree with the justice of Mr. Hood's concluding remarks on this transaction:—

"It is one of the most flagrant cases, certainly, which has come under our notice, of the unfair treatment the Polynesian islanders too often experience at the hands of the Papalangis; and in this particular instance it is the more intolerable when it is considered that H.M.S. *Elk* took away from Uvea thirteen shipwrecked British subjects, saved by the natives. A vessel having foundered at sea off Savaii, the crew constructed a raft, upon which they were driven before the strong south-east wind towards the island, which they in vain endeavoured to reach. They were observed helplessly drifting past its shores by the natives, who swam out, and towed the raft through the breakers into the reef: no slight undertaking even for Polynesian swimmers. Many of the men were so exhausted that they could not walk, and were carried by them kindly into their houses, where all the thirteen were hospitably taken care of, and supplied with all the luxuries within reach, until they were afforded the means of leaving. For this they were munificently rewarded with the sum of one dollar and a half for each man, the estimated value of an English sailor by his countrymen who inflicted the severe penalty of nearly a year's whole produce of the island upon the people of Uvea because one or two of them had appropriated a few dollars' worth of goods floating about the reef."

It is difficult to imagine what must have been the effect on the simple congregation of a sermon which Mr. Hood heard in one of the Samoan Islands, which consisted of a tirade against the " Poor Pope," as the preacher called him, and the catholic missionaries of the island, for withholding the Bible from the natives, geologists also receiving their share of the anathemas, being in some mysterious way chargeable with the same offence. The Protestants seem, however, no way behind the Catholics in the use of weapons, which have been frequently supposed peculiarly Romish. In another island of this group—

"A girl was being carried to the grave by her friends, having been, to all appearance, dead for some time, when suddenly she awoke from the trance in which she had been.   When recovered a little, being asked what she had seen, she told her wondering friends that she had been at the gate of heaven, and was met there by an angel, whom she described with the most imaginative minuteness, convincing all the superstitious people that she had actually seen all she related.   She was told by this celestial being that there was but one religion only, and that the people who alone could gain admittance at the gate were Protestants.   Many of the Roman Catholics here it is said have taken the alarm, and left their priest."

The Christian religion seems to sit but lightly upon any of them, for they will throw off their profession for a time when tempted to indulge in any of their national customs, too flagrantly in contradiction with its precepts, and quietly return to their profession when they have carried out their purpose.   The cruise of the *Faron* extended from Sydney to the Samoan Islands and back by the Feejees and New Caledonia.   The account of the domestic politics of these small archipelagoes, of their productions, and inhabitants, given by Mr. Hood, is very full and impartial ; and we regret that our space will not admit of a fuller notice of his book, to which he has appended—what ought always to be published with every account of a sea voyage—a track chart of the route followed by the ship.   It is not, however, lettered in such exact conformity with the text as could be desired, and falls very short of the admirable completeness of German maps of a similar character, as all will acknowledge who remember the admirable one which accompanied the account of the voyage of the Austrian frigate the *Novara* in these seas.

Miss Cobbe has collected into a little volume those papers on Baalbec, Cairo, Rome, the Dead Sea, Athens, and Jerusalem, which she first published in " Fraser's Magazine.[12]   Many of our readers are no doubt already familiar with them.   No one, however, can regret that they are thus brought together in a more handy form.   The subjects might be supposed worn and threadbare, but how little this is the case will soon be found by those who take up this charming collection of *Impressions de Voyage.*   As she very justly remarks, everyone brings home different impressions ; and those who cannot, for want of means, leisure, or opportunity, gather them for themselves, could hardly have a better introduction to the scenes visited than that here afforded by Miss Cobbe.   The freshness and originality of her remarks, the genuine sympathy for every human feeling, and the sharp observation which allows no characteristic feature to escape, however different the forms of civilization under which they display themselves, make this a very delightful book.   There is, perhaps, a certain tone of affectionate feminine enthusiasm about the author which one at first sight hardly knows whether to love or laugh at ; but the sound sense and large charity that pervade all her reflections make it impossible to do the latter, and the great extent and accuracy of her information often gives them a fulness and depth that is not usually found in a lady's chronicle of foreign travel.

---

[12] " The Cities of the Past."   By F. P. Cobbe.   London : Trübner and Co. 1864.

An "old bushman's'" account of a spring and summer in the most northern province of Sweden[13] will be of most interest to the practical naturalist and especially to the ornithologist, as the main purpose of his journey was to collect fine specimens of the birds which frequent these high latitudes in the early summer; but his description of a very interesting country that is but little known to southern Europeans gives his book a general interest which will render it attractive to a larger circle of readers. It has one of the first requisites of all such descriptions, an air of unexaggerated truthfulness, especially in the account he gives of adventurous expeditions among the forests and on the hills or high lands which form the chief features of the country. The rule he laid down, never to recount any traveller's tales, however probable in themselves, but to restrict himself to his own personal experience, if it has deprived his pages of many of an animated story of hunting exploits with bears and gluttons, has at least had this good effect—the reader feels that he can put the fullest confidence in what he has before him. We have never met with a more excellent account of the suffering endured in a sub-arctic snowstorm than that given in this volume. For purposes of sport it is sufficient to start from England late in the spring; but as the author wished to be on the spot as soon as the birds began to build,—for it was part of his purpose to make a collection of their eggs—he was obliged to make a winter journey, by sledging up the whole length of the country to Luleä, at the head of the Gulf of Bothnia, and from thence inland to Quickiock, close under the mountain ridge which divides Sweden from Norway. The first and much longer part of this journey is rendered so easy by the excellent postal arrangements of the Government, that no one need be deterred from undertaking it who wishes to find employment for either gun or fishing-rod in a country which gives full opportunity of good sport for either. The fullest directions are given in this volume for the necessary equipment, and a cheaper or more enjoyable trip can hardly be imagined. In the middle and southern districts the elk is to be found, in private forests it is true, but the hospitable landowners are always ready to invite a stranger to their annual hunts. The lakes and streams in this most watery country abound in salmon, trout, grayling, and char, the last especially of great weight; if these things in the wildest landscape, and among the simplest people, are attractive to any, they cannot do better than avail themselves of the instructions of an "old bushman."

We do not know of any book more calculated to interest the young in the geography of the British Empire than the excellent compilation lately published by Mrs. Bray.[14] It is an enormous advance upon the usual bare list of isolated facts with which children are too often tormented under the name of geography. Not only is this the most complete work of its kind within the necessary limits of a schoolbook,

---

[13] "A Spring and Summer in Lapland: with Notes on the Fauna of Luleä Lapmark." By an old Bushman, author of "Bush Wanderings in Australia." London: Groombridge and Sons. 1864.
[14] "The British Empire." By Caroline Bray, author of "Physiology for Schools." London: Longman and Co. 1863.

but its arrangement is so good that the memory is relieved of half the burthen usually imposed upon it by manuals on the subject. The progress of the nation is first rapidly sketched, and then every colony and dependency of the Empire is treated of in appropriate groups. Though primarily a geographical book, the natural and political features of each of the numerous countries subject to the British Crown are added with so much judgment, that a strong and interesting impression can hardly fail to be the result on the minds of the young people for whose use it is intended. Though the result of very wide reading and great labour, the style is so clear and fresh that we should be much surprised if it did not soon assume a place among the most popular educational works of the day.

The first volume of a history of the United States, by Herr Karl Neumann,[15] which brings the narrative down to the Presidentship of Jefferson, may be recommended as a very clear and careful account of one of the most instructive periods of the world's political history. In spirit it is more a constitutional history than a pageant of events. With great judgment the author goes back to the colonial system, out of which the power of the Union was ultimately to be evolved ; and traces, with a sure hand, how early the seeds of the present struggle were sown in the Constitution itself. The second volume, which is nearly finished, will bring down the narrative to the Presidentship of Andrew Jackson, and the third will contain the events of the present day. By confining himself, as he does, to the essential social facts of American history, he is enabled, in the small compass of these volumes, to give a most useful guide through a complicated series of party manœuvres that is even now too little understood in Europe ; but the magnitude of the issue involved in and interests connected with them must, before long, force a more intelligent appreciation upon spectators who were, at first, but too willing to be misled by an apparently simple issue drawn from a supposed right of revolt. This argument, at first adopted to cloak an ignorance—at the time too general—has ever since been a weight round the necks of those who sought relief in it. If revolt is a political right, it must be always ready to show its grounds ; but those who have likened the present rebellion in the United States to the revolt from the Mother-country in which they originated as a nation, have been very careful to avoid a comparison of the causes which brought about each. With better knowledge, a truer and more charitable judgment will form itself in England and on the Continent of the events now taking place in America ; and every candid lover of the truth must be glad to welcome any effort to bring about so desirable a state of things. On this account, as well as on the ground of its own very great merits, we strongly recommend the present history.

There are few books more worthy of attention from the light they throw on the state of public opinion in America, than a collection of Speeches by Wendell Phillips, recently published at Boston.[16] They

---

[15] "Geschichte der Vereinigten Staaten von Amerika." Von Karl F. Neumann. Berlin: C. Heymann. London : Williams and Norgate. 1863.

[16] "Speeches, Lectures, and Letters." By Wendell Phillips. Boston, U.S. : J. Redpath. 1863.

cover, in some sort, the progress of the best democratic thought of the last quarter of a century, and seldom has greater progress been made in any country in so short a time. Nothing can be more easy than to find fault with their style, which is very different from the political oratory of our own country. All that is needed is to put out of sight the first consideration of every orator—namely, the public he addresses, and to substitute another of which he is not thinking, and it may then be conclusively shown that the canons of taste appealed to utterly condemn the performance thus criticized. Violence, bitterness, and personal invective have been thought graces in the oratorical triumphs of the Ancients; but in the mouth of an American they are too often the only thing attended to, while the purpose and animating spirit is cautiously kept out of view, that nothing may interfere with the judgment pronounced by polite indifference on a man struggling with all his might in a cause to which he has given every feeling of his heart. The almighty dollar has become a catch-word with many writers among us, as if Americans were the first who ever hesitated between God and Mammon. But this is the way in which an American abolitionist speaks to his fellow-countrymen on the election of the present President :—

" The saddest thing in the Union meetings of last year was the constant presence in all of them of the chink of coin—the whirr of spindles—the dust of trade. I must confess those pictures of the industrial value of the Union made me profoundly sad. I look, as beneath the skilful pencil trait after trait leaps to glowing life, and ask at last—Is this all? Where are the nobler elements of national purpose and life? Is this the whole fruit of ages of toil, sacrifice, and thought?—those cunning fingers, the overflowing lap, labour vocal on every hillside, and commerce whitening every sea—all the dower of one haughty and overbearing race. The zeal of the Puritan, the faith of the Quaker, a century of colonial health, and then this large civilization; does it result only in a workshop? Oh, no! not such the picture which my glad heart sees when I look forward."

And in another place, when, last year, describing the task which must be heartily undertaken, he meets the great problem of the future of America in the only way in which it can possibly be solved, and shrinking from no tittle of its magnitude, exclaims—

" We cannot expect in hours to cover the place of centuries. It is a great problem before us : we must take up the South and organize it anew. It is not the men we have to fight—*it is the state of society that produces them.* He would be a fool who, having a fever, scraped his tongue and took no medicine. Killing Davis is only scraping the tongue; killing Slavery is taking a wet sheet-pack, destroying the very disease. But when we have done it, there remains behind it the still greater and more momentous problem, whether we have the strength, the balance, the virtue, the civilization, to absorb six millions of ignorant, embittered, bedevilled Southerners, and transmute them into honest, decent, well-behaved, Christian mechanics, worthy to be the brothers of New England Yankees—that is the real problem."

There can be no doubt of it, and insight is the first step towards success. Nothing is more remarkable than the growing confidence with which these speeches are animated; what in 1837 and up to the eve of the last election was pleaded for by every constitutional device, and defended by every resource of legal fence, now steps boldly forward on the ground of its own inherent principles of justice, which it is manifest are felt to be sufficient and no longer to need any collateral support. If it were necessary to show that the violence of language which so often appears in these addresses is but the necessary tone to be adopted to a democratic assembly when a party question has to be discussed before them, it would be sufficient to refer to the only one in this volume which touches on a subject beyond the circle of party organizations, to that on the Rights of Women, in which a subject so often disfigured by enthusiastic declamation is treated with a clearness of philosophical insight and temperate command, both of thought and language, that leave nothing to be desired.

The " Diplomatic History of the years 1813, 14, 15," just published by F. A. Brockhaus, of Leipsic,[17] is a very well written account, from the German point of view, of the events of the War of Liberation. There is considerable advantage in making treaties and conventions the turning-points of any historical summary, comprising, as they usually do, the definite results attained at their respective dates. These volumes are a curious mixture of patriotic boasting and querulous complaint, that Germany was ultimately deprived of what she looked upon as not only a just retribution on her enemy, but as the only adequate condition of her future safety. A very different view is, of course, taken by M. Capefigue in his introduction to a collection of all the treaties and conventions connected with the settlement of Europe at Vienna, which forms two bulky volumes of the " Bibliothèque des Archives Diplomatiques," published by the Count d'Angeberg.[18] An interesting map is added to the first of these volumes, from the papers of Talleyrand, in which the demands of the German Powers for an improved frontier are very clearly laid down, together with those points ultimately yielded by France.

The manner in which the Liberal party in the French Legislative Chamber has taken advantage of the relinquishment by the Emperor of the power of increasing the floating debt of the country by the issue of supplementary credits, and the general financial tone of their opposition to the Government, give a special interest to two recent books on French finance. The first of these, by M. Casimir Perier,[19] is a programme of the Liberal party, and may be usefully studied as covering nearly the whole of that field to which they have, in the present state of French opinion, very judiciously restricted their common action. It is to be hoped that on such simple issues as are here raised, the many shades of free opinion in France may acquire a habit of mutual support which will with every succeeding session give coherence and force to their influence on the Government. M. Perier's essays originally appeared, for the most part, in the " Revue des Deux Mondes,"

---

[17] " Diplomatische Geschichte der Jahre 1813, 14, 15." Leipzig : F. A. Brockhaus. London : D. Nutt. 1863.
[18] " Le Congrès de Vienne et les Traités de 1815. Bibliothèque des Archives Diplomatiques." Paris : Amyot. London : D. Nutt. 1863.
[19] " Les Finances et la Politique." Par M. Casimir Perier. Paris : Lévy frères. London : D. Nutt. 1863.

and are directed to a general consideration of the character of the control exercised by the French Chambers from the times of Louis Phillipe. They also contain a review of the financial reforms of 1861, and of the subsequent budgets, with an estimate of the present debt and sinking fund; the whole closing with a very cautious aspiration to the *beau idéal*, yet so distant, of collective Ministerial responsibility, and a budget open to detailed amendments.

The second, and much longer work, by the Baron de Nervo,[20] with its epigraph, "Facta loquuntur," is an extended history of French finance from the times of Jacques Cœur to those of Mollien. Its purpose is to inculcate, by the examples of Sully, Colbert, and the First Consul, the necessity of a firm and able hand to sweep away the ruins of former disorder, and reconstruct the financial edifice on a new basis. As might have been expected, it is much more concerned with the administrative than with the Constitutional side of the question, and is a commentary on the epigram of Baron Louis: "Give me a good government, and I will answer for a good financial system." It is not surprising that the adversaries of the Imperial system look upon this view as putting the cart before the horse; nor is it to be expected that they will be led by patriotic admiration of successful administration to an implicit confidence in the working of a system which they cannot even bring themselves to look upon as good in itself, or be misled by examples which they refuse to consider applicable to the wants of the present moment. But whatever may be thought of its political intention, the Baron de Nervo's book will be welcome to those who appreciate the difficulties of research he has overcome; while the clear manner in which he handles a subject not usually very attractive to any but those political students who know how necessary such labours are for the correct appreciation of the cotemporary events they underlie and so powerfully influence, deserves the highest praise.

A manual of the current gold and silver coins of all countries, compiled by Messrs. Leopold C. Martin and Charles Trübner,[21] is, since the publication of that by Messrs. Eckfeldt and Dubois of the United States Mint, the most useful volume of its kind; and in the number and beauty of its fac-similes of the coins described, excels that well-known work. This volume cannot but be of great use to all connected with the trade in bullion, and, though from the impossibility of correctly valuing the silver coins of other countries in the terms of own currency, owing to the operation of the seignorage on the silver coinage, the values given cannot be made the basis of any extended calculation, they are yet sufficiently accurate as approximations to the value of single pieces, while the accompanying quotation of the amount of fine silver they contain obviates any difficulty with those who engaged in exchange operations.

---

[20] "Les Finances Françaises." Par M. Le Baron de Nervo. Paris: M. Levy frères. London: D. Nutt. 1863.

[21] "The Current Gold and Silver Coins of all Countries." By Leopold C. Martin and Charles Trübner. London: Trübner and Co. 1863.

SCIENCE.

THE book which, from its comprehensive nature, we must place first amongst the few scientific works which have reached us, appears under the somewhat ambitious title of " Kosmos." [1] The object of its author, Dr. A. N. Böhner, is to point out the evidences of the power and beneficence of the Deity to be found in cosmical and terrestrial phenomena, and to a certain extent to demonstrate the harmony existing between the testimony obtained from these phenomena and the written Word. In his attempt at the latter, however, he does not seem to have been very sure of his grounds, and accordingly his arguments prove but little. In his chapter specially devoted to the consideration of the " Harmony of the Book of Nature and the Bible," he confines himself to adducing examples from the latter in which the prophets and Christ himself appeal to surrounding objects for picturesque illustrations of their meaning, or for demonstrations of the power and glory of the Deity ; and although his numerous quotations from the Bible, many of which are adopted as mottoes for his chapters, are often most happily chosen, his views, particularly on one important point, are so completely at variance with the literal interpretation of the Scripture, that the orthodox reader will find but little comfort in his pages. To our earth he gives an antiquity of many millions of years, and he also adopts for the human race a period of existence of at least 100,000 years, accepting as fully established the data afforded by Horner's researches in the valley of the Nile, Dowler's calculations upon the length of the human period in that of the Mississippi, and the facts and deductions obtained by the investigation of valley deposits, bone-caves, and lake-dwellings in Europe—and all this with his pages swarming with quotations from the Bible and from devotional poems and hymns, and with pietistic ejaculatory passages on his own account, worked up with an unction worthy of the most evangelical of preachers. Apart from this theological element, which some would be inclined to regard as introduced for the purpose of blinding the faithful and deluding them into heretical paths, Dr. Böhner has furnished his readers with a most interesting *résumé* of the present state of our knowledge of the leading phenomena of the Cosmos. The primitive condition of the universe is described in accordance with the nebular theory, and the emission of light and heat by the cosmical bodies during their condensation is regarded as the fulfilment of the first volition of the Creator as recorded in Genesis—" Let there be light." The gradual evolution of the system of the heavens and the mutual relations of the celestial bodies, form the subject of his first book. The second book is devoted to the consideration of light and the correlated forces ; and the third to the geological development of our earth and its inhabitants. In the latter, we suppose by way of an attempt at a

---

[1] " Kosmos —Bibel der Natur." Von Dr. August Nathanael Böhner. Erster Band. 8vo. Hannover : Carl Rümpler. 1864. Pp. 570.

reconciliation with the so-called Mosaic narrative, the geological history is divided into seven periods,—namely, 1. Primitive (Gneiss, &c.); 2. Transition (Palæozoic); 3. Triassic; 4. Jurassic; 5. Cretaceous; 6. Molasse (Tertiary); 7. Diluvial (Human period). In the last of these the author assumes that the changes in the surface of the earth have gone on with far less violence than in former periods, and he finds in this supposed fact an illustration of the Jewish traditional origin of Sabbatical observances.

The second part of Professor Roscoe's translation of Kirchhoff's "Researches on the Solar Spectrum"[2] has just appeared. In the first part the author described that portion of the solar spectrum which includes Fraunhofer's lines D and F; the investigation is now continued on the same plan and with the same instruments on the two extremities of the spectrum from D to A and from F to G. By the comparison of the spectra of the chemical elements with the solar spectrum, the coincidence of the iron, calcium, and nickel bright lines with Fraunhofer's lines is further demonstrated, and new coincidences of the same kind were observed in the spectra of barium, copper, and zinc. These results strengthen the evidence as to the presence of the metals in question in the solar atmosphere, but the existence of cobalt therein still remains uncertain, as "many cobalt lines between C and D, and between F and G, are coincident with Fraunhofer's lines, whilst others, equally bright, have no coincident solar line." A few coincidences were observed in the spectra of cadmium and strontium, but not sufficient to warrant the conclusion that these metals are present. On the other hand, the closer investigation of the potassium spectrum has thrown great doubt upon the existence of that metal in the sun's atmosphere—the supposed red potassium line regarded by Bunsen and Kirchhoff as coincident with Fraunhofer's line A, is now proved to consist of two lines, both of which are less refrangible than A, and the second double potassium line, although near, is not coincident with B. Independent of the interest attaching immediately to these researches, Professor Kirchhoff and his pupil, Dr. Hofmann, merit the thanks of future observers in the field of spectrum analysis for the careful and admirable manner in which, in the plates appended to this memoir, they have as it were mapped out the solar spectrum with its almost innumerable Fraunhofer's lines, rendering the identification of the position of lines produced in chemical spectra a matter of perfect certainty.

We need do little more than notice the appearance of a fifth edition of Professor Phillips's "Guide to Geology,"[3] which has just been published, as its reputation, like that of its author, is already well established. We notice that Professor Phillips still adheres to his former views as to the equivalence of the beds between the Cornbrash and the Dogger in Yorkshire with the Great Oolite series of the south-

[2] "Researches on the Solar Spectrum and the Spectra of the Chemical Elements." By G. Kirchhoff. Translated by H. E. Roscoe, B.A., Ph.D., F.R.S. Second Part. 4to. Cambridge: Macmillan. 1863.
[3] "A Guide to Geology." By John Phillips, M.A., LL.D., F.R.S., F.G.S., &c. Fifth Edition. 12mo. London: Longmans. 1864.

west of England, in opposition to the opinion now generally entertained that the whole of the Yorkshire Oolites below the Cornbrash belong to the Inferior Oolite. In general the results of recent geological research have been carefully incorporated by the author in the present edition of his work, and the whole subject is treated in a philosophical spirit and with a close reference to personal observations, that render this book a most valuable manual of the principles of geology. To those who are beginning the practical study of this science it will prove an excellent guide.

Another little book on the same great subject with the one just noticed is Mr. Page's " Philosophy of Geology."[4] The author's object in its preparation was to direct the attention of geologists " to some of the higher aims of their science, to the principles that ought to guide them in their generalizations, and to what may be ultimately anticipated of Geology in her true and onward progress." The views here expressed are doubtless familiar to most geologists, but it is as well to have even familiar things occasionally brought prominently before us, as, when set in a new light, they not unfrequently impress our minds with greater force. The sections relating to the general hypotheses of geology and indicating the dangers of a too hasty generalization will be read with especial profit by the young geologist, and the observations on the uncertainty of calculations of geological time from any data at present at our command are also deserving of attention. With regard to the value of Palæontological evidence in determining the cotemporaneity of distant deposits, the author endorses the views of Professor Huxley, considering that we may by its means " establish a similarity of order between the strata of different regions, but similarity of order is not to be confounded with synchrony of deposit." With regard to the manifestations of life during geological periods, Mr. Page maintains the doctrine of progression, but at the same time indicates the difficulties in the way of the demonstration of the supposed gradual ascent, from Palæontological evidence. In discussing the mode by which this progression has been effected, the author, whilst admitting the probability of a developmental relation between organized bodies, indicates that none of the hypotheses hitherto proposed seem to satisfy all the conditions of the question ; he requires some higher law than any of those recognised in the Darwinian theory. The whole of this portion of the work, and of that treating of the origin and antiquity of man, is written in a liberal and philosophical spirit, which indeed is manifested by the author whenever he has occasion to touch upon those pseudo-theological questions which appear as serious stumbling-blocks to many minds.

M. Louis Figuier's " Earth and Sea,"[5] is the second of that series of scientific manuals with which he hopes to displace fairy tales

---

[4] " The Philosophy of Geology : a Brief Review of the Aim, Scope, and Character of Geological Inquiry." By David Page, F.R.S.E, F.G.S. 12mo. Edinburgh : Blackwood. 1863.
[5] " La Terre et les Mers, ou Description Physique du Globe." Par Louis Figuier. 8vo. Paris : Hachette. 1864.

from the hands of the rising generation. It contains, as indicated in its title-page, a popular account of the physical geography of the globe, with especial reference to the more picturesque details which may be so easily engrafted on the dry bones of the science. In this respect it must be regarded as a more successful effort than its predecessor (which was devoted to geology) towards the author's desired end, as the descriptions of Alpine adventures, disastrous earthquakes, and cave explorations, possess a general charm for the young mind with which it is perhaps more difficult to invest many of the facts of geological investigation.

In those anthropological researches which are now occupying so much attention both in this country and abroad, the investigation of the languages of different peoples forms by no means an unimportant element, but one which, owing to the various and arbitrary modes of spelling adopted by different authors in reducing the sounds of exotic languages to European terms, is surrounded by the most vexatious difficulties. With the view of getting rid of some of the obstacles in the way of reducing different languages to a common mode of spelling —the necessity of which is felt by missionaries as much, or perhaps more, than by scientific investigators—Professor Lepsius was induced, by several of the London Missionary Societies, to undertake the preparation of a "Standard Alphabet," in which each known sound employed in any language whatsoever, should be represented by its own character. The result of Professor Lepsius's labours is the work of which a second edition is now before us,[6] and for the production of which we are indebted to the English Church Missionary Society. It includes a historical account of previous attempts to express exotic languages in European characters, and a full discussion both of the objects to be attained by the adoption of a uniform standard alphabet, and of the means by which such an alphabet may be formed, the latter portion including a minute examination of the nature of the various sounds in use among different nations, and leading naturally to the development of the system proposed for adoption by the author. The alphabet, from the number of shades of sound which it has to express, is necessarily somewhat complicated ; but it is founded on so thorough an investigation of the subject, that it can hardly fail to prove practically useful : indeed, the examples of numerous languages given by the author in his second part, and the wide adoption of this alphabet by the Missionaries—especially in reducing the African languages to a written form—prove its applicability. The remarks upon the languages of which illustrations are given, often contain interesting information.

Mrs. Ward's "Microscope Teachings"[7] will furnish a simple and useful guide to those who wish to amuse themselves a little with the

---

[6] "Standard Alphabet for reducing Unwritten Languages and Foreign Graphic Systems to a Uniform Orthography in European Letters." By C. R. Lepsius. Second edition. 8vo. London : Williams and Norgate. 1863.
[7] "Microscope Teachings." By the Hon. Mrs. Ward. Square 8vo. London : Groombridge. 1864.

microscope, giving them a good deal of information as to the use of the instrument, the objects the examination of which will be most interesting to the beginner, and the modes of preparing and preserving them for inspection. Mrs. Ward makes no pretence to be an authority in science, as is the wont of too many of those who write books similar in their nature to her own; but she has an advantage over most of these authors in that she appears to have personally examined the greater part of the objects which she here describes. The little volume is illustrated with numerous coloured plates, from the author's own pencil, the figures in which are generally good.

Since the meeting of the Peace Congress at Brussels and the celebrated visit of Mr. Pease to the Emperor Nicholas of Russia, the world has been fuller of wars and rumours of wars than at any time during the memory of the present generation, and at no period perhaps has the general aspect of continental politics been more threatening than it is at present. How long this country may keep out of any greater embroilment than those which she has now upon her hands is a question that may receive a practical solution at any moment, and it is therefore a matter of no small importance to know how we should stand in the event of our being drawn into a struggle with any strong power. Among the points to be considered in order to arrive at a conclusion upon this subject, the condition of our artillery service and of the relation of our guns to armour-plated ships must occupy the first place. Those who wish for information as to the result of the efforts which have been made of late years in this country for the improvement of projectile weapons will find a most admirable summary of the whole series of experiments in Sir James Emerson Tennent's "Story of the Guns,"[8]—a little book which, whilst dealing apparently with the driest details, is at the same time, from its style and the mode in which its subject is arranged, as attractive reading as any novel. The author first of all indicates the comparatively stationary condition of all firearms up to a very recent period, the absence of improvement being so complete in the case of the ordinary soldier's musket, that the weapons borne by our men at Waterloo cannot be regarded as more effective than those used in the wars of Marlborough. The first step in advance was the introduction of the Minié rifle in 1851, and this gave way in 1853 to the Enfield musket. The further experiments of Mr. Whitworth led him to the invention of the rifle which bears his name, and the leading principles of which consist in its possessing a polygonal instead of a grooved bore, and a rather rapid twist, and in its being fired with a bullet made to fit the bore of the gun instead of one forced into an irregular figure in order to fill up the rifling. The demonstrated result of this arrangement is a decided superiority over the Enfield and indeed any other rifle; it possesses great accuracy, a very long range, and a remarkably low trajectory, the latter a condition of the very greatest importance in firing at a distant mark. It appears from the evidence that this weapon might be produced at

---

[8] "The Story of the Guns." By Sir James Emerson Tennent, K.C.B. 8vo. London : Longmans. 1864.

about the same cost as the Enfield rifle; the only obstacle to its introduction into the British army seems to be the expense of altering the machinery at the Enfield Government works to enable it to produce the new arm. The whole course of the experiments leading to the invention of these rifles, and to the general adoption for military purposes of a conical or elongated form of projectile, is described fully by Sir James Tennent,—the effect produced in the art of war by the introduction of weapons which would kill, and even admitted of good shooting, at a range of 1000 yards, may be easily understood when we remember that the old fighting rule for the soldier when armed with "Brown Bess" was to reserve his fire until he could distinguish the whites of his enemies' eyes, and that Napoleon and his marshals regarded 450 yards as a perfectly safe distance from any small arms in use in their day. It is also easy to see that with this improvement in the weapons carried by the infantry of the line, the position of artillerymen became far less secure than formerly, as they were now liable to be picked off when engaged in handling their guns at a distance which had previously been regarded as perfectly safe. Accordingly, the efforts which had previously been made to improve the larger guns were redoubled, and a series of experiments was made both by the Government and by private individuals, with the view of obtaining an arm which should maintain the old superiority of the ordnance over the muskets of the line. The attempts made in this direction, both in this country and on the continent, are discussed by Sir James Tennent, and the peculiarities and defects of the different guns proposed are thoroughly explained. The principle to which all the inventors had recourse in order to give increased range and accuracy to their projectiles, consists in rifling the bore of the gun : the difficulty of adapting the ball to the new mode of construction, and in the case of heavy ordnance, the apparent impossibility of obtaining a material strong enough to resist the force of the explosion, formed the chief obstacles to the realization of the various projects. Among the crowd of inventors two names stand conspicuous—those of Mr. Whitworth and of Sir W. Armstrong. The latter adopted a cylindrical bore, rifled with grooves, to be used with lead-coated projectiles : a necessary condition of this construction is that the gun should be a breech-loader, in order that the ball may be forced to occupy the grooves, and this necessity has led to the introduction in the Armstrong guns of a complicated arrangement of screws about the breech, and especially of a loose vent-piece, which cannot but weaken the weapon at the very point where it requires to be strongest. It appears that unless the greatest care be taken the vent-piece of the Armstrong gun may be blown out by the force of its discharge, and several naval officers have declared that both they and their men regard the new guns with considerable distrust. Mr. Whitworth, in his ordnance, simply reproduced on a larger scale the model which had guided him in the construction of his rifle—a polygonal twisted bore, with an iron projectile moulded so as to fit accurately to the interior of the barrel. His gun, therefore, loads in the ordinary way, at the mouth, in itself no small advantage, and when he has adopted a breech-loading arrangement in the smaller cannon, the whole breech screws firmly on the hinder extremity of the barrel, so as to avoid all loose vent-pieces and other complications. In fact, in simplicity Mr. Whitworth's invention is so far preferable to the Armstrong gun, that one is surprised that the Committee of 1858 should have adopted the latter without further inquiry, and even without visiting Mr. Whitworth's works, an omission of which no satisfactory explanation has been given. The advantages of the Whitworth gun over all its competitors as far as they have yet been tried, consist in its greater range and accuracy and its low trajectory, and in proof of its penetrating power it has sent both shot and shell through armour-plates, which, as Sir W. Armstrong himself admits, no gun in the service could touch. Under these circumstances every one must agree with Sir James Tennent in thinking that further trials of these and other guns are absolutely necessary, and that the Committee appointed for the purpose should not be exclusively composed of naval and military men.

Lieutenant Forsyth, in his work on " The Sporting Rifle,"[9] takes a different view of the subject of projectiles, maintaining that while great range is undoubtedly an advantage in military rifles, the sportsman rather requires a weapon which will carry true nearly point blank to a distance of 150 or 200 yards. For sporting purposes he disapproves of the conical bullet, and recommends a return to the spherical form, which, he says, is more certain than any other to disable an animal when hit. The rifle for shooting with spherical balls should have but little twist in its grooves, according to the author. In his concluding chapter, Lieutenant Forsyth describes some percussion shells which he has invented for sporting purposes, and gives full directions for making them.

In medical literature we have but little that is new to notice ; the few books before us being chiefly new editions of well-known works. Amongst them we have a third edition of Gray's Descriptive and Surgical Anatomy, edited by Mr. Holmes.[10] The easy familiarity of its style, and the admirable illustrations with which it abounds, cannot fail to render this work popular with students of anatomy. A third edition of Dr. Althaus' work on the treatment of certain forms of Paralysis and Neuralgia by the Galvanic Current,[11] gives us a fair *résumé* of the present state of our knowledge of the therapeutic value of the various modifications of this agent. It is needless to say that on this subject Dr. Althaus is our best authority.

Few medical works written for the general reader are worthy of notice : we have, however, a notable exception to this rule, in the truly useful work by Mr. Chavasse, which has already reached a seventh edi-

[9] " The Sporting Rifle and its Projectiles." By Lieut. James Forsyth, M.A. 8vo. London : Smith, Elder, and Co. 1863.
[10] " Anatomy, Descriptive and Surgical." By H. Gray, F.R.S. Third Edition. By T. Holmes, M.A., Cantab. London : Longman, Green, Longman, & Co. 8vo. 1864.
[11] " On Paralysis, Neuralgia, and other Affections of the Nervous System, and their Successful Treatment by Galvanization and Faradization." By J. Althaus, M.D. Third Edition. London : Trübner & Co. 1864. 12mo.

tion.[12] Were it possible to impress mothers with the value and importance of the advice contained in it and to ensure their acting upon it, we should not long have to deplore the high rate of infant mortality which the reports of the Registrar-General record, more than half of which, we believe, is due to preventible causes, and especially to the ignorance and neglect of the few simple principles which ought to guide mothers in the management of their infants which are so clearly set forth in this unpretending little volume.

Topics of the Day is the title of a volume of essays on various subjects, medical and social.[13] The work contains nothing that is new either in fact or theory, nevertheless in a pleasant, gossiping manner it runs over a variety of interesting themes, as for example, Atmospheric Phenomena in relation to Cholera, History and Practice of Vaccination, Ethnological Psychology, The Indian Rebellion, &c. Many of the essays are elegantly written, and indicate a wide field of observation.

A volume on the sanitary condition of the army in India is a reprint in a separate form of Miss Nightingale's observations, communicated by request to the Royal Commission.[14] The author has in a concise form given a summary of the evidence contained in the "stational reports." These reports show that at almost every station there is an utter neglect of the simplest sanitary precautions; bad water, often filthy, no drainage, the soil soaked with refuse and filth—baths either wanting or imperfect—inducements to intemperance, and a want of any means for healthy recreation and amusement are the normal conditions with which the soldier in India is surrounded. Need we wonder that disease and death are their constant companions? The more we know of India and its diseases, the more are we convinced that if close attention were paid to the sanitary condition of our military stations—if efforts were made to secure for the men the advantages of a plentiful supply of pure water, good drainage, and efficient ventilation of hospitals and barracks, together with the means for healthy recreation and amusement, and, if possible, the diminution of those temptations to intemperance which everywhere exist, we should have less of the fearful mortality which prevails amongst our troops than we do now. The British soldier is an expensive article, and if humanity and a sense of duty are not sufficient incentives to preserve his health by better attention to the sanitary conditions with which he is surrounded, notions of economy might have some weight.

A second medical report of the hospital for consumption contains much valuable information, chiefly in a statistical form, having

---

[12] "Advice to a Mother on the Management of her Offspring, and on the Treatment of some of their more Urgent Diseases." By P. H. Chavasse, F.R.C.S. Seventh Edition. London : Churchill & Sons. 1864.

[13] "Topics of the Day, Medical, Social, and Scientific." By J. A. Hingeston, M.R.C.S. London: Churchill & Sons. 1863. 12mo.

[14] "Observations on the Evidence contained in the Stational Reports submitted to her by the Royal Commission on the Sanitary State of the Army in India." By Florence Nightingale. Reprinted from the Report of the Royal Commission. London : E. Stamford, 1863. 8vo.

reference to all the more prominent features of interest in this disease.[15] Amongst other facts, these tables show that by far the greater proportion of cases of consumption occur between the ages of twenty and thirty. On the question of hereditary predisposition they reveal an interesting fact—namely, that this predisposition follows to a considerable extent sexual relations, the daughters of phthisical mothers being more prone to disease than the sons, that is, in cases where the father is healthy; whilst the sons of consumptive fathers are more prone to the disease than daughters in cases where the mother is healthy: the existence of this hereditary predisposition is shown to exist in more than three-fourths of the cases admitted. In addition to statistics on these points of general interest, there are many of special value in a medical point of view. The general result shown by this report is cheering, and clearly indicates how much may be done by judicious treatment, not only towards relieving but curing the scourge of our country. The report is a valuable contribution to the literature of this disease.

Two small pamphlets by Dr. Beale,[16] set forth, in a concise form, his views on the formation of the tissues, the value of nutriment, and the use of alcohol in certain acute diseases. The value of alcohol in the treatment of acute diseases—as, for example, pneumonia—he thinks arises from the fact that it diminishes or assists the active reproduction of morbid cell growth, and then puts an end to the process which constitutes the essential element in the diseased arteries. The truth or fallacy of this theory depends, to a great extent, if not entirely, on the truth or otherwise of the author's theory of growth and nutrition.

HISTORY AND BIOGRAPHY.

REGARDING the career of Charles the Bold as capable of supplying material for an historical construction, rather than as forming "merely a romantic episode" in European history, Mr. Kirk has availed himself of the recent researches of the students of the period, has examined the chronicles and memoirs which illustrate it, and from various novel sources opened up in Belgium, Switzerland, and Austria, has derived valuable evidence relating to the chief actors and notable events of the time, and for final result has combined the information and knowledge he has obtained into one "symmetrical

---

[15] "The Second Medical Report of the Hospital for Consumption and Diseases of the Chest." Presented to the Committee of Management by the Physicians to the Institution. London : J. Churchill & Son. 1863. 8vo.
[16] "On Deficiency of Vital Power in Disease, and on Support ; with Observations upon the Action of Alcohol in Serious Cases of Acute Disease." By L. S. Beale, M.B., F.R.S. 12mo. London : T. Richards. 1863.
"First Principles—Observations upon the Essential Changes occurring in Inflammation." A Lecture by L. S. Beale, M.B., F.R.S. Dublin : Thomas Day. 1863. 12mo.

narrative."[1]   The two published volumes of this work, designed to be completed by a third now in course of preparation, indicate a scholarly diligence, real understanding of the subject, and an undoubted historical ability.   It is true that with all its merits the book before us is not a great book.   We find in it no philosophical thought of a high order, nor does its author seem to us to possess the historical imagination in any very eminent degree.   If we look to the style which he has adopted, we should say that though writing with vigour and animation, he is deficient in grace, simplicity, and illuminating force.

His composition is sometimes laboured and verbose; in the subjoined sentence his language seems wild :—

" Feudalism, though endued with a centrifugal force ever fruitful of alarming phenomena, and though engaged—at what seemed the period of its rampant strength, but what was in truth the period of its feebleness and decline—in a desperate contest with monarchical power, was nevertheless the chief source from which that power derived its nutriment and growth, weaving the countless threads that when grasped by a skilful hand drew together all the revolving particles and atoms, and distilling all the copious fountains of loyalty that were at length to overflow and mingle in a common reservoir."

In spite, however, of defects or deficiencies, Mr. Kirk has produced a really valuable book—a book which is entitled to a place in our library beside the volumes of the friend who aided him in procuring the requisite materials for his literary enterprise, the late William H. Prescott; a distinction which is in itself no mean praise.

Commencing with a description of France at the close of the fourteenth and in the first half of the fifteenth century, Mr. Kirk rapidly delineates the struggles of feudalism with royalty, the long prevailing anarchy and ultimate regeneration of France, when the English had abandoned, not only their recent acquisitions, but their earliest possessions, and when Calais alone saw " the standard of St. George still floating over French soil."   The account of the dominions, court and policy of Philip the Good, which follows, abounds in interesting and picturesque details.   In the third chapter we are introduced to Charles the Bold, the inheritor of that renowned sovereignty, which had no fewer than five successive phases, and which Charles proposed to restore to its ancient splendour, as the kingdom of the Rhine,—" the counterpart of that earlier Burgundian kingdom which, leaning on the Vosges, the Jura, and the Alps, had guarded the waters of the Rhine to their junction with the sea."   Charles, the hero of Mr. Kirk's history, and the rival of Louis XI., has hitherto been pronounced deficient in sagacity and deliberative foresight, and as the Terrible, the Rash, the Bold, and by anticipation, the Idiot, has been held to have played rather a conspicuous than distinguished part, in the drama of European history.   To this conception of Charles's character Mr. Kirk objects, not without grounds.   He does not, indeed, claim for him transcendent genius, or versatile talent, or ready adaptiveness, but he contends that he had eminent, though not pre-eminent intelligence;

[1] " History of Charles the Bold, Duke of Burgundy." By John Foster Kirk. With Portraits.   Vols. I. and II.   London : John Murray.   1863.

that "his vision, within a limited range, was singularly clear," and that while, without the profound and foreseeing intellect and the inventive faculty of his antagonist, he had powers of reasoning that were rare and admirable, and principles of action that were consistent and sound. That Charles was not wanting either in the faculty that discerns or that which appropriates opportunity is manifest, from the promptitude with which he took advantage of the existing weakness, discord, and embarrassments of neighbouring states, and which is attested by the downfall of Liége, the purchase of Alsace, the annexation of Gueldres, and the establishment of a military protectorate over Lorraine.

Of this sincere, straightforward and impetuous prince Louis XI. was the natural enemy. As Mr. Kirk undertakes to correct the popular impression of Charles's character, so he revises the traditionary portrait of the French king. Far from denying, however, the reality of the historical element that enters into the received representation, he insists that "most of the particulars are indubitable facts. The cages and the steel-traps, the cunning, the cruelty, the suspicions, the bigotry are authentically established." Yet a monarch of whom it can be truly said that he strove to win the sympathy and co-operation of his people, that he appealed to and created public opinion, that he granted charters liberally to Communes, must have had some remarkable qualities—qualities that justified the admiration of so able and comparatively impartial a judge as Philippe de Commines. A vigorous mind, Mr. Kirk explains, united with a bad heart, is not necessarily an instrument of evil. Louis found the French nobility insubordinate. Deprived by royal enactment of the privileges of the chase, they were dreadfully *bored*, and partly out of pure *ennui*, it would seem, formed a combination—the so-called League of the Public Weal—which might have resulted in the dismemberment of France. The unity of the country was imperilled, and the existence of the Monarchy menaced by the rebellious vassals of the Crown. With a firm grasp, Louis held the power which legitimately belonged to him, crushed feudal anarchy, and saved France. And this great and necessary work "was effected, not with the aid of fortune or by a preponderance of strength, but through the efforts of an intellect ever watchful and never dispirited, contending against enormous difficulties and overwhelming odds—an intellect so keen and so vivacious as to compel our sympathy, and render dormant that aversion which its choice of means would otherwise inspire." Such are the two principal actors in events which have in them a deep and permanent interest. We have shown how Mr. Kirk regards the rival princes and the work one of them did, and one of them tried to do. We cannot follow him in his narrative of the double career of Charles the Bold, which, beginning with an attempt to undermine the French monarchy, ended with an effort "to establish a power which should rise beside and overtop that monarchy." Among the passages of this history which have struck us most are those which describe the scenery, the institutions, the resources, and the usages of Liége, Bruges, Ghent, the analysis of the characters of Charles and Louis, the story of the counter-revolution in England, in which some light is thrown on the conduct of the king-making Earl of Warwick, and the episode of Hagenbach's rise and fall. We shall welcome the conclusion of Mr. Kirk's most praiseworthy labours. He is evidently a thoughtful and diligent writer, and gives such evidences of reading and research that we are quite at a loss to conjecture how he, in common with another recent historian, can confound Gregory I. with Gregory VII., as he assuredly does in the note to p. 288, vol. i.

To form a close alliance with the Duke of Burgundy was the obvious policy of the head of the House of York, which gained additional popularity in England from its maintenance of the claims advanced by Edward III. to the crown of France. Edward IV., though he reconquered none of the lost territory, compelled Louis XI. to pay him tribute, and stipulated that the Dauphin should marry his eldest daughter. The treaty of Arras, however, directly set aside this stipulation. On the death of Edward no resentment was manifested in England, and Richard III., who had enough to do at home, had neither motive nor inclination for a quarrel with France.

Such is the view at least of Mr. James Gairdner, who, in the preface to a second and final volume of letters and papers illustrative of the reigns of Richard III. and Henry VII.,[2] has taken an interesting survey of the period, or rather of some of its leading events, discussing such questions as Richard's criminality, Perkin Warbeck's identity, and James the Fourth's character. We notice that in the present volume Mr. Gairdner recalls the opinion which he expressed in the former volume, on the authorship of the Latin History of Richard III., which he was at one time disposed to attribute, not to Sir Thomas More, but, following the tradition mentioned by Harrington in Queen Elizabeth's reign, to Cardinal Morton. The difficulty of supposing More to be the author of the " History," which arises from the consideration that if he were only three years old at Richard's accession he could not possibly have written the passage in which he says that he remembers an anecdote then told to his father, Mr. Gairdner endeavours to surmount by antedating More's birth by four years. But would a boy of seven have been much more likely than a child of three years of age to have retained in his memory the circumstances recorded in page xxi. of the preface: or is it certain that he would have even understood the report?

There are three other volumes of the Record Office, publications which we can but briefly notice here. " The Annales Monastici,"[3] edited by Mr. Luard, contains the Margan Annals, beginning with the death of Edward the Confessor, and in part, perhaps, derived from William of Malmesbury's History; the Annals of the Monastery of

[2] "Letters and Papers illustrative of the Reigns of Richard III. and Henry VII." Edited by James Gairdner. Published by the authority of the Lords Commissioners of Her Majesty's Treasury, under the direction of the Master of the Rolls. Vol. II. London: Longman, Green, and Co. 1863.

[3] "Annales Monastici." Vol. I. &c. Edited by Henry Richards Luard, M.A., Fellow and Assistant-Tutor of Trinity College, &c. Published by the authority, &c. London: Longman, Green, and Co. 1864.

Tewkesbury, which also begin with Edward's death; and the Annals of Burton, the most valuable portion of which, says the editor, "relates to the Provisions of Oxford and the revolution, which in fact almost dethroned the King" (Henry III.).

"The Magna Vita S. Hugonis Episcopi Lincolniensis,"[4] admirably edited by Rev. James F. Dimock, from manuscripts in the Bodleian Library, Oxford, and the Imperial Library, Paris, is a circumstantial biography of an illustrious saint, written by one Adam, a Benedictine monk, and a retainer of Hugh's household. "The Life," which has always been held in high estimation, appears to be of considerable value. It should have a particular attraction for Somersetshire antiquarians, as it contains various details relating to Witham Friary, near Frome, where Henry II. founded a Carthusian monastery, of which Hugh was appointed prior, being the third in order of succession. Witham, or the "House of Understanding," as Adam interprets it, out of compliment to Hugh, has gone the way of many another picturesque village, and hears the profane railway scream where once it heard the monks' pious chant.

The remaining volume is a very curious one, but its lengthy title,[5] which we give below, will sufficiently explain its nature. In the preface, Mr. Oswald Cockayne has collected many quaint and instructive details respecting charms, witches, and magic in general.

Among the more remarkable persons accused of practising the Black Art was Gerbert, or Silvester II., one of the most learned of popes. In a valuable and attractive study called "The Pope-Fables of the Middle Age," Döllinger, the celebrated Roman Catholic writer, explains the origin of this and several other singular papal myths, including the most singular of all, that of Pope Joan.[6] In the 13th century, a saga which had perhaps been *in the air* for some little time assumed a definite shape, and took its place as a *fact* in history. The story went that a woman of surpassing knowledge had succeeded in procuring her own elevation to the papal chair; that she performed the various functions of her sublime position; brought scandal on the Church by giving birth to a child in the streets, and, according to one account, was stoned immediately after. The street in which the little accident happened has been avoided since, it is added, and processions take a circuitous route, in order to shun that spot of shame. Now, the strange circumstance about this fable is, that it is not a weak invention of the Protestant enemy. It was current in the 13th century, arose in Rome, and was propagated, not by the Valdenses, but by their most

---

[4] "Magna Vita S. Hugonis Episcopi Lincolniensis," &c. Edited by the Rev. James F. Dimock, M.A., Rector of Barnbury, Yorkshire. Published by the authority, &c. London: Longman, Green, and Co. 1864.

[5] "Leechdoms, Wort-cunning, and Star-craft of Early England." Being a collection of documents, for the most part never before printed, illustrating the history of science in this country before the Norman Conquest. Collected and edited by the Rev. Oswald Cockayne, M.A. Cantab. Vol. I. Published by the authority, &c. London: Longman, Green, and Co. 1864.

[6] "Die Papst-Fabeln des Mittelalters. Ein Beitrag zur Kirchengeschichte." Von Joh. Jos. Ign. V. Döllinger. London: D. Nutt. 1863.

determined opponents, the Dominicans and Minorites, in the time of Boniface VIII., who was not over-favourably disposed to these orders, and whose disesteem inspired them with a personal dislike, which was extended to the papal office itself, so far, at least, that they found a gratification in indicating the holes in his predecessors' coat. After tracing with great learning and research the literary history of this marvellous myth, the accomplished author offers what appears to us a perfectly satisfactory explanation of it. The constituent elements of the story are, the customary use of a perforated chair, believed to afford particular facilities for the ascertainment of the sex of the newly-elected pope, who never again occupies it ; a stone with an inscription, which was mistaken for a monument ; a supposed female statue, and the practice of avoiding a particular street already mentioned. For the manner in which these real materials were combined into a fabulous whole we must refer the reader to the essay itself ; merely observing that the stone seat was chosen for its beautiful colouring, and not for its perforations ; that the statue was probably that of a priest of Mithras, in flowing robes and with an attendant youth, and that the P.P.P. inscription, which was understood to mean

"Papa Pater patrum peperit papissa papillum,"

or something like it, may, and perhaps does, signify Papirius pater patrum propriâ pecuniâ posuit—pater patrum being a recognised appellation of a priest of Mithras ; while, in conclusion, the avoidance of the street is to be ascribed simply to its inconveniently narrow dimensions. There are, it would seem, eight other similarly "true tales" similarly dealt with in this curiously learned investigation. We extremely admire the dexterity with which the author converts what has been taken for history into its mythical elements, and heartily recommend his researches to Catholics and Protestants alike.

About the end of the eighth century appeared that collection of Ecclesiastical Canons now usually known as the "False Decretals." They were given to the world under the name of Isidore, an unknown person, who borrowed in part from a previous and genuine collection of canons. The supremacy of Rome over the various national churches rested for centuries on these spurious decretals. Two compact volumes, from the Leipsic press, contain these memorable documents.[7] In the treatise which introduces them an account seems to be given of the different MSS. of the Decretals, of their character and composition, and an inquiry is instituted into their authorship, date, and derivation. Though we have spoken above of two compact volumes, we judge of the nature of the first from that of the second, having seen the latter only.

In this place a few words may be appropriately given to Hasse's "Manual of Church History," a work which shows some research, and

---

7 "Decretales Pseudo-Isidorianæ et capitula Angilramni. Ad fidem librorum manuscriptorum recensuit fontes indicavit commentationem de collectione Pseudo-Isidori præmisit Paulus Hinschius." Pars Posterior. Ex officina Bernardi Tauchnitz. London : Williams and Norgate. 1863.

displays a real acquaintance with the subject of which it treats, but which is not distinguished by bold or original criticism.[8] The plan of the work precludes anything like detailed exposition, and thus, perhaps, we ought hardly to expect the distinction between the later and earlier Ophitæ, a Gnostic sect, to be preserved. In the account of the Paschal controversy the conformity of Apollinaris to the usage of Asia Minor, asserted by our author, is a misconception. Apollinaris agreed with the Western view, which was that of the fourth Gospel, but which was *not* that of the Asiatic Church traditionally founded on the authority of the Apostles John and James, and supported by the evidence of the Synoptic Gospels. The first part only of Dr. Hasse's work is before us: it brings us down to the time of St. Augustine, passing in rapid review the doctrine, government, and discipline of the Church; its struggle with Paganism, Judaism, &c.; its relations to the state, and its ceremonial, ritual, and philosophy.

The historical researches, in ancient, mediæval, and modern times, of Dr. Friedrich Kortüm, consist of detached papers: an anti-Cleonic essay on the demagogue Cleon, one on Agis IV., one on Pindar's political and philosophical view of life, one on Thucydides, and one on the history of ancient art.[9] A seventh treats of peculiarities in the Hispano-Roman poetry of the second half of the first century after Christ, and traces the characteristics of Silius Italicus, Lucan, and Martial. The two mediæval essays are on Ezzelino da Romano, and the royal power, serfdom, and land-allotments of the old Germans; while the subjects of the essays relating to modern times are: I. the Duke of Alba as commander of the projected expedition against Geneva and the Evangelical Swiss Confederacy; and II., the Lady Jane Grey, whom Herr Kortüm appears to regard as a kind of Protestant saint and martyr.

M. Alfred Maury, noting the existence of an historical element in the sciences, and wishing to impress on the public mind a conviction of the superiority of scientific truth to literary ornamentation, has attempted, in "Les Académies d'Autrefois," to sketch the history of two remarkable societies, L'ancienne Académie des Sciences, and L'ancienne Académie des Inscriptions et Belles Lettres, choosing the former for the scientific illustration which it supplies, and discerning in both alike a certain historical interest.[10] The present volume deals only with the Académie des Sciences. This institution was the creation of Colbert. Under the patronage of the Grand Monarque it began its sittings on

---

[8] "Kirchengeschichte von Friedr. Rud. Hasse," weil. Consistorialrath Dr. z. ord. Prof. der evangel. Theologie in Bonn. Herausgegeben von Lic. Dr. August Kohler, a. o. Prof. der Theologie in Erlangen. Erster Band. London: David Nutt. 1864.

[9] "Geschichtliche Forschungen im gebiete des Altertbums, des Mittelalters und der Neuzeit von Dr. Friedrich Kortüm," &c. Nach dessen Tode herausgegeben von Dr. Karl Alexander Freiherrn von Reichlin-Meldegg offentl. ordentl. Professor der Philosophie ebendaselbst. London: David Nutt. 1863.

[10] "Les Académies d'Autrefois. L'ancienne Académie des Sciences." Par L. F. Alfred Maury, Membre de l'Institut, Professor d'Histoire et Morale au Collège de France. London: David Nutt. 1864.

the 22nd December, 1666, in one of the rooms of the royal library. A peculiarity of this society, and one which supplied our author with an additional motive for the preparation of this work, lay in its cosmopolitan character.   It availed itself from the first of the suggestions and co-operation of foreigners.   Huyghens, Cassini, Newton, were early associated with it.   At the commencement, it enrolled as its correspondents Flamsteed, Briggs, Eisenschmid, Viviani (the pupil of Galileo), Marchetti (the successor of Borelli), Bayle, Basnage, and Papin.   It will be readily understood that the most illustrious names in science, the great mathematicians, the great astronomers, the famous chemists, the most renowned physicists and physiologists, are all registered in M. Maury's historical table.   The work they did is briefly indicated, and thus we are furnished with an outline of scientific progress.   It is quite impossible to give the details here.   After a brilliant career of more than a century and a quarter, the Academy was suppressed by the Republican Government on the 8th August, 1793.   It may be said, however, to have been represented in the National Institute, founded by the same government about two years after, and to have been re-established in 1816, as a branch of that magnificent corporation.   M. Maury has produced in his sketch of its origin and development a volume that is both pleasant and instructive.

M. Maury's countryman, Amédée Gabourd, has published the first volume of a history of our own times,[11] in which, while giving the lion's share to France, as the directress of the social movement, the initiative power, the apostle of thought and intelligence, he records the leading events that have taken place in other countries since the Revolution of 1830.   Notwithstanding his admiration for France, which, with an almost Jewish enthusiasm he regards as divinely chosen to serve as the instrument with which the Supreme works out his majestic purposes, he seems to us to write with considerable freedom and impartiality. His religious predilections necessarily lead to conclusions which we cannot accept ; nor have we any sympathy with that extension of the Catholic domain, or that military guardianship of Rome, which he so proudly eulogizes.   In spite, however, of this patriotic and theological partizanship, M. Gabourd tells the story of European contemporary history with certainly a proximate accuracy, and as he "retains the old habit of loving liberty and welcoming its conquests," we find ourselves generally in sufficient accordance with his views, and quite willing to concede that, if he does look through a pair of French spectacles, he sees other countries in the world besides his own.   The portion of this contemporaneous "History" before us falls into three principal divisions.   Having in an introduction characterized the Restoration and the Bourbon government, from 1814 to the catastrophe which drove Charles X. from his throne, he describes the situation of France and of Europe, down to the period of dissatisfaction and disorder which followed the establishment of the bourgeois monarchy of July.   The subject of the second book is

---

11 " Histoire Contemporaine, comprenant les principaux Événements qui se sont accomplis depuis la Revolution de 1830, jusqu'à nos Jours," &c.   Par Amédée Gabourd.   Tome premier.   London : David Nutt.   1863.

the reaction, not only in France, but in Europe, against the revolutionary movement. As the separation of Belgium from Holland was related in the first book, so the Polish insurrection is a leading topic of the second. The third book relates the events connected with the progress of the revolutionary movement, and the new expedients employed for keeping it down. The Bristol riot, the insurrection at Lyons, the affairs of Greece, are discussed in the final section of the volume, which closes with the death of Casimir Perier. M. Gabourd undertakes to delineate the social, artistic, and literary movement, as well as the political events of the period which he has chosen to illustrate. To some extent the social characteristics of the times are almost unavoidably noticed; but we presume that he reserves for a future occasion the formal statement of his views on this, as well as on the other complementary subjects of his historical essay.

The insurrection of Greece, which receives some notice in M. Gabourd's pages, is treated at great length by its appropriate historian, Spiridion Tricoupi; a second and corrected edition of whose comprehensive work, written in a sort of *classical* modern Greek, invites the attention of the studious and sanguine Philohellenist, more especially at a new crisis in the fate of the land in which he is interested.[12] Believing in the regeneration of Greece, and in the justice and grandeur of her cause, the historian pronounces her struggle for liberty to be an event that confers honour on humanity, and bids us hear in the blast of her battle-trumpet an angel's hymn to the Most High. Turning to the passage in which he discusses the character of the Greek Governor, Capo d'Istria, we see that while he recognises his worth he is by no means blind to his faults. In vindicating his patriotism, he maintains that the President did not seek the government of Greece for the sake of Russia, but courted Russia for the sake of Greece. The chief aim of his administration was the promotion of the material improvement of Greece, as the basis and necessary preliminary of all other and all higher improvement. Tricoupi gives him credit for many serviceable qualities and admirable gifts; for courteous and conciliating diplomacy, vigilance and economy in government, a persuasive tongue and a charming pen. On the other hand, he attributes to him an exaggerated self-esteem. He did not hesitate to speak of himself as the saviour of Greece, while he reviled his predecessors in office, and went so far as to call the Phanariots and others all sorts of vituperative names. Possessing little faith in the capacity of the Greeks for constitutional government, he would have preferred the establishment of an absolute rule as better adapted, in his own judgment, to a people in a state of transition from slavery to freedom.

This view of the character of Capo d'Istria is confirmed by Dr. Karl Mendelsohn-Bartholdy, the eldest son, we believe, of the celebrated musical composer, who has written a complete memoir of the

---

[12] Σπυριδῶνος Τρικούπη. Ἱστορία τῆς Ἑλληνικῆς Ἐπαναστάσεως. Ἔκδοσις δευτέρα ἐπιθεωρηθεῖσα καὶ διορθωθεῖσα. In 4 vols. London: Taylor and Francis. 1862.

famous Corfiote count.[13] Equally with Tricoupi he testifies to his respectable church-going conduct, his finished diplomacy, and ready pen, but complains that he belongs to the school of "enlightened despotism," that wanted to do everything *for* the people, nothing *by* it, and fancied, as it were, that *much* governing was the same as *good* governing. Dr. Karl Mendelsohn-Bartholdy, however, appears to us to consider Capo d'Istria to have been less patriotic than Tricoupi does. Though allowing that in general he supported Russian views only where the common advantage of both countries justified his support, he accuses him of subserviency to the Czar, and, on one occasion at least, of a decided postponement of the interests of Greece. There was one thing, however, which our author thinks Capo d'Istria preferred to the welfare of either Greece or Russia—his own personal aggrandizement; and when Northern pretensions conflicted with his own claims, he grew discontented with his ally, though Russia was now his sole resource for putting down the constitutional party in Greece. His egoism, our author contends, was not a strong masculine egoism like that of Richelieu, which might have saved his country, but a weak feminine egoism which, after unchaining the passions of the people, left it long a prey to a fearful confusion. Accordingly he holds that the dagger of Mauromichalis struck the self-seeking President at the right moment, enabling him to fall with the glory of a martyr and procuring him the honourable posthumous distinction of the new Timoleon. Born 11th February, 1776, he died 9th October, 1831.

We have given the son precedence of the father, as an author, not the subject of a biography.[14] The letters of Felix Mendelsohn, (1833—1847), of which Karl is one of the editors, have been translated by Lady Wallace, in what seems to be very readable English. Commencing directly after the termination of the former volume which contained the letters from Switzerland and Italy, the present volume brings us down to the last scene of all, the great composer's death. In addition to a good deal of musical criticism that will attract only those who cultivate the glorious art, there are notices of Mendelsohn's life and vocation, as the account of his appointment at Berlin, that will interest the general reader. We particularly admire the fine answer of Mendelsohn when he felt unable to comply with the royal request to compose music for the Eumenides : "I will always obey the commands of a sovereign so beloved by me, even at the sacrifice of my personal wishes and advantage. If I find I cannot do so with a good artistic conscience, I must endeavour candidly to state my scruples or my incapacity, and if that does not suffice, then I must go," &c.

---

[13] " Graf Johann Kapodistrias. Mit benutzung handschriftlichen Materials." Von Dr. Karl Mendelsohn-Bartholdy. London : David Nutt. 1864.
[14] " Letters of Felix Mendelsohn Bartholdy. From 1833 to 1847." Edited by Paul Mendelsohn-Bartholdy, of Berlin, and Dr. Karl Mendelsohn-Bartholdy, of Heidelberg. With a catalogue of all his musical compositions, compiled by Dr. Julius Rietz. Translated by Lady Wallace. London : Longman, Green, and Co. 1863.

The first volume of a Life of Karl Ritter, by Dr. Kramer, describes the boyhood and early education of that well-known geographer, his travels, his residence in Florence, Rome, and Naples; his maturer studies and occupations, and his marriage and settlement in Berlin.[15] It seems agreeably and intelligibly written; but could not the biographer tell the story of his hero's life in half the number of pages?

In a somewhat heterogeneous selection of German books, the next that "occurs," as the geologists say, is Dehnel's Reminiscences of German officers engaged in the British service, from the year of grace, or, as our author says, of war, 1805, to 1816.[16] The papers comprised in this volume are very miscellaneous. The first section begins with the Copenhagen affair in 1807, includes an account of the battle of Busaco and the lines of Torres Vedras, and ends with a drive in a waggon drawn by bullocks, from Burgos to Viseu. In a second division we find a notice of the siege of Ciudad Rodrigo and the battle of Waterloo. The storming of Badajos is a leading topic of the third division, and various exploits and different military trans- actions, chiefly relating to the Peninsular War, are described in the remaining sections.

The last German publication that we have to acknowledge, is Gustav de Veer's sketch of the life and times of the renowned Portuguese navigator, Prince Henry, introduced by an historical essay on the Portuguese trade and maritime affairs from the earliest period, the opening of the twelfth century, to the commencement of the fifteenth.[17] The discoverer of the Island of Madeira, the Azores, and various places on the west coast of Africa, has every title to have his history told and retold, in all the dialects of articulate-speaking men.

The life of the theologian Calixtus, Danish by allegiance and Hanoverian by position, has been drawn up, not without ability, though also not without a certain quaint affectation and perhaps unavoidable impotency of conclusion, by his ardent admirer, the Rev. W. C. Dow- ding,[18] a gentleman who is sanguine enough to nourish the hope that the conciliating theology of Calixtus may possibly have the same in- fluence on the mind of England now, it had on that of Germany formerly. George Calixtus was born at Flensburg, in Schleswig, in the autumn of 1586. At twelve years of age he was received into the Latin school of Flensburg. In his seventeenth year he entered the university of Helmstadt, of the student life of which in those good

---

[15] " Carl Ritter. Ein Lebensbild nach seinem handschriftlichem Nachlass dargestellt von. G. Kramer. Erster Theil. Nebst einem Bildniss Ritters. London : Williams and Norgate. 1864.

[16] " Erinnerungen deutscher Officiere in Britischen Diensten aus den Kriegs- jahren 1805 bis 1816, nach aufzeichnungen und mündlichen Erzählungen," &c. Von H. Debnel, Königlich-hannoverischer Oberst. London : David Nutt. 1864.

[17] " Prinz Heinrich der Seefahrer und seine Zeit." Von Gustav de Veer. Mit einem portrait, &c. London : David Nutt. 1864.

[18] " German Theology during the Thirty Years' War." The Life and Corre- spondence of George Calixtus, Lutheran Abbot of Königslutter, and Professor Primarius in the University of Helmstadt. By the Rev. W. C. Dowding, M.A. &c. Oxford and London : John Henry and James Parker. 1863.

old times Mr. Dowding gives us an edifying description. An excellent classic, and an accomplished Hebrew scholar, Calixtus was promoted to the office of ordinary professor of Theology in Jan. 1615, and a few years after, he married Catherine Gairtner, the daughter of a rich burgher of Helmstadt. A life of professional usefulness and learned leisure, spiced or peppered with frequent theological discussion, closed in a peaceful death in 1657. A man who like Calixtus lived amid the stirring scenes of the Thirty Years' War, who was associated in power and intellect with Casaubon, Vossius, and Grotius, and is mentioned with respect by Bossuet, must have been no common man. Opposed to the predominant stringent and exclusive Lutheranism, and favouring " the Melancthonian humanities," Calixtus seems to have represented the Broad Church of his own times. His efforts for comprehension, however, had precisely the success that might have been anticipated in days when men gravely disputed whether the blood of Christ, being inconceivably precious, the world's salvation had been purchased by *one* drop or by the *whole* of it—days when it was held by the vulgar that " God and Nature no longer did anything, but the witches did it all," and princes insisted that the magistrates should proceed against the imaginary crime of sorcery—the very same princes, perhaps, who "assumed to themselves the decision of theological truth, and embodied their dicta in some *corpus* or summary which was presented to their people upon the point of the sword." Mr. Dowding holds up Calixtus as a model ; but what did Calixtus accomplish ? Such was the force of bigotry, that at the Congress of Thorn, the Reformed party could not even record a statement of their faith, nor the Lutheran obtain a hearing. Nay, so opposed was Calovius, a Lutheran zealot, to any plan for the inclusion of the Calvinists, that Calixtus gave up the discussion. Thus, though present in Thorn, the man who had made peace the object of his life took no part in the Conference. After it had cost the citizens 50,000 florins, it failed, and " what before was said of Dort was repeated with justice of this wasted effort."

> " Quid synodus ? nodus.   Patrum chorus integer ? æger.
>   Conventus ? Ventus.   Gloria ? stramen, amen."

So intractable is the spirit of theology ; so indefinable, evasive, and undemonstrable is its dogma!

Happily, " where Luther preached another preacher came whom we know as Goethe !" The life of this high-priest of truth and beauty has been pourtrayed, as the life of such a man rarely is pourtrayed, by Mr. Lewes.[19] His record of the career of the greatest European poet since Shakespeare will occupy a permanent place in the biographical section of our libraries. For fidelity, research, narrative ability, clearness and completeness of exposition, critical insight, and transparent purity of language, it deserves almost unqualified praise. The sale of thirteen thousand copies of this work in England and Germany is a proof of the estimation in which it is held. In the cheaper and

---

[19] " The Life of Goethe." By George Henry Lewes. Second Edition. Partly rewritten. London : Smith, Elder, and Co. 1864.

more compact form which it has assumed, in the new English edition, it is likely to become still more popular. To enhance its value Mr. Lewes has partly rewritten it, introducing new material, as well as correcting and reconstructing it. By means of personal corroboration, by actual consultation of those "who lived under the same roof" with the poet, by the inspection of a mass of printed testimony, controlled and completed by the evidence of unprinted papers, Mr. Lewes has "sought to acquire and reproduce a definite image of the living man, and not simply of the man as he appeared in all the reticence of print." Occasional alterations, additions, or omissions may be discovered in the pages of this revised "Biography," as in the explanation of the love-affair with Frederica, the extract from a letter humorously describing the backward state of historical study at the University of Tübingen at the end of the eighteenth century, the sentences at the commencement of the now separate chapter on Goethe's wife, and the modifications in the magnificent survey of "The Poet as a Man of Science;" but the book is essentially the same book now that it was when it was first published some ten or twelve years ago, so that we may greet it as an old friend, finding the old memories and old associations undisturbed.

Mr. George Ticknor's Life of Mr. Prescott, in an illustrated quarto volume, has some agreeable and interesting pages, but is surely unnecessarily long.[20] The blind historian, as we learn from it, had many estimable qualities. He was amiable, patient, and persevering. Naturally gay and volatile, he broke himself into habits of regularity and industry. The accident by which he became ultimately blind, or all but blind, occurred at college—the result of a frolic or chance-medley. The author of "Ferdinand and Isabella," "The Conquest of Mexico," and "Philip II.," had many English friends and acquaintances, among them Macaulay, Milman, Lord Carlisle, and Sir Charles Lyell. His merits as an historian were recognised by Hallam and others whose praise is honour. When the late Mr. Thackeray visited him, he saw "on the library-wall of one of the most famous writers of America, two crossed swords which his relatives wore in the great War of Independence," and noted the fact, to Mr. Prescott's gratification, at the commencement of "The Virginians." There are many pleasing incidents recorded in Mr. Ticknor's volume. He shows us faithfully his hero's characteristics, discloses his ways of life and work, and registers his opinions. Mr. Prescott twice instituted an inquiry into Christianity, and in both instances came to a similar conclusion—that is, he rejected the orthodox version of that religion for a sort of vague Unitarianism. One of the most sweeping literary censures that we ever read is pronounced by this author on a book which we venture to think testifies to the possession of undoubted genius on the part of its writer, if ever book did. Speaking of "*The French Revolution*," Mr. Prescott says: "Carlyle is even a bungler at his own business; for his creations, or rather combinations, in this way, are the most discordant and awkward possible. As he runs altogether for dramatic, or rather picturesque effect, he is not to be

[20] "Life of William Hickling Prescott." By George Ticknor. Trübner and Co. 1864.

challenged, I suppose, with want of original views. This forms no part of his plan. His views certainly, as far as I can estimate them, are trite enough. And, in short, the whole thing, in my humble opinion, both as to *forme* and to *fond*, is perfectly contemptible." After this we can only add that William Hickling Prescott, who was born in Salem, New England, on the fourth day of May, 1796, died the twenty-eighth of January, 1859.

We must content ourselves with a simple recognition of the biographical existence of two other transatlantic worthies—John Winthrop, the Governor of Massachusetts, A.D. 1630, but an Englishman by birth,[21] and Edward Livingstone, the adviser of Jackson,[22] when President of the United States, and the legislator to whose lot, Mr. Bancroft tells us, it fell "to adjust the old municipal laws, derived from France and Spain, to the new condition of the connexion with America."

The same year which saw Winthrop installed as Governor of Massachusetts witnessed the imprisonment of Sir John Elliot, the leader of that patriotic assembly, of which Hallam says:—"In asserting the illegality of arbitrary detention, of compulsory loans, of tonnage and poundage levied without consent of Parliament, they stood in defence of positive rights won by their fathers, the prescriptive inheritance of Englishmen." A sketch of the life of Sir John Eliot, designated by the same authority the most illustrious confessor in the cause of liberty whom that time produced, was included by Mr. Forster in his "British Statesmen," published many years ago.[23] The present Life of this champion of English freedom cannot be described as an expansion of that miniature biography. It is an entirely new work, demanding inordinate labour in preparation, and extreme care and diligence in execution. Loaded with fact, and oppressive with detail, this valuable contribution to the history of the Stuart period will at once invite curiosity and exhaust patience. Based on Eliot's hitherto inherited papers, in the possession of his descendant Lord St. Germans, it professes to reflect what is important in his correspondence, and in the abstracts of his speeches, and on the memoirs drawn up by himself. In addition to materials supplied by these papers, often decipherable only after the most persevering inspection, Mr. Forster has derived information from public documents, as well as from a private collection of his own. The result is a complete and circumstantial biography of the great Cornishman, not only exhibiting the personal characteristics of the man, but presenting such a picture of the opening of the struggle against the government of Charles I, as the author may well suppose to be "in many respects more detailed and accurate than has yet been afforded." In relating the incidents of the hero's life, Mr.

---

[21] "Life and Letters of John Winthrop, Governor of the Massachusett's Bay Company at their Emigration to New England, 1630." By Robert C. Winthrop. Boston: Ticknor and Fields. 1864.
[22] "Life of Edward Livingstone." By Charles Havens Hunt. With an Introduction by George Bancroft. New York: D. Appleton and Co. 1864.
[23] "Sir John Eliot: a Biography, 1590-1632." By John Forster. In Two Vols. London: Longman, Green, and Co. 1864.

Forster has not neglected the opportunity of vindicating him against both the misrepresentations of party spirit and the perversions of the elder D'Israeli, to whom portions of the papers were submitted about thirty years ago, when he was engaged in preparing his Commentaries on the Life of Charles the First. In the volumes before us, the entire story of Eliot's life from his youthful days is set forth. His early tastes and pursuits, his conduct as Vice-Admiral of Devon, his career as member for Newport, his views on politics, religion, literature, indicating, with a certain allowance for his age, a sound philosophy, and perhaps irrespectively of all allowance, a commendable scholarship : the part he took as the great opposition leader in the impeachment of the Duke of Buckingham, in the resistance to the Forced Loan, and the assertion of the Petition of Right, and lastly his imprisonment and death, are all recorded in these volumes, which attest the indomitable diligence, the unfailing power of investigation, the enduring patience in composition, and the masculine thought and sound sense of their author. Our chief apprehension is that Mr. Forster has lost in breadth what he has gained in length, that his readers will sometimes be reminded of the epigrammatic saying of the Greek poet, and think how much better *one* of these volumes, if it had told the tale of Eliot's life, with discreet omission and wise condensation, would have been than *both*.

It is scarcely possible to institute a parallel between the representative of the expansive spirit of English liberty and the defender of the oligarchical Roman constitutionalism.[24] Yet Cicero, weak and vacillating as he often was, no doubt took what was the patriotic side, in opposing the ambition of Cæsar, and desiring, we can hardly say endeavouring, to establish the rotten aristocratical republic of Rome on its old foundations. Cicero justified and gloried in the overthrow of the man who, with all his shortcomings, more truly represented humanity than the sentimental stoic Marcus Brutus, who, according to Mr. George Long, " became an assassin in the name of freedom, which meant triumph of his party, and in the name of virtue, which meant nothing." A "Life of Cicero " written by a competent scholar and in wholesome every-day English is a book which, we think, will prove a valuable addition to our vernacular classical biography. Mr. Forsyth has, in calling up once more this great Roman writer, made a successful effort to show us not only the orator and the politician, but the father, the husband, the friend, the gentleman. An admirer of Cicero, he is no apologist for his frailties, his vanities, his insincerities. Thus he admits that to oblige Brutus, who was evidently a man who had an eye to the main chance, Cicero abused his proconsular authority, when he declined to allow the Cyprians to deposit the sum really due to that judicious money-lender, though nominally to Matinius and Scaptius, his friends, the latter of whom first tried to cheat his debtors by pretending that they owed him more than they actually did, and

[24] "Life of Marcus Tullius Cicero." By William Forsyth, M.A., Q.C., Author of "Hortensius, &c., and late Fellow of Trinity College, Cambridge. In Two Vols. With Illustrations. London : John Murray. 1864.

who when his allegation was disproved, entreated Cicero to let the matter stand over, hoping apparently that under a new governor he might get the illegal percentage, to which by the contract he had undeniably a right, though he had no right to increase the interest by refusing to take the offered principal. Nor was this the only instance in which, to please Brutus, Cicero abused his official power, though the case of Ariobarzanes was far less flagrant. So again Mr. Forsyth expresses a fear that in his hollow reconciliation with Vatinius and Gabinius he sacrificed not only his previous enmities but his principles; forfeiting his own self-respect and losing his influence in the senate and the rostra. On the other hand, Mr. Forsyth calls attention to the general excellence of Cicero's government. He says, and says with truth, that his administration deserved almost unqualified praise. " It is no light merit in Cicero to have been in advance of the morality of his age, and amidst the darkness of Paganism (?) to have exhibited the equity and self-denial of a Christian statesman. But a government was just a sphere in which he was fitted to shine. His love of justice, his kindness, his humanity, his disinterestedness were qualities which all there came into play without the disturbing causes which at Rome misled him more than once ' to know the best and yet the worse pursue,' " Mr. Forsyth's estimate of Cicero's moral character seems to us fair, and his critical judgment of his writings correct. But is not the assertion that he is the greatest master of the music of speech that has ever yet appeared among mankind, somewhat sweeping? Is he really superior to Plato, for instance? Or are the great poets of Greece, Italy, England, less melodious than the first essayist and orator of Rome?

The last book on our list carries us back into the twilight of history, describing the manners and customs, warlike and pacific, of the people of Asshur, to whom Mr. Rawlinson assigns an antiquity of more than 1800 years B.C.[25] This antiquity is divisible into two periods, one marked by the commencement of the empire about B.C. 1260, and continuing to its close, and the other distinguished by the seemingly dependent existence of the Assyrian people as far back, if we may trust the date, as B.C. 1820, when "Shamas-Iva, the son of Ismi-Dagon. King of Chaldea, built a temple to Anü and Iva at Asshur, which was then the Assyrian capital." Asshur was not only the name of the country—it was also the name of the supreme god of the country. This god Mr. Rawlinson supposes to have been the deified descendant of Noah, the so-called son of Shem. It is more probable that the writer, or the antecedent tradition which he followed, *euhemerized* the god into a man; but our author's account of this deity is, from paucity of material, extremely unsatisfactory. One thing, however, comes out with great clearness, if we may rely on

---

[25] "The Five Great Monarchies of the Ancient Eastern World; or, the History, Geography, and Antiquities of Chaldea, Assyria, Babylon, Media, and Persia, collected and illustrated from ancient and modern sources. By George Rawlinson, M.A., Camden Professor of Ancient History in the University of Oxford, late Fellow and Tutor of Exeter College. In Four Vols. Vol. II. London: Murray. 1864.

the inscription-interpreters; we mean the intensely theological
Jewish character of the Assyrian mode of thought. With the
Assyrians, Asshur was the national god, as Jehovah was with the
Jews. Thus, as Asshur's people, they are appointed to the government of the four regions: the fear of Asshur falls upon their defeated
and flying enemies: at the invitation of Asshur, an expedition into
a neighbouring land is undertaken; and when a country not previously
subject to Assyria is attacked, it is because the inhabitants do not
acknowledge Asshur. In addition to the historical and chronological
elements of interest, there is much in Mr. Rawlinson's present volume
which it is agreeable to read about, and the numerous woodcuts scattered over the pages help us to realize the life of this ancient people,
who, it appears, anticipated us in the use of the magnifying-glass, who
constructed tunnels and aqueducts, employed the pulley, the lever, and
the roller, enamelled, cut gems, and inlaid. If we are not always convinced of the correctness of Mr. Rawlinson's views, and are inclined to
look with a suspensive scepticism on the pictures of the past which
archæological enthusiasm revives for us, we are still grateful to him
for writing a readable and pleasant book which embodies our real or
supposed knowledge of the world's ancient empires.

BELLES LETTRES.

SINCE the Paris Exposition of 1855 disclosed to our neighbours the
hitherto unsuspected fact that a school of English painting existed,
the subject has attracted considerable attention among French art-
critics, by whom, for the most part, its special merits have been amply
recognised. According to M. Ernest Chesneau,[1] his countrymen, in
their surprise at the unexpected discovery that the dull Briton could
paint at all, have fallen into the opposite extreme, and have not only
been betrayed into exaggerated admiration, but have given way to a
ridiculous dread of possible rivalry between the artists of France and
England. Such a contingency he dismisses as too preposterous to be
seriously entertained by any one who is acquainted with the past history and present prospects of art in the two countries. For, as he
conclusively affirms, the special characteristic of English art is the
absence of genius; whereas the distinguishing peculiarity of the French
school is that profound love of truth, subordinating all things to itself,
which is a quality "*tout à fait Française.*" But there is also in M.
Chesneau's book not a little sound criticism, and, on the whole, a fair
and judicious estimate of the chief works by the best masters on both
sides of the Channel. Many chapters are devoted to the examination
in detail of the French Exhibition of last year, but the earlier part of
the volume contains a rapid review of the progress of painting in

---

[1] "L'Art et les Artistes Modernes en France et en Angleterre." Par Ernest
Chesneau. Paris: Didiér. London: Nutt. 1864.

France and England, and is well worthy of perusal, although the remarks on English art are sometimes more true than flattering, as may be seen by the following passage:—

"From whatever point of view we regard it, the English school reveals one striking peculiarity of the British mind. The works of this school do not indicate the faintest recognition of the value of painting for its own sake, considered as one of the fine arts. The art of painting appears to answer to no intellectual need of the English—to no real sentiment of beauty or of artistic expression. It is evident to me that for them a picture is an object of luxury; the acquisition of a *chef d'œuvre* is a sign of wealth and distinction which must therefore be produced. but they promise themselves no delight in the contemplation of such a masterpiece. This is at the bottom of the artistic taste of England, and this explains why the buyers of pictures care much more for singularity than for simple beauty; hence their painters, whatever may be their natural tendency, think themselves bound to sacrifice everything to eccentricity and, in consequence, to bad taste. This submission to the caprice of the public is much greater and more apparent in British art than in our own, where there is, nevertheless, far too much of it. Thanks to the accumulation of large fortunes, the artist on the other side of the Channel knows beforehand which is his true public—that which pays; he knows perfectly well that there is but one class which will encourage and reward his efforts; and to this end he becomes a courtier. Was Hogarth any other than the courtier of the Puritan society of his time? On this score, it ought not to surprise us that art has flourished so little hitherto in England. It is true she professes the liveliest admiration for her great men. But do not let us be the dupes of the tombs in Westminster Abbey, nor of the columns nor statues set up in the public squares; the English have but a moderate esteem for their contemporaries while they are only on the road to greatness, and their courtesy barely extends to men of taste. Artists, in their eyes, are machines made for the express purpose of amusing and enlivening the aristocracy. Is that a fitting estimate of the great and the elevated in art? Hence the words grandeur, elevation, should be banished when the British painter is under consideration. They have a firm *naïveté* which soon becomes monotonous; they are prodigal of effects—effects literary as well as pictorial. Nevertheless the qualities they have are thoroughly their own. Thus, in *genre* pieces they display powers of observation; in landscape they are great in skies, in which they show a marked superiority; they render those ever-varying effects with great care, and seize the uncounted varieties of aspect. Nor, lastly, should we forget that they number among them illustrious portrait-painters, nor that portrait-painting is one of the most difficult of arts. But there is no evidence in the English school of any serious efforts (?); the latest school of all, rich in the experience of the past, it has produced very little, and originated nothing whatever."—p. 108.

But in spite of these severe strictures, M. Chesneau does ample justice to the rare and great beauties of Gainsborough, Reynolds, and Turner; and shows that he can admire as heartily as he can censure.

The works of another French writer, well known in England by his translation of "Childe Harold," and his "Etudes sur l'Angleterre," contributed to the "Revue des Deux Mondes," are in course of publication by his widow.[2] The sudden death of M. de Pontès, at the age of fifty-

---

[2] "Etudes sur l'Orient. Par Lucien Davesiès de Pontés. Paris: Michel Lévy, Frères. 1864.

three, in 1859, cut short a career which had seemed to promise a greater eminence than he lived to attain. Madame de Pontès has set herself the task of collecting and printing all his writings contributed on various subjects to different Reviews, and the present volume is the first that has yet appeared. It contains notes upon Greece written while the author was an officer in the French navy, and essays on the East reprinted from the "Revue des Deux Mondes" and other periodicals. They are well written, fresh, and graphic, and convey the impression of accurate knowledge and personal observation. The short introductory memoir which occupies the first forty pages of the volume, by "Bibliophile Jacob" (Paul Lacroix), slightly sketches a life and character of no ordinary interest, and excites the wish for the more complete biography which the writer intimates an intention to undertake at some future day.

The valuable works on Indian Literature of the late Boden Professor of Sanscrit,[3] are in course of publication under the editorship of Dr. Reinhold Rost. Of the four volumes already published, the two first consist of Essays and Lectures on the Religion of the Hindus, and the remaining two are upon Sanscrit Literature, with translations and abstracts of noted works of fiction and poetry. Nearly fifty years have elapsed since Professor Wilson, then assistant-surgeon in the service of the East India Company, published a translation of the Meghadúta, and from that time until his death in 1860, he pursued the study of Oriental literature with indefatigable zeal. A complete edition of his works, many of which are scarce and not accessible, from having been originally published in the Transactions of Oriental Societies, will form a most valuable and important work, and brings within the reach of the English reader much which has hitherto been known only to Sanscrit scholars. Volumes iv., v., and vi., on the Books of the Rig-Veda, are preparing for publication.

A Tamil Drama,[4] translated by a native of Ceylon, barrister-at-law of Lincoln's Inn, and member of Her Majesty's Legislative Council of Ceylon, is a curiosity in the history of letters. In a graceful and admirably well expressed dedication to the Queen, the translator claims to be the first who has sought that honour "of those millions of Orientals over whom you have been declared the first British Empress, and to whom by the proclamation last issued under the sanction of your august name, you have accorded a charter of rights which opens up to them new careers of usefulness and happiness." The introduction, which is written in perfectly idiomatic English, is the composition of one well versed in ancient and modern letters and languages, and briefly and clearly explains the origin of the drama of *Arichandra.* Although it is extremely popular both in Southern India and Tamil-Ceylon, no recognised text exists. "The manuscripts are chiefly written on the leaves of the Palmyra palm, and the facility which

[3] "Re-issue of the principal Works of the late Horace Hayman Wilson." Collected and edited by Dr. Reinhold Rost. Trübner & Co. 1864.
[4] "Arichandra, the Martyr of Truth." A Tamil drama, translated into English by Mutu Coomára Swámy, Mudeliár, M.R.A.S. London : Smith, Elder, & Co. 1863.

manuscripts always offer for interpolation and alteration has enabled the inhabitants of the various districts which constitute the immense *Tamil-land* of India to modify the original, without, however, completely recasting it, in such a manner as to suit the peculiar tastes and fancies of different classes at different periods." Even the date of this play is unknown; it is only conjectured to have been in existence for about 500 years. It is the history of the greatness, the virtues, the sufferings, and the invincible constancy of Arichandra, King of Ayòdiah (supposed to be Oude), who undergoes all the trials of Job and all the tortures of a Christian martyr rather than tell a lie, and who is at last restored to greatness and honour, blest by Siva in these words:—"You have borne your severe trials most heroically, and have proved to all men that virtue is of greater worth than all the vanities of a fleeting world." This is the high moral throughout this singular and most interesting drama, and the surprise with which we receive it, suggests how much we have yet to learn of the Eastern mind. With some little irony, the accomplished translator justly observes :—

" It may be a source of some encouragement to those who inculcate the desirability of improving the benighted Indians with a better code of morals than that which their own systems of philosophy teach, that even amongst them are to be found admirers of such characters as Arichandra, who, though persecuted for his persistent adherence to truth and virtue, yet maintains his constancy to the last, regardless of consequences, in the midst of the most excruciating tortures, and in the presence of death itself. The story of Arichandra may be a myth ; but the response which its representation meets with in the hearts of a large section of the Hindus is a fact."

The original play is partly in prose and partly in verse of different metres, and the absence of scenery is made up for by the actors, who describe what the spectators are to imagine they see. The dialogue is often eloquent, poetical, and impassioned, and every line conveys some eastern image or thought. In the history of the trials and temptations of the hero, it is impossible not to be reminded of the story of Job, but through all a deep abiding fatalism may be traced. It is thus that Sattyakirti, the faithful minister, seeks to console Arichandra when the unhappy monarch has been compelled to sell even his Queen to enable him to keep his word :—

" Most noble king! succumb you, then, to misfortune ? Is this, after all, the fruit of your knowledge and wisdom ? Oh, no ! Forget not that truth is more precious than all earthly happiness—that it must be maintained anyhow, at the risk of life, even in the face of Death himself. Sire, by far easier is it to count the number of the sands which cover the shores whence rebound the mighty waves of the ocean, or to ascertain the number of the atoms which constitute *Meru*, the loftiest mountain of the universe, than to enumerate the number of the births which our sins have already necessitated, and which we shall yet be compelled to pass through before final rest awaits us. Poor souls ! we are tossed hither and thither, washed by the waves of Destiny from world to world, sphere to sphere, age to age, bounding from death to life, and from life rebounding to death ; children once—fathers again ; a husband now—a wife anon ; now a king—now a slave ; now a man—now a beast ; till our merits and demerits are cancelled off—till the heavenly *sàyncchya* [absorption of the soul into God] welcomes us to eternal bliss. Foolish man clings to this earth, and cries out, 'Oh, this is my land, this my field, this my home—who dare take it from me? How can I part with it?' Knows he how many worlds have already owned him, and disown him now? He hugs his wife closely, and proclaims, 'Oh, this is my partner, this my love! who dare remove her from me? How can I exist separated from her?' Know you how many thousands of women have called themselves your wives, and how many millions of children have cried out to you, 'Father! father?' When such is life, why weep you? Battle with Fate itself. What must be done will be done. Grieve not because evils beset you and unhappiness is your lot; but grasp the sword of wisdom, demolish the wild phantasies of the wicked mind, then mount the winged horse of reason, scale the heights of knowledge, and learn that where happiness is, there also unhappiness must necessarily be. Seek the one, and you seek the other as well: for pleasure ever ends in pain, whilst pain ever leads to pleasure. Such is the common lot of humanity."—p. 163.

The author of an Essay on Beauty explains that he found his subject too much for him, and has therefore postponed the examination of poetic and picturesque beauty until he can prepare another volume.[5] Meanwhile he publishes his first Essay on Natural Beauty, and propounds a theory on the subject as harmless as it is naïve. Having discovered that in the Septuagint version of the book of Genesis, that passage in the narrative of the creation which our version renders " behold it was very *good*," is there translated " behold it was very *beautiful*," and, remembering also that we use the expression "good-looking," he has satisfied himself that beauty is goodness and goodness is beauty, and proceeds to apply and develope his discovery. It is not easy to feel the force of the arguments by which Mr. Purton imagines that he has demonstrated the absolute coincidence of moral and spiritual with natural and visible beauty, or, as he expresses it, "The fruits of the Spirit are love, joy, peace beyond and above long-suffering; and the virtues of our warfare, and their perfectly reflected image or expression are—light, life, and harmony." But the subject of Natural Beauty has drawn the author into " much that seems connected with it," and an appendix which fills nearly half the book is devoted to these kindred themes. The reader will be hardly prepared to find that they consist of a discussion on the nature of the fall of man—a theory on the personality of the devil or devils—a very remarkable discovery that before man was degraded by polygamy " for children to be born twins, male and female, *i.e.*, husband and wife, was the original law of nature "—and an examination of the causes which have produced the unequal standard by which society judges of different moral offences. We must own our inability to trace the connexion between these dark and mysterious themes and the abstract nature of beauty, although it is clear that the author writes in sober seriousness and earnest good faith.

The same theory of beauty is expressed far more dogmatically, and applied to the human face and form with uncompromising logic, in an

---

[5] " Philocalia: Elementary Essays on Natural, Poetic, and Picturesque Beauty." By Wm. Purton, M.A. London: Whitaker. 1864.

amusing little essay " On Ugly People,"[6] which asserts that " all that is morally good is physically beautiful. All that is morally bad is physically ugly ; *ergo*, every man and woman may be beautiful if they like, and no man or woman has a right to be ugly.—Q. E. D." It would be perhaps nearer the truth, to say that ugliness is too often the undeserved penalty of wronged humanity, caused by the inherited sins of progenitors, and intensified by bad food, bad air, starved heart and brain, and the lack of all that gives joy and beauty to life : who has not shuddered at the hideous countenances of even infants which swarm in the dark alleys of great towns ? But our author has more to say against the inexcusable and unnecessary fault of ugliness :—

" Take the case of my excellent friend Mr. Towers. Look at his nose, and his nose only—at that nose, rubicund and Bardolphian, out of all proportion to any ordinary face ; a nose pimpled and freckled, bearing blossoms like a tree, and of the colour of the peony—a nose that is a *bonâ-fide grogometer*—and judge him by that only, and you shall, at a casual glance, pronounce him ugly. But Mr. Towers is not ugly. The physical deformity is, no doubt, obvious enough, and suggests ugliness enough to the passer-by. But hear him talk. Listen to his wit. Let him unlock in your presence the abundant stores of his learning. See him pile a brick of wisdom here and another there. See him ransack all the brick-kilns of the ancients and the moderns, and watch the house of Fancy or of Learning that he will build with them. Go with him into private life and see what a joyous companion he is, what a good friend, what a good husband, what a kind father, what a pure-minded citizen,—and in the light of his moral and intellectual excellence, you will look at his ugly nose and admit that the face is beautiful—aye, that the nose itself is more beautiful than many a nose that Phidias or Praxiteles delighted to model, but which belonged to a countenance that was not impermeated with and moulded by these noble qualities.

" Take Trimmles, another man I know, and look at him as he walks along the street—small, spare, and with a slight and scarcely perceptible hunch on his back ; and at the first glance you shall call him ugly. But you will be in error if you do. Physically, he may seem to be ugly ; but his mind is a melody and a harmony. He is a logician who could argue with Euclid. He sees daylight in the darkest corners of disputation with a mental eye, over which there is no film or darkness. He talks with eloquent tongue, and neither woman nor man can resist the fascination of his company. How can such a person be called ugly ? In spite of his small stature and his hunch, Trimmles is handsomer than silly Captain Fitz-Mortimer of the Rifles, who has a straight back, a Roman nose, and a beard that Methuselah might envy.

" Then take the case of Theodosia Perkins—fresh, fair, twenty-three, and passably rich. She has a face and a form that a sculptor might love to imitate. But she is pert—she flirts—she has a bad opinion of her own sex and of the other—she has no education of the heart or of the mind—she has no taste for colour, for tune, for propriety—she is 'fast'—she is 'loud'—she is eaten up with vanity and conceit, and thinks herself the very cream and quintessence of the world. In one word, she is ugly in spite of her face and form. To look at her is sufficient to know that she will find no one to marry her, except for her money ; and to prophesy, that after she is married her husband will detest her.

---

[6] " The Gouty Philosopher ; or the Friends, Acquaintances, Opinions, Whims and Eccentricities of John Wagstaff, Esq." By Charles Mackay. London : Saunders and Otley. 1864.

"Take also the case of young Master Wigram. He was born a pretty child, aud might have grown up to be a beautiful boy; but he is intensely ugly. He has been humoured and fondled without reason one day, and punished without reason the next; he has been indulged in all his caprices in the morning, and denied his just and natural requirements in the evening. He has been coaxed and petted, coerced and punished, equally without justification; and the result is, that he is the plague of every one who comes near him. He is built up of evil passions. There is not a good thing about him. He is a slave one minute and a tyrant the next; niggardly and extravagant—clement and cruel. Though but fifteen years of age, he is ugly in the extreme, because he has not a single moral or intellectual quality to keep his physical qualities in good countenance. It comes to this—that whatever physical nature may have done, or may have neglected to do for us, the power of being beautiful remains with ourselves. . . . . I know an old woman, of seventy-three years of age, of a beauty as much superior to that of seventeen as that of snowy Mont Blanc to verdant Primrose Hill. Lovely are the snow-white locks, neatly parted over her serene forehead; lovely are the accents of her soft voice, that speaks loving-kindness to all the world; lovely is the smile that starts from her eyes, courses to her lips, and lights up all her countenance, when she fondles a child, or gives counsel of wisdom to young man or maid; lovely is she even in her mild reproof of a wrong-doer—so mild and gentle —so more than half-divine,—that he or she who relapses afterwards into wickedness, is reckless and hardened indeed."—p. 191.

Mr. Wagstaffe has views not less positive and as strongly expressed on various other subjects, especially on smoking, or the use of slang words by persons who should know better; and on the twenty-five capital offences of criticasters. He is always racy and sensible, and we recommend the lucubrations of the Gouty Philosopher to all who can appreciate his plain-spoken wisdom, and who will not quarrel with his lamentations over modern degeneracy in thought, manners, and language. On this last head some few useful remarks will be found in Dean Alford's notes on the Queen's English,[7] which make their third public appearance in a neat, pleasant little gossiping volume. They first did duty as lectures to the Church of England Young Men's Literary Association, at Canterbury, were then printed in *Good Words*, and now, with some alterations and emendations, they form a small, separate book. The author explains that they were written in odd moments of time, as when waiting for the train at railway stations, which accounts for their superficial and often trivial character, and almost tempts the question, Why were they thought worth preserving? Some of the passages which had called forth the animadversions of critics have been altered, and the misquotation from the Book of Numbers, which gave the dean's pertinacious censor, Mr. Moon, an excuse for so much indignant vituperation, has been left out, and a verse from the Psalms substituted, that justifies the dean's appeal to "the great storehouse of good English" as his authority for placing the adverb before the verb. Mr. Moon was invited to hear the third lecture and to enjoy the hospitality of the dean, who thus, with

[7] "The Queen's English : Stray Notes on Speaking and Spelling." By Henry Alford, D.D. London : Strahan and Co. 1864.

more good-humour than dignity, laughs at the antagonist whose criticism he sagaciously disarmed :—

" I did what I could. I wrote a letter, inviting the chief of my censors to come to Canterbury and hear my third lecture. I wrote in some fear and trembling. All my adverbs were (what I should call) misplaced, that I might not offend him. But at last I was obliged to transgress, in spite of my good resolutions. I was promising to meet him at the station, and I was going to write, ' if you see on the platform *an old party in a shovel*, that will be I.' But my pen refused to sanction (to *endorse*, I believe I ought to say, but I cannot) the construction. ' *That will be me*' came from it, in spite, as I said, of my resolve of the best possible behaviour.'

We, nevertheless, protest against the dean's maxim that usage can excuse bad grammar, and trust that no one will be convinced by his reasoning in behalf of such expressions as "it is me," " I was going to," which he declares may be used colloquially without blame.

Mr. Cox has followed up his "Tales of the Gods and Heroes" with another little volume of Greek Legends,[8] in which the spirit of the original myth is well preserved, and the story given as nearly in the original form as the conflicting versions of poets will allow. The author is an earnest student of comparative mythology, and believes that a better understanding of it will cleanse the ancient classic myths of much that has seemed gross and revolting in their later forms. In a long and not very clearly-written Introduction, Mr. Cox seeks to establish the identity of Indian, Greek, and Scandinavian myths, and also to show how many of the Greek stories are but different versions of one and the same legend. Thus he writes :—

" If we can trace this recurrence of the same ideal in different heroes, and of the same imagery in the recital of their adventures in Hellenic mythology alone, the marvel is intensified a thousandfold when we compare this mythology with the ancient legends of Northern Europe or of the far distant East. There is scarcely an incident in the lives of the great Greek heroes which cannot be traced out in the wide field of Teutonic or Scandinavian tradition ; and the complicated action of the Iliad, or rather of the whole legend of which the Iliad forms a part, is reproduced in the Eddas and the lays of the Volsungs and the Nibelungs. If the Greek tales tell us of serpent slayers and the destroyers of noxious monsters, the legends of the ice-bound north also sing of heroes who slay the dragons that lie coiled round sleeping maidens. If the former recite the labours of Heracles and speak of the bondage of Apollo, Sifrit and Sigurdr are not less doomed to a life of labour for others, not for themselves. If Heracles alone can rescue Hesionê from a like doom with Andromeda, or bring back Alkêstis from the land of Hades, it is Sigurdr only who can slay the serpent Fafnir, and Ragnar Lodbrog alone who can deliver Thora from the dragon's grasp. If, at the end of his course, Heracles once more sees his early love—if Œnônê comes again to Paris in his death hour—so Brenhyldr lies down to die with Sigurdr, who had forsaken her. If Achilleus and Baldr can only be wounded on a single spot, Isfendiyar, in the Persian epic, can only be killed by the thorn thrown into his eye by Rustem. If Paris forsakes Œnônê, and Theseus leaves Ariadne mourning on the barren shore, so also Sigurdr deserts Brenhyldr, and Gudrun to him supplies the place of Aiglê or of Helen. If the tale

---

[8] "Tales of Thebes and Argos." By the Rev. Geo. W. Cox, M.A. London : Longmans. 1864.

of Perseus is repeated in the career of Heracles, the legend of Ragnar Lodbrog is also a mere echo of the nobler story which told of the sunbright Sigurdr. * * * The name of Heracles brings us to the strange border ground in which the character of some of the gods assumes a jovial or even a comic aspect. The language of the Vedic hymns at once shows why this should be the portion of some among the greater gods, and not of others. Phœbus, Athenê, and Orpheus, as representing the pure effulgence of the sun, Hestia, as the unsullied fire upon the hearth; Dêmêtêr, as the nourishing mother of all living things; Poseidon, as the lord of the mysterious sea; Hades and Persephonê, as rulers of the unseen land, pass under no conditions which may detract from their purity or their majesty. It was far otherwise with Ouranos or Zeus, the heaven and the sky, whose relations to the earth, when described under anthropomorphic forms, exhibit a mere unbounded licence and its results of envy, jealousy, and strife in the home of the gods."—p. 43.

In this manner our author traces the allegorical meaning of later stories, and finds it easy to establish the complete identity of Perseus, Bellerophon, Theseus, Kephalos, Paris, and Apollo. Indeed, all Greek mythology is easily reduced by his method to poetical forms of expression for the various aspects and processes of nature, and the Iliad ceases to be a tale of gods and heroes, being resolved into " a magnificent solar epic, telling us of a sun rising in radiant majesty (Achilles), soon hidden by the clouds, yet abiding his time of vengeance, when from the dark veil he breaks forth at last in more than his early strength, scattering the mists and kindling the ragged clouds which form his funeral pyre, nor caring whether his brief splendour shall be succeeded by a darker battle as the vapours close again over his dying glory. The feeling of the old tale is scarcely weakened when the poet tells us of the great cairn which the mariner shall see from afar, on the shore of the broad Hillespontos." This may be so : Homer cannot vindicate or explain himself ; but we may imagine the same mode of interpretation applied by some future scholar to Dante or Milton, when we, our beliefs and our language, will be things of the past ; and the inference seems obvious, that it would fail utterly to elicit the true thought that inspired either poet.

While the legends of ancient Greece are thus being resolved into a kind of meteorological fable, their modern representatives have been for the first time collected and edited. The author of two volumes of Greek and Albanian fairy tales[9] has accomplished a work as praiseworthy as that which Mr. Campbell performed for the folk-lore of the Highlands. During his residence at Jannina in 1848, Herr Hahn conceived the happy thought of employing some of the pupils of the Gymnasium in aiding him to carry out a favourite project. He commissioned a dozen of the most intelligent to collect for him during their holiday time, all the fairy tales they could gather from the lips of mothers, grandmothers, and sisters. He had great difficulty in procuring any contributions from Syra, until at last he was fortunate enough to find a young damsel who could write, and

---

[9] "Griechische und Albanesishe Märchen." Gesammelt übersetzt und erläutert von J. G. v. Hahn, K.K., Consul fur das östliche Griechenland. Leipzig: Engelmann. London : Nutt. 1864.

who was willing to exercise her uncommon talent in his service. By these means, a hundred and forty tales and fables were obtained, of which the author has now published a translation. He has carefully collated and classified his materials, and prefaces them by an introduction almost as elaborate as that of Mr. Cox upon the nature, growth, and origin of those short chapters of primitive romance which are found with such unvarying constancy among people the most widely severed, and which point to some common source far back in the infancy of our race. Under the heading, "Märchen and Sagformeln," forty different groups of subjects are given, and the corresponding tale, legend, or fable indicated in the folk-lore of nine other nations, thus enabling the reader to see at a glance the comparative frequency and prevalence of each. There are also abundant notes critical and explanatory, which testify to the painstaking industry of the author, and which will be of interest to the philological student. It is a striking peculiarity of by far the greater number of these hitherto unwritten fairy tales, that they possess so little local colouring ; now and then in a more modern composition, the influence of Christian and ecclesiastical ideas is discernible, but in general they are cast in the mould with which we are all familiar, and the child of Epirus or Tinos listens to the same stereotyed history of marvels that are the delight of our own nurseries—the king who has three sons who go to seek their fortunes, or the queen, long childless, who at last becomes the mother of the wonderful princess. But many of the tales are singularly unmeaning and as devoid of beauty as of wit.

The story of Niobe has been made the subject of a work[10] by Professor Stark, of Heidelberg, which friends will pronounce exhaustive, and which critics may be pardoned if they call it exhausting. In this ponderous volume, all that German industry could collect is brought together, and the whole mass pitilessly turned out again, with that lack of any distinct theory or animating purpose, and that calm unconsciousness of the ordinary limits of human patience, which belong to the true German scholar. The plates of the various statues, sculptures, reliefs, and vases in which the story of Niobe and her children are represented, are well executed, beginning with the sitting figure on Mount Sipylos which still exists, and is supposed to be the very same that Pausanias mentions, and ending with the well-known Niobe group at Florence. Every author who has mentioned or alluded to Niobe, from Homer to Dante, and from Dante downwards, contributes a line or a sentence to this elaborate, shadowless piece of Mosaic work, which is a work of immence industry, but which would have been far more useful and readable had the materials been better arranged, and selected with more discrimination.

The present quarter yields but few novels of any special interest. In "Mr. and Mrs. Faulconbridge,"[11] the stale old expedient of col-

---

[10] "Niobe und die Niobiden in ihre Literarischen, Künstlerischen, und Mythologischen Bedeutung." Von Dr. K. B. Stark. Leipzig: Engelmann. London: Nutt. 1863.

[11] "Mr. and Mrs. Faulconbridge." By Hamilton Aïdé. London: Smith and Elder. 1864.

lecting a number of ladies and gentlemen in a large country house, and developing a plot by means of private theatricals, has been adopted, but with the addition of an intricate mystery which is ingeniously kept up, and gives a certain novelty to the well-worn materials. The author, like Mr. Wilkie Collins, from whom he has taken other hints, begs the reviewers to respect the secret which ought not to be divulged before the fulness of time has come in the second volume; we must therefore observe a discreet silence with regard to it, although it is not always so well kept by the author as to elude the penetration of an experienced novel reader. The mystery, which certainly fulfils its purpose of keeping up the sense of a coming catastrophe, and an uncomfortable state of increasing embroilment, is not, however, the only noticeable feature. There is in this tale the same evidence of close observation, knowledge of the world, and aptitude for portraying certain types of the modern lady and gentleman which have distinguished the previous works of the author of " Rita," and there is also a refinement of feeling and tone of good society which give a certain ease and grace to his compositions. The people are real ; their conversation almost painfully true to nature, and most real and well described is the oppression which will overtake even the virtuous when their stay in a country house is prolonged beyond the expected time. We quote a scene which is a fair sample of the easy style and light quality of the story — a "five o'clock tea" at Stourton Towers, the seat of Sir Richard Stourton, uncle of the hero George (who is disabled by an accident which has compelled the postponement of the play) and of the charming Lady Trevelyan. Mr. and Mrs. Faulconbridge have come in a professional character to manage the theatricals :—

" It had grown so dark that faces were no longer distinguishable. Some one came in—a tall figure with a heavy tread—and approached George's sofa. 'Who is that ?' said Lady Trevelyan. 'It's me, Diana.' The grammar was everybody's, but the voice was Sir Richard's. 'How d'ye feel this evening, Georgy ?' He sat himself down heavily in a chair, and took out his snuffbox.' 'Oh! fresh as a two-year old, uncle Dick. I'm thinking of offering to ride in the grand military steeple chase on Saturday, sir.' 'Gad ! you madcap !' said his uncle, 'I believe we shall have to put a strait-waistcoat on you, if you're to be kept on that sofa for a week.' Then followed a sound which told that Sir Richard was taking a pinch of snuff; after which, in laying his box down on the table, his hand encountered the teatray. Sir Richard always waged war against this barbarous innovation on the habits of his day, and always affected extreme surprise on every fresh occasion that he saw a teacup before dinner. 'God bless my soul ! What's this ? Tea ? *Tea* at this hour !' You don't mean to say, Georgy, that you're taking to that absurd habit—only fit for women. Destroy your appetite for dinner—injure your digestion. If you must take anything, have a glass of sherry and bitters. Not that *I* ever require anything from breakfast to dinner. It wasn't the fashion of my time to be eating all day long.' 'Only to drink all night long ?' said George, laughing. 'Aye, George, a gentleman then wasn't afraid of his couple of bottles or so. You young men now are such a set of mollycoddles, you want to be off to the ladies after a couple of glasses.' 'You see, uncle Dick,' said George, with mock humility, 'I'm ashamed to own it—it's a shocking horrid vice, I know, but I'm fond of my cup of tea.' 'Pshaw !' said Sir

Richard, with a lofty good humour. 'Don't chaff your uncle, sir. Diana, where are you? Impossible to see a soul in this Trophonius's cave of yours. That is another ridiculous custom, not to have lights as soon as it gets dark. What is the use of sitting like so many ghosts there? Why don't you ring for a lamp?' 'Those last rays of sunset are so beautiful from this window,' said his niece. 'It seems a pity to shut them out. Besides, no one ever does anything at this hour.' 'And that is such a blessing,' chimed in George. 'It is the only time of the day one sits down without a fidgety desire to get up and do something else.' 'I didn't know, Master George,' observed his uncle, 'there was ever one hour in the twenty-four when you were free from that affliction—ha! ha! except, by-the-by, when you're sitting by a pretty woman. Is there any one else here, Diana? Do I see some one opposite there, in the arm-chair?' 'It is Mr. Faulconbridge, uncle.' 'Oh!' There was a formality in the way that interjection was exhaled—a perceptible change at once in the baronet's manner. Those jokes and sportive family ways were not for such as the 'young man who is down here, you know, to superintend the plays, and so forth.' 'I am glad to find from my nephew that this *congtretong*, Mr. Faulconbridge, will not deprive him and the company in general of your services—very valuable I am sure—for these plays . . . The theatres are sadly changed since my day. I remember the time when the stage was supported by the first people in the land. What a galaxy of talent there was then! Betterton—the Kembles—Mrs. Siddons! I seldom enter a theatre now—the low buffoonery, and then the audience! Even the opera. When I think what the pit of the opera was in my day. Fop's alley is gone! Now there is only a mass of tailors and bootmakers, who push and elbow you. By gad! it's intolerable!' 'Yes,' said George, 'the pit of the opera resembles, in one particular, that bottomless pit, where so much gnashing of teeth goes on' . . . 'The Elizabethan drama has utterly departed. No such thing as a five-act tragedy in blank verse is ever given now, I believe. A few enterprising persons, who are fond of low, *very* low, wit, go down to some place in the Strand, where they sit, jammed in a vice they call a stall, and listen to a vulgar set of dogs in a burlesque, and that's what they call "going to the theatre" in the present day!' 'You wouldn't call it going to chapel, sir?' said George. The door opened at that moment, and the figures of two ladies loomed in the dusk. 'We thought we should find some one here,' said Miss Skipton's brisk voice, 'and tea going on, I declare. We have had *such* a walk. Is Lady Trevelyan here? because it's impossible to tell. Mrs. Faulconbridge and I *are so* tired—a cup of tea, please, Gracious! Mr. Faulconbridge, I beg your pardon! I was going to sit down, not seeing your knee. It really is so dark.' 'Of course it is,' said Sir Richard's pompous voice, out of the darkness, 'I wonder you don't all tumble over each other. Miss Skipton, I thought you were a woman of more sense than to drink slops at this hour.' 'We must make some *more* slops for her, I see,' laughed Lady Trevelyan, 'for we have drained the teapot. Mr. Faulconbridge, if you can find the silver teabox anywhere on the table, you may empty it in here, and put in some water. Uncle Richard, I want to speak to you before you go.'

* * * * * * * * * * * *

"Sir Richard was interrupted by something that nearly approached a shriek from Miss Skipton. 'Oh! oh! ugh! Gracious goodness! What on earth is there in this tea? Oh! Of all the horrible—horrible—ugh!' Amid general exclamations of astonishment, enters Mr. Millet, with a lamp. 'By Jove!' shouted George, with a roar of laughter, 'By Jove! Sir Richard, here's Faulconbridge has been and emptied your snuffbox into the teapot. Poor Miss Skipton!' That was it. The empty snuffbox beside the teapot left it beyond all doubt. All gathered round the unfortunate sufferer except Sir Richard, who as he left the room, took occasion to say—'This comes of your drinking your slops at this hour, and sitting in the dark. I'm not the least surprised. I always told you how it would be!'"—Vol. i. p. 279.

Dr. Sandwith has drawn upon his recollections and experience of the east for the subject-matter of "Hekim Bashi," [12] and the result is two entertaining volumes which bear the stamp of faithful adherence to facts, only so far trimmed and pruned as to render them fit for use in the form of an imaginary autobiography. The hero of the story is an Italian doctor, who confesses to having played the part of cheat, traitor, and renegade in the pursuit of wealth, but who repents of his evil ways, and is found by an English traveller in the Hospital of Incurables at Pinerolo, in Sardinia, in the character of a Cistercian monk devoted to charitable works. He relates how he arrived at Constantinople in 1858, as a young doctor seeking his fortune, and he thus describes the medical school of Galata Serail :—

"My medical brethren were as various in their nationalities as in their garments. Italy furnished the majority of the foreigners, France a goodly number, Germany several, and England a few ; but these mostly of the highest position. Of natives, there were a few genuine Turks, enjoying but little of the confidence of their fellow countrymen. The Greeks swarmed, and some of them occupied the best medical appointments in the palace and the public service. There were also a few Armenians, who did not, however, possess a great reputation even amongst their own people. These Christian Asiatic nationalities furnished a great number of professors of small surgery : there were numbers of barbers, who were bleeders, tooth-drawers, cuppers, and dressers of wounds. Some years before my arrival in Constantinople, all the doctors possessed of diplomas were foreigners, or natives who had studied abroad ; but latterly the Sultan had founded a medical university of his own, and a curious exotic it was. The pupils were clothed, fed, and paid, and yet but few of the Turks would face the horrors of learning anatomy. Moreover, all the lessons were given in French, which the students had to learn while listening to the lectures. The Sultan, however, was determined that the lecture-rooms should be filled, so peasants were captured in the interior, and brought in chains to learn the science of medicine. This plan, however, did not succeed, as the brains of these rustics were found impermeable to both French and physiology, besides which many of them were only too glad to settle for life at the school when they found themselves fed, clothed, and paid, and disliked the idea of leaving it. Compulsory attendance was, therefore, given up, and (with the peculiar advantages held out) there was no lack of Greeks, Jews, and Armenians, with a few Ottomans, which latter were highly encouraged in their studies, some of them being made colonels as soon as they had passed a very indulgent examination. The professors were, in the beginning, first-rate men and highly paid, from France and Austria ; these were in time gradually replaced by Greeks and Armenians, who neglected their duties, and made a traffic of the emoluments and appointments connected with their posts."—Vol. i. p. 45.

Dr. Sandwith has evidently but small faith in the much talked of reforms that have taken place in the Turkish Government and administration, in consequence of the pressure of European, and especially of English, interference of late years ; and according to his pictures of

---

[12] "The Hekim Bashi ; or, the Adventures of Giuseppe Antonelli, a Doctor in the Turkish Service." By Humphry Sandwith, C.B., D.C.L., author of "The Siege of Kars." London : Smith and Elder. 1864.

provincial misrule, corruption, and injustice, the improvement has not spread into Asia, nor does he believe in any change for the better in the universal system of bribery and extortion from the highest official to the meanest slave, while he is loud in his condemnation of the recent policy of England, which has always taken the side of the Mussulman against the Christian. The following is one of the notes to the second volume: the statement is bold, to say the least—

"When I was in Turkey in 1860, it was notorious that the British consuls had received hints from the embassy to refrain from reporting anything that could tell against the Turkish Government. I was once conversing with a consul, and he told me stories of Turkish oppression that aroused my indignation. 'At least,' I remarked, 'you have the satisfaction of reporting these horrors to your Government.' 'By no means,' was his answer; 'I dare not report anything unfavourable to the Turks; such a course would be fatal to my career, since Sir H. Bulwer has given us to understand that we are always to take the part of the Turks.'"

Another two volume novel, called "Uncle Crotty's Relations,"[13] would have been more aptly named "Aunt Crotty's Will," since the chief interest of the story relates to the two wills of a remarkably disagreeable lady of that name, by one of which the heroine would possess 3000*l.* a-year, and by the other only 3000*l.*, the hero becoming the heir in her stead; but as it is plain from the first that they are lovers, and intended to come together in happiness and prosperity, the reader is disturbed by no misgivings about the money, and knows that it will ultimately come to the two deserving cousins. The story is a quiet, cheerful little picture of common life, with which the attempt to interweave a darker thread of crime and tragedy does not harmonize, as the author seems to have become suddenly conscious, and cuts it short in a somewhat abrupt manner. In fact, the work is a series of incomplete schemes and surprises, not alway expressed in good English; but there are a few well-sketched scenes, and one or two characters sufficiently interesting to redeem it from dulness and insipidity.

"Le Maudit"[14] is the title of a book in three large volumes, devoted to the exposure of the cruelties of the Inquisition and the corruptions of the Romish clergy, especially of the disciples of Loyola. The author quotes clerical precedents for adopting the form of composition which he considers the best suited to the popular taste, and justifies his choice by the examples of Fénélon and Cardinal Wiseman. The nature of his work hardly bears out the assertion that it is neither polemical nor religious, but "a work of art," for there is very little art displayed in the voluminous narrative, but there are pages of argumentation, and whole chapters of religious discussion. The main object of the book is to trace the fortunes of a young Abbé—high minded and irreproachable—who starts in life with the shadow of priestly disfavour upon him, and who becomes the cruelly persecuted victim of the Holy Office, undergoing a lifelong persecution from the Jesuits both on account of

---

[13] "Uncle Crotty's Relations." By Herbert Glyn, Author of "The Cotton Lord." Smith, Elder, and Co. 1863.
[14] "Le Maudit." Par l'Abbé * * * Quatrième Édition. Paris: Libraire Internationale. London: Williams and Norgate. 1864.

his avowed liberal opinions, and because he has endeavoured, although vainly, to recover his own and his sister's rightful inheritance of which the Jesuits had possessed themselves by means of flattery and intimidation patiently exercised for ten years, winning at last a will in their favour. There is nothing new in the disclosures of the intricate chicanery and perfect organization by which the Society of Jesus obtains its ends and circumvents its unfortunate victims, but so earnest and outspoken a protest against clerical domination and the corruption of faith and practice in the Church of Rome, is expressive of the growing impatience of thinking men under a yoke which has long lost its sanctity in the eyes of those who are not blinded by bigotry. The story is of the present time, and among his various adventures, the hero escapes from the prison of the Inquisition in Rome by the help of a Garibaldian irregular. There are passages in his life as a quiet curé in a remote mountain district which have all the air of being sketches from life ; but it must be the inherent interest of the subject more than the artistic skill of the author which has caused this somewhat clumsy performance to go through four editions, unless, indeed, the fact of its having been prohibited be not a sufficient explanation.

"Lloyd Pennant "[15] and "Die von Hohenstein,"[16] are not otherwise remarkable than as giving a tolerably accurate idea of two very distinct phases of life ; the first is an Irish story of the time of the French invasion under Hoche, the second is a history of personages not particularly moral or well conducted or interesting, during the revolutionary days of 1848. A cheap edition of Mrs. Gaskell's "Sylvia's Lovers" [17] in one volume will no doubt obtain deserved popularity, but the very inferior illustrations do not add to its attractions.

Among illustrated gift books we have to notice two very beautiful volumes adorned with photographs many of which are admirable. "Our English Lakes,"[18] is a well chosen selection from Wordsworth's poems, with exquisite photographic illustrations of many of the loveliest spots commemorated by or associated with them. The poet's modest home at Rydal Mount forms the frontispiece, and the simple stone which marks the last resting-place of William and Mary Wordsworth, in Grasmere churchyard, is the appropriate finish of a volume which has every form of artistic and typographic excellence to recommend it. The other work is the second series of "Ruined Abbeys and Castles,"[19] for which Mr. Howitt supplies the descriptive letter-press. The softness, minute delicacy, and richness of tint in these photographs, many of them extremely small, are remarkable, and the exterior of the volume is a triumph of bookbinding decoration.

---

[15] "Lloyd Pennant, a Tale of the West." By Ralph Neville. London : Chapman and Hall. 1864.
[16] "Die von Hohenstein." Roman von Friedrich Spielhagen. Berlin: Otto Janke. London : Nutt. 1864.
[17] "Sylvia's Lovers." By Mrs. Gaskell. Illustrated Edition. Smith, Elder, and Co. 1863.
[18] "Our English Lakes, Mountains, and Waterfalls, as seen by William Wordsworth." London : Alfred W. Bennett.
[19] "Ruined Abbeys and Castles of Great Britain and Ireland." By William Howitt. London : Alfred W. Bennett, 5, Bishopsgate-street Without. 1864.

Mr. Richard Doyle's " Bird's-eye Views of Society,[20] which first appeared in the *Cornhill Magazine*, are now published in a separate volume, with a page or two of very tame letter-press to each engraving. As specimens of Mr. Doyle's extraordinary power of delineating the human face and form in every possible variety of grotesque ugliness and distressing vulgarity these drawings are matchless, and perhaps the almost unprecedented absence of grace and fitness in the style of costume now in fashion, deserves to be recorded in these grim unsparing satires. But the constant repetition of the same vacant, vapid, meaningless faces, with only just enough of variety to prove the artist's skill, becomes at last more painful than diverting, and the effect is less that of a caricature than of a sneering libel. Even in the Juvenile Party there is scarcely a face that is not distorted by evil passion or mean feeling, while in the State Party we are shown sixteen ladies and gentlemen engaged in demolishing delicacies out of season, each with a scowling malignity or an inane insipidity of expression which it is simply a penalty to look upon. But there is one scene in which none of these defects intrude themselves, and where Mr. Doyle's marvellous power of drawing has full play—The Science and Art Conversazione. Here every face, however ugly, has a true individual expression, and the various attitudes of the learned and inquisitive company are truly comic, without being dismally ungainly. The contrast between the artist's pencil and his pen is striking: the letter-press is somewhat flat, but full of amiable benignity—the drawings might have been the work of a cynical monomaniac, whose brain had been turned on the subject of overcrowding at evening parties.

We are shown ourselves in detail in two volumes of sketches;[21] the descriptions are by various authors, including the late Mr. Thackeray and Douglas Jerrold; the drawings are by Kenny Meadows, and are of the coarsest rudest character, little if at all superior to the wood engravings in the cheapest periodicals.

A dainty little volume on Palms[22] is adorned with glowing illustrations from drawings by the authoress, and in addition to a good deal of botanical and miscellaneous information, there is a vein of religious sentiment, and a section devoted to " Scripture Notices of Palms," which redeems the work from the suspicion of being dangerously scientific, and which will recommend it to the timidly pious, who are afraid of any reading that is not plentifully sprinkled with Scripture texts.

Two picture-books[23] for children, containing between them thirty-eight engravings, illustrate the question What should you like to be ? Each trade and profession is illustrated by a typical scene which at once tells its own story. The drawings are excellent, both in design

---

[20] " Bird's-eye Views of Society." Taken by Richard Doyle. Smith, Elder, and Co. 1864.

[21] " Heads of the People ; or, Portraits of the English." Henry G. Bohn. 1864.

[22] "The Palm Tree." By S. Moody. London: Nelson and Sons. 1864.

[23] " Was willst du werden ?" Von Oscar Pletsch. Berlin: Weidmann. London: Williams and Norgate.

and execution, and bit off minor nicities of expression with much cleverness and sly humour without caricature.

Mr. Charles Mackay's new volume of poems[24] evinces his usual vigour and warmth of feeling in the treatment of themes of modern life and experience, but he is less at home in classical ground, and never ceases to be the Englishman of to-day even in "Momus" and "Cassandra."

The "Tales of a Wayside Inn"[25] will hardly satisfy those who remember what Mr. Longfellow has written, although there is the true ballad clang and thunder in the Saga of King Olaf.

The chief poem in another volume of American poetry[26] is entitled an "Idyl of the Great War," and if the author does not promise to write war-songs like those of Körner, he has at least seized one of the forms of tragic interest which bring a national struggle within the circle of personal feelings and sorrows; and the tone of plaintive sadness which quenches the fire out of the battle-scenes may be well excused in one who is or who tries to be patriotic in the midst of civil war. There is real poetic feeling and taste in this poem, but there is also a certain faintness and hesitation, in which no trace of hearty enthusiasm, as for a cause wholly believed in, can be traced. Thus it concludes :—

> "'Daughter,' the man replied (his face was bright
> With the effulgent reflex of that light,)
> The time shall come, by merciful Heaven will'd,
> When these celestial omens shall be fulfill'd,
> Our strife be closed, and the nation purged of sin,
> And a pure and holier union shall begin ;
> And a jarring race be drawn throughout the land,
> Into new brotherhood by some strong hand ;
> And the baneful glow and splendour of war shall fade
> In the whiter light of love, that, from sea to sea,
> Shall soften the rage of hosts in arms array'd,
> And melt into share and shaft each battle blade,
> And brighten the hopes of a people great and free.
> But in the story told of a nation's woes,
> Of the sacrifices made for a century's fault,
> The fames of fallen heroes shall ever shine,
> Serene, and high, and crystalline as those
> Fair stars which reappear in yonder vault ;
> In the country's heart their written names shall be,
> Like that of a single one in mine and thine."

A new volume of sacred verse,[27] by the author of "Lyra Eucharistica," contains a large and choice selection of devotional poetry from

---

[24] "Studies from the Antique and Sketches from Nature." By Charles Mackay. Virtue. 1864.
[25] "Tales of a Wayside Inn." By Henry Wadsworth Longfellow. Routledge. 1864.
[26] "Alice of Monmouth, an Idyll of the Great War, with other Poems." By Edmund C. Stedman. New York : Carleton. 1864.
[27] "Lyra Messianica : Hymns and Verses on the Life of Christ. Ancient and Modern." Edited by the Rev. Orby Shipley. Longman. 1864.

various sources and of every age of the Christian Church. Ancient breviaries and mediæval missals furnish some of the hymns, and in their quaint symbolism betray their origin through their English dress, and scarcely harmonize with the English hymns by living writers. The translations are well done, and many of the Latin and Greek hymns are now first published in verse. The collection is well deserving a place beside the beautiful " Lyra Germanica" of Miss Winkworth, and is printed and bound in the same antique style.

INDEX.

END OF VOL. XXV.

CPSIA information can be obtained
at www.ICGtesting.com
Printed in the USA
BVHW061015280819
556932BV00017B/2505/P

9 781318 535972